The Wiley Handbook of Memory, Autism Spectrum Disorder, and the Law

Edited by

Jonni L. Johnson

Gail S. Goodman

Peter C. Mundy

WILEY Blackwell

This edition first published 2018

Registered Offices
John Wiley & Sons, Inc., 111 River Street, Hoboken, NJ 07030, USA
John Wiley & Sons Ltd, The Atrium, Southern Gate, Chichester, West Sussex, PO19 8SQ, UK

Editorial Office
The Atrium, Southern Gate, Chichester, West Sussex, PO19 8SQ, UK

For details of our global editorial offices, customer services, and more information about Wiley products visit us at www.wiley.com.

Wiley also publishes its books in a variety of electronic formats and by print-on-demand. Some content that appears in standard print versions of this book may not be available in other formats.

Library of Congress Cataloging-in-Publication Data

Names: Johnson, Jonni L., 1986– author.
Title: The Wiley handbook of memory, autism spectrum disorder, and the law / edited by Jonni L. Johnson, Gail S. Goodman, Peter C. Mundy.
Other titles: Handbook of memory, autism spectrum disorder, and the law
Description: Hoboken, NJ : Wiley, [2018] | Includes bibliographical references and index. |
Identifiers: LCCN 2017057974 (print) | LCCN 2017061831 (ebook) | ISBN 9781119158400 (pdf) | ISBN 9781119158370 (epub) | ISBN 9781119158264 (cloth)
Subjects: LCSH: Autism spectrum disorders–Handbooks, manuals, etc. | Autobiographical memory–Handbooks, manuals, etc.
Classification: LCC RC553.A88 (ebook) | LCC RC553.A88 J62 2018 (print) | DDC 616.85/882–dc23
LC record available at https://lccn.loc.gov/2017057974

Cover image: © Maksim Kabakou/Shutterstock
Cover design: Wiley

Set in 10/12pt Galliard by SPi Global, Pondicherry, India

Printed in Singapore by C.O.S. Printers Pte Ltd

10 9 8 7 6 5 4 3 2 1

Contents

Notes on Contributors

Andrea Arndorfer is Assistant Professor of Criminology at California State University, Fresno. She received her Ph.D. in Psychology from Florida International University in 2016. Her research interests center on various topics at the intersection of psychology and the law such as criminal interrogation and confessions, eyewitness memory, and the social and cognitive factors influencing lineup identification decisions and post-decision judgments.

Daniel Bederian-Gardner, Ph.D., graduated from the University of California, Davis, studying various issues relating to children's involvement as witnesses in the legal system, such as the interplay of children's moral development and testimony. He has studied and authored chapters about characteristics of child witnesses that influence judgments of their credibility. Dr. Bederian-Gardner has also conducted research on true and false memory across development. He is currently addressing the impact of foster care on mental health outcomes.

Dermot M. Bowler graduated from Trinity College Dublin in 1976 and gained his Ph.D. from the University of London in 1986. After working at the Thomas Coram Research Unit, and subsequently, with Dr. Lorna Wing at the Medical Research Council, he joined City, University of London in 1990. At City, he set up the Autism Research Group and currently holds the position of Professor of Psychology. He has also held an adjunct professorship at McGill University, Montreal, as well as a European Union-funded visiting chair at the University of Caen and the French National Institute for Medical and Health Research (INSERM). His research interests center on the neuropsychology of memory across the lifespan in individuals with autism spectrum disorders.

Neil Brewer, Ph.D., is the Matthew Flinders Distinguished Professor of Psychology at Flinders University, South Australia. He is an experimental psychologist with broad interests in the psychology-law area, including eyewitness identification and reporting, determinants of testimonial credibility, and cognitive and social characteristics that may contribute to naive involvement in criminal activity by ASD individuals. He is on the editorial boards of *Law and Human Behavior* and *Psychology, Public*

Policy and Law, and has served on the editorial boards of all of the major psychology-law journals. Professor Brewer is just completing his term as Editor of the *Journal of Experimental Psychology: Applied*.

Lorinda B. Camparo, Ph.D., is Professor in the Department of Psychological Sciences at Whittier College, where she has taught and conducted research on enhancing children's narrative reports since 1997. Dr. Camparo has published numerous articles and book chapters, and recently co-authored the book *Evidence-based child forensic interviewing: The Developmental Narrative Elaboration Interview* (Oxford University Press, 2014) with Dr. Karen Saywitz. Dr. Camparo has also conducted workshops on interviewing children for lawyers, judges, police officers, and social workers, and she has served as an expert witness on cases involving children alleging sexual abuse.

Michael Carlin, Ph.D., attended Peabody College of Education and Human Development of Vanderbilt University for his graduate training, and worked with Dr. Sal Soraci and Dr. Alan Baumeister at the John F. Kennedy Center. Upon graduation, he moved to Massachusetts to work at the Eunice Kennedy Shriver Center from 1994 to 2007. He then accepted a faculty position at Rider University, where he teaches courses in Cognitive and Developmental Disabilities, Statistics, and Cognitive Psychology.

Yoojin Chae, Ph.D., is Assistant Professor in Human Development and Family Studies at Texas Tech University. Her research focuses on children's abilities as witnesses, including children's eyewitness memory and suggestibility, trauma and memory, attachment and memory, language and memory, forensic interview techniques, and adults' evaluations of children's autobiographical memory. She received her doctorate in human development from Cornell University.

Laura Crane, Ph.D., is Senior Teaching and Engagement Fellow at the Centre for Research in Autism and Education (CRAE) at the University College London Institute of Education in the United Kingdom. Dr. Crane completed her undergraduate and postgraduate training in Psychology at Goldsmiths, University of London, before taking postdoctoral research positions at City, University of London and Goldsmiths, University of London. Dr. Crane's research focuses on supporting children and adults on the autism spectrum within the criminal justice system as well as exploring the educational and healthcare experiences of autistic adults, parents of children on the autism spectrum, and professionals working in the field of autism.

Deborah Davis, Ph.D., is Professor of Psychology at the University of Nevada, Reno, and a member of the faculty of the National Judicial College. She has published widely in the areas of witness memory, police interrogation and confessions, communicating and understanding sexual intentions, and other areas as well. She worked for more than 20 years as a trial consultant, has testified as an expert witness in close to 150 trials, and is a frequent speaker at Continuing Legal Education seminars across the country.

Sebastian B. Gaigg, Ph.D., joined the Autism Research Group at City, University of London in 2001 and has since then pursued two primary research interests. One strand of his work focuses on understanding learning and memory processes across the autism spectrum, with projects ranging from the examination of episodic memory in autistic adults who live relatively independent lives to studies of basic learning processes in young autistic children who have very significant language and intellectual impairments. His second strand of work seeks to develop a better understanding of the emotional lives of individuals with autism, particularly concerning the mechanisms underlying the unusually high prevalence of anxiety disorders in this population.

Lorna Goddard, Ph.D., is a senior lecturer at Goldsmiths, University of London. She has published over 20 articles and chapters related to theoretical research on autobiographical memory in autism. She is also a registered cognitive behavior therapist involved in researching and delivering intervention service for individuals with autism spectrum disorder.

Deborah Goldfarb, J.D., is a developmental psychology doctoral candidate at the University of California, Davis. Prior to attending graduate school, Deborah worked as an attorney, including two years as a law clerk to a federal district court judge. She graduated *cum laude* with a Juris Doctor degree from the University of Michigan Law School and a Bachelor of Science degree in Psychology from the University of Illinois, Urbana-Champaign. She has published research on children's legal involvement in law reviews, books, and journals, and has presented this work internationally.

Alejandra Gonzalez is a researcher at the University of California, Davis, currently conducting studies on trauma and memory. She received a Bachelor of Arts degree in Psychology and a Bachelor of Science degree in Genetics and Genomics from the University of California, Davis, and she has published about the topic of child suggestibility in the courtroom. Her interests include trauma-related psychopathology as well as challenges faced by disadvantaged populations in the legal system.

Gail S. Goodman, Ph.D., is Distinguished Professor of Psychology at the University of California, Davis. Her research concerns such topics as children's and adults' eyewitness memory, child maltreatment, forensic interviewing, victimization, legal involvement, and trauma and memory. She has served as President of several divisions of the American Psychological Association (e.g., Developmental Psychology, American Psychology-Law Society, Child and Family Policy and Practice). She is internationally known for her research on victims and witnesses, which has been cited multiple times by the U.S. Supreme Court. Dr. Goodman has published widely and received numerous national awards and grants for her research and writings.

Catherine Grainger, Ph.D., is a lecturer at the University of Stirling. Her research focuses on understanding the nature of autism spectrum disorder. In particular, she is interested in understanding self-awareness, theory of mind, and memory in autism.

Ambar Guzman, ACSW, is a clinical social worker and recent graduate of the University of California Los Angeles, where she was also a trainee for the University of California Leadership Education in Neurodevelopmental and Other Related Disabilities (UC-LEND). She worked as a therapist for adolescents, and then most recently, transitioned to serving the community as a medical social worker. Her experience in the forensic interviewing field includes her past work as the project director of a child interviewing lab and serving as a bilingual forensic interviewer for a local Children's Advocacy Center.

Sue D. Hobbs, Ph.D., is a developmental psychologist, Assistant Professor at Sacramento State University in the Child Development Area of the College of Education, and a member of the American Psychological Association Division 7 (Developmental Psychology) Executive Committee. Her research focuses on two key areas of child development as they relate to child victims and witnesses: 1) children's eyewitness testimony, specifically, suggestibility, memory development, and secret-keeping; and 2) factors influencing the outcomes of foster youth once they emancipate from care.

Jonni L. Johnson is completing her Ph.D. at the University of California, Davis, with research interest in developmental psychology, autism spectrum disorder, and the law. Funded by the National Science Foundation, American Psychological Association, and American Psychology-Law Association, her dissertation examines memory functions in youths with and without autism spectrum disorder and the utility of forensic memory interviewing protocols. She has published and presented scientific papers on the development of children's eyewitness abilities, perceptions of children's eyewitness abilities, and more recently, eyewitness abilities in individuals with autism spectrum disorder.

Elisa Krackow, Ph.D., is Associate Professor of Psychology at West Virginia University. She earned her doctorate in clinical psychology from Binghamton University, SUNY. She conducts research on eyewitness memory relevant to clinical issues and populations.

Julia Landsiedel is completing her Ph.D. at the University of Kent and will begin a postdoctoral research position at Bangor University in November 2017. Her research focuses on the typical and atypical development of prospective memory and social interaction.

Sophie E. Lind, Ph.D., is a Senior Lecturer in Psychology and member of the Autism Research Group at City, University of London. Her research explores cognition in autism, and her key interests include self-referential cognition, episodic memory, episodic foresight, and metacognition in people with this disorder.

Arthur MacNeill Horton, Jr., received his Ed.D. degree from the University of Virginia in 1976, holds ABPP Diplomates in Clinical and Behavioral Psychology and an ABN Diplomate in Neuropsychology, and is the author/editor of 15 books. He is a past-president of the National Academy of Neuropsychology (NAN) and the Maryland Psychological Association (MPA). Previously, Dr. Horton was a Program Officer with the National Institutes of Health (NIH). Currently, Dr. Horton is Editor in Chief of *Applied Neuropsychology*. He recently co-edited (with Danny Wedding, Ph.D.), *The Neuropsychology Handbook* (3rd edition).

Lindsay C. Malloy, Ph.D., is Associate Professor of Psychology at the University of Ontario Institute of Technology in Oshawa, located in Ontario, Canada. Her research addresses questions concerning children's and adolescents' disclosure of negative or traumatic experiences, cognitive and sociocontextual influences on children's memory and narratives, and implications of research findings for the legal system.

Katie Maras, Ph.D., is a Lecturer in Psychology at the University of Bath in the United Kingdom. She has an international reputation for her research in the field of autism and forensic psychology in which she takes a theoretically informed, applied approach with a particular focus on memory and cognition. Much of her research to date has focused on how the specific memory difficulties of adults with autism affect the evidence that they provide in the criminal justice system, and how police interviewing techniques can be adapted to support their difficulties.

Haylie L. Miller, Ph.D., is an experimental psychologist and Assistant Professor in the Department of Physical Therapy at the University of North Texas Health Science Center in Fort Worth, Texas. Her training in cognitive development and expertise in autism spectrum disorder (ASD) support two key areas of study: gist-based information processing and memory, and sensorimotor integration. Dr. Miller currently directs a federally funded (National Institutes of Health, National Science Foundation) program of research on the development of visual information processing and attention in ASD, and their impact on functional movement.

Rebecca Milne, Ph.D., is Professor of Forensic Psychology at the Institute of Criminal Justice Studies at the University of Portsmouth. The main focus of her work over the past 20 years concerns the examination of police interviewing and investigation that improve the quality of interviews administered. She is also Director of the Centre of Forensic Interviewing and a member of the Association of Chief Police Officers' Investigative Interviewing Strategic Steering Group. Notably, she was part of a writing team that developed the 2007 version of *Achieving Best Evidence: National Guidelines for Interviewing Vulnerable Groups.*

Allison P. Mugno is Assistant Professor of Psychology at Huntingdon College in Montgomery, Alabama. She received her Ph.D. in Psychology from Florida International University in 2017. Her research interests focus on issues at the intersection of developmental and legal psychology, with a particular emphasis on the cognitive and sociocontextual factors that affect the honesty and accuracy of children's eyewitness testimony.

Peter C. Mundy, Ph.D., is Distinguished Professor of Education and the Lisa Capps Professor of Neurodevelopmental Disorders and Education at the MIND Institute and the School of Medicine's Department of Psychiatry and Behavioral Sciences at University of California, Davis. He is an expert in the education and development of children with autism. As a developmental and clinical psychologist, Mundy has been working on defining the major dimensions of autism for the past 32 years.

Timothy N. Odegard, Ph.D., is Professor of Psychology and holds the endowed Chair of Excellence in Dyslexic Studies at Middle Tennessee State University (MTSU). He oversees the efforts of the Tennessee Center for the Study and Treatment of Dyslexia, which is a research center housed on the MTSU campus. He earned his Ph.D. in Experimental Psychology from the University of Arkansas in 2004. His research in cognitive development has focused on semantic and episodic memory development, and the acquisition of reading skills.

Matilda Ohlsson, Ph.D., received her Bachelor of Science degree in Psychology from The University of York, followed by a Master of Science degree in Memory and Memory Disorders from the University of Leeds. After this, she completed her training in clinical psychology at the University of Hull. Currently, she is a practicing clinical psychologist working across neuropsychology and neurorehabilitation services in Leeds.

Valerie Reyna, Ph.D., is Professor and Director of the Human Neuroscience Institute at Cornell University. She has been elected to the National Academy of Medicine and the Society of Experimental Psychologists, and served as President of the Society for Judgment and Decision Making. Her research integrates brain and behavioral approaches to understand and improve judgment, decision-making, and memory across the lifespan. Her recent work has focused on the neuroscience of risky decision-making and its implications for health and well-being, especially in adolescents; applications of artificial intelligence to understanding cancer genetics; and medical and legal decision-making (e.g., jury awards, medication decisions, and adolescent crime).

Joanne Richards, Ph.D., worked in special education for 20 years, and set up units and outreach services for children with multisensory impairment and teenagers with complex communication needs. She is a lecturer at the University of Portsmouth for the Institute of Criminal Justice and a member of the Centre of Forensic Interviewing.

Karen J. Saywitz, Ph.D., is Professor at the UCLA, School of Medicine, Department of Psychiatry and Bio-behavioral Sciences and a developmental and clinical psychologist. For over 25 years, she has directed programs providing mental health services to families and taught normative child development to students in medicine, law, psychology, social work, and nursing. She is an expert on the capabilities, limitations, and needs of children involved in the legal system, authoring articles applying developmental science to legal decision-making that have been cited by the U.S. Supreme Court. Dr. Saywitz has won national awards for research, teaching, advocacy, and clinical service; she has chaired blue-ribbon panels on public health strategies to prevent child maltreatment in primary care settings; and authored handbooks for judges and forensic interviewers on the efficacy of child interview strategies and preparing child witnesses for court.

Henry V. Soper received his Bachelor's degree from Yale University; he then received his M. A. and Ph.D. from the University of Connecticut. He has served as a reviewer for *Perceptual and Motor Skills, Psychological Reports, Applied Neuropsychology*, both *Adult* and *Child*. He is a Fellow of the National Academy of Neuropsychology and the Psychonomic Society, and on the Editorial Board of *The Encyclopedia of Neuropsychological Disorder*. He has published over 130 abstracts, papers, chapters, and books in the neurosciences, neuropsychology, and related fields in medicine and psychology, and chaired over 40 dissertations.

Céline Souchay is a Senior Researcher at Le Centre National de la Recherche Scientifique (CNRS) in France. After completing her Ph.D. on metacognition in Alzheimer's disease in Tours in 2000, she held posts in Montreal, Strasbourg, Plymouth, and Leeds. She moved back to France in 2012 and to Grenoble in 2015. She is on the editorial board of the journal *Memory* and is co-director of a national research group on memory. She has a broad interest in the higher-order contributions to episodic memory in various clinical populations.

David M. Williams, Ph.D., is Professor of Developmental Psychology and head of the Developmental Research Group at the University of Kent. His research focuses on theory of mind, metacognition, and language development in people with autism and the neurotypical population.

Diane L. Williams, Ph.D., CCC-SLP is Professor and Head of the Department of Communication Sciences and Disorders at Pennsylvania State University. She has authored numerous peer-reviewed publications and book chapters on the neurobiological and neuropsychological basis of Autism Spectrum Disorders (ASD) with an emphasis on language, cognition, and memory. Dr. Williams has worked extensively with individuals with ASD across the age span in her clinical practice as a speech-language pathologist.

Emily F. Wood is pursuing her Ph.D. in Interdiscplinary Social Psychology at the University of Nevada, Reno. She investigates topics related to decision-making, stigma, prejudice, and injustices in the legal system.

Robyn L. Young, Ph.D., has published widely in peer-reviewed journals, such as *Journal of Autism and Developmental Disorders, Autism Research*, and *Psychological Assessment*, with over 30 papers published in the field of autism spectrum disorder (ASD). Her initial research involved the development of an early screening tool and intervention programs for young children with ASD. Currently, she is often asked to assess older individuals and provide expertise as an expert witness and submit reports to the court, specifically concerning whether ASD may be considered as a mediating factor in criminal activity. This has led to the study of adults with ASD, focusing on diagnostic issues and on ASD adults' interactions with the criminal justice system. This work stimulated a book with co-author Neil Brewer entitled *Crime and Autism Spectrum Disorder: Myths and Mechanisms* (Brewer & Young, 2015).

Tiziana Zalla, Ph.D., is Research Director at the Centre National de la Recherche Scientifique (CNRS) and head of the Social Cognition group at the Jean Nicod Institute, in the Department of Cognitive Studies at the École normale supérieure in Paris. Her work mainly focuses on social cognition in people with autism spectrum disorders and people who fall within the typically developing population, using a multidisciplinary approach bringing together concepts and methodologies from social psychology, neuropsychology, cognitive neuroscience, and biological psychiatry.

Irina Zilberfayen has been a Licensed Professional Counselor since 2000, and is currently pursuing a Ph.D. in Clinical Psychology with a Neuropsychology concentration at Fielding Graduate University. Her interest in developmental disorders grew out of her teaching background, clinical training, and counseling experience with children and their families with learning and developmental disorders in schools and community mental health clinics.

Acknowledgment

Dr. Goodman's contributions here were supported in part by grants from the National Science Foundation (Nos. 1424420 and 1627297). Any opinions, findings, conclusions, or recommendations expressed in her contributions to this book are those of hers as author and do not necessarily reflect the views of the National Science Foundation.

Autism Spectrum Disorder, Memory, and the Legal System: Knowns and Unknowns

Jonni L. Johnson, Gail S. Goodman, and Peter C. Mundy

Autism Spectrum Disorders (ASD) are neurodevelopmental disorders represented on a continuum of severity and marked by repetitive/restricted behaviors and difficulties in social interactions and communications (American Psychiatric Association, 2013). In this book, we offer integrative, theory-rich, and science-based discussions of how the particular cognitive and social deficits associated with ASD create unique challenges in assessing autobiographical memory, especially in the legal context.

Throughout the book, authors demonstrate why *autobiographical* memory, versus other forms of memory, requires specialized empirical attention and nuanced understanding for individuals with ASD. This is particularly true when individuals with ASD become involved in the legal system. With this consideration in mind, authors discuss how the legal system, with its formal social infrastructure and primary goal of justly balancing the needs of accused and accusers, can meet societal duties of offering appropriate accommodations for individuals with ASD. The discussions will surely spark debate on theoretical, empirical, and ethical conflicts that should be resolved.

Autobiographical memory theories and ASD

Autobiographical memories are recollections of one's past experiences. Memory theorists offer varying definitions of autobiographical memory, but generally such memories give a sense of remembering that the self previously experienced certain events (e.g., "I remember I was sick on my last birthday"), sometimes even mentally reliving what happened as opposed to simply knowing semantic de-contextualized facts about the self (e.g., "I know my birthday is January 14"), although by some definitions both "remembering" and "knowing" are involved in autobiographical memory (Conway & Rubin, 1993). Autobiographical memory is especially distinct in ASD: The scientific evidence, discussed by many of the contributors of this book, reveals autobiographical memory deficits in those with versus without ASD. However, as this is an

The Wiley Handbook of Memory, Autism Spectrum Disorder, and the Law, First Edition.
Edited by Jonni L. Johnson, Gail S. Goodman, and Peter C. Mundy.

emerging field of research, agreement on theoretical mechanisms underlying these shortfalls in memory performance in ASD has yet to be reached.

We have arranged the first section of the book to reflect differing theoretical viewpoints. Part 1 begins with how memory operates or is organized. Gaigg and Bowler address this important topic in their chapter on relational processing theory (Chapter 1), Miller and colleague's chapter offers an alternative view in their application of fuzzy trace theory (Chapter 2), and Williams outlines a third view for information processing and executive function theory that uniquely contends that memory function in ASD is a derivation, not deviation, of memory functioning (Chapter 3). Chapters 4 and 5 provide a specific focus on theoretical mechanisms that may influence autobiographical memory functioning in ASD in the domains of Theory of Mind (Souchay, Ohlsson, & Zalla) and the development of the self (Lind, Williams, Grainger, & Landsiedel), respectively, as both Theory of Mind and self-development are known to be diminished or underdeveloped in ASD. Soper and colleagues' chapter rounds out the section by discussing ways in which multiple mechanisms and individual differences potentially integrate together to influence the functioning of autobiographical memory and how this could create difficulties within the legal system (Chapter 6).

Empirical findings and methodological assessments

Part 2 of the book offers readers thorough summaries of research on autobiographical and eyewitness memory in those with and without ASD. In each chapter, when research is recounted, specific details about the samples are described as possible. For example, information is provided for each study about the samples tested in regard to ASD diagnosis/severity, age, gender, and cognitive functioning levels (e.g., IQ) when such information is available. In most research on autobiographical memory in ASD, individuals who can provide verbal memory reports are assessed, as reflected in the chapters here as well. Although, in the future, research on memory in nonverbal or limited-verbal individuals with ASD will provide vital new knowledge, the legal system largely relies on verbal eyewitness reports, which is our book's focus.

The chapters by Goddard (Chapter 7) and Crane and Maras (Chapter 8) present a developmental perspective on what is currently known about autobiographical memory functioning in children and adults with ASD, respectively. These contributions are then followed by two chapters that review factors known to influence eyewitness memory and eyewitness identification in typically developing (TD) children (Chae, Hobbs, & Bederian-Gardner, Chapter 9) and adults (Wood & Davis, Chapter 10). These chapters are meant to provide grounding in eyewitness memory research, in general, which may be especially helpful for readers who are more familiar with the ASD literature. These chapters reveal that eyewitness memory is not perfect, even in TD individuals. Chae and colleagues, particularly, emphasize how development during childhood can influence memory accuracy. Wood and Davis discuss many issues in adult eyewitness identification research that ASD memory researchers have not begun to address (e.g., influences on the reliability of eyewitness identification). We end this section with a contribution by Carlin (Chapter 11) that offers a critical lens on experimental methodology, demonstrating the field's need for consistent, well-designed, and transparent study findings. Overall, Parts 1 and 2 of the book address theories and empirical findings of how memory operates in ASD compared to TD individuals, setting the stage for the third and final section of the book that addresses the practical, legal side of this topic.

Investigative tools and legal application

In a legal setting, autobiographical recollection of an experienced event that is criminal in nature is called eyewitness memory. Witnessing a store robbery would require one to tell what the self or others experienced while at the store, ideally in a way that aids in the pursuit of justice. Understanding the accuracy of such memories—their creation, malleability, preservation, and retrieval—is of utmost importance from a legal perspective. In legal application examples, eyewitness memory serves as the basis of a victim's outcry to police officers, forensic interviewers, educators, and clinicians about wrong doings; a witness's testimony during a deposition or hearing; or a defendant's answers to questions during an interrogation.

Unfortunately, some areas of the legal system are unequipped to provide adequate legal services to individuals with ASD and stagnant in instilling ample, appropriate training for legal professionals. Legal professionals have pulled together anecdotal collections and case studies to assist in training investigators on how to interact with and investigate cases involving individuals with ASD (e.g., Taylor, Mesibov, & Debbaudt, 2009), yet they lack important information from scientific studies to facilitate this training (Smith, Polloway, Patton, & Beyer, 2008).

Given this applied need, we have arranged the third part of the book to address existing forensic techniques for interviewing individuals with ASD as well as to address other legal considerations. Brewer and Young (Chapter 12) introduce readers to situations where difficulties arise within the legal system due to misunderstood and misinterpreted characteristics of ASD, highlighting that most of our knowledge on meeting the needs of individuals with ASD in the legal system comes from a few observations and case studies. Thus, providing tools that trained professionals could use to collect accurate eyewitness statements would be a starting point in delivering adequate services to individuals with ASD.

The next three chapters address this starting point by discussing three forensic interview protocols currently in use by professionals. Each chapter outlines the conceptual and research basis of the protocol, and offers suggestions and evidence as to why the protocol may be effective for use with individuals with ASD or may need to be further tested and modified. Richards and Milne (Chapter 13) review the use of the Cognitive Interview protocol in ASD, identifying many of the theoretical mechanisms discussed early on in the book as having influence on the Cognitive Interview's administration. Camparo, Guzman, and Saywitz (Chapter 14) present the Narrative Elaboration Technique highlighting the need to limit cognitive demands on executive functioning and verbal skill when interviewing individuals with ASD. Malloy, Mugno, and Arndorfer (Chapter 15) review the use of the National Institute of Child Health and Human Development (NICHD) Investigative Interview and the Ten-Step Investigative Interview protocols, describing how these protocols may minimize difficulties for those with ASD by addressing the social demands imposed by a forensic interview. Although these latter two chapters describe protocols that have yet to be empirically tested in an ASD sample, the authors provide evidence of the use of these protocols with children with developmental disabilities. Overall, the authors of the three chapters encourage future researchers to incorporate novel experimental designs examining the efficacy of these protocols for individuals with ASD.

The final two chapters address remaining concerns from clinical and legal points of view. Krackow (Chapter 16) offers a clinical viewpoint, describing such topics as how mandated reporters should respond when collecting eyewitness accounts from individuals with ASD as well as describing how characteristics of ASD (e.g., co-morbidity) present further challenges for mandated reporters. The book ends with several thought-provoking issues, raised by Goldfarb and Gonzalez (Chapter 17), for the legal system to tackle, such as the challenges an individual with ASD would face in taking the stand to testify and whether or not individuals with ASD can tell a lie. These are vital issues that future studies will need to address.

Concomitant Concerns

Overall, from this book, readers will gain a sense of what is known about autobiographical memory in ASD, especially when such memory becomes an eyewitness account as well as a sense of the existing forensic interview tools available. This information is essential so that discourse among researchers, practitioners, and legal professionals results in dissemination of valid, scientific findings. It is also vital for future research in this budding area of psychology.

Yet, on the horizon, looms what we have identified to be two large storms that future researchers must address and that readers should consider. The first consideration is one of urgency: The growing prevalence rate of ASD underscores the importance of future research on topics discussed in the chapters. The second consideration addresses the difficulty of implementing policy changes given a continuously reclassified and heterogeneous population. These considerations, discussed, in turn, next, contextualize evidence presented in this book

Prevalence of ASD

Within the past 20 years, the prevalence rate of ASD diagnoses has increased by more than 200%, from 1 in 150 to 1 in 68 in the United States ("Autism Spectrum Disorder," 2014; Christensen et al., 2012), with increases in prevalence rates also being noted globally elsewhere. This prevalence spike may be indicative of increased awareness of ASD, availability of services, and training to diagnose the disorder as well as a societal acknowledgment of the disorder's spectrum form. These prevalence rates in society foretell increased numbers of individuals with ASD becoming involved in the legal system as eyewitnesses, victims, or perpetrators (e.g., Brewer & Young, 2014; Cheely, Carpenter, Letourneau, Nicholas, Charles, & King, 2012; King & Murphy, 2014). Compared to those without, individuals with disabilities, including ASD, are seven times more likely to have interaction with legal professionals, most often police officers (Debbaudt, 2001), yet empirically derived and scientifically validated tools and trainings to meet these challenges are virtually non-existent.

From a moral standpoint, being ill-prepared to offer accommodations can lead to psychological harm to individuals who are not afforded available means to pursue justice, and from an economic, risk management standpoint, this can also lead to civil suits. Further, the legal system's possible misinterpretation of statements provided by individuals with ASD raises concerns about false confessions, false allegations, and false imprisonment, all of which hold moral and economic costs. Other societal systems (e.g., educational, medical) have made strides in providing training to their work forces as well as implementing curriculums, services, and general care for individuals with ASD. If the legal system continues to show little recognition of increased ASD prevalence, then it is essentially and knowingly excluding this population from a crucial part of society. Yet, the legal system is quite unique in its need to balance three important forces at once (e.g., needs of the accuser, the accused, and society at large). Thus, the legal system requires *consistent* empirical backing to make changes while remaining balanced. Presently, science falls short of the legal requirement of consistency, as described, in turn, next.

Evolving classification and heterogeneity of ASD

Since its earliest descriptions more than 70 years ago (e.g., Baker, 2013; Masi, DeMayo, Glozier, & Guastella, 2017), ASD has had an ever-evolving classification. Fortunately, professionals have developed a greater understanding of what individuals with ASD are or are not able to do. Only in 1980 did the American Psychiatric Association (APA) include in the *Diagnostic and Statistical Manual for Mental Disorders* (DSM-3) a description of autism disorder as being a *spectrum* disorder. This, in turn, permitted the diagnosis and development of treatment plans for individuals displaying detached emotional responses and difficulties with social communication and interactions. In 1994, the DSM-4 added Asperger syndrome as a separate classification, mainly displaying difficulties in social interaction; however, in the most recent version, the DSM-5 has collapsed Asperger syndrome to be included in the spectrum of autism disorders, described as a higher functioning form of ASD marked with greater verbal abilities (APA, 2013). An examination of the historical classification of ASD is important when thinking through ideas or results described in the chapters, and in thinking about the full challenge for deriving findings to a "group" who, *diagnostically speaking*, may no longer "exist" (for a historical review, see Baker, 2013; Ousley & Cermek, 2014).

For example, the DSM-4, which included the separate classification of Asperger syndrome from autism, distinguished between Asperger syndrome and high-functioning ASD; the former indicated that the main deficit was social interaction and communication, whereas the latter indicated deficits in social interaction and communication coupled with early childhood language delay (Autism Speaks, 2010). Thus, researchers at the time who examined memory abilities in group of individuals with Asperger syndrome did not need to account for how verbal ability might influence participant responses to suggestive questions, but researchers examining these same abilities in a group of individuals with high-functioning ASD would (or should). By today's standard, both groups would be called high-functioning ASD. This has clear implications for determining whether accommodations to limit the cognitive and social demands should be permitted for all individuals with ASD or just those who qualify for assistance. Who will determine who qualifies? Or what level of deficit qualifies for what type of accommodation? How will these variations in accommodations for "the population of individuals with ASD" be perceived by societal members (e.g., jurors)?

The heterogeneity of the ASD population has some researchers arguing in favor of subgroups within the ASD population (e.g., Masi et al., 2017; Ousley & Cermek, 2014). In response, the research community has begun using biomarkers as a way to identify subgroups of the ASD population that respond to certain kinds of treatments as well as experience greater or lesser degrees of difficulties in selective cognitive domains. Biomarkers range from being genetic variations to neurological patterns of activation to aberrant behavioral tendencies. Stratifying the ASD population with biomarkers sounds promising for the field in developing useful tools and training programs that would be supported by psychological theory. Although this use may, in part, limit the generalizability of past research, a definite advantage to identifying accurate subgroups permits formation of appropriate expectations about cognitive and social capabilities. Thus, the field can create more precise tools, services, and training to better meet the needs of individuals with ASD. That said, the hope is that the biomarker approach will result in coherent and useful subgroup classifications.

A similar concern for researchers applying memory findings in ASD to the legal system is accounting for the effects of co-morbid diagnoses, which may further exacerbate ASD symptoms. Individuals with ASD experience co-morbidity with several psychiatric disorders, including attention deficit (hyperactivity) disorder, anxiety disorders, phobias, learning disabilities, depression, oppositional defiant disorder, intellectual disabilities, and conduct disorder (e.g., Salazar, Baird, Chandler, Tseng, O'Sullivan, Howlin, … & Simonoff, 2015; Simonoff, Pickles, Charman, Chandler, Loucas, & Baird, 2008). It is estimated that approximately 70% of individuals experience co-morbid issues (e.g., Mazzone, Rua, & Reale, 2012); others have reported summaries of studies indicating a range from 63% to 96% comorbidity rate (Van Steensel, Bögels, & de Bruin, 2013). Although not a topic thoroughly covered in this volume, we recognize that co-morbidity is an additional concern for researchers moving forward in this field; unfortunately, the effects of co-morbid types is presently overlooked in memory and ASD studies.

Overall, the ever-evolving classification of individuals with ASD, coupled with their hallmark heterogeneity in cognitive and social abilities, delays the development of adequate accommodations, postponing recommendations for policy changes.

Concluding Remarks

The study of memory in ASD is not new (e.g., Boucher & Bowler, 2008), yet many would contend that we are just beginning to understand specifically how *autobiographical* memory develops and operates in ASD. Although the evidence is often presented to argue in favor of different theories and mechanisms, instances of overlap in the cited research of this book demonstrate the dire need for empirical attention to this area of study. Moreover, the legal application of autobiographical memory is relatively new and has had little empirical attention, although interest is currently growing. This emerging field requires an integration of expertise from multiple areas of study: autism, autobiographical memory, and the law.

We are thankful to the contributors of this edited volume whose efforts in summarizing these disparate fields are to be commended. Traversing a new empirical frontier, one with immense ethical considerations, is a daunting task. We hope this book will propel discussion forward, foster a network of researchers developing expertise in this area of study, and lead to new scientific discoveries that ultimately improve the lives of individuals with ASD.

References

American Psychiatric Association (2013). *Diagnostic and statistical manual of mental disorders: DSM-5*. Washington, D.C.: American Psychiatric Association.

Autism Speaks: How are Asperger Syndrome and high functioning Autism Spectrum Disorder different? (2010). Retrieved from https://www.autismspeaks.org/sites/default/files/documents/as-hfa/diff_as-hfa_tool_kit.pdf

Autism Spectrum Disorder: Data and statistics (2014). Retrieved from https://www.cdc.gov/ncbddd/autism/data.html

Baker, J. (2013). Autism at 70: Redrawing the boundaries. *New England Journal of Medicine*, *369*, 1089–1091. doi:10.1056/NEJMp1306380

Boucher, J., & Bowler, D. (Eds.). (2008). *Memory in autism: Theory and evidence*. Cambridge, England: Cambridge University Press.

Brewer, N., & Young, R. (2014). *Crime and autism spectrum disorder: Myths and mechanisms*. London, England: Jessica Kingsley Publishing.

Cheely, C. A., Carpenter, L. A., Letourneau, E. J., Nicholas, J. S., Charles, J., & King, L. B. (2012). The prevalence of youth with autism spectrum disorders in the criminal justice system. *Journal of Autism and Developmental Disorders*, *42*, 1856–1862.

Christensen, D. L., Bilder, D. A., Zahorodny, W., Pettygrove, S., Durkin, M. S., Fitzgerald, R. T., … & Yeargin-Allsopp, M. (2016). Prevalence and characteristics of Autism Spectrum Disorder among children aged 8 years: Autism and developmental disabilities monitoring network, 11 sites, United States, 2012. *Surveillance Summaries*, *65*(3), 1–23.

Conway, M., & Rubin, D. (1993). The structure of autobiographical memory. In A. F. Collins, S. E. Gathercole, M. A. Conway, & P. E. Morris (Eds.), *Theories of memory* (pp. 103–137). Hillsdale, NJ: Erlbaum.

Debbaudt, D. (2001) *Autism, advocates, and law enforcement professionals recognizing and reducing risk situations for people with autism spectrum disorders*. London, England: Jessica Kingsley Publishing.

King, C., & Murphy, G. H. (2014). A systematic review of people with autism spectrum disorder and the criminal justice system. *Journal of Autism & Developmental Disorders*, *44*, 2717–2733.

Masi, A., DeMayo, M. M., Glozier, N., & Guastella, A. J. (2017). An overview of Autism Spectrum Disorder, heterogeneity and treatment options. *Neuroscience Bulletin*, *33*(2), 183–193. http://doi.org/10.1007/s12264-017-0100-y

Mazzone, L., Ruta, L., & Reale, L. (2012). Psychiatric comorbidities in Asperger Syndrome and high functioning Autism: Diagnostic challenges. *Annals of General Psychology*, *11*, 16. doi:10.1186/1744-859X-11-16

Ousley, O., & Cermak, T. (2014). Autism Spectrum Disorder: Defining dimensions and subgroups. *Current Developmental Disorders Reports*, *1*, 20–28. http://doi.org/10.1007/s40474-013-0003-1

Salazar, F., Baird, G., Chandler, S., Tseng, E., O'Sullivan, T., Howlin, P., … & Simonoff, E. (2015). Co-occurring psychiatric disorders in preschool and elementary school-aged children with autism spectrum disorder. *Journal of Autism & Developmental Disorders*, *45*, 2283–2361.

Simonoff, E., Pickles, A., Charman, T., Chandler, S., Loucas, T., & Baird, G. (2008) Psychiatric disorders in children with autism spectrum disorders: Prevalence, comorbidity, and associated factors in a population-derived sample. *Journal of the American Academy of Child Adolescent Psychiatry*, *47*, 921–929. doi:10.1097/CHI.0b013e318179964f

Smith, T., Polloway, E. A., Patton, J. R., & Beyer, J. F. (2008). Individuals with intellectual and developmental disabilities in the criminal justice system and implications for transition planning. *Education & Training in Developmental Disabilities*, *43*, 421–430.

Taylor, K., Mesibov, G., & Debbaudt, D. (2009). Autism in the criminal justice system. *North Carolina Bar Journal*, *14*, 32–36.

Van Steensel, F. J., Bögels, S. M., & de Bruin, E. I. (2013). Psychiatric comorbidity in children with autism spectrum disorders: A comparison with children with ADHD. *Journal of Child & Family Studies*, *22*, 368–376.

Part I

Autobiographical Memory Theories and Autism Spectrum Disorder

1

A Relational Processing Framework of Memory in Autism Spectrum Disorder

Sebastian B. Gaigg and Dermot M. Bowler

Ever since the seminal studies of Beate Hermelin and Neil O'Connor during the 1960s and 1970s, it has been known that individuals with autism spectrum disorder (ASD), compared to typically developing individuals, learn and remember things differently. They tend not to benefit from meaningful relations among stimuli to facilitate memory (e.g., Tager-Flusberg, 1991), their memory is often void of contextual details that situates past events in a particular place and time in personal history (e.g., Lind & Bowler, 2010a), and they often find it difficult to spontaneously recall information without aids for retrieval (Bowler, Gardiner, & Berthollier, 2004). At the same time, many individuals with ASD can also demonstrate exceptional memory skills. Autistic savants such as Stephen Wiltshire, for example, draw cityscapes in intricate detail following just a few minutes of exposure (Treffert, 1988, 2009)[1] and although such eidetic memory is rare, it is not uncommon for individuals with ASD to demonstrate superior rote memory skills (Hermelin & O'Connor, 1970)[2] or to remember details of events that would escape almost everyone else (e.g., Grandin, 2006). This pattern of strengths and difficulties is neither a unique nor a necessary feature of ASD, but interest in this topic is growing because of the functional consequences that memory difficulties can have for an individual. This is, perhaps, nowhere as evident as in the context of the criminal justice system.

Whether it is as a victim, witness, or even a suspected perpetrator of crime, individuals who come into contact with the criminal justice system will often be required to provide accurate accounts of past events that should be rich in relevant detail and provide a coherent narrative of the unfolding of events over time (i.e., who did what

1 See also http://www.stephenwiltshire.co.uk/

2 *Rote memory* describes memory for material that is relatively meaningless, either by virtue of the material per se (e.g., abstract shapes; arbitrary sequences of letters, numbers, or words), or by virtue of the relations between the material and its context (e.g., remembering train time-tables without a need to travel on relevant routes).

The Wiley Handbook of Memory, Autism Spectrum Disorder, and the Law, First Edition.
Edited by Jonni L. Johnson, Gail S. Goodman, and Peter C. Mundy.

to whom, where, and when). Recent evidence is beginning to shed light on how individuals with ASD cope with such demands and how their particular profile of memory strengths and weaknesses impacts their ability to give evidence. To provide a broader context for this emerging literature, the present chapter provides an overview of the memory profile in ASD from the perspective of the distinctions between *relational* and *item-specific* memory processes on the one hand, and between *recollection* and *familiarity* on the other. After a brief introduction to these distinctions, three lines of evidence are summarized, which suggest that *relational* memory and *recollection* are compromised in ASD whereas *item-specific* memory and *familiarity* are relatively preserved. A final section then considers what the implications of this pattern are for how individuals with ASD should be supported in the context of the criminal justice system. It is important to note, however, that the evidence summarized in this chapter primarily concerns individuals with ASD who do not have significant intellectual and/or language impairments.

Distinctions in memory

It is now well established that our ability to remember the past is the result of a number of interacting processes that govern how memories are initially formed, how securely they are retained, and how likely it is that they can be retrieved at a later stage. A detailed overview of the various distinctions that have been drawn in this context is beyond the scope of this chapter (see Neath & Suprenant, 2003, for comprehensive overviews). Instead, we focus on two related distinctions that have proven useful for understanding the memory profile associated with ASD: between *relational* and *item-specific* processing on the one hand, and *recollection* versus *familiarity* on the other.

The distinction between relational and item-specific processing was first formalized in a pair of publications by Einstein and Hunt (1980) and Hunt and Einstein (1981) to integrate two influential perspectives of the time about which information people needed to process effectively in order to ensure successful memory. One view held that memory crucially depended on the processing of commonalities between to-be-remembered elements or events, which could serve to organize material around a common theme that would subsequently aid retrieval (Tulving, 1966; Tulving & Patkau, 1962). Evidence for the operation of such organizational processes stemmed from the observation that participants generally remembered sets of interrelated items better than unrelated items (Cofer, 1965; Hyde & Jenkins, 1969) and that this memory advantage was predicted by the extent to which participants spontaneously organize to-be-remembered stimuli into clusters of categorically (e.g., fruit) or associatively (e.g., table-chair) related items during retrieval (Tulving, 1962, 1966). There was also evidence for a rather different view, however, which emphasized the processing of the unique details of to-be-remembered stimuli as important for successful memory. Specifically, it was well established that memory is better when stimuli are processed for their meaning instead of their perceptual properties (e.g., Tresselt & Mayzner, 1960). According to the *Levels of Processing* (LoP; Craik & Lockhart, 1972) account, this is because meaning is represented at a deeper level of an information processing hierarchy than more superficial perceptual information, and deeper levels of processing render memory traces more elaborate and distinct, and thus, more readily accessible for retrieval.

Organizational and LoP accounts of memory seemed antithetical because they each emphasized the processing of *relational* versus *item-specific* information as important for successful memory. However, Einstein and Hunt (1980) argued that both processes could be operating in parallel and contribute independently to successful memory. They argued that the extent to which people spontaneously process either type of information depends on the nature of the to-be-remembered material. Highly interrelated stimuli, such as categorically related words or objects that are commonly found together in a particular room, would naturally encourage relational processing, whereas stimuli that are more distinctive (e.g., a knife in a bathroom rather than a kitchen) would encourage item-specific processing. Einstein and Hunt (1980) reasoned that if both types of information contribute independently to successful memory, encouraging relational processing should be most effective for material that would spontaneously give rise to item-specific processing. Conversely, encouraging item-specific processing should be most effective for material that would otherwise stimulate relational processing. These predictions were confirmed in a series of experiments in which participants were asked to study lists of related and/or unrelated words under conditions that either drew attention to relational (e.g., sorting words into categories) or item-specific (e.g., rating words on pleasantness) information (Einstein & Hunt, 1980; Hunt & Einstein, 1981; Hunt & Seta, 1984). In all experiments, words that were obviously related were better remembered following item-specific processing, whereas less obviously related words were better remembered following relational processing. It is interesting to note that memory was best overall when participants engaged both processes together, confirming that relational and item-specific information contribute *additively* to memory success. Another important observation was that study instructions that directed participants' attention to relational information were most beneficial for facilitating their ability to freely recall material, whereas instructions that directed attention to item-specific information were most beneficial for their ability to discriminate studied from non-studied items in tests of recognition (Einstein & Hunt, 1980) or to retrieve items in response to cues such as category labels (Hunt & Mcdaniel, 1993; Hunt & Smith, 1996). This finding was important because it established a functional independence between relational and item-specific processing with the former serving an organizational function that can guide unaided retrieval (e.g., Tulving, 1962, 1966), while the latter serves a discriminative function that renders items more distinct, and thus, more easily identifiable on tests of recognition or accessible in response to relevant cues. To put this into context, relational processing would be expected to enhance an eye-witnesses ability to freely describe the appearance of a perpetrator of a crime or any weapons or objects that may have been involved. By contrast, item-specific processing would be expected to benefit the identification of a perpetrator among similar individuals in a line-up, or to identify a specific knife among many as the weapon involved in a crime.

Since the early studies of Hunt and colleagues, a wealth of behavioral and neuropsychological evidence has accumulated to support the distinction between relational and item-specific processing (Davachi, 2006), which has proved useful not only for explaining typical memory functions, but also the memory difficulties that are associated with older age (Old & Naveh-Benjamin, 2008) and disorders such as schizophrenia (Ranganath, Minzenberg, & Ragland, 2008) and ASD (e.g., Bowler, Gaigg, & Lind, 2011). A complementary distinction that has proven equally useful in these contexts is that between *recollection* and *familiarity,* which differentiates between distinct ways of retrieving memories rather than the processes involved during memory formation. Recollection describes the retrieval of contextually rich memories that involve details about where, when, and how a particular experience occurred and how different elements of that experience relate to one another. A prototypical example of recollection is brought to life in Marcel Proust's *In Search of Lost Time* (1946), where the protagonist, upon tasting a Madeleine, re-lives the following experience from his childhood (see also Hobson & Hermelin, 2008):

> And suddenly the memory revealed itself. The taste was that of the little piece of Madeleine which on Sunday mornings at Combray (because on those mornings I did not go out before mass), when I went to say good morning to her in her bedroom, my aunt Léonie used to give me, dipping it first in her own cup of tea or tisane (p.68).

In contrast to such vivid recollections, familiarity describes the process of retrieving knowledge that is not bound to a particular place or time in our past such as knowing the boiling point water, or recognizing our butcher on the bus without realizing where we know him from. As these descriptions suggest, the distinction between recollection and familiarity is closely related to that between relational and item-specific processing in so far as that recollection involves the retrieval of relational information whereas familiarity is primarily based on the retrieval of item-specific information. Although there are nuances to this parallel that are beyond the scope of this chapter (see Mayes, Montaldi, & Migo, 2007), considerable evidence corroborates a close link between these processes. First, neural evidence indicates that the brain areas that support relational processing during memory formation are also involved in retrieval in the form of recollection while the areas that support item-specific processing are involved in retrieval in the form of familiarity (Davachi, 2006; Mayes et al., 2007). In other words, the brain mechanism recruited by both relational processing and by recollection is different from the one broadly shared by item-specific processing and familiarity. This particular pattern of functional separation and overlap is further supported by evidence from several patient populations who demonstrate parallel impairments in relational processing and recollection while item-specific processing and familiarity are spared (Ragland et al., 2012). Perhaps more relevant for the present purposes, evidence also shows that recollection critically underpins free recall, whereas recognition memory can be mediated by recollection or by familiarity (see Yonelinas, 2002). Returning to the earlier example above, witnesses might be able to pick out a perpetrator from a line-up because one of the individuals feels distinctly more familiar or because they can recollect seeing that individual in the specific context of the witnessed crime (e.g., where they stood, what they wore, who they were arguing with, etc.). By contrast, a sense of familiarity would not suffice for witnesses to freely describe the appearance of a perpetrator because such a description would critically depend on the ability to recollect the combination of details (skin tone, height, eye color, etc.) that identify a specific individual.

To sum up these somewhat tedious technicalities, the processing of relations among the elements of unfolding events serves to organize material in memory, which is particularly important when we subsequently try to freely recall the events or bring back to mind rich contextual detail (i.e., recollection). The processing of individual elements of events, by contrast, serves to aid the discrimination of previously encountered versus new material on tests of recognition through a sense of familiarity. In most situations, people process both relational and item-specific information in parallel, and thus, retrieve memories through a combination of recollection and familiarity. However, as the following sections illustrate, several lines of evidence suggest that individuals with ASD may find it relatively more difficult to process relational than item-specific information, and therefore, rely more heavily on familiarity rather than recollection when retrieving past events.

Familiarity, recollection, and remembering the personal past

A general observation in memory studies of individuals with ASD is that they tend to experience greater difficulties on tests of free recall than tests of recognition or cued recall (Boucher, Mayes, & Bigham, 2012). In its own right, this pattern suggests greater difficulties with retrieval through recollection than through familiarity, but there is also more direct evidence for this dissociation. Specifically, several studies have taken advantage of the fact that the distinction between recollection and familiarity is respected in natural language where we differentiate between events that we *remember* and facts that we *know*. In a typical experiment that draws on this distinction, participants would be asked to study a set of stimuli, and subsequently, indicate whether they *remember* or *know* the items they recognize. Participants are told that remembering must entail recognition of the item along with additional contextual information, such as remembering where, when, or how it was presented, or remembering any thoughts that might have come to mind at the time of studying it. Knowing, by contrast, must entail recognition of the item without any additional contextual information.

The "Remember/Know" paradigm has been used extensively in the study of typical memory function (Gardiner, 2001; Gardiner, Ramponi, & Richardson-Klavehn, 2002; Yonelinas, 2002), and several studies of ASD have revealed relatively specific difficulties with remembering but not knowing (Bowler, Gardiner, & Gaigg, 2007; Bowler, Gardiner, & Grice, 2000; Cooper et al., 2015; Souchay, Wojcik, Williams, Crathern, & Clarke, 2013). For example, Bowler, Gardiner, and Grice (2000) asked participants with and without ASD to study a list of high- and low-frequency words, and found that the ASD group reported fewer remember but more know experiences than comparison participants. Both groups demonstrated a well-established word-frequency effect, whereby low-frequency words were better remembered than high-frequency words, and only recognition in the form of remembering but not knowing was affected by word frequency in both groups. This observation was important because it confirmed that experiences of remembering were quantitatively reduced but not qualitatively different in ASD compared to non-ASD participants, which was further corroborated by Bowler, Gaigg, and Gardiner (2008) across three experiments (but see Massand & Bowler, 2015; Massand, Bowler, Mottron, Hosein, & Jemel, 2013, for relevant neurophysiological data). In other words, when individuals with ASD say that they "remember" or "know" something, they tend to describe qualitatively similar experiences to individuals without ASD. Souchay et al. (2013) further extended this finding to recognition memory for pictures, where individuals with ASD again reported fewer remembering experiences in the context of overall preserved levels of recognition. Finally, Tanweer, Rathbone, and Souchay (2010) showed that even when individuals with ASD retrieve experiences about their personal pasts, they are less likely to *remember* these experiences in vivid contextual detail while they have no difficulties *knowing* which events occurred. This last finding has been replicated across a number of studies investigating autobiographical memory retrieval (Crane & Goddard, 2008; Crane, Goddard, & Pring, 2009; Crane, Lind, & Bowler, 2013; Lind & Bowler, 2010b; Lind, Williams, Bowler, & Peel, 2014). Such findings carry the important implication that witnesses with ASD can be expected to "know" what they have witnessed even if they would have difficulties furnishing this knowledge with concrete contextual detail. Converging evidence from so-called source memory studies lend further support to this conclusion.

In a typical source memory experiment, participants are asked to study items that are presented in different formats or contexts. For instance, stimuli might be presented in different fonts, in different locations on a screen, in different lists or by different people. Alternatively, participants might be asked to do different things with the stimuli such as simply reading them, thinking about actions related to them or generating rhymes. The former constitute examples of *external* source information in that the participant plays no active role in influencing the contextual details that define the presentation of the item. The latter constitute *internal* source information because the participants' thoughts or behavior define the context under which the items are studied. In line with the observation of attenuated recollection in other paradigms, a number of studies have shown that individuals with ASD often have difficulties remembering such contextual details (Bigham, Boucher, Mayes, & Anns, 2010; Lind & Bowler, 2009; Ring, Gaigg, & Bowler, 2015; Russell & Jarrold, 1999), particularly when these details need to be freely recalled. For instance, Bowler et al., (2004) asked participants to study lists of words either by actively performing one of four encoding tasks (e.g., think about a rhyme) or by passively studying words that were presented on the top or bottom of the screen or in a male or female voice. On a subsequent recognition test, participants first needed to indicate whether or not they recognized words from the previous study lists. If they did, they were then either asked to recall how the word was presented or what encoding task they had performed, or to choose the relevant contextual detail from a list. The findings showed that individuals with ASD were worse than comparison participants at recalling contextual details, but they were as good as comparison participants in recognizing them. Bowler, Gaigg, and Gardiner (2015) extended this observation to show that ASD participants benefit significantly more than a comparison group from retrieval support to remember in which of three screen locations words had been studied earlier. Similarly, difficulties in recalling the sequential order in which dots are presented on a screen are also ameliorated in ASD when relevant screen locations are highlighted for the participant to choose from (Bowler, Poirier, Martin, & Gaigg, 2016). In other words, whereas the free recall of contextual source information often proves difficult for individuals with ASD, source recognition often does not, which is generally in line with difficulties in recollection rather than familiarity processes during retrieval.

Although the evidence outlined thus far suggests that ASD is characterized by difficulties with recollection but not familiarity during memory retrieval, none of the studies outlined above provide evidence that this difference is linked to abnormalities with the processing of relational versus item-specific information during memory formation. The next sections set out evidence that addresses this issue directly, but first it is useful to note another aspect of the source memory literature that lends indirect support. As previously noted, overall levels of recognition memory are generally preserved in ASD. This is true for studies that have employed the Remember/Know recognition procedure (e.g., Bowler et al., 2007; Gaigg, Bowler, Ecker, Calvo-Merino, & Murphy, 2015), and the majority of studies that have tested recognition for single items (see Boucher et al., 2012, for a comprehensive review). It may seem surprising therefore that in the context of source memory studies, individuals with ASD often demonstrate recognition memory difficulties for the to-be-remembered items. For instance, in the study by Bowler et al. (2004) outlined earlier, the authors observed a small but nevertheless significant recognition memory decrement in the ASD relative to the comparison group. In a source memory experiment by Massand and Bowler (2015) that required participants to study line drawings presented in one of two different colors, results also revealed marginally attenuated recognition memory in ASD alongside difficulties in remembering the color of the pictures that were recognized. Substantially attenuated item recognition was also observed by Ring, Gaigg, and Bowler (2016) when participants were asked to study various sets of abstract images that were presented in different locations on a screen. These observations may seem at odds with the finding of generally preserved recognition memory in ASD, but as the Remember/Know procedure illustrates, recognition performance can be mediated by recollection or by familiarity. Unlike other recognition memory paradigms, source memory paradigms may direct participants' attention to the relations between items because of the source properties they share (e.g., the screen locations). This relational information could augment item recognition through recollection, thus disadvantaging individuals with ASD vis-a-vis comparison groups. Admittedly, this is a rather speculative interpretation, but it serves to highlight that individuals with ASD must not be assumed to have preserved memory for item information in all circumstances.

The encoding of item-specific and relational meaning

When Hermelin and O'Connor first investigated memory functions in ASD, one of their earliest observations was that autistic children did not seem to demonstrate a memory advantage for meaningful over nonmeaningful material. For instance, whereas children without autism could recall sequences of words that formed grammatically intact sentences far better than randomly ordered word sequences, children with autism recalled both types of sequence equally well (Hermelin & O'Connor, 1967). Similarly, children without autism could recall sequences of conceptually related words or pictures better than unrelated sequences while children with autism could not (Hermelin & O'Connor, 1967). Many subsequent studies have corroborated these initial observations (e.g., Maister, Simons, & Plaisted-Grant, 2013; Tager-Flusberg, 1991), but a number of studies have also demonstrated similar memory benefits for meaningful over non-meaningful material in ASD (Ameli, Courchesne, Lincoln, Kaufman, & Grillon, 1988). The distinction between item-specific and relational memory processes has helped to resolve this apparent inconsistency by suggesting that individuals with ASD have relatively few difficulties drawing on the meaning of individual items to facilitate memory, whereas difficulties arise when meaning can be derived from relations among the items.

One of the first studies to suggest that item-specific meaning facilitates memory relatively typically in ASD was a study by Ameli et al. (1988), who asked children with and without ASD to study sets of either meaningful pictures or abstract line drawings. During subsequent test trials, children needed to identify new images that had been inserted in the original study sets, and both groups of children found this substantially easier for the meaningful pictures rather than the abstract shapes. Further evidence for preserved processing of item-specific meaning in ASD has come from studies employing levels of processing manipulations. As noted earlier, memory is generally superior following the processing of stimuli for their meaning instead of more superficial perceptual properties. Mottron, Morasse, and Belleville (2001) examined this in ASD by drawing participants' attention either to semantic (e.g., "show me the name of a vegetable") or perceptual (e.g., "Show me the word starting with NA") properties of different words. On a subsequent free-recall test, individuals with and without ASD demonstrated a similar memory advantage for the words encoded for their meaning. However, while comparison participants benefited more from semantic than perceptual cues to retrieve additional items they had not spontaneously recalled, ASD participants benefitted equally from both types of cues. Instead of suggesting an impairment in processing items for their meaning, this indicates an enhanced ability to process perceptual properties of stimuli in ASD, which was further corroborated by Toichi and Kamio (2002). These authors also asked participants to study words by drawing attention to their meaning (e.g., "Is it a drink?") or their perceptual features (e.g., "Does it sound like *table*?"). On a subsequent recognition memory test, comparison participants again demonstrated a clear memory advantage for the words encoded for their meaning. Although individuals with ASD did not demonstrate this advantage, this was not because of poorer memory for words encoded for their meaning, but because of superior memory for words processed for their perceptual properties. Thus, LoP studies suggest not only that the encoding of item-specific meaning is preserved in ASD, but also that the encoding of item-specific perceptual properties may be enhanced, which could make witnesses with ASD a particularly useful source of information about perceptual details of witnessed events that might escape a typical observer. For instance, witnesses with ASD may be better able to identify the specific colors of clothing, objects, or vehicles involved in a crime and they may be able to report details of the environment that might not necessarily be relevant to the crime per se (i.e., the central meaning of the event), but that could serve other witnesses as retrieval cues for further relevant details.

Studies examining associatively generated memory illusions further support the idea that the processing of item-specific meaning and perceptual details are preserved in ASD, while the processing of relational meaning is compromised. Specifically, when asked to study lists of words comprising items that are highly associated with a target word that is not on the list (e.g., *bed, pillow, night, dream*, and *tired* for the target word *sleep*), adults with ASD are as likely as comparison participants to falsely recall this target word (Bowler, Gardiner, Grice, & Saavalainen, 2000; Hillier, Campbell, Keillor, Phillips, & Beversdorf, 2007; but see Beversdorf et al., 2000, for subtle differences). At the same time, however, they tend to recall fewer of the actual items that are on the to-be-remembered list (Bowler et al., 2000). This apparent paradox is resolved when considering the fact that memory illusions are predicted primarily by the associative strength between each to-be-remembered list item and the critical target word, whereas veridical recall of the list items is predicted by the associative strength between the list items themselves[3] (Roediger, Watson, McDermott, & Gallo, 2001). In other words, memory illusions are elicited by virtue of the fact that all list items share an item-specific meaning, whereas free recall of list items is dependent on the utilization of this meaning to relate the items to one another. The pattern of preserved memory illusions alongside reduced recall of list items in ASD therefore suggests sufficient processing of item-specific meaning to elicit memory illusions, but difficulties utilizing this meaning to relate the to-be-remembered items to one another to facilitate veridical recall. It is interesting to note that in one of the experiments by Hillier et al. (2007), memory illusions were elicited for abstract shapes rather than meaningful words, and in that study, individuals with ASD were less likely to demonstrate illusory memories. Similar to the LoP studies, therefore studies of memory illusions suggest that the encoding of perceptual information may be enhanced in ASD.

A final line of evidence, which links difficulties in the processing of relational meaning to the difficulties individuals with ASD experience in recollection rather than familiarity during retrieval, stems from comparisons of tests of free recall, cued recall, and recognition. As noted earlier, relational processing serves an organizational function that is particularly important for free recall, whereas item-specific processing serves a discriminative function that aids performance on tests of recognition and cued recall (Hunt & Smith, 1996). The majority of studies that have demonstrated reduced memory benefits from meaningful relations between stimuli in ASD have employed tests of free recall (Bowler, Matthews, & Gardiner, 1997; Gaigg, Gardiner, & Bowler, 2008; Loth, Gómez, & Happé, 2011; Maister et al., 2013; Tager-Flusberg, 1991). On such tests, individuals with ASD also demonstrate reduced category clustering (Bowler, Gaigg, & Gardiner, 2009; Gaigg et al., 2008; Minshew & Goldstein, 1993), which indexes the type of organizational function that relational memory processes serve. By contrast, studies employing cued-recall (Bowler, Gaigg, & Gardiner, 2010; Mottron et al., 2001) or recognition procedures (Bowler et al., 2008) tend to find no ASD related impairment in using meaning to aid memory. For example, Tager-Flusberg (1991) found that children with autism benefited less than comparison children from categorical relations among words to facilitate free recall, but when memory was cued with appropriate category labels, no group differences were found. Similarly, Bowler and colleagues (2008) asked participants to study words that were presented either alongside related or unrelated context words (e.g., Crop-Grain vs. Crop-Screen). When memory was subsequently tested through free recall, only comparison participants demonstrated a memory advantage for words presented alongside related words, but when recognition memory was tested, both groups demonstrated a similar memory advantage for the words encoded in a meaningful context. Finally, a number of studies using the California Verbal Learning Test (CVLT) also show that individuals with ASD have difficulties drawing on meaningful relations among stimuli to facilitate primarily free recall rather than recognition or cued recall. The CVLT asks participants first to learn a list of categorically related words over five successive free-recall trials before cued-recall and recognition memory is assessed. Minshew and Goldstein (1993; also Minshew, Goldstein, Muenz, & Payton, 1992) found that ASD participants experienced difficulties during the free-recall learning trials while their

[3] *Associative strength*, in this context, refers to the probability with which the presentation of an item leads participants to respond with another item (i.e., the target word or another list item) during free association where participants are simply asked to say the first words that come to mind.

performance on the recognition test was virtually identical to that of a comparison group. Although findings on the cued-recall part of the CVLT are somewhat mixed (Minshew & Goldstein, 1993 vs. Minshew et al., 1992 and Minshew & Goldstein, 2001), many other studies have reported preserved cued recall for related material in ASD (Boucher & Warrington, 1976; Bowler et al., 1997; Bowler et al., 2010; Gardiner, Bowler, & Grice, 2003; Mottron et al., 2001; Tager-Flusberg, 1991). Overall, therefore, there is considerable evidence to suggest that individuals with ASD only struggle to benefit from meaningful relations among items to facilitate their free recall but not their cued recall or recognition.

Direct evidence for relational memory difficulties in ASD

The evidence outlined thus far is in line with the suggestion that difficulties in relational rather than item-specific processing contribute to the difficulties individuals with ASD experience in contextually rich recollection. The evidence, however, is rather circumstantial. Recently, a number of studies have tested this hypothesis more directly by manipulating encoding conditions to direct participants' attention either to relational or item-specific information. For example, Gaigg et al. (2008) followed the original paradigms developed by Hunt and Seta (1984) outlined earlier, and asked participants to study two lists of words that were made up of varying instances of different categories (e.g., 2 Sports, 4 Clothing, 8 Weapons, 12 Countries, and 16 Animals). For the first list, participants were simply asked to try to remember the words before recalling as many as they could. Since Hunt and Seta (1984) demonstrated that relational processing primarily benefits the recall of less obviously related items, the prediction for individuals with ASD was that they should have difficulties in recalling items of the smaller categories, which is precisely what was observed. For the second list, participants were instructed to study the list either by rating each item in terms of pleasantness (promoting item-specific processing) or by sorting the items into their respective categories (promoting relational processing). Here, the ASD group performed worse than the comparison group only following the relational orienting task and a number of indices that could be derived from the participants' recall responses further supported the idea that individuals with ASD rely more heavily on item-specific rather than relational processing during memory formation (see also Bowler et al., 2009). A subsequent study furthermore established a direct link between these relational processing difficulties during study and attenuated recollection during retrieval. Gaigg et al. (2015) asked people with and without ASD to study word triplets while deciding whether none, two, or all three words were categorically related (i.e., a relational orienting task). During a subsequent forced choice recognition test, participants needed to discriminate studied from non-studied triplets and indicate whether their choices were based on *remembering*, *knowing*, or *guessing*. Replicating earlier work, remember responses were reduced in ASD in the context of overall preserved recognition rates. Critically, only the proportion of remember but not know responses increased as a function of the number of categorical links in the word triplets in both groups, implicating difficulties in the processing of such relations as a source of attenuated recollection in ASD.

Although the above experiments link relational processing difficulties in ASD to problems in recollection, the implications for the criminal justice system are not immediately clear. Studies that have employed associative recognition tests may make these implications more transparent because of the use of more ecologically valid stimulus materials than the somewhat arbitrary word lists in the previously mentioned studies. For instance, Bowler, Gaigg and Gardiner (2014) used an experimental paradigm that emulates the problem eyewitnesses face when they try to re-construct accurate details about an event (e.g., where a blue car was parked) from fragmentary memories. Specifically, they asked participants to study sets of 22 colored line drawings of common objects that were arranged in various positions of a 6x6 grid. During a first experiment, participants were asked simply to remember certain features of this grid, such as the colors that were presented, the locations that were occupied by objects, or the identities of these objects. On subsequent forced choice recognition tests for these features, ASD and comparison participants performed equally well. In other words, both groups retained specific details of the to-be-remembered grid of objects equally well. In a second experiment, however, participants were required to remember the precise object-color and object-location combinations because a subsequent recognition test would require them to identify objects that were presented in their original colors or locations from those that had their features recombined (e.g., a *yellow ball* and *green shoe* might turn at test into a *green ball* and *yellow shoe*). In this experiment, participants with ASD performed substantially worse. Thus, while their memory for item-specific features of stimuli was preserved, their memory for the relations between these features was compromised. Ring et al. (2015) extended these observations to more naturalistic scenes by requiring participants to remember in which of three plausible room locations, certain objects were presented. For example, participants needed to remember that, in a picture of a bathroom, a hairbrush was presented on a sink, rather than a shelf, and that a sponge was on the corner of a bath rather than the sink. During subsequent item recognition tests, ASD and comparison participants performed equally well at recognizing the objects and the locations that had been studied earlier. However, when participants were asked to put the objects either back into their original locations or into different locations, the ASD participants performed worse. Note that the recognition of the items and locations could be achieved through a combination of recollection and familiarity, whereas the requirement to put objects back into their original or new locations relies on the ability to accurately recollect exactly where the specific objects were originally presented. Thus, the observations confirm that at least the explicit recollection of object-location relations[4] is a source of difficulty for individuals with ASD. Cooper et al. (2015) further corroborated this finding by showing that ASD participants also experience difficulties detecting whether objects have either been substituted or moved in pictures of rooms they were asked to remember. Interesting to note in the Cooper et al. study is that participants were asked to specify whether they *remembered* or *knew* that objects had been substituted or relocated and group differences were driven primarily by reduced remembering in ASD. Thus, a number of recent studies now confirm a close link between relational processing difficulties during memory formation in ASD and the recollection of contextually rich information at retrieval.

[4] Aspects of the data suggested that individuals with ASD retain similar implicit knowledge of object-location relations in memory as comparison participants.

Conclusions and Implications

There is now a considerable body of evidence that supports the idea that memory in ASD is characterized by a relative bias to process item-specific rather than relational information during memory formation, with the consequence that retrieval in the form of contextually rich recollection is compromised whilst the process of familiarity is relatively preserved. As noted at the outset of this chapter, this pattern is neither a necessary nor a unique feature of ASD, but it has important implications for how individuals with this disorder should be supported in the criminal justice system. The memory profile in ASD suggests that witnesses on the autism spectrum should ideally not be required to freely recall events from the past, but be supported in their retrieval through the provision of relevant cues or tests of recognition that would allow them to draw on item-specific memory to retrieve information. Even with such support, however, individuals with ASD would be expected to find it difficult to retrieve relational information that could be vital to criminal investigations. Remembering the spatial or temporal relations among elements of a prior event inevitably relies heavily on the ability to encode and recollect relevant relations, and therefore, individuals on the autism spectrum would often find it difficult to retrieve exactly where things were in relation to one another, and exactly how events unfolded over time when trying to recount a previous event. At the same time, individuals with ASD may find it easier to remember some important details about events that might escape others. As we have shown, the processing of item-specific information may be enhanced in ASD in so far as that certain perceptual features of stimuli are retained very well. If interviewed about a crime they witnessed, therefore individuals with ASD should have no more difficulties than other people in identifying the objects that were involved or in remembering how many individuals were involved—in fact, they may report details about the event that would escape most others (e.g., colors of clothing, particular furniture in the room, etc.).

Take-Home Points

- Individuals with ASD tend to have more fragmented memories of complex events because of a bias to process details specific to individual elements of those events (*item-specific processing*) rather than how those elements relate to one another and to the wider context in which they are situated (*relational processing*).
- As a result of their bias for item-specific rather than relational processing, individuals with ASD tend to find it more difficult to freely recall information than to identify previously seen information among new information on tests of recognition. This is because relational information serves an organizing function in memory that is particularly important for free recall, whereas item-specific information serves a discriminating function that can aid recognition.
- It is important to appreciate, however, that individuals with ASD may also experience difficulties on tests of recognition memory, particularly when such tests require the identification of particular relational details or when recognition of single items might benefit from relational information pertaining to that item.

References

Ameli, R., Courchesne, E., Lincoln, A., Kaufman, A. S., & Grillon, C. (1988). Visual memory processes in high-functioning individuals with autism. *Journal of Autism & Developmental Disorders, 18*(4), 601–615.

Beversdorf, D. Q., Smith, B. W., Crucian, G. P., Anderson, J. M., Keillor, J. M., Barrett, A. M., … Heilman, K. M. (2000). Increased discrimination of "false memories" in autism spectrum disorder. *Proceedings of the National Academy of Sciences of the United States of America, 97*(15), 8734–8737. https://doi.org/10.1073/pnas.97.15.8734

Bigham, S., Boucher, J., Mayes, A., & Anns, S. (2010). Assessing recollection and familiarity in autistic spectrum disorders: Methods and findings. *Journal of Autism & Developmental Disorders, 40*(7), 878–889. https://doi.org/10.1007/s10803-010-0937-7

Boucher, J., Mayes, A., & Bigham, S. (2012). Memory in autistic spectrum disorder. *Psychological Bulletin, 138*(3), 458–496. https://doi.org/10.1037/a0026869

Boucher, J., & Warrington, E. K. (1976). Memory deficits in early infantile autism: some similarities to the amnesic syndrome. *British Journal of Psychology, 67*(1), 73–87. https://doi.org/10.1111/j.2044-8295.1976.tb01499.x

Bowler, D. M., Gaigg, S. B., & Gardiner, J. M. (2008). Effects of related and unrelated context on recall and recognition by adults with high-functioning autism spectrum disorder. *Neuropsychologia, 46*(4), 993–999. https://doi.org/10.1016/j.neuropsychologia.2007.12.004

Bowler, D. M., Gaigg, S. B., & Gardiner, J. M. (2009). Free recall learning of hierarchically organized lists by adults with Asperger's syndrome: Additional evidence for diminished relational processing. *Journal of Autism & Developmental Disorders, 39*(4), 589–595. https://doi.org/10.1007/s10803-008-0659-2

Bowler, D. M., Gaigg, S. B., & Gardiner, J. M. (2010). Multiple list learning in adults with autism spectrum disorder: Parallels with frontal lobe damage or further evidence of diminished relational processing? *Journal of Autism & Developmental Disorders, 40*(2), 179–187. https://doi.org/10.1007/s10803-009-0845-x

Bowler, D. M., Gaigg, S. B., & Gardiner, J. M. (2014). Binding of multiple features in memory by high-functioning adults with autism spectrum disorder. *Journal of Autism & Developmental Disorders, 44*(9), 2355–2362. https://doi.org/10.1007/s10803-014-2105-y

Bowler, D. M., Gaigg, S. B., & Gardiner, J. M. (2015). Brief report: The role of task support in the spatial and temporal source memory of adults with autism spectrum disorder. *Journal of Autism & Developmental Disorders, 45*(8), 2613–2617. https://doi.org/10.1007/s10803-015-2378-9

Bowler, D.M., Gaigg, S.B., & Lind, S. (2011). Memory in autism: Binding, self and brain. In I. Roth & P. Rezaie (Eds.), *Researching the Autism Spectrum* (pp. 316–346). Cambridge: Cambridge University Press. https://doi.org/10.1017/CBO9780511973918.013

Bowler, D. M., Gardiner, J. M., & Berthollier, N. (2004). Source memory in adolescents and adults with Asperger's syndrome. *Journal of Autism & Developmental Disorders, 34*(5), 533–542. https://doi.org/10.1007/s10803-004-2548-7

Bowler, D. M., Gardiner, J. M., & Gaigg, S. B. (2007). Factors affecting conscious awareness in the recollective experience of adults with Asperger's syndrome. *Consciousness & Cognition, 16*(1), 124–143. https://doi.org/10.1016/j.concog.2005.12.001

Bowler, D. M., Gardiner, J. M., & Grice, S. J. (2000). Episodic memory and remembering in adults with Asperger syndrome. *Journal of Autism & Developmental Disorders, 30*(4), 295–304. https://doi.org/10.1023/A:1005575216176

Bowler, D. M., Gardiner, J. M., Grice, S., & Saavalainen, P. (2000). Memory illusions: False recall and recognition in adults with Asperger's syndrome. *Journal of Abnormal Psychology, 109*(4), 663–672. https://doi.org/10.1037//0021-843X.109.4.663

Bowler, D. M., Matthews, N. J., & Gardiner, J. M. (1997). Asperger's syndrome and memory: Similarity to autism but not amnesia. *Neuropsychologia*, *35*(1), 65–70. https://doi.org/10.1016/S0028-3932(96)00054-1

Bowler, D. M., Poirier, M., Martin, J. S., & Gaigg, S. B. (2016). Nonverbal short-term serial order memory in autism spectrum disorder. *Journal of Abnormal Psychology*, *125*(7), 886–893. https://doi.org/10.1037/abn0000203

Cofer, C. N. (1965). On some factors in the organizational characteristics of free recall. *American Psychologist*, *20*, 261–72.

Cooper, R. A., Plaisted-Grant, K. C., Hannula, D. E., Ranganath, C., Baron-Cohen, S., & Simons, J. S. (2015). Impaired recollection of visual scene details in adults with autism spectrum conditions. *Journal of Abnormal Psychology*, *124*(3), 565–575. https://doi.org/10.1037/abn0000070

Craik, F. I. M., & Lockhart, R. S. (1972). Levels of processing: A framework for memory research. *Journal of Verbal Learning & Verbal Behavior*, *11*(6), 671–684. https://doi.org/10.1016/S0022-5371(72)80001-X

Crane, L., & Goddard, L. (2008). Episodic and semantic autobiographical memory in adults with autism spectrum disorders. *Journal of Autism & Developmental Disorders*, *38*(3), 498–506. https://doi.org/10.1007/s10803-007-0420-2

Crane, L., Goddard, L., & Pring, L. (2009). Specific and general autobiographical knowledge in adults with autism spectrum disorders: The role of personal goals. *Memory (Hove, England)*, *17*(5), 557–576. https://doi.org/10.1080/09658210902960211

Crane, L., Lind, S. E., & Bowler, D. M. (2013). Remembering the past and imagining the future in autism spectrum disorder. *Memory*, *21*(2), 157–166. https://doi.org/10.1080/09658211.2012.712976

Davachi, L. (2006). Item, context and relational episodic encoding in humans. *Current Opinion in Neurobiology*, *16*(6), 693–700. https://doi.org/10.1016/j.conb.2006.10.012

Einstein, G. O., & Hunt, R. R. (1980). Levels of processing and organization: Additive effects of individual-item and relational processing. *Journal of Experimental Psychology: Human Learning & Memory*, *6*(5), 588–598. https://doi.org/10.1037/0278-7393.6.5.588

Gaigg, S. B., Bowler, D. M., Ecker, C., Calvo-Merino, B., & Murphy, D. G. (2015). Episodic recollection difficulties in ASD result from atypical relational encoding: Behavioral and neural evidence. *Autism Research*, *8*(3), 317–327. https://doi.org/10.1002/aur.1448

Gaigg, S. B., Gardiner, J. M., & Bowler, D. M. (2008). Free recall in autism spectrum disorder: The role of relational and item-specific encoding. *Neuropsychologia*, *46*(4), 983–992. https://doi.org/10.1016/j.neuropsychologia.2007.11.011

Gardiner, J. M. (2001). Episodic memory and autonoetic consciousness: A first-person approach. *Philosophical Transactions of the Royal Society of London. Series B, Biological Sciences*, *356*(1413), 1351–1361. https://doi.org/10.1098/rstb.2001.0955

Gardiner, J. M., Bowler, D. M., & Grice, S. J. (2003). Further evidence of preserved priming and impaired recall in adults with Asperger's syndrome. *Journal of Autism & Developmental Disorders*, *33*(3), 259–269. https://doi.org/10.1023/A:1024450416355

Gardiner, J. M., Ramponi, C., & Richardson-Klavehn, A. (2002). Recognition memory and decision processes: A meta-analysis of remember, know, and guess responses. *Memory (Hove, England)*, *10*(2), 83–98. https://doi.org/10.1080/09658210143000281

Grandin, T. (2006). *Thinking in pictures*. New York: Vintage Press.

Hermelin, B., & O'Connor, N. (1970). *Psychological experiments with autistic children*. Oxford, England: Pergamon Press.

Hermelin, B., & O'Connor, N. (1967). Remembering of words by psychotic and subnormal children. *British Journal of Psychology*, *58*(3–4), 213–218. https://doi.org/10.1111/j.2044-8295.1967.tb01075.x

Hillier, A., Campbell, H., Keillor, J., Phillips, N., & Beversdorf, D. Q. (2007). Decreased false memory for visually presented shapes and symbols among adults on the autism spectrum. *Journal of Clinical & Experimental Neuropsychology*, *29*(6), 610–616. https://doi.org/10.1080/13803390600878760

Hobson, P., & Hermelin, B. (2008), Preface, in J. Boucher & D. Bowler (Eds) *Autism and Memory.* Cambridge, U.K.: Cambridge University Press.

Hunt, R. R., & Einstein, G. O. (1981). Relational and item-specific information in memory. *Journal of Verbal Learning & Verbal Behavior, 20*(5), 497–514. https://doi.org/10.1016/S0022-5371(81)90138-9

Hunt, R. R., & Mcdaniel, M. A. (1993). The enigma of organization and distinctiveness. *Journal of Memory & Language, 32*(4), 421–445. https://doi.org/10.1006/jmla.1993.1023

Hunt, R. R., & Seta, C. E. (1984). Category size effects in recall: The roles of relational and individual item information. *Journal of Experimental Psychology: Learning, Memory, & Cognition, 10*(3), 454–464. https://doi.org/10.1037/0278-7393.10.3.454

Hunt, R. R., & Smith, R. E. (1996). Accessing the particular from the general: The power of distinctiveness in the context of organization. *Memory & Cognition, 24*(2), 217–225. https://doi.org/10.3758/BF03200882

Hyde, T. S., & Jenkins, J. J. (1969). Differential effects of incidental tasks on the organization of recall of a list of highly associated words. *Journal of Experimental Psychology, 82*(3), 472–481. https://doi.org/10.1037/h0028372

Lind, S. E., & Bowler, D. M. (2009). Recognition memory, self-other source memory, and theory-of-mind in children with autism spectrum disorder. *Journal of Autism & Developmental Disorders, 39*(9), 1231–1239. https://doi.org/10.1007/s10803-009-0735-2

Lind, S. E., & Bowler, D. M. (2010a). Episodic memory and episodic future thinking in adults with autism. *Journal of Abnormal Psychology, 119*(4), 896–905. https://doi.org/10.1037/a0020631

Lind, S. E., & Bowler, D. M. (2010b). Impaired performance on see-know tasks amongst children with autism: Evidence of specific difficulties with theory of mind or domain-general task factors? *Journal of Autism & Developmental Disorders, 40*(4), 479–484. https://doi.org/10.1007/s10803-009-0889-y

Lind, S. E., Williams, D. M., Bowler, D. M., & Peel, A. (2014). Episodic memory and episodic future thinking impairments in high-functioning autism spectrum disorder: An underlying difficulty with scene construction or self-projection? *Neuropsychology, 28*(1), 55–67. https://doi.org/10.1037/neu0000005

Loth, E., Gómez, J. C., & Happé, F. (2011). Do high-functioning people with autism spectrum disorder spontaneously use event knowledge to selectively attend to and remember context-relevant aspects in scenes? *Journal of Autism & Developmental Disorders, 41*(7), 945–961. https://doi.org/10.1007/s10803-010-1124-6

Maister, L., Simons, J. S., & Plaisted-Grant, K. (2013). Executive functions are employed to process episodic and relational memories in children with autism spectrum disorders. *Neuropsychology, 27*(6), 615–27. https://doi.org/10.1037/a0034492

Massand, E., & Bowler, D. M. (2015). Atypical neurophysiology underlying episodic and semantic memory in adults with autism spectrum disorder. *Journal of Autism & Developmental Disorders, 45*(2), 298–315. https://doi.org/10.1007/s10803-013-1869-9

Massand, E., Bowler, D. M., Mottron, L., Hosein, A., & Jemel, B. (2013). ERP correlates of recognition memory in autism spectrum disorder. *Journal of Autism & Developmental Disorders, 43*(9), 2038–2047. https://doi.org/10.1007/s10803-012-1755-x

Mayes, A., Montaldi, D., & Migo, E. (2007). Associative memory and the medial temporal lobes. *Trends in Cognitive Sciences, 11*(3), 126–135. https://doi.org/10.1016/j.tics.2006.12.003

Minshew, N. J., & Goldstein, G. (1993). Is autism an amnesic disorder? Evidence from the California Verbal Learning Test. *Neuropsychology, 7*(2), 209–216. https://doi.org/10.1037/0894-4105.7.2.209

Minshew, N. J., & Goldstein, G. (2001). The pattern of intact and impaired memory functions in autism. *Journal of Child Psychology & Psychiatry, and Allied Disciplines, 42*(8), 1095–1101. https://doi.org/10.1111/1469-7610.00808

Minshew, N. J., Goldstein, G., Muenz, L. R., & Payton, J. B. (1992). Neuropsychological functioning in nonmentally retarded autistic individuals. *Journal of Clinical & Experimental Neuropsychology*, *14*(5), 749–761. https://doi.org/10.1080/01688639208402860

Mottron, L., Morasse, K., & Belleville, S. (2001). A study of memory functioning in individuals with autism. *Journal of Child Psychology & Psychiatry, and Allied Disciplines*, *42*(2), 253–260. https://doi.org/10.1017/S0021963001006722

Neath, I., & Surprenant, A. M. (2003). *Human memory: An introduction to research, data, and theory, 2nd ed.* Belmont, CA: Wadsworth. ISBN: 0534595626

Old, S. R., & Naveh-Benjamin, M. (2008). Differential effects of age on item and associative measures of memory: a meta-analysis. *Psychology & Aging*, *23*(1), 104–118. https://doi.org/10.1037/0882-7974.23.1.104

Proust, M. (1946) Du côté de chez Swann. Paris: Gallimard (original edition, 1913, Paris: Grasset).

Ragland, J. D., Ranganath, C., Barch, D. M., Gold, J. M., Haley, B., MacDonald, A. W., … Carter, C. S. (2012). Relational and item-specific encoding (RISE): Task development and psychometric characteristics. *Schizophrenia Bulletin*, *38*(1), 114–124. https://doi.org/10.1093/schbul/sbr146

Ranganath, C., Minzenberg, M. J., & Ragland, J. D. (2008). The cognitive neuroscience of memory function and dysfunction in schizophrenia. *Biological Psychiatry*, *64*(1), 18–25. https://doi.org/10.1016/j.biopsych.2008.04.011

Ring, M., Gaigg, S. B., & Bowler, D. M. (2015). Object-location memory in adults with autism spectrum disorder. *Autism Research*, *8*(5), 609–619. https://doi.org/10.1002/aur.1478

Ring, M., Gaigg, S. B., & Bowler, D. M. (2016). Relational memory processes in adults with autism spectrum disorder. *Autism Research*, *9*(1), 97–106. https://doi.org/10.1002/aur.1493

Roediger, H. L., Watson, J. M., McDermott, K. B., & Gallo, D. A. (2001). Factors that determine false recall: A multiple regression analysis. *Psychonomic Bulletin & Review*, *8*(3), 385–407. https://doi.org/10.3758/BF03196177

Russell, J., & Jarrold, C. (1999). Memory for actions in children with autism: Self versus other. *Cognitive Neuropsychiatry*, *4*(4), 303–331. https://doi.org/10.1080/135468099395855

Souchay, C., Wojcik, D. Z., Williams, H. L., Crathern, S., & Clarke, P. (2013). Recollection in adolescents with autism spectrum disorder. *Cortex*, *49*(6), 1598–1609. https://doi.org/10.1016/j.cortex.2012.07.011

Tager-Flusberg, H. (1991). Semantic processing in the free recall of autistic children: Further evidence for a cognitive deficit. *British Journal of Developmental Psychology*, *9*(3), 417–430. https://doi.org/10.1111/j.2044-835X.1991.tb00886.x

Tanweer, T., Rathbone, C. J., & Souchay, C. (2010). Autobiographical memory, autonoetic consciousness, and identity in Asperger syndrome. *Neuropsychologia*, *48*(4), 900–908. https://doi.org/10.1016/j.neuropsychologia.2009.11.007

Toichi, M., & Kamio, Y. (2002). Long-term memory and levels-of-processing in autism. *Neuropsychologia*, *40*(7), 964–969. https://doi.org/10.1016/S0028-3932(01)00163-4

Treffert, D. A. (1988). The idiot savant: A review of the syndrome. *American Journal of Psychiatry*, *145*(5), 563–572.

Treffert, D. A. (2009). The savant syndrome: An extraordinary condition. A synopsis: past, present, future. *Philosophical Transactions of the Royal Society of London Series B, Biological Sciences*, *364*(1522), 1351–1357. https://doi.org/10.1098/rstb.2008.0326

Tresselt, M. E., & Mayzner, M. S. (1960). A study of incidental learning. *Journal of Psychology: Interdisciplinary & Applied*, *50*, 339–347. https://doi.org/10.1080/00223980.1960.9916451

Tulving, E. (1966). Subjective organization and effects of repetition in multi-trial free-recall learning. *Journal of Verbal Learning & Verbal Behavior*, *5*(2), 193–197. https://doi.org/10.1016/S0022-5371(66)80016-6

Tulving, E., & Patkau, J. (1962). Concurrent effects of contextual constraint and word frequency of immediate recall and learning of verbal material. *Canadian Journal of Psychology*. https://doi.org/10.1037/h0083231

Yonelinas, A. P. (2002). The nature of recollection and familiarity: A review of 30 years of research. *Journal of Memory & Language*, *46*(3), 441–517. https://doi.org/10.1006/jmla.2002.2864

2

Autobiographical Memory in Autism Spectrum Disorder through the Lens of Fuzzy Trace Theory

Haylie L. Miller, Timothy N. Odegard, and Valerie Reyna

Autobiographical memory is a form of memory intricately linked to the self, which requires integration of episodic, semantic, and procedural information (Marsh & Roediger, 2013). It provides an individual with a means of replaying specific past self-referential events in the mind's eye (Conway & Pleydell-Pierce, 2000; Cosentino, 2011). Forensically, it is of interest due to its importance in legal situations reliant on eyewitnesses to provide accounts of past events. Memory reports of events can make or break legal proceedings, and the veracity of memory reports is critical (Brainerd & Reyna, 1990a). Yet, some populations are viewed as having unreliable memories, for example, children (Block et al., 2012). These views can negatively impact how players in the legal system (e.g., judges, jurors, attorneys) value testimony provided from these sources. This has motivated research on factors that influence autobiographical memory in specific subgroups, such as children and the elderly, two of the most vulnerable populations (Odegard, Cooper, Holliday, & Ceci, 2010a; Toglia, Ross, Pozzulo, & Pica, 2014).

Our focus is on individuals with autism spectrum disorder (ASD), who represent a vulnerable population historically viewed as having impoverished memory function. Empirical data suggest that some individuals with ASD struggle to remember personally experienced events (Boucher, 1981; Boucher & Lewis, 1989; Kaney et al., 1999; Klein et al., 1999; Millward et al., 2000). However, the current literature on episodic memory in ASD is an amalgam of seemingly conflicting findings that do not clearly define which individuals will and will not have difficulty in this area (e.g., Crane, Lind, & Bowler, 2013b; Millward et al., 2000). The confusion stems from both methodological differences and heterogeneity of symptom profiles in the ASD community.

The Wiley Handbook of Memory, Autism Spectrum Disorder, and the Law, First Edition.
Edited by Jonni L. Johnson, Gail S. Goodman, and Peter C. Mundy.

There is considerable need for a clearer understanding of factors that undergird memory function in this population. This will, in turn, aid in identifying boundary conditions to better gauge the reliability of their memories.

Here, we attempt to unpack one specific domain of episodic memory—autobiographical memory. We present current evidence within a well-established theoretical framework—Fuzzy Trace Theory (FTT)—that may account for some of the performance differences observed in individuals with ASD (see also Reyna & Brainerd, 2011). FTT describes the developmental shift from reliance on *verbatim representations*, or detailed encoding of information as it was presented, to *gist representations*, or broader encoding of the pattern of associated concepts related to the original input (Brainerd & Reyna, 1992; Reyna & Brainerd, 1991a, 1991b) and is supported by established process models (Bauer, Larkina, & Deocampo, 2011; Howe, 2011; Raj & Bell, 2010; Schneider, 2011; Shing & Lindenberger, 2011).

Within the framework of Fuzzy Trace Theory (FTT), there are three levels of processing at which autobiographical memory in ASD may break down: (a) encoding (was it stored), (b) availability (is it stored in a way that can be retrieved), and (c) retrieval (what cues are needed to access it). Two types of memory trace—verbatim and gist—support these processes. Verbatim-based versus gist-based influences on encoding, accessibility, and retrieval appear to be domain-specific in ASD, rather than global. Therefore, it is more straightforward to examine these processes as they pertain to each of the component skills required for autobiographical memory. In the following sections, we discuss the component skills required for autobiographical memory-language and narrative construction, spatiotemporal binding and self-projection backward in time, self-concept, and source-monitoring—and the evidence of dysfunction in ASD as it relates to aspects of FTT.

Overview of Fuzzy Trace Theory

FTT proposes that cognition consists of seven core components accounting for processes from perception and encoding to storage and retrieval. They are: (a) gist extraction, (b) fuzzy-to-verbatim continuum, (c) fuzzy-processing preference, (d) reconstructive short- and long-term memory, (e) output interference, (f) resource freedom, and (g) ontogenesis. Each of these components uniquely contributes to an individual's ability to interpret and maintain information for later use.

Within an FTT framework, information is encoded either as general, vague representations of the whole (fuzzy or gist traces) or as detailed, exact representations of a target (verbatim traces). Individuals sift through information in search of patterns or elements that characterize the whole (Brainerd & Reyna, 1990b; Reyna, 1995, Reyna, 2008; Reyna et al., 2014). This is the *fuzzy* end of the fuzzy-to-verbatim continuum. Across the lifespan, humans rely less on verbatim retrieval and more on fuzzy traces to remember and make inferences. An increased reliance on fuzzy traces stems from the fact that these traces are meaningful as well as easier to retrieve, process, and alter. Throughout the past two decades, researchers have amassed a great deal of evidence in support of this proposed developmental trajectory (Brainerd, Holliday, & Reyna, 2004; Brainerd, Reyna, & Zember, 2011; Farrar & Goodman, 1992; Ghetti & Angelini, 2008; Ghetti, Qin, & Goodman, 2002; Odegard, Cooper, Lampinen, Reyna, & Brainerd, 2009; Odegard, Jenkins, &

Koen, 2010b; Reyna, Chick, Corbin, & Hsia, 2014; Reyna & Kiernan, 1994; Reyna, Wilhelms, McCormick, & Weldon, 2015b).

Verbatim traces are more vulnerable to decay and interference than gist traces, perhaps in part, because of underlying differences in the neurological structures that support these separate forms of information (Brainerd, Reyna, & Brandse, 1995; Dennis, Kim, & Cabeza, 2008; Kintsch, Welsch, Schmalhofer, & Zimny, 1990; McDermott, 1996; Stäubli, Ivy, & Lynch, 1984; Toglia, Neuschatz, & Goodwin, 1999). Verbatim traces also suffer from the constraint of encoding specificity, which requires highly detailed retrieval cues and makes them more difficult to access (Tulving, 1983). Thus, a search for the most detailed and accurate information found in verbatim traces requires a significant amount of time and is subject to interference (Malmberg & Shiffrin, 2005; Reyna & Mills, 2007; Tun, Wingfield, Rosen, & Blanchard, 1998).

Although verbatim traces are limited in duration due to decay, enduring gist traces may contain the information necessary to overcome lost information and produce a successful response. Reyna and Brainerd (1995) posited that gist traces are more likely than verbatim traces to be fully encoded, and that they are more robust against the effects of forgetting. In fact, as Brainerd and Reyna (1988; 1990a; 1990b) proposed, humans have a bias toward the use of gist traces in cognition, using gist for both memory retrieval and information processing. In essence, this means that individuals search for the simplest, most readily accessible solution, which leads them to the preferential use of gist-based information.

However, as is the case with most heuristics, reliance on gist to "fill in the blanks" puts an individual at risk for error. Error may be introduced by way of content borrowing when associated information is activated during retrieval. Wrongly activated information may be reconsolidated into an existing trace, particularly if the original trace is weak because of forgetting or limited learning events, expanding the reach of the trace and allowing interference during subsequent retrievals (Brainerd & Reyna, 1990a; Ceci & Bruck, 1993; Ceci, Toglia, & Ross, 1988; Loftus, Miller, & Burns, 1978; Marche & Howe, 1995; Titcomb & Reyna, 1995). This reconsolidation process leads to strong feelings of familiarity with the falsely retrieved information, which becomes incorporated into the original memory as though it were present at the time of encoding (Bransford & Franks, 1971; Lampinen, Meier, Arnal, & Leding, 2005; Reyna, Corbin, Weldon, & Brainerd, 2016). This is particularly important to consider when attempting to elicit eyewitness or autobiographical memories from a person, especially when he or she is vulnerable to suggestion (e.g., children, certain clinical populations). Wrongly-activated information can taint related traces, interfering with a person's ability to accurately reconstruct a memory, and the process of reconsolidation during retrieval increases confidence in that memory regardless of its accuracy.

Neither type of trace is superior to the other across all domains, as noted by Acredolo (1995), but, rather, both gist and verbatim memory traces support learning and information processing in unique and vital ways, and their relative strength depends largely on task demands and availability of cognitive resources. When considering the relation between FTT and autobiographical memory, it is important to appreciate that FTT specifies both the memory structure at a representational level and processes that act on these traces. Reliving a past event can arise from directly accessing a verbatim trace for a specific past event. Direct access to a verbatim trace leads to highly reliable memory reports with considerable detail. However, as we highlighted, these traces are vulnerable to forgetting through a host of mechanisms that limit direct access to verbatim traces.

At the same time, an event can be relived through reconstruction of the past using gist representations. In this regard, individuals reconstruct the past using a fuzzy representation and their general understanding of the nature of the event that took place. Under these circumstances memory reports can contain accurate information but can also contain less than reliable details. In many contexts, such as comprehending a narrative or making a decision, knowing the gist of what took place can be highly functional, in spite of not having access to specific details (Reyna, Weldon, & McCormick, 2015a). Reconstructed memories are of concern in forensic settings because such settings are among the few times that accuracy in the details of a memorial experience is of utmost importance.

Autobiographical Memory in ASD

Autobiographical memory develops throughout childhood, beginning around age 2 or 3 (Fivush et al., 1987; Nelson & Fivush, 2004). However, while the literature on autobiographical memory in typical development is rich, there is a paucity of evidence available to support conclusions about autobiographical memory ability in ASD.

Within the broader body of evidence for memory deficits in ASD, some have suggested that individuals with ASD have differences in episodic memory across both encoding and retrieval processes, despite preserved function in semantic memory (Ben Shalom, 2003). Others have posited that deficits in elaborative encoding limit the availability of to-be-remembered information (Beversdorf et al., 2007; Bowler et al., 2000; Bowler, Gaigg, & Gardiner, 2014; Bowler, Gardiner, & Berthollier, 2004; Meyer, Gardiner, & Bowler, 2014), in turn, driving performance differences on memory tasks. To effectively support availability for retrieval, information must be encoded in a way that is both durable (i.e., resistant to decay), and accessible (e.g., cross-referenced with appropriate associative nodes in order to maximize retrieval through spreading activation). Specifically, individuals with ASD may not have difficulty with the durability of memory traces, but may instead have difficulty with elaborative encoding processes, including feature and temporal binding, that limit the availability of memory traces (Beversdorf et al., 2007; Bowler, Gaigg, & Gardiner, 2014; Meyer, Gardiner, & Bowler, 2014; for review, also see Miller, Odegard, & Allen, 2014). In particular, as we discuss in further detail, studies requiring narrative-based recall may present a unique set of challenges to individuals with ASD.

This topic is particularly relevant to eyewitness testimony, given that individuals are often asked to produce free-recall narratives when giving evidence. In the case of an individual with ASD, the narrative representing an autobiographical memory may appear disjointed and incoherent—a scattered set of details rather than a coherent story—in turn, undermining the credibility of the eyewitness. However, as we outline here, this reflects the difficulty that individuals with ASD have with spatiotemporal binding, narrative coherence, and gist-based processing, rather than indicating unreliability and inaccuracy in this population.

In our view, a combination of differences in spontaneous encoding, accessibility, and retrieval of verbatim and gist-based memory traces and differences in the development of self-concept likely drive autobiographical memory impairments in ASD.

Gist-based processing allows an individual to represent the world in a broader categorical or contextual fashion, and to subsequently use that representation to reconstruct the past when access to verbatim traces breaks down. If individuals with ASD do not adhere to a typical balance of reliance on gist and verbatim information, they may differ qualitatively in the way that they reconstruct autobiographical memories and the type of information those reconstructions contain.

To fully appreciate autobiographical memory in ASD, we must unpack the ability of individuals with ASD to construct personal narratives, to engage in spatiotemporal binding and project their self-concept backward in time to previously experienced events (Cosentino, 2011), and to form and maintain a sense of self (i.e., autonoetic consciousness; Powell & Jordan, 1993).

Language and narrative construction

Nelson and Fivush (2004) proposed a central role of language and narrative construction in autobiographical memory formation and recollection. They suggested that autobiographical memory results from sharing narratives about past events, which in turn, provides opportunity for elaboration and rehearsal, strengthening memory traces (see also Nelson, 1995). However, individuals with ASD have differences in the use of gist to reconstruct narratives in a way that is consistent with the temporal order and relative importance of events (Diehl, Bennetto, & Young, 2006), which may impact coherent recall of autobiographical memories.

To effectively communicate and construct narratives, individuals must use the core processes described in FTT. To explore the influence of key FTT processes on language and narrative construction, consider the following examples:

1 **Gist impairment**: If a breakdown occurs at the level of gist extraction, the context of a memory will be obscured and may not be available to support spatiotemporal binding (connecting the features of an event with their spatial and temporal context in memory), source memory (memory for the source of learned information), contextualization (remembering the context of an event or piece of information), and coherent construction of a narrative during encoding. This will, in turn, negatively impact accessibility. In this instance, an individual would be compelled to rely heavily on the verbatim end of the fuzzy-to-verbatim continuum at retrieval.
2 **Gist intact, but over-reliance on verbatim**: If the fuzzy-processing preference is not strong in ASD, individuals may still be able to encode and retrieve gist-based traces, but they are not likely to do so in a typical manner. They may produce a highly detailed recounting of events, but without sufficient attention to temporal order or context, relying heavily on the verbatim end of the fuzzy-to-verbatim continuum.
3 **Gist impairment, forcing over-reliance on verbatim**: If an individual primarily encodes verbatim traces without also encoding gist-based traces, the result is likely to be difficulty with accessibility and retrieval. Verbatim traces may not be durable enough (i.e., inaccessible or unavailable) depending on the amount of time that elapses and the strength of the original encoding. If gist traces are not available to support the reconstructive nature of autobiographical memory, the resultant memory may be incomplete, riddled with information gaps.

4 **Gist intact, but output interference**: If the use of gist is intact, but there is too much output interference at retrieval, an individual may produce autobiographical memories laden with technically inaccurate information activated by relying on the gist of the situation. Insufficient encoding or accessibility of verbatim traces will increase this vulnerability to interference.

People with ASD consistently appear to struggle with spontaneous use of gist and heavily rely on verbatim traces, which are susceptible to decay. For example, Bruck et al. (2007) observed that children with ASD had generally poorer performance than controls during retrospective reporting of personally experienced events and interviews following staged events. The ASD group made more errors of omission, rather than errors of commission, during autobiographical memory recall, especially for early-life events. This suggests that gist-based traces were unavailable to (a) aid in retrieval of less-accessible information, or (b) produce output interference that would lead to errors of omission. However, Bruck and colleagues noted that core deficits in autobiographical memory persisted in their sample, independent of the question or response format. On the surface, this pattern of results could arise from primarily verbatim-based responding and limited access to gist representations. In addition, children with ASD were suggestible to the same degree as typically developing (TD) controls, incorporating inaccurate information from misleading questions.

McCrory, Henry, and Happé (2007) presented similar results, finding that adolescents with ASD were no less accurate and no more suggestible than TD controls when recalling personally experienced staged events in a classroom setting. Further, they found strong evidence of impaired gist-based memory in their sample, with the ASD group reporting significantly less gist-based information about salient aspects of the event (e.g., the actors had a broken piece of equipment) than controls during free recall. In addition to highlighting the role of gist in autobiographical memory, this finding underlines the importance of testing or interview format for assessing the memory ability of people with ASD, who may struggle with expressive language or narrative construction needed for free recall.

Evidence also suggests that individuals with ASD do not reconstruct personal narratives in the same self-referential context as TD peers, providing further evidence of impaired gist processing. Brown and colleagues (2012) asked children and adolescents to report their earliest memories, one positive emotional experience, and one negative emotional experience. They found that individuals with ASD included fewer emotional, cognitive, and perceptual terms when recounting personally-experienced events. Similarly, Tanweer and colleagues (2010) noted that adults with Asperger's lacked specificity and self-reference when recalling personally experienced events from three time points in their lives. Chaput et al. (2013) also observed that adults with ASD recalled fewer and less-detailed autobiographical memories, and used fewer possessive pronouns and fewer family-related words (e.g., *mother*, *father*, *sister*), than TD controls.

In contrast, Bang, Burns, and Nadig (2013) reported that adolescents with ASD were able to appropriately use cognitive terms to describe mental states, despite producing fewer personal narratives during conversations than TD peers. They were, in essence, able to effectively engage in source monitoring to identify and describe their own mental states, but less able to place those mental states into the context of personal narratives. This pattern of evidence underscores the importance of dissociating between the ability to use self-concept to support source monitoring from the ability to spontaneously produce narratives, personal or otherwise. It is especially important to consider this distinction when considering eyewitness memory reconstruction. For example, individuals with ASD may be able to reliably identify the source of information, regardless of their ability to effectively and spontaneously place that information or its source into a coherent narrative context. Given the age difference between ASD and TD adolescents, it is also possible that developmental factors drive the discrepancy in results.

Most recently, Losh and Gordon (2014) observed that high-functioning children with ASD produced personal narratives that were similar in content to those produced by controls, despite being of lower semantic quality. Narratives of lower semantic quality, as measured by Latent Semantic Analysis (Landauer & Dumais, 1997), were those which contained irrelevant or tangential remarks, disjointed narrative timelines, and heavy reliance on external prompts. This finding, along with others (e.g., Lind, Williams, et al., 2014), suggests that autobiographical memory differences in ASD are somewhat independent of language and narrative construction difficulties.

Spatiotemporal context for episodic memory

Spatiotemporal binding may prove difficult for people with ASD. The ability to bind features of an environment or event based on temporal contingencies adds specificity and enriched context to memorial traces. Inefficient or absent temporal binding disrupts coherence in episodic memories, in turn, posing challenges to accurate retrieval. Inefficient or absent spatial memory may result in missing details about objects or persons in a scene that could prove valuable to eyewitness accounts. Broadly, difficulty with spatiotemporal binding at encoding can leave memories susceptible to output interference, or render them partially or entirely inaccessible. With respect to FTT, spatiotemporal binding offers this enriched context for both verbatim and gist-based traces, but may especially aid in cueing reconstruction of gist-based information when other verbatim information is absent or inaccessible by facilitating "mental time travel." Spatiotemporal context may also aid in source monitoring, or the ability to differentiate personally experienced events from others' experiences, which is a key component of autobiographical memory. With respect to eyewitness memory, spatiotemporal binding is especially important for enriched cueing of gist-based memory. The use of "mental time travel" offers an opportunity for context reinstatement, which increases opportunities for retrieval of gist-based spatial (e.g., location, elements of a scene, persons relative to objects in a scene) or temporal (e.g., duration of an event, sequence of events) elements of the memory.

Some studies have found evidence of intact or superior temporal binding in children and adolescents with ASD (Mostofsky et al., 2000; Wallace & Happé, 2008), while others report impairments in children and adolescents (Szelag et al., 2004; Bennetto, Pennington, & Rogers, 1996) and adults (Crane & Goddard, 2008; Gowen & Miall, 2005; Martin, Poirier, & Bowler, 2010) with Asperger's or high-functioning autism. These studies employed a variety of measures of temporal processing, including reproducing intervals of time (Gowen & Miall, 2005; Martin et al., 2010; Szelag et al., 2004) and estimation or production (Wallace & Happé, 2008).

Reproduction—storing the original stimulus information in memory and reproducing it at the time of recall—is perhaps the most relevant to the discussion of eyewitness testimony, given its reliance on memory to maintain an accessible representation of the interval of time to be reproduced at retrieval. Notably, this is also the domain in which individuals with ASD have consistently demonstrated difficulty.

Crane and Goddard (2008; Crane, Goddard, & Pring, 2009) found that adults with ASD relied atypically on temporally nonspecific representations of events much like TD younger children. For example, individuals with ASD might be able to remember that an event occurred, but may be unable to place that event or its elements on a timeline (i.e., the memory is lacking temporal context). They recalled personal semantic memories at rates equal to TD controls, despite lower specificity for personal episodic memories in a narrative recall task. Crane and Goddard further observed that individuals with ASD did not demonstrate the typical reminiscence bump–enhanced recall for events of adolescence and early adulthood—often observed in the typical developmental literature (Conway & Pleydell-Pearce, 2000). They suggested that atypical development of self-concept may produce limitations in autobiographical memory for individuals with ASD, specifically with respect to recall of events in temporal context (Crane & Goddard, 2008; Crane, Goddard, & Pring, 2009). Recently, Goddard et al. (2014) replicated many of these findings, observing that individuals with ASD had difficulty retrieving autobiographical memories across the lifespan, with specific difficulty retrieving and referring to information in remote memories. Further study of this tendency under multiple retrieval conditions (e.g., manipulating the type and amount of cueing) might aid in determining whether this information is available but difficult to access in ASD, or entirely unavailable for retrieval.

The relation between temporal information processing and episodic memory is bidirectional, such that intact traces for temporal context (e.g., duration of an event) are necessary for accurate episodic memory, and complete episodic memory recall includes information about temporal context (Sederberg, Gershman, Polyn, & Norman, 2011). The same is true for many forms of temporal information (e.g., order of events, onset and offset of an event). This temporal information, like any other feature of an episodic memory, may be retrieved directly or inferred. Absent, incomplete, or decayed verbatim traces for temporal information are vulnerable to gist-based errors, in which inference is made based on a broader, conceptual reconstruction of the event. Inferences are made about information for which a precise verbatim trace is and is not present, but the latter encourages reliance on gist (Reyna et al., 2016). Bennetto et al. (1996) reported poor performance of children and adolescents with high-functioning autism on tasks requiring retrieval or inference of temporal information from remembered events, including temporal order judgments and recency discrimination. Thus, the results of Bennetto et al.'s study suggest that gist-based processing is limited in ASD, but the degree of limitation remains unknown. Frith and colleagues' weak central coherence hypothesis also has been the impetus for research supporting a similar distinction between unimpaired processing of details and impaired processing of meaningful inferences (Happé & Frith, 2006; see also Reyna & Brainerd, 2011).

More recently, Maister and Plaisted-Grant (2011) conducted a study of temporal perception in children with ASD wherein participants were required to reproduce short (4–30 sec) and long (45 sec) durations, with the novel addition of a concurrent task that prevented chronometric counting, a technique which may scaffold performance on duration-reproduction tasks. Duration reproduction is particularly relevant to autobiographical memory in instances where eyewitness recall of a timeline or duration of a given event is needed. Like Mostofsky et al. (2000) and Martin et al. (2010), Maister and Plaisted-Grant did not find any differences in perception of short time durations (i.e., 4–30 sec) between individuals with ASD and TD controls. However, they did observe impairments in the ASD group for long durations of 45 seconds, which did not relate to measures of attentional variability. Mimura et al. (2000) and others have suggested that durations of >30 seconds (especially with an interfering task) are reliant on episodic, rather than short-term, memory. Thus, Maister and Plaisted-Grant concluded that this difference reflected impairments in episodic memory in the ASD group. Further supporting their conclusion, long-duration performance in the TD, but not ASD, group was correlated with greater reorganization in a free-recall episodic memory task.

Maister and Plaisted-Grant noted that methodological differences between their study and those that do not control for chronometric counting (e.g., Wallace & Happé, 2008) may explain the discrepant results reported in the literature. They suggested that not only do individuals with ASD struggle to retain episodic memories; they also neglect the typical strategy of spontaneously reorganizing and re-encoding temporal information. This reorganization and re-encoding of information in typical development is most efficiently done in a gist-based manner (e.g., encoding the approximate duration of an event based on one's own perception of time vs. chronometric counting), and supports episodic memory retrieval by providing context for inferences required during gist-based reconstruction. With respect to eyewitness memory, the failure to spontaneously and accurately re-encode the approximate duration of an event in a gist-based manner may hinder the ability of individuals with ASD to recall temporal context or duration of an event accurately, especially in situations where attentional resources are taxed.

Lind and colleagues (Lind & Bowler, 2010; Lind & Bowler, 2008, Lind, Bowler, & Raber, 2014a) have previously hypothesized that difficulty with temporal self-projection might drive episodic memory and spatial memory challenges. However, Lind et al. (2014a, 2014b) demonstrated that children and adults with ASD displayed equal impairment in spatial memory for fictitious scenes, which do not require self-projection. Lind and colleagues (2014a, 2014b) suggested that this pattern of results in ASD represents difficulty with generating cognitive maps of the environment and scene construction. Both of these skills are related to autobiographical memory in that they provide context for episodes, and in the case of eyewitnesses, spatial memory may contain important information about the presence and location of key objects or persons.

Spatial memory for specific scenes requires encoding and accessibility of both verbatim traces for details of the scene and gist-based traces that aid in reconstructing the scene as a whole. Of importance, the pattern of results observed by Lind et al. (2014a, 2014b) occurred independent of narrative ability. Thus, impaired scene reconstruction may drive spatial memory and episodic memory difficulties in ASD, rather than autonoetic consciousness or the ability to self-project. Others have found additional evidence of the ability to engage in "mental time-travel" to some degree (Bowler et al., 2007). Given this limited body of work, questions remain regarding the specific degree to which the ability to project self-concept forward and backward in time to support autobiographical memory is present in individuals with ASD, how these abilities differ between children and adults, and what measures could be used to differentiate subtypes of ASD based on this ability.

Self-concept and source monitoring

As a person's self-concept becomes more complex, opportunities for memory organization increase in complexity. Thus, memory performance is typically facilitated by involvement of the self (Rogers, Kuiper, & Kirker, 1977). However, the typical advantage that self-referential information has in memory (Baker-Ward, Hess, & Flannagan, 1990) appears to be reduced or absent in adolescents and adults with ASD (Grisdale et al., 2014), Asperger's/high-functioning autism (Jackson, Skirrow, & Hare, 2012; Toichi et al., 2002), and a co-morbid diagnosis of ASD and intellectual disability (Hare, Mellor, & Azmi, 2007).

Self-awareness is a critical factor in the ability to engage in accurate source monitoring, which is important for correctly identifying the actor(s) or agent(s) in an autobiographical memory (Gardiner, 2001; Naito, 2003). Self-awareness may be generally impaired in ASD, which could impact the effectiveness of self-reference or source monitoring during encoding (Bowler, Gardiner, & Grice, 2000; Crane, Goddard, & Pring, 2009; for review, also see Lind, 2010). In support of this hypothesis, studies have reported reduced activity in ventromedial prefrontal cortex, an area related to judgments of self, when making self- versus other-judgments about personality traits or behavioral characteristics, in adults with ASD (Kennedy & Courchesne, 2008; Lombardo et al., 2010).

When considered in total, the developmental literature on self-awareness and self-concept in ASD reports somewhat mixed findings. Several studies have found intact self-recognition and metarepresentational ability in young children with ASD (Dawson & McKissick, 1984; Dissanayake, Shembrey, & Suddendorf, 2010), with exceptions for children functioning at a mental age lower than their chronological age (Ferrari & Matthews, 1983). However, Carmody and Lewis (2012) found that some children with ASD had deficits in self-representation ability that could not be explained by mental age alone. Thus, it may be that only a subset of children with ASD has reduced ability to form or maintain a typical self-representation or self-concept.

Although evidence suggests that many adults with ASD have the ability to perform just as well on memory tasks and some self-representation tasks as their TD counterparts, they may not report memories with the same confidence, perhaps because of differences in their self-awareness. For example, Elmose and Happé (2014) observed that adults with ASD and TD controls were comparably accurate in memory for both social and nonsocial information. However, individuals with ASD were better at judging their memory accuracy for nonsocial than social stimuli. Conceptualization of agency and the ability to self-conceptualize from another's perspective also appears to differ in adolescents with ASD, as reported by Farley et al. (2010) and others.

Adults with ASD appear able to engage in source monitoring and affirm or deny whether a behavior or an observable characteristic is attributable to self versus other, despite difficulty differentiating between internal (e.g., psychological, personality) and external (e.g., physical) traits (David et al., 2010; Farrant et al., 1998; Kennedy & Courchesne, 2008; Lind, 2010). Some children with ASD also demonstrate the "enactment effect" observed in TD children—that is, self-performed actions are better-remembered than other-performed actions (Hare, Mellor, & Azmi, 2007; Lind & Bowler, 2009; Williams & Happé, 2009). They are able to monitor source accurately (Hala et al., 2005; Hill & Russell, 2002), perhaps due to the tendency to encode verbatim memory traces more readily than error-prone gist (Reyna & Brainerd, 2011).

However, Lind and Bowler (2010) reported that, in their sample, adults with ASD were less likely than TD controls to re-experience past events from their own point of view, tending to recount events from the perspective of a third-person observer. They also demonstrated impaired episodic memory at a general level. Zalla et al. (2010) found mixed results with respect to the enactment effect. In their sample, adults with ASD did not consistently experience memory advantages for self-performed actions. However, Zalla et al. noted that their results may reflect difficulties specific to processing and encoding motor actions and proprioceptive signals rather than to memory in general.

Of interest, Crane and colleagues (Crane, Goddard, & Pring, 2010, 2013a; Crane, Pring, Jukes, & Goddard, 2012) have suggested that autobiographical memory differences in ASD may result in part from a failure to use personally experienced events to update the self. They observed that adults with ASD correctly distinguished between memories for self-defining events and memories for everyday events (Crane et al., 2010), despite extracting less meaning from their narratives and generating fewer specific memories than TD controls. This finding was paired with similar qualitative reports of memories between the two groups. Crane and colleagues (2012) further demonstrated differences in speed and specificity of recall for individuals with ASD versus controls, despite qualitative similarities in the memories retrieved. This important body of work suggests that individuals with ASD may not have broad episodic or autobiographical memory deficits, but rather differences in the availability, degree of recollective specificity, and perceived importance of memory traces for personally experienced events.

An earlier study of source monitoring further muddies the waters of this body of work, reporting that adults with ASD had greater reliability during recall of other- than self-performed actions (Russell & Jarrold, 1999). It has since been suggested that this differing finding may be due in part to sample characteristics—namely, that the sample reported in Russell and Jarrold's study had significantly greater cognitive impairments. At this time, a larger preponderance of evidence is needed to resolve the question of whether differences in self-concept impact memory for personally experienced events, and whether these differences vary in any systematic way within the ASD population.

Additional Factors That May Influence Autobiographical Memory in ASD

Theory of Mind

The relation between theory of mind (ToM) and autobiographical memory has been discussed elsewhere in the literature, but results have yet to clearly distinguish whether autobiographical memory impairments hinder ToM task performance, or whether underlying ToM deficits affect autobiographical memory encoding. The ability to distinguish self-knowledge from others may influence a person's ability to generate or elaboratively encode self-related memories. Adler and colleagues (2010) and Kristen,

Rossmann, and Sodian (2014) have reported a relation between ToM and autobiographical memory in ASD but not in TD controls. In Adler et al.'s (2010) sample, adolescents and young adults with ASD were less specific than age-matched controls in their references to time intervals and had lower overall performance on an autobiographical memory task, despite an equal number of references to self. This finding highlights the distinction between largely intact self-concept and impairment in temporal binding that likely produces impairments in autobiographical memory encoding and recall. Adler and colleagues concluded that differences in autobiographical memory ability in ASD drive impaired performance on ToM tasks.

Psychiatric co-morbidities

Some have drawn a theoretical link between atypical autobiographical memory and delusions in ASD and other psychiatric populations, with delusions attributed in part to difficulty with source monitoring (Corcoran, 2001; Kaney et al., 1999). However, the evidence presented here suggests that source monitoring is largely intact in adults with ASD. Abell and Hare (2005) found support for previous work suggesting that adolescents and adults with Asperger's/high-functioning autism experience more delusions than the general population, but fewer than people with psychosis. However, Abell and Hare did not find support for a link between delusions and autobiographical memory. Thus, the negative correlation between persecutory delusions and autobiographical memory recall observed by Kaney and colleagues (1999) may be due to clinical features of other psychiatric conditions and not necessarily relevant to ASD.

Recommendations for Facilitating Effective Retrieval of Autobiographical Memory in ASD

Some have suggested that adults with ASD may have atypically strong resistance to memory interference (Mottron et al., 1998), perhaps in part, due to a preference for the verbatim end of the fuzzy-to-verbatim continuum (although research suggests that verbatim is more susceptible to interference than gist memory; Reyna & Brainerd, 1995a, 1995b). Bruck and Ceci (1995, 1999, 2004) have described the circumstances that influence suggestibility in TD children (Brainerd et al., 2011). However, less is known about suggestibility of individuals with ASD, particularly with regard to autobiographical memory. Extrapolating from Bruck and Ceci's work, key factors influencing the suggestibility of individuals with ASD might include weak traces (whether due to less elaborative encoding, limited durability, or difficulty with retrieval), difficulty with source monitoring and self versus other distinctions, and limitations related to language and production of personal narratives. We have discussed the extant literature pertaining to these factors, but important questions remain regarding the degree to which development influences suggestibility in ASD.

For both TD children and adults, social demands can increase suggestibility (Bjorklund et al., 2000; Holliday, Douglas, & Hayes, 1999). Individuals with ASD who have intact autobiographical memory may have decreased sensitivity to social cues and pressures, thus reducing their susceptibility to suggestion. Conversely, individuals with ASD who have deficits in autobiographical memory may be more susceptible due to impoverished verbatim memory traces for an event because they must rely on gist traces to fill in the gaps (e.g., Howe, 1991; Marche, 1999; Pezdek & Roe, 1995). In addition to the ability of individuals with ASD to monitor the source of information (e.g., their own experience versus suggestion from others), it is important to consider whether they would be able to accurately judge the credibility of a given source and resist suggestion from noncredible sources or those in positions of authority. This has important implications for the weight given to testimony provided by individuals with ASD, particularly in instances where information is obtained from another source rather than from direct experience. Several groups have demonstrated age-related trends in ability to judge credibility, resistance to suggestion from noncredible sources, and vulnerability to suggestion from credible sources in typical development (Lampinen & Smith, 1995; Skagerberg & Wright, 2008; French, Garry, & Mori, 2011). Ceci and colleagues (Ceci & Leichtmann, 1995; Ceci, Ross, & Toglia, 1987) also identified vulnerability to suggestion in younger and older children when misled by adult authority figures. These paradigms would be a useful addition to the ASD literature to answer questions about the specific circumstances under which suggestibility is increased for this clinical population.

From a complementary perspective proposed by Brezis (2015) and others, perhaps individuals with ASD do not spontaneously use self-concept as a tool in organizing episodic memories (e.g., Crane et al., 2009) and binding relevant features, potentially leading to deficits in autobiographical memory (see also Lind et al., 2014; Zmigrod et al., 2013). However, some advantages in memory accuracy may accompany a limited use of self-concept in memory organization. It may be the case that the tendency of TD individuals to rely on gist-based memory traces also supports a broader and more malleable self-concept, in turn, facilitating a positivity bias and leading indirectly to overconfidence in one's own memory accuracy. Thus, individuals with ASD who organize memories in a less self-referential way may be better able to avoid adjusting their memories for previously experienced events to avoid cognitive dissonance and fit their current self-concept, in the way that TD people often do.

Individuals with ASD may be less prone to strategic alterations to self-presentation under neutral conditions (Scheeren et al., 2010). Scheeren et al. noted that individuals with ASD did not strategically alter their self-presentation in response to information about audience preferences. However, positivity biases in self-presentation did surface in the presence of sufficient reward-based motivation. Of interest, Scheeren et al. noted that some individuals with ASD in their sample accurately identified a social expectation to modify self-presentation in response to task demands, but stated that they chose not to do so because it was dishonest. This particular study did not include direct examination of autobiographical memory or suggestibility, but the results reinforce the importance of using appropriate interviewing techniques in legal and law-enforcement settings to probe autobiographical memory in persons with ASD. Interviewers must remain neutral, avoiding any coercion or introduction of incentives, and should rely predominantly on open-ended questions to avoid reward-based motivation that could increase the likelihood of alterations to self-presentation. These aims can be achieved by using the cognitive interview (CI) (Fisher & Geiselman, 1992) or the NICHD structured interview (Lamb, Orbach, Hershkowitz, Esplin, & Horowitz, 2007). Under certain circumstances, evidence suggests that individuals with ASD are equally reliable, and perhaps even more so, compared to those who are TD (Maras & Bowler, 2014). Interviewers must be sensitive to the fact that a person with ASD may only produce disjointed elements of a scene or event, rather than a coherent narrative, when presented with open-ended prompts. It is important to note that this approach may not be appropriate for all people with ASD, particularly in cases of nonverbal or minimally verbal individuals with marked expressive language deficits who might become easily frustrated by not being able to answer open-ended questions. For these individuals, a less verbally-dependent approach may be more appropriate (e.g., "show me," drawing, writing, using picture cards or assistive communication devices to respond) depending on the situation and the specific strengths and challenges of the witness.

One possible technique for obtaining information about autobiographical memories is the cognitive interview (Fisher & Geiselman, 1992; Geiselman et al., 1984), which has demonstrated efficacy as a form of eliciting accurate eyewitness information from adults, children, the elderly, and individuals with learning disabilities (Davis et al., 2005; Bartlett & Memon, 2007; Milne et al., 1999; Wright & Holliday, 2007). The cognitive interview consists of context reinstatement, imagery-guided questioning, and changes to the order and perspective of recall.

However, Maras and Bowler (2010, 2012) suggested that the cognitive interview is not an appropriate tool for use in ASD. In one study (Maras & Bowler, 2010), they found that use of the cognitive interview reduced accuracy in the ASD group, an effect not observed when using a structured interview. It is possible that the scaffolding provided by context-reinstatement and imagery-guided aspects of the cognitive interview does not offer optimal support for those with ASD. As we have discussed here and elsewhere (Miller, Odegard, & Allen, 2014), individuals with ASD may not benefit from such scaffolding because of their tendency to rely heavily on individual verbatim memory traces for information not bound by features or context.

Indeed, in a later study, Maras and Bowler (2012) reported that individuals with ASD only benefitted from context reinstatement when the physical environment matched the contextual cues provided in the interview. This is not surprising given that individuals with ASD often have difficulty with remembering context or source during recall, relative to recognition, tasks (Bowler et al., 2004; Bowler, Gaigg, & Gardiner, 2008). Maras, Gaigg, and Bowler (2012) further observed that individuals with ASD had stronger recall and diminished forgetting for emotionally arousing events, similar to age-matched controls. However, the precise effect of emotional arousal on recall remains unclear since others have reported that negative emotion does not produce enhanced recall in ASD as in typical development (Deruelle et al., 2008).

It is notable that many of the studies discussed here were conducted using either videotaped events or photographic scenes, rather than personally experienced real or staged events. Results presented by Sigman et al. (2003) and Corona et al. (1998) suggested that individuals with ASD do not have equivocal emotional responses to videotaped versus real-life events. Indeed, Maras and colleagues (2013) found that adults with ASD demonstrated the enactment effect during recall for live, personally experienced events, despite several other studies failing to find this typical advantage for self- versus other-experienced events in ASD when using videos or photographs. This finding is in line with work demonstrating that reality monitoring—determining whether a memory is derived from actual experience or imagination—and source monitoring during enacted versus imagined events promotes greater encoding of kinesthetic details, which can provide additional context for memory reconstruction (Foley & Johnson, 1985; Foley,

Aman, & Gutch, 1987; Goff & Roediger, 1998; Johnson, Foley, Suengas, & Raye, 1988; Lindsay, Johnson, & Kwon, 1991; Sussman, 2001).

In light of somewhat mixed findings regarding the importance of context and personal experience, future study is needed to examine the efficacy of the cognitive interview for individuals with ASD. Specific attention should be paid to autobiographical memories for personally experienced events, which may have greater salience and emotional arousal and thereby lead to more effective feature- or temporal-binding at encoding. The NICHD structured interview protocol, which has an established record of productivity in TD populations (Lamb et al., 2007; Sternberg et al., 2001), may be a more appropriate alternative to the cognitive interview given the collective findings of Maras and colleagues (2010, 2012, 2013, 2014). In the structured interview, interviewers rely on open-ended prompts in an effort to elicit free recall. Free recall is less susceptible to commission errors—due to greater reliance on verbatim retrieval in standard free recall of unrelated items—than to errors of omission resulting from the absence, decay, or inaccessibility of verbatim traces (Brainerd et al., 2009). The more conservative approach of open-ended prompting may provide a means of eliciting more accurate, although perhaps less, information from a person with ASD.

Regardless of interview format, it is important to note that investigators who are not highly trained may become frustrated when a person with ASD does not produce a detailed, coherent narrative during free recall. The tendency may be to transition to more leading questions or context reinstatement as an attempt to elicit gist-based reconstruction. However, whereas gist-based reconstruction is generally less literally accurate regardless of whether a person is typically or atypically developing, it may be extremely difficult or even impossible under some circumstances for a person with ASD.

A lineup or photo book offers a tool to cue recognition memory. In a detailed meta-analysis, Steblay et al. (2001) found strong support for the use of sequential lineups, which may produce fewer correct identifications of targets, but fewer false-positives relative to simultaneous lineups. They are essentially a more conservative method in that they require individuals to make an absolute judgment for each target as it is presented. The use of sequential lineups is particularly appropriate for use when neither the witness nor the administrator knows how many photos are in the deck (Greathouse & Kovera, 2009). Simultaneous lineups, on the other hand, encourage relative judgments. While they are likely to yield higher rates of target identification, they may also result in more false positives by leading witnesses with weak memory traces to choose the target that is the best match to their memory, in essence constituting a calculated guess. Steblay et al. (2001) highlighted the possibility that these guesses might then be considered as evidence by the police or courts, which would be ill-advised. Recent evidence from real-world studies (vs. staged laboratory experiments) suggests that in typical development, simultaneous lineups may have an advantage over sequential lineups in terms of their overall results when considered with corroborating evidence (Amendola & Wixted, 2015; Wixted, Mickes, Dunn, Clark, & Wells, 2016). Since correct rejection rates are significantly higher for sequential than simultaneous lineups, and correct identification rates are nearly equal, especially when real-world conditions are approximated, Steblay and colleagues (2001) advocated for the use of sequential lineups in most situations. Given the recent questions surrounding best practices in target identification lineup procedures, it is important to consider the risks and benefits of each approach when working with individuals with ASD who may be vulnerable to suggestion or susceptible to feeling pressured to guess under certain circumstances.

Ideally, these tools could be administered on a computer in order to limit the social demands of the situation. Although individuals with ASD do not spontaneously modify their responses to meet social demands as readily as TD peers, they are not completely immune to this pressure. Computer administration would also be appropriate for minimally or nonverbal individuals, provided their receptive language skills were strong enough to understand task instructions because they could behaviorally indicate a response (pointing/touching/clicking) rather than having to produce responses heavily dependent on expressive language or narrative production ability.

Drawing offers another possible method of eliciting information independent of expressive language skills. Mattison, Dando, and Ormerod (2015) recently tested the efficacy of a novel retrieval tool, sketch reinstatement of context. For sketch reinstatement of context, individuals are provided with paper and pencil, and asked to draw the event that they witnessed in as much detail as they wish and describe each element as they draw it, with no time limit (see also Dando, Wilcock, & Milne, 2009). Mattison et al. found that this approach was more effective than mental context reinstatement (i.e., the technique employed in the cognitive interview) or no support for recall. Although the sketch reinstatement approach was developed with TD individuals and traditionally involves a verbal description during sketching, it may be modifiable to meet the needs of individuals with ASD who have limited expressive language skills. Further work is needed to determine whether this approach is valid in the ASD population. Mental context reinstatement may prove challenging for individuals with ASD who have receptive language challenges or difficulty with imagination, spatiotemporal reconstruction, and abstract thinking. Alternative approaches are important to consider, so that the needs of a wide spectrum of individuals with ASD can be met during both memory research in laboratory settings and eyewitness interviews in investigative contexts.

Conclusion

Despite having some general impairments in autobiographical memory in the domain of errors of omission, people with ASD may actually be more reliable eyewitnesses when expressive language deficits do not limit their ability to provide detailed reports, consistent with predictions of FTT. In addition, extant data suggest that people with ASD are less susceptible to the biases inherent to self-concept and gist-based processing that lead to errors of commission in TD people. Errors of omission in ASD are likely related to over-reliance on verbatim traces, which are susceptible to (a) unavailability due to decay, and/or (b) inaccessibility due to impaired binding during encoding or difficulty activating appropriate retrieval cues.

The reconstructive nature of autobiographical memory is of critical importance to understanding ASD through the lens of FTT. Gist-based reconstruction is a double-edged sword for people with ASD. It can serve the purpose of binding features together to make a cohesive memory, but it can also introduce error. For individuals who are able to use gist-based processing in a more typical manner, the risk of commission errors and suggestibility may be heightened. Although current evidence does not suggest that people with ASD are hyper-suggestible, as some previously thought, it is still important to monitor suggestibility and use appropriate interview techniques when eliciting autobiographical memories from people with ASD. As in typical development, suggestibility is especially important to consider when working with children with ASD; there is a dearth of literature on age-based differences in autobiographical memory in this population.

Verbatim traces are also interesting as related to reliability of memory in ASD. People with ASD seem to have intact verbatim memory traces, but these traces are often inaccessible. Contributing to issues with accessibility, verbatim traces may not be bound correctly with other episodic features because individuals with ASD do not seem to engage in spontaneous feature binding like TD people. Given the critical nature of elaborative retrieval processes, the remaining challenge for researchers and clinicians is finding ways to teach this skill to people with ASD.

Researchers must also find means to test autobiographical memory in ways that are not so dependent on language or narrative production skills. Language does not appear to be directly related to the *ability* to accurately recall personally experienced events, despite its significant role in the semantic sophistication of the recollective response. Therefore, a more appropriate means of testing autobiographical memory in ASD would be to use paradigms other than think-aloud or narrative reconstructions that are less dependent on language skills. This would enable researchers to determine the true nature of autobiographical memory in people with a wider range of ASD symptoms.

Take-Home Points

- Children and adults with ASD have notable differences in the way that they spontaneously encode and retrieve autobiographical memories.
- Autobiographical memory in ASD is less rooted in overarching self-concept than in specific facts or elements of episodic memories for personally experienced events.
- People with ASD are less susceptible to the biases inherent to self-concept and gist-based processing that lead to errors of commission.
- Errors of omission in ASD are likely related to over-reliance on verbatim traces, which may be unavailable or inaccessible.
- Source monitoring appears to be intact in ASD, but personally experienced events may be reported from the perspective of a third-party observer rather than in a self-referential manner.
- Children and adults with ASD can be reliable witnesses, but should be interviewed under carefully structured conditions to reduce suggestibility.

References

Abell, F., & Hare, D. J. (2005). An experimental investigation of the phenomenology of delusional beliefs in people with Asperger syndrome. *Autism*, *9*(5), 515–531.

Acredolo, C. (1995). Intuition and gist. Special issue: a symposium on fuzzy-trace theory. *Learning & Individual Differences*, *7*(2), 83–86.

Adler, N., Nadler, B., Eviatar, Z., & Shamay-Tsoory, S. G. (2010). The relationship between theory of mind and autobiographical memory in high-functioning autism and Asperger syndrome. *Psychiatry Research, 178*(1), 214–216.

Amendola, K. L., Wixted, J. T. (2015). Comparing the diagnostic accuracy of suspect identifications made by actual eyewitnesses from simultaneous and sequential lineups in a randomized field trial. *Journal of Experimental Criminology, 11*(2), 263–284.

Baker-Ward, L., Hess, T. M., & Flannagan, D. A. (1990). The effects of involvement on children's memory. *Cognitive Development, 5*(1), 55–69.

Bang, J., Burns, J., & Nadig, A. (2013). Brief report: Conveying subjective experience in conversation: production of mental state terms and personal narratives in individuals with high functioning autism. *Journal of Autism & Developmental Disorders, 43*(7), 1732–1740.

Bartlett, J. C., & Memon, A. (2007). Eyewitness memory in young and older adults. In R. C. L. Lindsay, D. F. Ross, J. D. Read, & M. P. Toglia (Eds.), *Handbook of eyewitness testimony* (Vol. *II*, pp. 309–338). New York, NY: Psychology Press.

Bauer, P. J., Larkina, M., & Deocampo, J. (2011). Early memory development. In U. Goswami (Ed.), *The Wiley-Blackwell handbook of childhood cognitive development* (2nd ed., pp. 153–179). Oxford, England: Wiley-Blackwell Publishers.

Begeer, S., Banerjee, R., Lunenburg, P., Meerum Terwogt, M., Stegge, H., & Rieffe, C. (2008). Brief report: Self-presentation of children with autism spectrum disorders. *Journal of Autism & Developmental Disorders, 38*(6), 1187–1191.

Bennetto, L., Pennington, B. F., & Rogers, S. J. (1996). Intact and impaired memory functions in autism. *Child Development, 67*(4), 1816–1835.

Ben Shalom, D. (2003). Memory in autism: Review and synthesis. *Cortex, 39*(4–5), 1129–1138.

Beversdorf, D. Q., Narayanan, A., Hillier, A., & Hughes, J. D. (2007). Network model of decreased context utilization in autism spectrum disorder. *Journal of Autism & Developmental Disorders, 37*(6), 1040–1048.

Bjorklund, D. F., Cassel, W. S., Bjorklund, B. R., Brown, R. D., Clark Park, C. L., Ernst, K., & Owen, F. A. (2000). Social demand characteristics in children's and adults' eyewitness memory and suggestibility: The effect of different interviewers on free recall and recognition. *Applied Cognitive Psychology, 14*, 421–433.

Block, S. D., Shestowsky, D., Segovia, D. A., Goodman, G. S., Schaaf, J. M., & Alexander, K. W. (2012). "That never happened": Adults' discernment of children's true and false memory reports. *Law & Human Behavior, 36*(5), 365–374.

Boucher, J. (1981). Memory for recent events in autistic children. *Journal of Autism & Developmental Disorders, 11*(3), 293–301.

Boucher, J., & Lewis, V. (1989). Memory impairments and communication in relatively able autistic children. *Journal of Child Psychology & Psychiatry & Allied Disciplines, 30*(1), 99–122.

Bowler, D. M., Gaigg, S. B., & Gardiner, J. M. (2008). Effects of related and unrelated context on recall and recognition by adults with high-functioning autism spectrum disorder. *Neuropsychologia, 46*(4), 993–999.

Bowler, D. M., Gaigg, S. B., & Gardiner, J. M. (2014). Binding of multiple features in memory by high-functioning adults with autism spectrum disorder. *Journal of Autism & Developmental Disorders, 44*(9), 2355–2362.

Bowler, D. M., Gardiner, J. M., & Berthollier, N. (2004). Source memory in adolescents and adults with Asperger's syndrome. *Journal of Autism & Developmental Disorders, 34*(5), 533–542.

Bowler, D. M., Gardiner, J. M., & Gaigg, S. B. (2007). Factors affecting conscious awareness in the recollective experience of adults with Asperger's syndrome. *Consciousness & Cognition, 16*(1), 124–143.

Bowler, D. M., Gardiner, J. M., & Grice, S. J. (2000). Episodic memory and remembering in adults with Asperger syndrome. *Journal of Autism & Developmental Disorders, 30*(4), 295–304.

Brainerd, C. J., Holliday, R. E., & Reyna, V. F. (2004). Behavioral measurement of remembering phenomenologies: So simple a child can do it. *Child Development, 75*, 505–522.

Brainerd, C. J., & Reyna, V. F. (1990a). Inclusion illusions: Fuzzy-trace theory and perceptual salience effects in cognitive development. *Developmental Review, 10*, 365–403.

Brainerd, C. J., & Reyna, V. F. (1990b). Gist is the grist: Fuzzy-trace theory and the new intuitionism. *Developmental Review, 10*, 3–47.

Brainerd, C. J., & Reyna, V. F. (1992). Explaining "memory-free" reasoning. *Psychological Science, 3*, 332–339.

Brainerd, C. J., & Reyna, V. F. (2005). *The science of false memory.* New York, NY: Oxford University Press.

Brainerd, C. J., Reyna, V. F., & Brandse, E. (1995). Are children's false memories more persistent than their true memories? *Psychological Science, 6*, 359–364.

Brainerd, C. J., Reyna, V. F., & Howe, M. L. (2009). Trichotomous processes in early memory development, aging, and cognitive impairment: A unified theory. *Psychological Review, 116*, 783–832.

Brainerd, C. J., Reyna, V. F., & Zember, E. (2011). Theoretical and forensic implications of developmental studies of the DRM illusion. *Memory & Cognition, 39*, 365–380.

Bransford, J. D., & Franks, J. J. (1971). The abstraction of linguistic ideas. *Cognitive Psychology, 2*, 331–350.

Brezis, R. S. (2015). Memory integration in the autobiographical narratives of individuals with autism. *Frontiers in Human Neuroscience, 9*, 76.

Brown, B. T., Morris, G., Nida, R. E., & Baker-Ward, L. (2012). Brief report: Making experience personal: Internal states language in the memory narratives of children with and without Asperger's disorder. *Journal of Autism & Developmental Disorders, 42*(3), 441–446.

Bruck, M., & Ceci, S. J. (1999). The suggestibility of children's memory. *Annual Review of Psychology, 50*(1), 419–439.

Bruck, M., & Ceci, S. J. (2004). Forensic developmental psychology: Unveiling four scientific misconceptions. *Current Directions in Psychology, 13*, 229–232.

Bruck, M., London, K., Landa, R., & Goodman, J. (2007). Autobiographical memory and suggestibility in children with autism spectrum disorder. *Development & Psychopathology, 19*(1), 73–95.

Carmody, D. P., & M. Lewis (2012). Self representation in children with and without autism spectrum disorders. *Child Psychiatry & Human Development, 43*(2), 227–237.

Ceci, S. J., & Bruck, M. (1993). The suggestibility of the child witness: A historical review and synthesis. *Psychological Bulletin, 113*, 403–439.

Ceci, S. J., & Bruck, M. (1995). *Jeopardy in the courtroom: A scientific analysis of children's testimony.* Washington, D.C.: American Psychological Association.

Ceci, S. J., Toglia, M.P., & Ross, D.F. (1987). Suggestibility of children's memory: Psycholegal implications. *Journal of Experimental Psychology: General, 116*(1), 38–49.

Ceci, S. J., Toglia, M.P., & Ross, D.F. (1988). On remembering…more or less: A trace strength interpretation of developmental differences in suggestibility. *Journal of Experimental Psychology: General, 117*, 201–203.

Chaput, V., Amsellem, F., Urdapilleta, I., Chaste, P., Leboyer, M., Delorme, R., & Gousse, V. (2013). Episodic memory and self-awareness in Asperger Syndrome: Analysis of memory narratives. *Research in Autism Spectrum Disorders, 7*(9), 1062–1067.

Conway, M. A., & Pleydell-Pearce, C. W. (2000). The construction of autobiographical memories in the self-memory system. *Psychology Review, 107*(2), 261–288.

Corcoran, R. (2001). Theory of mind and schizophrenia. In P. W. Corrigan & D. L. Penn (Eds.), *Social cognition and schizophrenia.* Washington, D.C.: American Psychological Association.

Corona, R., Dissanayake, C., Arbelle, S., Wellington, P., & Sigman, M. (1998). Is affect aversive to young children with autism? Behavioural and cardiac responses to experimenter distress. *Child Development*, *69*, 1494–1502.

Cosentino, E. (2011). Self in time and language. *Consciousness & Cognition*, *20*(3), 777–783.

Crane, L., & Goddard, L. (2008). Episodic and semantic autobiographical memory in adults with autism spectrum disorders. *Journal of Autism & Developmental Disorders*, *38*(3), 498–506.

Crane, L., Goddard, L., & Pring, L. (2009). Specific and general autobiographical knowledge in adults with autism spectrum disorders: The role of personal goals. *Memory*, *17*(5), 557–576.

Crane, L., Goddard, L., & Pring, L. (2010). Brief Report: Self-defining and everyday autobiographical memories in adults with autism spectrum disorders. *Journal of Autism & Developmental Disorders*, *40*(3), 383–391.

Crane, L., Goddard, L., & Pring, L. (2013a). Autobiographical memory in adults with autism spectrum disorder: The role of depressed mood, rumination, working memory and theory of mind. *Autism*, *17*(2), 205–219.

Crane, L., Lind, S. E., & Bowler, D. M. (2013b). Remembering the past and imagining the future in autism spectrum disorder. *Memory*, *21*(2), 157–166.

Crane, L., Pring, L., Jukes, K., & Goddard, L. (2012). Patterns of autobiographical memory in adults with autism spectrum disorder. *Journal of Autism & Developmental Disorders*, *42*(10), 2100–2112.

David, N., Rose, M., Schneider, T. R., Vogeley, K., & Engel, A. K. (2010). Brief report: Altered horizontal binding of single dots to coherent motion in autism. *Journal of Autism & Developmental Disorders*, *40*(12), 1549–1551.

Davis, M. R., McMahon, M. & Greenwood, K. M. (2005). The efficacy of mnemonic components of the cognitive interview: Towards a shortened variant for time-critical investigations. *Applied Cognitive Psychology*, *19*, 75–93.

Dawson, G., & McKissick, F. C. (1984). Self-recognition in autistic children. *Journal of Autism & Developmental Disorders*, *14*(4), 383–394.

Dennis, N. A., Kim, H., & Cabeza, R. (2008). Age-related differences in brain activity during true and false memory retrieval. *Journal of Cognitive Neuroscience*, *20*, 1390–1402.

Deruelle, C., Hubert, B., Santos, A., & Wicker, B. (2008), Negative emotion does not enhance recall skills in adults with autistic spectrum disorders. *Autism Research*, *1*, 91–96.

Diehl, J. J., Bennetto, L., & Young, E. C. (2006). Story recall and narrative coherence of high-functioning children with autism spectrum disorders. *Journal of Abnormal Child Psychology*, *34*(1), 87–102.

Dissanayake, C., Shembrey, J., & Suddendorf, T. (2010). Delayed video self-recognition in children with high functioning autism and Asperger's disorder. *Autism*, *14*(5), 495–508.

Elmose, M., & Happé, F. (2014). Being aware of own performance: How accurately do children with autism spectrum disorder judge own memory performance? *Autism Research: Official Journal of the International Society for Autism Research*, *7*(6), 712–719.

Farley, A., Lopez, B., & Saunders, G. (2010). Self-conceptualisation in autism: Knowing oneself versus knowing self-through-other. *Autism*, *14*(5), 519–530.

Farrant, A., Blades, M., & Boucher, J. (1998). Source monitoring by children with autism. *Journal of Autism & Developmental Disorders*, *28*(1), 43–50.

Farrar, M. J., & Goodman, G. S. (1992). Developmental changes in event memory. *Child Development*, *63*(1), 173–187.

Ferrari, M., & Matthews, W. S. (1983). Self-recognition deficits in autism: Syndrome-specific or general developmental delay? *Journal of Autism & Developmental Disorders*, *13*(3), 317–324.

Fisher, R. P., & Geiselman, R. E. (1992). *Memory enhancing techniques for investigative interviewing: The cognitive interview*. Springfield, IL: Charles C. Thomas.

Fivush, R., Gray, J. T., & Fromhoff, F. A. (1987). Two-year-olds talk about the past. *Cognitive Development, 2*, 393–409.

Foley, M. A., Aman, C., & Gutch, D. (1987). Discriminating between action memories: Children's use of kinesthetic cues and visible consequences. *Journal of Experimental Child Psychology, 44*(3), 335–347.

Foley, M. A., & Johnson, M. K. (1985). Confusions between memories for performed and imagined actions: A developmental comparison. *Child Development, 56*, 1145–1155.

French, L., Garry, M., & Mori, K. (2011). Relative—not absolute—judgments of credibility affect susceptibility to misinformation conveyed during discussion. *Acta Psychologica, 136*(1), 119–128.

Gardiner, J. M. (2001). Episodic memory and autonoetic consciousness: a first-person approach. *Philosophical Transactions of the Royal Society (Biological Sciences), 356*, 1351–1361.

Geiselman, R. E., Fisher, R. P., Firstenberg, I., Hutton, L. A., Sullivan, S., Avetissian, I., & Prosk, A. (1984). Enhancement of eyewitness memory: An empirical evaluation of the cognitive interview. *Journal of Police Science & Administration, 12*, 74–80.

Ghetti, S., & Angelini, L. (2008). The development of recollection and familiarity in childhood and adolescence: Evidence from the dual-process signal detection model. *Child Development, 79*(2), 339–358.

Ghetti, S., Qin, J., & Goodman, G. S. (2002). False memories in children and adults: Age, distinctiveness, and subjective experience. *Developmental Psychology, 38*, 705–718.

Goddard, L., Dritschel, B., Robinson, S., & Howlin, P. (2014). Development of autobiographical memory in children with autism spectrum disorders: Deficits, gains, and predictors of performance. *Development & Psychopathology, 26*(1), 215–228.

Goff, L. M., & Roediger, H. L. (1998). Imagination inflation for action events: Repeated imaginings lead to illusory recollections. *Memory & Cognition, 26*(1), 20–33.

Gowen, E., & Miall, R. C. (2005). Behavioural aspects of cerebellar function in adults with Asperger syndrome. *Cerebellum, 4*(4), 279–289.

Greathouse, S. M., & Kovera, M. B. (2009). Instruction bias and lineup presentation moderate the effects of administrator knowledge on eyewitness identification. *Law & Human Behavior, 33*, 70–82.

Grisdale, E., Lind, S. E., Eacott, M. J., & Williams, D. M. (2014). Self-referential memory in autism spectrum disorder and typical development: Exploring the ownership effect. *Consciousness & Cognition, 30*, 133–141.

Hala, S., Rasmussen, C., & Henderson, A. M. (2005). Three types of source monitoring by children with and without autism: The role of executive function. *Journal of Autism & Developmental Disorders, 35*(1), 75–89.

Happé, F., & Frith, U. (2006). The weak coherence account: Detail-focused cognitive style in autism spectrum disorders. *Journal of Autism & Developmental Disorders, 36*(1), 5–25.

Hare, D. J., Mellor, C., & Azmi, S. (2007). Episodic memory in adults with autistic spectrum disorders: Recall for self- versus other-experienced events. *Research in Developmental Disabilities, 28*(3), 317–329.

Hill, E., & Russell, J. (2002). Action memory and self-monitoring in children with autism: Self versus other. *Infant & Child Development, 11*, 159–170.

Holliday, R. E., Douglas, K., & Hayes, B. K. (1999). Children's eyewitness suggestibility: Memory trace strength revisited. *Cognitive Development, 14*, 443–462.

Howe, M. L. (1991). Misleading children's story recall: Forgetting and reminiscence of the facts. *Developmental Psychology, 27*, 746–762.

Howe, M. L. (2011). *The nature of early memory: An adaptive theory of the genesis and development of memory.* New York, NY: Oxford University Press.

Jackson, P., Skirrow, P., & Hare, D. J. (2012). Asperger through the looking glass: An exploratory study of self-understanding in people with Asperger's syndrome. *Journal of Autism & Developmental Disorders, 42*(5), 697–706.

Johnson, M. K., Foley, M. A., Suengas, A. G., & Raye, C. L. (1988). Phenomenal characteristics of memories for perceived and imagined autobiographical events. *Journal of Experimental Psychology: General, 117*(4), 371–376.

Kaney, S., Bowen-Jones, K., & Bentall, R.P. (1999). Persecutory delusions and autobiographical memory. *British Journal of Clinical Psychology, 38*(1), 97–102.

Kennedy, D. P., & Courchesne, E. (2008). Functional abnormalities of the default network during self- and other-reflection in autism. *Social Cognitive & Affective Neuroscience, 3*(2), 177–190.

Kintsch, W., Welsch, D., Schmalhofer, F., & Zimny, S. (1990). Sentence memory: A theoretical analysis. *Journal of Memory & Language, 29*, 133–159.

Klein, S. B., Chan, R. L., & Loftus, J. (1999). Independence of episodic and semantic self-knowledge: The case from autism. *Social Cognition, 17*(4), 413–436.

Kristen, S., Rossmann, F., & Sodian, B. (2014). Theory of own mind and autobiographical memory in adults with ASD. *Research in Autism Spectrum Disorders, 8*(7), 827–837.

Lamb, M. E., Orbach, Y., Hershkowitz, I., Esplin, P. W., & Horowitz, D. (2007). Structured forensic interview protocols improve the quality and informativeness of investigative interviews with children: A review of research using the NICHD Investigative Interview Protocol. *Child Abuse & Neglect, 31*(11–12), 1201–1231.

Lampinen, J. M., Meier, C. R., Arnal, J. D., & Leding, J. K. (2005). Compelling untruths: Content borrowing and vivid false memories. *Journal of Experimental Psychology: Learning, Memory, & Cognition, 31*(5), 954–963.

Lampinen, J. M., & Smith, V. L. (1995). The incredible (and sometimes incredulous) child witness: Child eyewitnesses' sensitivity to source credibility cues. *Journal of Applied Psychology, 80*(5), 621–627.

Landauer, T. K., & Dumais, S. T. (1997). A solution to Plato's problem: The latent semantic analysis theory of acquisition, induction, and representation of knowledge. *Psychological Review, 104*(2), 211–240.

Leichtman, M. D., & Ceci, S. J. (1995). The effects of stereotypes and suggestions on preschoolers' reports. *Developmental Psychology, 31*(4), 568–578.

Lind, S. E. (2010). Memory and the self in autism: A review and theoretical framework. *Autism, 14*(5), 430–456.

Lind, S. E., & Bowler, D. M. (2008). Episodic memory and autonoetic consciousness in autistic spectrum disorders: The roles of self-awareness, representational abilities and temporal cognition. In J. Boucher & D. M. Bowler (Eds.), *Memory in autism: Theory and evidence* (pp. 166–187). New York, NY: Cambridge University Press.

Lind, S. E., & Bowler, D. M. (2009). Delayed self-recognition in children with autism spectrum disorder. *Journal of Autism & Developmental Disorders, 39*(4), 643–650.

Lind, S. E., & Bowler, D. M. (2010). Episodic memory and episodic future thinking in adults with autism. *Journal of Abnormal Psychology, 119*(4), 896–905.

Lind, S. E., Bowler, D. M., & Raber, J. (2014a). Spatial navigation, episodic memory, episodic future thinking, and theory of mind in children with autism spectrum disorder: Evidence for impairments in mental simulation? *Frontiers in Psychology, 5*, 1411.

Lind, S. E., Williams, D. M., Bowler, D. M., & Peel, A. (2014b). Episodic memory and episodic future thinking impairments in high-functioning autism spectrum disorder: An underlying difficulty with scene construction or self-projection? *Neuropsychology, 28*(1), 55–67.

Lindsay, D. S., Johnson, M. K., & Kwon, P. (1991). Developmental changes in memory source monitoring. *Journal of Experimental Child Psychology, 52*(3), 297–318.

Loftus, E. F., Miller, D. G., & Burns, H. J. (1978). Semantic integration of verbal information into a visual memory. *Human Learning & Memory, 4*, 19–31.

Lombardo, M. V., Chakrabarti, B., Bullmore, E. T., Sadek, S. A., Pasco, G., Wheelwright, S. J., … Baron-Cohen, S. (2010). Atypical neural self-representation in autism. *Brain, 133*(Pt 2), 611–624.

Losh, M., & Gordon, P. C. (2014). Quantifying narrative ability in autism spectrum disorder: A computational linguistic analysis of narrative coherence. *Journal of Autism & Developmental Disorders, 44*(12), 3016–3025.

Maister, L., & Plaisted-Grant, K. C. (2011). Time perception and its relationship to memory in Autism Spectrum conditions. *Developmental Science, 14*(6), 1311–1322.

Malmberg, K. J., & Shiffrin, R. M. (2005). The "one-shot" hypothesis for context storage. *Journal of Experimental Psychology: Learning, Memory, & Cognition, 31*(2), 322–336.

Maras, K. L., & Bowler, D. M. (2010). The cognitive interview for eyewitnesses with autism spectrum disorder. *Journal of Autism & Developmental Disorders, 40*, 1350–1360.

Maras, K. L., & Bowler, D. M. (2012). Context reinstatement effects on eyewitness memory in autism spectrum disorder. *British Journal of Psychology, 103*(3), 330–342.

Maras, K. L., & Bowler, D. M. (2014). Eyewitness testimony in autism spectrum disorder: A review. *Journal of Autism & Developmental Disorders, 44*(11), 2682–2697.

Maras, K. L., Gaigg, S. B., & Bowler, D. M. (2012). Memory for emotionally arousing events over time in autism spectrum disorder. *Emotion, 12*(5), 1118–1128.

Maras, K. L., Memon, A., Lambrechts, A., & Bowler, D. M. (2013). Recall of a live and personally experienced eyewitness event by adults with autism spectrum disorder. *Journal of Autism & Developmental Disorders, 43*(8), 1798–1810.

Marche, T. A. (1999). Memory strength affects reporting of misinformation. *Journal of Experimental Child Psychology, 73*, 45–71.

Marche, T. A., & Howe, M. L. (1995). Preschoolers report misinformation despite accurate memory. *Developmental Psychology, 31*, 554–567.

Marsh, E. J., & Roediger, H. L., III. (2013). Episodic and autobiographical memory. In A. F. Healy & R. W. Proctor (Eds.), *Handbook of psychology: Vol. 4, Experimental Psychology* (2nd ed., pp. 472–494). New York, NY: John Wiley & Sons.

Martin, J. S., Poirier, M., & Bowler, D. M. (2010). Brief report: Impaired temporal reproduction performance in adults with autism spectrum disorder. *Journal of Autism & Developmental Disorders, 40*(5), 640–646.

Mattison, M. L., Dando, C. J., & Ormerod, T. C. (2015). Sketching to remember: Episodic free recall task support for child witnesses and victims with autism spectrum disorder. *Journal of Autism & Developmental Disorders, 45*(6), 1751–1765.

McCrory, E., Henry, L. A., & Happé, F. (2007). Eye-witness memory and suggestibility in children with Asperger syndrome. *Journal of Child Psychology & Psychiatry & Allied Disciplines, 48*(5), 482–489.

McDermott, K. B. (1996). The persistence of false memories in list recall. *Journal of Memory & Language, 35*, 212–230.

Meyer, B. J., Gardiner, J. M., & Bowler, D. M. (2014). Directed forgetting in high-functioning adults with autism spectrum disorders. *Journal of Autism & Developmental Disorders, 44*(10), 2514–2524.

Miller, H. L., Odegard, T. N., & Allen, G. (2014). Evaluating information processing in autism spectrum disorder: The case for Fuzzy Trace Theory. *Developmental Review, 34*, 44–76.

Millward, C., Powell, S., Messer, D., & Jordan, R. (2000). Recall for self and other in autism: children's memory for events experienced by themselves and their peers. *Journal of Autism & Developmental Disorders, 30*(1), 15–28.

Milne, R., Clare, I. C. H., & Bull, R. (1999). Using the cognitive interview with adults with mild learning disabilities. *Psychology, Crime & Law, 5*, 81–100.

Mimura, M., Kinsbourne, M., & O'Conner, M. (2000). Time estimation by patients with frontal lobe lesions and by Korsakoff amnesics. *Journal of the International Neuropsychological Society, 6*, 517–528.

Mostofsky, S. H., Goldberg, M. C., Landa, R. J., & Denckla, M. B. (2000). Evidence for a deficit in procedural learning in children and adolescents with autism: Implications for cerebellar contribution. *Journal of the International Neuropsychological Society, 6*, 752–759.

Mottron, L., Belleville, S., Stip, E., & Morasse, K. (1998). Atypical memory performance in an autistic savant. *Memory, 6*(6), 593–607.

Naito, M. (2003). The relationship between theory of mind and episodic memory: Evidence for the development of autonoetic consciousness. *Journal of Experimental Child Psychology, 85*(4), 312–336.

Nelson, K. (1995). The dual category problem in lexical acquisition. In W. Merriman & M. Tomasello (Eds.), *Beyond names for things* (pp. 223–250). Hillsdale, NJ: Erlbaum.

Nelson, K., & Fivush, R. (2004). The emergence of autobiographical memory: A social cultural developmental theory. *Psychological Review, 111*(2), 486–511.

Odegard, T. N., Cooper, C. M., Holliday, R. E., & Ceci, S. J. (2010a). Interviewing child victims: Advances in the scientific understanding of child eyewitness memory. In J. M. Lampinen & K. Sexton-Radek (Eds.), *Protecting children from violence: Evidence based interventions* (pp. 105–127). New York, NY: Psychology Press.

Odegard, T. N., Cooper, C. M., Lampinen, J. M., Reyna, V. F., & Brainerd, C. J. (2009). Children's eyewitness memory for multiple real-life events. *Child Development, 80*(6), 1877–1890.

Odegard, T. N., Jenkins, K. M., & Koen, J. D. (2010b). Developmental differences in the use of recognition memory rejection mechanisms. *Developmental Psychology, 46*, 691–698.

Pezdek, K., & Roe, C. (1995). The effect of memory trace strength on suggestibility. *Journal of Experimental Child Psychology, 60*, 116–128.

Powell, S. D., & Jordan, R. R. (1993). Being subjective about autistic thinking and learning to learn. *Educational Psychology, 13*(3–4), 359–370.

Raj, V., & Bell, M. A. (2010). Cognitive processes supporting episodic memory formation in childhood: The role of source memory, binding, and executive functioning. *Developmental Review, 30*, 384–402.

Reyna, V. F. (1995). Interference effects in memory and reasoning: A fuzzy-trace theory analysis. In F. N. Dempster & C. J. Brainerd (Eds.), *Interference and inhibition in cognition* (pp. 29–59). San Diego, CA: Academic Press.

Reyna, V. F. (2008). A theory of medical decision making and health: Fuzzy Trace Theory. *Medical Decision Making, 28*(6), 850–865.

Reyna, V. F., & Brainerd, C. J. (1991a). Fuzzy-trace theory and children's acquisition of scientific and mathematical concepts. *Learning & Individual Differences, 3*, 27–60.

Reyna, V. F., & Brainerd, C. J. (1991b). Fuzzy-trace Theory and framing effects in choice: Gist extraction, truncation, and conversion. *Journal of Behavioral Decision Making, 4*, 249–262.

Reyna, V. F., & Brainerd, C. J. (1995a). Fuzzy-trace theory: An interim synthesis. *Learning & Individual Differences, 7*(1), 1–75.

Reyna, V. F., & Brainerd, C. J. (1995b). Fuzzy-trace theory: Some foundational issues. *Learning & Individual Differences, 7*(2), 145–162.

Reyna, V. F., & Brainerd, C. J. (2011). Dual processes in decision making and developmental neuroscience: A fuzzy-trace model. *Developmental Review, 31*, 180–206.

Reyna, V. F., Chick, C. F., Corbin, J. C., & Hsia, A. N. (2014). Developmental reversals in risky decision-making: Intelligence agents show larger decision biases than college students. *Psychological Science, 25*(1), 76–84.

Reyna, V. F., Corbin, J. C., Weldon, R. B., & Brainerd, C. J. (2016). How fuzzy-trace theory predicts true and false memories for words, sentences, and narratives. *Journal of Applied Research in Memory & Cognition, 5*(1), 1–9.

Reyna, V. F., & Kiernan, B. (1994). The development of gist versus verbatim memory in sentence recognition: Effects of lexical familiarity, semantic content, encoding instruction, and retention interval. *Developmental Psychology, 30*, 178–191.

Reyna, V. F., & Mills, B. A. (2007). Converging evidence supports fuzzy-trace theory's nested sets hypothesis (but not the frequency hypothesis). *Behavioral & Brain Sciences, 30*, 278–280.

Reyna, V. F., Weldon, R. B., & McCormick, M. J. (2015a). Educating intuition: Reducing risky decisions using fuzzy-trace theory. *Current Directions in Psychological Science, 24*(4), 392–398.

Reyna, V. F., Wilhelms, E. A., McCormick, M. J., & Weldon, R. B. (2015b). Development of risky decision making: Fuzzy-trace theory and neurobiological perspectives. *Child Development Perspectives, 9*(2), 122–127.

Rogers, T. B., Kuiper, N. A., & Kirker, W. S. (1977). Self-reference and the encoding of personal information. *Journal of Personality & Social Psychology, 35*, 677–688.

Russell, J., & Jarrold, C. (1999). Memory for actions in children with autism: Self versus other. *Cognitive Neuropsychiatry, 4*(4), 303–331.

Scheeren, A. M., Begeer, S., Banerjee, R., Meerum Terwogt, M., & Koot, H. M. (2010). Can you tell me something about yourself? Self-presentation in children and adolescents with high functioning autism spectrum disorder in hypothetical and real life situations. *Autism, 14*(5), 457–473.

Schneider, W. (2011). Memory development in childhood. In U. Goswami (Ed.), *The Wiley-Blackwell handbook of childhood cognitive development* (2nd ed., pp. 347–376). West Sussex, England: Wiley-Blackwell Publishers.

Sederberg, P. B., Gershman, S. J., Polyn, S. M., & Norman, K. A. (2011). Human memory reconsolidation can be explained using the temporal context model. *Psychonomic Bulletin & Review, 18*(3), 455–468.

Shing, Y. L., & Lindenberger, U. (2011). The development of episodic memory: Lifespan lessons. *Child Development Perspectives, 5*, 148–155.

Sigman, M., Dissanayake, C., Corona, R., & Espinosa, M. (2003). Social and cardiac responses of young children with autism. *Autism, 7*, 205–216.

Skagerberg, E. M., & Wright, D. B. (2008). Susceptibility to postidentification feedback is affected by source credibility. *Applied Cognitive Psychology, 23*(4), 506–523.

Stäubli, U., Ivy, G., & Lynch, G. (1984). Hippocampal denervation causes rapid forgetting of olfactory information in rats. *Proceedings of the National Academy of Sciences, 81*, 5885–5887.

Steblay, N., Dysart, J., Fulero, S., & Lindsay, R. C. L. (2001). Eyewitness accuracy rates in sequential and simultaneous lineup presentations: A meta-analytic comparison. *Law & Human Behavior, 25*(5), 459–473.

Sternberg, K. J., Lamb, M. E., Orbach, Y., Esplin, P. W., & Mitchell, S. (2001). Use of a structured investigative protocol enhances young children's responses to free-recall prompts in the course of forensic interviews. *Journal of Applied Psychology, 86*, 997–1005.

Sussman, A. L. (2001). Reality monitoring of performed and imagined interactive events: Developmental and contextual effects. *Journal of Experimental Child Psychology, 79*, 115–138.

Szelag, E., Kowalska, J., Galkowski, T., & Poppel, E. (2004). Temporal processing deficits in high functioning children with autism. *British Journal of Psychology, 95*, 269–282.

Tanweer, T., Rathbone, C. J., & Souchay, C. (2010). Autobiographical memory, autonoetic consciousness, and identity in Asperger syndrome. *Neuropsychologia, 48*(4), 900–908.

Titcomb, A. L., & Reyna, V. F. (1995). Memory interference and misinformation effects. In F. N. Dempster & C. J. Brainerd (Eds.), *Interference and inhibition in cognition* (pp. 263–294). San Diego, CA: Academic Press.

Toglia, M. P., Neuschatz, J. S., & Goodwin, K. A. (1999). Recall accuracy and illusory memories: When more is less. *Memory, 7*(2), 233–256.

Toglia, M. P., Ross, D. F., Pozzulo, J., & Pica, E. (Eds.). (2014). *The elderly eyewitness in court.* New York, NY: Psychology Press.

Toichi, M., Kamio, Y., Okada, T., Sakihama, M., Youngstrom, E. A., Findling, R. L., & Yamamoto, K. (2002). A lack of self-consciousness in autism. *American Journal of Psychiatry, 159*(8), 1422–1424.

Tulving, E. (1983). *Elements of episodic memory.* New York, NY: Oxford University Press.

Tun, P. A., Wingfield, A., Rosen, M. J., & Blanchard, L. (1998). Response latencies for false memories: Gist-based processes in normal aging. *Psychology & Aging, 13*(2), 230–241.

Wallace, G. L., & Happé, F. (2008). Time perception in autism spectrum disorders. *Research in Autism Spectrum Disorders, 2*, 447–455.

Williams, D. M., & Happé, F. (2009). What did I say? Versus what did I think? Attributing false beliefs to self amongst children with and without autism. *Journal of Autism & Developmental Disorders, 39*(6), 865–873.

Wixted, J. T., Mickes, L., Dunn, J. C., Clark, S. E., & Wells, W. (2016). Estimating the reliability of eyewitness identifications from police lineups. *Proceedings of the National Academy of Sciences of the United States of America, 113*(2), 304–309.

Wright, A. M., & Holliday, R. E. (2007). Enhancing the recall of young, young-old, and old-old adults with cognitive interviews. *Applied Cognitive Psychology, 21*, 19–43.

Zalla, T., Daprati, E., Sav, A. M., Chaste, P., Nico, D., & Leboyer, M. (2010). Memory for self-performed actions in individuals with Asperger syndrome. *PLoS ONE, 5*(10), e13370.

Zmigrod, S., de Sonneville, L. M., Colzato, L. S., Swaab, H., & Hommel, B. (2013). Cognitive control of feature bindings: Evidence from children with autistic spectrum disorder. *Psychological Research, 77*(2), 147–154.

3

Executive Function and Complex Processing Models

Diane L. Williams

One of the most striking aspects of autism spectrum disorders (ASD) is the heterogeneity of presentation across individuals diagnosed with the disorder. Professionals who work with individuals with ASD frequently say, "If you've seen one person with autism, you've seen one person with autism." Many models of ASD have sought to move past this heterogeneity to identify a common, underlying problem that will characterize all individuals with this disorder. However, information processing models of ASD accept the heterogeneity as an expected result given the basic tenet that individuals with ASD are essentially learning and processing information differently than most people, but not necessarily the same as each other.

This chapter describes the challenges individuals with ASD have with autobiographical memory based on an information processing model of cognitive function. Information processing models of cognitive function are patterned after computer models of learning with emphasis on the dynamic nature of the learning process or HOW learning occurs rather than on WHAT is learned. Processing models attempt to explain how the brain handles incoming and outgoing information—how it interprets or makes sense of information, how it organizes and stores the information, and how information is retrieved from the brain for sharing with others. To understand the information processing of individuals with ASD, the general cognitive mechanisms that support memory from the perspective of individuals with typical development is explained. Although memory function in ASD differs from that of individuals with typical development, it appears to be a derivation of these normative processes, not a deviation, so we must first understand how these normative processes function. Next, how the cognitive mechanisms supporting memory are affected in individuals with ASD is discussed in more detail. The chapter concludes with a discussion of the implications of problems with memory and information processing when individuals with ASD encounter representatives of the legal system.

The Wiley Handbook of Memory, Autism Spectrum Disorder, and the Law, First Edition.
Edited by Jonni L. Johnson, Gail S. Goodman, and Peter C. Mundy.

General cognitive mechanisms for information processing

Before discussing the executive function and information processing models of ASD, this chapter first describes memory processes from the perspective of information processing models of cognitive function in individuals with typical development. Memory function in ASD is a variation of what is observed in typical development; therefore, what we know about typical memory function will help us to understand the less typical memory function seen in individuals with ASD.

According to information processing models, memory is a general cognitive resource that is part of the learning process for all types of information. Memory is commonly thought of as the store house of all that we have experienced and thought; however, it is much more than a static storage area in the brain. Memory is a dynamic process involved in each of the four primary stages of information processing—attention, encoding, storage, and retrieval. Furthermore, memory processing can affect cognitive functioning across the neurocognitive domains.

Neurocognitive domains

The six primary neurocognitive domains, as delineated in the *Diagnostic and Statistical Manual of Mental Disorders, 5th Edition* (DSM-5; American Psychiatric Association, 2013), are complex attention, executive function, language, learning and memory, social cognition, and perceptual-motor function. The first four of these are discussed in more detail in the next sections because they are the ones most relevant to our consideration of autobiographical memory in ASD.

Complex attention

Attention is a general learning mechanism through which individuals control where to direct and how to use cognitive resources. We generally describe attention in relation to how it is being used. For example, *selective attention* is a reaction to the perceptual aspects of incoming stimuli that draw our notice such as a light that is suddenly bright or an unexpected loud sound. *Selective attention* may also occur through a more deliberative process in which the individual focuses on certain stimuli to the exclusion of others (e.g., watching a football game rather than listening to the conversation of your companions). *Sustained attention* allows us to devote cognitive resources to a task over time (e.g., focusing on a report that needs to be completed to meet a deadline). *Divided attention* occurs as we process stimuli of differing types or focus on multiple tasks at the same time (e.g., watching that football game and listening to your friends). *Processing speed*, or the time it takes a person to complete a cognitive task, is also generally considered under the neurocognitive domain of complex attention because it is related to the dedication and use of cognitive resources.

Because of the functional nature of attention, we typically specify what stimulus is being attended to and for what purpose. For example, an individual may *selectively attend* by directing cognitive resources to a license plate and may *sustain* that attention to memorize the numbers to later report to the authorities. They are therefore choosing to attend to these numbers to the exclusion of other stimuli that are in the environment and are devoting the needed memory resources for a period of time to accomplish the information processing task.

Executive functions

Executive functions are cognitive processes that are thought to manage all the other cognitive resources as they are allocated to accomplish the processing of information to attain a future goal (Welsh & Pennington, 1988). These functions, which arise from the frontal lobe of the brain, particularly the prefrontal cortex (Baddeley & Wilson, 1988; Knight, Staines, Swick, & Chao, 1999; Stuss & Benson, 1986), coordinate cognitive processing so that tasks are accomplished and work gets done. Executive functions include, but are not limited to, planning, working memory, response inhibition, and cognitive flexibility or goal switching (Ozonoff, 1997; Pennington & Ozonoff, 1996; Roberts, Robbins, & Weiskrantz, 1998). These "higher-order" functions allow us to use our cognitive resources efficiently and to accomplish tasks such as problem solving and navigating changing environmental demands.

Working memory

One of the executive functions, working memory, is considered in more detail given our overall interest in memory in ASD. The label for this process "working memory" can lead to some confusion as to what it is and why it is considered an executive function and not part of the neurocognitive domain of learning and memory. Whereas *memory* is commonly thought of as storage of information, no information is stored in a person's working memory. Rather, it is an active process by which information is actively maintained and manipulated so that it can be moved into long-term storage (Baddeley, 2002).

Several models of working memory have been proposed; the most commonly adopted one was proposed by Baddeley (1986). According to this model, working memory consists of three "slave" systems (the phonological or articulatory loop, the visuospatial sketchpad, and the episodic buffer) and a central executive that directs the work of these systems (Baddeley, 1996). Working memory is a relatively brief process lasting only a few seconds after which the memory trace rapidly disappears unless the information is updated. The phonological loop processes and stores material in a short-lived verbal code and is important for listening to language and reading written words. Memory items in the processes of listening and reading are thought to be represented in terms of their phonological structure or the sounds of a language. The phonological loop has an auditory component (for the maintenance of spoken language that was heard) and an articulatory rehearsal component (for the maintenance of language that is repeated to oneself aloud or silently) (Baddeley, 2003). The visuospatial sketchpad processes and stores visual and spatial information including material encoded as visual imagery (Baddeley, 1986). The episodic buffer holds larger pieces of verbal and visual information before storing them in long term memory (Baddeley, 2000). The central executive regulates the flow of information through working memory and oversees storage and retrieval of information from long term memory (Baddeley, 1996). As mentioned earlier, the central executive is responsible for the control and regulation of the three "slave" systems.

Language

Language, including both spoken and written forms, is a powerful cognitive domain that interacts with the other domains; it facilitates the creation of thoughts and the sharing of ideas. Whereas, language is a separate neurocognitive domain from learning and memory, which we consider next, the two domains are intrinsically linked. It is possible to learn and store visual information without encoding it verbally or putting it into words as evidenced when someone can draw a scene that they cannot describe in words. However, in individuals with typical development, experiences are quickly translated into a verbal form experienced as inner speech or thinking in words. Automatic verbal encoding of information reduces the cognitive processing load when managing large amounts of information. Putting information into words helps make it possible to store related information together, to later retrieve the information efficiently, and then to share it with others. The left hemispheric language regions are thought to be automatically engaged to interpret stimuli and assimilate them into comprehensible events (Wolford, Miller, & Gazzaniga, 2000). This automatic storytelling allows for elaboration and generalization of information such that the left hemisphere creates order from chaos (Gazzaniga, 2012). The left hemispheric language network provides a narrative and relates information to the other remembered events, whereas the right hemisphere is thought to maintain a record of the events that is more representative of the actual occurrence (Wolford et al., 2000).

Much of what we have learned is retrieved and shared with others by encoding this information into words and either speaking or writing these words. Because we cannot directly access an individual's memory, we depend on this verbal translation process to determine what information is stored there. An individual's facility with spoken and written language will therefore be an important factor in their ability to retrieve and share remembered information, such as when responding to police who are questioning witnesses at a scene or when reporting an incidence of domestic violence or sexual abuse.

Learning and memory

At first glance, memory would seem to be a rather one-dimensional cognitive domain that is the storage of all the information that an individual has processed. However, storage is actually the result of a process of learning and memory, a process that is very complex, and despite decades of research, is still not fully understood. Memory is thought to occur in three primary stages: encoding, storage, and retrieval (Melton, 1963).

Encoding is the acquisition stage when incoming information is first *acquired* through inputs to the sensory systems and then *consolidated* (Gazzaniga, Ivry, & Mangun, 2013). Despite the name, a memory that is undergoing consolidation is not fixed at the moment of encoding, rather it becomes more stable over time and becomes stronger when it is repeatedly retrieved and stored so that forgetting is disrupted (Squire, 1986). Another interesting aspect of memory function in the learning process is that learned information may actually be changed the more times the information is retrieved and then stored again in memory. That is, while retrieval and restorage of information makes the memory trace stronger, and subsequently, easier to retrieve, it may also alter the original information, linking details from the current experience that may over-ride details from the original experience (Bridge & Paller, 2012). For example, every time a witness retells an event, the original memory for the event may be altered as new details are added. The added details may arise from a true memory of the event or they may result from the incorporation of suggested or unconsciously integrated false information (Gallo, 2010).

The second stage of memory processing, storage, is when the information that has been attended to, processed in the working memory system, and encoded into a neurochemical signal, is then moved into long-term memory, waiting and available for future use by the learner. Long-term memory, as indicated by its name, is the cognitive mechanism by which we store data for extended periods of time.

The last stage of memory occurs when the stored information is retrieved by the learner. Retrieval capacity is dependent on critical factors such as the presence of cues or information that may trigger the stored information, the frequency with which an item is retrieved, the recency with which the information has been learned (or how long it has been since the information was stored), and competition from other similar items in memory (Tulving, 1974).

For learners with typical development, the more frequently an item has been retrieved, the greater its "retrieval strength" (Roediger & Butler, 2011). That is, the less time it will take the learner to access this information. How well information is retrieved will depend on how often we have accessed and retrieved it. Frequently used information is much easier to recall; information that we have not "thought about" since it was first encountered becomes more difficult to retrieve with the passage of time. This is why accounts of experiences from long ago or ones that have never been shared with others are generally questioned as to their accuracy.

The more recently an item has entered long term memory, the easier it is to access this information. Information that is requested from a learner after only a brief delay is more likely to be retrieved and is more likely to be in the form with which was stored, not altered by competition from similar information or as subject to the loss of information from a decay of the memory trace. This is why it is generally recommended that witnesses be interviewed as soon after an event as possible.

In typical development, we attend more to novel events which means that we depend on our store of prior events to determine what is novel or has not been encountered before. When encoding this information, we associate it with previously stored related information. How well information is stored depends on what is already in our memory storage. However, a result of this association with previously stored information is that if we have many examples that are similar to the information we are currently encountering, it becomes difficult to distinguish among these individual examples in the storage system. For example, it may be difficult to recall a specific, uneventful trip to work from among all the other very similar trips to work that we have stored. Individuals who have experienced repeated incidents of victimization may have difficulty recalling the details from one specific event—all their related experiences may become incorporated into a more generalized memory of victimization.

Organization of memory

Memory processing also tends toward efficiency, with data reduction mechanisms that alleviate the need to store the myriad amounts of information that we encounter on a daily basis. Rather than remembering every detail of an event, we create a *gist* or a type of synopsis or shortened version containing the central ideas of the event. A gist allows us both to access the memory more easily and to relate the event to others in an efficient manner. For example, when telling your friend what happened on the way to work one morning, your friend wants to hear the highlights of the traffic accident you witnessed, not the sequential details starting with when your alarm went off that morning. New information should be quickly integrated into already learned information, not retained as an unrelated detail.

Memory processing also tends to impose an organizational structure on information—grouping like items together and relating new information to previously stored information. Of interest, this feature of memory processing is also what is thought to create false memories when information activates the previously stored information so strongly that it affects what we think we have heard or observed (Gallo, 2010). For example, in a classic experiment on false memories, the way the participants recalled the details of a video of a car collision was more affected by the verb used to describe the crash (e.g., bumped vs. smashed) than what was actually witnessed on the video (Loftus & Palmer, 1974). That is, when asked "About how fast were the cars going when they *smashed* into each other?", the participants recalled seeing broken glass, although no glass was actually broken in the video.

Autobiographical memory

Autobiographical memory, which is the focus of this text, is a particular type of memory content within the episodic memory system (personally experienced events) and within the semantic memory system (self-related information) (Lind, 2010). Episodic memory and semantic memory are both forms of *declarative* memory (Squire & Zola, 1998). Declarative memory ("knowing what") is memory of facts and events and refers to those memories that can be consciously recalled or "declared."

Summary

In sum, even for individuals without learning difficulties, memory processes are not a pure recording of an actual experience. What is stored in memory is initially determined by the individual's attentional processing. The form of the memory that is stored is affected by the individual's previously stored experiences, the use of organizational strategies, how frequently the information has been retrieved and stored, and the presence of competing experiences. The retrieval of the stored information so that it can be shared with others is affected by "retrieval strength" or how easily the information is to access in the memory stores and the ability of the individual to translate the stored information into a form that can be shared. This translated form is usually spoken or written words.

Allocation of cognitive resources

An important aspect of an information processing model of cognitive function is what is referred to as the *allocation of cognitive resources.* Cognitive processing is a neural or brain network function. That is, it is accomplished by a network of neural processors that are used for a whole host of cognitive functions. However, these cognitive processes are a limited resource. If the brain is expending cognitive resources doing one task, it limits the available resources for another cognitive task. No matter how many cognitive resources one might have, at times, the demands for processing will exceed the available cognitive resources. Therefore, one fundamental characteristic of cognitive processing is the necessity to allocate the available resources to the demands of the processing tasks. The effects of the limits are task and learner specific. For example, if a learner is using attentional resources to watch a television program, there is a reduction in the available resources for reading a book. Even though the tasks involve different mediums, one auditory and visual and the other a graphic representation of phonological and semantic language, the same general attentional resources are used for both, and therefore, must be divided between the tasks. If neither task is heavily resource demanding, such as watching a rerun of a familiar program or reading a light-hearted book, then both tasks may be successfully accomplished. However, if the television program has a confusing plot or large amounts of dense dialogue or the book is about an unfamiliar academic subject, then one of the tasks will consume the attentional and information processing resources at a cost to performance of the other task. Similarly, if the attention of a witness is on a bloody knife in a person's hand, he or she may allocate less attentional resources to details of the person's face or clothing (Kramer, Buckhout, & Eugenio, 1990).

Information processing models of ASD

Now that we have a better understanding of the cognitive mechanisms related to memory processing in typical development, we next discuss how these cognitive mechanisms are affected in individuals with ASD. Before proceeding, it is important to understand that memory processing may not be affected in all individuals with ASD in exactly the same way. Because of underlying differences in brain development and brain functioning, individuals with ASD must use other cognitive resources to learn about their world and to respond to demands of their environment. As stated earlier, memory function in ASD appears to be a derivation of typical memory processes, but what that derivation is may vary among individuals with ASD depending on their overall level of cognitive functioning and their innate abilities.

We now turn our attention to the application of information processing models of cognitive functioning to ASD. The two primary information processing models of ASD are the *Executive Function* (or dysfunction) model and the *Complex Information Processing* model.

Executive function model

Executive function models of ASD are based on a body of research that has focused specifically on this neurocognitive domain and documented difficulty in this area in verbal individuals with ASD with overall cognitive function in the average or above average range (Hill, 2004). This theory or model was originally proposed when the symptoms of individuals with ASD were observed to be similar to those of patients with frontal lobe injuries (Damasio & Maurer, 1978). For example, behaviors such as repetitive movements, an insistence on sameness, a lack of impulse control, difficulty with initiation of unfamiliar activities, and a deficit in cognitive flexibility are characteristic of individuals with ASD and patients with frontal lobe injuries (Robinson, Goddard, Dritschel, Wisley, & Howlin, 2009). Other executive functions, such as working memory, attention, planning, response inhibition, set shifting, and goal monitoring, have also been reported to be relatively impaired in individuals with ASD (Pennington & Ozonoff, 1996; Russell, 1997).

Difficulty in all aspects of executive function has not been a universal finding for individuals with ASD, however. For example, individuals with ASD have been reported to perform verbal working memory (Williams, Goldstein, Carpenter, & Minshew, 2005), attention (Goldstein, Johnson, & Minshew, 2001), response inhibition (Kana, Keller, Minshew, & Just, 2007; Ozonoff, 1997), and shifting tasks (Williams, Goldstein, & Minshew, 2013) similar to age and ability-matched individuals particularly when these tasks do not have significant processing demands.

Other areas of executive function such as planning are consistently reported as difficult for individuals with ASD, especially when complex plans have to be devised to accommodate a number of factors or in unfamiliar situations (see review in Hill, 2004). Difficulties in the executive functions of planning, response inhibition, and self-monitoring are thought to be characteristic of ASD and appear to be independent of verbal ability and IQ (Robinson et al., 2009). Supporting the centrality of the executive function deficit in ASD is research demonstrating that relative weaknesses in executive function are highly related to outcomes in adaptive functioning for adults with ASD (Williams, Mazefsky, Walker, Minshew, & Goldstein, 2014). Cognitive inflexibility, or changing thoughts and actions in response to changes in a context or situation, has consistently been reported to be affected in individuals with ASD (e.g., Bennetto, Pennington, & Rogers, 1996; Geurts, Verté, Oosterlaan, Roeyers, & Sergeant, 2004; Ozonoff, 1997; Rumsey & Hamburger, 1988). This finding has been so consistent that cognitive flexibility has been proposed as an area that represents a core deficit in ASD (Ozonoff, Strayer, McMahon, & Filloux, 1994).

Rather than damage to the frontal lobe, the executive function difficulty in ASD is thought to be related to differences in frontal lobe maturation. For example, in a behavioral study with 61 verbal children, adolescents, and adults with ASD as compared with the same number of participants with typical development, individually matched by age and cognitive ability, all the ASD age groups had difficulty with response inhibition and spatial working memory (Luna, Doll, Hegedus, Minshew, & Sweeney, 2007). However, consistent with an abnormal developmental trajectory, speed of sensorimotor processing and voluntary response inhibition were less affected in the older age groups with ASD.

Complex Information Processing model

Another model that attempts to explain the cognitive profile associated with ASD is the Complex Information Processing model (Minshew & Goldstein, 1998; Williams, Goldstein, & Minshew, 2015). The term *complex* in the name of this model does not refer to the type or content of the information, but rather to the *level and/or type of demand* on the brain's processing system from the tasks or situations within which the processing is occurring. An individual with ASD may or may not successfully process the information depending on whether or not they have the cognitive resources to meet the demands of the task. Individuals with ASD may encounter these processing difficulties in cognitive domains beyond language and social cognition. Based on the results of neuropsychological profile studies with adults and older children and adolescents with ASD, individuals with ASD are thought to have a particular profile of strengths and weaknesses across the cognitive domains (Minshew, Goldstein, & Siegel, 1997; Williams, Goldstein, & Minshew, 2006a). In these studies, individuals with ASD were reported to have relative impairments in skilled motor, complex memory, complex language, concept formation, and reasoning domains with intact performance in attention, simple memory, simple language, rule learning, and visuospatial domains (Minshew et al., 1997; Williams et al., 2006a).

The results of the neuropsychological profile studies also revealed that the individuals with ASD performed as well as the age and ability-matched controls with typical development when the tasks did not require integrative processing, imposition of order, or other higher order cognitive skills (Minshew et al., 1997; Williams et al., 2006a). Whereas a decrement in performance with increasing demands is typical of any learner, the individuals with ASD began to have difficulty at a lower level of demand than predicted based on their overall level of cognitive functioning and as compared to age- and ability-matched controls with typical development (Minshew, Williams, & McFadden, 2008). Furthermore, the overall cognitive ability of the adults with ASD did not predict their performance in the same way that it did for the controls; therefore, a related assumption of this model is that individuals with ASD accomplish information-processing tasks using lower order abilities and that this results in inefficiencies in learning and other differences in behavioral performance that are associated with ASD (Minshew et al., 2008). For example, an individual with ASD who can use spoken language may respond appropriately to short, simple questions that have been practiced and learned through association (a lower order ability) such as: "What is your name?" or "Where do you live?" However, that same individual may be unable to respond to a novel, more complex question such as "Why are you so agitated?" that requires comprehension of abstract language, integration of linguistic and emotional information, and formulation of a grammatically complex sentence or sentences (all higher order abilities). Similarly, when witnessing a crime, an individual with ASD may be able to name or to recognize what the observed persons were wearing in great detail—a simple lower order visual memory task. However, this same individual may have difficulty with relating what happened between those individuals—a complex memory that involves the higher order skills of schematic organization and forming a gist or synopsis of the events. According to a Complex Information Processing model of ASD, there is a mismatch between the demands of the information processing task and the ability of the individual with ASD to meet these demands due to an underlying neurobiological constraint. This neurobiological constraint has been conceptualized as a problem with "functional connectivity," or the failure of key brain regions to work together in a highly synchronized manner, based on a number of functional magnetic resonance imaging studies with children and adults with ASD (e.g., Just, Cherkassky, Keller, & Minshew, 2004; Just, Cherkassky, Keller, Kana, & Minshew, 2007; Kana et al., 2015; Mason, Williams, Kana, Minshew, & Just, 2008; Villalobos, Mizuno, Dahl, Kemmotsu, & Müller, 2005). Children and adults with ASD have been reported to differ from age- and ability-matched controls with typical development in the degree of network coordination, the distribution of the workload among the nodes of network, and the recruitment of brain regions in response to contextual demands during cognitive and linguistic processing tasks (Williams et al., 2013). These abnormalities of neural coordination are thought to result in the behavioral task difficulty that occurs when individuals with ASD are engaged in processing tasks that require a high level of integration or a high computational demand, regardless of the task domain (Minshew et al., 2008).

ASD and memory

Even individuals who know little about ASD can recount stories they have heard about individuals with this diagnosis who reportedly have a prodigious memory for detailed information whether it be facts such as the statistics for baseball players from the backs of trading cards, the schedule of arrivals and departures for municipal bus routes, or encyclopedia entries that were read decades earlier. Dustin Hoffman's portrayal of Raymond, a young man with ASD in the movie *Rain Man* (Hoffman et al., 2004) is centered on his ability to recall a myriad of facts that he has encountered during his lifetime. These stories lead individuals to conclude that memory is an enhanced ability in individuals with ASD and to expect that anyone with this diagnosis should be able to recall verbatim prior events with a reliability and validity that may not be expected of individuals without ASD. However, the function of memory for individuals with an ASD diagnosis cannot be characterized in such a simplistic manner.

First, the overall cognitive functioning level of the individual with ASD will have an impact on both the individual's ability to attend to, encode, and store an experience

(Boucher, Mayes, & Bingham, 2012). Similarly, the individual's ability to communicate using spoken language will affect his or her ability to retrieve and convey these experiences to others.

Individuals with ASD who have significant cognitive challenges may be less aware of ongoing events and/or may have substantial difficultly relating this information to others in a form that is comprehensible to their listener. These types of difficulties are usually not subtle and are therefore not surprising or unanticipated even by individuals who are less experienced in interacting with individuals with significant intellectual disabilities. Of concern when officials are interacting with individuals with ASD who are minimally verbal is that they might not initially be recognized as being someone who has a developmental disorder, and instead, they will be treated as if they are being uncooperative or nonresponsive. Police officers who are not trained to recognize the signs that these individuals have ASD may fail to provide appropriate accommodations for these individuals.

Less appreciated is that individuals with ASD who are verbal with overall cognitive ability in the average or above average range may also have challenges in storing, retrieving, and sharing experiences. However, these challenges may be less obvious, and therefore, unanticipated by the communication partner. We review some of the research that both documents and attempts to understand the nature of the memory processes in verbal, cognitively able individuals with ASD and discuss these findings in relation to the information processing models of ASD.

Organizational strategies

In general, verbal individuals with ASD with cognitive functioning in the average range have been found to have good rote memory (Rutter, 1974). That is, they can learn and retrieve information that is presented to them in a form that is essentially ready to encode in long-term storage (e.g., recalling the dialog from a movie that they have viewed a number of times). For example, adults with ASD with cognitive functioning and general language skills in the average range have been reported to have no difficulty recalling stories that are read to them (Ambery, Russell, Perry, Morris, & Murphy, 2006; Boucher et al., 2005; Williams, Goldstein, & Minshew, 2005); however, they have more difficulty than age- and ability-matched adults with typical development at recalling information from pictured scenes of individuals performing different activities of daily living (Williams et al., 2005). Both tasks required memorization of relatively large amounts of information; however, in the former task, the information was already verbally encoded and ready for storage, whereas in the latter task, the adults with ASD had to generate a strategy to facilitate encoding. These findings suggest that verbal individuals with ASD have difficulty spontaneously using organizational strategies to support remembering of information leading to decreasing memory performance as the complexity of the information increases (Minshew & Goldstein, 2001; Williams, Goldstein, & Minshew, 2006b).

Prior encoding of information is not necessarily enough for younger individuals with ASD to recall the material. Unlike the adults in the studies cited above, older children and adolescents with ASD had difficulty with relating narratives that were presented to them orally *when no picture support was provided* as compared to age- and ability-matched controls (Minshew & Goldstein, 2001; Williams et al., 2006b). One interpretation of these findings is that, unlike for the adults, prior verbal encoding was not sufficient to alleviate the information processing load for this task in the children with ASD who had relatively less developed language abilities than the adults with ASD.

Difficulty with the spontaneous use of organizational strategies is also evidenced by the problems individuals with ASD have in creating and relating the gist of an orally heard story or an observed event (Diehl, Bennetto, & Young, 2006). Adolescents with Asperger syndrome (a form of ASD with a relatively high level of verbal ability) not only had difficulty with reporting the gist of a scripted live event, but also recalled fewer details than the children with typical development (McCrory, Henry, & Happé, 2007). Lack of inherent organizational strategies or schema is thought to interfere with the ability of individuals with ASD to remember more complex linguistic material (i.e., integrate the elements into a coherent whole) and to tell a comprehensive story or sequence of events (for reviews, see Boucher et al., 2012; Williams, Goldstein, & Minshew, 2008). Therefore, individuals with ASD could be expected to have difficulty with giving a coherent eyewitness account to an officer at the scene of a crime or with providing testimony in open court.

Verbal encoding

Results from a recent functional imaging study of children with and without ASD provide some insight into the nature of the difficulty individuals with ASD have with remembering episodic information (Carter, Williams, Lehman, & Minshew, 2012). Functional imaging uses magnetic resonance imaging (MRI) technology to examine the use of oxygenated blood during a cognitive processing task. Neurons that are doing the processing work need oxygen; therefore, following the uptake of oxygenated blood allows researchers to make some assumptions about what regions of the brain are being used during a cognitive task. The regions of the brain that are using relatively greater levels of oxygenated blood are said to be "activated." For this particular study, Carter and her colleagues (2012) were interested in investigating the ability of children with ASD to make judgments about pictured social interactions. The pictured scenarios did not require the use of language and both the children with ASD and those with typical development accurately identified the situations that depicted inappropriate social interactions. However, the children with typical development had robust activation in their language processing network when performing the task; they appeared to be spontaneously verbally encoding the information from the scenes that they were viewing. In contrast, the children with ASD had activation in a network associated with the processing of social information but no significant use of neural resources in the language network. This result suggested that the children with ASD were not spontaneously encoding the information into a verbal form. This pattern of results was consistent with that of an earlier functional imaging study of verbal working memory in ASD that found a lack of verbal encoding for adults with ASD during a task that is known to elicit use of a verbal working memory network (Koshino et al., 2005).

Difficulty with spontaneous verbal encoding of information would affect the ability of an individual with ASD to recall and report events that were observed. In fact, several behavioral studies of episodic memory or memory for personally experienced events by individuals with ASD have reported results that are consistent with a difficulty with spontaneous verbal encoding. For example, children with ASD, 10–16 years of age, reported less information than children with typical development and children with intellectual disability about a set of activities in which they had participated earlier in the day (Boucher, 1981). Another group of children with ASD recalled significantly less information about events experienced over the previous year than children without ASD. However, in both studies, the children with ASD were reported to have good recall when cued with leading questions (Boucher, 1981; Boucher &

Lewis, 1989). One interpretation of these results is that the children with ASD had stored information about the experienced events, but had difficulty accessing and relating the information until verbal cuing was provided.

Facilitation of recall of events with cueing has been demonstrated in other studies with children with ASD. For example, adolescents, ages 11–14 years, with Asperger syndrome were reported to have difficulty verbally recalling a passively-observed, scripted live event involving people; however, when asked both general and more specific questions, the adolescents with ASD provided more details about the observed event (McCrory et al., 2007).

Task support

The facilitatory effect on retrieval of personal episodic memories when cues are provided to individuals with ASD led Bowler and colleagues to propose the ***task support hypothesis*** (Bowler, Gardiner, & Berthollier, 2004; Bowler, Matthews, & Gardiner, 1997). According to this proposition, the relative difficulty individuals with ASD have with recall of personal experiences is due to difficulty with retrieval not diminished memory for these events. When individuals with ASD are provided support for retrieval in the form of cued recall or the use of recognition tests rather than free recall, the performance differences as compared to individuals with typical development are no longer obtained (Bowler et al., 2004). The task support hypothesis predicts that when memory is tested using free recall, then individuals with ASD will recall fewer details. However, when support is provided at recall, individuals with ASD perform comparable to age- and ability-matched controls.

The task support hypothesis is consistent with an impairment in executive function in ASD and a resulting difficulty in employing flexible strategies to recall details of an event (Maras & Bowler, 2014). The provision of external support provides the triggers or strategies that increase the recall of the event for the individual with ASD.

The task support hypothesis is also consistent with other information processing difficulties in ASD, particularly the proposed difficulty with verbal encoding in individuals with ASD with cognition in the average range (Carter et al., 2012) or the proposed problems with limitations in cognitive resources (Minshew et al., 2008). In the former case, the support at recall would be facilitating the translation of the remembered information into a verbal form so that it can be expressed by the individual with ASD. In the latter case, the support at recall would be freeing up cognitive processing resources allowing for the re-allocation of resources to retrieval and verbal encoding. Both of these explanations suggest that the problem with autobiographical memory in ASD is one of retrieval of stored information. The assumption is that the individual with ASD has encoded the experience, but supportive retrieval mechanisms may be needed to access the stored information.

Implications

According to executive function and information processing models, even if individuals with ASD remember the same information as individuals with typical development, the way in which they have learned that information is assumed to be different. This difference may affect the nature of the memories themselves, but will especially affect access to those memories. Individuals with ASD may have difficulty freely recalling and relating information that was not received in a verbal form. They may have difficulty reporting events that happened to others that they did not personally experience and may even have difficulty relating personally experienced events (Maras, Memon, Lamrechts, & Bowler, 2013).

Free-recall techniques may be less effective with an individual with ASD. More specific questioning may be required to provide the support the individual with ASD needs to relate an episodic memory. In addition, the type of support may be particularly important. For example, a cognitive interview technique that incorporates context reinstatement and imagery-guided questions was reported to result in the reporting of more incorrect details by adults with ASD than a structured interview using free recall with follow-up questions based on what the participant said in the free recall (Maras & Bowler, 2010). Accessing the information first in a visual format may also be necessary. For example, children with ASD (average age 12 years) recalled more details with less inaccurate information when they were first given unlimited time to draw about a video that they had previously viewed (Mattison, Dando, & Ormerod, 2015).

The executive function and information processing problems associated with ASD not only affect the encoding, storage, and retrieval of episodic information. Individuals with ASD also have difficulty with organization of information, meaning that they have difficulty with the organization of narratives or verbally-relating personal events (e.g., Diehl et al., 2006; Losh & Capps, 2003). Even if individuals with ASD remember and are supported in the recall of an autobiographical memory or personal event narrative, they may relate that information in a form that is difficult for their communication partner to understand with shorter, less grammatically complex sentences and reduced use of descriptive language (King, Dockrell, & Stuart, 2013).

Given the challenges previously described, obtaining autobiographical memories from individuals with ASD will require particular skill on the part of the interviewer. Retrieval strategies will need to be used to facilitate both the quantity and the accuracy of details recalled. Scaffolding will need to be used to promote organization of the spoken narrative. Individuals with ASD learn and think differently than typically developing individuals, and these differences will need to be appreciated and accommodated by the communication partner to obtain reliable information.

Take-Home Points

- Information processing models of ASD emphasize the dynamic nature of the learning process
- Although individuals with ASD may easily retell pre-organized, detailed information, they may have a relative weakness in relating more complex, unorganized episodic information
- Individuals with ASD lack organizational schemas that reduce large amount of information to more manageable forms
- Individuals with ASD may have difficulty converting their memories into spoken or written language
- Supportive retrieval mechanisms such as cued-recall may be needed to help individuals with ASD access their stored memories
- Obtaining autobiographical memories from individuals with ASD requires a skilled interviewer who can implement strategies to accommodate the challenges in retrieving and relating stored information that these individuals experience

References

Ambery, F. Z., Russell, A., Perry, K., Morris, R., & Murphy, D. (2006). Neuropsychological functioning in adults with Asperger syndrome. *Autism, 10*, 551–564.

American Psychiatric Association. (2013). *Diagnostic and statistical manual of mental disorders* (5th ed.). Washington, DC: Author.

Baddeley, A. D. (1986). *Working memory.* Oxford, England: Clarendon.

Baddeley, A. (1996). Exploring the central executive. *Quarterly Journal of Experimental Psychology, 44A*, 1–31.

Baddeley, A. (2000). The episodic buffer: A new component of working memory? *Trends in Cognitive Science, 4*, 417–423.

Baddeley, A. (2002). Is working memory still working? *European Psychologist, 7*, 85–97.

Baddeley, A. (2003). Working memory: Looking back and looking forward. *Nature Reviews Neuroscience, 4*(10), 829–839.

Baddeley, A., & Wilson, B. (1988). Frontal amnesia and the dysexecutive syndrome. *Brain & Cognition, 7*, 212–230.

Bennetto, L., Pennington, B. R., & Rogers, S. J. (1996). Intact and impaired memory functions in autism. *Child Development, 67*, 1816–1835.

Boucher, J. (1981). Memory for recent events in autistic children. *Journal of Autism & Developmental Disorders, 11*, 293–302.

Boucher, J., Cowell, P., Howard, M., Broks, P., Farrant, A., Roberts, N., & Mayes, A. (2005). A combined clinical, neuropsychological, and neuroanatomical study of adults with high functioning autism. *Cognitive Neuropsychiatry, 10*, 165–213.

Boucher, J., & Lewis, V. (1989). Memory impairments and communication in relatively able autistic children. *Journal of Child Psychology & Psychiatry, 30*, 99–122.

Boucher, J., Mayes, A., & Bigham, S. (2012). Memory in autism spectrum disorders. *Psychological Bulletin, 138*, 458–496.

Bowler, D. M., Gardiner, J. M., & Berthollier, N. (2004). Source memory in adolescents and adults with Asperger's syndrome. *Journal of Autism & Developmental Disorders, 34*(5), 533–542.

Bowler, D. M., Matthews, N. J., & Gardiner, J. M. (1997). Asperger's syndrome and memory: Similarity to autism but not amnesia. *Neuropsychologia, 35*, 65–70.

Bridge, D. J., & Paller, K. A. (2012). Neural correlates of reactivation and retrieval-induced distortion. *Journal of Neuroscience, 32*, 12144–12151.

Carter, E.J., Williams, D.L., Lehman, J., & Minshew, N.J. (2012). Is he being bad? The roles of social and language brain networks during social judgment in children with autism. *PLOS One, 7*, 1–9.

Damasio, A. R., & Maurer, R. G. (1978). A neurological model for childhood autism. *Archives of Neurology, 35*, 777–786.

Diehl, J. J., Bennetto, L., & Young, E. C. (2006). Story recall and narrative coherence of high-functioning children with autism spectrum disorders. *Journal of Abnormal Child Psychology, 34*, 83–98.

Gallo, D. A. (2010). False memories and fantastic beliefs: 15 years of the DRM illusion. *Memory & Cognition, 38*, 833–848.

Gazzaniga, M. S. (2012). *Who's in charge? Free will and the science of the brain.* New York, NY: HarperCollins.

Gazzaniga, M. S. Ivry, R, & Mangun, G. R. (2013). *Cognitive neuroscience: The biology of mind* (4th ed.). New York, NY: W. W. Norton.

Geurts, H. M., Verté, S., Oosterlaan, J., Roeyers, H., & Sergeant, J. A. (2004). How specific are executive functioning deficits in attention deficit hyperactivity disorder and autism? *Journal of Child Psychology & Psychiatry, 45*, 836–854.

Goldstein, G., Johnson, C. R., & Minshew, N. J. (2001). Attentional processes in autism. *Journal of Autism & Developmental Disorders, 31*, 433–440.

Hill, E. L. (2004). Executive dysfunction in autism. *Trends in Cognitive Sciences, 8*, 26–32.

Hoffman, D., Cruise, T., Golino, V., Johnson, M., Levinson, B., Morrow, B., Bass, R., ... MGM Home Entertainment Inc. (2004). *Rain man*. Santa Monica, CA: MGM Home Entertainment.

Jones, W., & Klin, A. (2013). Attention to eyes is present but in decline in 2-6-month-old infants later diagnosed with autism. *Nature, 504*, 427–443.

Just, M. A., Cherkassky, V. L., Keller, T. A., Kana, R. K., & Minshew, N. J. (2007). Functional and anatomical cortical underconnectivity in autism: Evidence from an fMRI study of an executive function task and corpus callosum morphometry. *Cerebral Cortex, 17*, 951–961.

Just, M. A., Cherkassky, V. L., Keller, T. A., & Minshew, N. J. (2004). Cortical activation and synchronization during sentence comprehension in high-functioning autism: Evidence of underconnectivity. *Brain, 127*, 1–11.

Kana, R. K., Keller, T. A., Minshew, N. J., & Just, M. A. (2007). Inhibitory control in high-functioning autism: Decreased activation and underconnectivity in inhibition networks. *Biological Psychiatry, 62*, 198–206.

Kana, R. K., Maximo, J. O., Williams, D. L., Keller, T. A., Schipul, S. E., Cherkassky, V. L., Minshew, N. J., & Just, M. A. (2015). Aberrant functioning of the Theory-of-Mind network in children and adolescents with autism. *Molecular Autism, 6*, 59.

King, D., Dockrell, J. E., & Stuart, M. (2013). Event narratives in 11–14 year olds with autistic spectrum disorder. *International Journal of Language & Communication Disorders, 48*, 522–533.

Knight, R. T., Staines, W. R., Swick, D., & Chao, L. L. (1999). Prefrontal cortex regulates inhibition and excitation in distributed neural networks. *Acta Psychologica, 101*, 159–178.

Koshino, H., Carpenter, P. A., Minshew, N. J., Cherkassky, V. L., Keller, T. A., & Just, M. A. (2005). Functional connectivity in an fMRI working memory task in high-functioning autism. *NeuroImage, 24*, 810–821.

Kramer, T. H., Buckhout, R., & Eugenio, P. (1990). Weapon focus, arousal, and eyewitness memory: Attention must be paid. *Law & Human Behavior, 14*, 167–183.

Lind, S. E. (2010). Memory and the self in autism: A review and theoretical framework. *Autism, 14*, 430–456.

Loftus, E. F. and Palmer, J. C. (1974). Reconstruction of automobile destruction: An example of the interaction between language and memory. *Journal of Verbal Learning & Verbal Behavior, 13*, 585–589.

Losh, M., & Capps, L. (2003). Narrative ability in high-functioning children with autism or Asperger's syndrome. *Journal of Autism & Developmental Disorders, 33*, 239–251.

Luna, B., Doll, S. K., Hegedus, S. J., Minshew, N. J., & Sweeney, J. A. (2007). Maturation of executive function in autism. *Biological Psychiatry, 61*, 474–481.

Maras, K. L., & Bowler, D. M. (2010). The cognitive interview for eyewitnesses with autism spectrum disorder. *Journal of Autism & Developmental Disorders, 40*, 1350–1360.

Maras, K. L., & Bowler, D. M. (2014). Eyewitness testimony in autism spectrum disorder: A review. *Journal of Autism & Developmental Disorders, 44*, 2682–2697.

Maras, K. L., Memon, A., Lambrechts, A., & Bowler, D. M. (2013). Recall of a live and personally experienced eyewitness event by adults with autism spectrum disorder. *Journal of Autism & Developmental Disorders, 43*, 1798–1810.

Mason, R. A., Williams, D. L., Kana, R. K., Minshew, N. J., & Just, M. A. (2008). Theory of mind disruption and recruitment of the right hemisphere during narrative comprehension in autism. *Neuropsychologia, 46*, 269–280.

Mattison, M. L., Dando, C. J., & Ormerod, T. C. (2015). Sketching to remember: Episodic free recall task support for child witnesses and victims with autism spectrum disorder. *Journal of Autism & Developmental Disorders*, *45*, 1751–1765.

McCrory, E., Henry, L. A., & Happé, F. (2007). Eye-witness memory and suggestibility in children with Asperger syndrome. *Journal of Child Psychology & Psychiatry*, *48*, 482–489.

Melton, A. W. (1963). Implications of short-term memory for a general theory of memory. *Journal of Verbal Learning & Verbal Behavior*, *2*, 1–21.

Minshew, N. J., & Goldstein, G. (1998). Autism as a disorder of complex information processing. *Mental Retardation & Developmental Disabilities Research Reviews*, *4*, 129–136.

Minshew, N. J., & Goldstein, G. (2001). The pattern of intact and impaired memory functions in autism. *Journal of Child Psychology & Psychiatry*, *42*, 1095–1101.

Minshew, N. J., Goldstein, G., & Siegel, D. (1997). Neuropsychologic functioning in autism: Profile of a complex information processing disorder. *Journal of the International Neuropsychological Society*, *3*, 303–316.

Minshew, N. J., Williams, D. L., & McFadden, K. (2008). Information processing, neural connectivity and neuronal organization. In A. Zimmerman (Ed.), *Autism: Current theories and evidence* (pp. 381–405). Totowa, NJ: Humana Press.

Ozonoff, S. (1997). Components of executive function in autism and other disorders. In J. Russell (Ed.), *Autism as an executive disorder* (pp. 179–211). Oxford, England: Oxford University Press.

Ozonoff, S., Strayer, D. L., McMahon, W. M., & Filloux, F. (1994). Executive function abilities in autism and Tourette syndrome: An information processing approach. *Journal of Child Psychology & Psychiatry*, *35*, 1015–1032.

Pennington, B. F., & Ozonoff, S. (1996). Executive functions and developmental psychopathology. *Journal of Child Psychology & Psychiatry*, *37*, 51–87.

Robinson, S., Goddard, L., Dritschler, B., Wisley, M., & Howlin, P. (2009). Executive functions in children with autism spectrum disorders. *Brain & Cognition*, *71*, 362–168.

Roediger, H. L., & Butler, A. C. (2011). The critical role of retrieval practice in long-term retention. *Trends in Cognitive Sciences*, *15*, 20–27.

Rumsey, J. M., & Hamburger, S. D. (1988). Neuropsychological findings in high-functioning men with infantile autism, residual state. *Journal of Clinical & Experimental Neuropsychology*, *10*, 201–221.

Russell, J. (1997). *Autism as an executive disorder*. New York, NY: Oxford University Press.

Rutter, M. (1974). The development of infantile autism. *Psychological Medicine*, *4*, 147–163.

Squire, L. R. (1986). Mechanisms of memory. *Science*, *232*, 1612–1619.

Squire, L. R., & Zola, S. M. (1998). Episodic memory, semantic memory, and amnesia. *Hippocampus*, *8*, 205–211.

Stuss, D. T., & Benson, D. F. (1986). *The frontal lobes*. New York, NY: Raven.

Tulving, E. (1974). Cue-dependent forgetting: When we forget something we once knew, it does not necessarily mean that the memory trace has been lost; it may only be inaccessible. *American Scientist*, *62*, 74–82.

Villalobos, M. E., Mizuno, A., Dahl, B. C., Kemmotsu, N., & Müller, R. A. (2005). Reduced functional connectivity between V1 and inferior frontal cortex associated with visuomotor performance in autism. *NeuroImage*, *25*, 9161925.

Welsh, M. C., & Pennington, B. F. (1988). Assessing frontal lobe functioning in children: Views from developmental psychology. *Developmental Neuropsychology*, *4*, 199–230.

Williams, D. L., Cherkassky, V. L., Mason, R. A., Keller, T.A., Minshew, N. J., & Just, M. A. (2013). Brain function differences in language processing in children and adults with autism. *Autism Research*, *6*, 288–302.

Williams, D. L., Goldstein G., Carpenter, P. A., & Minshew N. J. (2005). Verbal and spatial working memory in autism. *Journal of Autism & Developmental Disorders*, *35*, 747–756.

Williams, D.L., Goldstein, G., & Minshew, N. J. (2005). Impaired memory for faces and social scenes in autism: Clinical implications of the memory disorder. *Archives of Clinical Neuropsychology, 20*, 1–15.

Williams, D. L., Goldstein, G., & Minshew, N. J. (2006a). Neuropsychologic functioning in children with autism: Further evidence for disordered complex information processing. *Child Neuropsychology, 12*, 279–298.

Williams, D. L., Goldstein G., & Minshew, N. J. (2006b). Profile of memory function in children with autism. *Neuropsychology, 20*, 21–29.

Williams, D. L., Goldstein, G., & Minshew, N. J. (2013). The modality shift experiment in adults and children with high functioning autism. *Journal of Autism & Developmental Disorders, 43*, 794–806.

Williams, D. L., Goldstein, G., & Minshew, N. J. (2015). Further understanding of complex information processing in verbal adolescents and adults with ASD. *Autism* (Special issue on adults with ASD), 1–9.

Williams, D. L., Mazefsky, C. A., Walker, J. D., Minshew, N. J., & Goldstein, G. (2014). Association between conceptual reasoning, problem solving, and adaptive ability in high-functioning autism. *Journal of Autism & Developmental Disorders, 44*, 2908–2920.

Williams, D.L., Minshew, N.J., & Goldstein, G. (2008). Memory within a complex information processing model. In J. Boucher & D. Bowler (Eds.), *Memory in autism* (pp. 125–142). New York, NY: Cambridge University Press.

Wolford, G., Miller, M. B., & Gazzaniga, M. S. (2000). The left hemisphere's role in hypothesis formation. *Journal of Neuroscience, 20*, 1–4.

4

The Self in Autism and Its Relation to Memory

Sophie E. Lind, David M. Williams, Catherine Grainger, and Julia Landsiedel

The Multifacted Nature of Memory and the Self

Among psychologists and philosophers alike, it is widely assumed that memory, particularly autobiographical memory, and the self are inextricably linked (e.g., Conway, 2005; Hume, 1739, 2003; James, 1890; Locke, 1690, 1995; Prebble et al., 2013; Wilson & Ross, 2003). Indeed, the relation between the two constructs is generally thought to be bidirectional in nature. Without memory for one's past personal experiences, one's sense of self—one's personal identity—would be impoverished. In Wilson and Ross's (2003) words, "We are what we remember" (p. 137). But equally, without a sense of self, one would be unable to appreciate the personal significance of the events that one experiences. That there is a link between the two is undeniable. However, the precise nature of the relation requires careful consideration, and is likely to be far more complex and subtle than one might imagine at first glance. This is, in no small part, because memory and the self are not unitary entities, but multifaceted in nature (despite what introspection tells us). Hence, the relation between memory and the self requires careful unpacking.

In this chapter, we start by considering some definitions of memory and the self. We then consider in some detail how memory and the self might be related on the psychological level. We next consider the relevance of these theories to autism spectrum disorder (ASD), providing a critical review of relevant research on the self in autism, followed by some hypotheses concerning how diminished sense of self might predict and explain the unique memory profile we see in the ASD population.

Facets of memory

The idea that memory consists of multiple systems is now widely accepted (e.g., Schacter & Tulving, 1994). For the current purposes, one of the most important distinctions to have been drawn is between episodic and semantic memory (e.g., Tulving, 2001). Broadly, these hypothetical, functionally distinct, but interactive neuro-cognitive systems are thought to underpin long-term memory for personally

The Wiley Handbook of Memory, Autism Spectrum Disorder, and the Law, First Edition.
Edited by Jonni L. Johnson, Gail S. Goodman, and Peter C. Mundy.

experienced events and objective, factual knowledge, respectively. By definition, episodic memories are associated with a unique spatial temporal context—they are memories of experiences that occurred in a particular *place* at a particular *time* (e.g., remembering celebrating your last birthday with friends at your favorite restaurant). Episodic retrieval is also uniquely associated with autonoetic awareness, a type of self-conscious awareness that gives rise to a sense of "mental time travel"—mentally re-experiencing a past event from a subjective perspective or mentally re-inhabiting a past state of self (e.g., feeling embarrassed at recalling everyone in the restaurant singing "Happy Birthday" to you). In contrast, semantic memories are not associated with any spatiotemporal context—they do not contain any information about when or where the memory was encoded (e.g., you may know precisely when and where you were born, without recalling anything about the context in which you learned that information). Semantic memories are characterized by noetic (knowing) rather than autonoetic (self-knowing) awareness, and do not involve any sense of mental time travel (Wheeler, Stuss, & Tulving, 1997).

Autobiographical memory—the focus of the current volume—has been defined in a variety of ways by different authors, but is frequently (and in our view, confusingly) considered to be synonymous with episodic memory (e.g., Gilboa, 2004). Here, we use the term *episodic* to refer specifically to the memory *system,* and the term *autobiographical* to refer specifically to a particular type of memory *content* (i.e., information pertaining to the self) (Lind, 2010). Thus, to ensure clarity, we distinguish (a) autobiographical episodic memory (e.g., remembering what happened on one's last birthday); (b) *non*-autobiographical episodic memory (e.g., remembering an article from the newspaper this morning); (c) autobiographical semantic knowledge (e.g., knowledge of one's place of birth); and (d) *non*-autobiographical semantic knowledge (e.g., knowledge of the alphabet). As we attempt to argue in this chapter, (a), (b), and (c) are likely to be related to sense of self, though the nature of the relation is likely to differ in each case.

Facets of the self

Several theories have proposed different aspects of the self (e.g., Lewis, 1995; Neisser, 1988; Rochat, 2003). The most well-known and widely accepted of these theories was originally proposed by William James (1890), who distinguished between the "I" (henceforth "I-self")—the self as the *subject* of experience—and the "me" (henceforth "me-self")—the self as the *object* of experience. Others have adopted the terms "self-experience" and "self-knowledge" to refer to these aspects, respectively. The I-self is arguably involved in all forms of conscious, mental activity. However, the me-self is involved only in certain contexts. The terms *self-awareness* and *self-concept* are frequently used in the literature and are generally thought to relate specifically to the me-self (e.g., Prebble et al., 2013). Here, we use the term *self-awareness* to refer to the *process* by which some aspect of the self becomes the object of consciousness, and the term *self-concept* to refer to the enduring, but continuously updated, mental *representation* of the self (i.e., a set of beliefs about the self). Through self-awareness, it is possible to focus one's attention on various aspects of the self, including physical sensations, emotions, thoughts, memories, and one's self-concept. It is through self-awareness that we gain self-knowledge or self-understanding, and this information may potentially become part of one's self-concept. Thus, a rich and accurate self-concept most likely relies on having a sufficient level of self-awareness.

In addition to considering the I-self and me-self as different aspects of the self, a further pertinent distinction, between "present" and "temporally extended" aspects of self, has been drawn by some theorists (e.g., Lemmon & Moore, 2001; Prebble et al., 2013). The present self refers to the self as it is experienced or known about in the present moment, whereas the temporally extended self refers to the self as it is experienced or known about across the present, past, and future, including a sense of personal continuity through time. Although it is undoubtedly an oversimplification to consider the self purely in terms of the I/me and present/temporally extended dimensions, this type of framework has clear utility for considering the relation between memory and the self (see Prebble et al., 2013). Hence, we have chosen to use this model to frame the following section, which attempts to broadly sketch the putative relation between memory and the self.

The Relation Between Memory and the Self

So how do these hypothetical aspects of self relate to the different types of memory discussed above? If we start from the assumption that the I-self must, by definition, be involved in all forms of conscious memory, that leaves us to consider if and how the me-self relates to these forms of memory. For example, Tulving (2001) considered episodic memory (for both autobiographical and non-autobiographical content) to be closely tied to the self insomuch as episodic *retrieval* entails autonoetic—or "self-knowing"—consciousness. Thus, it requires one to focus attention on one's mental representation (a memory) of a past state of self in order to mentally re-experience it. This clearly implies the involvement of the me-self (i.e., the self as the object of experience), given that one is consciously focusing attention on one's self.

Indeed, self-awareness is also likely to be crucial to the *encoding* of episodic memories. For a memory to be encoded from a subjective, first-person ("field") perspective, the original event must presumably be *experienced* from this perspective. Hence, self-awareness is thought to enable experiences to be encoded episodically. At the same time, episodic memory is said to underpin the *temporally extended* self. On some level, when we remember a past event, we recognize it as a *past* experience—we do not believe that we are currently experiencing it. Hence, episodic memory (and indeed, episodic foresight) may be necessary for the phenomenal experience of temporal continuity—the feeling that we are essentially the same person across time. Here, the bidirectional nature of the relation between memory and the self becomes apparent.

Furthermore, while semantic memory is likely to underpin the self-concept (another manifestation of the me-self—the self as the object of consciousness), episodic memories with autobiographical content may also be considered integral to the self-concept, providing "the detail needed for a rich and nuanced self-understanding" (Prebble et al., 2013, p. 827). Given that the temporally extended self-concept incorporates multiple, alternative representations of self that must be understood *as* alternative representations of the same enduring self, meta-representation (Perner, 1991) may also be a prerequisite (Povinelli & Simon, 1998).

From a developmental perspective, Howe and Courage (1993) proposed that the development of a self-concept is the cornerstone of the emergence of autobiographical episodic memory in early childhood. They argued that it acts as an organizational structure, which interprets and integrates events with respect to the self. Without a self-concept, it should not be possible to encode memories as personally relevant. The self-concept is said to reach a "critical mass" at around 2 years of age, coinciding with the onset of rudimentary autobiographical episodic memory, and indeed, there is some evidence to support this claim (Harley & Reese, 1999). This developmental approach complements the approach outlined thus far in this chapter: Semantic autobiographical memory may be integral to the development of the self-concept; this enables episodic autobiographical memory to emerge; this then feeds back to further elaborate on the self-concept. Once again, the bidirectional nature of the relation between memory and the self is highlighted.

Some evidence for the organizational properties of the self-concept on memory comes from studies that manipulated the extent to which the to-be-remembered material was self-relevant in some way. Within the neurotypical literature, it is well established that individuals show superior memory for information that is considered self-relevant, or that has been encoded in relation to the self (Symons & Johnson, 1997). This "self-reference effect" can be thought of as a type of depth-of-processing effect (Craik & Tulving, 1975), and is thought to occur because processing information in relation to the self-concept, which acts as an organizing structure, should facilitate deeper, more elaborate encoding of this information within memory. This deeper encoding, in turn, makes this information more likely to be retrieved, relative to information that has not been processed in relation to the self-concept.

Finally, in addition to the involvement of self in retrospective aspects of memory, "future-oriented" aspects of memory are also thought to require a me-self. For example, prospective memory is the ability to carry out intended, planned actions at the appropriate moment in the future (McDaniel & Einstein, 2007). Commonly, researchers distinguish between event-based, which involves carrying out a planned action upon the occurrence of a pre-specified event (e.g., taking food out of the oven *when the timer goes off*), and time-based prospective memory, which involves carrying out a planned action at a specific future point in time (e.g., taking food out of the oven *at 3pm*). On the one hand, a robust temporally-extended me-self allows one, at the stage of *encoding* one's plan to act in the future, to imagine oneself in the future actually carrying out the plan (e.g., when deciding to get milk on the way home from work, imagining approaching and entering the supermarket, and then buying the milk) (Atance & O'Neill, 2001). By utilizing autonoetic awareness to imagine oneself carrying out one's plan in the future, one's plan gets encoded deeply and is thus more likely to be retrieved at the moment it should be carried out (Brewer, Knight, Meeks, & Marsh, 2011; Brewer, Knight, Marsh, & Unsworth, 2010). On the other hand, at the stage of *retrieving* one's intention, one arguably needs to represent one's intention as such. That is, at the moment when one's planned action should be carried out, one needs to activate *and represent* one's previously formed intention to act (Ford, Driscoll, Shum, & Macaulay, 2012; Williams, Boucher, Lind, & Jarrold, 2013). In this way, one's me-self is also thought to contribute to prospective memory ability via the metacognitive ability to become aware of one's own mental states.

Having outlined a theoretical model for the relation between memory and the self, we now consider how this may apply to individuals with autism spectrum disorder (ASD), a disorder that a number of researchers have suggested is characterized by diminished self-awareness and self-knowledge (e.g., Frith, 2003; Hobson, 1990; Russell, 1997) and that is also characterized by a particular profile of strengths and weaknesses in memory (Boucher et al., 2012). We first review the relevant literature on self in ASD before considering the profile of memory strengths and difficulties in this disorder, and how limitations of self-awareness/self-concept may explain this profile.

The Self in Autism

A number of researchers have suggested that individuals with ASD have a diminished sense of self (e.g., Hobson, 1990; Lind, 2010; Lombardo & Baron-Cohen, 2010; Williams, 2010) or even an "absent self" (Frith, 2003). Our view is that although it is implausible to suggest that individuals with ASD have diminished I-selves (i.e., have attenuated subjective experiences of the world), they may have diminished me-selves. For example, they may have reduced or atypical self-awareness (i.e., attention to the self), and consequently, under-elaborated or inaccurate self-concepts (e.g., they may have overly positive or negative beliefs about themselves). In the following sections, we review evidence that is relevant to this proposal. Something important to flag up at this stage is the fact that if an individual performs poorly on a "self" task of some kind, it can be difficult to determine whether this is due to problems with the *process* of self-awareness (attention to self) or problems with their *mental representation* of self—it is very difficult to tease these apart experimentally (moreover, in some cases, people can perform atypically for reasons that have nothing to do with the self). However, in most cases, one can at least draw the broader conclusion that there is/is not a problem with the me-self. Although there are a considerable number of studies showing typical performance on some types of "self" task among people with ASD—notably visual self-recognition tests—on balance, existing evidence suggests that individuals with ASD have atypical me-selves.

Mirror self-recognition in autism

The mark test of mirror self-recognition (Amsterdam, 1972; Gallup, 1970) is widely considered to be the definitive test of self-awareness. The task involves surreptitiously marking a child's face with a spot of rouge (or placing a sticker on his or her hair) and assessing the child's behavioral response when he or she subsequently looks in a mirror. Touching the rouge or sticker is taken as evidence of self-recognition, and typically developing children generally show this reaction at around 18 months of age (e.g., Anderson, 1983). The developmental significance of such mark-directed behavior has been hotly debated, and there have been disagreements over the cognitive requirements of the task (e.g., Hobson, 1990; Mitchell, 1997). Nevertheless, the broad consensus is that mirror self-recognition implies that a child has a mental representation of what they typically look like and that this self-representation has become the object of their conscious awareness (Amsterdam, 1972; Neisser, 1995; Nielsen, Suddendorf, & Slaughter, 2006). Hence, successful mirror self-recognition implies both a sufficient *self-concept* (knowledge of one's own appearance) and the capacity for self-awareness (i.e., the me-self). Studies of mirror-self-recognition in autism (Dawson & McKissick, 1984; Ferrari & Matthews, 1983; Neuman & Hill, 1978) have tended to suffer from methodological weaknesses, making it difficult to draw absolute conclusions (see Lind, 2010). Notably, given that autism is rarely diagnosed or even suspected in children under 18 months (the mean age of passing the task in typical development), it is very difficult to establish whether there is any degree of developmental delay in this cognitive milestone. Nevertheless, older children with ASD (even those with significant intellectual difficulties) appear to be able to recognize themselves in mirrors (but see Carmody & Lewis, 2012). However, mirror self-recognition may only require very rudimentary self-awareness and self-knowledge. Note that even pigeons have been found to show mark-directed behavior in tests of mirror self-recognition (Epstein et al., 1981). Hence, it would be very surprising if children with ASD were *not* capable of mirror self-recognition. If we are to understand the me-self in ASD in more depth, it is necessary to look at tasks and situations that require a more sophisticated level of self-awareness.

Delayed video self-recognition in autism

Based on the assumption that mirror self-recognition measures the present self, Povinelli and colleagues (1996) adapted the paradigm to incorporate a temporal element in an attempt to chart the development of the temporally extended self. In this novel adaptation, which is known as the delayed video self-recognition paradigm, children were videotaped while they played a game with an experimenter. During the game, the experimenter surreptitiously placed a large sticker on the front of their hair. After the game was complete, the child was shown the recording, allowing them to see the sticker placement. As in the mirror self-recognition task, mark-directed behavior was the key variable of interest, but in this case, it was taken to imply that children had a *temporally extended* self-concept/self-awareness. The researchers argued that children need to reason that they are the same person as the person they see in the video and understand the temporal causal relation between their present self watching the video, and their past self being videoed, in order to realize that the sticker will still be on their head here and now, not just there and then. Povinelli et al. found that whereas 3-year-olds tended not to show mark-directed behavior in response to delayed video images of themselves, 4-year-olds did so reliably, and this was taken as evidence for the emergence of the temporally extended self at around age 4 years. To our knowledge, only two published studies have explored delayed video self-recognition in ASD (Lind & Bowler, 2009; Dissanayake et al., 2010). Each of these studies found intact performance, relative to matched typically developing comparison children (average $\phi = .25$, average $p = .35$). However, on the basis of existing data, we cannot be sure that delayed video self-recognition is not delayed relative to chronological age—neither of these studies tested young enough children to establish this (Lind et al.'s sample included only a handful of children aged under 4 years, and the youngest child in Dissanayake et al.'s study was aged 4). Nevertheless, these findings echo those obtained in studies of mirror self-recognition, implying that both the present and temporally extended me-self are sufficient to enable visual self-recognition among young people with ASD.

Response to own name and first-person pronoun use in autism

The two lines of evidence discussed thus far have suggested that the me-self is intact in ASD—insofar as tasks requiring a fairly low level of self-awareness are unproblematic for people with the disorder. However, there are other sources of evidence that may be considered to the contrary. One striking example is reduced responsiveness to name. It is frequently noted that many children with ASD fail to orient to their name (e.g., Nadig et al., 2007). For neurotypical individuals, hearing one's own name—whether someone is trying to get our attention or whether we overhear someone talking about us with other people—has a powerful and immediate effect, causing us to "prick up our ears." In ASD, although there are probably several factors that contribute to an attenuated response to one's name (e.g., social-cognitive and social-motivation factors), it seems likely that it is also a reflection of a diminished me-self—a failure to appreciate that this word you are hearing is *your* name and refers to *your* self (Lombardo & Baron-Cohen, 2010).

Other potential indicators of diminished self-awareness include difficulty using first-person pronouns such as *I*, *me*, and *my* (including substituting third-person pronouns for first-person pronouns) among children with ASD (Jordan, 1996; Lee, Hobson, & Chiat, 1994; Lind & Bowler, 2009a). For example, a child may say, "You want a drink" to request a drink for themselves. There may even be some subtle differences in first-person pronoun use among intellectually high-functioning *adults* with ASD. For example, Lombardo et al. (2007) found that such individuals used the terms moderately less frequently ($d = 0.56$, $p = .04$) than sex, age, and IQ matched neurotypical individuals in a self-focus sentence completion task. This finding implies that participants with ASD were focusing attention on themselves (i.e., becoming self-aware—part of the me-self) less frequently than their neurotypical counterparts.

Self-conscious emotion, awareness of own emotions, alexithymia, and interoception in autism

Several studies have suggested that people with ASD are less likely than their neurotypical counterparts to experience so-called "self-conscious" emotions (i.e., emotions that arise through self-evaluation, such as embarrassment, shame, pride, and guilt). For example, although children with ASD clearly experience pleasure, they are less likely to experience pride in response to a personal achievement (Kasari, Sigman, Baumgartner, & Stipek, 1993). In the context of mirror-self-recognition tasks, behavior such as blushing, shy smiling, gaze aversion, and preening are taken to indicate embarrassment and pride, and they are frequently noted among young typically developing children (Amsterdam, 1972). However, studies of mirror self-recognition in ASD have generally noted the absence of these behavioral indicators of self-conscious emotion. Diminished expression of self-conscious emotion may *potentially* be attributable to a diminished me-self—the experience of these emotions involves self-evaluation; these emotions are *about* the self, and therefore, involve self-awareness, and necessarily, some form of self-representation. However, diminished self-conscious emotion may also be explained by difficulties with social cognition (notably, they are often referred to as "social" rather than "self-conscious" emotions). Thus, it is a possibility that children with ASD have the capacity for self-evaluation, but lack awareness of (or are unconcerned by) socially accepted standards and behaviors. Hence, they may have no clear benchmark for how one is "supposed to be or behave" to compare to their own self-representation. It is also interesting to note that despite showing fewer outward expressions of self-conscious emotion, at least some studies have shown that children with ASD are perfectly able to describe past instances in which they have experienced such emotions (Hobson et al., 2006; Williams & Happé, 2010; but see Losh & Capps, 2006; Capps, Yirmiya, & Sigman, 1992).

In addition to evidence regarding expression of self-conscious emotion in ASD, research on emotional self-awareness in people with this disorder is highly relevant in the current context. Individuals with autism tend to self-report elevated levels of alexithymia, that is, they consider themselves to have difficulty identifying and describing their own emotions (e.g., Berthoz & Hill, 2005; Lombardo et al., 2007). However, there is something a little paradoxical about asking someone—whether they have ASD or not—to rate how self-aware they are using a self-report method that surely relies on a certain level of self-awareness (Williams, 2010; but see Gaigg et al., 2016). Nevertheless, there is some limited empirical support for the idea that people with ASD have diminished emotional self-awareness.

Using a more objective approach, Ben Shalom et al. (2006) found that compared to approximately age- (but not IQ-) matched typically developing children, intellectually high-functioning children with ASD showed normal physiological responses to pleasant, unpleasant, and neutral pictures (taken from the International Affective Picture System [IAPS]), as indicated by changes in skin conductance (unfortunately the precise descriptive and inferential statistics were not reported), but their self-reported ratings of the pleasantness of the pictures were significantly or marginally significantly different (higher for pleasant pictures, $p = .04$; lower for unpleasant, $p = .03$, and neutral, $p = .05$, pictures) from those given by comparison children (unfortunately, no descriptive statistics or effect sizes were reported). In an extension of this method, Bölte et al. (2008) presented images from the IAPS designed specifically to elicit fear, anger, disgust, happiness, and sadness to intellectually high-functioning adults with ASD and neurotypical comparison adults (only roughly matched for age and IQ). They obtained objective, physiological measures (heart rate and blood pressure) as well as subjective, self-report measures of valence and arousal. Replicating Ben-Shalom et al.'s findings, only small (and nonsignificant) effect sizes were observed between the groups for the physiological measures (ds = 0.03 to 0.66, ps = .06 to .99). However, several medium-to-large between-group effects were observed on the self-report measures (these were not always statistically significant, but this was most likely due to the small sample size of $N = 20$). Specifically, participants with ASD gave more positive valence scores for fear ($d = .67$, $p = .13$), anger ($d = .51$, $p = .49$), and sadness ($d = .63$, $p = .08$) pictures (with only small differences for neutral, disgust, and happiness pictures; ds = .20 to .40, ps = .13 to .48) than comparison participants, and reported a higher level of arousal for neutral pictures ($d = 0.70$, $p = .04$) and a lower level of arousal for sadness pictures ($d = 1.18$, $p = .02$) (with only small differences on other picture types; ds = 0.10 to 0.40, ps = .12 to .33). Although Ben-Shalom et al.'s and Bolte et al.'s studies suffer from some weakness, particularly with regard to loose matching procedures and small sample sizes, they nevertheless provide suggestive evidence that although people with ASD have typical physiological emotional reactions to "emotional" stimuli, they may have diminished awareness of these reactions (a function of the me-self). These findings complement research documenting self-reported alexithymia, which in isolation may not be considered particularly compelling. Intriguingly, research exploring "interoception" (awareness of internal bodily sensations) has shown that children and adolescents with ASD are able to judge their own heart rate as accurately as neurotypical individuals (unfortunately, precise inferential statistics were not reported) (Schauder et al., 2015). Although further research is needed, this study fits the emerging picture that self-awareness in ASD may involve several peaks and troughs.

Metacognitive skills and attribution of mental states to self in autism

There is extensive evidence that individuals with ASD have diminished awareness of others' mental states, including their beliefs and intentions (so-called "mindreading" or "mentalizing"). For example, children with ASD tend to have difficulty with so-called "false belief tasks, such as the "Sally-Anne" task (Baron-Cohen et al., 1989). Here, the child watches a scenario in which one doll, Sally, places her marble in a basket and then leaves the scene. While she is gone, another doll, Anne, transfers the marble to a box. The key test question for the participant is, when Sally returns, where will she look for her marble? To correctly predict that Sally will look in the (now empty) basket, the child must attribute a mistaken belief (that the marble is still in the basket) to Sally. The difficulty that children with ASD have in generating correct predictions in such tasks is widely thought to reflect their diminished awareness of *others'* mental states in general.

Despite the enormous body of literature exploring awareness of other people's mental states in ASD, there exists comparatively little research regarding awareness of one's *own* mental states (so-called "metacognition"; e.g., taking a large gulp of liquid from a glass only to discover that it is wine, and becoming aware of your previous mistaken belief that the glass contained water) in this disorder. What research into metacognition in ASD does exist, however, points to an equivalent difficulty with this ability and with mindreading (e.g., Grainger et al., 2014a, 2016). Children with ASD are as likely to fail self-versions of classic mindreading tasks in which participants are required to explain their *own* behavior in terms of mental states (e.g., beliefs and intentions) as they are likely to fail mindreading tasks in which participants are required to explain others' behavior in terms of mental states (e.g., Phillips et al., 2001; Williams & Happé, 2008). For instance, in the classic "Smarties" false belief task, a child is shown a tube of Smarties (a popular type of children's candy in the United Kingdom) and asked what is inside. The vast majority of children (with or without ASD) appropriately respond "Smarties." The experimenter then reveals that the tube contains something unexpected, such as a pencil and then asks the child the key test question, "What did you think was in the tube before you saw inside?" Children with ASD tend to incorrectly answer, "A pencil," thereby showing a lack of awareness of their previous false belief about the tube's contents (i.e., that it contained Smarties). Such a difficulty in forming a meta-representation of one's own mental states (an aspect of the me-self) should have consequences for many aspects of memory, as we discuss later in the chapter.

Awareness of own social skills, ASD traits, and personality traits in autism

Studies that compare self-ratings to informant ratings of social skills (e.g., a person's ability to engage in chit-chat or make friends), ASD traits (e.g., a person's ability to notice small details or their difficulties with changes in routine), and personality traits (e.g., whether a person is curious, lazy, or reliable) are another potentially illuminating source of evidence with respect to self-awareness. Several such studies have found that children with ASD give themselves significantly higher ratings than do their parents on equivalent self/informant versions of social skills questionnaires, but not all of these studies have included a comparison group (e.g., Knott et al., 2006; Lerner et al., 2012). Without a comparison group, one cannot conclude that this represents a diminution of self-awareness—perhaps all individuals, neurotypical and autistic alike, show this type of positive bias. However, on balance, those studies that *have* included comparison participants suggest this is probably not the case.

Koning and MacGill-Evans (2001) found that adolescent boys with ASD rated their social skills significantly higher than parents ($d = 1.26$) or teachers ($d = 0.83$) rated them. In contrast, the self-ratings of an age- and vocabulary-matched neurotypical comparison group did not significantly differ from parent ($d = 0.49$) or teacher ($d = 0.14$) ratings. More recently, Johnson et al. (2010) found, on the one hand, that children and adolescents with ASD gave themselves significantly *lower* scores ($d = 1.76$, $p < .001$) on the Autism-spectrum Quotient (Baron-Cohen et al., 2001) and significantly *higher* scores ($d = 1.79$, $p < .001$) on the Empathizing Quotient (Baron-Cohen & Wheelwright, 2004) than their parents did, although there were no significant self-parent differences in scores ($d = 0.27$, $p > .05$) on the Systemizing Quotient (Baron-Cohen et al., 2003). On the other hand, sex, age, and IQ matched typically developing children did not score themselves significantly differently from their parents on these three measures (all $ds \leq 0.37$; all $ps > .05$). More recently, Kalyva (2010) found a more mixed pattern of results. Children and adolescents with ASD rated their own social skills significantly higher than their teachers rated them ($d = 0.99$, $p > .001$), but significantly lower than their fathers rated them ($d = 0.95$, $p > .001$). Within this group, the discrepancy between self and mother ratings was small and non-significant ($d = 0.31$, $p = .25$). Among a typically developing comparison group (who were matched closely on age, but had somewhat higher verbal IQs, $d = 0.60$, $p = .06$), it was found that self-ratings of social skills corresponded closely with mother ratings, ($d = 0.07$, $p = .25$), were somewhat lower than father ratings ($d = 0.52$, $p = .08$), and were considerably higher than teacher ratings ($d = 0.69$, $p = .01$),

In a recent study, Schriber et al. obtained self and parent reports of personality using the Big Five Inventory. Children and adolescents with ASD were compared to typically developing children matched on age but who had significantly higher full scale IQs ($d = 0.88$, $p < .01$). An interesting pattern of results emerged. In the ASD group, participants gave themselves more favorable ("self-enhancing") ratings than did their parents, associated with effect sizes ranging from small to large in magnitude, across all five of the Big Five dimensions; extraversion ($d = 0.27$, $p > .05$); agreeableness ($d = 0.15$, $p > .05$), conscientiousness ($d = 0.83$, $p < .01$), neuroticism ($d = 0.89$, $p < .01$), and openness ($d = 0.44$, $p < .05$), with differences reaching statistical significance on three out of the five dimensions. However, the opposite pattern was observed in the comparison group: Typically developing participants tended to give themselves less favorable ("self-diminishing") ratings than their parents did, associated with effect sizes ranging from small to medium in magnitude, across all five dimensions (extraversion: $d = 0.23$, $p > .05$; agreeableness: $d = 0.70$, $p < .01$; conscientiousness: $d = 0.27$, $p > .05$; neuroticism: $d = 0.43$, $p < .01$; openness: $d = 0.44$, $p < .05$), with differences reaching statistical significance on two out of the five dimensions. Thus, although the evidence is not totally clear-cut and further research is warranted, it does seem to suggest that young people with ASD are less aware of their social skills and ASD traits than typical individuals are.

Self-concept in autism

Developing a self-concept is thought to rely on a sufficient degree of self-awareness: If one cannot become aware of a feature of oneself, then that feature simply cannot become part of one's concept of self. The fact that children with ASD are able to pass tests of visual self-recognition suggests that they have representations of what they look like. However, this is a very basic level of self-knowledge and it cannot be assumed on the basis of this evidence alone that the quantity or accuracy of self-knowledge is typical in ASD.

Self-concept in ASD has been explored in several studies that have employed Damon and Hart's (1988) self-understanding interview. This interview assesses various domains of self-knowledge, which are separated into the categories of self-as-subject/I-self (including continuity, distinctiveness, and agency domains) and self-as-object/me-self (including physical, active, psychological, and social domains). It is worth highlighting that the "self-as-subject/I-self" category is a misnomer in this context. This component of the interview cannot be regarded as a measure of pre-reflective self-*experience*. Rather, it measures self-*knowledge* of one's temporal continuity through time ("continuity"), one's distinctiveness from other people ("distinctiveness"), and formation, existence, and control of self ("agency"). Thus, data obtained from both strands of the interview shed light purely on the me-self.

Lee and Hobson (1998) were the first to adopt this method among people with ASD. They employed a sample of adolescents with ASD who had low verbal ability, and age- and verbal ability-matched "mentally retarded" comparison adolescents. With respect to the self-as-subject category, participants from both groups produced very few self-descriptive statements relating to continuity, distinctiveness, or agency (possibly because of verbal limitations). However, the researchers noted that the majority of references to continuity among the ASD group referred to "recollections" of early infancy, whereas none of those referred to by comparison participants concerned early infancy. With respect to the self-as-object category, the researchers found that relative to comparison adolescents, adolescents with ASD reported significantly more self-descriptive statements about physical and active characteristics, equal numbers of psychological characteristics (though qualitative differences were noted), and fewer social characteristics (again, qualitative differences were noted).

Farley et al. (2010) administered the self-as-subject portion of the self-understanding interview only, 6 to a verbally able group of adolescents with ASD, and age- and verbal mental age-matched typically developing adolescents. They found significant differences in numbers of self-descriptive statements, favoring the typically developing group, in the agency domain, but not the distinctiveness or continuity domains. Intriguingly, Jackson et al. (2012) found the reverse pattern of results in the self-as-subject portion of the interview among a sample of intellectually high-functioning *adults* with ASD and age (but not IQ) matched neurotypical adults: They found significant differences in the continuity and distinctiveness domains but not the agency domain. Jackson et al. also explored the self-as-object component of the interview and found that adults with ASD produced significantly fewer self-descriptions than neurotypical adults in the social and psychological domains, but not the physical or active domains. Overall, then, across studies, there does not appear to be a clear pattern of between-group differences in the self-as-subject domain of the self-understanding interview. However, participants with ASD appear to have typical (or even enhanced) self-concepts in the physical and active domains, but diminished self-concepts in the psychological and social domains.

Conclusions about the self in autism

It is clear that people with ASD are not completely self-unaware. The existing evidence suggests they are capable of visual self-recognition using mirror images and delayed videos of themselves. They also appear to have typical, or even enriched, self-concepts with respect to physical traits and abilities. However, there is accumulating evidence to indicate that the me-self is atypical in ASD. Research suggests that people with ASD show reduced response to their own names, have difficulties using first-person pronouns, express fewer self-conscious emotions, show diminished awareness of their own emotions and mental states, have reduced awareness of their own social skills and ASD traits, and have atypical self-concepts.

How Might a Diminished Me-Self Explain the Memory Profile in Autism?

If we refer back to the framework set out earlier in this chapter, we can apply this, taking into account the evidence previously considered, to predict and explain patterns of memory strengths and difficulties that we see/might see in ASD. If the me-self is diminished in ASD, we should expect it to have several consequences for memory functioning. Specifically, if people with ASD have diminished self-awareness, it should negatively influence episodic memory (including episodic autobiographical memory), episodic future thinking, and prospective memory. Moreover, if individuals with ASD lack self-*knowledge* and have under-elaborated/inaccurate self-concepts because they have diminished self-*awareness,* we should predict atypical patterns of performance on self-referential memory tasks. That is, people with ASD should not, on average, show the kind of memory advantage for self-related information that neurotypical individuals show. On the other hand, we would not expect to see any deficits in semantic memory per se—since this should not require the me-self. However, we might expect to see specific deficits in *autobiographical* semantic memory. Thus, although problems with self-awareness should not affect the *process* of semantic memory, they may affect the *content* that gets encoded within it. In the following sections, we explain these predictions in full and provide a review of existing evidence from each of these areas.

Episodic memory and episodic foresight in autism

There is now a considerable amount of evidence to suggest that individuals with ASD have impaired episodic memory (Bowler et al., 2011). Retrieval from episodic and semantic memory are said to be associated with autonoetic (self-knowing) and noetic (knowing) awareness, respectively. Autonoetic and noetic awareness are associated with their own distinct experiential qualities, and it is possible to distinguish them through introspection. Episodic (autonoetic) retrieval, or *remembering,* is associated with a rich recollective experience in which one mentally re-lives the previously experienced event and has a quality of "warmth and intimacy" (James, 1890). Semantic (noetic) retrieval, or *knowing*, is associated with a feeling of familiarity but no sense of re-living a past episode. Researchers have capitalized on this ability to introspectively distinguish between these different states of awareness during memory retrieval in order to gauge the relative contributions of episodic and semantic memory, respectively, to performance on laboratory memory tasks. The widely used "remember-know" task (Tulving, 1985) is the classic example of this.

In a typical remember-know task, participants are asked to complete a recognition memory test, and for each test item they identify as previously seen during the study phase of the experiment, they are asked to judge whether they actually *remember* the item being presented at study or just *know* that it was presented at study. Neurotypical adults generally provide a mixture of *remember* and *know* responses in such tests, reflecting the contribution of both episodic and semantic memory to task performance. Thus, if individuals with ASD have impaired self-awareness, and consequently, impaired autonoetic consciousness, they should show less *remembering* and more *knowing* in such tests.

Indeed, this is what Bowler and colleagues showed across two studies (Bowler, Gardiner, & Grice, 2000; Bowler et al., 2007). Compared to age- and IQ-matched neurotypical adults, adults with ASD showed diminished rates of remembering, despite undiminished levels of item recognition. The findings imply that adults with ASD experience autonoetic awareness less frequently than people without ASD. Thus, individuals with ASD appear to have marked difficulties with non-autobiographical episodic memory, and as we might expect, these extend to autobiographical episodic memory. Several studies have shown reduced to autobiographical episodic memory specificity in adults with ASD (e.g., Crane et al., 2013; Goddard et al., 2007; Lind & Bowler, 2010; Tanweer et al., 2010) and reduced accuracy in children with ASD (Lind, Bowler, & Raber, 2014), relative to age- and IQ-matched neurotypical comparison participants.

There is now widespread agreement and considerable empirical support for the idea that the episodic memory system is involved not only in recalling past experiences, but also in imagining possible future experiences (e.g., Atance & Martin-Ordas, 2014; Schacter & Addis, 2007; Suddendorf & Redshaw, 2013; Wheeler et al., 1997). This latter ability has been referred to as episodic future thinking, episodic simulation, prospection, and episodic foresight by various authors. Episodic foresight is said to involve future-oriented mental time travel, and like episodic remembering, involves autonoetic awareness. Hence, if people with ASD have problems with self-awareness generally and autonoetic awareness specifically, we should expect to see difficulties with episodic foresight as well as episodic memory. Indeed, recent research shows that both children (Terrett et al., 2013; Lind, Bowler, & Raber, 2014) and adults (Lind & Bowler, 2010; Lind, Williams, Bowler, & Peel, 2014; but see Crane et al., 2012, for counterevidence) with ASD have difficulty with episodic foresight. The verbal reports of possible future personal experiences produced by people with ASD have been found to be less specific (Lind & Bowler, 2010), less elaborate (Lind, Williams, Bowler, & Peel, 2014; Terrett et al., 2013), and less plausible (Lind, Bowler, & Raber, 2014) than those produced by neurotypical individuals. These findings overall are consistent with the notion that autonoetic awareness is diminished in ASD.

Semantic autobiographical memory in autism

The vast majority of studies of autobiographical memory in ASD have explored *episodic* autobiographical memory, but a limited number have investigated semantic autobiographical memory—or factual knowledge about the self. This research was sparked by a case study by Klein et al. (1999) who documented that a young, intellectually able man with ASD had detailed semantic knowledge of his personality traits, but had great difficulty in generating episodic memories of occasions when he had demonstrated those traits. Crane and Goddard (2008) systematically investigated both episodic and semantic autobiographical memory in a series of tasks among a sample of intellectually high-functioning *adults* with ASD and neurotypical comparison adults. Whereas adults with ASD evinced impairments in episodic autobiographical memory (e.g., recounting what they did on their last birthday), there was no evidence of difficulties with semantic autobiographical memory (e.g., recalling the name and address of their secondary school). This otherwise methodologically rigorous study did, however, suffer from one limitation—accuracy of responses was not independently verified. Participants in this study—both with and without ASD—may potentially have reported entirely spurious information. This approach is not uncommon in studies of autobiographical memory, but it does make it difficult for us to draw clear conclusions about whether these results imply a diminished or undiminished me-self in ASD.

In contrast, Bruck, London, Landa, and Goodman (2007) found that intellectually high-functioning *children* with ASD showed significantly less accurate semantic autobiographical knowledge (responses were verified by parents), as assessed with questions about personal facts such as "What's your mother's name?" However, this finding should be interpreted with a degree of caution because the typically developing comparison group from the study had a significantly higher mean IQ than the ASD group. This IQ decrement could potentially account for significant group differences in semantic autobiographical knowledge. Thus, although there is some suggestive evidence that autobiographical semantic memory is impaired in ASD, any conclusions at this stage would be quite tentative without further research.

Prospective memory in autism

Strikingly, the study of prospective memory in ASD is an emergent research field with only a handful of studies published to date. However, given the theoretical relation between the me-self and prospective memory, there are good reasons to suspect that (at least certain aspects of) this ability will be diminished in ASD. Two forms of prospective memory are commonly distinguished. Event-based prospective memory involves remembering to carry out an intended action (e.g., take the food out of the oven) on the occurrence of a specific event (e.g., when the timer goes off). Time-based prospective memory involves remembering to carry out an intended action (e.g., take the food out of the oven) at a specific point in the future (e.g., in 10 minutes).

A typical time-based prospective memory paradigm requires participants to perform a specific action (e.g., press a pre-specified keyboard key) at specific time intervals (e.g., every 2 minutes) while being engaged in an ongoing task such as categorizing images. Throughout, participants can monitor the elapsed time by pressing a specific key. A typical event-based PM task requires participants to perform a specific action (e.g., press a pre-specified keyboard key) when a specific event occurs (e.g., an image of an animal appears as part of the ongoing task). The crucial difference between the two is that event-based prospective memory is thought to rely less than time-based prospective memory on *self-initiated* retrieval of one's intention (McDaniel & Einstein, 2007). This is because retrieval of one's intended action is cued in an event-based task by the event itself (e.g., hearing a timer go off cues retrieval of one's intention to take the food out of the oven). In contrast, in time-based prospective memory tasks, retrieval of one's intended action must be self-initiated because there is no cue (i.e., event) to remind one of it. This is important because self-initiated retrieval may depend (in part, at least) on the me-self (and/or temporally-extended self-awareness). It has been argued that retrieving one's intentions relies on the ability to recognize one's own intentions in the first place (Williams et al., 2013); thus, a difficulty with metacognition in ASD could lead to a time-based prospective memory deficit in ASD. In fact, this is exactly what we see with regard to prospective memory in ASD.

Evidence from research under both naturalistic and laboratory conditions has revealed a clear impairment of time-based prospective memory in both children and adults with ASD in comparison to typically developing peers (Altgassen, Koban, & Kliegel, 2012; Altgassen, Williams, Bölte, & Kliegel, 2009; Henry et al., 2014; Kretschmer, Altgassen, Rendell, Bolte, & Bölte, 2014; Williams et al., 2013; Williams, Jarrold, Grainger, & Lind, 2014). This unambiguous result is remarkable, given that the studies differed considerably in their methodological approach and that most of the studies showed that participants with ASD *were* able to monitor time appropriately (thus, time-based prospective memory deficits cannot be merely the result of limitations in time-processing).

Event-based prospective memory paradigms also require participants to perform an ongoing task (e.g., press a pre-specified keyboard key). However, the prospective memory action needs to be executed on the appearance of a pre-specified prospective memory cue/event that is embedded into the ongoing task (e.g., press the key *when the screen color changes from white to yellow*). Although some studies have found that event-based prospective memory is diminished in ASD (Altgassen et al., 2012; Brandimonte, Filippello, Coluccia, Altgassen, & Kliegel, 2011; Kretschmer et al., 2014; Yi et al., 2014), most of these studies suffer from methodological issues that may have confounded results (e.g., failure to match groups for age and IQ, failure to match groups for ongoing task performance, failure to check that the prospective memory instruction was even encoded appropriately; see Landseidel et al., under review). When more controlled studies have been conducted, they have always found event-based prospective memory to be unimpaired in ASD (even in samples that show a clear time-based prospective memory deficit) (Altgassen & Koch, 2014; Altgassen, Schmitz-Hubsch, & Kliegel, 2010; Henry et al., 2014; Williams et al., 2013; Williams et al., 2014).

This pattern of impaired time-based, but unimpaired event-based, prospective memory in ASD is important in relation to the topic of the current chapter, because event-based prospective memory is thought to rely less than time-based prospective memory on *self*-initiated retrieval of one's intention (McDaniel & Einstein, 2007). This is because retrieval of one's intended action is *cued* in an event-based task by the event itself (e.g., hearing a timer go off cues retrieval of one's intention to take the food out of the oven). In contrast, in time-based prospective memory tasks, retrieval of one's intended action must be *self-initiated* because there is no cue (i.e., event) to remind one of it. Therefore, self-awareness/temporally extended self may be less crucial for event-based prospective memory than for time-based prospective memory (see Altgassen et al., 2015; Neroni, Gamboz, & Brandimonte, 2014). Thus, even if it turns out that event-based prospective memory is unimpaired in ASD, this does not show that a limitation of the me-self does not contribute to diminished time-based prospective memory in ASD.

The self-reference and ownership effects in autism

Studies of self-referential memory provide a direct test of the capacity of individuals with ASD to encode material in relation to their self-concept, and may provide further evidence regarding whether or not individuals with ASD have intact or impaired me-selves. As such, if self-concept is diminished among individuals with ASD, they should show diminished self-reference effects, relative to neurotypical individuals.

Several studies have examined the "self-reference effect" in ASD, each showing a diminished (Lombardo et al., 2007) or absent (Henderson et al., 2009; Toichi et al., 2002) effect in this population. For example, in one study, Lombardo and colleagues employed a typical self-referential memory paradigm with adults with ASD as well as age- and IQ-matched neurotypical adults. In this study, individuals were presented with psychological trait adjectives and asked to rate the extent to which each word described themselves, a close friend, or Harry Potter. After a delay, participants were given a surprise recognition test, in which they were presented with the adjectives from the previous study phase of the task alongside new lure adjectives. Both groups showed self-reference effects (Harry Potter < Close Friend < Self), but the effect was stronger in the neurotypical group than the ASD group.

Additional evidence of difficulties with self-referential processing in ASD comes from a recent study exploring "ownership" in this population (Grisdale et al., 2014). Previous research with neurotypical individuals indicates that objects people feel they own hold a privileged status in memory and people are more likely to remember objects they "own" compared to objects they do not own (see Cunningham et al., 2008). One explanation for this "ownership effect" is that owned objects are treated almost as an extension of one's self within memory (see Beggan, 1992). If so, individuals with ASD might be expected to demonstrate a reduced ownership effect. To test this prediction, Grisdale et al. employed a task where participants were required to sort pictures of objects that people commonly buy in supermarkets into two shopping baskets. It was explained that they "owned" the objects in one of the baskets, while the objects in the other basket belonged to the experimenter. It was found that neurotypical adults recalled cards belonging to the self significantly better than cards belonging to the experimenter. However, in keeping with studies of self-reference effect in ASD, adults with ASD recalled self- and other-owned cards equally well. Thus, while neurotypical adults showed a clear ownership effect, this effect was absent in the ASD group.

Summary and Conclusions

In our view, it is uncontroversial to conclude that aspects of self-awareness and self-concept are diminished in ASD. Also, it is relatively clear that people with ASD have a particular memory profile of memory strengths (e.g., in semantic memory) and limitations (e.g., in episodic memory, prospective memory). How and to what extent difficulties with self and memory limitations are causally related is somewhat less clear. Certainly, we are not claiming that limitations of the me-self are the only possible causes of memory difficulties; memory (like the self) is multifaceted and has multiple underlying bases. Thus, a number of difficulties (other than with self-awareness/self-concept) among people with ASD probably contribute to impairments of memory. However, there is a relatively large body of evidence that a diminution of the me-self contributes to memory difficulties in this disorder. The findings of reduced self-reference and ownership effects in ASD suggest strongly that the self-concept does not have the same organizational properties/effects in memory.

If our conclusions are correct and people with ASD do have attenuated me-selves, this may have practical implications, particularly for eyewitness testimony and forensic interviewing. The quality of eyewitness memory depends on both the quantity and quality of the information provided by the witness—in court, one is asked to tell the "whole truth" (quantity) and "nothing but the truth" (quality) (Koriat et al., 2001; Maras & Bowler, 2014). In fact, a diminished me-self could potentially result in less complete *and* less accurate testimony. In this chapter, we argue that an attenuated me-self at least contributes to episodic memory difficulties in ASD. Difficulty with episodic memory should, in turn, lead to less complete eyewitness testimony, which by its very nature relies on recollection of a specific event, including details such as what happened, who was there, and where and when it occurred. As well as being less complete, the testimony of people with ASD may potentially also be less accurate than that of neurotypical people. Several studies have shown that even intellectually able individuals with ASD have difficulty judging the accuracy of their own memories—a clear example of diminished self-awareness. This may mean they have difficulties "screening out" potentially inaccurate event details when they are providing eyewitness accounts. Clearly, then, an attenuated me-self has potentially far-reaching consequences for individuals. Having said all this, we are reluctant to draw *firm* conclusions—particularly with respect to the eyewitness testimony of people with ASD—without further, more direct research on the topic.

Take-Home Points

- Several theories propose that the self and memory are multifaceted and have a complex and bidirectional relation with one another.
- Such theories have clear applications to the case of autism—a large body of research suggests impairments in aspects of self and aspects of memory in this disorder.
- We conclude that impairments in self-awareness and self-representation are likely to contribute to the memory difficulties that many individuals with autism experience.

References

Amsterdam, B. (1972). Mirror self-image reactions before age two. *Developmental Psychobiology*, *5*, 297–305.

Anderson, J. R. (1983). The development of self-recognition: A review. *Developmental Psychobiology*, *17*, 35–49.

Atance, C. M., & Martin Ordas, G. (2014). Projecting the self into the future. In P. J. Bauer & R. Fivush (Eds.), *The Wiley handbook on the development of children's memory*, (1st ed., Vol. *2*, pp. 645–664). Chichester, England: Wiley.

Baron-Cohen, S., Leslie, A. M., & Frith, U. (1985). Does the autistic child have a "theory of mind"? *Cognition*, *21*(1), 37–46.

Baron-Cohen, S., & Wheelwright, S. (2004). The empathy quotient: An investigation of adults with Asperger syndrome or high functioning autism, and normal sex differences. *Journal of Autism & Developmental Disorders*, *34*(2), 163–175.

Baron-Cohen, S., Wheelwright, S., Skinner, R., Martin, J., & Clubley, E. (2001). The Autism-Spectrum Quotient (AQ): Evidence from Asperger syndrome/high-functioning autism, males and females, scientists and mathematicians. *Journal of Autism & Developmental Disorders*, *31*(1), 5–17.

Baron-Cohen, S., Richler, J., Bisarya, D., Gurunathan, N., & Wheelwright, S. (2003). The systemizing quotient: An investigation of adults with Asperger syndrome or high-functioning autism, and normal sex differences. In U. Frith & E. Hill (Eds.), *Autism: Mind and brain* (pp. 161–186). New York, NY: Oxford University Press.

Beggan, J. K. (1992). On the social nature of nonsocial perception: The mere ownership effect. *Journal of Personality & Social Psychology*, *62*(2), 229–237.

Ben Shalom, D., Mostofsky, S.H., Hazlett, R.L., Goldberg, M.C., Landa, R.J., Faran, Y., … Hoehn-Saric, R. (2006). Normal physiological emotions but differences in expression of conscious feelings in children with high-functioning autism. *Journal of Autism & Developmental Disorders*, *36*, 395–400.

Berthoz, S., & Hill, E. L. (2005). The validity of using self-reports to assess emotion regulation abilities in adults with autism spectrum disorder. *European Psychiatry*, *20*(3), 291–298.

Bölte, S., Feineis-Matthews, S., & Poustka, F. (2008). Brief report: Emotional processing in high-functioning autism—physiological reactivity and affective report. *Journal of Autism & Developmental Disorders*, *38*(4), 776–781.

Boucher, J., Mayes, A., & Bigham, S. (2012). Memory in autistic spectrum disorder. *Psychological Bulletin*, *138*(3), 458–496.

Bowler, D. M., Gardiner, J. M., & Gaigg, S. B. (2007). Factors affecting conscious awareness in the recollective experience of adults with Asperger's syndrome. *Consciousness & Cognition*, *16*(1), 124–143.

Bowler, D. M., Gaigg, S. B., & Lind, S. E. (2011). Memory in autism: Binding, self and brain. In I. Roth & P. Rezaie (Eds.), *Researching the autism spectrum: Contemporary perspectives* (pp. 316–346) Cambridge, England: Cambridge University Press.

Bowler, D. M., Gardiner, J. M., & Grice, S. J. (2000). Episodic memory and remembering in adults with Asperger syndrome. *Journal of Autism & Developmental Disorders*, *30*, 295–304.

Bruck, M., London, K., Landa, R., & Goodman, J. (2007). Autobiographical memory and suggestibility in children with Autism Spectrum Disorder. *Development & Psychopathology*, *19*, 73–95.

Capps, L., Yirmiya, N., & Sigman, M. (1992). Understanding of simple and complex emotions in non-retarded children with autism. *Journal of Child Psychology & Psychiatry*, *33*(7), 1169–1182.

Carmody, D. P., & Lewis, M. (2012). Self representation in children with and without Autism Spectrum Disorders. *Child Psychiatry & Human Development*, *43*(2), 227–237.

Conway, M. A. (2005). Memory and the self. *Journal of Memory & Language*, *53*(4), 594–628.

Crane, L., & Goddard, L. (2008). Episodic and semantic autobiographical memory in adults with autism spectrum disorders. *Journal of Autism & Developmental Disorders*, *38*, 498–506.

Crane, L., Goddard, L., & Pring, L. (2013). Autobiographical memory in adults with autism spectrum disorder: The role of depressed mood, rumination, working memory and theory of mind. *Autism, 17*(2), 205–219.

Crane, L., Lind, S. E., & Bowler, D. M. (2013). Remembering the past and imagining the future in autism spectrum disorder. *Memory, 21*(2), 157–166.

Cunningham, S. J., Turk, D. J., Macdonald, L. M., & Macrae, C. N. (2008). Yours or mine? Ownership and memory. *Consciousness & Cognition, 17*(1), 312–318.

Damon, W., & Hart, D. (1988). *Self-understanding in childhood and adolescence.* New York, NY: Cambridge University Press.

David, N., Gawronski, A., Santos, N., Huff, W., Lehnhardt, F. G., Newen, A., & Vogeley, K. (2008). Dissociation between key processes of social cognition in autism: Impaired mentalizing but intact sense of agency. *Journal of Autism & Developmental Disorders, 38*, 593–605.

Dawson, G., & McKissick, F. C. (1984). Self-recognition in autistic children. *Journal of Autism & Developmental Disorders, 14*, 383–394.

Dissanayake, C., Shembrey, J., & Suddendorf, T. (2010). Delayed video self-recognition in children with high Vo functioning autism and Asperger's disorder. *Autism, 14*(5), 495–508.

Epstein, R., Lanza, R. P., & Skinner, B. F. (1981). Self-awareness in the pigeon. *Science, 212*(4495), 695–696.

Farley, A. J., Lopez, B., & Saunders, G. (2010). Self-conceptualisation in autism: Knowing oneself versus knowing self-through-other. *Autism, 14*, 519–530.

Frith, U. (2003). *Autism: Explaining the enigma* (2nd ed.). Malden, MA: Blackwell.

Gaigg, S. B., Cornell, A. S., & Bird, G. (2016). The psychophysiological mechanisms of alexithymia in Autism Spectrum Disorder. *Autism*, Advance online publication https://doi.org/10.1177/1362361316667062

Gallup, G. G. (1970). Chimpanzees: Self-recognition. *Science, 167*, 86–87.

Gilboa, A. (2004). Autobiographical and episodic memory—one and the same? Evidence from prefrontal activation in neuroimaging studies. *Neuropsychologia, 42*, 1336–1349.

Goddard, L., Howlin, P., Dritschel, B., & Patel, T. (2007). Autobiographical memory and social problem-solving in Asperger syndrome. *Journal of Autism & Developmental Disorders, 37*, 291–300.

Grainger, C., Williams, D. M., & Lind, S. E. (2014a). Metacognition, metamemory, and mindreading in high-functioning adults with autism spectrum disorder. *Journal of Abnormal Psychology, 123*(3), 650–659.

Grainger, C., Williams, D. M., & Lind, S. E. (2014b). Online action monitoring and memory for self-performed actions in autism spectrum disorder. *Journal of Autism & Developmental Disorders, 44*(5), 1193–1206.

Grainger, C., Williams, D. M., & Lind, S. E. (2016). Metacognitive monitoring and control processes in children with autism spectrum disorder: Diminished judgement of confidence accuracy. *Consciousness & Cognition, 42*, 65–74.

Grisdale, E., Lind, S. E., Eacott, M. J., & Williams, D. M. (2014). Self-referential memory in Autism Spectrum Disorder and typical development: Exploring the ownership effect. *Consciousness & Cognition, 30*, 133–141.

Harley, K., & Reese, E. (1999). Origins of autobiographical memory. *Developmental Psychology, 35*, 1338–1348.

Henderson, H. A., Zahka, N. E., Kojkowski, N. M., Inge, A. P., Schwartz, C. B., Hileman, C. M., … Mundy, P. C. (2009). Self-referenced memory, social cognition, and symptom presentation in autism. *Journal of Child Psychology & Psychiatry, 50*(7), 853–861.

Hobson, R.P. (1990). On the origins of self and the case of autism. *Development & Psychopathology, 2*, 163–181.

Hobson, R. P., Chidambi, G., Lee, A., Meyer, J., Müller, U., Carpendale, J. I. M., … Racine, T. P. (2006). Foundations for self-awareness: An exploration through autism. *Monographs of the Society for Research in Child Development*, i–166.

Howe, M.L., & Courage, M.L. (1993). On resolving the enigma of infantile amnesia. *Psychological Bulletin, 113*, 305–326.

Hume, D. (2003). *A treatise of human nature*. Retrieved from http://www.gutenberg.org/files/4705/4705-h/4705-h.htm (Original work published 1739).

Jackson, P., Skirrow, P., & Hare, D. J. (2012). Asperger through the looking glass: an exploratory study of self-understanding in people with Asperger's syndrome. *Journal of Autism & Developmental Disorders, 42*(5), 697–706.

James, W. (1890). *The principles of psychology*. New York, NY: Holt.

Johnson, S. A., Filliter, J. A., Murphy, R. R. (2009). Discrepancies between self- and parent-perceptions of autistic traits and empathy in high functioning children and adolescents on the autism spectrum. *Journal of Autism & Developmental Disorders, 39*, 1706–1714.

Jordan, R. R. (1996). Pronouns and autism. *International Journal of Psychology, 31*, 169–172.

Kalyva, E. (2010). Multirater congruence on the social skills assessment of children with Asperger Syndrome: Self, mother, father, and teacher ratings. *Journal of Autism & Developmental Disorders, 40*(10), 1202–1208.

Kasari, C., Sigman, M. D., Baumgartner, P., & Stipek, D. J. (1993). Pride and mastery in children with autism. *Journal of Child Psychology & Psychiatry, 34*(3), 353–362.

Klein, S. B., Chan, R. L., & Loftus, J. (1999). Independence of episodic and semantic self-knowledge: The case from autism. *Social Cognition, 17*, 413–436.

Knott, F., Dunlop, A. W., & Mackay, T. (2006). Living with ASD How do children and their parents assess their difficulties with social interaction and understanding? *Autism, 10*(6), 609–617.

Koning, C., & Magill-Evans, J. (2001). Social and language skills in adolescent boys with Asperger syndrome. *Autism, 5*(1), 23–36.

Koriat, A., Goldsmith, M., Schneider, W., & Nakash-Dura, M. (2001). The credibility of children's testimony: Can children control the accuracy of their memory reports? *Journal of Experimental Child Psychology, 79*, 405–437.

Lee, A., & Hobson, R.P. (1998). On developing self-concepts: A controlled study of children and adolescents with autism. *Journal of Child Psychology & Psychiatry, 39*, 1131–1144.

Lee, A., Hobson, R.P., & Chiat, S. (1994). I, you, me, and autism: An experimental study. *Journal of Autism & Developmental Disorders, 24*, 155–176.

Losh, M., & Capps, L. (2006). Understanding of emotional experience in autism: Insights from the personal accounts of high-functioning children with autism. *Developmental Psychology, 42*(5), 809–818.

Moore, C., & Lemmon, K. (Eds.) (2001). *The self in time: Developmental perspectives*. Mahwah, NJ: Lawrence Erlbaum Associates.

Lerner, M. D., Calhoun, C. D., Mikami, A. Y., & De Los Reyes, A. (2012). Understanding parent–child social informant discrepancy in youth with high functioning autism spectrum disorders. *Journal of Autism & Developmental Disorders, 42*(12), 2680–2692.

Lewis, M. (1995). Aspects of self: From systems to ideas. In P. Rochat (Ed.), *The self in infancy: Theory and research* (pp. 95–115). Amsterdam, the Netherlands: North Holland/Elsevier Science.

Lind, S. (2010). Memory and the self in autism: A review and theoretical framework. *Autism, 14*, 430–456.

Lind, S. E., & Bowler, D. M. (2009a). Delayed self-recognition in children with autism spectrum disorder. *Journal of Autism & Developmental Disorders, 39*, 643–650.

Lind, S. E., & Bowler, D. M. (2010). Episodic memory and episodic future thinking in adults with autism. *Journal of Abnormal Psychology, 119*(4), 896–905.

Lind, S. E., Williams, D. M., Bowler, D. M., & Peel, A. (2014a). Episodic memory and episodic future thinking impairments in high-functioning autism spectrum disorder: an underlying difficulty with scene construction or self-projection? *Neuropsychology, 28*(1), 55–67.

Locke, J. (1995). *An essay concerning human understanding*. Retrieved from https://ebooks.adelaide.edu.au/l/locke/john/l81u/contents.html (Original work published 1690).
Lombardo, M. V., Barnes, J. L., Wheelwright, S. J., & Baron-Cohen, S. (2007). Self-referential cognition and empathy in autism. *PlosOne*, *2*, e883.
Lombardo, M. V., & Baron-Cohen, S. (2010). Unraveling the paradox of the autistic self. *Wiley Interdisciplinary Reviews: Cognitive Science*, *1*(3), 393–403.
Maras, K. L., & Bowler, D. M. (2014). Eyewitness testimony in autism spectrum disorder: A review. *Journal of Autism & Developmental Disorders*, *44*(11), 2682–2697.
McDaniel, M. A., & Einstein, G. O. (2007). *Prospective memory: An overview and synthesis of an emerging field*. Thousand Oaks, CA: Sage Publications.
Mitchell, R. W. (1997). A comparison of the self-awareness and kinesthetic-visual matching theories of self-recognition: Autistic children and others. *Annals of the New York Academy of Sciences*, *818*, 39–62.
Nadig, A. S., Ozonoff, S., Young, G. S., Rozga, A., Sigman, M., & Rogers, S. J. (2007). A prospective study of response to name in infants at risk for autism. *Archives of Pediatrics & Adolescent Medicine*, *161*(4), 378–383.
Neisser, U. (1988). Five kinds of self-knowledge. *Philosophical Psychology*, *1*, 35–59.
Neisser, U. (1995). Criteria for an ecological self. In P. Rochat (Ed.), *The self in infancy: Theory and research* (pp.17–34). Amsterdam, the Netherlands: North Holland/Elsevier Science.
Neuman, C. J., & Hill, S. D. (1978). Self-recognition and stimulus preference in autistic children. *Developmental Psychobiology*, *11*, 571–578.
Nielsen, M., Suddendorf, T., & Slaughter, V. (2006). Mirror self-recognition beyond the face. *Child Development*, *77*, 176–185.
Perner, J. (1991). *Understanding the representational mind*. Cambridge, MA: MIT Press.
Povinelli, D. J., & Simon, B. B. (1998). Young children's understanding of briefly versus extremely delayed images of the self: Emergence of the autobiographical stance. *Developmental Psychology*, *34*(1), 188–194.
Povinelli, D. J., Landau, K. R., & Perilloux, H. K. (1996). Self-recognition in young children using delayed versus live feedback: Evidence of a developmental asynchrony. *Child Development*, *67*(4), 1540–1554.
Prebble, S. C., Addis, D. R., & Tippett, L. J. (2013). Autobiographical memory and sense of self. *Psychological Bulletin*, *139*(4), 815–840.
Rochat, P. (2003). Five levels of self-awareness as they unfold early in life. *Consciousness & Cognition*, *12*, 717–731.
Russell, J. (1997). How executive disorders can bring about an inadequate "theory of mind." In J. Russell (Ed.), *Autism as an executive disorder* (pp. 256–304). Oxford, England: Oxford University Press.
Schacter, D. L., & Addis, D. R. (2007). The cognitive neuroscience of constructive memory: remembering the past and imagining the future. *Philosophical Transactions of the Royal Society B: Biological Sciences*, *362*(1481), 773–786.
Schacter, D. L., & Tulving, E. (1994). *Memory systems 1994*. Cambridge, MA: MIT Press.
Schauder, K. B., Mash, L. E., Bryant, L. K., & Cascio, C. J. (2015). Interoceptive ability and body awareness in autism spectrum disorder. *Journal of Experimental Child Psychology*, *131*, 193–200.
Schriber, R., Robins, R., & Solomon, M. (2014). Personality and self-insight in individuals with autism spectrum disorder. *Journal of Personality & Social Psychology*, *106*, 112–130.
Suddendorf, T., & Redshaw, J. (2013). The development of mental scenario building and episodic foresight. *Annals of the New York Academy of Sciences*, *1296*(1), 135–153.
Tanweer, T., Rathbone, C. J., & Souchay, C. (2010). Autobiographical memory, autonoetic consciousness, and identity in Asperger syndrome. *Neuropsychologia*, *48*(4), 900–908.

Terrett, G., Rendell, P. G., Raponi-Saunders, S., Henry, J. D., Bailey, P. E., & Altgassen, M. (2013). Episodic future thinking in children with autism spectrum disorder. *Journal of Autism & Developmental Disorders, 43*(11), 2558–2568.

Toichi, M., Kamio, Y., Okada, T., Sakihama, M., Youngstrom, E. A., Findling, R. L., & Yamamoto, K. (2002). A lack of self-consciousness in autism. *American Journal of Psychiatry, 159*, 1422–1424.

Tulving, E. (1985). Memory and consciousness. *Canadian Psychology, 26*, 1–12.

Tulving, E. (2001). Episodic memory and common sense: How far apart? *Philosophical Transactions of the Royal Society of London Series B-Biological Sciences, 356*, 1505–1515.

Wheeler, M. A., Stuss, D. T., & Tulving, E. (1997). Toward a theory of episodic memory: The frontal lobes and autonoetic consciousness. *Psychological Bulletin, 121*, 331–354.

Williams, D. (2010). Theory of own mind in autism Evidence of a specific deficit in self-awareness? *Autism, 14*(5), 474–494.

Williams, D. M., & Happé, F. (2009). Pre-conceptual aspects of self-awareness in autism spectrum disorder: The case of action-monitoring. *Journal of Autism & Developmental Disorders, 39*, 251–259.

Williams, D. M., & Happé, F. (2010). Recognizing "social" and "non-social" emotions in self and others: A study of autism. *Autism, 14*, 285–304.

Wilson, A. E., & Ross, M. (2003). The identity function of autobiographical memory: Time is on our side. *Memory, 11*, 137–149.

5

Autobiographical Memory and Theory of Mind in Autism Spectrum Disorder

Céline Souchay, Matilda Ohlsson, and Tiziana Zalla

Autism spectrum disorder (ASD) is a neurodevelopmental disorder characterized by repetitive patterns of behavior, and impairments in social reciprocal interaction and in verbal and nonverbal communication, all present from early childhood (American Psychiatric Association, 2000; World Health Organization, 1993). Autism is also characterized by atypical functioning within the domain of memory (Boucher, Mayes, & Bigham, 2012). Because of its clear everyday importance for the healthy functioning of individuals (Conway, 2005), autobiographical memory in autism has now been investigated extensively. However, despite clear difficulties to retrieve autobiographical memories in autism, the factors explaining those difficulties remain a matter of debate. Deficits in autobiographical memory have been explained as the result of many different factors, including deficits in executive function (Goddard, Dritschel, & Howlin, 2014), autonoetic consciousness (Bowler et al., 2000), memory binding (Lind, 2010), and scene construction (Lind et al., 2014). In this chapter, we review how source memory and theory of mind (ToM), two different but interlinked potential causal factors, might explain why individuals with autism exhibit autobiographical memory deficits.

Autobiographical Memory in Autism

Autobiographical memory allows individuals to define themselves in relation to others and to their own personal life stories. According to the Self-Memory-System (SMS) framework reviewed by Conway (2005), autobiographical memory is structured hierarchically. Lifetime periods (e.g., being a student at a university) can be used to access more specific autobiographical knowledge called general events (e.g., writing lab reports). These general events are then used as a cue to access event-specific knowledge (ESK), defined as sensory-perceptual episodic memories (e.g., arriving at university with your parents and feeling nervous).

The Wiley Handbook of Memory, Autism Spectrum Disorder, and the Law, First Edition.
Edited by Jonni L. Johnson, Gail S. Goodman, and Peter C. Mundy.

Studies investigating autobiographical memory in children with ASD support the idea that both episodic and semantic autobiographical memories are impaired, as children with autism have difficulties in recalling events and facts from their personal life (Bon et al., 2013; Bruck, London, Landa, & Goodman, 2007; Goddard et al., 2014). For example, Bruck et al. investigated autobiographical memory in children with ASD (ranging in age from 5 to 10 years) using a questionnaire in which children were asked to provide life facts (e.g., "What is your mother's name?") and narratives of life events (e.g., "What happened at your last birthday party?"). Results showed that fewer episodic events were retrieved by children with ASD compared to healthy controls and that these memories were characterized by a lack of detail. Moreover, compared to their memories for recent events, their memories for early life events were poor. Children with ASD also had difficulties recalling personal factual knowledge (Buck et al., 2007).

By adulthood, children with ASD show a relative preservation of semantic autobiographical memory despite still having difficulties to retrieve episodic autobiographical memory (Goddard, Howlin, Dritschel, & Patel, 2007). Klein et al. (1999) reported the case of a 21-year-old high-functioning individual with autism (R.J.), who clearly showed a preserved semantic autobiographical memory despite having difficulties recalling episodic autobiographical memories. This dissociation between intact semantic autobiographical knowledge and autobiographical episodic memory was later confirmed in group studies. For example, Crane and Goddard (2008) assessed both personal facts and episodic memories in a group of adults with autism and a matched comparison group using an autobiographical memory interview (Bekerian, Dhillon, & O'Neill, 2001), an episodic memory narrative task, and an autobiographical fluency task (Dritschel, Williams, Baddeley, & Nimmo-Smith, 1992). The fluency and episodic memory narrative tasks revealed a personal episodic memory deficit in the ASD group. However, on tests of personal semantic memory individuals with ASD performed comparably to controls.

Autobiographical Memory and the Self in Autism

Lee and Hobson (1998) assessed semantic autobiographical memory in a group of children with ASD with low verbal ability. Although they were found to produce qualitatively similar descriptions of their physical characteristics when compared to controls, differences appeared in their descriptions of psychological and social self-descriptive statements. Indeed, children with ASD produced significantly fewer psychological or social self-statements. This study clearly highlights the question of the relation between psychological self and memory, and how one might influence the other. In fact, these findings fit with the SMS (Conway, 2005; Conway & Pleydell-Pearce, 2000) according to which autobiographical memory is structured hierarchically at different levels of specificity. In this hierarchy, the first type of memory representation is the more general semantic autobiographical memory. The second type of autobiographical memory representation is specific episodic autobiographical memories. These are sensory perceptual memories for personally experienced events (Conway, 2005; Tulving, 1972). In the SMS, episodic and semantic autobiographical memories are thought to provide the content for various self-images. In line with this idea, it has been found that autobiographical memories, which are cued by self-images, tend to cluster temporally around the time of emergence for that particular self-image, a phenomenon known as the reminiscence bump (Rathbone, Moulin, & Conway, 2008). For example, people have a tendency to recall more personnel events from their adolescence or adulthood. In the context of our research, we decided to explore further the relation between self-images, autobiographical memory, and future thinking in autism. Indeed, the SMS holds that normal autobiographical memory function is crucial for a well-functioning self-concept (Conway, 2005). As such, impairments in autobiographical memory like those observed in ASD samples, might have detrimental effects on self-concept development, and indeed, research on the self and memory has provided indirect evidence for this idea.

For example, previous studies have revealed reduced self-reference effect (Millward et al., 2000; Toichi et al., 2002) and a lack of the enactment effect in autism (i.e., a facilitation effect in retrieving self-performed actions; Zalla et al., 2010). This suggests that memory in individuals with ASD does not improve when information is processed in relation to the self. To assess more directly the links between autobiographical memory and the self, we tested individuals with ASD on the Twenty Statements Test (TST) (Rathbone et al., 2008). Participants were asked to generate I AM statements (e.g., I AM a mother) and then to recall episodic autobiographical memories to some of those statements. We also decided to test adolescents with ASD (unpublished data) as self-identity formation has been suggested as the main developmental task of adolescence (Erikson, 1968).

A total of 14 adolescents with ASD (male = 13, female = 1; mean age = 15.1, SD = 2.41; age range = 12–19; full scale IQ = 113.00, SD = 13.76) and 12 control participants (male = 10, female = 2; mean age = 14.9, SD = 2.97, age range = 11–19; full scale IQ = 115.08, SD = 10.11) took part in the study. There were no significant differences: gender [$t(24) = 0.74$, $p = .469$], age [$t(24) = 0.21$, $p = .832$], or full scale IQ [$t(24) = 0.43$, $p = .669$] indicating close matching. Inclusion criteria for ASD participation was a clinician confirmed diagnosis of either Asperger syndrome (AS) or high-functioning autism (HFA) with no language impairment and a full scale IQ of >70 as assessed by Weschler abbreviated intelligence scale (WASI; Weschler, 1999). Ethical approval was obtained from Leeds University Institute of Psychological Sciences Ethics Committee (ethics reference code 12-0067). Prior to their participation, all participants gave their informed consent. In addition, parental consent was obtained if the participant was below 18 years of age.

To measure the current self-concept a modified version of the TST (Kuhn & McPartland, 1954) was used. Participants were instructed to generate 20 self-statements (under no time pressure) until 20 statements had been produced or until they knew with certainty that no more self-statements could be generated. The task employed to measure participant's future self can be thought of as an extension of the TST, which allows the assessment of a person's future self-concept. The procedure and format of the future self-task were identical to those of the current self-task with the modification that this task required participants to provide statements describing their future self-beginning with "I will be." As was the case in the current self-task, participants were provided with possible categories (social roles, personality traits, physical traits, or interests) of responses and examples of these categories (e.g., "I will be a mother for a future social role"). All participants were informed that the future self-statements provided were to be plausible and realistic.

Following the TST task, participants were asked to select the three self-statements they felt best described their current self-concept from the ones they had generated in the current self-task. Each of these three statements was then used to cue three episodic autobiographical memories of related events. Participants were instructed that the memory should be of a personally experienced event that occurred over one year ago and reflected an event where the particular self-image was present (e.g., if the I am statement was musician, then the memories needed to be of an event relating to being a musician). Participants described their memories verbally and were asked to provide as much details as they could possibly recall. Following the I Will Be task, participants were asked to select from their future self-statements the three future self-images they felt would best come to describe their future self. Participants were then asked to imagine three specific future events linked to each of these three future self-statements and to provide as much details as possible about the imagined future event.

Self-strength was first measured as the mean total number of current and future self-statements generated per group (max = 20). A 2 (group; ASD/control) × 2 (condition; current/future) mixed ANOVA generated a significant main effect of condition, $F(1, 23) = 4.83$ $p = .03$, such that both groups generated more current ($M = 17.8$, $SD = 4.35$) than future self-statements ($M = 16.48$, $SD = 4.79$). The main effect of group was not significant, $F(1, 23) = 1.31$, $p = .26$. The Group × Condition interaction was also non-significant, $F(1, 23) = 0.27$, $p = .61$.

Moreover, a measure of self-quality was created using both current and future self-concepts statements. These statements were coded using an extensive self-statement coding scheme developed for use with the TST by Rhee, Uleman, Lee, and Roman (1995). Following this method, each statement was categorized as either autonomous (denoting self-statements that were "stable over time and context and that represented internalized feelings, beliefs, or abilities") or social (denoting self-statements that include reference to others, specific locations, or social context). Independently of this, each statement was also coded as either specific (denoting self-statements, which were qualified by specific details) or abstract (denoting self-statements lacking in specific details). This permitted a measure of self-quality.

To assess group differences in social versus autonomous current self-quality, an independent samples *t*-test was carried out on social responses. This revealed a significant effect showing that the controls generated a higher proportion of social statements (M = .36, SD = .13) than the ASD group (M = .26, SD = .12), $t(23) = 2.02$, $p = .05$. An independent samples *t*-test was also carried out in order to assess group differences in the proportion of abstract versus specific statements. This showed that controls generated significantly more abstract responses (M = .33, SD = .13) than did the ASD-group (M = .23, SD = .12), $t(23) = 2.06$, $p = .05$. For future self-statements, an independent samples *t*-test revealed no significant group differences in the proportion of social responses provided (Control group M = .37, SD = .09, ASD-group M = .38, SD = .15), $t(23) = 0.164$, $p = .871$. The independent samples *t*-test on the proportion of abstract responses did however reveal that controls generated a significantly higher proportion of abstract self-statements (M = .17, SD = .07) than the ASD group (M = .08, SD = .09), $t(23) = 2.73$, $p = .012$.

The findings in both current and future self-quality motivated a more in depth analysis on self-quality. As such, a set of independent samples *t*-tests were carried out on the proportion of statements that fell into four of the categories (Rhee et al., 1995). The analysis of current self-statements revealed a number of trends showing that the ASD group produced more physical descriptive statements, $t(23) = 1.84$, $p = .07$, and more specific attributes, $t(23) = 1.87$, $p = .07$, but fewer trait-based

Table 5.1 Mean proportion of current trait, social identity, specific attribute, and physical descriptive statements for each group (SDs in parentheses).

	Trait	*Social identity*	*Specific attributes*	*Physical description*
ASD	0.23(.15)	0.21(.15)	0.19(.18)	0.15(.07)
Control	0.34(.15)	0.26(.18)	0.08(.07)	0.10(.07)

Table 5.2 Mean proportion of future trait, social identity, specific attribute, and physical descriptive statements for each group (SD in parentheses).

	Trait	*Social identity*	*Specific attributes*	*Physical description*
ASD	0.07(.08)	0.28(.15)	0.15(.15)	0.21(.19)
Control	0.16(.06)	0.28(.11)	0.07(.06)	0.16(.10)

statements, $t\,(23) = -1.82$, $p = .08$. For future self-statements, the independent samples *t*-tests revealed that controls generated significantly more trait based statements, $t\,(23) = -3.08$, $p = .005$, and significantly less specific attribute statements, $t\,(23) = 2.18$, $p = .04$.

Data from the autobiographical memory and future experience tasks were coded according to the methodology employed by Lind and Bowler (2010). In accordance with this coding scheme, a past or future event was classified as episodic if it met three criteria. First, it needed to be a specific personal event that lasted, or would last, less than one day and had occurred or would occur on only one occasion. Second, the event needed to be situated in time to within a two-year range (such as 8 or 9 years old). Third, the event needed to be situated in space. This criterion was considered met if participants provided a specific location such as, "my classroom in school." Simply stating a town or a country was regarded insufficient. A future experience or autobiographical memory was coded as non-episodic if the participant was unable to remember or imagine any event associated with the particular self-statement used as a cue, if the event lasted or would last longer than a day, had occurred or would occur on repeated occasions, or was not located in time and space.

A second rater, blind to participant group, independently coded 50% of the autobiographical memories and future experiences. Cohen's Kappa indicated that inter-rater reliability was substantial at 0.96 for autobiographical memory and 0.93 for future experiences. Episodic scores for both autobiographical memories and future events were generated by assigning a score of 1 to any autobiographical memory or event classified as episodic and a 0 to events and autobiographical memories classified as non-episodic. Thus, a proportion of episodic autobiographical memories and episodic future events could be calculated by dividing the number of truly episodic autobiographical memories and future events by the total autobiographical memories and future events provided. As such, the maximum episodic score for both was 1.00.

The mean episodic scores for autobiographical memories and future events were generated by calculating the mean proportion of strictly episodic autobiographical memories and future events per group (max = 1.00). A 2 (group; ASD/controls) × 2 (condition; past/future) mixed ANOVA revealed a significant main effect of group,

Table 5.3 Mean proportion of autobiographical memories and future images classified as episodic in nature (max = 1.0).

	Episodic memories	*Future experiences*
ASD group	0.48(.28)	0.17(.22)
Control group	0.75(.17)	0.38(.25)

F (1, 23) = 10.04, p = 0.004) resulting from the greater proportion of episodic autobiographical memories and future events generated by controls than the ASD-group. There was also a significant main effect of condition, F (1, 23) = 38.30, p < .001) demonstrating that both groups obtained significantly higher episodic scores in the past (M = .61, SD = .27) than future condition (M = .27, SD = .26). The Group × Condition interaction was however nonsignificant, F (1, 23) = 0.27, p = .612. See table 5.3 for Means and SDs.

The results of this study are in line with the growing body of research that has already demonstrated that episodic autobiographical memory impairments are a common feature of the disorder (Bruck et al., 2007; Crane et al., 2009; Crane et al., 2011; Goddard et al., 2007; Lind & Bowler, 2010; Tanweer et al., 2010;). The impaired ability to use current self-images to cue episodic autobiographical memory was mirrored in the future condition by a reduced ability to use future self-images to cue episodic future events. This appears to confirm previous findings of impaired future thinking in ASD (Lind & Bowler, 2010). This result converges with previous research on ASD, which has shown that impairments in episodic autobiographical memory are associated with impairments in episodic future thinking (Lind & Bowler, 2010). Finally, these results are consistent with the wider literature, which demonstrates that the two abilities are closely interlinked (D'Argembeau, Raffard, & Van der Linden, 2008; Spreng & Levine, 2006).

The finding of impaired episodic autobiographical memory in the present study does also extend the literature in an interesting way. In the bidirectional self-memory relation, the self is thought of as a structure that controls the encoding and retrieval of autobiographical memories (Conway, 2005). Because the present study used current self-images to cue episodic autobiographical memories, the finding of impaired episodic autobiographical memory might suggest that individuals with ASD have a specific deficit in using the self to organize retrieval from autobiographical memory. That is, individuals with ASD might fail to use their self as an effective organizing structure in memory. This idea supports Crane and Goddard (2009), who suggested that the reduced ability of individuals with ASD to use self-relevant cues to access episodic autobiographical memories indicated a deficit in using the self to organize memory retrieval.

However, the hypothesis of a reduced ability to use self-relevant cues clearly contrasts with our findings showing that adolescents (and adults, Tanweer et al., 2010) are able to produce as many self-images as controls, and therefore, do not show a diminished self. In other words, despite the impairments in episodic autobiographical memory, adolescents with ASD appear to develop a strong and accessible self. As previous studies have shown that individuals with ASD might have intact semantic autobiographical memory (Crane & Godard, 2008; Tanwer et al., 2010), one potential explanation of such findings is that patients with impaired episodic autobiographical memory simply rely on their intact conceptual semantic autobiographical memory to maintain or develop a strong sense of self (Conway et al., 2004; Rathbone, Moulin, & Conway, 2009). One possibility is that in the same way that the current self might be supported by the intact semantic autobiographical memory in ASD, the future self-concept can be supported by semantic future thoughts. In this way, the simple knowledge of events that may occur in the future could support retrieval of episodic future events (Atance & O'Neill, 2005). For example, it is conceivable that cultural life scripts (Berntsen & Rubin, 2004), which can be thought of as a schema of normative life events and their usual timing (e.g., leaving school or having children) might support the future self-concept in ASD.

Autobiographical Memory Specificity in Autism and Source Memory

Autobiographical memory is characterized by the retrieval of episodic details such as spatial, time, self, or visual information. However, one constant finding in the autism literature is the lack of specificity, and therefore, details in autobiographical memories (Bruck et al., 2007; Goddard et al., 2014; Tanweer et al., 2010). This could seem surprising as several studies suggest that individuals with autism perceive the world more intensely and perceive more details (Markram & Markram, 2010).

However, being able to detect more details and remembering those details could be differentially impaired in ASD. The capacity to remember contextual details, for example, as related to source memory, has only recently been explored in autism. Such studies (cited later) give us a window into whether or not individuals with autism can retrieve specifics or detailed information.

Starting with temporal processing and memory, several studies have shown clear difficulties exhibited by individuals with autism performing tasks such as serial recall (e.g., Poirier et al., 2011). Bennetto et al. (1996) used temporal intrusions as a measure of source memory. Participants (adolescents with ASD and TD controls) were given the California Verbal Learning Test (CVLT, Delis et al., 1987), and participants were asked to give recency judgments. Participants with ASD had difficulties judging which items had been presented most recently. However, using a similar recency task with picture stimuli, Gras-Vincendon et al. (2007) found no deficit in adults with ASD compared to controls. However, Bigham et al. (2010) demonstrated recency judgment impairments in low functioning children/adolescents with ASD. Therefore, whether or not temporal source memory is impaired in autism is not a clear-cut answer.

Bowler et al. (2004) suggested that the *Task Support Hypothesis* previously proposed to explain episodic memory deficits in autism (Bowler, Matthews, & Gardiner, 1997) could also apply to temporal source memory. In other words, temporal source memory would be impaired only in tasks with unsupported test procedures, such as recall, but not supported tests, like recognition. In a first study comparing recall and recognition performance of source memory, Bowler et al. (2004) showed impaired recall but intact recognition of studied item location, voice of presentation, and item-related actions. A more recent study (Bowler, Gaigg, & Gardiner, 2015) confirmed these first findings, but also showed that environmental support might be less important for temporal source memory than for any other type of source.

In support of the *Task Support Hypothesis* for source memory, Souchay et al. (2013), using supported recognition questions (e.g., "Was the item in the beginning of the list, the middle of the list, or the end of the list?"), showed that adolescents with ASD could recall different types of source information correctly (voice, color, spatial, and temporal localization). Similarly, Bowler, Gaigg, and Gardiner (2014) showed that individuals with ASD could recognize different source features such as color or location but could not recognize object-location or object-color combinations. Altogether, these findings therefore suggest that apart from temporal information, individuals with autism can retrieve contextual information. However, individuals with autism might have difficulties using such contextual information to form an autobiographical memory (as it is the case for self-cues) or even bind the contextual information to the gist information to create an autobiographical memory (Bowler, Gardiner, & Berthollier, 2014). Of particular interest to the autobiographical literature, other studies have suggested that source memory might be more impaired in ASD when the contextual information involves a social aspect, as impairments in social functioning are a primary characteristic of ASD (O'Shea et al., 2005). Similarly, numerous studies now demonstrate memory in autism, specifically recollective experiences, might be characterized by a lack of rich detail related to the self (Bowler et al., 2000a, 2000b; Bowler et al., 2007; Souchay et al., 2013; Tanweer et al., 2010). To summarize, a lack of social and/or self-contextual information as well as a difficulty to bind the contextual information to the gist information might contribute to explain the autobiographical memory deficits in autism.

Autobiographical Memory Specificity in Autism and Theory of Mind

Episodic specificity, and therefore, autobiographical episodic specificity has been recently proposed as an important component of a range of cognitive tasks that involve memory and imagination. For example, Madore and Schacter (2014) showed that improving specificity (i.e., the amount and quality of details that people retrieve), improved performance on a problem-solving task in normal young and older adults. According to the "episodic simulation hypothesis" (Schacter et al., 2008) retrieval of past episodic experiences is needed to imagine future events and is crucially involved in means-end problem solving.

In this context, Ciaramelli, Bernardi, and Moscovitch (2013) suggested that episodic simulation would also support theory of mind (ToM) tasks as well as in general most tasks involving self-projection. In ASD, impaired ToM for oneself and others appears to be closely related to an impaired episodic autobiographical memory (Adler et al., 2010). This suggests that diminished level of self-consciousness and diminished social insight might reflect a common underlying deficit in autism (Frith & Happé, 1999).

As largely documented, children and adults with ASD exhibit diminished or delayed abilities to decode affective and mental states in themselves and others (Baron-Cohen et al., 1985). The first-order false belief tasks, such as "The Sally & Anne" task, usually employed to assess ToM ability, consist in a story in which the character Sally does not witness character Anne transferring a ball from a basket to a box, and thus, she falsely believes it is still in its original location. Contrary to the more severe forms of autism, individuals with HFA may pass false belief tasks successfully. Specifically, they often solve first-order (e.g., "Sally thinks it's x, when really it's y") and second-order false beliefs tests (e.g., "Sally thinks Mary thinks x, but both Sally and Mary are wrong"; Bowler, 1992; Dahlgren & Trillingsgaard, 1996; Happé, 1995), although they might fail more "advanced" ToM tests, based on detection of sarcasm, irony, or bluff (Happé, 1994) as well as fail on recognition of *faux pas* (Baron-Cohen et al., 1999; Zalla et al., 2009).

In everyday life, individuals with ASD find mindreading of both themselves and others relatively difficult, slow, and unreliable, and often attain only a fragmentary and incomplete grasp of knowledge of their own and others' mental states. However, while it is commonly acknowledged that explicit ToM, which refers to the abilities to overtly attribute and consciously reason on mental states, might be delayed and not totally disrupted in individuals with HFA or AS, implicit ToM reasoning, which refers to the spontaneous and automatic sensitivity to others' mental states, is generally impaired in ASD (Senju et al., 2009), and not alleviated by compensatory strategies (Senju, 2012). Because ASD individuals are thought to lack a devoted implicit ToM system (Senju, 2009, 2012), it is likely that in these individuals with normal intellectual functioning, access to both self- and other knowledge can be achieved by means of general learning mechanisms or compensatory cognitive strategies that differ from those applied by individuals with typical development (Happé, 1995).

Difficulties encountered in individuals with ASD when presented with advanced explicit ToM tests also suggest that impairments might concern the ability to integrate different types of information about the social scenario and to use them to infer the characters' mental states (Zalla et al., 2009). Further empirical support for this hypothesis is provided by studies investigating the relation between intentional judgment and moral reasoning in adults with ASD (Buon et al., 2013; Moran et al., 2011; Zalla & Leboyer, 2011; Zalla et al., 2011). These studies reported difficulties in using information about the agent's intentions for moral reasoning in this population (Buon et al., 2013; Zalla & Leboyer, 2011), even when the agent's intention is not misattributed. Along the same line, Zalla and collaborators (2011) reported difficulties providing appropriate moral justifications and evaluating the seriousness of normative transgressions in adults with HFA. The authors explained these results by a failure in integrating and using normative knowledge and information about the agent's intentions and affective states in conscious moral reasoning.

Two non-exclusive hypotheses can be proposed to account for these difficulties: The first one—The *Weak Theory of Mind* hypothesis—relates to the lack of robustness of mental states representations; the second one points to the dysfunction in the integration process of multiple types of information due to a diminished cognitive control in the ASD population.

With respect to the first hypothesis, several studies have shown that even when individuals with ASD pass first- and second-order ToM tasks, they still show considerable variations in their ability to use intentions in social reasoning (e.g., Buon et al., 2013). Thus, even when they correctly attribute mental states, they might fail to appeal to the agent's psychological states when justifying their judgments (Zalla & Leboyer, 2011). As shown by a neuroimaging study (Young & Saxe, 2009), the strength of activation in the temporo-pariental junction region strongly correlated with participants' ability in ToM reasoning (i.e., the exculpation of an agent causing accidental harm). This finding suggests that the more participants have robust mental states representations, the more they are able to use them in social reasoning task.

With respect to the second hypothesis, previous studies have shown severe impairments in cognitive control and mental flexibility in individuals with ASD (Barbalat, Leboyer, & Zalla, 2014; Geurts, Corbett, & Solomon, 2009; Hill & Bird, 2006). Of note, the ability to flexibly and consciously reason about a wide range of perceptual, contextual, verbal, and knowledge-based information, as required for the explicit forms of ToM, might be cognitively demanding. While, in people with typical development, a considerable part of this work can be done automatically by implicit ToM processes, in individuals with ASD, who lack an early developing implicit ToM system, this might rely on generalized mechanisms, and in particular, through a process of explicit recollection of prior personal memories about the situation.

Corcoran and Frith (2003) found robust correlations between the strength of autobiographical memory retrieval and ToM functioning in individuals with schizophrenia, and proposed that, when people attempt to infer another's mental state, they refer initially to autobiographical episodic memory and make use of past events to inform ongoing situations. Thus, understanding another's mental state and self-introspection may rely on autobiographical memory and inductive or analogical reasoning in order to retrieve analogous events from the past that might help to disambiguate a social scenario.

More recently, Barbalat, Leboyer and Zalla (2014) investigated the temporal organization of cognitive control in adults with ASD by adapting an experimental paradigm that modelled (a) the sensory responses that were most appropriate for processing the incoming stimuli; (b) the contextual control information (i.e., the incoming signal is adapted in time within a specific context), and (c) the episodic control processes (i.e., incoming signal is temporally distant from the subject's response; see Koechlin et al., 2003). As in the seminal study, we used information theory to vary the demands of these control processes by modulating the amount of information conveyed by each control signals that is required for selecting appropriate representations for action.

For example, at the basic sensory level, the phone rings (stimulus), which usually triggers the appropriate behavior of picking up the phone (motor response). The contextual control level is involved in selecting appropriate stimulus-response associations according to the immediate contextual information that accompany the occurrence of stimuli. For example, if on its screen, the phone displays the number of a close friend (context 1) while ringing (stimulus), people will pick it up (response), but if it displays the number of a co-worker (context 2), the same stimulus might be associated to a different response, people might let it ring. In other words, the stimulus-response associations depend on the immediate context accompanying the occurrence of the stimulus. The episodic control level is the higher level of this control hierarchy, which is involved in selecting consistent sets of stimulus-response associations evoked in the same immediate context according to the temporal episode in which the stimuli occur. Here, an episode is defined as a particular situation in which the person is acting, and which is based on past events, instructions or ongoing internal goals. For example, in the situation where a person is at home (episode 1), a call from a close friend (context 1) will be associated to a pick up response, but a call from a work colleague (context 2) will lead to a nonresponse.

In accordance with studies showing that individuals with ASD were impaired in the control of information conveyed by past events (Hare et al., 2007; Lind & Bowler, 2010), Barbalat et al. (2014) found that ASD adults perform as well as comparison participants when they were required to control information conveyed by sensory and context control. However, they demonstrated decreased accuracy when they had to control information conveyed by episodic signals. Of interest, this specific deficit in controlling episodic information (and not of a general cognitive control deficit) correlated with the severity of autistic symptomatology, as measured by the Autistic Spectrum Quotient (AQ) in both the ASD and the comparison groups: The more participants were impaired in episodic control processes, the more severe their symptoms were. This study suggests an interesting relation between two consistent findings in ASD: executive dysfunctions (Geurts et al., 2009; Hill, 2004) and episodic memory deficits (Hare et al., 2007; Lind & Bowler, 2010). Episodic control allows the updating of specific association rules between immediate contextual signals and tasks-sets to be performed in a subsequent temporal episode.

Such association rules are thought to be stored in episodic memory (Buckner & Koutstaal, 1998; Koechlin et al., 2003) and temporarily in working memory. Episodic control is the executive component that supervises the retrieval of such information stored in the long-term memory, and temporarily represented it as integrated, coherent, multimodal, episodic bindings in the Episodic Buffer (Baddeley, 2000). The episodic control plays a crucial role in complex tasks such as learning, comprehension, and reasoning both in the intrapersonal and social domains: It is capable of retrieving prior information in the form of conscious awareness, and of manipulating and reflecting on that information. In doing so, the episodic control system allows the use of episodic memories and makes such memories available for other cognitive operations. It also serves the ToM system for understanding intentions and mental states as well as executive functions for the selection of specific action plans and flexible switching between appropriate behaviors. The selective disruption of this episodic control system may explain why, in the absence of episodic information, both the explicit understanding of other mental states and the self-knowledge might be impaired in individuals with ASD.

Because of the reduced use of episodic autobiographical memory in social and intrapersonal judgments, children and adolescents with ASD fail to fully develop an interpersonal and narrative self. As suggested by Crane and Goddard (2009), the reduced ability of individuals with ASD to use self-relevant cues to access episodic autobiographical memories indicates a deficit in using the self to organize memory retrieval. Of interest, Powell and Jordan (1993) noted that the development of personal episodic memories depends on the existence of an "experiencing self" that codes events as part of a personal dimension. If the self is not constructed and involved as an agent in the process of memory retrieval, events are experienced and encoded at the perceptual stage in a nonsubjective way, that is, "individuals with autism would be aware of what was happening, but not aware that it was happening to them" (Powell & Jordan, 1993).

The hypothesis of a selective impairment in episodic control is consistent with a more general Bayesian model of signal processing (Pellicano & Burr, 2012). This model depicts perception as a process of probabilistic, knowledge-driven inference that matches incoming external (sensory) signals with a cascade of top-down predictions biased by prior experience (the "prior"). According to Pellicano and Burr (2012), in individuals with ASD, priors are attenuated ("hypo-priors") with fewer internal constraints on perception, leading to increased sensory accuracy, but diminished performance in situations where priors help resolve ambiguity. Social event prediction might be particularly difficult if one preponderantly relies on external, observable evidence only, without being able to call on precise prior beliefs and memories to reduce the intrinsic uncertainty of social behaviors (i.e., to reduce the many-to-one mappings between causes and sensory inputs that characterize these behaviors; Lawson et al., 2014). Hence, in individuals with ASD, impoverished prior knowledge, and in particular, episodic information, would result in an incapability to reduce the pervasive uncertainty of the social world and make social interaction and action prediction more difficult, as recently demonstrated by Chambon et al. (in press). The disruption in the inferential mechanism that integrates sensory evidence into prior beliefs could ultimately be responsible for social disorders and reduced self-knowledge.

Conclusion

To conclude, in this chapter, we reviewed how source memory and theory of mind might explain why individuals with autism exhibit autobiographical memory deficits. We also demonstrated the impact of autobiographical memory deficits on the development of the self and how a reduced episodic specificity could interfere with social behaviors. We suggest that future research should tackle how to improve autobiographical memory in autism and assess the impact on a wide range of self-projection tasks, including theory of mind tasks, reasoning tasks, or future thinking tasks. Such research could lead to the development of rehabilitation training programs and improve the quality of life for individuals with autism.

Take-Home Points

- Autobiographical memory is impaired in autism spectrum disorder.
- Source memory and theory of mind can explain some autobiographical deficits.
- Reduced autobiographical memory specificity can interfere with social behaviors.

References

Adler, N., Nadler, B., Eviatar, Z., & Shamay-Tsoory, S. G. (2010). The relationship between theory of mind and autobiographical memory in high-functioning autism and Asperger syndrome, *Psychiatry Research*, *178*, 214–216.

Atance, C., & O'Neill, D. (2005). The emergence of episodic future thinking in humans. *Learning and Motivation*, *36*, 126–144.

Baddeley, A. (2000). The episodic buffer: A new component of working memory? *Trends in Cognitive Sciences*, *4*, 11.

Barbalat, G., Leboyer, M., & Zalla, T. (2014). A specific impairment in cognitive control in adults high-functioning autism disorders, *Journal of Psychiatric Research*, *58*, 26–35.

Baron-Cohen, S., Leslie, A., & Frith, U. (1985). Does the autistic child have a theory of mind? *Cognition*, *21*, 37–46.

Baron-Cohen, S., O'Riordan, M., Stone, V., Jones, R., & Plaisted, K. (1999). Recognition of faux pas by normally developing children and children with Asperger syndrome or high-functioning autism. *Journal of Autism & Developmental Disorders, 29*(5), 407–418.

Bennetto, L., Pennington, B. F., & Rogers, S. J. (1996). Intact and impaired memory functions in autism. *Child Development, 67*(4), 1816–1835.

Bekerian, D., Dhillon, D., & O'Neill, M. H. (2001). The children's autobiographical memory inventory, poster presentation. Valencia: Third International Conference on Memory.

Berntsen, D., & Rubin, D. C. (2004). Cultural life scripts structure recall autobiographical memory. *Memory and Cognition, 32*(3), 427–442.

Bigham, S., Boucher, J., Mayes, A., & Anns, S. (2010). Assessing recollection and familiarity in autistic spectrum disorders: Methods and findings. *Journal of Autism & Developmental Disorders, 40*(7), 878–889.

Bon, L., Baleyte, J. M., Piolino, P., Desgranges, B., Eustache, F., & Guillery-Girard, B. (2013). Growing up with Asperger's syndrome: Developmental trajectory of autobiographical memory. *Frontiers in Psychology*, Jan 11; *3*, 605.

Boucher, J., Mayes, A., & Bigham, S. (2012). Memory in autistic spectrum. *Psychonomic Bulletin, 138*(3), 458–496.

Bowler, D. M. (1992). Theory of mind in Asperger's syndrome. *Journal of Child Psychology & Psychiatry, 33*(5), 877–893.

Bowler, D. M., Gaigg, S. B., & Gardiner, J. M. (2015). Brief Report: The Role of task support in the spatial and temporal source memory of adults with autism spectrum disorder. *Journal of Autism & Developmental Disorder, 8*(3), 317–327.

Bowler, D. M., Gardiner, J. M., & Gaigg, S. B. (2007). Factors affecting conscious awareness in the recollective experience of adults with Asperger's syndrome. *Consciousness & Cognition, 16*, 124–143.

Bowler, D. M., Gardiner, J. M., & Berthollier, N. (2014), Source memory in adolescents and adults with Asperger's syndrome. *Journal of Autism & Developmental Disorders, 34*(5), 533–542.

Bowler, D. M., Gardiner, J. M., & Grice, S. (2000). Episodic memory and remembering in high-functioning adults with autism. *Journal of Autism & Developmental Disorders, 30*, 295–304.

Bowler, D. M., Gardiner, J. M., Grice, S., & Saavalainen, P. (2000). Memory illusions: False recall and recognition in high functioning adults with autism. *Journal of Abnormal Psychology, 109*(4), 663–672.

Bowler, D. M., Matthews, N. J., & Gardiner, J. M. (1997). Asperger's syndrome and memory: Similarity to autism but not amnesia *Neuropsychologia, 35*(1), 65–70.

Buckner, R. L., & Koutstaal, W. (1998). Functional neuroimaging studies of encoding, priming, and explicit memory retrieval. *Proceedings of the National Academy of Sciences, 95*(3), 891–898.

Bruck, M., London, K., Landa, B., & Goodman, J. (2007). Autobiographical memory and suggestibility in children with autism. *Development & Psychopathology, 17*, 73–95.

Buon, M., Dupoux, E., Jacob, P., Chaste, P., Leboyer, M., & Zalla, T. (2013). The role of causal and intentional judgments in moral reasoning in individuals with high-functioning autism, *Journal of Autism & Developmental Disorders, 43*(2), 458–470.

Chambon, V., Farrer, C., Pacherie, E., Jacquet, P., Leboyer, M., & Zalla, T. (in press). Reduced sensitivity to social priors during action prediction in adults with autism spectrum disorders, *Cognition*.

Conway, M. A. (2005). Memory and the self. *Journal of Memory & Language, 53*(4), 594–628.

Conway, M. A., & Pleydell-Pearce, C. W. (2000). The construction of autobiographical memories in the self memory system. *Psychological Review, 107*, 261–288.

Corcoran, R., & Frith, C. D. (2003). Autobiographical memory and theory of mind: Evidence of a relationship in schizophrenia. *Psychological Medicine, 33*, 897–905.

Crane, L., & Goddard, L. (2008). Episodic and semantic autobiographical memory in adults with autism spectrum disorders. *Journal of Autism & Developmental Disorders, 38*(3), 498–506.

Dahlgren, S. O., & Trillingsgaard, A. (1996). Theory of mind in non-retarded children with autism and Asperger's syndrome. *Journal of Child Psychology & Psychiatry and Allied Disciplines, 37*(6), 759–763.

D'Argembeau, A., Raffard, S., & Van der Linden, M. (2008). Remembering the past and imagining the future in schizophrenia. *Journal of Abnormal Psychology, 117*(1), 247–251.

Dritschel, B. H., Williams, J. M., Baddeley, A. D., & Nimmo-Smith, I. (1992). Autobiographical fluency: A method for the study of personal memory. *Memory & Cognition, 20*(2), 133–140.

Frith, U., & Happé, F. (1999). Theory of Mind and self consciousness: What is it like to be autistic? *Mind & Language, 14*(1), 82–89.

Geurts, H. M., Corbett, B., & Solomon, M. (2009). The paradox of cognitive flexibility in autism. *Trends in Cognitive Sciences, 13*(2), 74–82.

Goddard, L., Howlin, P., Dritschel, B., & Patel, T. (2007). Autobiographical memory and social problem-solving in Asperger syndrome. *Journal of Autism & Developmental Disorders, 37*(2), 291–300.

Goddard, L., Dritschel, B., Howlin, P. (2014). A preliminary study of gender differences in autobiographical memory in children with an autism spectrum disorder. *Journal of Autism & Developmental Disorders, 44*(9), 2087–2095.

Gras-Vincendon, A., Mottron, L., Salame, P., Bursztejn, C., & Danion, J.-M. (2007). Temporal context memory in high-functioning autism. *Autism, 11*(6), 523–534.

Happé, F. G. E. (1994). An advanced test of theory of mind: Understanding of story characters' thoughts and feelings by able autistic, mentally handicapped and normal children and adults. *Journal of Autism & Developmental Disorders, 24*, 129–154.

Happé, F. G. E. (1995). The role of age and verbal ability in the theory of mind task performance of subjects with autism. *Child Development, 66*, 843–855.

Hare, D. J., Mellor, C., & Azmi, S. (2007). Episodic memory in adults with autistic spectrum disorders: Recall for self-versus other-experienced events. *Research in Developmental Disabilities, 28*(3), 317–329.

Hill, E. L., & Bird, C. M. (2006). Executive processes in Asperger syndrome: Patterns of performance in a multiple case series. *Neuropsychologia, 44*(14), 2822–2835.

Hill, E. L. (2004). Executive dysfunction in autism. *Trends in Cognitive Sciences, 8*, 26–32.

Klein, S. B., Chan, R. L., & Loftus, J. (1999). Independence of episodic and semantic self–knowledge: The case from autism. *Social Cognition, 17*, 413–436.

Koechlin, E., Ody, C., & Kouneiher, F. (2003). The architecture of cognitive control in the human prefrontal cortex. *Science, 302*(5648), 1181–1185.

Kuhn, M. H., & McPartland, T. S. (1954). An empirical investigation of self-attitudes. *American Sociological Review, 19*(1), 68–76.

Lawson, R. P., Rees, G., Friston, K. J. (2014). An aberrant precision account of autism. *Frontiers in Human Neuroscience, 8*, 302.

Lee, A., & Hobson, R. (1998). On developing self concepts: Controlled study of children and adolescence with autism. *Journal of Child Psychology and Psychiatry, 39*(8), 1131–1144.

Lind, S. (2010). Memory and the self in autism. *Autism, 14*(2), 1–27.

Lind, S., & Bowler, D. M. (2010). Episodic memory and episodic future thinking in adults with autism. *Journal of Abnormal Psychology, 119*(4), 896–905.

Lind, S., Bowler, D. M., & Raber, J. (2014). Spatial navigation, episodic memory, episodic future thinking, and theory of mind in children with autism spectrum disorder: Evidence for impairments in mental simulation? *Frontiers in Psychology, 5*, 1411.

Millward, C., Powell, S., Messer, D., & Jordan, R. (2000). Recall for self and other in autism: Children's memory for events experienced by themselves and their peers. *Journal of Autisim & Developmental Disorders, 30*(1), 15–28.

Minshew, N. J., Meyer, J., & Goldstein, G. (2002). Abstract reasoning in autism: A dissociation between concept formation and concept identification. *Neuropsychology, 16*(3), 327–334.

Moran, J. M., Young, L. L., Saxe, R., Lee, S. M., O'Young, D., ... Mavros, P. L. (2011). Impaired theory of mind for moral judgment in high-functioning autism. *Procedures of the National Academy of Science USA, 108*(7), 2688–2692.

O'Shea, A. G., Fein, D. A., Cillessen, A. H. N., Klin, A., & Schultz, R. T. (2005). Source memory in children with autism spectrum disorders. *Developmental Neuropsychology, 27*(3), 337–360.

Pellicano, E., & Burr, D. (2012). When the world becomes "too real": A Bayesian explanation of autistic perception. *Trends in Cognitive Science, 16*(10), 504–510.

Powell, S. D., & Jordan, R. R. (1993). Being subjective about autistic thinking and learning to learn. *Educational Psychology, 13*, 359–370.

Perner, J., Kloo, D., & Gornik, E. (2007). Episodic memory development: Theory of mind is part of re-experiencing experienced events. *Infant & Child Development, 16*, 471–490.

Poirier, M., Martin, J. S., Gaigg, S. B., & Bowler, D. M. (2011). Short-term memory in autism spectrum disorder. *Journal of Abnormal Psychology, 120*(1), 247–252.

Rathbone, C. J., Moulin, C. J. A., & Conway, M. A. (2008). Self-centered memories: The reminiscence bump and the self. *Memory & Cognition, 36*(8), 1403–1414.

Rathbone, C. J., Moulin, C. J. A., & Conway, M. A. (2009). Autobiographical memory and amnesia: Using conceptual knowledge to ground the self. *Neurocase, 15*(5), 405–418.

Rhee, E., Uleman, J. S., Lee, H. K., & Roman, R. J. (1995). Spontaneous self descriptions and ethnic identities in individualist and collective cultures. *Journal of Personality & Social Psychology. 69*, 142–152.

Senju, A., Southgate, V., White, S., & Frith, U. (2009). Mindblind eyes: An absence of spontaneous theory of mind in Asperger syndrome. *Science, 325*, 883--885.

Senju, A. (2012). Spontaneous theory of mind and its absence in autism spectrum disorders. *Neuroscientist, 18*(2), 108–113.

Souchay, C., Wojcik, D. Z., Williams, H. L., Crathern, S., & Clarke, P. (2013). Recollection in adolescents with autism spectrum disorder. *Cortex, 49*(6), 1598–1609.

Spreng, R. N., & Levine, B. (2006). The temporal distribution of past and future autobiographical events across the lifespan. *Memory & Cognition, 34*(8), 1644–1651.

Tanweer, T., Rathbone, C. J., & Souchay, C. (2009). Autobiographical memory, autonoetic consciousness, and identity in Asperger syndrome. *Neuropsychologia, 48*(4): 900–908.

Toichi, M., Kamio, Y., Okada, T., Sakihama, M., Youngstrom, E., Findling R. L., & Yamamoto, K. (2002). A lack of self-consciousness in autism. *American Journal of Psychiatry, 159*, 1422–1424.

Wechsler, D. (1999). *Abbreviated scale of intelligence (WASI)*. New York, NY: Harcourt.

Young, L., & Saxe, R. (2009). Innocent intentions: A correlation between forgiveness for accidental harm and neural activity. *Neuropsychologia, 47*, 2065–2072.

Zalla, T., Daprati, E., Chaste, P., Nico, D., & Leboyer, M. (2010). Memory for self-performed actions in individuals with Asperger syndrome, *PLoS One, 5*(10).

Zalla, T., Sav, A.-M., Stopin, A., Ahade, S., & Leboyer, M. (2009). Faux pas detection and intentional action in Asperger syndrome: A replication on a French sample, *Journal of Autism & Developmental Disorders, 39*, 373–382.

Zalla, T., Barlassina, L., Buon, M., & Leboyer, M. (2011). Moral judgment in adults with autism spectrum disorders. *Cognition, 121*(1), 115–126.

Zalla, T., & Leboyer, M. (2011). Judgment of intentionality and moral evaluation in individuals with high-functioning autism. *Review of Philosophy & Psychology, 2*(4), 681–698.

6

Autism Spectrum Disorders and Autobiographical Memory in the Forensic Setting

Henry V. Soper, Irina Zilberfayen, and Arthur MacNeill Horton, Jr.

Working with people with autism spectrum disorder (ASD) in the forensic arena can be very challenging for two related reasons. This is true regardless of whether the proband is a defendant, a witness, or anything else. First, the world of the person with ASD is not the same as that for others, for mindblindness (inability to read the minds of others) shuts out a large source of information. Second, and related to this, the language content of those with ASD is often quite different and perplexing to others. Many, including prosecutors, will say they understand ASD and its language, whereas in real life, they often have no idea what is going on. We discuss the problems those with ASD have, especially with reference to autobiographical language. After this, we discuss other aspects of those with autism that play a role in autobiographical recall and memory, specifically theory of mind (ToM) on narrative speech. Although some feel executive dysfunction is endemic to ASD, in fact, it really is not, although being a neurological disorder, it has a high co-occurrence with ASD. We discuss the effects of executive functions on adaptive functioning impairments in ASD, followed by the roles of social reciprocity, executive functioning, and language delays in ASD. At the very end, we have an example of the troubles someone with ASD can have when essential autobiographical information does not come out in the forensic arena.

There are two areas that contribute to the difficulty. Lorna Wing (1991) described many high-functioning people with ASD as "Innocents," in that they are very vulnerable to the wiles of others, who can talk them into doing things that are illegal with the threat that if they do not do it they will no longer be their friend. Related to this, many with ASD, even if they understand what they did is wrong, have no idea of how bad it was. One young man was conned by his "partner" into the kidnap, rape, and murder of a young woman, and later when asked what he thought his punishment was going to be, he said he thought he was going to have to pay a fine, since that is what

The Wiley Handbook of Memory, Autism Spectrum Disorder, and the Law, First Edition.
Edited by Jonni L. Johnson, Gail S. Goodman, and Peter C. Mundy.

happened last time. (Last time, it turns out, the arrest was for throwing rocks at trucks.) Another young man became very agitated when his father was pulled over for speeding. He was sure that after the arrest his father was going to be taken to jail and he would be left alone on this unfamiliar road.

Difficulties abound due to the lack of general knowledge about the ASD presentation. A quick look on the internet found the names of several people who have been diagnosed with ASD, including Albert Einstein, Sir Isaac Newton, Stephen Speilberg, Harry Truman, Vincent van Gough, and the wild boy of Aveyron, most of whom are highly doubtful to have had or have ASD (with the possible exception of the wild boy). However, the consensual definition seems to be closer to acting unusual, not socially adroit, and having consuming interests that preclude many social interactions. Therefore, we begin by discussing just what autism is and the aspects critical to us now.

Autism spectrum disorder (ASD)

It is presumed within the autism field that autism lies along a spectrum, ranging from more to less severe. Many of those afflicted in the less severe range can appear, for the most part, to be neurotypical except for occasional oddities. Autism spectrum disorder (ASD) is a neurological disorder, and hence, it is not surprising that, among those in the more severely afflicted range, there are frequently co-morbid neurological disorders, such as epilepsy, developmental delay/intellectual disability, and attention deficit hyperactivity disorder (ADHD). The core feature of ASD is a deficit in the "autos" or in reciprocal interpersonal interactions. These individuals have difficulty comprehending that other people can have a different perspective, or knowledge, of the world. Although individuals with ASD do not necessarily have difficulty with processing right-hemisphere gestaltic information, they do when this kind of processing is used with interpersonal expression. For example, an individual may have no difficulty with processing the various forms of visual gestaltic processing, yet find it impossible to interpret facial expressions, body language, and prosody, all of which can produce exceedingly poor pragmatics. As an example, these people gain little information from the expressions of the eyes, and as a result, will tend to have poor eye contact, for the same reason the rest of us do not generally try to find out what is going on with our car by "reading" the headlights. This difficulty gives rise to the multitude of other features often seen with ASD.

ASD is a neurodevelopmental condition that is characterized by the impairments in social, communication functioning as well as restricted and repetitive behaviors (American Psychiatric Association, 2013). It is widely known that children with ASD experience significant impairments with social communication and social interaction, delayed verbal and nonverbal development, and restricted or repetitive patterns of behavior since early developmental period as stated in *The Diagnostic and Statistical Manual of Mental Disorders, 5th Edition* (*DSM–5*; American Psychiatric Association, 2013).

Although memory deficits are not included in the diagnostic criteria, autobiographical memory difficulties have been documented for individuals with ASD (Crane et al., 2012, Bordiignon et al., 2015; Crane et al., 2011; Boucher & Mayes, 2012; Kristen, 2014). Theoretical models of autobiographical memory system suggest that multiple components contribute to the normal functioning of the memory about self and personal past. Understanding autobiographical memory deficits in these disorders is important for further conceptualization of ASD.

Previous research attributed many of these difficulties to a lack of theory of mind (as excellently described by Baron-Cohen, 1989), or an inability to understand the thoughts and mental states of others. More accurately, most of those with ASD are unable to appreciate that there are truths they are not privy to but that others are, so if they know there is spaghetti in the cookie jar, everyone should know that. It is not as if they feel something is missing, somewhat like most of us who are unable to echolocate. We do not miss it any more than someone with ASD misses not being able to take the perspective of another. In a way, this other perspective does not exist, and hence, is not missed.

Recent studies have also looked at the involvement of executive functioning in narrative construction, or storytelling ability. The literature highlights findings in these aspects of narrative language development and executive functioning: social, linguistic, and neurobiology. Mirror neurons, often tied to theory of mind neurobiologically, appear to be nested within the inner chambers of the ventrolateral prefrontal area, an area involved in speech production and regulation of speech affect (especially in affective speech output vs. prosody). The association between theory of mind and executive functioning has been suggested by several studies (Barnes & Baron-Cohen, 2012; Kimhi et al., 2014). These studies indicate that the use of language necessitates mechanisms that would organize thoughts along with personal goals, regulate attentional control, and cope with interferences as well as regulate cognitive, motor, sensory, and memory system, and the neuronal networks of language and executive control are reported to partially overlap (Ye & Zhou, 2009). We need more information on the role of executive functioning in the information processing in children with ASD with regard to narrative (expressive) speech.

This is one aspect of the development of narrative, but there is another aspect which is well recognized by those who work with those with ASD. Often expressive speech and the narrative can become unintelligible because of a lack of desire on the part of the proband to be understood. The person is talking, but not in a manner that ideas are communicated. Often a prompt such as, "Say it again so I can understand you," will be effective. This is a parallel to someone talking to themselves, making sounds they may like, but not with the intent of communicating ideas to others.

Theory of mind (ToM)

In the late 1980s, Italian scientists found that there were cells which would act as if the individual were actually performing an action that it was observing. Somewhat simplistically, these neurons were called mirror neurons because they would mirror the activity expected if the animal itself were performing the action(s) it was just observing. Through such information, the animal could, in a sense, "feel" what the other animal was "feeling" or possibly thinking. In other words, these neurons were mirroring what was going on in the "mind" of the other animal. Through such a mechanism, certain animals or humans can "read" what is going on in the mind of the other individual, a kind of "I know what I would be thinking if I were experiencing this, and that is probably what that other animal/person is thinking." Also essential to this is the individual's potential for understanding that others can think things that differ from what this individual is thinking is the understanding that others have minds of their own, which is very close to a theory of mind (ToM). Regardless of the exact physiology, the idea of such mirror neurons permit a ToM in which an individual appreciates that others can think things that differ from what the individual knows or thinks, and without that ability the person could be called mind blind (Baron-Cohen, 1995). Such a theory goes a long way in explaining the minds of those with ASD. Not having such a ToM means that there is a lot that goes on in the world that those with ASD are simply not privy to. It also results in many common symptoms (some of which have become diagnostic criteria), such as inability to read body and facial gestures, poor language development, and stereotypies.

Memory

Although as we know certain individuals with ASD can have incredibly good rote memory (and are often referred to as savants), many others have memorized information that gives them the appearance of having exceedingly good memory, such as certain calendar savants and those who have memorized the multiplication tables up to 100 times 100, although even here, their difficulties are often displayed (Question: "If Tom will turn 40 years old next month, how many months old is he now? Answer: "About 480," and repeated questioning did not help). Another factor is that which is important to the person with ASD, and hence, that which is retained in memory, may not be the most salient information to one who is neurotypical. On the other hand, the apparently trivial information retained by the person with ASD can at times make them appear to have very large memories, even though they have no memory for what to the rest of us seems more important information.

Autobiographical memory

Autobiographical memory is explicit self-referential memory of past events. It has been defined as a constantly maintained and updated record of "salient public and private events" (McCarty & Warrington, 1990, p. 296).

According to the Bordignon's et al. (2015) review of memory functions in ASD, especially working memory, the most impairments were evident in autobiographical memory, memory for faces, and prospective and associative memory for names and people. Memory is one of the cognitive functions responsible for clinical impairment in ASD that constitute executive dysfunction (Williams, Goldstein, & Mishew, 2006b).

Deficiencies in autobiographical memory in ASD are linked to multisystem dysfunctions in various memory systems (Bordignon et al., 2015), ToM and self-representation (Hill, 2004), narrative structure and content as well as executive dysfunction (Nelson & Fivush, 2004).

Autobiographical memory serves self-reflection, self-definition, and self-regulation systems (Baddeley, 1988). Recently, theorists started pointing out usage and functions of autobiographical memory, which include but are not limited to organization and retrieval of personal information, self-definition, interpretation of actions, relationship maintenance, mood regulation (Robinson & Swanson,1990), communication, guidance, and self-direction (Pillemer, 2003).

It is important to understand gradual emergence of the autobiographical memory in early life in the context of normal development of language, memory, and social skills. Even though autobiographical memory has been studied for over a century (Galton), much of the controversy continues to revolve around theoretical approach and its division on to the subsystems (Baddeley, 1988). According to memory theorists, memory is constructed of multiple systems, such as working memory, declarative, procedural, semantic, and episodic memory (Baddeley, 1988; Tulving, 1972).

The first dichotomous pair is declarative and procedural memory, where declarative memory, sometimes known as explicit, is the ability to recall or recognize previously experienced or intentionally learned information. On the other hand, procedural memory, which is sometimes called implicit, refers to performance improvement without conscious recall of learning experience (Baddeley, 1988; Nelson & Fivush, 2004). Other two distinct subsystems—semantic and episodic memory were first introduced by Tulving (1972), with the semantic memory referring to the general and linguistic knowledge, and the episodic memory consisting of memories of personal experiences. Autobiographical memory is conceptualized as declarative and episodic types of memory. It requires personal awareness and recollection of earlier life episodic memories constructed through experiences on the bases of self-concept (Baddeley, 1988). Autobiographical memories include information about self and consist of semantic memory (personal information such as addresses, names), and episodic memory that contains information about experienced events (Goddard et al, 2014).

Autobiographical memories are embedded in social and cultural context. All knowledge is memories created from learning experiences, which takes narrative form and requires certain levels of linguistic abilities (Howard, 1991). Thus, autobiographical memory appears to be intricate interplay of different abilities, which includes but are not limited to memory systems alone.

Theoretical Model of Autobiographical Memories

The sociocultural developmental theory of autobiographical memory (Nelson & Fivush, 2004) proposed that autobiographical memory is linked to gradual early childhood development of self-concept, language, and memory systems. The theory is comprised of the major arguments: gradual emergence of autobiographical memory in early childhood; language as a sociocultural tool for development of autobiographical memory; and importance of culture, gender, and individual differences in autobiographical memories throughout the life span. The multicomponent developmental theory accounts for gender and cultural variations in autobiographical memory across the life span. The contributing components include memory systems, expressive and receptive language acquisition, narrative speech and communication, social relationships, self-representation, and understanding thoughts and mental states of others (ToM). It provides a dynamic model of emergence and interaction of the elements of the system. Nelson and Fivush (2004) postulated that autobiographical memory is the outcome of a social cultural cognitive system, with all its components available to varied experiences over time and context, where social and cognitive sources are combined on the bases of the unique personal history. The sociocultural developmental theory provides explanations and clearly portrays the important role each component plays in the development of an intact autobiographical memory system. The theory also explains qualitative changes in childhood across social and cognitive development, which are not simply the results of different "inputs," but rather drastic change and maturation of neurocognitive structures, language development, change in concept of self in the society, which lead to integration of autobiographical memory system. In ASD, the disruption of one or more elements leads to malfunction of the autobiographical memory process. The sociocultural developmental theory provides explanation of the variability in developmental outcomes of autobiographical memory based on level of development of each component and its integration.

Developmental Perspective of Autobiographical Memory and Atypical Development in ASD

Hobson (2010), in his theoretical paper, provided an explanation of ASD in terms of atypical development in ASD, including lack of structure of self-experience. The missing component of self-experience affects an individual's emotional engagement and social relatedness, which impacts pragmatic aspects of communication. Because self-experience is associated with emotional connection with others and understanding of others experiences, ToM explains "self-other engagement" (p. 394) and how these contribute to sophisticated and linguistically based components of self-experience. Based on Vygotsky (1962), sociocultural relationships impact social and cognitive development that occurs through self-regulation and narrative speech building executive functioning which draws on self-experience.

Verbal development, especially expressive speech and narratives production, is the area of significant struggle for children with ASD (Tager-Flusburg, 1996; Loveland et al., 1990; Loveland & Tunali, 1994; King et al., 2014; Barnes & Baron-Cohen, 2012; Suh et al., 2014). Language and communication processes rely on reciprocity and an understanding of other's perspective (ToM), which are compromised in individuals with ASD. Clinical manifestations of ASD are also characterized by impaired reciprocity and lack of joint attention (Leekam & Ramsden, 2006; Mundy et al., 1986) as well as deficiencies in emotional identification and understanding mental states of others (Baron-Cohen, 1988; Happé, 2003; Hobson, 2010; Klin et al., 2009). Difficulties with language, communication, and social experiences disrupt the transformation into autobiographical memories (Nelson & Fivush, 2004).

Memory Dysfunction and Autism

The literature reports impairments in autobiographical memory in individuals with ASD however the research on the subject remains scarce (Kristen, Rossman, & Sodian, 2014; Bordignon et al., 2015). The existing studies reported that ASD individuals showed greater difficulties with memory retrieval (memories for collection of events) and recalling specific memories to word cues, especially emotions (Goddart et al., 2007; Goddart et al., 2014).

Autobiographical Memories in ASD

The study by Goddard, Dritschel, Robinson, and Howlin (2014) assessed 63 children with ASD (6–17 years old) focusing on recall of specific event, recent and remote past, and semantic versus episodic memories over a life span. The results showed that children with ASD exhibited difficulties in "retrieving specific memories to word cues and had poorer access to the remote past as well as problems in retrieving episodic and semantic AMs [autobiographical memories] across the life span were also evident." The study performed qualitative analysis of memory, which suggested that children with ASD were more likely to describe emotions in recent memories as opposed to refer to emotion in their remote memories. The study reported that executive abilities were important predictors of AM performance in the ASD group, specifically cognitive flexibility and verbal fluency (Goddart et al., 2014).

Another study by Kristen, Rossman, and Sodian (2014) explored differential self and other related ToM and cognitive skills as related to autobiographical memory. The study examined two groups of individuals, 20 adults with ASD and 20 matched controls. Participants were tested individually, first administered ToM tasks short stories and mindedness task as well as eyes task, followed by episodic and semantic memory interview task and control measures (IQ measures and WMS-R scale). The results of the study suggested presence of the deficits in episodic autobiographical memory in ASD, especially in regards to inability to retrieve specific memories. The deficits were observed on a conceptual and constructive level so that individuals were unable to describe their emotional states, or understand the meaning of certain social interactions (white lie, deception). The study reported that relationship between episodic autobiographical memories and the mindedness for oneself. Overall, the results indicated the connection between episodic memory and semantic autobiographical memories and ToM, without association with verbal or nonverbal IQ (Kristen, 2014).

Along with these findings, Lind (2010) explored autobiographical episodic memory in autism, and suggested that "under-elaborated self-concept may correspond with diminished psychological and intact physical self-knowledge" (Hobson, 2010, p. 387), eluding to bidirectional relationship between memory and the self, such that re-experiencing the self in the past consolidates the development of a temporally extended self, and vice versa. Despite being able to recognize themselves in the mirror and in delayed video images, the study reported that relationship between episodic autobiographical memories and the mindedness for oneself. Overall, the results indicated the connection between episodic memory and semantic autobiographical memories and theory of mind, without association with verbal or nonverbal IQ (Kristen, 2014). Crane et al. (2012) examined autobiographical memories especially at specificity and retrieval latency. The results suggested that individuals with ASD generated fewer specific memories as well as took longer time for constructing specific memories leading to reduction in autobiographical memory retrieval. Even though previous research results regarding mechanisms associated with autobiographical memory retrieval are inconclusive, Crane et al. (2012) reported the patterns of memory retrieval are similar to typical individuals. However, as related to cued recall, significant cues related to self or emotions were processed differently in ASD (Goddart et al., 2007; Crane et al., 2012). Individuals with ASD struggle to access and recall specific memories in social conversations, which appears awkward and causes difficulties in social situations and relationship difficulties. Autobiographical memory serves as a data bank for resolving social problems from the past, which is not readily available for ASD individuals and cause further social problems and contribute to emotional difficulties. As related to the neural causes of episodic impairment in high functioning individual with ASD with intact IQ and language function, Boucher and Meyers (2012) proposed that neural disconnectivity is the underlying cause for these dysfunctions.

Theory of Mind and Narrative Speech

Language delays and difficulties in social interaction in children with ASD, such as inability to understand thoughts and mental states of others, were captured by ToM (Baron Cohen, 1989). A number of studies documented disruption in ToM processing in children with ASD (Loveland, & Tunali, 1994, King et al, 2014; Barnes & Baron-Cohen, 2012; Mason et al., 2008).

These deficits interfere with the ability to construct cohesive narratives and exchange meaningful information. Furthermore, autistic children showed pragmatic deficits and used a smaller number of communicative acts (Loveland et al., 1988). Social interaction and narrative construction are the essential components of communication and basis for daily conversational interaction as well as a predictor of academic achievement, and in turn, adaptive abilities (King et al., 2014).

The study by Barnes and Baron-Cohen (2012) performed qualitative analysis of narratives produced by 27 individuals with high-functioning autism (ASD) as compared to narratives of 27 typically developing controls matched by age, gender, verbal IQ, and writing ability. Participants were administered verbal scales of standardized measures (WASI, Wechsler Abbreviates Scales of Intelligence, Wechsler 1999) and writing passage about their interest to obtain the matching criteria. Written narratives were generated from the movie-based clips, which contained a moral dilemma or a conflict. Two independent raters coded the data, with assessed high inter-rater reliability. The results of one-way ANOVA indicated significant differences between individuals with ASD and typically developing controls in ability to provide global information in the narrative, specifically concentrating on a "big picture" (Baron-Cohen, 2012, p. 1563). When retelling stories about the movie clips, individuals with ASD fixated on the details of the setting, characters, or story plot, and had difficulties in ability to communicate a larger structure. They also had difficulties prioritizing story elements and their relevance to the big picture. These results were attributed to the weak central coherence theory, which is focused on one of the cognitive symptoms of autism—the perceptual bias toward details over the large picture. Additionally, the researchers attributed these results to the executive functioning difficulties assigning significance to the story elements according to the big picture, organizing these, and creating a structure of the story. The study appeared to be methodologically strong with meaningful results, which warrant further research on the role of executive functioning in narrative production in ASD.

Another study by King, Dockrell, and Stuart (2014) examined the differences in fictional narrative between children with ASD and typically developing controls. The results revealed significant structural, global, and evaluative differences in narratives produced by children with ASD as compared to typically developing matched controls. The comparison groups were matched on nonverbal ability and expressive language scores yielded by the standardized measures of nonverbal and language abilities, such as BAS II (British Ability Scales, second edition, Elliot, Smith, & McCullouch, 1996), the BPVSII (British Picture Vocabulary), and CELF IV. The total sample comprised 81 participants. The stories constructed by 27 high-functioning children with ASD ages 11–14 were compared with stories generated by typically developing language matched children of younger age as well chronological age-matched peers. Participants were asked to produce stories from given two-story stems. The stories were coded and analyzed using two transcription programs, such as the SALT program as well as coded using NSS coding scheme, which were reportedly utilized in previous research.

The stories were shorter with fewer causal statements and less grammatically complicated sentences. However, the study reported no differences in vocabulary use. Consistent with previous research, the study attributed shorter length of the narratives to the language delays and ToM (Brown & Klein, 2011) as well as associated difficulties of managing competing tasks to the model of cognitive overload.

Researchers reported that less grammatically complicated sentences were a reflection of previously reported less complex syntax and syntactic diversity (Tager-Flusberg, 1995). Additionally, the study also reported that the narratives of ASD children contained significantly fewer causal statements and included fewer explanations of events, emotions, and thoughts, which is similar to previous findings (Loveland & Tunali, 1993). Researchers reported that less grammatically complicated sentences were a reflection of previously reported difficulties with complex syntax and syntactic diversity (Tager-Flusberg, 1995). Consistent with previous reports, the narratives of ASD children contained significantly fewer causal statements and included fewer explanations of events, emotions, and thoughts (Loveland & Tunali, 1993). The study linked these shortcomings to difficulties of compiling ideas together to form a narrative.

Moreover, the study proposed that the reported deficits cannot only be attributed to language development alone, but also to social difficulties which point to ToM deficits (Baron-Cohen et al., 1985) as well as structural and organizing deficits leading higher order processing (Luria, 1966) and impairment of executive functioning processes (Pennington & Ozonoff, 1996). However, the results need to be interpreted with caution due to the multiple shortcomings in data gathering such as lack of psychometric information for the coding programs, a majority of the coding conducted by the study researcher, and the moderate to low inter-rater reliability.

Language delays and difficulties in social interaction in children with ASD, such as the inability to understand thoughts and mental states of others, were captured by ToM (Baron Cohen, 1989). A number of studies documented disruption in ToM processing in children with ASD (Loveland, & Tunali, 1994; King et al., 2014; Barnes & Baron-Cohen, 2012; Mason et al., 2008).

Many years ago, one of us (HVS) noted the paucity of global or big picture processing in the narratives of children with ASD, a symptom often seen following right hemisphere trauma. We decided to see how much these people present as people with such right trauma. At about this time, there were reports of higher functioning ASD being associated with nonverbal learning disorders. It turns out the latter is not true, but we looked at the more pure sensory aspects of processing in such higher functioning ASD. Using tests often proven difficult for people with right trauma (e.g., figure ground tests), we found no particular deficits in these are among those with ASD, and in fact, some did rather well on these tests. The gestaltic deficits appear to be restricted to the social emotional realms of information processing. The well-known high-quality art work (buildings, horses, roosters, flowers) produced by some who are otherwise quite compromised by their autistic features is further evidence of a lack of a general gestaltic sensory deficit within this condition.

Effects of Executive Functions on Adaptive Functioning Impairment in ASD

It is important to mention that adaptive functioning is affected by executive deficits as these prevent individual adjustment to environmental demands and independent functioning. The study by Peterson and colleagues (2015) examined the relationships between executive functions and adaptability by analyzing the archival data of 120 individuals with ASD, using BRIEF (executive functioning questionnaire) and ABAS II (adaptive functioning questionnaire) scores. The results revealed significant relationships among executive control, specifically behavior regulation, initiation, monitoring, metacognition, and global and adaptive functioning. Adult individuals with ASD suffering from executive functioning deficits are at a greater risk of social difficulties and isolation, lower ability for independence, and unemployment regardless of their cognitive abilities and education level. This study provides evidence of the importance of addressing life skills training and executive functions cognitive remediation starting at a young age.

Social Reciprocity, Executive Functioning, and Language Delays in ASD

A number of severe developmental issues and delays accompany ASD. Verbal development, especially expressive speech and narratives production, is an area of significant struggle for children with ASD (Tager-Flusburg, 1996; Loveland et al., 1990; Loveland & Tunali, 1994; King et al., 2014; Barnes & Baron-Cohen, 2012; Suh et al., 2014). Further, children with ASD manifest deficiencies in emotional identification and understanding mental states of others (Baron-Cohen, 1988; Happé, 2003; Hobson, 2010; Kelin et al., 2009). Language and communication processes rely on reciprocity and an understanding of other's perspective (ToM), which are all compromised in individuals with ASD. Clinical manifestations of ASD are also characterized by impaired reciprocity and lack of joint attention (Leekam & Ramsden, 2006; Mundy et al., 1986). Difficulties with language, communication, and social experiences disrupt memory construction, transformation, and retrieval into autobiographical memories in ASD (Nelson & Fivush, 2004).

Hobson (2010) provided an explanation of ASD in terms atypical development, including lack of structure of self-experience. Deficits in self-experience affect an individual's emotional engagement and social relatedness, which impacts pragmatic aspects of communication. Because self-experience is associated with emotional connection with others and understanding of others' experiences, ToM explains "self-other engagement" (p. 394) and how these contribute to sophisticated and linguistically based components of self-experience. Based on Vygotsky (1962), sociocultural relationships impact social and cognitive development. Children learn self-regulation facilitated by executive functions such as inhibition, shifting, attention, and memory. Such learning to self-regulate is based on self-experience and occurs through language and narrative ability to give verbal description of context and instructions to oneself.

Cumulatively, executive dysfunction appears to be strongly involved in the majority of symptoms of ASD, including memory, social reciprocity, and language deficits.

Even though overwhelming evidence is available regarding impairment of executive functions in ASD, O'Hern and colleagues (2008) reported that the age-related improvements are possible during the window of opportunity in childhood to adolescent years due to brain plasticity. However, complex executive functioning deficits could still be present in adulthood due to dysfunction in information processing associated with abnormalities in various brain networks (O'Hearn et al., 2008). Further research is necessary to elucidate the specific mechanisms of executive functioning and its involvement in each cognitive function to provide further information, which could be used in early cognitive and behavioral interventions and treatment of ASD.

Executive Functioning in Autism

Literature revealed that executive functions play an important role in neurodevelopment as well as language development and social interaction (Luria, 1966; Barkley, 2011; King et al., 2014; Ye & Zhou, 2009; O'Hearn et al., 2008; Joseph et al., 2005).

Some believe autism to be an executive function disorder (Russel, 1997), and it may even play a causal role in ASD (Joseph et al., 2005). Executive functioning is an umbrella term for different functions such as working memory, planning and organization, and inhibitory function. Even though there is abundant research available regarding the important role of executive function in ASD, not all components of executive functioning are impaired. The majority of research has documented consistent dysfunctions in several components of the executive functioning such as inhibitive function (perseverative behavior and shifting), and planning and organization, whereas impairment in other components of executive functioning still remain inconclusive (Hill, 2004). Research design of the studies mostly included testing single executive functions, using different measures (Russell, 1997; Hill, 2004). Executive dysfunctions may explain impairments and variations in the severity of autism symptoms in individual differences in ToM (Taeger-Flusberg, 2004), communication, and language impairments (Mazuka, Jincho, & Oishi, 2009).

Even though overwhelming evidence is available regarding impairment of executive functions in ASD, O'Hern and colleagues (2008) reported age related improvements are possible during childhood and adolescent years due to brain plasticity. However, executive dysfunction was traced to abnormalities in various brain networks, especially in frontal lobe regions (Hill, 2004), which lead to impaired complex information processing across multiple domains (O'Hearn et al., 2008)

Executive functioning studies generally investigate planning, mental flexibility, inhibition, and self-monitoring functions (Hill, 2004). In the last decade the studies mostly concentrated on the relationship between executive dysfunction, memory, social functioning, ToM, and language in individuals with ASD.

The executive functions involve higher-order cognitive operations such as planning, working memory, inhibition, and attention shifting that guide human behavior, participate in problem solving, and generate solutions based on existing information (Joseph et al., 2005; Landa & Godberg, 2005; Kimhi et al., 2014). Previous research reported that children with autism exhibited deficits in executive function working memory and inhibitory control domains as well as planning (Joseph et al., 2005; Landa & Godberg, 2005).

Although memory deficits are not included in the diagnostic criteria of ASD, working memory and autobiographical memory difficulties are attributed to executive function are reported in individuals with autism (Crane et al., 2012; Bordignon et al., 2015; Crane et al., 2011; Boucher & Mayes, 2012; Kristen, 2014; Hill, 2004).

Today, it is quite clear that many who suffer from ASD have attention deficit disorder/hyperactivity. Some work by O'Hanlon (2016) suggested that the types of ADHD seen in and outside ASD may be different. He found that the most effective medication for those without ASD was methylphenidate, but for those with ASD it was guanfacine. He concludes that the pathophysiological processes that produce hyperactivity in ASD and ADHD may be different, or maybe more accurately, the predominant subtypes of hyperactivity differ.

Executive Functioning and Autobiographical Memory

Even though previous research pointed out the important role of executive function in language development (Luria, 1966; Barkley, 2011; Mazuka, 2009; Ye & Zhu, 2009; Kimhi et al., 2014; Joseph et al., 2005), the results are inconclusive. The relationship between executive linguistic and social functioning is poorly understood.

Executive functioning is really a manner of processing information and it utilizes predominantly the prefrontal areas of the brain. These frontal areas take in information: sensory, affective, reinforcement, and memory from the various areas of the brain and process this information in order to make the best motor response. These functions are often listed by the types of tasks or operations they are involved in (v.i.).

The executive functions consist of higher-order cognitive operations such as planning, working memory, inhibition, and attention shifting that guide human behavior, participate in problem solving, and generate solutions based on existing information (Joseph et al., 2005; Landa & Godberg, 2005; Kimhi et al., 2014). Previous research reported that children with autism exhibited deficits in executive function working memory and inhibitory control domains as well as planning (Joseph et al., 2005; Landa & Godberg, 2005). The connection between ToM and executive function was suggested by several studies (Barnes & Baron-Cohen, 2012; Kimhi et al., 2014). It was speculated that executive functioning mediates or indirectly contributes to language production, sentence processing, and nonlinguistic information (Barkley, 2011; Mazuka et al., 2009; Joseph et al., 2005). Additionally, the study by Kimhi et al. (2014) suggested that verbal ability plays an important role in the relationship between executive function and ToM skills in ASD as well as playing a causal role in the development of ToM abilities in both ASD and typically developing children.

The following is a recent example of someone with ASD whose difficulties are very much related to deficits in producing accurate and effective autobiographical memories, in part, due to executive difficulties, and in part, due to an intellectual disability/developmental delay. Lou was a 22-year-old young man with severe autism, intellectual disability, and ADHD. He was clearly a special needs person who did not understand much of what was going on around him. He was wandering around one evening when two thugs, recognizing an innocent when they saw one, put him in a headlock and started banging him on the concrete. A woman drove by and saw the action and was able to see that Lou was special needs, and got the two men to stop beating him. As she went back to her car, Lou followed her and put his arm on her shoulder to thank her. She was surprised, but then understood and drove off. The two men went after Lou and attacked him again. When the police came the men said they were preventing him from raping the woman. Then the police tried to Mirandize Lou (but did it inappropriately). Lou clearly had no idea of the consequences of his conversation with the police, where he reiterated the story about the intended rape (though he clearly does not have the ability to plan such an action). The police then arrested him. In fact, Lou was afraid of sex, having been molested several times in various facilities by people of both genders. While in prison, he had difficulty reporting his own medical condition, and suffered several seizures and dehydration. The evening after I saw him, another inmate launched into him and beat him so severely that his head was black and blue and one eye was closed. These beatings continued. He was protected a bit by the prison psychiatrist. Lou understood full well that reporting the names of the beaters would make it even worse. Then the prison guards started beating him. His parents (and I) knew full well that only death would cause an end to the beatings, but for some reason, the judges refused to take any action that could preserve Lou's life. He was deemed incompetent to stand trial, but even though clearly no amount of training would make him competent, he is waiting in jail for a place in a state hospital that will try to train him to become competent. Although we have problems with the initial thugs, the other people involved just do not seem to have the foggiest idea of the difficulties of such ASD people, especially those with ADHD and intellectual disabilities/developmental delays, to provide autobiographical memory that is accurate and helpful to themselves. And the others in the judicial system do not understand the difficulties people like Lou have.

Take-Home Points

- There are autobiographical memory impairments in autism.
- The theoretical model of autobiographical memory portrays the connection of ToM, narrative speech, and executive functions in encoding and memory formations.
- The research revealed impairments in episodic and semantic memories, memories for faces, and prospective and associative memories for names and people (Bordignon et al., 2015).
- The results for working memory deficits are inconclusive and warrants further research.
- Additionally, the links among memory, narrative abilities, ToM, and executive functioning provide information for connection between brain networks and warrants further exploration for functional connectivity.
- Incorporation and integration of developmental, cognitive, social approaches, and neuroimaging approaches will provide additional information on the brain development and autobiographical memories in individuals with autism.

References

American Psychiatric Association. (2013). *Diagnostic and statistical manual of mental disorders* (5th ed.). Washington, DC: Author.

Barkley, R. A. (2011). *Barkley deficits in executive functioning scale (BDEF)*. New York, NY: Guilford Press.

Barnes, J. L., & Baron-Cohen, S. (2012). The big picture: Storytelling ability in adults with autism spectrum conditions. *Journal of Autism & Developmental Disorders, 42*(8), 1557–1565.

Baron-Cohen, S. (1988). An assessment of violence in a young man with Asperger's syndrome. *Journal of Child Psychology & Psychiatry, 29*, 351–360.

Boucher, J., & Mayes, A. (2012). Memory in ASD: Have we been barking up the wrong tree? *Autism, 16*, 603–611.

Brown, H. M., & Klein, P. D. (2011). Writing, Asperger syndrome and theory of mind. *Journal of Autism & Developmental Disorders, 41*(11), 1464–1474.

Crane, L., Goddard, L., & Pring, L. (2013). Autobiographical memory in adults with autism spectrum disorder: The role of depressed mood, rumination, working memory and theory of mind. *Autism, 17*, 205–219.

Crane, L., Pring, L., Jukes, K., & Goddard, L. (2012). Patterns of autobiographical memory in adults with autism spectrum disorder. *Journal of Autism & Developmental Disorders, 42*(10), 2100–12.

Goddard, L., Dritschel, B., & Howlin, P. (2014). A preliminary study of gender differences in autobiographical memory in children with an autism spectrum disorder. *Journal of Autism & Developmental Disorders, 44*(9), 2087–2095.

Goddart, L., Howlin, P., Dritschel, B., & Patel, T. (2007). Autobiographical memory and social problem solving in young adults with ASD. *Journal of Autism & Developmental Disorder, 37*, 291–300.

Goldman, S., & DeNigris, D. (2015). Parents' strategies to elicit autobiographical memories in autism spectrum disorders, developmental language disorders and typically developing children. *Journal Autism & Developmental Disorders, 45*, 1464–1473.

Happé, F. (2003). Theory of mind and the self. *Annals of the New York Academy of Sciences, 1001*, 134–144.

Hill, E. L. (2004). Evaluating the theory of executive dysfunction in autism. *Developmental Review, 24*, 189–233.

Hill, E. L. (2004). Executive dysfunction in autism. *Trends in Cognitive Science, 8*, 26–32.

Hill, E. L. (2004). Evaluating the theory of executive dysfunction in autism. *Developmental Review, 24*, 189–233.

Hobson, R. P. (2010). Explaining autism: Ten reasons to focus on the developing self. *Autism, 14*, 391–407.

Howard, G. S. (1991). Culture tales. A narrative approach to thinking, cross-cultural psychology, and psychotherapy. *American Psychologist, 46*, 187–197.

Joseph, R. M., McGrath, L. M., & Tager-Flusberg, H. (2005). Executive dysfunction and its relation to language ability in verbal school-age children with autism. *Developmental Neuropsychology, 27*(3), 361–378.

Kimhi, Y., Shoam-Kugelmas, D., Agam Ben-Artzi, G., Ben-Moshe, I., & Bauminger-Zviely, N. (2014). Theory of mind and executive function in preschoolers with typical development versus intellectually able preschoolers with autism spectrum disorder. *Journal of Autism & Developmental Disorders, 44(9)*, 2341–2354.

King, D., Dockrell, J., & Stuart, M. (2014). Constructing fictional stories: A study of story narratives by children with autistic spectrum disorder. *Research in Developmental Disabilities, 35*(10), 2438–2449.

Klein, C., Travers, B., Klinger, L., Klinger, M., & Kana, R. (2009). *Neural bases of self- representation in higher functioning autism.* Paper presented at the International Meeting of Autism Research, Chicago, May 7.

Kristen, S., Rossmann, F., & Sodian, B. (2014). Theory of own mind and autobiographical memory in adults with ASD. *Research in Autism Spectrum Disorders*, 827–837.

Landa, R. J., & Goldberg, M. C. (2005). Language, social, and executive functions in high functioning autism: A continuum of performance. *Journal of Autism & Developmental Disorders, 35*(5), 557–573.

Leekam, S. R., & Ramsden, C. A. (2006). Dyadic orientation and joint attention in preschool children with autism. *Journal of Developmental Disorders, 36*, 185–197.

Loveland, K. A., McEvoy, R. E., & Tunali, B. (1990). Narrative story telling in autism and Down's syndrome. *British Journal of Developmental Psychology, 8*(1), 9–23.

Loveland, K., & Tunali, B. (1994). *Narrative language in autism and the theory of mind hypothesis: A wider perspective. Understanding other minds: Perspectives from autism.* (pp. 247–266). New York, NY: Oxford University Press.

Luria, A. R. (1966). *Higher cortical functions in man.* New York, NY: Basic Books.

Mason, R. A., Williams, D. L., Kana, R. K., Minshew, N., & Just, M. A. (2008). Theory of mind disruption and recruitment of the right hemisphere during narrative comprehension in autism. *Neuropsychologia, 46*(1), 269–280.

Mazuka, R., Jincho, N., & Oishi, H. (2009). Development of executive control and language processing. *Language & Linguistics Compass, 3*(1), 59–89.

McCarthy, R., & Warrington, E. (1990). The dissolution of semantics. *Nature, 343*, 599.

Mundy, P., Gwaltney, M., & Henderson, H. (2010). Self-referenced processing, neurodevelopment and joint attention in autism. *Autism, 14*, 408–429.

Nelson, K., & Fivush, R. (2004). The emergence of autobiographical memory: A social cultural developmental theory. *Psychological Review, 111*, 486–511.

O'Hanlon, J. (2016). What drug is best for treating hyperactivity in autism spectrum disorder (ASD)? *TriLine (fall), 14.*

O'Hearn, K., Asato, M., Ordaz, S., & Luna, B. (2008). Neurodevelopment and executive function in autism. *Development & Psychopathology, 20*(4), 1103–1132.

Pennington, B. F., & Ozonoff, S. (1996). Executive functions and developmental psychopathology. *Journal of Child Psychology & Psychiatry, 37*(1), 51–87.

Peterson, R. K., Noggle, C. A., Thompson, J. C., & Davis, J. J. (2015). Everyday executive functioning influences adaptive skill in autism spectrum disorders. *Neuropsychological Trends, 18*, 31–37.

Pillemer, D. (2003). Directive functions of autobiographical memory: The guiding power of the specific episode. *Memory, 11*, 193–202.

Robinson, J. A., & Swanson, K. L. (1990). Autobiographical memory, the next phase. *Applied Cognitive Psychology, 4*, 321–335.

Russell, J. (1997). *Autism as an executive disorder.* New York, NY: Oxford University Press.

Suh, J., Eigsti, I., Barton, M., Kelley, E., & Dain, D. (2014). Narrative performance of optimal outcome children and adolescents with a history of an autism spectrum disorder (ASD). *Journal of Autism & Developmental Disorders, 44*(7), 1681–1694.

Tager-Flusberg, H. (1996). Brief report: Current theory and research on language and communication in autism. *Journal of Autism & Developmental Disorders, 26*(2), 169–172.

Tager-Flusberg, H. (2004). Strategies for conducting research on language in autism. *Journal of Autism & Developmental Disorders, 34*, 75–80.

Tulving, E. (1972). Episodic and semantic memory. In E. Tulving & W. Donaldson (Eds.), *Organization of memory* (pp. 382–403). New York, NY: Academic Press.

Vygotsky, L. S. (1962). *Thought and language.* Cambridge, MA: MIT Press.

Ye, Z., & Zhou, X. (2009). Executive control in language processing. *Neuroscience & Biobehavioral Reviews, 33*(8), 1168–1177.

Part II

From Autobiographical Memory to Eyewitness Memory: Empirical Findings and Methodological Assessments

7

Development of Autobiographical Memory in Autism Spectrum Disorders

Lorna Goddard

Remembering our past is a key component of psychological well-being, serving several important personal and social functions. Memories provide us with an understanding of who we are, maintaining our sense of self over time (Conway, 2005). They assist us in personal problem solving by providing a database from which we can reason and develop effective strategies (Williams, 1996). Drawing on past experience can play a role in emotion regulation, as low moods may be tempered by recalling positive memories (Wilson, Gunn, & Ross, 2009). Memory also supports our social world, as sharing our life story with others allows us to forge and cement new attachments (Neisser, 1978; Nelson, 1993).

Given the substantial role that autobiographical memory plays in psychological health, it is not surprising that a considerable amount of research on the topic has occurred within the context of different mental health conditions. In this respect, autism spectrum disorder (ASD) has been highlighted, and there is now a substantial research base demonstrating a variety of autobiographical memory deficits that characterise this condition and underlie some of the difficulties associated with it. The aim of this chapter is to review the current status of knowledge on autobiographical memory in children with autism. I begin by reflecting on the concept of autobiographical memory and review theoretical perspectives on its emergence in typical development in order to provide a setting for considering how autism may affect this process. I then discuss the findings arising from autism developmental research, focusing on autobiographical memory access, accuracy, content, and detail. Finally, I review some of the mechanisms that underlie impairments in autobiographical memory and consider the research implications for best practice in eliciting the memory reports from children with autism.

Autobiographical Memory: The Concept

Central to our current understanding of autobiographical memory development is the knowledge that memory is made up of several dynamically integrated systems.

The Wiley Handbook of Memory, Autism Spectrum Disorder, and the Law, First Edition.
Edited by Jonni L. Johnson, Gail S. Goodman, and Peter C. Mundy.

Of particular relevance is Tulving's (1972) distinction between sematic and episodic memory. The former refers to factual knowledge, for example, knowing that Madrid is the capital of Spain. The latter describes event memories where knowledge is contextualized within time and place (e.g., "the last party I attended"). A further requirement of episodic memory (Tulving, 2002) is that its retrieval is accompanied by autonoetic consciousness, that is, an awareness of self during the processing of the event giving rise to a felt sense of "remembering" at recall. In contrast, semantic memory, involves noetic consciousness leading to a sense of "knowing" where self-referential information at encoding is unavailable at retrieval.

Historically, autobiographical memory was viewed as synonymous with episodic memory, but there are several reasons why this assumption is no longer valid. First, the semantic/episodic distinction has its counterpart within autobiographical memory. Semantic personal memory contains personal facts such as date of birth, the names of schools attended, and knowledge of the personality traits we possess. Episodic autobiographical memory comprises all personal experiences located in time and place (Conway & Rubin, 1993). We might then conclude that it is personal event memory that is synonymous with episodic memory, but while it undoubtedly provides a foundation for autobiographical memory (Nelson & Fivush, 2004), there are several ways in which autobiographical event memory can be distinguished from episodic memory per se. First, the *content* of autobiographical memory is essentially self-referential; it contains information about "me." Thus, while my memory of the steps involved in preparing dinner last night is episodic in nature, it is unlikely to become part of my autobiographical memory as it does not have relevance to me and for my life history. Indeed, some (e.g., Fivush, 2011) have argued for a distinction between "truly autobiographical" and "purely episodic" with the former recalled in reference to a continuous sense of self, and the latter, a sequence of events remembered independently of self-involvement. Thus, while babies and toddlers are capable of remembering events encoded at a single time point (e.g., Rovee-Collier & Hayne, 2000), these memories are not attached to a representation of a continuous self (Fivush, 2011) and are therefore not examples of autobiographical memory. The reconstructive nature of autobiographical memory provides a second argument for demarcating it from episodic memory. Unlike paradigms within nonpersonal episodic memory, research often focuses on quality of recall rather than whether it is an accurate representation of events. For example, autobiographical memories can be recalled at different levels of abstraction from a specific memory of an individual event (e.g., my first day at work) to a more general memory that summaries experience by category (e.g., returning to boarding school after a holiday) or across extended time frames (my holiday in Sri Lanka) (Conway & Rubin, 1993).

Theories of Autobiographical Memory Development: Implications for Autism

Our ability to remember our past develops gradually, and it has been commonly reported that our very early life experience yields no enduring memories. A period originally referred to as infantile amnesia, the phenomenon has attracted a long history of research. One of the earliest studies by Henri and Henri (1898) found that adults' earliest recollections usually pertained to the ages between 2 and 4 years, a subsequently robust and reliable finding. Freud (1963) believed that much earlier event memories existed, but were repressed due to inappropriate sexual content, rendering them inaccessible. A contrasting popular view was that earlier event memories were not possible as biological immaturity or a lack of language representation prevented the encoding, storing, or retrieval of events. We now know that this is not the case. It has been demonstrated in the laboratory that even babies as young as 6 months have the memory capability of recalling a sequence of events, learned at one particular time (Rovee-Collier, 1999). However, while we now know that very young, preschool children can remember events, these memories do not persist over time and memories are only deemed autobiographical if they have some element of perseverance. Using a longitudinal design, Peterson, Warren, and Short (2011) showed that while young children's earliest memories could date prior to the age of two years, these memories were unlikely to be recalled at a later testing time two years later.

Infantile amnesia is now more commonly referred to as "childhood amnesia," reflecting adults' fewer memories relating to the period between 2 and 7 years of age than can be explained by normal rates of forgetting (Pillemer & White, 1989). In general, theories subscribe to the view that memories of early life do not endure because the brain has not sufficiently developed to support the cognitive, emotional, and social developments associated with autobiographical memory's onset. Theories vary in the importance they give to key features in development. These include self-representation, the ability to mentally travel in time, a theory of mind (ToM), language, the ability to use narrative structure, and the quality of social interactions. Developmental deficits in many of these variables have been reported in autism leading to the prediction of a development trajectory that is both delayed and/or qualitatively different.

The importance of self

The notion of self as intrinsic to autobiographical memory is evident in Brewer's (1986) widely accepted definition, "memory for information related to the self." The notion of a qualitatively different self in autism has a long history, with the early descriptions of Kanner (1943) and Asperger (1944) referring to a condition of extreme self-focus or egotism. Disruptions in autobiographical memory might therefore be expected in children with this condition since some version of self is a ubiquitous hypothesized mechanism in autobiographical memory development. However, since the self is multifaceted and as not all aspects are impaired in autism (Lind, 2010), the extent of impairment would depend on which particular aspect of self is implicated.

Howe and Courage (1993, 1997) gave the "cognitive self," embodying the "I" and the "me," the primary status in the emergence of autobiographical memory. The self acts as a medium through which events are understood as happening to "me" and forms a base around which to organize and retrieve experiences. Rudimentary elements of a cognitive self in typical development appear at approximately 18 months to 2 years of age as toddlers show the ability to recognize themselves in the mirror (Lewis & Brooks-Gunn, 1979). Self-recognition is further signalled by language development, in particular, correct first-person pronoun usage ("I" and "me") denoting the child's capacity to self-reference. In autism, while mirror-self recognition is largely intact in children from 3.5 years of age, problems with correct pronoun usage are common and can persist into adulthood (Lind, 2010).

Supporting Howe and Courage's cognitive self-theory is the finding that there are some reports of adults' earliest memories that date back to the second year of life (Usher & Neisser, 1993). Nonetheless, memories from this early period of around two years of age are extremely sparse, suggesting a rudimentary self-concept as signalled by visual self-recognition, which is not a sufficient condition for a fully functioning autobiographical memory system. This early self-concept is rooted in the present moment and other theorists (e.g., Perner & Ruffman, 1994; Povinelli, 2001; Klein, Cosmides, German, & Gabriel, 2004) have argued that an understanding of oneself as extending in time is required for autobiographical memory development. An extended self-concept denotes the ability to understand and represent change over time, a process referred to as diachronic thought (Suddendorf & Corballis, 1997). Using an adapted mirror recognition task, Povinelli, Landaux, & Perriloux (1995) showed this ability to reliably emerge around the ages of 4–5 years as typically developing children became able to recognize delayed video images of themselves. According to Povinelli (2001), children are only able to develop a fully functioning autobiographical memory once they are able to recognize themselves from the past because "remembering" requires the ability to project oneself backward through mental representation.

Children with autism can also recognize themselves from delayed video images (Lind & Bowler, 2009) and would therefore have the capacity for early autobiographical memory if delayed self-recognition was the definitive test of an extended self. However, children with autism fail to benefit from encoding material self-referentially (vs. phonologically) (Toichi et al., 2002), and it has been suggested that this denotes a disruption in extended self in a psychological sense (Lind, 2010) and that this would have implications for the emergence of a fully functioning autobiographical memory system.

The growing complexity of the typically developing self is intertwined with a deepening understanding of mind; the capacity for meta-representational thought and a theory of mind enable the child to understand the perceptual origins of their own (and others') knowledge. These latter metacognitive developments have also been highlighted as forming the basis for true autobiographical memory recollection (Perner & Ruffman, 1995). Autobiographical memory and theory of mind are related through meta-representation, which allows the linking of psychological states from the past to present. There is a significant amount of support for Perner and Ruffmans' theory; for example, the findings that demonstrate children's ability on theory of mind tasks to relate to the extent to which they participate in conversations with their mother about the past (Welch-Ross, 1997).

The theory of mind hypothesis of autism has of course stimulated a vast amount of research; while children with autism make developmental gains in this skill, its acquisition is certainly delayed (Steele, Joseph, & Tager-Flusberg, 2003). Furthermore, while some autistic children can pass certain theory of mind tests, they are more likely to be using problem-solving mechanisms than social insight as evidenced by research demonstrating the activation of different brain areas during these tasks compared to typically developing children (Tager-Flusberg, 2007). Thus, a theory of mind deficit is likely to delay and impair autobiographical memory in autism.

Moreover, self-awareness and autonoetic consciousness have also been implicated in autobiographical memory development and deficits in these other metacognitive abilities are also reported in children with autism. For example, recognition of their own psychological state is impaired (Williams, 2010), and they report a reduced self-understanding (Dritschel, Wisley, Goddard, Robinson, & Howlin, 2010).

Theory of mind, self-awareness, and autonoetic consciousness share a common developmental pathway, and there is considerable (but not total) overlap in the brain regions recruited during their activation (Spreng, Mar, & Kim, 2009; Rabin et al., 2010). Separating the trajectory of these processes in order to identify the primary mechanism that underlies onset of autobiographical memory has proved difficult due to their symbiosis. Together, the cognitive theories point toward the important metacognitive developments in the first four to five years of life as the crucial mechanisms underlying the onset of autobiographical memory (Souchay, Guillery-Girard, Pauly-Takacs, Wojcik, & Eustache, 2013). Since autism is associated with deficits in these metacognitive abilities, some degree of autobiographical memory impairment would be expected. However, another set of theories have focused on autobiographical memory function rather than mechanisms and argue that while cognitive developments are necessary, they alone are not sufficient; autobiographical memory develops and functions within a sociocultural as well as personal context.

Social factors: Interaction, narrative construction, and attachment

Much of remembering involves verbal communication, and as children develop the rudiments of language, they begin to talk about their pasts (Reese, 2002). Social-cultural theories argue that social interaction is fundamental to autobiographical memory development because it is through interaction with caregivers, that the child learns what is socially significant, and therefore, memorable (Nelson, 1993). These theories (e.g., Nelson & Fivush, 2004) draw support from the plethora of studies demonstrating a link between the quality and quantity of mothers' memory talk and their children's memory development. In particular, "elaborative" mothers who engage their preschool children in detailed conversation about the past and ask open-ended questions resulting in rich memory representations produce children who develop detailed and coherent autobiographical memories. In contrast, low elaborative mothers who encourage children in memory talk with closed questions requiring yes/no responses produce children who develop less detailed and coherent autobiographical memories (see Bauer, 1997, for review).

Deficits in social communication, a core feature of autism, will most likely impact on the quality of social interaction between parent and child. For example, children with autism are more likely than typically developing children to ignore mothers' attempts at communication (Doussard-Roosevelt, Joe, Bazhenara, & Porges, 2003; Jones & Schwartz, 2009) and research shows how this might affect the reminiscence style of mothers of children with autism. Goldman and DeNigris (2015) compared mother-child dyads involving autistic, other (non-autistic) developmentally disabled, and typically developing children in the strategies they used to encourage conversation about the past. Although there were no differences in the number of events, length of conversations, and turns taken, mothers of autistic children were more likely to ask direct questions and make more factual corrections than mothers of typically developing children. Goldman and DeNigris suggested that these mothers asked more questions than comments because the former were less likely to be ignored than the latter.

Sharing memories is facilitated by language, which in turn, enables an understanding of both self and others in a social context. Language is therefore purported to be an essential ingredient of autobiographical memory. Although language is sometimes absent or impaired in children with autism, this generally occurs with mental retardation (Boucher, 2003), and many children with autism and normal IQ have well-developed language form and vocabularies (Rumpf, Kamp-Becker, Becker, & Kauschke, 2012). However, more nuanced aspects of language such as narrative structure and use of internal state language are affected, and these deficits may help elucidate difficulties in both talking about the past and building a coherent life story. It has been argued that the ability to use narrative is critical because it provides a structure for understanding the meaning of events in relation to self and others (e.g., Fivush, Habermas, Waters, & Zaman, 2011). In turn, single narrative events form the basis for refinements in self-understanding by contributing to the development of a personal life narrative (Habermas & Bluck, 2000) and this emerges during adolescence as the individual begins to reason about the past rather than merely retrieve it (Habermas & Paha, 2001). Internal state language is also critical to the development of the self-memory system (Fivush & Nelson, 2006). This proposition is supported by research demonstrating that as mothers' place greater reflection on the thoughts and emotions of past events, their children show better theory of mind skills (Bird & Reese, 2006) and richer autobiographical memories featuring more references to internal states (Rudek & Haden, 2005). Research examining narrative ability in children with autism has revealed a mixed pattern of intact and impaired skills. In general, structure, length, and syntactic complexity are largely unaffected, but the narratives are less coherent compared to those of typically developing children (Diehl, Bennetto, & Young, 2006); references to cognitive and emotional states within narratives are also reduced (e.g., Rumpf et al., 2012).

More recently, the social perspective on autobiographical memory development has been extended to include the influence of social emotional bonds on remembering. For example, Chae, Goodman, and Edelstein (2014) presented a model that emphasized parent/child attachments. Drawing attention to the finding that early memories more often represent negative than positive events, they argue that remembering has an evolutionary role that enhances the chances of survival through keeping safe attachments. Accordingly, the encoding, organization, and retrieval of negative events are key and how children process negative events varies according to how their needs have been met and their subsequent attachment to caregiver. Avoidant-attached children, for example, regulate negative affect during an event by reduced encoding, resulting in impoverished recall. Conversely, securely attached children have parental support in down-regulating negative experiences that enables greater attentional resources to be deployed during the encoding of events.

Debate regarding the parent-child attachment in autism has a long history, and a full consideration of this issue is beyond the scope of this chapter. Suffice to say, Bettelheim's (1967) controversial "refrigerator mother" hypothesis of autism has been widely discredited, and research shows mothers of children with autism to be equally sensitive as mothers of children without autism (van Ijzendoorn et al., 2007). However, less secure attachments to caregivers are evident in children with autism compared to comparison children (Rutgers, Bakermans-Kranenburg, van Ijzendoorn, & van Berckalaer-Onnes, 2004). While attachment insecurity becomes less apparent in more cognitive-able children, it has been suggested that high functioning children might be attaching in a different way, using effortful cognitive strategies to compensate for difficulties (Taylor, Target, & Charman, 2008). Difficulties in emotion processing that are fundamental to autism (Uljarevic & Hamilton, 2013) are also likely to impact on ability to emotionally connect, and together, these factors may contribute to a delayed onset of autobiographical memory.

The sociocultural theories previously discussed have contributed an understanding of both how we organize our experiences and why we remember. Language, narrative skill, and the desire to attach and communicate with others are proposed as key mechanisms in autobiographical memory development. Given the social impairments, together with the cognitive deficits associated with autism, it would be extremely surprising if remembering the personal past was not in some way affected. In typical development, research has highlighted age-related changes in the quality and quantity of autobiographical event memories. Although young children are able to recall the gist of events their memories resemble ***generalized scripts*** rather than specific memories (Nelson, 1978). Ageing brings greater memory specificity, and detail as representations become based more on autonoetic consciousness (Picard, Reffuveille, Eustance, & Piolino, 2009). Here, the self, autobiographical memory, and social communication develop in symbiosis. However, in autism, there is some evidence in adults that the self-memory links may be more tenuous as correlations between event memory access and social functioning are less apparent (Crane, Goddard, & Pring, 2013). Understanding how these links fail to integrate in childhood could have valuable implications for intervention, but first we need to gather a comprehensive description of how autobiographical memory development is characterized.

Autobiographical Memory in Children with Autism

Access, accuracy, and detail

Our understanding of how autism affects a child's personal memory is still relatively limited with very few research studies devoted to this area. The first recorded investigation of past event memory in autism was conducted by Boucher (1981) and focused on children's ability to remember a sequence of events in which they had participated earlier on in the day. Children with autism performed more poorly than language-matched controls when asked freely to recall activities such as "What did we/you do?" However, when cued, (e.g., "I bought a pencil and some paper, what did you have to do?"), their performance was no different to controls. Results were replicated in a later study (Boucher & Lewis, 1989) that examined memory for activities undertaken several months previously. Once again, children showed difficulties with free recall of events that were ameliorated when recall conditions were supported by cues. Deficits therefore appeared to be one of retrieval rather than encoding.

As these studies were conducted within a broader context of episodic memory with their focus on accurate recall of a sequence of events, it was not possible to ascertain whether findings reflected a general episodic memory impairment or a particular memory deficit for personal events. A later study by Millward, Powell, Messer, and Jordan (2000) provided evidence suggesting the latter. They were interested in how involvement of the self affected memory processes. Using a similar paradigm to

Boucher and Lewis (1989), Millward et al. investigated recall of activities undertaken during a trip to the park. Events were experienced either personally or vicariously in children (aged 12–16 years) with ASD and severe language delay compared to typically developing control children (aged 5–6 years) matched on language ability. In typically developing children (and adults), we would expect memory for personally experienced events to be superior since the self represents a deeper level of encoding than processing events in relation to others (Rogers, Kuiper, & Kirker, 1977). Whereas this was indeed the case for control children, the ASD group had greater difficulty recalling activities they had performed themselves than activities they had observed another child perform. The authors concluded that autobiographical memory difficulties in autism were therefore due to a "lack of experiencing self." This landmark study paved the way for understanding how the interdependency of self and memory may be disrupted in autism.

The methodologies of Boucher and Lewis (1989) and Millward et al. (2001) employed controlled stimuli, and free and cued recall to assess the accuracy of encoding. The experimental control that these methodologies offer has several benefits, in particular, the accuracy of recall can be established. Recall accuracy may be a particularly appropriate measure of memory in groups with moderate-severe language difficulties where memory narratives are limited by poor verbal ability. However, in real life, the investigator has no control over the encoding situation with personal event memories accrued naturally. Therefore, an alternative, and arguably more ecological approach to examining children's memories of events is to probe how children recall their own idiosyncratic life experiences. It is, of course, much more difficult to assess the veridicality of these accounts, but in the context of autobiographical memory's social and personal functions, while "truth" is a crucial consideration, reconstruction nevertheless that influences ongoing behavior. Examining autobiographical memory in this context has meant a focus on high-functioning autism as the methodologies employed typically rely on verbal reports.

There is now a substantial body of autism research concerning adults' memories of naturally occurring personal events. Findings have been consistent in demonstrating a difficulty in accessing specific events (i.e., individual events recalled within context and usually referring to one particular day). There are few empirical studies devoted to children, but the evidence that does exist suggests that specific memory difficulties appear in childhood. Specific memory difficulties have frequently been characterized in terms of over generality and as lacking in detail. Losh and Capps' (2003) investigation into narrative thinking in autism provided an initial insight into how autism might impact the recall of naturally accumulating event memories. Twenty-eight high-functioning children with autism between the ages of 8 and 14 years were compared with typically developing controls on narrative ability in two contexts: accounts of personal experience and construction of a story in response to a picture book. For the personal narrative task, children were asked to tell a story about themselves. Various prompts were offered when necessary, and when responses were overly general, they were prompted for specific events. Losh and Capps reported the narrative ability of both groups to share many similarities. For example, they produced a similar number of narratives that were of similar length, and both groups' narratives were longer for personal experiences than for the picture book story. However, children with autism required more prompts for elaboration, and while not explicitly stated, this appears to suggest a difficulty in accessing specific events in the absence of retrieval support.

Bruck, London, Landa, and Goodman (2007) conducted one of the first explicit investigations of autobiographical memory in children with autism and explored semantic and episodic autobiographical memory as well as suggestibility. For the purposes of this chapter, I refer only to their findings on autobiographical event memory. They probed memory for recent (within the past 6 months) and remote (prior to 2 years) events using a semi-structured interview, in 30 children with high-functioning autism (i.e., IQ above 70) aged between 5 and 10 years. They compared both the quality and accuracy of their reports with age-matched (but not IQ-matched) typically developing children. Target events to be recalled were specified by the experimenter (e.g., first day at kindergarten) and by parents who selected from a list of typical childhood events (e.g., going on an airplane trip) that were pertinent to their child. Event memory was also explored with a yes/no recognition procedure where judgments were made as to whether specified events (e.g., getting lost in the park) had occurred. Accuracy was assessed for both the event recollections and the yes/no recognitions by parents' stating whether their own memory of the event was consistent or inconsistent with their child's. Bruck et al. reported impaired memory access in autism relative to typically developing children as their event memory narratives were less detailed (i.e., contained fewer mean number of utterances). This provides some contrast to Losh and Capps' (2003) findings described earlier. The younger age of Bruck et al.'s participants and/or the greater constraints of their retrieval task that specified the types of memories required may provide some explanation for the differences between the studies when assessing level of detail.

With respect to accuracy, Bruck et al. (2007) reported that children with autism were more likely to have forgotten that an event had occurred (as established by their parents), but they were not more likely, relative to typically developing controls, to confabulate. Bruck et al.'s study has been particularly valuable in demonstrating that asking children with autism to report on their past experience can produce reliable information as their recollections, while limited in information, nonetheless related to "true" events. The study also indicated a delayed onset of autobiographical memory in autism as younger children were particularly prone to forgetting, and impoverished memory reports were particularly apparent for the distant past. One limitation of the study was that the control group was not IQ-matched, although analysis of covariance revealed no effect of IQ on memory.

The aforementioned studies helped form the basis for my colleagues and my research into the developmental trajectory of autobiographical memory in autism (Goddard, Dritschel, & Howlin, 2014a; Goddard, Dritschel, Robinson, & Howlin, 2014b). We wanted to know more about specific memory difficulties, for example whether they were affected by the richness of cues offered at retrieval. Our research benefited from a relatively large sample of 63 children between the ages of 8 and 17 years with an autism spectrum diagnosis and 63 typically developing children matched on age, IQ, and receptive vocabulary. We used three methods for eliciting specific event memories. The cueing task paradigm is the most commonly used test of specific memory retrieval. Originally devised by Galton (1879), this task requires respondents to produce, at speed, memories of individual events cued by single words. In our study, cues pertained to positive and negative emotions, and neutral words and children's understanding was first established through the accuracy of their definitions of these words.

The strength of this ubiquitous assessment tool is that it provides a reliable index of specificity and it has been extremely useful for understanding how autobiographical memory is organized (Conway & Bekerian, 1987). Its emphasis on speed and specificity means that it is a cognitive demanding task that is highly dependent on executive processes; it requires the elaboration of a cue into a description with which to search and identify appropriate cases within memory. However, its ecological validity is somewhat questionable since in everyday life memories frequently pop into mind (Bernsten, 1996) rather than requiring a strategic search through the memory stores. Therefore, in addition to this task, we developed a semi-structured interview that prompted children to recall in much detail as possible recent events that had happened over the past week and more distant memories, including the very first thing that they could remember. Episodic autobiographical memory was further compared with its semantic counterpart via the Children's Autobiographical Memory task (Bekerian, Dhillon, & O'Neil, 2001) that systematically questions children about facts and events from different lifetime periods (for the purposes of this chapter, I refer only to the event memory data). Data were analyzed in order to compare children in terms of autism diagnosis and age, with children grouped into younger (8–12.4 years) versus older (12.5–17 years) age groups.

Across all memory tasks, children with autism showed significant difficulties in recalling autobiographical events that were manifested in several ways. They were significantly more likely than typically developing children to fail to retrieve any experience that matched the demands of the various tasks, and when they did recall, they showed a significant propensity toward retrieving categorical general memories where control children were more able to retrieve specific memories. Other research has also demonstrated specific memory deficits in autism. For example, Maister, Simons, and Plaisted-Grant (2013) asked 14 high-functioning children with autism and 14 typically developing controls between the ages of 11 and 13 to recall three specific autobiographical memories in as much detail as possible. They scored specificity in a slightly different way; memory narratives were analyzed for both episodic details and general details where no specific spatiotemporal context was given. Results demonstrated that the narratives of the autism group contained significantly fewer episodic and more general utterances. There is therefore a growing research base demonstrating specific memory deficits in autism to emerge in childhood. The question arises as to why these difficulties manifest.

In the context of emotion understanding, research has shown a tendency for children with autism to refer to nonspecific time frames. Losh and Capps (2006) asked children to discuss with an experimenter times when they had experienced both simple and complex emotions. They noted a tendency to recall emotional experience in a much more schematic, nonspecific way compared to typically developing children, and concluded that this was likely due to an impoverished emotional experience. Our data, however, suggested that nonspecific memory is a more universal than an emotion specific effect, as word valence on the cueing task had no effect on the specificity of memories retrieved. Our data showed that neutral cues were just as likely to elicit nonspecific memories.

Moreover, reduced specificity was apparent across all tasks including those without an obvious emotion component. We might argue that children with autism have a more restricted lifestyle yielding fewer life experiences on which to draw. Insistence on "sameness" might mean that nothing much stands out as memorable and explains the tendency toward retrieving categoric memories, where similar experiences are subsumed into a thematic representation. However, reduced life experience cannot explain difficulty in recognizing a match between life experience and a memory cue. We found that while children with autism required a greater number of prompts than typically developing children, they were frequently able to use these prompts to retrieve memories that previously seemed inaccessible. Difficulties here then appear to be more one of access than encoding and are consistent with Bowler, Matthew, and Gardiner's Task Support Hypothesis (1997). This states that individuals with autism have inefficient memory organizing strategies as they fail to encode and store relational aspects of information. Therefore, providing support at recall with cues to the initially encoded material can improve their memory performance. More recently, support has been qualified to exclude temporal information because research within an episodic memory paradigm found performance was facilitated with location cues but not with temporal cues (Bowler, Gaigg, & Gardiner, 2015). The authors argue that temporal source is unhelpful because of the inherent difficulties with diachronic thinking (Boucher, Pons, Lind, & Williams, 2007) and time perception (Martin, Poirier, & Bowler, 2010) in autism. Unfortunately, we did not systematically examine the kinds of prompts given in our study, but prompts were aimed at providing a richer context for retrieval. Interestingly, prompts often featured temporal cues (e.g., when asking for the earliest memory, prompting with before you went to school) as well as emotion/activity cues (e.g., "a special day out doing something you really liked"). The relative support that different cues to autobiographical memory retrieval provide in autism is a fruitful line of further investigation.

Examining the level of details in memories in autism has produced inconsistent findings. Maister et al. (2013) reported no group effect with respect to the number of overall details contained within memories, and this is similar to the findings of Losh and Capps (2003) who found no reduction in length of personal narratives in autism. Conversely, other studies have reported more impoverished memory reports in autism. For example, our findings (Goddard et al., 2014b), like those of Bruck et al. (2007), showed that even when children with autism generated specific memories, they were still significantly less detailed than their control counterparts. Methodological differences across studies may well explain these inconsistencies. Studies reporting no reduction in detail allowed greater freedom in the types of memories to be recalled, whereas those reporting reduced detail used more restrictive cues of memory. This corresponds with verbatim reports, particularly those of parents of children with autism, who often indicate that their children are capable of producing highly detailed memory accounts. Often, however, these are not in response to parental questioning, but arise seemingly spontaneously. Thus, children with autism may be able to experience involuntary retrieval of events on which they can report in detail, but rigid and inflexible thinking may reduce their ability for voluntary retrieval where an effortful match between target cue and experience is required. Deficits may then manifest in situations where memory has a functional role such as where memories are required in response to a social interaction or where memories are required for personal problem solving or mood repair.

How maturation might affect memory in autism is unclear. Deficits could become more pronounced as emerging meta-memory skills give typically developing children a greater advantage with the use of more complex memory strategies. Alternatively, deficits may ameliorate as language and cognitive development in autism support the development of compensatory strategies. The cross-sectional nature of research to date has limited conclusions in this area. There is one longitudinal study that has attempted to address this issue. A single case study reported by Bon, Baleyte, Piolino, Desgranges, Eustache, and Guillery-Girard (2013) described Simon, a high-functioning boy with autism at three time points—initially at 8 years, 14 months later, and finally, after a further 17-month gap. They tested autobiographical memory by prompting for target events across three different lifetime periods— the current year, previous year, and early school years. Results were compared with existing data from typically developing groups. Simon displayed memory deficits at all three testing sessions. Memory for events pertaining to the current year was particularly poor, and memory for events in the past year impaired to a lesser extent, but memory for the early years showed no significant differences. The authors argued that the early autobiographical memories of Simon showed no impairment because, like the comparison group, they were not truly autobiographical but rather fragments of events. They concluded that Simon's autobiographical memory remained developmentally delayed from age 7 years onward and that this extended to the final testing session. Developmental delay was indicated by a lack of detail and lack of specificity in his personal memories.

Other research has attempted to address the developmental question with age group comparisons and within group differences in recalling recent and remote events. This cross-sectional research has also provided evidence for a later onset of autobiographical memory. In our research, we asked children to estimate their age at earliest memory. Age reports were comparable to typically developing children in both younger and older age groups. Moreover younger children, regardless of autism diagnosis reported being younger at the time of their earliest memory than older children, an effect previously found in typical development (Peterson et al., 2011). These data are in line with Bon et al.'s (2013) findings, and also suggest early episodic memory processes to be intact in autism. These early memories are unlikely to reflect truly autobiographical recollections; indeed, in our research, the early memories were typically dated between the ages of 2 and 3 years, earlier than the often assumed onset of autobiographical memory. Qualitative analyses of memory narratives from remote time periods demonstrate impairments in autism (Bruck et al., 2007; Goddard et al., 2014b), suggesting a delay in onset of true autobiographical memory. There is evidence, however, that developmental gains are then in line with those of typically developing children. In our research, we observed age effects on several of our memory indices with older children outperforming their younger counterparts; however, none of these effects were qualified by autism status, suggesting a similar rate of development in both typically developing and autistic children.

Of interest, our research revealed that asking children with autism to report what they had done over the past week did not reveal access problems (Goddard et al., 2014a; Goddard et al., 2014b). These memories might be of a different quality, more reflective of episodic memories, inasmuch as describing a sequence of events than truly autobiographical events. However, one finding that runs counter to this suggestion is that these recent memories frequently contained references to emotion states apparently demonstrating the critical involvement of self, the quintessential ingredient of autobiographical memory. It is difficult to know whether or not these memories would consolidate and persist. It would seem unlikely given that the events pertained to generally routine behaviors (e.g., "What happened before going to bed last night?").

Memory for internal states

Autobiographical memories are accompanied by key phenomenological characteristics that distinguish them from nonpersonal episodic memories. They are frequently vivid, emotional, contain references to internal states, and embody self-reflection and personal temporality (Klein et al., 2004). These features contribute to the felt sense of reliving or mental time travel associated with autobiographical retrieval (Rubin, 1986). Emotion has been shown to particularly enhance autobiographical memory, yielding more durable (Brown & Kulik, 1977) and detailed accounts of events (St. Jacques & Levine, 2007). Emotion gives meaning to memories, and emotional memories are often associated with the pursuit of personal goals (Conway & Pleydell-Pearce, 2001).

We know that children with autism are characterized by difficulties in understanding both their own and others' emotions, particularly when emotions are complex (Losh & Capps, 2006). Research examining the use of internal state language has produced mixed results and inconsistent findings may be explained by the context within which internal state language has been explored (Kristen, Vuori, & Sodian, 2015). In the autobiographical memory domain, findings are also inconsistent with some research reporting reduced mental state references in event narratives (King, Dockerell, & Stuart, 2013) and other research (Goddard et al., 2014a; Goddard et al., 2014b) demonstrating internal state language (thoughts, beliefs, but excluding emotions) to not be affected by autism diagnosis. When considering emotions in isolation, however, a more consistent pattern of difficulty is seen, with fewer references to emotions in memory narratives (Brown, Morris, Nida, & Baker-Ward, 2012) particularly when pertaining to early experiences (Goddard et al., 2014a; Goddard et al., 2014b).

A lack of emotion in memory narratives may be connected to more general problems in narrative style where children with autism have difficulty contextualizing emotions within "causal explanatory frameworks" (Losh & Capps, 2006). Goldman (2008) elicited personal narratives of events such as "a visit to the hospital" and "last weekend" from children with autism, typically developing children, and a group of children with a developmental language disability. Narratives were coded across a range of qualitative dimensions. Of particular relevance to autism were references to evaluative states (i.e., how the narrator felt about aspects of events). This was significantly reduced compared to both control groups, demonstrating that reduced emotion in narratives to be specific to autism rather than a concomitant of language difficulties. Furthermore, Goldman noted that whereas an appreciation of narrative structure was apparent in children with autism, their personal narratives lacked high points making the relevance of their life stories unclear.

The evidence to date shows memory for emotional experiences to be impaired in children with autism, particularly in relation to early memories. In line with social interactional theories, emotion difficulties in autism may contribute to a delayed onset of autobiographical memory. In neurotypical populations, emotion valence acts as an important dimension in organizing autobiographical memory (Schulkind & Woldorf, 2005). Although maturation in autism facilitates emotion encoding (as evidenced by increased reference to emotion states in recent memories; Goddard et al., 2014a; Goddard et al., 2014b), the paucity of emotional information when recalling the past suggests that emotion is a less powerful tag for children with autism.

Cognitive mechanisms underlying event memory deficits

Few studies have considered autobiographical memory deficits in the context of general memory abilities. Despite a large body of research on general memory in autism, findings have been inconsistent. This is likely due to the heterogeneity of the condition, and the diversity of intellect and autism severity in research samples. However, some inconsistency can be explained by the complexity of the to-be-remembered material that different studies have employed. Generally, memory for relatively low-level verbal and visual material is intact with impairments emerging when stimuli becomes increasingly complex and where organizational strategies (such as applying semantic relatedness) would be beneficial (Williams, Goldstein, & Minschew, 2006).

Our research examined the correlations between verbal and visual general memory, and indices of autobiographical memory performance. We thought that visual memory processing might be of particular importance since visual images frequently accompany autobiographical memory retrieval and impairments in autobiographical memory have been reported in individuals with compromised visual ability due to either neurological damage (e.g., Ogden, 1993) or because they are born blind (Goddard & Pring, 2001). Our data revealed no verbal memory impairment in children with autism, being equally able to recall lists of random words both immediately after presentation and after a delay; a finding consistent with previous studies also suggesting intact verbal memory in autism (Diehl, Bennetto, & Young, 2006; Williams et al., 2006).

With respect to story recall, a more complex verbal stimuli, there was also no impairment. This contrasted with performance on the visual memory tasks: Here, the ability to recognize previously presented faces and learn spatial locations was impaired in our children with autism, which was apparent when tested both at short and longer intervals. However, visual memory did not seem to be the underlying cause of their autobiographical memory deficits. Regression analyses with visual and verbal memory as predictors of indices of specific event autobiographical memory were nonsignificant for both typically developing and autism groups. Thus, while children with autism exhibit both deficits in visual general memory and difficulties in accessing specific autobiographical memories, these impairments are relatively independent.

The executive function theories of autism (Pennington & Ozonoff, 1996; Russell, 1997) explain problems associated with social and everyday behaviors in terms of frontal lobe dysfunction. Problems in cognitive flexibility, inhibition, planning, and self-monitoring have all been reported (although findings tend to vary and depend on task difficulty and presentation; Robinson, Goddard, Dritschel et al., 2009). Executive deficits are also proposed to be at the core of general memory problems in autism (Bennetto, Pennington, & Rogers, 1996) and in autobiographical memory retrieval, executive resources are involved where retrieval requires the formation of a memory description for searching and verifying target matches to a memory cue (Shallice, 1988).

Two studies, to date, have examined how executive function deficits relate to autobiographical memory difficulties in children with autism. Maister et al. (2013) examined working memory, set shifting, verbal fluency, and inhibition as correlates of the number of episodic details contained with memories. Set shifting was the only variable emerging as significant—the better children with autism were on this task, the more episodic details they produced within their memories. We also examined set shifting, verbal fluency, and inhibition as predictors of autobiographical memory albeit with some slightly different findings. While we also found set shifting to predict some aspects of autobiographical memory performance, namely, the ability to remember very recent events (Goddard et al., 2014b), verbal fluency proved to be the most prominent predictor of access to specific event memories (Goddard et al., 2014a; Goddard et al., 2014b). It is arguable what verbal fluency really is a measure of; it is probably comprised of several facets, including set shifting and generativity. It involves the spontaneous generation of many exemplars to a given cue. Our autobiographical memory retrieval tasks also involved retrieving a specific memory to a cue. It would seem then that generating suitable descriptions of a target cue is problematic in autism. In the context of autobiographical memory, children with autism may find it difficult to see the relevance of their past in response to cues within their current environment.

As noted previously, research in this area is in its infancy, and there are many other potential mechanisms underlying autobiographical memory deficits in children with autism that, as yet, remain unexplored. Symptom heterogeneity also provides new avenues for exploring individual differences in autobiographical memory performance. There is already some evidence that being female offers protection against deficits and that this may be related to improved social communication abilities (Goddard et al., 2014b). Protection may also be proffered by intact cognitive flexibility (Maister et al., 2013). While autobiographical memory deficits in autism often appear subtle, a comprehensive understanding of their underlying mechanisms will help to inform interventions aimed at improving the personal and social lives of children and adults with autism.

Summary of Findings and Implications for Eliciting Event Memories in Autism

Difficulties in generating specific events memories in autism emerge at around the age of 5 years with memory narratives characterized by a paucity of detail and lack of both emotion references and causal links between event sequences. It is difficult to unequivocally establish whether impairments lie at encoding, storage, or retrieval stages as separating these processes is problematic (Roediger & Guynn, 1996). However, one primary barrier to retrieval appears to be in identifying target memories to match retrieval cues that might arise out of the cognitive rigidity that is characteristic of autism. Within a forensic setting, narrative questioning might therefore be met with a failure to spontaneously retrieve key elements of an event. Since there is evidence that prompting can ameliorate this difficulty, interviewers might be advised to use more directed questioning in order to increase both the specificity and detail of memories retrieved. We do not know for certain what kinds of prompts are likely to be most beneficial and research is needed to discover whether temporal information serves to facilitate or constrain retrieval in autism. However, it is clear that eliciting event memories from children with autism can be maximized by questioning that seeks to enrich and broaden retrieval cues.

With respect to encoding processes, our research suggests that recognition of emotional states leads to an increase in memory for recent events (Goddard et al., 2014a,

2014b). We do not know whether our observation of increased emotion recognition and preserved recent memory in autism was due to natural development or the result of interventions being delivered within the school settings. Nevertheless self-monitoring is an intervention worth exploring; encouraging children with autism to observe and record specific events may serve to enhance their autobiographical memory that could have a subsequent positive impact on their social function. Self-management interventions that focus on increasing self-awareness has already proved effective for managing stereotypies (i.e., repetitive or ritualistic movements) and decreasing disruptive behaviour (Yeung & Yeung, 2015). Training in self-managing memory processes so that events are encoded in reference to their meaning for the self, could also have positive effects on remembering.

One limitation of the findings reviewed here is that they are based on data collected within a social interaction between a child and stranger that requires a verbal exchange. The social demands of this paradigm will almost certainly be increased for the child with autism and the pressures of social interaction may deflect their attention from the task of retrieval and obscure their true abilities. Moreover, the target of memory retrieval is often determined by the investigator, and accordingly, based on events that are memorable within the context of neurotypical individuals. Memories arise from a focus of attention, and children with autism may well focus on different things. These issues have particular implications for interviewing children with autism in a forensic setting where the presence of an unknown interviewer is likely to create additional stress. Alternate modes that do not rely on verbal interaction may lessen the additional demands placed on the child. For example, requesting written or pictorial responses to questions presented in written form or orally by a familiar other will reduce the social demands of the interview situation and may facilitate memory recall.

We have not as yet captured all of the nuances of remembering in children with autism, and future research would benefit from creative methods of inquiry that can most accurately reflect this process in real life. Many questions remain unanswered, for example, the extent to which children with autism experience involuntary recollection, engage in silent reflection, and potentially develop compensatory strategies for their autobiographical memory difficulties. Understanding how children with autism remember their personal lives will not only aid the development of interview techniques for eliciting accurate memory reports, but will also permit us to devise optimal interventions for improving well-being.

Take-Home Points

- Children with autism have difficulty in accessing specific autobiographical memories.
- The specific memories that they recall in response to adults' elicitations are less detailed, contain fewer references to their own emotions and cognitive states, and are less coherent.
- Specific personal memory impairments in autism are independent of general memory function, but related to poor cognitive flexibility.
- Autobiographical memory difficulties may be ameliorated by providing prompts that steer children toward appropriate retrieval cues.
- Interview techniques that minimize the demands of a social setting are more likely to be successful in evoking detailed event memories.

References

Asperger, H. (1944). "Die 'Autistischen Psychopathen' im Kindesalter." *Archiv fur Psychiatrie und Nervenkarnkheiten*, 117(1), 132–135.

Bauer, P. J. (2007). *Remembering the times of our lives: Memory in infancy and beyond.* Mahwah, NJ: Erlbaum.

Bekerian, D., Dhillon, D., & O'Neill, M. H. (2001). The children's autobiographical memory interview. *Paper presented at the 3rd International Conference on Memory*, Valencia, Spain.

Bennetto, L., Pennington, B. F., & Rogers, S. J. (1996). Intact and impaired memory functions in autism. *Child Development*, 67, 1816–1835.

Bernsten, D. (1996). Involuntary autobiographical memories. *Applied Cognitive Psychology*, 10, 435–454.

Bettelheim, B. (1967). *The empty fortress: Infantile autism and the birth of the self.* New York, NY: The Free Press.

Bird A., & Reese E. (2006). Emotional reminiscing and the development of an autobiographical self. *Developmental Psychology*, 42, 613–626.

Bon, L., Baleyte, J. M., Piolino, P., Desgranges, B., Eustache, F., & Guillery-Girard, B. (2013). Growing up with Asperger's syndrome: Developmental trajectory of autobiographical memory. *Frontiers in Psychology*, 11(3), 605.

Bonnicci, H. M., Chadwick, M. J., Lutti, A., Hassabis, D., Weiskopf, N., & Maguire, E. A. (2012). Detecting representations of recent and remote autobiographical memories in vmPFC and hippocampus. *Journal of Neuroscience*, 32(47), 16982–16991.

Boucher, J. (1981). Memory for recent events in autistic children. *Journal of Autism & Developmental Disorders*, 11(3), 293–301.

Boucher, J., & Lewis, V. (1989). Memory impairments and communication in relatively able autistic children. *Journal of Child Psychology & Psychiatry*, 30(1), 99–122.

Boucher, J., Pons, F., Lind, S., & Williams, D. (2007). Temporal cognition in children with autistic spectrum disorders: Tests of diachronic thinking. *Journal of Autism & Developmental Disorders*, 37, 1413–1429.

Boucher, J. (2003). Language development in autism. *International Journal of Pediatric Otorhinolaryngology*, 67(1), 159–163.

Bowler, D. M., Matthew, N. J., & Gardiner, J. M. (1997). Asperger's syndrome and memory: Similarity to autism but not amnesia. *Neuropsychologia*, 35, 65–70.

Bowler, D. M., Gaigg, S. B. & Gardiner, J. M. (2015). Brief report: The role of task support in the spatial and temporal source memory of adults with autism spectrum disorder. *Journal of Autism & Developmental Disorders*, 45(8), 2613–2617.

Brewer, W. F. (1986). What is autobiographical memory? In D. C. Rubin (Ed.), *Autobiographical memory* (pp. 25–49). Cambridge, England: Cambridge University Press.

Brown, B. T., Morris, G., Nida, R. E., & Baker-Ward, L. (2012). Brief report: Making experience personal: Internal states language in the memory narratives of children with and without Asperger's disorder. *Journal of Autism & Developmental Disorder*, 42, 441–446.

Bruck, M., London, K., Landa, R., & Goodman, J. (2007). Autobiographical memory and suggestibility in children with autism spectrum disorder. *Development & Psychopathology*, 19, 73–95.

Chae, Y., Goodman, G. S., & Edelstein, R. S. (2011). Autobiographical memory development from an attachment perspective: The special role of negative events. *Advances in Child Development & Behavior*, 40, 1–49.

Conway, M. (2005). Memory and the self. *Journal of Memory & Language*, 53, 594–628.

Conway, M. A., & Bekerian, D. A. (1987). Organization in autobiographical memory. *Memory & Cognition*, 15, 119–132.

Conway, M. A., & Pleydell-Pearce, C. W. (2000). The construction of autobiographical memories in the self-memory system. *Psychological Review*, 107, 261–288.

Conway, M. A., & Rubin, D. C. (1993). The structure of autobiographical memory. In A. E. Collins, S. E. Gathercole, M. A. Conway, & P. E. M. Morris (Eds.), *Theories of memory* (pp. 103–137). Hove, Sussex, England: Erlbaum.

Crane, L., Goddard, L. & Pring, L. (2013). Autobiographical memory in adults with autism spectrum disorder: The role of depressed mood, rumination, working memory and theory of mind. *Autism*, 17, 205–219.

Diehl, J. J., Bennetto, L., & Young, E. C. (2006). Story recall and coherence of high functioning children with autism spectrum disorders. *Journal of Abnormal Child Psychology*, 34, 1, 87–102.

Dritschel, B., Wisley, M., Goddard, L., Robinson, S., & Howlin, P. (2010). Judgements of self-understanding in adolescents with Asperger syndrome. *Autism*, 14(5), 509–518.

Doussard-Roosevelt, J. A., Joe, C. M., Bazhenova, O. V., & Porges, S. W. (2003). Mother–child interaction in autistic and nonautistic children: Characteristics of maternal approach behaviours and child social responses. *Development & Psychopathology*, 15, 277–295.

Fivush, R., & Nelson, K. (2006). Parent-child reminiscing locates the self in the past. *British Journal of Developmental Psychology*, 24(2), 35–51.

Fivush, R., Habermas, T., Waters, T. E. A., & Zaman, W. (2011). The making of autobiographical memory: Intersections of culture, narratives and identity. *International Journal of Psychology*, 46(5), 321–345.

Freud, S. (1963). Three essays on the theory of sexuality. In J. Strachey (Ed.), *The standard edition of the complete works of Freud*, Vol. 7, London, England: Hogarth Press.

Galton, F. (1879). Psychometric experiments. *Brain*, 2, 149–162.

Gilboa, A., Winocur, G., Grady, C. L., Hevenor, S. J., & Moscovitch, M. (2004). Functional neuroanatomy of recollection of recent and very remote personal events. *Cerebral Cortex*, 14(11), 1214–1225.

Goddard, L., & Pring, L. (2001). Autobiographical memory in the visually impaired: Initial findings and impressions. *British Journal of Visual Impairment*, 19(3), 108–113.

Goddard, L., Dritschel, B., & Howlin, P. (2014a). A preliminary study of gender differences in autobiographical memory in children with an autism spectrum disorder. *Journal of Autism & Developmental Disorders*, 44(9), 2087–2095.

Goddard, L., Dritschel, B., Robinson, S., & Howlin, P. (2014b). Development of autobiographical memory in children with autism spectrum disorders: Deficits, gains, and predictors of performance. *Development & Psychopathology*, 26(1), 215–228.

Goldman, S. (2008). Brief report: Narratives of personal events in children with autism and developmental language disorders: Unshared memories. *Journal of Autism & Developmental Disorder*, 38, 1982–1988.

Goldman, S., & DeNigiris, D. (2015). Brief Report: Parents' strategies to elicit autobiographical memories in autism spectrum, language impaired and typically developing children. *Journal of Autism & Developmental Disorder*, 45(5), 1464–1473.

Habermas, T., & Bluck, S. (2000). Getting a life: The emergence of the life story in adolescence. *Psychological Bulletin*, 126(7), 48–69.

Habermas, T., & Paha, C. (2001). The development of coherence in adolescents' life narratives. *Narrative Inquiry*, 11, 35–54.

Henri, V., & Henri, C. (1898). Earliest recollections. *Popular Science Monthly*, 53, 108–115.

Howe, M. L., & Courage, M. L. (1993). On resolving the enigma of infantile amnesia. *Psychological Bulletin*, 113, 305–326.

Howe, M. L., & Courage, M. L. (1997). The emergence and early development of autobiographical memory. *Psychological Review*, 104, 499–523.

Jones, C. D., & Schwartz, I. S. (2009). When asking children questions is not enough: An observational study of social communication differences in high functioning children with autism. *Journal of Autism & Developmental Disorder*, 39, 432–443.

Kanner, L. (1943). Autistic disturbances of affective contact. *Nervous Child*, 2, 217–250.

King, D., Dockrell, J., & Stuart, M. (2013). Event narratives in children with autistic spectrum disorders. *International Journal of Language & Communication Disorders*, 48(5), 522–533.

Klein, S. B., German, T. P., Cosmides, L., & Gabriel, R. (2004). A theory of autobiographical memory: Necessary components and disorders resulting from their loss. *Social Cognition*, 22(5), 460–490.

Kristen, S., Vuori, M., & Sodian, B. (2015). "I love the cute caterpillar!" Autistic children's production of internal state language across contexts and relations to joint attention and theory of mind. *Research in Autism Spectrum Disorders*, 12, 22–33.

Lewis, M., & Brooks-Gunn, J. (1979). *Social cognition and the acquisition of the self.* New York, NY: Plenum Press.

Lind, S. E. (2010). Memory and the self in autism: A review and theoretical framework. *Autism: International Journal of Research & Practice*, 14(5), 430–456.

Lind, S., & Bowler, D. (2009). Delayed recognition in children with autism spectrum disorder. *Journal of Autism & Developmental Disorders*, 39, 643–650.

Losh, M., & Capps, L. (2003), Narrative ability in high-functioning children with autism or Asperger's syndrome. *Journal of Autism & Developmental Disorder*, 33 (3), 239–251.

Losh, M., and Capps, L. (2006). Understanding of emotional experience in autism: Insights from the personal accounts of high functioning children with autism. *Developmental Psychology*, 42, 809–818.

Maister, L., Simons, J. S., & Plaisted-Grant, K. (2013). Executive functions are employed to process episodic and relational memories in children with autism spectrum disorders. *Neuropsychology*, 27, 615–627.

Martin, J. S., Poirier, M., & Bowler, D. M. (2010). Brief report: Impaired temporal reproduction performance in adults with autism spectrum disorder. *Journal of Autism & Developmental Disorders*, 40, 640–646.

Millward, C., Powell, S., Messer, D., & Jordan, R. (2000). Recall for self and other in autism: Children's memory for events experienced by themselves and their peers. *Journal of Autism & Developmental Disorders*, 30, 15–28.

Neisser, U. (1978). Memory: What are the important questions? In M. M. Gruneberg, E. E. Morris, & R. N. Sykes (Eds.), *Practical aspects of memory* (pp. 3–24). San Diego, CA: Academic Press.

Nelson, K. (1978). How young children represent knowledge of their world in and out of language. In R. S. Siegler (Ed.), *Children's thinking: What develops?* (pp. 225–273). Hillsdale, NJ: Erlbaum.

Nelson, K. (1993). The psychological and social origins of autobiographical memory. *Psychological Science*, 4, 1–8.

Nelson, K., & Fivush, R. (2004). The emergence of autobiographical memory: a social cultural developmental theory. *Psychological Review*, 111, 486–511.

Ogden, J. A. (1993). Visual object agnosia, prosopagnosia, achromatopsia, loss of visual imagery and autobiographical amnesia following recovery from cortical blindness: Case M. *H Neuropsychologia*, 31, 571–589.

Pennington, B. F., & Ozonoff, S. (1996). Executive functions and developmental psychopathology. *Journal of Child Psychology &Psychiatry*, 37, 51–87.

Perner, J., & Ruffman, T. (1995). Episodic memory or autonoetic consciousness: Developmental evidence and a theory of childhood amnesia. *Journal of Experimental Child Psychology*, 59, 516–548.

Peterson, C., Warren, K. L., & Short, M. M. (2011). Infantile amnesia across the years: A 2-year follow-up of children's earliest memories. *Child Development*, 82, 1092–1110.

Picard, L., Reffuveille, I., Eustache, F., & Piolino, P. (2009). Development of autonoetic autobiographical memory in school-age children: genuine age effect or development of basic cognitive abilities? *Consciousness & Cognition*, 18, 864–976.

Pillemer, D. B., & White, S. H. (1989). Childhood events recalled by children and adults. In H. W. Reese (Ed.) *Advances in child development and behavior* (Vol. 21, pp. 297–340). San Diego, CA: Academic Press.

Povinelli, D. J. (2001). The self: elevated in consciousness and extended in time. In C. Moore & K. Lemmon (Ed.), *The self in time: Developmental perspectives* (pp. 75–96). Mahwah, NJ: Erlbaum.

Povinelli, D. J., Landau, K. R., Perilloux, H. K. (1996). Self-recognition in young children using delayed versus live feedback: Evidence of a developmental asynchrony. *Child Development*, 67, 1504–1554.

Rabin, J. S., Gilboa, A., Stuss D. T., Mar, R. A., & Rosenbaum, R. S. (2010). Common and unique neural correlates of autobiographical memory and theory of mind. *Journal of Cognitive Neuroscience*, 22, 1095–1111.

Reese, E. (1999). What children say when they talk about the past. *Narrative Inquiry*, 9, 1–27.

Reese, E. (2002). Social factors in the development of autobiographical memory: The state of the art. *Social Development*, 11(1), 24–42.

Robinson, S., Goddard, L., Dritschel, B., Wisley, M., & Howlin, P. (2009). Executive functions in children with autism spectrum disorder. *Brain & Cognition*, 71, 363–368.

Roediger, H. L., & Guynn, M. J. (1996). Retrieval processes. In E. L. Bjork & R. Bjork (Eds), *Memory* (pp. 197–236). San Diego, CA: Academic Press.

Rogers, T. B., Kuiper, N. A., & Kirker, W. S. (1977). Self-reference and the encoding of personal information. *Journal of Personality & Social Psychology*, 35, 677–688.

Rovee-Collier, C. (1999). The development of infant memory. *Current Directions in Psychological Science*, 8(3), 80–85.

Rudek, D., & Haden, C. A. 2005. Mothers and pre-schoolers' mental state language during reminiscing over time. *Merrill Palmer Quarterly*, 51, 557–583.

Rumpf, A.-L., Kamp-Becker, I., Becker, K., & Kauschke, C. (2012). Narrative competence and internal state language of children with Asperger syndrome and ADHD. *Research in Developmental Disabilities*, 33, 1395–1407.

Russell, J. (1997). How executive disorders can bring about an adequate theory of mind. In J. Russell (Ed.), *Autism as an executive disorder* (pp. 256–304). Oxford, England: Oxford University Press.

Rutgers, A. H., Bakermans-Kranenburg, M. J., van Ijzendoorn, M. H., & van Berckeleaer-Onnes, I. A. (2004). Autism and attachment: a meta-analytic review. *Journal of Child Psychology & Psychiatry*, 43(7), 885–900.

Shallice, T. (1988). *From neuropsychology to mental structure*. Cambridge, England: Cambridge University Press.

Souchay, C., Guillery-Girard, B., Pauly-Takacs, K., Wojcik, D., & Eustache, F. (2013). Subjective experiences of episodic memory and metacognition: a neurodevelopmental approach. *Frontiers in Behavioural Neuroscience*, 25(7), 212.

Spreng, R. N., Mar, R. A., & Kim, A. S. (2009). The common neural basis of autobiographical memory, prospection, navigation, theory of mind, and the default mode: A quantitative meta-analysis. *Journal of Cognitive Neuroscience*, 21, 489–510.

St. Jacques, P. L., & Levine, B. (2007). Aging and autobiographical memory for emotional and neutral events. *Memory*, 15(2), 129–144.

Steele, S., Joseph, R. M., & Tager-Flusberg, H. (2003). Brief report: Developmental change in theory of mind abilities in children with autism. *Journal of Autism & Developmental Disorder*, 3(4), 461–467.

Suddendorf, T., & Corballis, M. C. (1997). Mental time travel and the evolution of the human mind. *Genetic, Social, & General Psychology Monographs*, 123, 133–167.

Tager-Flusberg, H. (2007). Evaluating the Theory-of-Mind hypothesis of autism. *Current Directions in Psychological Science*, 16(6), 311–315.

Taylor, E., Target, M., & Charman, T. (2008). Attachment in adults with high functioning autism. *Attachment & Human Development*, 10, 143–163.

Toichi, M., Kamio, Y., Okada, T., Sakihama, M., Youngstrom, E., Findling, R, & Yamomoto, K. (2002). A lack of self-consciousness in autism. *American Journal of Psychiatry*, 159(8), 1422–1424.

Tulving, E. (1972). Episodic and semantic memory. In E. Tulving & W. Donaldson (Eds.), *Organization of memory* (pp. 382–403). New York, NY: Academic.

Uljaravek, M., & Hamilton, A. (2013). Recognition of emotions in autism: A formal meta-analysis. *Journal of Autism & Developmental Disorder*, 43, 1517–1526.

Usher, J. A., & Neisser, U. (1993) Childhood amnesia and the beginnings of memory for four early life events. *Journal of Experimental Psychology, General.* 122, 2, 155–165.

van Ijzendoorn, M. H., Rutgers, A. H., Bakermans-Kranenburg, M. J., Swinkels, S. H., van Daalen, E., Dietz, C., Naber, F. B., Buitelaar, J. K., & van Engeland, H. (2007). Parental sensitivity and attachment in children with autism spectrum disorder: Comparison with children with mental retardation with language delays and with typical development. *Child Development*, 78, 597–608.

Welch-Ross, M. K. (1997). Mother-child participation in conversation about the past: Relationships to preschoolers' theory of mind. *Developmental Psychology*, 33, 618–629.

Williams, D. (2010). Theory of own mind in autism: Evidence of a specific deficit in self awareness? *Autism*, 14, 474–494.

Williams, D. L., Goldstein, G., & Minschew, N. J. (2006). Neuropsychological functioning in children with autism: further evidence for disordered complex information-processing. *Child Neuropsychology, August*, 12(4–5), 279–298.

Williams, J. M. G. (1996). Depression and the specificity of autobiographical memory. In D. Rubin (Ed.), *Remembering our past: Studies in autobiographical memory.* Cambridge, England: Cambridge University Press, 244–267.

Wilson, A. E., Gunn, G. R., & Ross, M. (2009). The role of subjective time in identity regulation. *Applied Cognitive Psychology*, 23(8), 1164–1178.

Yeung, A. S., & Yeung, A. S. (2015). Self-management for autism spectrum disorders: A review. *North American Journal of Medical Science*, 8(3), 123–128.

8

General Memory Abilities for Autobiographical Events in Adults with Autism Spectrum Disorder

Laura Crane and Katie Maras

In this chapter, we review the literature on memory for autobiographical events in adults with autism spectrum disorder (henceforth, autism). We begin by addressing the importance of autobiographical memory (ABM), as well as its key characteristics, framed within a theoretical model of adult ABM. Various aspects of ABM in relation to autism are then covered, including: (a) the distinction between episodic and semantic ABM, (b) the role of the self in ABM, (c) the mechanisms underlying ABM in autism and (d) whether specific ABM difficulties in autism are due to encoding or retrieval issues. We then present a model of adult ABM in autism, utilizing a causal modelling framework. Finally, we present a summary of the preliminary work that has been conducted on eyewitness memory in autistic adults, and the practical implications of these results.

What is autobiographical memory and why is it important?

ABM comprises both personally experienced events (known as personal episodic memories, e.g., walking down the aisle on my wedding day) and self-related facts and information (known as personal semantic memories, e.g., my wedding day was November 26). ABM is one of our most important cognitive functions, the loss of which is demonstrated most profoundly in patients affected by forms of amnesia (Baddeley & Wilson, 1986) and dementia (Greene, Hodges, & Baddeley, 1995). The key functions of ABM can be broadly grouped into three distinct, but related, categories: social, self, and directive (Bluck & Alea, 2002; Pillemer, 1992). Atypicalities in any one of these categories—as may be the case in autism—could have a significant impact on memory encoding and/or retrieval, as is discussed next.

The Wiley Handbook of Memory, Autism Spectrum Disorder, and the Law, First Edition.
Edited by Jonni L. Johnson, Gail S. Goodman, and Peter C. Mundy.

Social functions of autobiographical memory

Arguably the most important function of ABM is in the social domain (Nelson, 1993), with ABMs providing relevant material for conversations and facilitating social interaction (Cohen, 1998). In the initiation of new social interactions, for instance, drawing on past experiences enables the listener to identify with the speaker, which aids in forming and maintaining social bonds. Likewise, for pre-existing social relationships, conversations about past events are commonplace and can serve to maintain and enhance the intimacy of a social relationship (Fivush, Haden, & Reese, 1996). Shared reminiscing can also enable an individual to better understand and empathize with others (Cohen, 1998), particularly if the listener relates a similar experience (Pillemer, 1992). This can also be evident when personal memories are not shared; for example, reminiscing about events involving those that have passed away serve to maintain a sense of intimacy with that person (Webster, 1995). Given these strong social functions of ABM, and the difficulties with social communication and interaction that form a key part of the diagnostic criteria for autism (American Psychiatric Association, 2013), it is perhaps unsurprising that issues with ABM have been noted in this group. This may even have cumulative effects, with a lack of memory rehearsal potentially compromising the strength of the original memory trace.

Self functions of autobiographical memories

ABMs are intrinsically related to the self (Brewer, 1986). Wilson and Ross (2003) proposed that there is a bi-directional link between ABM and self-identity: not only are current self-views and beliefs influenced by what we remember, but what we remember is strongly influenced by our appraisals of our former selves. For example, we may consider ourselves as hard working in light of memories of studying for exams recently. Similarly, when reflecting on our hardworking nature we may be more likely to retrieve memories of past effortful experiences over occasions when we have not put in as much effort as we could, or should, have done. As such, ABMs can serve a self-enhancement function in that past representations of the self can be judged as inferior to current self-perceptions, favoring our current self-view.

ABMs have also been implicated in the construction of a personal identity (Wilson & Ross, 2003), and in the formation of a group or societal identity (Holmes & Conway, 1999). This is thought to be of particular importance during the early adult years in which a person is beginning to develop a relatively stable self-representation (Holmes & Conway, 1999). Another important aspect of ABM is "self-defining memories"—memories of highly significant personal events that are particularly important in creating long-term goals and forming current views of the self; such as the death of a relative evoking a philosophy to live for the moment (Singer & Salovey, 1993). Self-defining memories are: vivid; evoke strong emotions; frequently thought about; and closely connected to other related memories, themes, or issues in one's life. An important feature of self-defining memories is the ability to use these events to learn lessons about the self, referred to as "meaning making" (Singer, 2004). This is an important marker of a functional ABM system. Studies exploring the self in autism (reviewed later in this chapter) have yielded mixed findings. Yet, given the interconnected nature of the self and ABM, even very subtle atypicalities regarding the self may have quite a profound impact on ABM in individuals on the autism spectrum.

Directive functions of autobiographical memories
The directive functions of ABM have tended to be less widely researched than the self or social functions (Pillemer, 2003), but involve using our knowledge of the past to guide our current and future thoughts and behaviours (Bluck, Alea, Habermas, & Rubin, 2005). Traditionally, general knowledge or semantic memory has been thought to be the most important source of direction or guidance (Pillemer, 1998). However, memories of specific autobiographical events have also been shown to play an important directive role (Pillemer, 1998), providing guidance as to how to act and behave in similar situations. Indeed, directives are most apparent when one is faced with novel situations that are similar to other previously experienced events (Pillemer, 2003). ABMs can also play a role in problem solving, providing a database of effective problem-solving solutions (Pillemer, 1998). This is especially important in relation to social problems, which are characteristically open-ended, with a number of effective solutions to each problem (Williams, 1996). Consistent with this, functional access to specific ABMs has been found to correlate with successful social problem solving (Goddard, Dritschel, & Burton, 1996; Goddard, Howlin, Dritschel, & Patel, 2007). Interestingly, however, this relationship is not observed in autism (Goddard et al., 2007). These findings suggest that ABM difficulties (such as those implicated in autism) can have far-reaching effects on other aspects of cognition and behavior.

Next, we review a theoretical model of adult ABM and reflect on how this may provide insights into ABM in autistic adults.

A model of adult autobiographical memory

Conway and Pleydell-Pearce's (2000) model of adult ABM highlighted how ABM is stored hierarchically, at three different levels of specificity: lifetime periods, general event knowledge, and event specific knowledge. Lifetime periods concern general knowledge about people, places, and activities as well as time periods with distinct beginnings and endings. These may be thematically and/or temporally related and are often combined to form higher-order themes (e.g., *relationships*, *work*). General event knowledge (also known as general memories) comprises both single and repeated events and include mini-histories (e.g., last job, holidays) and first-time memories (e.g., first boyfriend/girlfriend). They may be "categoric" memories of repeated instances (e.g., going to weddings), or "extended" memories of single events that last longer than a day (e.g., my honeymoon).

Unlike lifetime periods and general events, event-specific knowledge is not subject to pre-storage contextual organisation. Information stored here tends to be of individual events that are typically high in imagery, have associated sensory-perceptual details and tend to be remembered in forward temporal order (e.g., first day at school). They also incorporate "flashbulb memories" (Brown & Kulik, 1977), which are accurate and long-lasting memories of important events (e.g., the 2001 terrorist atrocities in New York on September 11). These three levels of specificity combine to form what Conway and Pleydell-Pearce termed the autobiographical knowledge base (see Figure 8.1).

As well as distinguishing between these three levels of autobiographical knowledge, Conway and Pleydell-Pearce (2000) stressed the importance of the self in ABM. They proposed that a component termed the "working self" coordinates memories into goal hierarchies, which constrain cognition and behavior according to current conceptions of the self. The use of the term *working self* here draws a direct analogy with

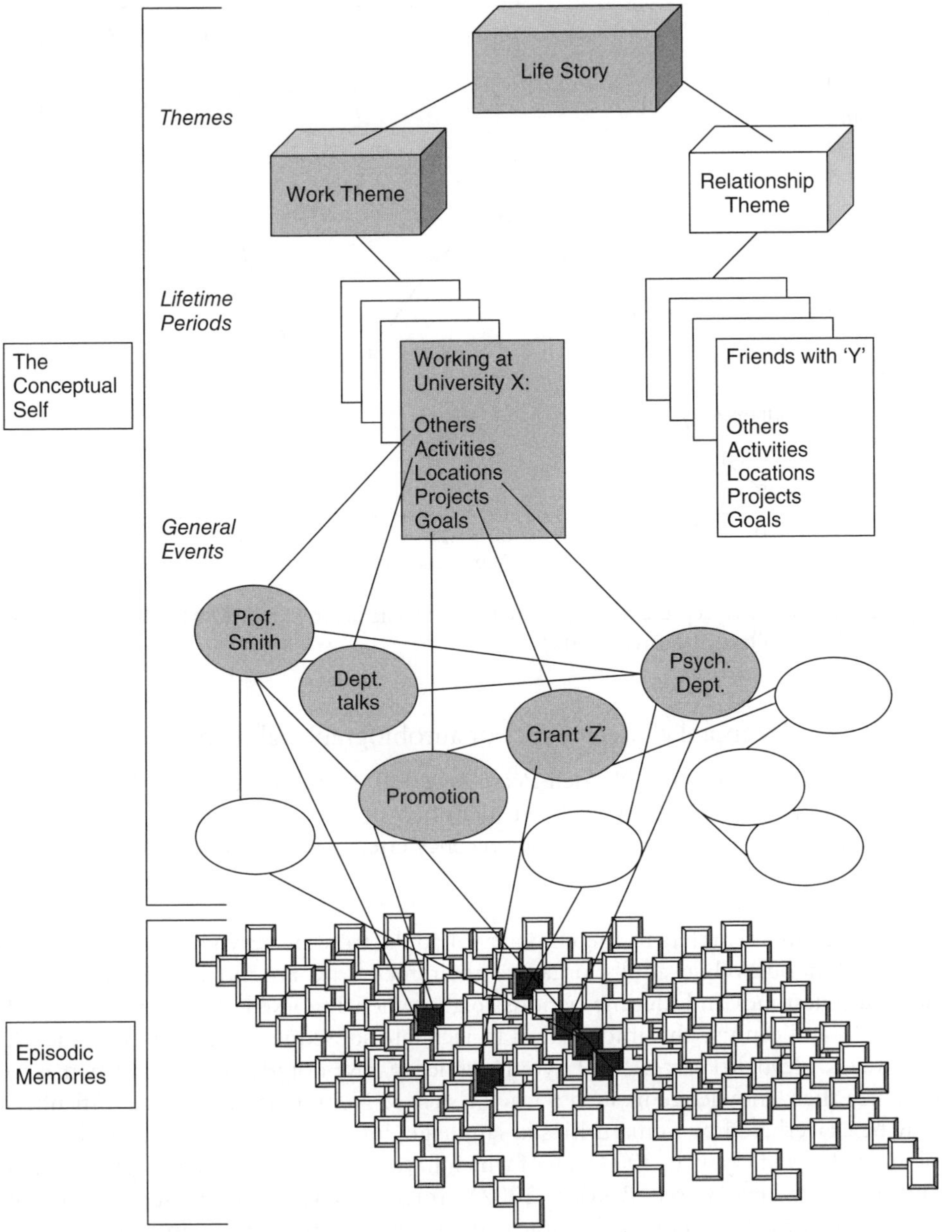

Figure 8.1 Knowledge structures in autobiographical memory. Source: © Elsevier Inc. Reproduced from Conway (2005) with permission.

Baddeley's (1986) model of "working memory—a temporary mental storage system. Consequently, a key premise of Conway and Pleydell-Pearce's model is that memories are temporary mental representations, coordinated by central executive processes. Consistent with this, executive resources have been implicated as a key component of successful autobiographical recall (Dalgleish et al., 2007) and have shown to be compromised in autism (Hill, 2004).

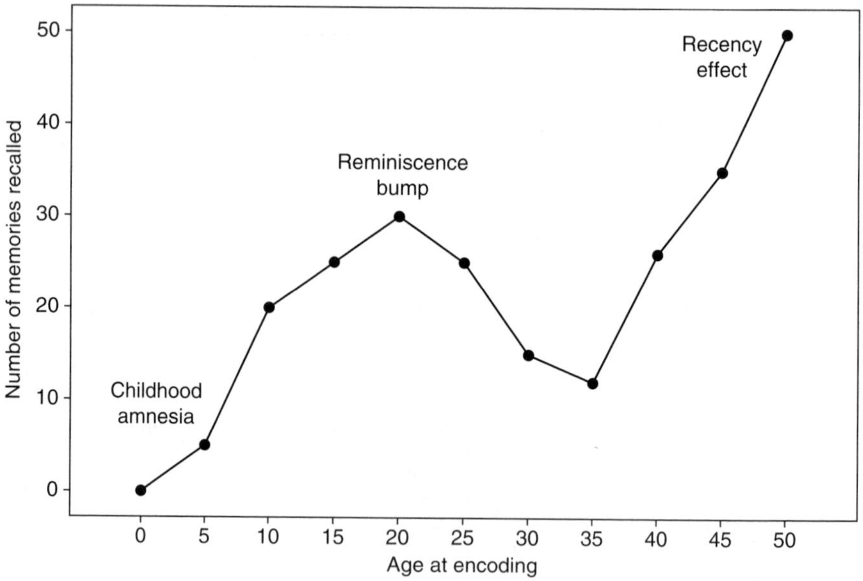

Figure 8.2 Idealised representation of the temporal characteristics of ABM. Source: Adapted from Conway & Pleydell-Pearce (2000).

Temporal characteristics of autobiographical memory

In addition to Conway and Pleydell-Pearce's (2000) framework, three robust temporal characteristics of ABM have been identified in adults: (a) childhood amnesia, (b) the reminiscence bump, and (c) the recency effect (see Figure 8.2).

Childhood amnesia

Childhood amnesia refers to the tendency of adults to recall very few memories from early childhood. While adults organize their memories around a series of clearly defined milestones and lifetime periods (e.g., "when I worked at X," "when I lived with Y"), and can use this information to facilitate subsequent memory retrieval (cf. Conway & Pleydell-Pearce, 2000), young children have not yet developed schemas to organize their knowledge in such a way (Usher & Neisser, 1993). These difficulties may be exacerbated by immaturities in language, information processing, and memory in childhood (Hayne, 2004); all of which have been shown to be compromised in autism (for a review, see Bowler, 2007). Interestingly, however, suggestions of enhanced ABMs for very early lifetime experiences have been noted in autistic adults (e.g., Lyons & Fitzgerald, 2005). In this respect, the "failure" of autistic adults to organize their memories "effectively" may, potentially, confer a cognitive advantage in this area.

Reminiscence bump

The reminiscence bump refers to the increase in the frequency of the number of life events recalled from the ages 10 to 30. There are several possible explanations for the emergence of a reminiscence bump concerning the adolescent and early adult lifetime periods. First, it is possible that this time period is characterized by highly novel experiences that enhance the memorability of events occurring during this time. Second, Berntsen and Rubin (2002) related the reminiscence bump to "culturally shared life scripts"—semantic knowledge about events that are typically expected to occur at a given time (e.g., marriage and childbirth are typically thought to occur during a person's twenties or thirties). A third account concerns the importance of the adolescent and early adult lifetime periods in the development of both a self and social identity. In support of this, reminiscence bumps have been found for favorite films (Sehulster, 1996), songs (Holbrook & Schindler, 1989), and books (Larsen, 1996). Given the atypicalities regarding the self and social domains in autism (as already noted), it is reasonable to presume that the reminiscence bump may be atypical in adults with autism. This has not, however, been explored fully.

Recency effect

The recency effect concerns how events from recent time periods (i.e., those encoded close to the time of recall) are highly accessible in memory. Conway and Bekerian (1987), for example, found 50% of adult participants' memories on a word cueing task to be from the past 12 months. The strength of this effect is such that memory recency has been shown to modulate hippocampal activation during ABM recall (Piefke, Weiss, Zilles, Markowitsch, & Fink, 2003). However, this effect does dissipate when recollective qualities (levels of detail, emotionality, and personal significance) are accounted for (Addis, Moscovitch, Crawley, & McAndrews, 2004). Although this suggests that these factors may be more important than memory recency, the recency effect still remains a highly robust temporal characteristic of ABM among adults. This has not, however, been systematically examined in autistic adults.

Overall, the literature on these temporal characteristics of ABM (particularly childhood amnesia and the reminiscence bump) highlights how several important factors underlie the successful recall of ABMs (most notably, the self). Given that many such aspects are thought to be compromised in autistic adults, one may expect that these may contribute to some of the ABM atypicalities noted in this group. In the next section, we review the research literature on ABM in autism, and the mechanisms that may underlie the distinctive pattern of recall found in adults with autism. This builds on the theoretical and empirical background to ABM that has already been presented.

Autobiographical Memory in Adults with Autism

ABM atypicalities in autism have been noted since the earliest clinical reports of the condition. Kanner (1943) documented how children with autism failed to voluntarily recall events that happened during their day, and the parents of these children reported how sharing experiences "seemed foreign" to them. He also noted that when these children were questioned about their experiences, their responses were often incorrect. In contrast, Asperger (1944, 1991) reported that children with autism did occasionally relay personal memories, but that these tended to be recalled in an odd or atypical context; for example, in Frith's (1991) annotation of Asperger's original paper "Autistic Psychopathy in Childhood," she commented on how responses on the "similarities" subtest of a standard intelligence scale (in which participants were asked to note how two words were similar) yielded a "seamless" mix of general knowledge and autobiographical experience. In contrast, typical children would be able to realize that an appropriate answer would involve providing a general knowledge response, rather than a specific ABM. Asperger (1944) also noted that when these children recalled events (usually in minute detail), they tended to forget information and to confuse details of the events. These early clinical reports of poor ABM were subsequently confirmed in empirical studies on autistic children.

In relation to autistic adults, findings from experimental studies (reviewed later in this chapter) appear at odds with the remarkably detailed and vivid accounts of past experiences documented in autobiographical writings. For example, Temple Grandin (2006, p. 102) describes in great detail some of her early school memories:

> I vividly remember learning about the solar system by drawing it on the bulletin board and taking field trips to the science museum. Going to the science museum and doing experiments in my third- and fourth-grade classrooms made science real to me. The concept of barometric pressure was easy to understand after we made barometers out of milk bottles, rubber sheeting, and drinking straws. We taped the straw onto the rubber sheeting, which covered the mouth of the milk bottle. Changes in the air pressure pushed the rubber membrane up and down and made the straw move.

A further paradox, as noted earlier, regards the retrieval of early ABMs being an area of relative strength in autism. While the literature on "childhood amnesia" suggests that typically developing individuals tend to recall their earliest memories from around the age of three and a half (Pillemer & White, 1989), Lyons and Fitzgerald (2005) noted that a number of individuals with autism possess a very early memory, from around 1 year of age (Lyons & Fitzgerald, 2005). This may relate to the utilization of different ABM organizational strategies in adults with autism (with typical adults relying more on pre-existing schemas than autistic adults). This is, however, speculative; this area is vastly under researched and requires rigorous and systematic investigation in future. Nevertheless, the question remains of how we account for these seemingly contradictory findings from experimental studies alongside this anecdotal data. Next, we review the experimental literature.

Episodic versus semantic autobiographical memory in autism

One of the first published group studies of ABM in adults with autism was by Goddard et al. (2007). In this study, the authors examined the recall of personally experienced events in adults with and without autism. This was achieved using the ABM cueing task (Williams & Broadbent, 1986), whereby participants were presented with a cue (in this case, a word) and were instructed to generate a specific ABM—a memory of a particular event, occurring in a particular place and time, lasting no longer than a day (Conway & Rubin, 1986)—at speed. There were two outcome measures on this task: (a) the number of specific memories retrieved to cue words, and (b) the time taken to retrieve a specific memory. Using positive, negative, and neutral word cues, Goddard et al. (2007) found that autistic adults recalled significantly fewer specific ABMs, and took considerably longer to do so, than a comparison group matched for age, gender and IQ.

Goddard et al.'s (2007) study provided three other important insights into the nature of ABM in this group. First, this study revealed that the ABM difficulties displayed by the autism group were independent of challenges with social-problem solving.

In typical adults, ABM and social-problem solving are closely linked, with past experiences being used to guide future behaviors. For example, when arguing with a friend, one may reflect on previous arguments (and what conflict resolution strategies worked well/did not work well) in order to decide on an appropriate course of action on this current occasion. In line with this, Goddard et al. found a correlation between ABM and social-problem solving in their sample of typical adults. In contrast, they found no correlation between ABM and social-problem solving abilities in adults with autism. This suggests that autistic adults may find it difficult to use their memories in an adaptive way (to guide future behaviors). For example, they may repeatedly make the same errors when resolving conflicts, without learning from their past experiences.

Second, Goddard et al. (2007) reported that the specific ABM difficulties displayed by the adults with autism appeared to be largely independent of a general memory deficit. However, visual memory difficulties were observed in their sample of autistic adults, and these were significantly (negatively) correlated with ABM performance. Indeed, ABMs are thought to be stored visually (Brewer, 1986) and this may be one potential mechanism underlying the ABM difficulties of autistic adults.

Third, Goddard et al.'s study provided insight into the role of emotion in ABM. Whereas the typical comparison group used emotion cue words (both positive and negative) to facilitate specific ABM retrieval, this pattern was not observed in the autism group (there were no differences between the number of memories retrieved or the latency to memory retrieval, depending on whether cues were positive, negative, or neutral). This finding does need to be treated with caution, however, as it was not replicated in a later study by Crane, Goddard, and Pring (2013). The role of emotion in ABM is discussed again later in this chapter.

Although Goddard et al.'s (2007) study was the first published group study to demonstrate ABM difficulties in autistic adults, only one aspect of ABM was explored—memories of specific autobiographical events. As previously noted, ABM comprises both personally experienced events (episodic ABM) and self-related information (semantic ABM), which combine to form a single ABM system. In an attempt to investigate both of these facets of ABM in autism, Klein, Chan, and Loftus (1999) reported the single case study of R.J., a 21-year-old man diagnosed with autism. R.J. had accurate knowledge of his personality traits (his semantic ABM) in the absence of access to the specific events on which this knowledge was based (his episodic ABM), suggesting a dissociation between episodic and semantic ABM in autism. However, as these conclusions were based on the results of a single case study, it was unclear whether the results generalized to individuals with autism more broadly (especially considering the wide heterogeneity characteristic of the autism spectrum). In addition, the researchers compared R.J.'s performance against that of a mental age-matched comparison group comprising three 12-year-old children. Therefore, the size and quality of the memory databases of participants was likely to be substantially different.

To overcome these methodological issues, Crane and Goddard (2008) examined episodic and semantic ABM in a group of 15 autistic adults and 15 comparison adults matched for age, gender, and IQ. Using ABM tasks indexing both episodic and semantic ABM (two semi-structured interview tasks and an autobiographical fluency task), the authors found evidence of episodic ABM difficulties in the autism group, coupled with preserved semantic ABM, a pattern consistent with that reported by Klein et al. (1999). Of interest, Crane and Goddard (2008) explored episodic and semantic memories across different lifetime periods and reported that although the adolescent and early adult lifetime periods facilitated memory retrieval in the typical adults (known as the "reminiscence bump"), this was not the case for the autism group. This therefore suggests that this group may not be using the self to facilitate memory in the same way as typical adults (Conway & Pleydell-Pearce, 2000). Following on from this finding, the next section further explores the relation between the self and ABM in autism.

The self and ABM in autism

Using predictions derived from Conway and Pleydell-Pearce's (2000) model of ABM and the self-memory system, Crane, Goddard, and Pring (2009) tested the suggestion that what we remember is strongly influenced by the goals of the "working self": a component of Conway and Pleydell-Pearce's (2000) self-memory system, which modulates access to autobiographical knowledge by successively shaping retrieval cues (via executive processes). These retrieval cues are then used to activate autobiographical knowledge structures, leading to the emergence of ABMs.

Using a paradigm adapted from Moberly and MacLeod (2006), Crane and colleagues (2009) asked autistic and non-autistic participants to select goals that they were currently pursuing (from a list of 50 items). For each goal selected, participants completed a questionnaire to determine whether the goal was self-concordant (i.e., they were pursuing the goal because they *wanted* to) or nonself-concordant (i.e., they were pursuing the goal because they *had* to). A subsample of three self-concordant, three nonself-concordant and three (random) nongoal items were then selected for each participant. First, a task indexing general ABMs was administered. Here, participants were shown (fairly quickly, in under 4000 ms) a series of short (two-word) phrases on a computer screen (e.g., romantic experiences). The participants had to respond (by pressing a Yes or No key) as to whether they had generally experienced that event in their own life, making their decision as quickly as possible, but ensuring that their response was considered. This task did not require participants to access a specific memory prior to making a decision (indeed, it was emphasized that there was no need to do this); rather, this task was purely related to their rough impressions of whether or not they had generally experienced the event. Memories of specific autobiographical events (referred to in Conway & Pleydell-Pearce's model as "event-specific knowledge") were also assessed, using a cue word task adapted from Moberly and MacLeod (2006). Here, participants were presented with three self-concordant and three nonself-concordant goal-related items, as well as three nongoal items, from which to retrieve memories of a single event, lasting no longer than a day (i.e., a specific ABM).

For the general memory task, Crane et al. (2009) found that the autism group took longer to respond, but both groups showed a similar pattern of responding as a function of the memory cue: General event knowledge accessed in relation to self-concordant goals was accessed quicker than that accessed to nonself-concordant goals, which was accessed quicker than knowledge retrieved to nongoals. However, a very different pattern appeared for event specific knowledge. For typical adults, specific memories retrieved in relation to goal cues were accessed faster than those retrieved in relation to nongoal cues. Goal self-concordance did not play a role, probably due to the crudeness of the measure of memory latency (timed via a stopwatch, rather than in ms). In contrast, the autistic group did not show this pattern. Of importance, this did not appear to be due to task demands. Administering a reverse version of the ABM cueing task (in which participants were given a cue and asked to respond with a general, as opposed to a specific, memory), Crane et al. (2009) found that adults with and without autism could use goal cues to facilitate general memory retrieval. Overall, these studies suggest that the general, but not specific, ABMs of autistic adults appear to be similar to those of typically developing individuals. Further, they suggest that the specific ABM difficulties of autistic adults may be related to problems in using the self as an effective memory organizational system. This may be compounded by the greater executive resources inherent in specific (opposed to general) ABM retrieval (Conway & Pleydell-Pearce, 2000), particularly given that executive functioning difficulties are well established in autism (Hill, 2004).

Crane, Goddard, and Pring (2010) further explored the role of the self and ABM by assessing "self-defining memories" in adults with autism. As previously noted, self-defining memories are a specific component of ABM that define our sense of self. In this study, Crane and colleagues (2010) found that, contrary to predictions, autistic adults were able to generate self-defining memories and the quality of these was similar to those recalled by typical adults. However, their self-defining memories were not as specific as those recalled by typical adults (they were less likely to be focused on one specific day). An exploration of memory narratives provided one possible explanation for this: Whereas the narratives of the typical adults commonly referred to events concerning achievement/mastery (to a greater extent than those of the autistic group), the memories of the autistic adults centered more heavily on recreation/exploration (consistent with the restricted and repetitive interests that form part of the autism diagnostic criteria; American Psychiatric Association, 2013). While recreation/exploration narratives were largely general in nature (e.g., "Skiing has always been a big part of my life"), achievement/mastery events often centered on one specific day (e.g., "when I received my exam results").

Perhaps a more important difference between the narratives of the autistic and comparison groups regards how the autistic adults extracted significantly less meaning from their narratives than their typical peers. This is illustrated in the following examples taken from the study by Crane et al. (2010). In this first example, the participant describes a situation involving one of her favorite interests (a band). While this autistic adult reports something quite out of character, she does not report learning any lessons from the event, nor does she explain how it may affect any of her future behaviors.

> **Example one: autistic adult.** My favourite band did their first show for something like fifteen years and it was the first time I'd ever seen them on tour and I was standing very near the front but when they came on, suddenly this crowd pushed in and shoved me right the way through and I was just jammed in and it was actually swelteringly hot, so much so that the security guards were handing out water to the audience and were getting quite concerned about the audience, some people fainted and things like that. And I kind of managed to enjoy it anyway, even though the conditions were absolutely horrific. I mean it's very out of character for me to enjoy big crowds and touch, it's just what I was prepared to do just to see this band.

In contrast, the non-autistic participant in the next excerpt describes the death of a relative and goes on to discuss the impact that it has had on her and how she has learned important lessons from the experience that will guide her future behaviors (meaning making).

> **Example two: typical adult.** Basically my uncle died of alcoholism last year in October, so that was about a year ago, the whole family were obviously devastated by the event, but the thing that I actually learnt from it was not to actually get addicted to a substance that could actually control me and to monitor the amount I drink, and also not to drink and drive and to seek help if I ever did wish to go down that avenue and it's also bought my family closer together because now we're kind of more open about how we really feel so no one will ever feel the need to shut themselves out to the world and let something like alcohol control them.

This finding of less "meaning" being derived from the narratives of autistic individuals is consistent with two theories of cognition in autism. First, the Enhanced Perceptual Functioning model of Mottron and colleagues (Mottron & Burack, 2001; Mottron, Dawson, Soulieres, Hubert, & Burack, 2006) stresses that the relation between high and low level cognitive processes is atypical in autism, with the superiority of perceptual processing in autism being disruptive to other higher level cognitive abilities. This reliance on lower level perceptual processing may result in a reduced tendency to extract high-order meaning from narratives. Second, Bowler and colleagues (Bowler & Gaigg, 2008; Gaigg, Gardiner, & Bowler, 2007) propose that relational memory (the ability to identify meaningful links between to-be-remembered items that is required for meaning making) is an area of difficulty in this group (see Chapter 1 for a review).

Nevertheless, one possibility that cannot be discounted is that the autism group were able to extract meaning from their memories, but opted not to report instances of lesson learning or gaining insight within their narratives. As stressed by Crane and colleagues (2010) in their original paper on this topic, the task instructions only asked participants to describe the memory—there was no explicit requirement to report instances of meaning making. This accords with White, Burgess, and Hill's (2009) suggestion that the difficulties faced by autistic people on open-ended cognitive tasks (i.e., tasks in which there are various potential approaches to responding, for which participants themselves must decide is the most appropriate course of action) may be due to a lack of "implicit mentalizing"—the ability to appreciate the inherent requirements of a task and respond to the social expectations of the experimenter. It is therefore important for future research to explore whether autistic adults can identify meaning from their narratives (by explicitly asking them to do so), and whether they can use this information in a functional and directive way.

Findings of a largely unimpaired "self-enactment effect" (whereby information processed in relation to the self is better remembered than information relating to, or actions performed by, another person) indicate that self-related information is processed at a deeper level by autistic individuals (e.g., Grainger, Williams, & Lind, 2014; Maras, Memon, Lambrechts, & Bowler, 2013; Williams & Happé, 2009; and see also Chapter 4; Lind, 2010; and Lind, Williams, Bowler, & Peel, 2014). Nevertheless, it is important to note that the atypical specific ABM relations with the self in autism (such as links to goals and extracting meaning from very salient narratives) are likely to be more sophisticated than the processes that underlie the self-enactment effect. Although some researchers have viewed episodic memories and ABMs as mutually exclusive, ABMs are thought to be much richer in nature, involving a greater degree of self-relevance and requiring the integration of events within one's personal past (Conway, 1990). Thus, an intact self-enactment effect may not simply equate to undiminished self-related ABMs, and further research is needed to disentangle the complex relation between the self and specific ABM in autism further.

Why do adults with autism take significantly longer than typical adults to retrieve specific ABMs?

As well as several studies highlighting that adults with autism struggle to retrieve specific ABMs, adults with autism have also been found to take considerably longer than typical adults to retrieve their memories. For example, Crane et al. (2013) used the ABM cueing task (with positive, negative, and neutral cue words) and showed that, despite larger variability in the performance of the autism group, the mean latency to specific memory retrieval in TD adults was 9.2s (*SD* = 5.8), whereas autistic adults took twice as long (mean = 19.2s, *SD* = 10.5). Similar findings were also reported by Goddard et al. (2007). There are a number of possible explanations for this. First, this might be due to the methodology used to assess response latencies. On the ABM cueing task (Williams & Broadbent, 1986), participants are penalized with a maximum latency of 60 seconds each time they fail to report a specific ABM to a cue word. Consequently, this would exacerbate the response latencies of participants who prematurely abort their memory search when they find retrieval too difficult. Although this penalty certainly increases the response latencies to memory retrieval in autistic adults, it should be noted that even when the autism group does retrieve specific ABMs to cue words, members take significantly longer to do so than the comparison group. Thus, there does seem to be a genuine reduction in the speed of memory retrieval in adults with autism, rather than problems regarding the measure of response latency.

A second possibility is that the increased latencies to specific memory retrieval in adults with autism reflect a general processing speed issue in this group. Indeed, successful performance on the ABM cueing task requires participants to respond to cue words as quickly as possible. Although adults with autism can retrieve corresponding general ABMs as quickly as typical adults on the cueing task (Crane et al., 2009), greater executive resources may be necessary for specific, relative to general, ABM retrieval (Conway & Pleydell-Pearce, 2000). This highlights the possibility that the specific memory profile of adults with autism might be due to a more generalized executive difficulty (see also Chapter 3; Maister, Simons, & Plaisted-Grant, 2013).

Third, the increased latency to memory retrieval in autism might reflect a genuine difference in the search strategies used by adults with and without autism. This is consistent with research suggesting that the organisation of memory is different between these two groups (e.g., Crane et al., 2009). Unfortunately, the ABM cueing task does not provide insight into the strategies that participants employ to generate specific ABMs. Instead, it focuses on rather shallow measures of performance (e.g., whether the memory is specific and how long it takes to access the memory). Future research could prompt participants to verbalize their thoughts during the memory retrieval process, so as to provide a preliminary investigation of task strategies in both typical adults and adults with autism. Alternatively, neuroimaging studies could identify whether similar neural regions are activated in these groups when retrieving specific ABMs. This would provide insight into whether adults with autism are employing the same strategies for memory retrieval as typical adults, or whether they are compensating by using different strategies to the same endpoint (Fassbender & Schweitzer, 2006).

A final explanation for this increase in memory response latencies regards participants with autism struggling to remain focused on the task. Anecdotal accounts from participants in Crane's research (see Crane, 2010) suggest sensory issues could have had a significant effect on task performance. For example, one autistic participant reported that she was struggling to respond with a specific memory on the ABM cueing task because she was distracted by the sound of a police car in the distance: "I can still hear it.... I couldn't think of anything else; I could just hear the sirens over and over again and I couldn't concentrate. I just kept thinking of that and couldn't get it out my mind." In addition, several other participants requested adjustments in the testing environment (e.g., turning down the lights, closing doors) to prevent any sensory processing difficulties affecting their ability to complete the task. Despite this, adults with autism did perform relatively well on other memory tasks presented to them (e.g., general ABM retrieval; Crane et al., 2009), which raises the question of why sensory atypicalities would affect performance during specific memory retrieval, but not on other memory tasks. One suggestion is that sensory sensitivities interact with task performance only when high levels of executive resources are necessary (e.g., during specific, but not general, ABM retrieval). This is consistent with research suggesting that nonverbal IQ negatively correlates with sensory processing difficulties in adults with autism, whereby individuals with lower attentional resources report greater effects of sensory processing on everyday skills and tasks (Crane et al., 2009). In addition, this may mean that autistic adults have better memory for sensory experiences. Although yet to be empirically tested, Crane et al. (2010) did find more sensory/perceptual elements reported in the memories of autistic adults. Heightened sensory processing may also go some way in explaining the reports of earlier (pre-language) memories in autistic adults (e.g., Lyons & Fitzgerald, 2005).

Overall, there are several potential factors that might account for the increased response latencies of the adults with autism when accessing specific ABMs. Further research is necessary to explore these suggestions further and to assess the relative effect of each variable on task performance. This has important implications for our understanding of ABM in adults with autism as well as task performance in this group more generally.

Despite autistic adults taking significantly longer to retrieve specific ABMs, the memories of autistic and non-autistic adults do share some similarities. Crane, Pring, Jukes, and Goddard (2012) presented two studies in which different stimuli were used as ABM cues. Both studies found that autistic adults generated fewer specific ABMs than typical adults and took significantly longer to do so. Despite this, experimental manipulations affected ABM similarly in both groups. Crane et al. (2012, Study One) showed that cue words high in imageability (i.e., the extent to which they evoked relevant images in the mind), but not frequency (i.e., how common the cue word was) facilitated the specificity of ABM retrieval in both adults with and without autism. Likewise, Crane et al. (2012, Study Two) demonstrated that adults with and without autism retrieved fewer specific memories in response to odor cues (relative to image or word cues) and took longer to do so, but there were no differences in ABM specificity between memories cued using auditory, image, or word cues. Comparable results (across both studies) were also observed when analyzing latencies to memory retrieval, illustrating the robustness of the results. Overall, these findings indicate that ABM in autistic adults may be underpinned by the same processes as in non-autistic adults, and that differences between groups may be more quantitative, rather than qualitative, in nature.

Mechanisms underlying autobiographical memory in autism

Many studies and reviews of ABM in autistic adults refer to ABM "impairments" or "deficits" (e.g., Crane & Goddard, 2008; Crane et al., 2009; Goddard et al., 2007; Klein et al., 1999). However, these "impairments" are often not as pronounced as one might think. Closer inspection of data presented by Crane et al. (2013), using the ABM cueing task with a sample of 28 autistic adults and 28 age-, gender-, and IQ-matched typical adults (Figure 8.3), highlights the total numbers of specific ABMs retrieved by both groups. Whereas 50% of the typical adults ($n = 14$) successfully retrieved either 14 or 15 specific ABMs to cue words, a significant proportion (36%) of adults with autism ($n = 10$) were also able to successfully access a significant number of ABMs. However, this must be considered in view of the fact that a fifth of adults with autism displayed very poor performance on the task, recalling just 6 or 7 specific ABMs to cue words. In contrast, none of the TD adults performed at this level. This raises two issues. First, some autistic adults clearly do not have ABM difficulties (at least not on the ABM cueing task). Second, it raises the question of which factors predict the autistic adults who will successfully retrieve specific ABMs, and which factors will identify those who will experience difficulties.

One study has suggested that theory of mind (ToM)—the understanding that other people can have thoughts, beliefs, and emotions that can differ from one's own, and also from reality (Premack & Woodruff, 1978)—is predictive of ABM difficulties in adults with autism (Adler, Nadler, Eviater, & Shamay-Tsoory, 2010). This is consistent with studies linking ToM and ABM retrieval in both typical (Perner & Ruffman, 1995) and clinical (Corcoran & Frith, 2003) samples. Given that not all individuals with autism fail ToM tasks (e.g., Dahlgren & Trillingsgaard, 1996; Prior, Dahlstrom, & Squires, 1990), this may go some way in accounting for the variability in ABM retrieval between autistic individuals. Crane et al. (2013) conducted a correlational analysis of ABM performance (assessed via a cueing task) and ToM performance and found significant relationships between these variables. However, ToM was not

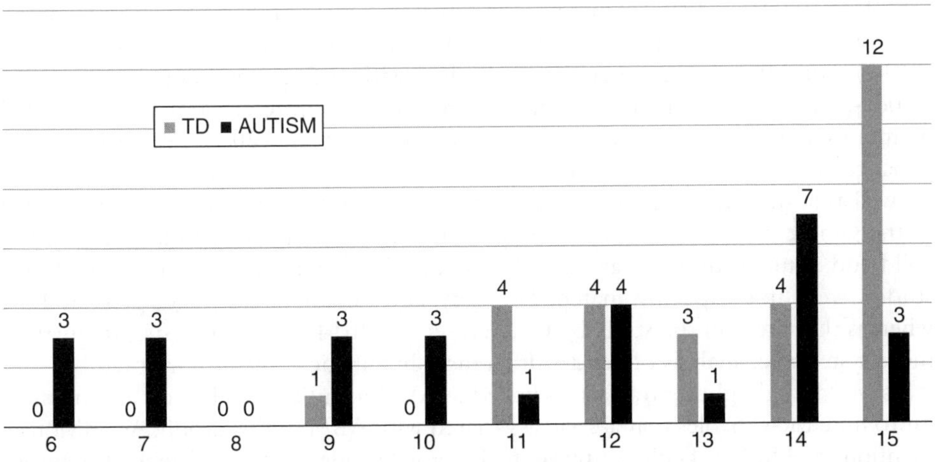

Figure 8.3 Performance of autistic (n =28) and non-autistic (n = 28) adults on the ABM cueing task. Source: data from Crane et al., 2013.

associated with specific ABM once the role of IQ had been partialled, indicating that general cognitive abilities may be driving this relationship. This is in line with the suggestion that autistic ToM "passers" may be using alternative compensatory routes in order to pass false belief tasks (Happé, 1995; Ozonoff, Pennington, & Rogers, 1991). It should also be noted that a regression analysis exploring the role of ToM on ABM by Adler et al. (2010) did not reach statistical significance in a sample of adults with autism ($p = .07$), and significant correlations were not found between all indices of ToM and ABM in their sample. These mixed findings highlight a need for more systematic investigation of this potential relationship (see Chapter 5).

Another possible correlate of ABM performance in autism is working memory—a "fundamental capacity required by complex activities" (Lépine et al., 2005, p. 165). In particular, a component of working memory termed the episodic buffer is thought to be involved in binding together disparate elements of an event to form a coherent long-term memory (Baddeley, 2000). Consistent with this suggestion, working memory performance has been associated with ABM in individuals with a range of clinical conditions as well as typical samples (e.g., Birch & Davidson, 2007; Ros, Latorre, & Serrano, 2010). This relationship is of particular interest given that relational binding is known to be atypical and linked to problems with episodic memory in autism (see Gaigg & Bowler, Chapter 1, for a review). Indeed, Crane et al. (2013) found some (albeit limited) evidence of a correlational relationship between working memory and categoric ABM in a sample of autistic adults. Executive functions more generally have, however, been implicated in ABM in children with autism (e.g., Goddard et al., 2014; Maister et al., 2013).

Another variable that may be involved in ABM in autism is gender. To date, no studies of autistic adults have systematically explored ABM as a function of gender differences. This is despite studies of sex differences in autism suggesting undiminished neurological responses when processing social information in females (Kirkovski, Enticott, Hughes, Rossell, & Fitzgerald, 2015), greater social interest in females (Attwood, 2007) as well as increased levels of self-awareness and insight in females (Lai et al., 2011). Taken together, these findings might imply "better" ABM abilities in autistic women (relative to autistic men), yet a series of studies by Crane et al. (2009, 2010, 2012, 2013) included approximately equal numbers of men and women and found no gender differences on any ABM indices. In contrast, Goddard, et al. (2014) found that ABM difficulties in children with autism were more characteristic of boys, with girls (with and without autism) recalling more emotional and detailed memories than their male counterparts. Goddard et al. (2014) also found that enhanced access to specific ABMs was related to verbal fluency performance in girls (as well as in the TD comparison group), but this failed to reach statistical significance in the sample of boys. One possible reason for these conflicting results between the child and adult studies is that the subsamples of men and women in Crane et al.'s studies were not explicitly matched on any key variables (e.g., age, gender, IQ), whereas they were in the study by Goddard et al. (2014). This suggests that further, more systematic, analysis of gender differences in autistic adults is warranted.

As well as highlighting the factors linked to ABM in autistic adults, it is also of interest to note the variables that are *not* associated with ABM in this group. As previously mentioned, ABM difficulties appear to be largely independent of general memory abilities in autism (Crane, 2010; Goddard et al., 2007). Further, Crane et al. (2013) found that although levels of depressed mood and rumination were associated with

ABM retrieval in typical adults (consistent with theoretical models such as Williams's, 2006, CarFAX model), corresponding relations were not noted in autistic adults. This is despite both high levels of depression and rumination being observed in this group. Although these results are correlational, and further research is necessary to confirm these findings, it does seem that the relation among depressed mood, rumination, and ABM may be different in autistic and non-autistic adults (see Crane et al., 2013, for further discussion and the presentation of relevant case studies).

Specific autobiographical memory difficulties in autism—an encoding or retrieval issue?

As well as identifying the mechanisms underlying specific ABM retrieval in autism, it is important to ascertain whether these difficulties are due to encoding or retrieval problems. In this section, evidence for each is reviewed in turn.

Encoding

On the one hand, the types of conscious awareness involved during the *encoding* of general and specific ABM might explain the dissociation between these two types of ABM. A key characteristic of specific ABMs is that they involve autonoetic encoding (an awareness of contextual details associated with a specific event) (Gardiner, 2001). In contrast, general ABMs rely more heavily on noetic awareness (awareness of knowledge in the absence of contextual details) (Gardiner, 2001).

One method of distinguishing between these phenomenological experiences is by giving participants a recognition test for a previously learned list, and asking them to make "remember" or "know" judgments for recognized items. A *remember* response would be accompanied by the retrieval of specific contextual information about the item from the study phase (e.g., the physical appearance of the word, what they were thinking at the moment that the word was initially presented). In contrast, a *know* response would reflect a general feeling of familiarity and recognition of the word (from the study list) in the absence of specific contextual or associative details from encoding (Rajaram, 1993; Tulving, 1985). Bowler and colleagues consistently demonstrated that autistic adults tend to make fewer *remember* and more *know* responses compared to typical individuals on these tasks (e.g., Bowler, Gardiner, & Gaigg, 2008; Bowler, Gardiner, & Grice, 2000; Bowler, Gardiner, Grice, & Saavalainen, 2000), suggesting a greater reliance on noetic awareness. Yet, it is not simply the case that autistic adults do not understand the difference between remember and know judgments—detailed information was given to participants, and their understanding was clarified in subsequent conversations (e.g., Bowler et al., 2000a). Rather, it indicates that adults with autism may preferentially encode memories at the general, opposed to the specific, memory level.

It should be stressed that Bowler and colleagues only examined self-awareness during the encoding of word lists (episodic memory), and it is difficult to generalize these studies to ABM. Therefore, a study by Tanweer, Rathbone, & Souchay (2010) sought to assess whether the ABMs of autistic adults was linked to atypical autonoetic awareness. Using an interview task, participants were asked to provide specific ABMs from three different lifetime periods (0–17 years, the last 5 years, and the last year) and were then asked to give a remember/know judgment for each memory (depending on whether or not they felt the memory was accompanied by conscious recollection). In line with previous studies (e.g., Goddard et al., 2007), the autistic sample retrieved fewer specific memories than the typical comparison group across all lifetime periods. Further, the autism group tended to provide fewer "remember" responses and more "know" responses than the comparison group across all lifetime periods (particularly the early lifetime period—aged 0–17 years). These findings therefore confirm previous studies suggesting reduced autonoetic awareness in autism, extending this work to ABM. It also suggests an intact recency effect in this group.

Together, these findings indicate that the specific ABM difficulties in autism may be related to issues during encoding. Further support for this supposition comes from Mottron et al.'s (2001) suggestion that autistic individuals have a "low level" bias that leads to reduced processing of contextual information. Diminished relational binding at encoding may also preclude intact retrieval of specific ABM (Bowler, Gaigg, & Gardiner, 2014). However, tasks that require greater attention to the context have been shown to be supportive for individuals with autism. Gaigg, Gardiner, and Bowler (2008), for instance, found that providing participants with global orienting tasks during encoding, such as sorting words into categories, improved free recall for individuals with autism to a similar extent as it did for their typical counterparts. That supportive procedures at encoding can enhance recall in autism provides further indication that the pattern of ABM findings observed may be explained—at least in part—by encoding mechanisms. However, caution is warranted in generalizing these findings from word lists to ABM more generally.

Retrieval

On the other hand, the reported difficulties across several facets of memory, such as the retrieval of specific ABMs and problems with utilizing the self as an effective memory cue, are somewhat dependent on the test procedure used. Converging findings suggest that autistic individuals' difficulties in retrieval are largely eliminated when more support for retrieval is provided at test (e.g., with the use of cued recall or recognition; see Craik & Jacoby, 1996). Bowler et al. (2004), for example, asked participants (with and without autism) to remember word lists. They found that when autistic participants previously generated a related word or were presented with the words in different formats at study, and were given "support" at test (with cues asking them to select the appropriate activity or presentation type as well as the word), they performed similarly to the comparison group. In contrast, in the "unsupported" condition, where participants were simply asked to recall the word without the corresponding action or presentation type, they performed significantly worse than the comparison group. This finding suggests that autistic individuals may simply require more support to retrieve specific memories (that may be otherwise intact), and difficulties could be related to retrieval, rather than encoding mechanisms. Such findings have led Bowler and colleagues to propose the task support hypothesis (Bowler, Gardiner, & Berthollier, 2004; Bowler, Matthews, & Gardiner, 1997).

The task support account is useful in accounting for the mixed pattern of findings regarding self-referential processing. Zalla et al. (2010), for example, reported that autistic participants did not show a self-enactment effect for self-performed actions on tests of free recall; however, they did show the effect on a recognition test. Similarly, Hare, Mellor, and Azmi (2007) reported that participants with autism did not show superior free recall for self-experienced over other-experienced events, but that they did show enhanced recall for self-experienced events when recall was cued. Lind and Bowler (2009) also observed an enactment effect in the autism group when they tested participants using a recognition test. Finally, in a personally experienced "live" eyewitness experiment, Maras et al. (2013) found that, although adults with autism recalled more self- than other-performed actions on a test of free recall, they also erroneously attributed more self-performed actions as being performed by someone else in their free recall, but these errors were diminished when cued follow-up questions were used.

Cued recall and recognition tests may be particularly effective in supporting retrieval difficulties in autism because they reduce demands on cognitive load and executive functions, which may free up cognitive resources required to elicit an appropriate search strategy. Indeed, as previously discussed, the dissociation between specific and general ABM in adults with autism might be due to the retrieval of specific ABMs being significantly more cognitively demanding than the retrieval of corresponding general memories (Dalgleish et al., 2007). Consistent with this suggestion, models of ABM (Conway & Pleydell-Pearce, 2000) propose that it is organized hierarchically, with memory cues first activating general memories (e.g., "studying at university," "living in halls of residence"), followed by more specific exemplars (e.g., "my first day at university"). Conway and Pleydell-Pearce (2000) therefore suggested that when accessing a general ABM, it is necessary to inhibit only a small subset of specific memories that are accessed directly. In contrast, when retrieving specific memories, an individual must inhibit each inappropriate general memory encountered during the retrieval search, to focus on a specific exemplar.

As is discussed in Chapter 1, researchers have posited that relational processing difficulties may underpin the diminished retrieval of specific ABMs in autism (e.g., Bowler et al., 2008, 2014; Gaigg et al., 2008). According to Moscovitch's (1992) dual process model, the retrieval of associatively related items (e.g., context-bound episodic ABMs) by typical individuals is a rapid, automatic, associative process. In autism, however, reduced spontaneous utilization of the semantic association among items in memory is well established (e.g., Boucher & Warrington, 1976; Bowler et al., 1997; Hermelin & O'Connor, 1967). Maister and colleagues (2013) argued that autistic individuals compensate for their reduced ability to automatically retrieve associative, contextually bound ABMs by using more effortful, controlled, retrieval processes. Despite this, executive difficulties prevail (e.g., Hill, 2004; Hill & Bird, 2006), leading to atypical performance on relational memory tasks among autistic people. Support for this supposition comes from Maister et al.'s finding that executive ability correlated with relational, but not item-based, memory retrieval in their autism group (and not the typical comparison group). Unfortunately, Bowler et al.'s task support hypothesis is limited to tasks that do not require complex relational binding; recent findings indicate diminished recognition of episodically defined (relational) combinations of features, even though recognition of the elements themselves is intact (Bowler et al., 2014).

In sum, evidence exists for both encoding and retrieval problems underlying the specific ABM difficulties of adults with autism, and it is therefore highly likely that both play a contributory role. For example, adults with autism might encode their memories with less self-awareness and autonoetic consciousness, which makes them harder to subsequently retrieve (at least when using self-related retrieval strategies). Members of this group may also struggle with the executive resources necessary to search for and retrieve their specific ABMs.

Emotion and autobiographical memory in autism

A further factor that may influence ABM in autism is emotion. Autistic atypicalities in emotion-related processes (such as understanding and responding to emotional stimuli and behaviors by others) have long been recognized (e.g., Hobson, 2002; Mazefsky et al., 2013; White et al., 2014). In recent years, work has emerged suggesting that these atypicalities may extend to the modulation of emotionally salient memories. Studies have shown, for instance, that unlike typical individuals, autistic individuals do not show diminished forgetting rates of emotionally arousing words (Gaigg & Bowler, 2008), reduced susceptibility to illusory memories of emotionally charged words (Gaigg & Bowler, 2009), or enhanced memory for emotionally charged sentences (Beversdorf et al., 1998) and images (Deruelle, Hubert, Santos, & Wicker, 2008). However, using more ecologically valid stimuli (a slide sequence with accompanying narrative and a video clip), Maras, Gaigg, and Bowler (2012) showed (over two experiments) that emotional events were remembered better and forgotten less over time than neutral events by autistic adults. This suggests that autistic individuals may be able to capitalize on an event's narrative structure to support an otherwise weakened automatic modulation of its emotional content with memory, and that the modulating effect of emotionally arousing information on memory may depend on the methodologies used to study it.

South et al. (2015) recently suggested that Bowler et al.'s contention that diminished relational processing underlies the episodic memory difficulties in autism may also account for patterns of atypical emotional processing in autism. Specifically, South et al. proposed that neural underconnectivity between brain regions associated with memory, sensory processes, and relational binding leads to atypical "pattern separation" (with poor or overgeneralized connections made between environmental stimuli), which in turn, correlates with higher emotional symptoms such as anxiety.

ABM has also been implicated in the development and maintenance of depressed mood in typical individuals (Williams, 2006). The pattern of ABM in adults with autism appears similar to that observed in individuals with depression (i.e., reduced access to specific ABMs and longer latencies to memory retrieval; Goddard et al., 2007; Williams, 1996). However, there are subtle differences between the ABM profiles of adults with autism and those of patients with depression. First, the reduction in memory specificity observed in adults with autism results in an increased incidence of *categoric* memories (repeated events) and a high proportion of memory failures (in which no memory was retrieved), but not *extended* memories (single events lasting longer than a day) (Crane et al., 2013; Goddard et al., 2007). Although this pattern is also seen in groups with depression (Williams, 1996), the levels of categoric memory retrieval in adults with autism are not as high as those typically noted in depressed samples (Crane et al., 2013; Goddard et al., 2007). Second, Goddard et al. (2007) found that adults with autism do not display a mood congruent bias (a facilitation of the recall of memories to negative cues), as is commonly observed in adults with depression (Williams, 1996). These observations therefore suggest that there is a distinctive profile of ABM in individuals with autism that is different from other clinical conditions.

Autobiographical Memory in Autism: A Causal Modelling Approach

Over the past decade, there has been a growing interest in ABM in autistic adults. In Table 8.1, we present a comprehensive review of all published studies on ABM in adults with autism, which demonstrates some of the key findings in the area—from Klein et al.'s (1999) case study demonstrating R.J.'s poor access to his episodic ABM through to more recent and well-controlled group studies. Despite these advances in our understanding of ABM in autism, there is still a long way to go to fully understand the nature of ABM in this group and the mechanisms underlying it. In Figure 8.4, we present a causal modelling approach to attempt to map the relations between biology, cognition, and behavior in this area. In this figure, some of the many findings concerning ABM in autistic adults have been included. It is clear that more research is needed to fully understand ABM in autism, but this figure provides an indication of the complexity of the research area. It is also important to note that one aspect of the model that has not been elaborated on is the environment. This is despite the environment being a key influence at all stages of the causal modelling approach (Morton, 2004). At present, little (if anything) is known about environmental influences on ABM in autism (e.g., parent-child reminiscing, memories of shared cultural events). However, given the importance of factors such as shared reminiscing and social conversations in consolidating ABMs, it is imperative that future work addresses this under-researched topic.

In the next section, we focus on how our knowledge of ABM in autistic adults may have strong practical implications within the justice system. We review the limited empirical work in this area and highlight some initial recommendations for justice professionals.

Eyewitness Testimony in Autism

An important limitation of ABM memory research is that, due to the nature of the tasks, it is rarely possible to verify the accuracy of memories retrieved. Eyewitness paradigms, by contrast, typically present participants with a standardized to-be-remembered event before asking them to recall the event at some point afterward, allowing recall accuracy to be objectively ascertained. Most studies of eyewitness memory in autism have used videos as the to-be-remembered "event"; however, three studies have used personally experienced live events: two in child samples (Bruck, London, Landa, & Goodman, 2007; McCrory, Henry, & Happé, 2007) and one in an adult sample (Maras et al., 2013). These studies provide measures of both memory accuracy (proportion of correct details from total details reported) and completeness (number of correct details reported), while still retaining a higher level of ecological validity than traditional lab-based memory tasks (using stimuli such as word lists). To date, studies of eyewitness memory in children and adults with autism have reported diminished recall under unsupported free-recall tests, either in terms of fewer correct details reported (e.g., Bruck et al., 2007; Maras & Bowler, 2011; Maras et al., 2012; Mattison, Dando, & Ormerod, 2014; McCrory et al., 2007), or increased errors (Maras & Bowler, 2011; Maras et al., 2012, 2013; Mattison et al., 2014).

Table 8.1 Review of published studies on ABM in autistic adults.

Reference	*Age*	*Gender (m:f)*	*Group matching*	*ABM task*	*ABM different in autism?*
Klein et al. (1999)	21 year old R.J. (case study)	All male	Mental age matched comparison group (comprised of three 12 year old children)	Episodic ABM was assessed using a modified ABM cueing task (personality trait words were used as memory cues). Semantic ABM was assessed by asking participants and their mothers to complete a personality trait questionnaire and looking at the degree of correspondence between the two.	Episodic ABM = yes (fewer specific ABMs retrieved); Semantic ABM = no (intact knowledge of personality traits).
Goddard et al. (2007)	18–35 years old	30:7 (autism), 31:8 (TD)	TD comparison group matched for age, gender and IQ	ABM cueing task (positive, negative, neutral cues)	Episodic ABM = yes (fewer specific ABMs retrieved and longer latencies to memory retrieval). Also, a significant effect of cue valence.
Crane and Goddard (2008)	18–64	12:3 (autism and TD)	TD comparison group matched for age, gender and IQ	Episodic and semantic interview task; ABM fluency task; Episodic memory narrative task	Episodic ABM = yes (fewer specific ABMs retrieved); Semantic = no (intact access to information about the self).
Crane et al. (2009) – Study One	Autism mean = 41.57 (SD = 16.49), TD mean = 40.53 (SD = 17.20)	14:14 (autism and TD)	TD comparison group matched for age, gender and IQ	General event knowledge task (computer-based measure of whether participants generally experienced events) and event specific knowledge task (ABM cueing task)	General event knowledge = autism group took longer to respond, but showed a similar pattern of ABM as the TD group (using the self to facilitate ABM retrieval). Event specific knowledge task = autism group retrieved fewer specific ABMs and took longer to do so; also did not use the self to facilitate memory retrieval (whereas the comparison group did).

Crane et al. (2009) – Study Two	Autism mean = 36.55 (SD = 11.62); TD mean = 35.45 (SD = 11.75)	10:10 (autism and TD)	TD comparison group matched for age, gender and IQ	Reverse version of the ABM cueing task (in which participants are asked to report general, rather than specific, ABMs)	General ABM = no (similar latencies to retrieval and patterns of performance as a function of cue type, using the self to facilitate memory performance).
Adler et al. (2010)	Autism mean = 21.87 (SD = 4.75), TD mean = 22.90, SD = 4.62)	15:1 (autism), 20:1 (TD)	TD comparison group matched for age, years of education and gender.	A personality trait questionnaire was administered, with participants selecting the traits that best described them. Then, participants were asked to provide ABMs about selected traits.	Episodic ABM = yes (fewer specific ABMs).
Crane et al. (2010)	Autism mean = 36.55 (SD = 11.62); TD mean = 35.45 (SD = 11.75)	10:10 (autism and TD)	TD comparison group matched for age, gender and IQ	Self-defining and everyday ABM task	Episodic ABM = no difference in numbers of memories retrieved, but memories of the autism group were less specific. Themes of memories differed, but other qualitative similarities (e.g., emotion, self/other references). autism group also less likely to extract meaning from narratives than TD group.
Tanweer et al. (2010)	18–65 years	9:2 (autism), 4:11 (TD)	TD comparison group matched for age and IQ	ABM interview task in which ABMs were provided for three different time periods; participants were then asked to give R/K judgements for each memory	Episodic ABM = yes (fewer memories overall, and fewer specific memories over all lifetime periods). Autism group tended to give fewer R responses and more K responses, particularly regarding memories from early life.

(*continued on p. 168*)

Table 8.1 (*Continued*)

Reference	*Age*	*Gender (m:f)*	*Group matching*	*ABM task*	*ABM different in autism?*
Crane et al. (2012) – Study One	19–65 years	12:6 (autism and TD)	TD comparison group matched for age, gender and IQ	ABM cueing task (high/low imageability/frequency cue words)	Episodic ABM = yes (fewer specific ABMs retrieved and longer latencies to memory retrieval). Similar patterns of memory retrieval though: both groups retrieved a higher number of specific memories in response to high imageability (but not high frequency) cue words.
Crane et al. (2012) – Study Two	18–65 years	10:8 (autism and TD)	TD comparison group matched for age, gender and IQ	ABM cueing task (sensory cues – odour, image, word, auditory)	Episodic ABM = yes (fewer specific ABMs retrieved and longer latencies to memory retrieval). Similar patterns of memory retrieval though: both groups retrieved a higher number of general (categoric) memories to odour cues, which were also from the more distant past. Auditory cues also elicited more emotional memories in both groups.
Crane et al. (2013)	Autism mean = 41.57 (SD = 16.49); TD mean = 40.53 (SD = 17.20	14:14 (autism and TD)	TD comparison group matched for age, gender and IQ	ABM cueing task (positive, negative, neutral cues)	Episodic ABM = yes (fewer specific ABMs retrieved and longer latencies to memory retrieval). No effect of cue valence (cf. Goddard et al., 2007).
Crane, Lind & Bowler (2013)	Autism mean = 40.12 (SD = 13.94), TD mean = 44.80 (SD = 11.59)	13:5 (autism and TD)	TD comparison group matched for age, gender and IQ	Sentence Completion of Events from the Past (SCEPT) test and Sentence Completion of Events from the Future (SCEFT) test	Episodic ABM (from past and future): No (no group differences for any measures).

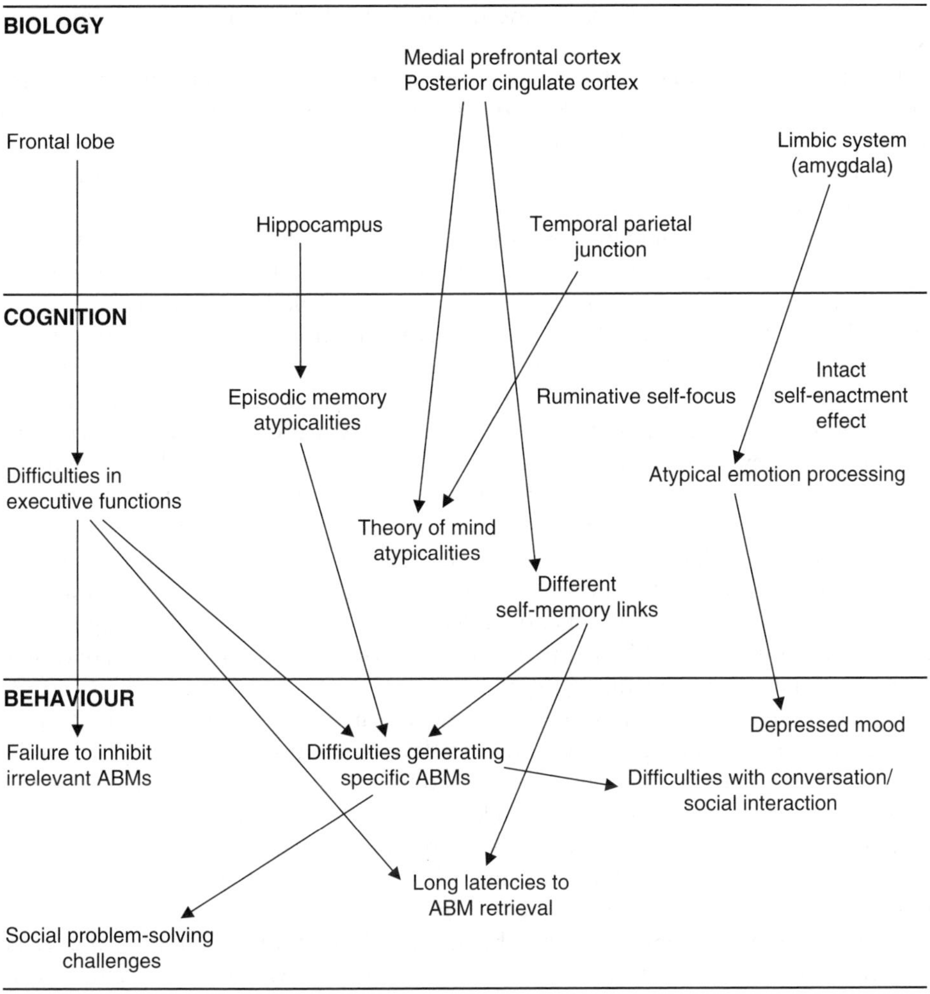

Figure 8.4 Illustration of the relation between ABM and autistic behaviours using the notation of the causal modelling approach (Morton, 2004). Full lines indicate relations identified in previous research (although not all relations are necessarily indicated); where no arrows are shown, no relation has yet been suggested. Relations between items in the model may be bi-directional (see also Hill, 2008). Although not shown in the illustration, the environment is thought to have an impact at all three levels of the model.

Four studies of eyewitness testimony in autism have specifically examined the role of retrieval support for witnesses with autism: three in adults (Maras & Bowler, 2010, 2012a; Maras, Mulcahy, Memon, Picariello, & Bowler, 2014) and one in children/adolescents (Mattison et al., 2014). The cognitive interview (see Chapter 13) is an evidence-based police interviewing technique that has been widely shown to increase both the quantity and the quality of witness recall (Memon, Meissner, & Fraser, 2010). In addition to social communication techniques, the cognitive interview contains various cognitive mnemonics, including instructions from the interviewer to mentally reinstate the context that was experienced during encoding as well as varied retrieval attempts such as recalling the details in a different order or changing the perspective of recall.

Based on the task support hypothesis (Bowler et al., 1997, 2004), one might predict that the cognitive interview would offer useful retrieval support for adults with autism. However, Maras and Bowler (2010) found that not only did it fail to increase the number of correct details reported by witnesses with autism; it actually increased their error reporting. The reinstatement of encoding context procedure in particular was ineffective, which could be related to one of two possibilities. Either autistic individuals failed to encode contextual detail during the encoding of an event (in which case any attempt to reinstate context during retrieval would be futile), or they experienced difficulty in retrieving the context under the traditional interview instructions. To elucidate whether this was more of an encoding or retrieval issue, Maras and Bowler (2012a) interviewed adults with autism with the context reinstatement instructions either in a different room from which they witnessed the event (as is usual for this type of eyewitness paradigm) or in the same room, to physically reinstate the context. When interviewed in a different room, the context reinstatement instructions once again resulted in diminished autistic performance relative to the typical comparison group. Physically returning to the encoding context at retrieval, however, led to improved recall in the autistic group, to the extent that there was no difference between groups in the number of correct details reported. These findings support the notion that autistic difficulties in utilizing context to enhance their retrieval are related to retrieval, rather than encoding issues.

Of course, returning to the scene of a crime in real life will rarely be practically possible or appropriate. Thus, it is important to develop methods of support that can be utilized in interviews. The self-administered interview (SAI) is a pen-and-paper evidence-based interview that was developed to allow an early, quality retrieval by witnesses in real life instances where there are multiple witnesses but limited police resources to interview each witness immediately (Gabbert, Hope, & Fisher, 2009). Crucially, the SAI contains some of the cognitive mnemonics of the cognitive interview, including context reinstatement, but being self-administered it removes the social communication techniques. As such, it offers potential for witnesses with autism, who may otherwise struggle with the inherently social nature of a police interview (see also White, 2013; White et al., 2009). Maras et al. (2014) tested the effectiveness of the SAI for witnesses with autism. Whereas the context reinstatement instructions remained to be ineffective in eliciting more detail (compared to a standard control written free-recall test), the "varied retrieval" component, whereby witnesses generate a sketch of the scene, increased recall, indicating a promising avenue to support retrieval in witnesses with autism. Similarly, a recent study by Mattison et al. (2014) found that a modification of sketching in order to reinstate context was effective in improving the number of correct details reported by children and adolescents with autism without a concomitant increase in error reporting (see Chapter 13 for more details).

Practical implications

Despite specific difficulties in the retrieval of certain autobiographical information (e.g., specific memories), autistic adults are capable of providing accurate and relevant information as witnesses if they are appropriately supported at interview.

For instance, autistic individuals tend to show diminished performance on most memory tasks when test procedures are unsupported (as is the case in free recall), but not on supported tests such as cued recall or recognition. This suggests that these difficulties do not always reflect an encoding problem and are open to effective support.

Although free recall is widely accepted as producing the most accurate, uncontaminated witness recall (Ministry of Justice, 2011), witnesses with autism may need more guided, focused, retrieval from the outset to (a) support memory retrieval (see Maras & Bowler, 2014), (b) reduce implicit social demands regarding what is relevant for recall (see White, 2013), and (c) minimize demands on executive resources (see Maister et al., 2013). Indeed, a recent survey of police officers in England and Wales indicated that police officers themselves recognized the importance of narrowing the parameters in their questioning (Crane, Maras, Hawken, Mulcahy, & Memon, 2016), for instance, by specifying the time frame, place, or event that the witness should focus on. Empirical, lab-based findings indicate that adults with autism (without accompanying intellectual impairment) are no more suggestible than those without autism (Maras & Bowler, 2011, 2012b; North, Russell, & Gudjonsson, 2008; see also Bruck et al., 2007; and McCrory et al., 2007 for similar findings with children); thus, more focused retrieval is unlikely to result in heightened suggestibility, provided it is nonleading. It is worth cautioning, however, that although no more suggestible, individuals *may* be more compliant (North et al., 2008; but see Maras & Bowler, 2012b).

On the basis of the research reviewed in this chapter, interviewers should also bear in mind that individuals with autism may:

- Need longer to process questions and recall their answers.
- Need more focused (nonleading) questions with set parameters.
- Have better memory for semantic and general information, but require more prompting to retrieve specific episodes.
- Find it difficult to focus due to sensory demands (e.g., in a noisy or brightly lit interview environment).

The Advocate's Gateway toolkits (2015a, 2015b) on autism provide further practical guidance for practitioners on such issues.

Take-Home Points

- Episodic ABM (memory for personal events), but not semantic ABM (memory for personal facts), appears to be atypical in autistic adults.
- While typical adults (primarily) tend to organize their ABMs around the self, this does not appear to be the case for adults with autism.
- Autistic adults appear to show some areas of strength regarding ABM; for example, they may recall ABMs for very early life events.
- Despite difficulties with some aspects of ABM retrieval and encoding, adults with autism are capable of providing accurate and relevant information as witnesses, if they are appropriately supported at interview.

References

Addis, D. R., Moscovitch, M., Crawley, A., & McAndrews, M. (2004). Recollective qualities modulate hippocampal activation during autobiographical memory retrieval. *Hippocampus, 14*, 752–762. doi:10.1002/hipo.10215

Adler, N., Nadler, B., Eviatar, Z., & Shamay-Tsoory, S. G. (2010). The relationship between theory of mind and autobiographical memory in high-functioning autism and Asperger syndrome. *Psychiatry Research, 178*(1), 214–216. doi:10.1016/j.psychres.2009.11.015

The Advocate's Gateway. (2015a). *Planning to question someone with an autism spectrum disorder including Asperger syndrome.* London, England: The Advocate's Gateway.

The Advocate's Gateway. (2015b). *Witnesses and defendants with autism: Memory and sensory issues.* London, England: The Advocate's Gateway.

American Psychiatric Association. (2013). *Diagnostic and statistical manual of mental disorders* (5th ed.). Washington, DC: Author.

Asperger, H. (1944/1991). "Autistic psychopathy" in childhood. In U. Frith (Ed.), *Autism and Asperger syndrome* (pp. 37–92). Cambridge, England: Cambridge University Press.

Attwood, T. (2007). *The complete guide to Asperger's syndrome.* London, England: Jessica Kingsley.

Baddeley, A. (1986). *Working memory.* Oxford, England: Oxford University Press.

Baddeley, A. (2000). The episodic buffer: A new component of working memory? *Trends in Cognitive Sciences, 4*(11), 417–423. doi:10.1016/S1364-6613(00)01538-2

Baddeley, A., & Wilson, B. (1986). Amnesia, autobiographical memory and confabulation. In D. C. Rubin (Ed.), *Autobiographical Memory* (pp. 225–252). New York, NY: Cambridge University Press.

Berntsen, D., & Rubin, D. C. (2002). Emotionally charged autobiographical memories across the lifespan: The recall of happy, sad, traumatic, and involuntary memories. *Psychology & Aging, 17*(4), 636–652. doi:10.1037/0882-7974.17.4.636

Beversdorf, D. Q., Anderson, J. M., Manning, S. E., Anderson, S. L., Nordgren, R. E., Felopulos, G. J., Nadeau, S., Heilman, K., & Bauman, M. L. (1998). The effect of semantic and emotional context on written recall for verbal language in high functioning adults with autism spectrum disorder. *Journal of Neurology, Neurosurgery & Psychiatry, 65*(5), 685–692. doi:10.1136/jnnp.65.5.685

Birch, L. S., & Davidson, K. M. (2007). Specificity of autobiographical memory in depressed older adults and its relationship with working memory and IQ. *British Journal of Clinical Psychology, 46*, 175–186. doi:10.1348/014466506X119944

Bluck, S., & Alea, N. (2002). Exploring the functions of autobiographical memory: Why do I remember the autumn? In J. Webster & B. Haight (Eds.), *Critical advances in reminiscence: From theory to application.* New York, NY: Springer.

Bluck, S., Alea, N., Habermas, T., & Rubin, D. C. (2005). A tale of three functions: The self-reported uses of autobiographical memory. *Social Cognition, 23*(1), 91–117. doi:10.1521/soco.23.1.91.59198

Boucher, J., & Warrington, E. K. (1976). Memory deficits in early infantile autism: Some similarities to the amnesic syndrome. *British Journal of Psychology, 67*(1), 73–87. doi:10.1111/j.2044-8295.1976.tb01499.x

Bowler, D. M. (2007). *Autism spectrum disorders: Psychological theory and research.* West Sussex, England: John Wiley & Sons Ltd.

Bowler, D. M., & Gaigg, S. B. (2008). Memory in ASD: Enduring themes and future prospects. In J. Boucher & D. Bowler (Eds.), *Memory in Autism* (pp. 330–349). Cambridge, England: Cambridge University Press.

Bowler, D. M., Gaigg, S. B., & Gardiner, J. M. (2008). Effects of related and unrelated context on recall and recognition by adults with high-functioning autism spectrum disorder. *Neuropsychologia, 46*(4), 993–999. doi:10.1016/j.neuropsychologia.2007.12.004

Bowler, D. M., Gaigg, S. B., & Gardiner, J. M. (2014). Binding of multiple features in memory by high-functioning adults with autism spectrum disorder. *Journal of Autism & Developmental Disorders, 44*(9), 2355–2362. doi:10.1007/s10803-014-2105-y

Bowler, D. M., Gardiner, J. M., & Berthollier, N. (2004). Source memory in adolescents and adults with Asperger's syndrome. *Journal of Autism & Developmental Disorders, 34*(5), 533–542. doi:10.1007/s10803-004-2548-7

Bowler, D. M., Gardiner, J. M., & Grice, S. J. (2000). Episodic memory and remembering in adults with Asperger syndrome. *Journal of Autism & Developmental Disorders, 30*(4), 295–304. doi:10.1023/A:1005575216176

Bowler, D. M., Gardiner, J. M., Grice, S., & Saavalainen, P. (2000). Memory illusions: False recall and recognition in adults with Asperger's syndrome. *Journal of Abnormal Psychology, 109*(4), 663–672. doi:10.1037/0021-843X.110.2.215

Bowler, D. M., Matthews, N. J., & Gardiner, J. M. (1997). Asperger's syndrome and memory: Similarity to autism but not amnesia. *Neuropsychologia, 35*(1), 65–70. doi:10.1016/S0028-3932(96)00054-1

Brewer, W. (1986). What is autobiographical memory? In D. C. Rubin (Ed.), *Autobiographical memory*. Cambridge, England: Cambridge University Press.

Brown, R., & Kulik, J. (1977). Flashbulb Memories. *Cognition, 5*, 73–99. doi:10.1016/0010-0277(77)90018-X

Bruck, M., London, K., Landa, R., & Goodman, J. (2007). Autobiographical memory and suggestibility in children with autism spectrum disorder. *Development & Psychopathology, 19*(1), 73–95. doi:10.1017/s0954579407070058

Cohen, G. (1998). The effects of ageing on autobiographical memory. In C. Thompson, D. Hermann, D. Bruce, J. Read, D. Payne, & M. Toglia (Eds.), *Autobiographical memory: Theoretical and applied perspectives* (pp. 67–93). Cambridge, England: Cambridge University Press.

Conway, M. A. (1990). *Autobiographical memory: An introduction*. Buckingham, England: Open University Press.

Conway, M. A. (2005). Memory and the self. *Journal of Memory & Language, 53*, 594–628. doi:10.1016/j.jml.2005.08.005

Conway, M. A., & Bekerian, D. A. (1987). Organization in autobiographical memory. *Memory & Cognition, 15*(2), 119–132. doi:10.3758/BF03197023

Conway, M. A., & Pleydell-Pearce, C. W. (2000). The construction of autobiographical memories in the self-memory system. *Psychological Review, 107*(2), 261–288. doi:10.1037/0033-295X.107.2.261

Conway, M. A., & Rubin, D. C. (1986). The structure of autobiographical memory. In A. Collins, S. Gathercole, M. A. Conway, & P. Morris (Eds.), *Theories of Memory* (pp. 103–137). Hillsdale, NJ: Lawrence Erlbaum Associates.

Corcoran, R., & Frith, C. D. (2003). Autobiographical memory and theory of mind: Evidence of a relationship in schizophrenia. *Psychological Medicine, 33*(5), 897–905. doi:10.1017/S0033291703007529

Craik, F. I. M., & Jacoby, L. L. (1996). Aging and memory: Implications for skilled performance. In W. A. Rogers, A. D. Fisk, & N. Walker (Eds.), *Aging and skilled performance: Advances in theory and applications. Rogers*. Hillsdale, NJ: Lawrence Erlbaum Associates.

Crane, L. (2010). *Autobiographical memory in adults with autism spectrum disorders (doctoral dissertation)*. University of London, England.

Crane, L., & Goddard, L. (2008). Episodic and semantic autobiographical memory in adults with autism spectrum disorders. *Journal of Autism & Developmental Disorders, 38*(3), 498–506. doi:10.1007/s10803-007-0420-2

Crane, L., Goddard, L., & Pring, L. (2009). Specific and general autobiographical knowledge in adults with autism spectrum disorders: The role of personal goals. *Memory, 17*(5), 557–576. doi:10.1080/09658210902960211

Crane, L., Goddard, L., & Pring, L. (2010). Self-defining and everyday autobiographical memories in adults with autism spectrum disorders. *Journal of Autism & Developmental Disorders, 40*(3), 383–391. doi:10.1007/s10803-009-0875-4

Crane, L., Goddard, L., & Pring, L. (2013). Autobiographical memory in adults with autism: The role of depressed mood, rumination, working memory and theory of mind. *Autism: The International Journal of Research and Practice, 17*(2), 205–219. doi:10.1177/1362361311418690

Crane, L., Lind, S. E., & Bowler, D. M. (2013). Remembering the past and imagining the future in adults with autism spectrum disorders. *Memory, 21*(2), 157–166. doi:10.1080/09658211.2012.712976

Crane, L., Maras, K. L., Hawken, T., Mulcahy, S., & Memon, A. (2016). Experiences of autism spectrum disorder and policing in England and Wales: Surveying police and the autism community. *Journal of Autism & Developmental Disorders, 46*(6), 2028–2041. doi:10.1007/s10803-016-2729-1

Crane, L., Pring, L., Jukes, K., & Goddard, L. (2012). Patterns of autobiographical memory in adults with autism spectrum disorder. *Journal of Autism & Developmental Disorders, 42*(10), 2100–2112. doi:10.1007/s10803-012-1459-2

Dahlgren, S. O., & Trillingsgaard, A. (1996). Theory of mind in non-retarded children with autism and Asperger's syndrome. A research note. *Journal of Child Psychology & Psychiatry, 37*(6), 759–763. doi:10.1111/j.1469-7610.1996.tb01469.x

Dalgleish, T., Williams, J. M. G., Golden, A. M. J., Perkins, N., Barrett, L. F.,...Barnard, P. J. (2007). Reduced specificity of autobiographical memory and depression: The role of executive control. *Journal of Experimental Psychology-General, 136*(1), 23–42. doi:10.1037/0096-3445.136.1.23

Deruelle, C., Hubert, B., Santos, A., & Wicker, B. (2008). Negative emotion does not enhance recall skills in adults with autistic spectrum disorders. *Autism Research, 1*(2), 91–96. doi:10.1002/aur.13

Fassbender, C., & Schweitzer, J. B. (2006). Is there evidence for neural compensation in attention deficit hyperactivity disorder? A review of the functional neuroimaging literature. *Clinical Psychology Review, 26*(4), 445–465. doi:10.1016/j.cpr.2006.01.003

Fivush, R., Haden, C., & Reese, E. (1996). Remembering, recounting and reminiscing: The development of autobiographical memory in social context. In D. C. Rubin (Ed.), *Remembering our past: Studies in autobiographical memory* (pp. 341–359). New York, NY: Cambridge University Press.

Gabbert, F., Hope, L., & Fisher, R. P. (2009). Protecting eyewitness evidence: Examining the efficacy of a self-administered interview tool. *Law & Human Behavior, 33*(4), 298–307. doi:10.1007/s10979-008-9146-8

Gaigg, S. B., & Bowler, D. M. (2008). Free recall and forgetting of emotionally arousing words in autism spectrum disorder. *Neuropsychologia, 46*(9), 2336–2343. doi:10.1016/j.neuropsychologia.2008.03.008

Gaigg, S. B., & Bowler, D. M. (2009). Illusory memories of emotionally charged words in autism spectrum disorder: Further evidence for atypical emotion processing outside the social domain. *Journal of Autism & Developmental Disorders, 39*(7), 1031–1038. doi:10.1007/s10803-009-0710-y

Gaigg, S. B., Gardiner, J. M., & Bowler, D. M. (2008). Free recall in autism spectrum disorder: The role of relational and item-specific encoding. *Neuropsychologia, 46*(4), 983–992. doi:10.1016/j.neuropsychologia.2007.11.011

Gardiner, J. M. (2001). Episodic memory and autonoetic consciousness: A first-person approach. *Philosophical Transactions of the Royal Society of London. Series B, Biological Sciences, 356*(1413), 1351–1361. doi:10.1098/rstb.2001.0955

Goddard, L., Dritschel, B., & Burton, A. (1996). Role of autobiographical memory in social problem solving and depression. *Journal of Abnormal Psychology, 105*(4), 609–616. doi:10.1037/0021-843X.105.4.609

Goddard, L., Dritschel, B., & Howlin, P. (2014). A preliminary study of gender differences in autobiographical memory in children with an autism spectrum disorder. *Journal of Autism & Developmental Disorders, 44*(9), 2087–2095. doi:10.1007/s10803-014-2109-7

Goddard, L., Howlin, P., Dritschel, B., & Patel, T. (2007). Autobiographical memory and social problem-solving in Asperger syndrome. *Journal of Autism & Developmental Disorders, 37*(2), 291–300. doi:10.1007/s10803-006-0168-0

Grainger, C., Williams, D. M., & Lind, S. E. (2014). Online action monitoring and memory for self-performed actions in autism spectrum disorder. *Journal of Autism & Developmental Disorders*, 1–14. doi:10.1007/s10803-013-1987-4

Grandin, T. (2006). *Thinking in pictures: My life with autism (expanded edition)*. New York, NY: Vintage.

Greene, J. D. W., Hodges, J. R., & Baddeley, A. (1995). Autobiographical memory and executive function in early dementia of Alzheimer type. *Neuropsychologia, 33*(12), 1647–1670. doi:10.1016/0028-3932(95)00046-1

Happé, F. G. E. (1995). The role of age and verbal ability in the theory of mind task performance of subjects with autism. *Child Development, 66*(3), 843–855. doi:10.2307/1131954

Hare, D. J., Mellor, C., & Azmi, S. (2007). Episodic memory in adults with autistic spectrum disorders: Recall for self- versus other-experienced events. *Research in Developmental Disabilities, 28*(3), 317–329. doi:10.1016/j.ridd.2006.03.003

Hayne, H. (2004). Infant memory development: Implications for childhood amnesia. *Developmental Review, 24*(1), 33–73. doi:10.1016/j.dr.2003.09.007

Hermelin, B., & O'Connor, N. (1967). Remembering of words by psychotic and subnormal children. *British Journal of Psychology, 58*(3), 213–218. doi:10.1111/j.2044-8295.1967.tb01075.x

Hill, E. L. (2004). Executive dysfunction in autism. *Trends in Cognitive Sciences, 8*(1), 26–32. doi:10.1016/j.tics.2003.11.003

Hill, E. L., & Bird, C. M. (2006). Executive processes in Asperger syndrome: Patterns of performance in a multiple case series. *Neuropsychologia, 44*(14), 2822–2835. doi:10.1016/j.neuropsychologia.2006.06.007

Hobson, R. P. (2002). *The cradle of thought*. London, England: Pan MacMillan.

Holbrook, M., & Schindler, R. (1989). Some exploratory findings on the development of musical taste. *Journal of Consumer Research, 16*, 119–124. doi:10.1086/209200

Holmes, A., & Conway, M. A. (1999). Generation identity and the reminiscence bump: Memories for public and private events. *Journal of Adult Development, 6*, 21–34. doi:10.1023/A:1021620224085

Kanner, L. (1943). Autistic disturbances of affective contact. *Nervous Child, 2*, 217–250.

Kirkovski, M., Enticott, P. G., Hughes, M. E., Rossell, S. L., & Fitzgerald, P. B. (2015). Atypical neural activity in males but not females with autism spectrum disorder. *Journal of Autism & Developmental Disorders*. doi:10.1007/s10803-015-2639-7

Klein, S. B., Chan, R. L., & Loftus, J. (1999). Independence of episodic and semantic self-knowledge: The case from autism. *Social Cognition, 17*(4), 413–436. doi: 10.1521/soco.1999.17.4.413

Lai, M. C., Lombardo, M. V, Pasco, G., Ruigrok, A. N. V., Wheelwright, S. J., Sadek, S. A., Charkrabarti, B., MRC AIMS Consortium, & Baron-Cohen, S. (2011). A behavioral comparison of male and female adults with high functioning autism spectrum conditions. *PloS One, 6*(6), e20835. doi:10.1371/journal.pone.0020835

Larsen, S. (1996). Memorable books: Recall of reading in its personal context. In M. McNealy & R. Kreuz (Eds.), *Empirical approaches to literature and aesthetics: Advances in discourse processes* (Vol. 52). Norwood, NJ: Ablex.

Lépine, R. I., Parrouillet, P., & Camos, V. (2005). What makes working memory spans so predictive of high-level cognition? *Psychonomic Bulletin & Review, 12*(1), 165–170. doi:10.3758/BF03196363

Lind, S. E. (2010). Memory and the self in autism: A review and theoretical framework. *Autism, 14*(5), 430–456. doi:10.1177/1362361309358700

Lind, S. E., & Bowler, D. M. (2009). Recognition memory, self-other source memory, and theory-of-mind in children with autism spectrum disorder. *Journal of Autism & Developmental Disorders, 39*(9), 1231–1239. doi:10.1007/s10803-009-0735-2

Lind, S. E., Williams, D. M., Bowler, D. M., & Peel, A. (2014). Episodic memory and episodic future thinking impairments in high-functioning autism spectrum disorder: An underlying difficulty with scene construction or self-projection? *Neuropsychology, 28*(1), 55–67. doi:10.1037/neu0000005

Lyons, V., & Fitzgerald, M. (2005). Early memory and autism. *Journal of Autism & Developmental Disorders, 35*(5), 683. doi:10.1007/s10803-005-0012-y

Maister, L., Simons, J. S., & Plaisted-Grant, K. (2013). Executive functions are employed to process episodic and relational memories in children with autism spectrum disorders. *Neuropsychology, 27*(6), 615–627. doi:10.1037/a0034492

Maras, K. L., & Bowler, D. M. (2010). The cognitive interview for eyewitnesses with autism spectrum disorder. *Journal of Autism & Developmental Disorders, 40*(11), 1350–1360. doi:10.1007/s10803-010-0997-8

Maras, K. L., & Bowler, D. M. (2011). Brief report: Schema consistent misinformation effects in eyewitnesses with autism spectrum disorder. *Journal of Autism & Developmental Disorders, 41*(6), 815–820. doi:10.1007/s10803-010-1089-5

Maras, K. L., & Bowler, D. M. (2012a). Context reinstatement effects on eyewitness memory in autism spectrum disorder. *British Journal of Psychology, 103*(3), 330–342. doi:10.1111/j.2044-8295.2011.02077.x

Maras, K. L., & Bowler, D. M. (2012b). Brief report: Suggestibility, compliance and psychological traits in high-functioning adults with autism spectrum disorder. *Research in Autism Spectrum Disorders, 6*(3), 1168–1175. doi:10.1016/j.rasd.2012.03.013

Maras, K. L., Gaigg, S. B., & Bowler, D. M. (2012). Memory for emotionally arousing events over time in autism spectrum disorder. *Emotion, 12*(5), 1118–1128. doi:10.1037/a0026679

Maras, K. L., & Bowler, D. M. (2014). Eyewitness testimony in autism spectrum disorder: A review. *Journal of Autism & Developmental Disorders, 44*, 2682–2697. doi:10.1007/s10803-012-1502-3

Maras, K. L., Memon, A., Lambrechts, A., & Bowler, D. M. (2013). Recall of a live and personally experienced eyewitness event by adults with autism spectrum disorder. *Journal of Autism & Developmental Disorders, 43*(8), 1798–1810. doi:10.1007/s10803-012-1729-z

Maras, K. L., Mulcahy, S., Memon, A., Picariello, F., & Bowler, D. M. (2014). Evaluating the effectiveness of the self-administered interview © for witnesses with autism spectrum disorder. *Applied Cognitive Psychology, 28*(5), 693–701. doi:10.1002/acp.3055

Mattison, M. L. A., Dando, C. J., & Ormerod, T. C. (2014). Sketching to remember: Episodic free recall task support for child witnesses and victims with autism spectrum disorder. *Journal of Autism & Developmental Disorders*. doi:10.1007/s10803-014-2335-z

Mazefsky, C. A., Herrington, J., Siegel, M., Scarpa, A., Maddox, B. B., Scahill, L., & White, S. W. (2013). The role of emotion regulation in autism spectrum disorder. *Journal of the American Academy of Child & Adolescent Psychiatry, 52*(7), 679–688. doi:10.1016/j.jaac.2013.05.006

McCrory, E., Henry, L. A., & Happé, F. (2007). Eye-witness memory and suggestibility in children with Asperger syndrome. *Journal of Child Psychology & Psychiatry, 48*(5), 482–489. doi:10.1111/j.1469-7610.2006.01715.x

Memon, A., Meissner, C. A., & Fraser, J. (2010). The cognitive interview: A meta-analytic review and study space analysis of the past 25 years. *Psychology, Public Policy, & Law, 16*(4), 340–372. doi:10.1037/a0020518

Ministry of Justice. (2011). *Achieving Best Evidence in Criminal Proceedings Guidance on interviewing victims and witnesses, and guidance on using special measures.* London: Ministry of Justice.

Moberly, N. J., & MacLeod, A. K. (2006). Goal pursuit, goal self-concordance, and the accessibility of autobiographical knowledge. *Memory*, *14*(7), 901–915. doi:10.1080/09658210600859517

Morton, J. (2004). *Understanding developmental disorders: A causal modelling approach.* Malden, MA: Blackwell Publishing.

Moscovitch, M. (1992). Memory and working-with-memory: A component process model based on modules and central systems. *Journal of Cognitive Neuroscience*, *4*, 257–267. doi:10.1162/jocn.1992.4.3.257

Mottron, L., & Burack, J. A. (2001). Enhanced perceptual functioning in the development of autism. In J. A. Burack, T. Charman, N. Yirmiya, & P. R. Zelazo (Eds.), *The development of autism: Perspectives from theory and research.* (pp. 131–148). Mahwah, NJ: Lawrence Erlbaum Associates Publishers.

Mottron, L., Dawson, M., Soulieres, I., Hubert, B., & Burack, J. (2006). Enhanced perceptual functioning in autism: An update, and eight principles of autistic perception. *Journal of Autism & Developmental Disorders*, *36*(1), 27–43. doi:10.1007/s10803-005-0040-7

Nelson, K. (1993). The psychological and social origins of autobiographical memory. *Psychological Science*, *4*(1), 7–14. doi:10.1111/j.1467-9280.1993.tb00548.x

North, A., Russell, A., & Gudjonsson, G. (2008). High functioning autism spectrum disorders: An investigation of psychological vulnerabilities during interrogative interview. *Journal of Forensic Psychiatry & Psychology*, *19*(3), 323–334. doi:10.1080/14789940701871621

Ozonoff, S., Pennington, B. F., & Rogers, S. J. (1991). Executive function deficits in high-functioning autistic individuals: Relationship to theory of mind. *Journal of Child Psychology & Psychiatry*, *32*(7), 1081–1105. Retrieved from 10.1111/j.1469-7610.1991.tb00351.x

Perner, J., & Ruffman, T. (1995). Episodic memory an autonoetic consciousness: Developmental evidence and a theory of childhood amnesia. *Journal of Experimental Child Psychology*, *59*(3), 516–548. doi:10.1006/jecp.1995.1024

Piefke, M., Weiss, P., Zilles, K., Markowitsch, H. J., & Fink, G. R. (2003). Differential remoteness and emotional tone modulate the neural correlates of autobiographical memory. *Brain*, *126*, 650–668. doi:10.1093/brain/awg064

Pillemer, D. (1992). Remembering personal circumstances: A functional analysis. In E. Winograd & U. Neisser (Eds.), *Affect and accuracy in recall: Studies of "flashbulb" memories* (pp. 236–264). New York, NY: Cambridge University Press.

Pillemer, D. (2003). Directive functions of autobiographical memory: The guiding power of the specific episode. *Memory*, *11*, 193–202. doi:10.1080/741938208

Pillemer, D., & White, S. (1989). Childhood events recalled by children and adults. In H. W. Reece (Ed.), *Advances in child development and behavior* (Vol. *21*, pp. 294–340). San Diego, CA: Academic Press.

Premack, D., & Woodruff, G. (1978). Does the chimpanzee have a theory of mind? *Behavioral & Brain Sciences*, *1*, 515–526. doi:10.1017/ S0140525X00076512

Prior, M., Dahlstrom, B., & Squires, T. L. (1990). Autistic children's knowledge of thinking and feeling states in other people. *Journal of Child Psychology & Psychiatry*, *31*(4), 587–601. doi:10.1111/j.1469-7610.1990.tb00799.x

Rajaram, S. (1993). Remembering and knowing: Two means of access to the personal past. *Memory & Cognition*, *21*(1), 89–102. doi:10.3758/BF03211168

Ros, L., Latorre, J. M., & Serrano, J. P. (2010). Working memory capacity and overgeneral autobiographical memory in young and older adults. *Aging, Neuropsychology, & Cognition*, *17*, 89–107. doi:10.1080/13825580903042650

Sehulster, J. (1996). In my era: Evidence for the perception of a special period of the past. *Memory*, *4*, 145–158. doi: 10.1080/096582196389013

Singer, J. (2004). Narrative identity and meaning making across the adult lifespan: An introduction. *Journal of Personality*, *72*(3), 437–459. doi:10.1111/j.0022-3506.2004.00268.x
Singer, J., & Salovey, A. (1993). *The remembered self.* New York, NY: The Free Press.
South, M., Stephenson, K. G., Nielson, C. A., Maisel, M., Top, D. N., & Kirwan, C. B. (2015). Overactive pattern separation memory associated with negative emotionality in adults diagnosed with autism spectrum disorder. *Journal of Autism & Developmental Disorders*, *45*(11), 3458–3467. doi:10.1007/s10803-015-2547-x
Tanweer, T., Rathbone, C. J., & Souchay, C. (2010). Autobiographical memory, autonoetic consciousness, and identity in Asperger syndrome. *Neuropsychologia*, *48*, 900–908. doi:10.1016/j.neuropsychologia.2009.11.007
Tulving, E. (1985). Memory and consciousness. *Canadian Psychology*, *26*(1), 1–12. doi:10.1037/h0080017
Usher, J. A., & Neisser, U. (1993). Childhood amnesia and the beginnings of memory for four early life events. *Journal of Experimental Psychology: General*, *122*(2), 155–165. doi:10.1037/0096-3445.122.2.155
Webster, J. (1995). Adult age differences in reminiscence functions. In B. Haight & J. Webster (Eds.), *The art and science of reminiscing: Theory, research, methods and applications.* Washington, DC: Taylor & Francis.
White, S. J. (2013). The Triple I Hypothesis: Taking another('s) perspective on executive dysfunction in autism. *Journal of Autism & Developmental Disorders*, *43*(1), 114–121. doi:10.1007/s10803-012-1550-8
White, S. J., Burgess, P. W., & Hill, E. L. (2009). Impairments on "open-ended" executive function tests in autism. *Autism Research*, *2*(3), 138–147. doi:10.1002/aur.78
White, S. W., Mazefsky, C. A., Dichter, G. S., Chiu, P. H., Richey, J. A., & Ollendick, T. H. (2014). Social-cognitive, physiological, and neural mechanisms underlying emotion regulation impairments: Understanding anxiety in autism spectrum disorder. *International Journal of Developmental Neuroscience*, *39*, 22–36. doi:10.1016/j.ijdevneu.2014.05.012
Williams, J. M. G. (1996). Autobiographical memory in depression. In D. C. Rubin (Ed.), *Remembering our past: Studies in autobiographical memory* (pp. 244–270). Cambridge, England: Cambridge University Press.
Williams, J. M. G., & Broadbent, K. (1986). Autobiographical memory in suicide attempters. *Journal of Abnormal Psychology*, *95*(2), 144–149. doi:10.1037/0021-843X.95.2.144
Williams, J. M. G. (2006). Capture and rumination, functional avoidance, and executive control (CaRFAX): Three processes that underlie overgeneral memory. *Cognition & Emotion*, *20*, 548–568. doi:10.1080/02699930500450465
Williams, D., & Happé, F. (2009). Pre-conceptual aspects of self-awareness in autism spectrum disorder: The case of action-monitoring. *Journal of Autism & Developmental Disorders*, *39*(2), 251–259. doi:10.1007/s10803-008-0619-x
Wilson, A., & Ross, M. (2003). The identity function of autobiographical memory: Time is on our side. *Memory*, *11*(2), 137–149. doi:10.1080/741938210
Zalla, T., Daprati, E., Sav, A.-M., Chaste, P., Nico, D., & Leboyer, M. (2010). Memory for self-performed actions in individuals with Asperger syndrome. *PloS One*, *5*(10), e13370. doi:10.1371/journal.pone.0013370

9

Eyewitness Memory Abilities in Typically Developing Children

Yoojin Chae, Sue D. Hobbs, and Daniel Bederian-Gardner

To understand the eyewitness memory abilities of children with autism, it is important to bear in mind the memory accuracies and inaccuracies of typically developing children. There have been heated debates about children's abilities to remember previous events and provide accurate and complete reports (McWilliams, Bederian-Gardner, Hobbs, Bakanosky, & Goodman, 2012). Although concerns that children are highly suggestible and inaccurate are long-standing, such concerns were heightened in recent years due to high-profile legal cases of alleged sexual abuse. In some of these cases (e.g., the McMartin Preschool case in Manhattan Beach, California), children were aggressively and repeatedly questioned using highly suggestive techniques that might have caused false reports (Garven, Wood, Malpass, & Shaw, 1998). Such problematic interview practices can not only result in false allegations of sexual abuse, but moreover, these practices also increase suspicions about the inaccuracy of children's eyewitness testimony generally. At the same time, there have been growing concerns over children's accurate testimony not being believed by fact finders in legal contexts or by adults responsible for children's well-being (e.g., Hobbs et al., 2013; McWilliams et al., 2012).

In a concerted effort to understand children's abilities to provide accurate reports, research on children's eyewitness memory has dramatically increased over the last few decades. Factors found to be associated with children's memory and suggestibility include types of to-be-remembered events, child interviewees' individual characteristics (e.g., cognitive skills, attachment, temperament), and situational factors (e.g., types and linguistic complexity of questions asked, repeated questioning/interviewing, rapport building). In this chapter, we address these factors as they pertain to eyewitness capabilities of typically developing children.

The Wiley Handbook of Memory, Autism Spectrum Disorder, and the Law, First Edition.
Edited by Jonni L. Johnson, Gail S. Goodman, and Peter C. Mundy.

Types of to-be-remembered events

Children's testimony is typically required for emotionally distressing incidents. Psycho-legal scholars have thus investigated whether children's memory for emotional experiences would be different from their memory for neutral experiences. Developmental patterns in memory for emotional events are not significantly different from those in memory for neutral events. That is, children's event memory improves as they develop regardless of emotional valence of the events (e.g., Peterson, 2012; Peterson & Whalen, 2001). However, children generally remember emotional events better than neutral ones. In a study by Fivush, Sales, Goldberg, Bahrick, and Parker (2004), children who experienced a hurricane when they were 3 to 4 years old were interviewed a few months later and again six years later. All children remembered the hurricane and its aftermath in vivid detail, even after a delay of six years. Also, in a laboratory study using aversive stimuli, 9- to 12-year-old children were presented with emotionally negative and neutral images, and asked to recognize these images one week later (Cordón, Pipe, Sayfan, Melinder, & Goodman, 2013). They remembered aversive images significantly better than neutral images. In another study using emotional stimuli, first-, third-, and fifth-grade children participated in a storytelling task involving emotional and neutral stories (Davidson, Luo, & Burden, 2001). Emotional behaviors depicted in the stories concerned happiness, sadness, and anger. Children remembered emotional behaviors significantly better than neutral behaviors, regardless of the valence of the emotions (see also Christianson, 1992; Goodman, Quas, & Ogle, 2009).

However, it is not always the case that children remember emotional events and stimuli better than those that are neutral. A variety of factors can influence children's memories for emotional events and stimuli. These include child interviewees' individual characteristics and interviewer factors that are discussed in the next section, along with the amount of stress children experienced during the event, whether central or peripheral details are being recalled, and the distinctiveness and personal significance of to-be-remembered information. These factors are interrelated.

The cue utilization hypothesis (Easterbrook, 1959) suggests that when exposed to personal threat or negative emotional stimuli, an individual's attention narrows to focus on the negative details central to the event. As a result, memory for peripheral details suffers. However, excessive distress can severely impair an individual's ability to process and encode emotional details, even resulting in memory impairments for central details (Deffenbacher, Bornstein, Penrod, & McGorty, 2004). This is consistent with the Yerkes-Dodson law (1908) that arousal and memory have a curvilinear relation, such that memory performance increases as arousal increases up to a point, but then decreases as arousal continues to increase. Research tends to support this theory. For example, in a study by Kensinger, Garoff-Eaton, and Schacter (2007), children who viewed emotionally negative and neutral pictures remembered more peripheral details in neutral pictures than in negative pictures, and remembered negatively arousing details better than neutral details. However, in a study on children's removal from home by the child protection services, children who demonstrated more distress during removal remembered fewer central details compared with children who demonstrated less distress (Baugerud & Melinder, 2011). It is reasonable to expect that removal from home would be much more distressing to children than viewing negative pictures would be.

The influence of distinctiveness was evident in a longitudinal study by Peterson (2012). In that study, 2- to 13-year-old children's memories for traumatic injuries and subsequent emergency room visits were examined. When children were interviewed five years later, all children who were 2 years old or older at the time of their injuries remembered the injuries nearly as well as they had five years previously. However, children's memory reports for the hospital treatment decreased in both accuracy and completeness. It is likely that because the hospital visits were similar to other doctors' appointments, they were not distinctive enough for children to remember clearly five years later, whereas the injuries themselves remained distinctive.

Interviewee factors

Developmental differences in memory and suggestibility

Age and/or development play a crucial role in children's memory, both at the time of encoding when an event occurs and at the time of retrieval when the stored information is recounted. In fact, age is an overarching predictor of children's memory performance. Age is related to or influences many factors involved in memory. For example, as children develop, so do their abilities to encode and store information (Brainerd & Ornstein, 1991; Saxe, Whitfield-Gabrieli, Scholz, & Pelphrey, 2009) and their abilities to report more overall information and details of their experiences (e.g., Bjorklund, Dukes, & Brown, 2008; Howe, 2011; Peterson, 2011).

Children's memory and suggestibility are often inversely related. That is, as memory abilities increase, suggestibility typically decreases. Generally, younger children, such as 3- to 5-year-olds, remember events less accurately and are more suggestible than older children and adults (Chae, Goodman, Eisen, & Qin, 2011; Eisen, Goodman, Qin, Davis, & Crayton, 2007; Hershkowitz & Terner, 2007; Malloy & Quas, 2009).

However, additional factors should be considered when discussing the reliability of children's eyewitness testimony. These include individual differences in cognitive abilities and socioemotional characteristics. We discuss these next.

Individual differences in memory development

The ability of children to correctly remember events they witnessed not only depends on the nature of the event, or solely on their age, but on their individual characteristics. These internal factors may be cognitive, such as executive function skills, or social, such as attachment. Research on the role of individual differences in predicting children's eyewitness memory informs the science regarding which of these factors increases or decreases memory accuracy. Such research also elucidates the reasons as to why there is inconsistency in the literature concerning how other variables, such as stress, influence memory. Much of the research on children's eyewitness memory has also examined suggestibility because the accuracy of their reports is not only the result of memory strength, but also the result of how vulnerable children are to suggestive interview (e.g., Blandón-Gitlin & Pezdek, 2009).

Cognitive factors. Individual differences are apparent in children's cognitive abilities, such as language and narrative skills and executive function, which have been identified as important predictors of children's eyewitness memory abilities. In this section, we discuss each of these cognitive individual-difference factors and review empirical findings on their contributions to children's memory and suggestibility.

Language skill is an important component of eyewitness memory because recounting events accurately requires understanding the questions asked and retelling what happened. Therefore, it is not surprising that children with higher language ability have more accurate memory (Burgwyn-Bales, Baker-Ward, Gordon, & Ornstein, 2001; Chae & Ceci, 2005; Young, Powell, & Dudgeon, 2003). Children with lower language ability may have difficulty verbally rehearsing an event and be less able to comprehend the interview context and the interviewer's questions. Psycho-legal scholars have thus investigated the effects of various interviewing strategies that can help children with language deficits overcome difficulties in recall. Studies have shown that interviewing techniques that were developed to scaffold children's performance indeed have beneficial effects on their eyewitness memory. For example, when interviewers used language that is easily comprehensible and syntactically noncomplex, young preschoolers' resistance to suggestive questions increased (e.g., Imhoff & Baker-Ward, 1999). In addition, a verbal labels procedure where children are asked in an open-ended manner to report information that pertains to story grammar categories, such as participants, actions, settings, and conversation/affective state (e.g., "Tell me more about the people who were there and how they looked" or "Tell me more about what the people said"), was found to be effective in improving children's performance (e.g., Brown & Pipe, 2003). Specifically, children who were given the verbal labels interview spontaneously produced more information and answer direct questions more accurately, compared with their counterparts in control condition (Kulkofsky, 2010). The beneficial effects of the verbal labels procedure were particularly pronounced for children with lower (vs. higher) vocabulary skills (Chae, Kulkofsky, Deberan, Wang, & Hart, 2014). Hence, such interviewing techniques seem to help reduce the negative impact of language deficits on children's memory.

Children's narrative skills are closely related to their language capabilities and predict both memory and suggestibility, even with age controlled. In research by Kulkofsky and Klemfuss (2008), preschool children who narrated a past event with greater volume, complexity, and cohesion were less suggestible about the event, compared with children who provided lower-quality narratives (but see Kulkofsky, Wang, & Ceci, 2008). In research with older children (Morris, Baker-Ward, & Bauer, 2010; Peterson, Morris, Baker-Ward, & Flynn, 2014), the coherence of children's narratives about personal experiences significantly predicted the likelihood that the memory would persist over the next two years. These findings were significant, even when age (also associated with narrative quality) was controlled in the statistical analyses.

Children's eyewitness memory has also been related to executive function, which refers to a multifaceted construct including problem solving ability, planning, inhibition of automatic and prepotent responses, sustained and selective attention, working memory, suppressing imitative behaviors, and shifting behavioral responses when task demands change (Garon, Bryson, & Smith, 2008; Lehto, Juujarvi, Kooistra, & Pulkkinen, 2003; Miyake et al., 2000). Different dimensions of executive functioning are intercorrelated. Theoretically, the ability to produce accurate memory is thought to involve executive function skills. For example, children with limited ability to inhibit prepotent responses or task-irrelevant thoughts may have difficulty attending to event details because they are distracted by irrelevant information (Harnishfeger & Bjorklund, 1994). Poorly encoded information may lead to weaker memory traces.

In addition, such children are likely to make memory errors during retrieval due to their tendency to produce immediate and impulsive statements before fully comprehending interview questions or conducting thorough memory searches (Alexander et al., 2002). They may not pay close attention to an interviewer's exact questions (Schaaf, Alexander, & Goodman, 2008).

Deficits in executive function may further influence children's vulnerability to interviewer pressure and suggestive questions (e.g., Karpinski & Scullin, 2009; Roberts & Powell, 2005). Children with less advanced executive function, who tend to respond quickly and without reflection to questions, are more likely to acquiesce to social pressure during forensic interviews and respond affirmatively to every question to please the interviewer instead of discounting misleading information. In contrast, children with well-developed executive function may eschew saying the first things that come to their mind. The ability to inhibit responses long enough to reflect on discrepancies between an interviewer's suggestions and their memory for an event may help children deny inaccurate inferences made by an interviewer.

A number of empirical studies have examined executive function skills in relation to children's memory and suggestibility. In a study by Karpinski and Scullin (2009), 3- to 5-year-old children were interviewed about a magic show in a highly suggestive manner. When age was controlled, children who obtained higher scores on planning (e.g., moving balls to make a tower look like a picture), working memory (e.g., recalling digit sequences), and inhibition (e.g., saying *day* when shown a moon card and *night* when shown a sun card) were less suggestible. Caprin and colleagues (2016) also showed that 6- to 11-year-olds' memory and suggestibility for a story about a conflict event were significantly associated with verbal working memory. Specifically, children with better working memory spontaneously recounted more correct information during free recall and were more accurate in answering specific nonleading questions concerning the story. In addition, such children were less likely to assent to misleading questions and less likely to change their responses following negative feedback from an interviewer. Children's ability to inhibit prepotent responses as measured by the day/night task significantly predicted fewer memory errors about personally significant life experiences as well, such as a painful medical procedure (Alexander et al., 2002; Schaaf et al., 2008). Further research should empirically identify the mechanisms whereby executive function skills contribute to children's eyewitness memory and specify beneficial techniques that can be used for children with deficits in executive function. For example, if limited ability to inhibit prepotent responses or impulsivity explain increased memory errors and suggestibility, children can be trained on delaying answers and reflect on interview questions to enhance their accuracy.

Socioemotional factors. Individual differences in socioemotional factors can also strongly affect the accuracy of children's eyewitness memory reports. Child memory is believed to be associated with individual differences in children's and parents' socioemotional characteristics. A prime example of such characteristics would be attachment. Children's attachment (Alexander et al., 2010; Belsky, Spritz, & Crnic, 1996; Chae & Goodman et al., 2014), and parents' attachment (Alexander, Goodman, Schaaf, Edelstein, Quas, & Shaver, 2002; Goodman, Quas, Batterman-Faunce, Riddlesberger, & Kuhn, 1997) have been related to children's memory. Alexander and colleagues (2010), for example, found that 8- to 12-year-old children's attachment security predicted more accurate memory for negative picture-story stimuli (e.g., separation). In a study by Chae, Goodman, and colleagues (2014), 3- to 6-year-old children's representations of close relationships were assessed using the Attachment Story Completion Task (ASCT; Bretherton, Ridgeway, & Cassidy, 1990). Children with more positive representations of parents (e.g., as protective, warm, affectionate) were more accurate in their memory about a painful medical procedure.

Adult attachment orientations can influence how parents interact with their children, especially during events that are traumatic or upsetting. For example, mothers with insecure-avoidant attachment are unlikely to comfort their children during upsetting events due to their efforts to keep their own attachment systems from activating. Children who do not have the support of parents must contend with the upsetting events along with lack of comfort and support. Combined, these increase the cognitive load and decrease the children's abilities to remember the upsetting events clearly in the future. Alexander and colleagues (2002) reported that an interaction between parental attachment avoidance and children's distress level during inoculations was a significant predictor of children's memory: Increased distress predicted increased memory accuracy for children whose parents scored low on avoidant attachment, but not for children whose parents scored high on avoidant attachment (see also Chae, Goodman et al., 2014). In a study by Goodman and colleagues (1997), children were interviewed about a Voiding Cystourethrogram Fluoroscopy (VCUG) examination, an invasive and stressful medical procedure involving urethral catheterization. Children whose parents were rated as more securely attached produced significantly fewer memory errors regarding the examination than did children whose parents were more insecurely attached (see also Quas et al., 1999). Taken as a whole, studies on attachment and children's memory point to the complex nature of the relation between the two variables. Attachment may directly influence memory accuracy in children's memory reports, but may also indirectly affect the accuracy through emotionality of the event and/or the amount of distress felt by the children. Much more research is needed to understand the relations of both child attachment and parental attachment with child memory for stressful and nonstressful events.

Attachment is not the only mechanism through which parents have been posited to influence child memory. Burgwyn-Bailes and colleagues (2001) investigated parenting style in relation to 3- to 7-year-old children's memory about surgeries they had received. Results indicated that children of more (compared with less) traditional parents, that is, parents who focus on obedience and respect for parental authority, recalled less information about their surgeries when interviewed one year post-surgery.

One mechanism through which attachment and parenting style affect children's memory is via parent-child conversations. Parents who are securely attached are more likely to provide a supportive environment for their children in which to discuss stressful events (Alexander et al., 2002). These children therefore have more experiences recounting such events and are thus better prepared to answer questions during memory interviews. Multiple studies have found significant relations between parent-child reminiscing conversations and children's memory (e.g., Fivush, Haden, & Reese, 2006; Reese, Haden, & Fivush, 1993). In these studies, the pattern of results indicates that children are likely to report more information if they have a history of communicating with their parents regarding stressful events.

Child temperament is another individual-difference factor that has been posited to relate to memory and suggestibility. For example, as noted by Chae and Ceci (2005), the level of children's inhibition might affect the children's willingness to respond during interviews. In their study, second-grade boys who were rated as shyer by their teachers reported less information spontaneously, compared with less shy boys. Endres, Poggenpohl, and Erben (1999) found that shyness predicted children's suggestibility as well: Shyer children were more suggestible in response to misleading yes-no questions than were less shy children. Another aspect of temperament, approach/withdrawal (i.e., the tendency to enter into new social situations readily vs. reluctantly) predicted younger children's (aged 3 years) recall to open-ended questions, but did not predict older children's (aged 5 years) recall (Gordon et al., 1993). In the same study, the 5-year-old children who expressed negative emotions more (vs. less) intensely produced more correct recall. However, Burgwyn-Bailes and colleagues (2001) did not uncover any significant relations between emotional intensity and memory. Emotionality and recall were not significantly associated in the study by Chae and Ceci (2005) either. Given the complex nature of the relations between the factors that compose child temperament (e.g., inhibition/shyness, approach/withdrawal, emotionality) and the factors involved in memory (e.g., open-ended recall, responses to yes-no questions, suggestibility), it is not surprising that the results have so far been inconsistent. Overall, there is evidence that child temperament does relate to memory, but that close attention must be payed to the aspect of memory being measured.

Situational factors

In addition to child interviewees' individual characteristics, adult interviewer factors and interviewing contexts also influence children's eyewitness memory (Larsson & Lamb, 2009). Interviewers need to elicit accurate and detailed information from children without evoking false reports (Lyon, 2014). A number of situational factors, including question types, linguistic complexity, repeated questioning/interviewing, and interviewer support and rapport building have been implicated as important predictors of the reliability of children's reports. We next discuss how each of these factors contributes to children's memory and suggestibility.

Question types

When young children are asked to produce free narratives or are given general open-ended prompts (e.g., "Tell me everything" or "What happened next?"), they tend to report relatively brief and sketchy accounts. Although their accuracy levels are usually high, their narratives lack details (for a review, see Pipe, Lamb, Orbach, & Esplin, 2004). Because children appear to have difficulty utilizing free-recall questions as effective retrieval cues to recount details, forensic interviewers often turn to direct questions (e.g., "What color hair did he have?") to elicit more information (Lamb et al., 1996; Orbach et al., 2000; Sternberg, Lamb, Esplin, & Baradaran, 1999; Sternberg et al., 1997). However, children typically give less accurate responses when answering such questions than when answering free-recall questions (e.g., Kulkofsky et al., 2008; Peterson, Dowden, & Tobin, 1999). Particularly, when asked forced-choice questions that require respondents to select between the options implied by interviewers (e.g., "Was it winter or spring?") or yes-no questions (e.g., "Did he touch your bottom?"), children are more likely to produce erroneous information (e.g., Lamb, Orbach, Hershkowitz, Horowitz, & Abbott, 2007). Such questions are considered leading or misleading. Studies have consistently shown that forced-choice and yes-no questions can bias children's responses. For example, when two-option, forced-choice questions were used, children are likely to choose the second option, which is called a "recency tendency," and this tendency is stronger for younger children (Mehrani & Peterson, 2015). Furthermore, children at times show a response bias of saying "yes" to yes-no questions (Rocha, Marche, & Briere, 2013). Although interviewers are advised to avoid forced-choice and yes-no questions, they still frequently use such questions with young children in forensic settings (Lamb, Orbach, Hershkowitz, Esplin, & Horowitz, 2007). For this reason, interviewing techniques to maximize the amount of information elicited from free-recall memory have been developed (e.g., a structured investigative protocol by researchers at the National Institute of Child Health and Human Development; NICHD).

Linguistic complexity

Another important factor that can influence the credibility of children's testimony concerns the linguistic complexity of questions posed by interviewers in a forensic context. Interviewers should match their language to children's level of functioning. However, forensic professionals who infrequently work with child witnesses are unlikely to ask developmentally appropriate questions (for a review, see Ceci, Markle, & Chae, 2005). Analyses of criminal court transcripts revealed that defense lawyers tend to use semantically and syntactically complex and unfamiliar language that children have difficulty understanding, grammatically confusing questions, and credibility-challenging questions (Davies & Seymour, 1998; Zajac, Gross, & Hayne, 2003). Young children are frequently asked lengthy questions including embedded clauses, difficult vocabulary, double negatives, and multiple prepositional phrases (Brennan & Brennan, 1988; Walker, 1994). In addition, preschool-aged children may not comprehend the meanings of common legal terms, such as *court*, *swear*, and *oath* (Saywitz, 1987; Warren-Leubecker, Tate, Hinton, & Ozbek, 1989). Even 11-year-old children do not fully understand such legal terms as *testify*, *jury*, and *attorney* that are commonly used in court (Saywitz, Jaenicke, & Camparo, 1990).

When questions are phrased in language beyond children's comprehension, children tend to try to answer the questions anyway and are as likely to respond incorrectly as correctly (Carter, Bottoms, & Levine, 1996; Saywitz, Snyder, & Nathanson, 1999; Zajac et al., 2003). However, children's performance can be significantly enhanced by facilitating their comprehension monitoring and response strategies (Saywitz et al., 1999). Specifically, when children were instructed to verbalize their lack of comprehension (e.g., saying, "I don't get it") before interviews and given the rationale that this response could elicit a more understandable question from an adult, they answered interview questions more correctly. Furthermore, when children practiced detecting and responding to incomprehensible questions with feedback, modelling, and praise in addition to receiving the instructions and rationale, they demonstrated even better interview performance. Therefore, although syntactic constructions and vocabulary that child witnesses do not fully understand may undermine their testimony accuracy, comprehension monitoring instructions and preparation can facilitate their performance.

Repeated questioning

In forensic settings, child witnesses are regularly exposed to repeated questions within a single interview. Forensic interviewers repeat questions to make their request clear, to follow-up ambiguous or unclear responses given by children, to encourage children who are anxious or reluctant to disclose, or to challenge children's previous responses

(Andrews & Lamb, 2014; La Rooy & Lamb, 2011). When a question is repeated, children may inappropriately infer that the interviewer wants to obtain additional information or that their initial answers are unsatisfactory or incorrect (Howie, Kurukulasuriya, Nash, & Marsh, 2009; Howie, Nash, Kurukulasuriya, & Bowman, 2012; Melinder, Scullin, Gravvold, & Iversen, 2007). Children may then reconsider and modify their answers. Repeated closed-ended questions such as "Are you sure you're telling me the truth?" are especially risky and more likely to elicit inconsistent and inaccurate information, compared with open-ended prompts such as "When did you say he hit you?" (Lamb & Fauchier, 2001; Memon & Vartoukian, 1996; Zajac et al., 2003; but see Quas, Davis, Goodman, & Myers, 2007). Although closed-ended question repetition can detrimentally affect the consistency of children's responses, repeated open-ended questioning can enhance children's reports. For example, when children were interviewed about a staged conflict event with repeated questioning, their recall improved on second questioning with open-ended prompts, whereas their accuracy deteriorated somewhat on repetition of closed-ended prompts (Memon & Vartoukian, 1996). Unfortunately, during forensic interviews with children, questions are most often repeated using closed-ended prompts that are likely to challenge children's previous responses rather than open-ended prompts that are used for clarification (Andrews & Lamb, 2014).

There are a handful of field studies in which transcripts of real forensic interviews with alleged child victims of sexual abuse were examined. La Rooy and Lamb (2011) found that, although most of the time interviewers repeated questions to challenge a previous response, children repeated their earlier answers 54% of the time and elaborated on what they had said previously 27% of the time. They contradicted themselves only 7% of the time. Similarly, Andrews and Lamb (2014) demonstrated that children alleging sexual abuse typically repeated or elaborated on their previous responses and seldom contradicted themselves, although closed-ended suggestive prompts (e.g., "Did that really happen?") were more likely to elicit self-contradictions (see also Lamb & Fauchier, 2001). In addition, the rate of self-contradictions increased dramatically as repetition frequency increased (Andrews, Lamb, & Lyon, 2015). Overall, findings from experimental and field studies suggest that repeated questions do not necessarily have an adverse effect on children's accuracy. Forensic interviewers should be given guidance on the appropriate use of repeated questions with children.

Repeated interviewing

Repetition can occur across interviews as well as within interviews. When children provide testimonial statements about a crime they witnessed or experienced, they might be questioned about the target event on multiple occasions. Repeated interviews are often conducted particularly when child witnesses disclose no relevant information or a limited amount of information in their prior interviews (Waterhouse, Ridley, Bull, La Rooy, & Wilcock, 2016).

Considerable controversy exists about how repeated interviews affect the accuracy of children's reports. Some researchers raised concerns regarding repeated interviewing based on their empirical findings that exposure to multiple interviews can make children's statements unreliable. In a study by Bruck, Ceci, and Hembrooke (2002), preschool children were interviewed five times about true and false events. The first interview was conducted in a neutral, nonleading manner and the other four interviews were conducted in a highly suggestive manner, each separated by one week. It was found that repeated suggestive interviews influenced the rate of assents over time: Children's false reports increased as a function of repeated interviewing. Peterson, Moores, and White (2001) examined consistency and accuracy of children's reports across multiple interviews. Children were interviewed four times about an injury that necessitated a trip to a hospital emergency room, namely, at 1 week, 6 months, 1 year, and 2 years, in a neutral manner. They were aged 2–13 years at time of injury. Children mostly provided the same information at each interview, displaying high consistency. Also, new information that was introduced after 6 months was reliably more accurate than chance. However, new information introduced at one or two years post-injury was just as likely to be inaccurate as accurate (except for 12- and 13-year-olds). Hence, according to this study's findings, new information introduced by young children after repeated interviews and after a long delay seems to have a relatively high probability of being inaccurate.

However, other researchers demonstrated beneficial effects of repeated interviews on the amount of children's reports. Waterhouse et al. (2016) examined the transcripts of first and second field interviews with 3- to 14-year-olds who were alleged child abuse victims. The majority of the details recounted by the children in second interviews were new and consistent with their prior testimony, implying that they might have "reminisced" through repeated interviews or become more willing to disclose traumatic events. Another field study with alleged child abuse victims found that increased production of new forensically relevant details in repeated interviews was particularly marked for younger children (5- to 10-year-olds) than older children (11- to 14-year-olds) and for children who had provided poor narratives in their first interviews (Katz & Hershkowitz, 2012). These findings support the use of repeated interviews to elicit further recall from children. A laboratory study by Quas et al. (2007) further showed that repeated interviews do not necessarily increase children's propensity to error. Preschool children experienced a play event and then were exposed either to three interviews, each separated by one week, or to one interview following a three-week delay. The children were questioned by either a suggestive interviewer or an unbiased interviewer. Children who were interviewed once in three weeks by a suggestive interviewer made the most errors. Children who were interviewed repeatedly were more accurate in their responses and less likely to make false reports, regardless of whether the interviews were suggestive or unbiased. These findings, consistent with the study by Peterson et al. (2001), suggest that repeated interviews that occur a short time after a target event do not cause increased errors. Instead, repeated interviews appear to serve as reminder cues to strengthen the memory of children who rehearsed the event each week. Factors that varied across the studies, such as delay and biased interviewing, should be considered to explain contradictory findings on the effects on repeated interviews on children's memory accuracy (for a review, see Goodman & Quas, 2008).

Rapport building and support

Many suspected victims undergoing forensic investigations may not disclose abuse due to anxiety and discomfort. Children who experienced sexual abuse perpetrated by family members are particularly reluctant to report their painful experiences (e.g., London, Bruck, Ceci, & Shuman, 2005; London, Bruck, Wright, & Ceci, 2008). It is of paramount concern to provide emotional support for such children so that they can overcome their distress and make valid allegations of abuse (for a review, see Saywitz, Larson, Hobbs, & Wells, 2015).

Field studies have documented the contribution of forensic interviewers' support and rapport building to increasing the richness of the testimony children provide.

Using transcripts of forensic interviews, Hershkowitz, Lamb, Katz, and Malloy (2015) explored the role of enhanced rapport building and supportive interviewing techniques in helping suspected child victims of intrafamilial abuse become less reluctant and more cooperative during forensic interviews. Half of the children were interviewed using the revised NICHD investigative interview protocol that emphasized rapport building and nonsuggestive support, whereas the others were interviewed using the standard NICHD protocol. In the revised NICHD protocol, interviewers express interest in children's personal experiences during the rapport-building phase (e.g., "I really want to know you better"), use the children's names, echo children's feelings, acknowledge such feelings, and explore them (e.g., "Tell me more about [the feeling]"). They also use positive reinforcement of children's efforts (e.g., "Thank you for sharing that with me") and expressions of empathy regarding the interview experience (e.g., "I know it is a long interview"). Children interviewed using the revised protocol showed reduced reluctance (e.g., fewer omissions, less resistance, fewer denials) throughout the interview, which in turn, predicted increased production of forensically relevant details. Similarly, Hershkowitz, Lamb, and Katz (2014) found that children suspected of having been abused by family members were more likely to make allegations when the revised protocol rather than the standard protocol was employed. All cases were corroborated by independent external evidence, including suspects' admissions, disinterested eyewitness testimony, and medical evidence. Hershkowitz (2009) additionally reported that the beneficial effects of interviewer's support and rapport building on the amount of forensic details about the alleged crimes were especially marked for less talkative children who might be in special need of support and rapport with interviewers.

In sum, existing field studies conducted with real forensic interviews imply that the provision of emotional support and better rapport building help children to cope with their distress and disclose traumatic experiences. These findings are consistent with laboratory analog studies showing that, compared with nonsupportive interviewers, supportive interviewers are more likely to obtain accurate reports from children (e.g., Bottoms, Quas, & Davis, 2007; Davis & Bottoms, 2002). It is important that children are interviewed in supportive conditions so they can overcome reluctance and feel comfortable enough to discuss painful experiences.

Conclusion

This chapter reviews a variety of factors associated with typically developing children's eyewitness abilities. Individual and situational factors identified thus far provide insight into potential sources of variability in the amount and accuracy of children's testimonial statements and help us learn about the complicated nature of memory and suggestibility. Further research that can precisely identify the context and conditions in which those factors contribute to children's eyewitness memory is warranted.

A detailed understanding of these individual and situational characteristics has important applied implications for legal, mental health, and social service professionals who interview and evaluate children's statements. As a substantiated number of children are brought to the attention of child protective services where their accounts serve as forensic evidence, it is crucial to ensure that interviews with children are conducted in appropriate contexts using up-to-date techniques. Children should be questioned in a manner consistent with their individual needs. This involves specifying and developing effective interviewing strategies that can maximize the quantity and accuracy of information provided by children in light of the children's characteristics.

References

Alexander, K. W., Goodman, G. S., Schaaf, J. M., Edelstein, R. S., Quas, J. A., & Shaver, P. R. (2002). The role of attachment and cognitive inhibition in children's memory and suggestibility for a stressful event. *Journal of Experimental Child Psychology*, *83*(4), 262–290. doi:10.1016/S0022-0965(02)00149-2

Alexander, K. W., O'Hara, K. D., Bortfeld, H. V., Anderson, S. J., Newton, E. K., & Kraft, R. H. (2010). Memory for emotional experiences in the context of attachment and social interaction style. *Cognitive Development*, *25*, 325–338. doi:10.1016/j.cogdev.2010.08.002

Andrews, S. J., & Lamb, M. E. (2014). The effects of age and delay on responses to repeated questions in forensic interviews with children alleging sexual abuse. *Law & Human Behavior*, *38*, 171–180.

Andrews, S. J., Lamb, M. E., & Lyon, T. D. (2015). The effects of question repetition on responses when prosecutors and defense attorneys question children alleging sexual abuse in court. *Law & Human Behavior*, *39*, 559–570.

Baugerud, G. A., & Melinder, A. (2011). Maltreated children's memory of stressful removals from their biological parents. *Applied Cognitive Psychology*, *26*, 261–270. doi:10.1002/acp.1817

Belsky, J., Spritz, B., & Crnic, K. (1996). Infant attachment security and affective-cognitive information processing at age 3. *Psychological Science*, *7*, 111–114. doi:10.1111/j.1467-9280.1996.tb00339.x

Bjorklund, D. F., Dukes, C., & Brown, R. D. (2008). The development of memory strategies. In N. Cowan, & C. Hulme (Eds.), *The development of memory in childhood* (pp. 145–169). New York, NY: Psychology Press Ltd.

Blandón-Gitlin, I., & Pezdek, K. (2009). Children's memory in forensic contexts. In B. L. Bottoms, C. J. Nadjowski, & G. S. Goodman (Eds.), *Children as victims, witnesses, and offenders: Psychological science and the law* (pp. 57–80). New York, NY: The Guilford Press.

Bottoms, B. L., Quas, J. A., & Davis, S. L. (2007). The influence of the interviewer-provided social support on children's suggestibility, memory, and disclosures. In M. E. Pipe, M. E. Lamb, Y. Orbach, & A. C. Cederborg (Eds.), *Child sexual abuse: Disclosure, delay, and denial* (pp. 135–157). Mahwah, NJ: Erlbaum.

Brainerd, C. J., & Ornstein, P. A. (1991). Children's memory for witnessed events: The developmental backdrop. In J. Doris (Ed.), *The suggestibility of children's recollections* (pp. 10–20). Washington, DC: American Psychological Association.

Brennan, M., & Brennan, R. (1988). *Strange language*. Wagga Wagga, Austrailia: Riverina Murry Institute of Higher Education.

Bretherton, L., Ridgeway, D., & Cassidy, J. (1990). Assessing internal working models of the attachment relationship: An attachment story completion task for 3-year-olds. In M. T. Greenberg, D. Cicchetti, & E. M. Cummings (Eds.), *Attachment in the preschool years: Theory, research, and intervention* (pp. 273–308). Chicago, IL: University of Chicago Press.

Brown, D. A., & Pipe, M.-E. (2003). Individual differences in children's event memory reports and the narrative elaboration technique. *Journal of Applied Psychology*, *88*, 195–206. doi:10.1037/0021-9010.88.2.195

Bruck, M., Ceci, S. J., & Hembrooke, H. (2002). The nature of children's true and false narratives. *Developmental Review*, *22*, 520–554.

Burgwyn-Bailes, E., Baker-Ward, L., Gordon, B. N., & Ornstein, P. A. (2001). Children's memory for emergency medical treatment after one year: The impact of individual difference variables on recall and suggestibility. *Applied Cognitive Psychology*, *15*, S25–S48. doi:10.1002/acp.833

Caprin, C., Benedan, L., Ciaccia, D., Mazza, E., Messineo, S., & Piuri, E. (2016). True and false memories in middle childhood: The relationship with cognitive functioning. *Psychology, Crime & Law*, *22*, 473–494.

Carter, C. A., Bottoms, B. L., & Levine, M. (1996). Linguistic and socioemotional influences on the accuracy of children's reports. *Law & Human Behavior*, *20*, 335–358.

Ceci, S. J., Markle, F., & Chae, Y. (2005). Children's understanding of the law and legal processes. In M. Barrett & E. Buchanan-Barrow (Eds.), *Children's understanding of society* (pp. 105–134). New York, NY: Psychology Press.

Chae, Y., & Ceci, S. J. (2005). Individual differences in children's recall and suggestibility: The effect of intelligence, temperament, and self-perceptions. *Applied Cognitive Psychology*, *19*, 383–407. doi:10.1002/acp.1094

Chae, Y., Goodman, G. S., Eisen, M. L., & Qin, J. (2011). Event memory and suggestibility in abused and neglected children: Trauma-related psychopathology and cognitive functioning. *Journal of Experimental Child Psychology*, *110*, 520–538. doi:10.1016/j.jecp.2011.05.006

Chae, Y., Goodman, G. S., Larson, R. P., Augusti, E.-M., Alley, D., VanMeenen, K. M.,... Coulter, K. P. (2014). Children's memory and suggestibility about a distressing event: The role of children's and parents' attachment. *Journal of Experimental Child Psychology*, *123*, 90–111. doi:10.1016/j.jecp.2014.01.005

Chae, Y., Kulkofsky, S., Deberan, F., Wang, Q., & Hart, S. L. (2014). Low-SES children's eyewitness memory: The effects of verbal labels and vocabulary skills. *Behavioral Sciences & the Law*, *32*, 732–745. doi:10.1002/bsl.2145

Christianson, S.-Å. (1992). Emotional stress and eyewitness memory: A critical review. *Psychological Bulletin*, *112*, 284–309.

Cordón, I. M., Melinder, A., Goodman, G. S. & Edelstein, R. S. (2013). Children's and adults' memory for emotional pictures: Examining age-related patterns using the Developmental Affective Photo System. *Journal of Experimental Child Psychology*, *114*, 339–356. doi:10.1016/j.jecp.2012.08.004

Davidson, D., Luo, Z., & Burden, M. J. (2001). Children's recall of emotional behaviors, emotional labels, and nonemotional behaviors: Does emotion enhance memory? *Cognition & Emotion*, *15*, 1–26. doi:10.1080/02699930125794

Davies, E., & Seymour, F. W. (1998). Questioning child complainants of sexual abuse: Analysis of criminal court transcripts in New Zealand. *Psychiatry, Psychology & Law*, *5*, 47–61.

Davis, S. L., & Bottoms, B. L. (2002). Effects of social support on children's eyewitness reports: A test of the underlying mechanism. *Law & Human Behavior*, *26*, 185–215.

Deffenbacher, K. A., Bornstein, B. H., Penrod, S. D., & McGorty, E. K. (2004). A meta-analytic review of the effects of high stress on eyewitness memory. *Law & Human Behavior*, *28*, 687–706. doi:10.1007/s10979-004-0565-x

Easterbrook, J. A. (1959). The effect of emotion on cue utilization and the organization of behavior. *Psychological Review*, *66*, 183–201. doi:10.1037/h0047707

Eisen, M. L., Goodman, G. S., Qin, J., Davis, S. L., & Crayton, J. (2007). Maltreated children's memory: Accuracy, suggestibility, and psychopathology. *Developmental Psychology*, *43*, 1275–1294. doi:10.1037/0012-1649.43.6.1275

Endres, J., Poggenpohl, C., & Erben, C. (1999). Repetitions, warnings and video: Cognitive and motivational components in preschool children's suggestibility. *Legal & Criminal Psychology*, *4*, 129–146. doi:10.1348/135532599167725

Fivush, R., Haden, C. A., & Reese, E. (2006). Elaborating on elaborations: Role of maternal reminiscing style in cognitive and socioemotional development. *Child Development*, *77*, 1568–1588.

Fivush, R., Sales, J. M., Goldberg, A., Bahrick, L., & Parker, J. (2004). Weathering the storm: Children's long-term recall of Hurrican Andrew. *Memory*, *12*, 104–118. doi:10.1080/09658210244000397

Garon, N., Bryson, S. E., & Smith, I. M. (2008). Executive function in preschoolers: A review using an integrative framework. *Psychological Bulletin*, *134*, 31–60.

Garven, S., Wood, J. M., Malpass, R. S., & Shaw, J. S. (1998). More than suggestion: The effect of interviewing techniques from the McMartin Preschool case. *Journal of Applied Psychology*, *83*, 347–359. doi:10.1037/0021-9010.83.3.347

Goodman, G. S., & Quas, J. A. (2008). Repeated interviews and children's memory: It's more than just how many. *Current Directions in Psychological Science*, *17*, 386–390.

Goodman, G. S., Quas, J. A., Batterman-Faunce, J. M., Riddlesberger, M. M., & Kuhn, J. (1997). Children's reactions to and memory for a stressful event: Influences of age, anatomical dolls, knowledge, and parental attachment. *Applied Developmental Science*, *1*, 54–75. doi:10.1207/s1532480xads0102

Goodman, G. S., Quas, J. A., & Ogle, C. M. (2009). Child maltreatment and memory. *Annual Review of Psychology*, *61*, 325–351. doi:10.1146/annurev.psych.093008.100403

Gordon, B., N. Ornstein, P. A., Nida, R. E., Follmer, A. Crenshaw, M. C., & Albert, G. (1993). Does the use of dolls facility children's memory of visits to the doctor? *Applied Cognitive Psychology*, *7*, 459–474. doi:10.1002/acp.2350070602

Harnishfeger, K. K., & Bjorklund, D. F. (1994). A developmental perspective on individual differences in inhibition. *Learning & Individual Differences*, *6*, 331–355.

Hershkowitz, I. (2009). Socioemotional factors in child sexual abuse investigations. *Child Maltreatment*, *14*, 172–181.

Hershkowitz, I., Lamb, M. E., & Katz, C. (2014). Allegation rates in forensic child abuse investigations: Comparing the revised and standard NICHD protocols. *Psychology, Public Policy, & Law*, *20*, 336–344.

Hershkowitz, I., Lamb, M. E., Katz, C., & Malloy, L. C. (2015). Does enhanced rapport-building alter the dynamics of investigative interviews with suspected victims of intra-familial abuse? *Journal of Police & Criminal Psychology*, *30*, 6–14.

Hershkowitz, I., & Terner, A. (2007). The effects of repeated interviewing on children's forensic statements of sexual abuse. *Applied Cognitive Psychology*, *21*, 1131–1143. doi:http://dx.doi.org/10.1002/acp.1319

Hobbs, S. D., Johnson, J. L., Goodman, G. S., Bederian-Gardner, D., Lawler, M. J., Vargas, I. D., & Mendoza, M. L. (2013). Eyewitness testimony in children. In I. B. Weiner & R. K. Otto (Eds.), *Handbook of forensic psychology* (4th ed., pp. 561–612). Hoboken, NJ: Wiley.

Howie, P., Kurukulasuriya, N., Nash, L., & Marsh, A. (2009). Inconsistencies in children's recall of witnessed events: The role of age, question format and perceived reason for question repetition. *Legal & Criminological Psychology*, *14*, 311–329.

Howie, P., Nash, L., Kurukulasuriya, N., & Bowman, A. (2012). Children's event reports: Factors affecting responses to repeated questions in vignette scenarios and event recall interviews. *British Journal of Developmental Psychology*, *30*, 550–568.

Imhoff, M. C., & Baker-Ward, L. (1999). Preschoolers' suggestibility: Effects of developmentally appropriate language and interviewer supportiveness. *Journal of Applied Developmental Psychology*, *20*, 407–429. doi:10.1016/S0193-3973(99)00022-2

Karpinski, A. C., & Scullin, M. H. (2009). Suggestibility under pressure: Theory of mind, executive function, and suggestibility in preschoolers. *Journal of Applied Developmental Psychology*, *30*, 749–763.

Katz, C., & Hershkowitz, I. (2012). The effect of multipart prompts on children's testimonies in sexual abuse investigations. *Child Abuse & Neglect*, *36*, 753–759.

Kensinger, E. A., Garoff-Eaton, R. J., & Schacter, D. L. (2007). Effects of emotion on memory specificity: Memory trade-offs elicited by negative visually arousing stimuli. *Journal of Memory & Language, 56*, 575–591. doi:10.1016/j.jml.2006.05.004

Kulkofsky, S. (2010). The effects of verbal labels and vocabulary skill on memory and suggestibility. *Journal of Applied Developmental Psychology, 31*, 460–466. doi: 10.1016/j.appdev.2010.09.002

Kulkofsky, S. & Klemfuss, J. Z. (2008). What the stories children tell can tell about their memory skill and young children's suggestibility. *Developmental Psychology, 44*, 1442–1456. doi:10.1037/a0012849

Kulkofsky, S., Wang, Q., & Ceci, S. J. (2008). Do better stories make better memories? Narrative quality and memory accuracy in preschool children. *Applied Cognitive Psychology, 22*, 21–38.

Lamb, M. E., & Fauchier, A. (2001). The effects of question type on self-contradictions by children in the course of forensic interviews. *Applied Cognitive Psychology, 15*, 483–491.

Lamb, M. E., Hershkowitz, I., Sternberg, K. J., Esplin, P. W., Hovav, M., Manor, T., & Yudilevitch, L. (1996). Effects of investigative utterance type on Israeli children's response. *International Journal of Behavioral Development, 19*, 627–638.

Lamb, M. E., Orbach, Y., Hershkowitz, I., Esplin, P. W., & Horowitz, D. (2007). A structured forensic interview protocol improves the quality and informativeness of investigative interviews with children: A review of research using the NICHD Investigative Interview Protocol. *Child Abuse & Neglect, 31*, 1201–1231.

Lamb, M. E., Orbach, Y., Hershkowitz, I., Horowitz, D., & Abbott, C. B. (2007). Does the type of prompt affect the accuracy of information provided by alleged victims of abuse in forensic interviews? *Applied Cognitive Psychology, 21*, 1117–1130.

La Rooy, D., & Lamb, M. E. (2011). What happens when interviewers ask repeated questions in forensic interviews with children alleging abuse? *Journal of Police & Criminal Psychology, 26*, 20–25.

Larsson, A. S., & Lamb, M. E. (2009). Making the most of information gathering interviews with children. *Infant & Child Development, 19*, 1–16. doi:10.1002/ICD.573

Lehto, J. E., Juujärvi, P., Kooistra, L., & Pulkkinen, L. (2003). Dimensions of executive functioning: Evidence from children. *British Journal of Developmental Psychology, 21*, 59–80.

London, K., Bruck, M., Ceci, S. J., & Shuman, D. W. (2005). Disclosure of child sexual abuse: What does the research tell us about the ways that children tell? *Psychology, Public Policy, & Law, 11*, 194–226.

London, K., Bruck, M., Wright, D. B., & Ceci, S. J. (2008). Review of the contemporary literature on how children report sexual abuse to others: Findings, methodological issues, and implications for forensic interviewers. *Memory, 16*, 29–47.

Lyon, T. D. (2014). Interviewing children. *Annual Review of Law & Social Science, 10*, 73–89. doi:10.1146/annurev-lawsocsci-110413-030913

Malloy, L. C., & Quas, J. A. (2009). Children's suggestibility: Areas of consensus and controversy. In K. Kuehnle & M. Connell (Eds.), *The evaluation of child sexual abuse allegations: A comprehensive guide to assessment and testimony* (pp. 267–297). Hoboken, NJ: John Wiley & Sons.

McWilliams, K., Bederian-Gardner, D., Hobbs, S. D., Bakanosky, S., & Goodman, G. S. (2012). Children's eyewitness memory and suggestibility: Revisiting Ceci and Bruck's (1993) review. In A. M. Slater & P. C. Quinn (Eds.), *Developmental psychology: Revisiting the classic studies* (pp. 101–117). Thousand Oaks, CA: Sage.

Mehrani, M. B., & Peterson, C. (2015). Recency tendency: Responses to forced-choice questions. *Applied Cognitive Psychology, 29*, 418–424.

Melinder, A., Scullin, M., Gravvold, T., & Iversen, M. (2007). The stability and generalizability of young children's suggestibility over a 44-month interval. *Psychology, Crime & Law, 13*, 459–468.

Memon, A., & Vartoukian, R. (1996). The effects of repeated questioning on young children's eyewitness testimony. *British Journal of Psychology, 87*, 403–415. doi:10.1111/j.2044-8295.1996.tb02598.x

Miyake, A., Friedman, N. P., Emerson, M. J., Witzki, A. H., Howerter, A., & Wager, T. D. (2000). The unity and diversity of executive functions and their contributions to complex "Frontal Lobe" tasks: A latent variable analysis. *Cognitive Psychology, 41*, 49–100.

Morris, G., Baker-Ward, L., & Bauer, P. J. (2010). What remains of that day: The survival of children's autobiographical memories across time. *Applied Cognitive Psychology, 24*, 527–544. doi:10.1002/acp.1567

Orbach, Y., Hershkowitz, I., Lamb, M. E., Sternberg, K. J., Esplin, P. W., & Horowitz, D. (2000). Assessing the value of structured protocols for forensic interviews of alleged child abuse victims. *Child Abuse & Neglect, 24*, 733–752.

Peterson, C. (2011). Children's memory reports over time: Getting both better and worse. *Journal of Experimental Child Psychology, 109*, 275–193. doi:10.1016/j.jecp.2011.01.009

Peterson, C. (2012). Children's autobiographical memories across the years: Forensic implications of childhood amnesia and eyewitness memory for stressful events. *Developmental Review, 32*, 287–206. doi:10.1016/j.dr.2012.06.002

Peterson, C., Dowden, C., & Tobin, J. (1999). Interviewing preschoolers: Comparisons of yes/no and wh- questions. *Law & Human Behavior, 23*, 539–555.

Peterson, C., Moores, L., & White, G. (2001). Recounting the same events again and again: Children's consistency across multiple interviews. *Applied Cognitive Psychology, 15*, 353–371.

Peterson, C., Morris, G., Baker-Ward, L., & Flynn, S. (2014). Predicting which childhood memories persist: Contributions of memory characteristics. *Developmental Psychology, 50*, 439–449. doi:10.1037/a0033221

Peterson, C., & Whalen, N. (2001). Five years later: Children's memory for medical emergencies. *Applied Cognitive Psychology, 15*, S7–S24. doi:10.1002/acp.832

Pipe, M.-E., Lamb, M. E., Orbach, Y., & Esplin, P. W. (2004). Recent research on children's testimony about experienced and witnessed events. *Developmental Review, 24*, 440–468.

Quas, J. A., Davis, E. L., Goodman, G. S., & Myers, J. E. B. (2007). Repeated questions, deception, and children's true and false reports of body touch. *Child Maltreatment, 12*, 60–67.

Quas, J. A., Goodman, G. S., Bidrose, S., Pipe, M.-E. E., Craw, S., & Ablin, D. S. (1999). Emotion and memory: Children's long-term remembering, forgetting, and suggestibility. *Journal of Experimental Child Psychology, 72*, 235–270. doi:10.1006/jecp.1999.2491

Quas, J. A., Malloy, L. C., Melinder, A., Goodman, G. S., D'Mello, M., & Schaaf, J. (2007). Developmental differences in the effects of repeated interviews and interviewer bias on young children's event memory and false reports. *Developmental Psychology, 43*, 823–837.

Reese, E., Haden, C. A., & Fivush, R. (1993). Mother-child conversations about the past: Relationships of style and memory over time. *Cognitive Development, 8*, 403–430.

Roberts, K. P., & Powell, M. B. (2005). The relation between inhibitory control and children's eyewitness memory. *Applied Cognitive Psychology, 19*, 1003–1018.

Rocha, E. M., Marche, T. A., & Briere, J. L. (2013). The effect of forced-choice questions on Children's suggestibility: A comparison of multiple-choice and yes/no questions. *Canadian Journal of Behavioural Science, 45*, 1–11.

Saxe, R. R., Whitfield-Gabrieli, S., Scholz, J., & Pelphrey, K. A. (2009). Brain regions for perceiving and reasoning about other people in school-aged children. *Child Development, 80*, 1197–1209. doi:10.1111/j.1467-8624.2009.01325.x

Saywitz, K. J. (1987). Children's testimony: Age-related patterns of memory errors. In S. J. Ceci, M. P. Toglia, & D. F. Ross (Eds.), *Children's eyewitness memory* (pp. 36–52). New York, NY: Springer Verlag.

Saywitz, K. J., Jaenicke, C., & Camparo, L. (1990). Children's knowledge of legal terminology. *Law & Human Behavior, 14*, 523–535.

Saywitz, K. J., Snyder, L., & Nathanson, R. (1999). Facilitating the communicative competence of the child witness. *Applied Developmental Science, 3*, 58–68.

Saywitz, K. J., Larson, R. P., Hobbs, S. D., & Wells, C. R. (2015). Developing rapport with children in forensic interviews: Systematic review of experimental research. *Behavioral Sciences & the Law, 33*, 372–389.

Schaaf, J. M., Alexander, K. W., & Goodman, G. S. (2008). Children's false memory and true disclosure in the face of repeated questions. *Journal of Experimental Child Psychology, 100*, 157–185.

Sternberg, K. J., Lamb, M. E., Hershkowitz, I., Yudilevitch, L., Orbach. Y., Esplin, P. W., & Hovav, M. (1997). Effects of introductory style on children's abilities to describe experiences of sexual abuse. *Child Abuse & Neglect, 21*, 1133–1146.

Sternberg, K. J., Lamb, M. E., Esplin, P. W., & Baradaran, I. P. (1999). Using a scripted protocol in investigative interviews: A pilot study. *Applied Developmental Science, 3*, 70–76.

Walker, A. G. (1994). *Handbook of questioning children: A linguistic perspective.* Washington, DC: American Bar Association.

Warren-Leubecker, A. R., Tate, C., Hinton, I., & Ozbek, N. (1989). What do children know about the legal system and when do they know it? First steps down a less traveled path in child witness research. In S. J. Ceci, D. F. Ross, & M. P. Toglia (Eds.), *Perspectives on children's testimony* (pp. 158–183). New York, NY: Springer Verlag.

Waterhouse, G. F., Ridley, A. M., Bull, R., La Rooy, D., & Wilcock, R. (2016). Dynamics of repeated interviews with children. *Applied Cognitive Psychology, 30*, 713–721.

Yerkes, R. M., & Dodson, J. D. (1908). The relation of strength of stimulus to rapidity of habit-information. *Journal of Comparative Neurology of Psychology, 18*, 459–482. doi:10.1002/cne.920180503

Young, K., Powell, M. B., & Dudgeon, P. (2003). Individual differences in children's suggestibility: A comparison between intellectually disabled and mainstream samples. *Personality & Individual Differences, 35*, 31–49. doi:10.1016/S0191-8869(02)00138-1

Zajac, R., Gross, J., & Hayne, H. (2003). Asked and answered: Questioning children in the courtroom. *Psychiatry, Psychology & Law, 10*, 199–209.

10

Perceptual, Cognitive, and Social Foundations of Eyewitness Identifications: Why Do Identifications Go Wrong?

Emily F. Wood and Deborah Davis

On September 18, 2015, Brandon Burnside became the most recently exonerated person in a long line of wrongly accused individuals sent to prison, even death row, in part because of mistaken eyewitness identifications. Burnside had spent almost five years in prison after being wrongfully convicted of the fatal parking lot shooting of Bryan Drake II just before 2 a.m. on August 11, 2010. Fortunately, Burnside eventually was granted a new trial, and ultimately, DNA evidence and eyewitness expert testimony led to his exoneration.

Cases similar to Brandon Burnside's are not rare. Studies of causes of wrongful conviction have consistently identified eyewitness errors as among the most common contributors to the convictions. Other contributors include mistaken, falsified, or misleading evidence, such as forensic errors or fabrications, false confessions, mistaken or dishonest witnesses, and snitch accounts. Some represent errors in trying the case, such as prosecutorial misconduct, defense counsel errors, inappropriate judicial rulings, and so on. But among all forms of error and misconduct, mistaken eyewitness identifications have been some of the most common. Indeed, most studies report eyewitness errors as the single most frequent contributor to wrongful convictions, present in 16% to 76% of their cases (e.g., Garrett, 2011; Scheck, Neufeld, & Dwyer, 2000; Wells et al., 1998).

Although the role of mistaken eyewitnesses may vary across crime types, their importance for the justice system is nevertheless clear. Misidentifications are harmful at all stages of the judicial process. They are harmful to innocent suspects, in that they can lead to the targeting, investigation, and prosecution of the wrong person (while the guilty perpetrator remains free), and ultimately, to conviction by jurors who tend to give great weight to eyewitness evidence (Wells, Memon, & Penrod, 2006). Misidentifications can also lead innocent suspects to facilitate their own prosecution/incarceration. They affect suspect decision-making by increasing suspects' sense of

The Wiley Handbook of Memory, Autism Spectrum Disorder, and the Law, First Edition.
Edited by Jonni L. Johnson, Gail S. Goodman, and Peter C. Mundy.

hopelessness in defending themselves against the allegations against them. Such a sense of hopelessness increases the likelihood that innocent suspects will falsely confess or falsely plead guilty (Ofshe & Leo, 1997).

Given that eyewitness misidentifications are prominently implicated as contributors to the prosecution and conviction of innocents, it is important to understand how often and for what reasons they occur. In this chapter, we examine causes of eyewitness errors in normal adults, with some attention to age differences and the performance of children. It is important to understand eyewitness memory performance in neurotypicals to fully understand how specific differences in the perceptual, cognitive, and social functioning of those on the autism spectrum might lead to greater accuracy in some circumstances and in less in others.

In this chapter, we first review evidence of the overall accuracy with which eyewitnesses are able to identify strangers. We offer data concerning accuracy under the best of conditions as context for subsequent discussion of how accuracy can be reduced by the nature of conditions under which the target person is originally encountered. We then turn to consideration of how memory for the actual perpetrator may change over time, as the result of processes both internal and external to the witness. Finally, we offer take-home points from our review.

Eyewitness Accuracy in Laboratory and Field Studies

Even under the best of circumstances, eyewitness identification of strangers is often inaccurate. To fully understand how difficult it is for eyewitnesses to correctly identify someone they do not know, it is useful to look at rates of accuracy of eyewitness performance in both laboratory and field studies.

Overall accuracy in laboratory studies

In laboratory studies, participants are exposed to a target individual either in person or via video. Often, the original target is viewed while committing a mock crime. He or she may also be viewed or encountered in other naturalistic settings, such as during stressful medical procedures (e.g., Petersen & Whalen, 2001) or military training drills (e.g., Morgan et al., 2004). Subsequently, participants take part in an identification procedure. They may be asked to look at a lineup of six or more potential targets and indicate whether the original target is or is not present (and if so, which is the target). This may be conducted with a lineup of photographs or a live lineup with all potential targets present in person. Alternatively, the participants may be asked to take part in a "show-up" procedure, during which they view a single individual (either in photo or in person) and indicate whether that individual is or is not the original target. Sometimes the original targets are included in the lineup or show-up presentation (a "target-present" procedure) and sometimes they are not (a "target-absent" procedure).

Several meta-analyses of laboratory studies have been conducted to assess performance in lineup and/or show-up procedures, both target-present and target-absent. Clark, Howell, and Davey (2008) conducted a meta-analysis based on a review of 94 experiments differentiating between studies that used simultaneous and sequential lineups. They found that in simultaneous lineups (i.e., all photographs or suspects are presented to the witness at the same time) when the target was present, participants correctly identified the target 47% of the time and incorrectly identified a foil (i.e., someone other than the target) 21% of the time. In target-present lineups, among the subset of participants who made any identification, 30.9% were of foils (if 68% identify someone and 21% of those identify a foil, 30.9% of all identifications were foil identifications). When the target was not included in the lineup, 49% of participants nevertheless misidentified a foil as the perpetrator. In sequential lineups (i.e., each photograph or suspect is presented one at a time to the witness), when the target was present, 40% of participants correctly identified the target and 17% incorrectly identified a foil. In target-present lineups, 29.8% of all identifications were of foils. When the target was not in the lineup, 32% identified a foil.

In another meta-analysis Steblay, Dysart, and Wells (2011) reviewed 72 experiments with 13,142 participant witnesses. In target-present simultaneous lineups, 52% of participants correctly identified the target and 24% identified a foil, resulting in 31.6% of all identifications being foils (if 76% identify someone and 24% of those identify a foil, 31.6% of all identifications were foil identifications). When the target was absent, 57% identified a foil. In sequential lineups when the target was present, 38% of participants identified the target, 24% identified a foil, and 34.8% of all identifications were foils. When the target was not included in the lineup, 36% identified a foil. A third meta-analysis (Steblay, Dysart, Fulero, & Lindsay, 2003) did not distinguish between type of lineup (sequential or simultaneous), but included over 3,000 witnesses from 12 experiments. Of all identifications, 34.8% were of foils.

Together, the results of these meta-analyses suggest that among those who do make a lineup identification, rates of misidentification are substantial, ranging from a high of 57% in target-absent simultaneous lineups to a low of 29.8% in target-present sequential lineups.

Overall accuracy in archival studies

There have also been a number of individual studies of witness accuracy in real life criminal cases, collectively involving over 6,000 eyewitness attempts (e.g., Behrman & Davey, 2001; Behrman & Richards, 2005; Horry, Halford, Brewer, Milne, & Bull, 2014; Horry, Memon, Wright, & Milne, 2012; Memon, Havard, Clifford, Gabbert, & Watt, 2011; Slater, 1994; Valentine, Pickering, & Darling, 2003; Wells, Steblay, & Dysart, 2011, 2014; Wright & McDaid, 1996; Wright & Skagerberg, 2007). Researchers obtained access to case records to identify instances in which one or more witnesses inspected lineups to attempt to identify the perpetrator. Such attempts were coded with respect to whether the witness identified the suspect, identified a known foil, or was not able to make an identification. Although the identity of the true perpetrator cannot be known, and thus, the accuracy of suspect identifications is unknown, foil identifications are misidentifications.

Across studies, 26% to 58% of witnesses identified the suspect (less than 45% in 9 of 11 studies). The percent of all identifications that were of known innocent foils ranged from roughly 23% to 49% (falling between 30%–41% in 7 of the 11 studies). An unknown number also chose an innocent suspect.

Eyewitness errors and estimator variables

Available laboratory and archival data have revealed similar rates of eyewitness error, at least for lineups. Among eyewitnesses who do make an identification, roughly one third or more identify an innocent foil. Moreover, laboratory studies have revealed that if the true perpetrator (or target) is not present in a lineup, between 32% and 57% nevertheless identified a foil. Overall rates of misidentification tend to be lower for show-up identifications, but depending on the suspect's resemblance to the perpetrator rates of misidentification ranged from 15% to 23% (approximately 1 in 5: Steblay et al., 2011). Overall, these rates of error are quite disturbing, and suggest that the excessive faith in and reliance on eyewitness identification of criminal perpetrators in our legal system should be tempered by greater skepticism and caution.

Errors in eyewitness identification can become even more problematic when we consider the number of innocent people who go to trial, in part, because of a mistaken identification. The vast majority of criminal cases (90%–95%) are settled before trial largely though guilty pleas and plea bargains (Bureau of Justice Statistics, 2005). However, innocent suspects who were misidentified by an eyewitness and who are ultimately charged will presumably be less likely to plead guilty and take a plea bargain (because they are innocent) compared to guilty suspects. This process of pleading before trial affects the proportion of guilty and innocent people who go to trial such that there is a higher proportion of innocent people among those who go to trial than among all who are charged (the "pleading effect"; Charman & Wells, 2006).

Eyewitness errors clearly represent a danger to innocents, one that has continued relatively unabated from the time they were first noted by scholars in the 1800s into the twenty-first century. But why do these errors occur? Researchers have identified factors contributing to errors of identification, ranging from circumstances of the original criminal event through many post-event influences that can change and distort memory to characteristics of official police identification procedures and in-court identifications.

In extant literature, both "estimator" and "system" variables can influence eyewitness identification (Wells, 1978). "Estimator" variables refer to factors not under the control of the justice system that can affect the quality and reliability of eyewitness memory (e.g., lighting, distance from the perpetrator, witness age, exposure to post-event publicity or conversations with other witnesses, internal cognitive processes that can distort memory over time). These variables are important to consider when evaluating the reliability and accuracy of eyewitness identifications. "System" variables are determinants of eyewitness accuracy that are subject to the control of the criminal justice system, such as the nature of lineup procedures or potentially biasing behaviors by investigators. We focus most of our review on estimator variables, ending with brief coverage of system variables specific to identification procedures.

What is There to be Seen?

Criminal events can be complex, involving many people, actions, sounds, conversations, and events. The amount of information available to the witness can be overwhelming. Amid this sea of information, one or more perpetrators commit the crime in question. Needless to say, they are the targets of interest for perpetrator identification procedures to come. Are there things about these perpetrators themselves that might affect accuracy in later identification procedures? Research has indeed identified several that tend to exert strong effects.

Distinctiveness and the relatively unique target

One of the things making eyewitness identification so difficult is the extraordinarily large number of people who grossly resemble almost any specific person, many of whom will closely resemble that specific person. Many others might easily be mistaken for the person in question, particularly when that person was seen briefly, only once, and in complex or stressful circumstances. This confusion is less likely, however, when the specific target is unusual or unique, possessing distinctive features that few others possess. Those features can cause the witness to pay more attention to the person at the time of the crime, and therefore, to remember him[1] better. It may also be difficult for police to find suitable foils for a lineup, making it easier for witnesses to distinguish the suspect.

Indeed, perpetrator distinctiveness (highly noticeable individual features) is related to accuracy in witness identifications (e.g., Badham, Wade, Watts, Woods, & Maylor, 2014). Carlson and Carlson (2012, 2014) found that the presence of distinctive features seemed to draw sufficient attention to the perpetrator's face as to eliminate the weapons focus effect (see later in this chapter).

In-group biases

When a perpetrator is similar to the witness in age, gender, or race, accuracy in identification is higher (known as in-group bias). The most prolifically researched of these biases concerns the "own-race bias" or "cross-race effect" (Brigham, Bennett, Meissner, & Mitchell, 2007). Among cases involving erroneous eyewitness identifications known to The Innocence Project, 42% involved a cross-race identification (i.e., the witness was a different race than the suspect). In a meta-analysis of 30 years of laboratory studies, Meissner and Brigham (2001) reviewed 91 independent samples, including 4,996 participants. Participants were 1.4 times more likely to correctly identify a previously viewed own-race face compared to an other-race face, and were 1.56 times more likely to incorrectly identify a novel other-race face compared to an own-race face. This effect has also been observed among children (e.g., Bar-Haim, Ziv, Lamy, & Hodes, 2006; Pezdek, Blandon-Gitlin, & Moore, 2003) and adolescents (e.g., Goodman et al., 2007), and in multiple ethnicities (e.g., Bothwell, Brigham, & Malpass, 1989).

Similar in-group bias occurs for age. A meta-analysis of 43 studies with over 4,000 participants found evidence of an own-age bias (Rhodes & Anastasi, 2012). Most of these studies tested the effect in college students. However, some studies used children, middle-aged adults, and older adults, and found that the effect was robust across samples. Participants identifying same-age targets were more likely to make

[1] Throughout this chapter, we use *him* for suspects because the majority of individuals arrested and the majority of exonerations due to mistaken identification involve male defendants. In 2015, according to the FBI Uniform Crime Statistics, 73% of all arrested persons were males. Furthermore, the National Registry of Exonerations reports that of exonerations that had mistaken identifications as a contributing factor, 98% of exonerees were male.

correct identifications and less likely to make incorrect identifications compared to participants identifying different-age targets.

Additionally, there has been some evidence of in-group bias for gender (although there is less consistency in own gender biases for males; Palmer, Brewer & Horry, 2013). Research has demonstrated a consistent own-gender bias for females; however, this was in part due to encoding of hair (Wright & Sladden, 2003).

What *Can* be Seen and How Easily?

What is there to be seen can only be perceived correctly with a clear view and adequate time to observe. Thus, it is no surprise that eyewitness researchers have widely investigated what they refer to as "witnessing conditions" that may affect this opportunity to observe clearly what must later be reported or identified. For the case of eyewitness identification, this means the opportunity to clearly observe the face (and sometimes other features) of the perpetrator(s). Several features of the perpetrator and the circumstances of the encounter affect this opportunity.

Angle of view, lighting, distance, and disguise

Face visibility during the criminal event is one of the most important issues affecting eyewitness accuracy because the face is what will be shown to witnesses in a lineup (most often a full frontal view of face and upper shoulders in a six-person photo lineup). Faces originally viewed from the front are identified with greater accuracy than those viewed from the side or back (e.g., Burton & Jenkins, 2011, for review) and descriptions of demographic features (e.g., race, gender, age; Afraz, Vaziri-Pashkam, & Cavanagh, 2010) are more accurate. But this depends on the correspondence between the angle of the original view and that during the identification procedure. Even subtle mismatches between angle at encoding and recognition can influence accuracy. Poor lighting conditions (e.g., Steidle, Werth, & Hanke, 2011) and longer distance between the witness and the to-be-remembered face also impair face visibility and accuracy (e.g., Lampinen et al., 2014; Loftus & Harley, 2005). Even if the face is near and in good lighting, it may nevertheless be obstructed by hats, hoodies, sunglasses, or explicit disguises such as bandanas or face masks. Hair is particularly important for stranger identification, and such clothing or disguises can obscure the hair. Any obstruction of facial features necessary to later identify or describe a perpetrator results in poorer accuracy. Moreover, as with angle of view, other changes in appearance between original viewing and identification procedures tend to impair accuracy (such as changes in hairstyle or color, or facial hair).

Exposure duration

Even in the best of lighting and at close distances, witnesses must still have adequate time to observe the perpetrator. Indeed, across laboratory studies, the proportion of correct identifications is significantly higher when duration of exposure is longer (66%) than when shorter (53%) (see meta-analysis by Bornstein, Deffenbacher, Penrod, and McGorty, 2012).

Archival analyses have examined effects of length of exposure to the perpetrator in real life crimes (e.g., Horry et al., 2003; Valentine, Pickering, & Darling, 2003). Horry et al. (2014) reviewed 833 real lineups seen by 709 witnesses. Again, longer exposure durations (more than 60 s) were related to higher suspect identification rates (57.53% for corroborated cases; 33.56% for uncorroborated cases) than shorter durations (38.67% for corroborated cases; 23.23% uncorroborated cases). Exposure duration was also negatively related to the rate of no identifications (25.6% vs. 48.7% for long and short durations, respectively, for corroborated cases). In general, to the extent that suspect identifications are correct in the field studies, it appears that witnesses who view a target for a long duration of time are more accurate in their identifications in both laboratory studies and real world crimes. It should be noted, however, that Morgan et al. (2004) found high rates of error among military cadets who were exposed to a target for a relatively long length of time (i.e., 40 min).

These viewing conditions reviewed above are usually studied in isolation, but in the case of real crimes, many estimator variables affect eyewitness identifications simultaneously. Unfortunately, we do not currently have studies varying lighting, duration, distance, and other witnessing conditions factorially, and therefore, cannot specify the degree of impairment resulting from the combination of poor conditions.

What *Did* the Witness Attend to and "See"

No matter what opportunity the witness might have to see the perpetrator clearly, he or she may or may not devote the necessary attention to successfully perceive and encode the perpetrator's features into memory. Additionally, the witness may fail to focus on the specific features of the perpetrator that will later allow him or her to distinguish that perpetrator from similar others. Researchers have devoted considerable attention to characteristics of the event and of the witness that might affect what is actually encoded.

Event characteristics and diversion of witness attention

Criminal events can be complex, involving many people, actions, and objects. The witness may also have goals that command attention, some existing before the crime is noticed (such as texting or talking to others), and other goals occasioned by the crime (such as the search for an escape route or attempts to protect others). All such things can draw attention away from the perpetrator, or specifically from his face, and the more complex the event, the less likely the witness is to later correctly identify the perpetrator (for review, see Davis & Loftus, 2018). However, one particular aspect of the criminal event has received particular attention—that of whether a weapon was or was not present.

The "weapon focus effect"

When a perpetrator wields a weapon, two effects of interest here can result, each with potential to affect attention to the perpetrator's face. That is, the weapon itself can draw attention away from the face (dubbed the "weapon focus effect"), or the weapon can increase fear, anxiety, and arousal in the witness (the focus of the next section).

Research on the weapon focus effect has aimed to demonstrate both cause (diversion of attention) and result (reduction in identification accuracy).

Research examining diversion of attention has used eye-tracking technology to assess where participants are focusing their attention when viewing a crime entailing use of a weapon versus one with no weapon. As expected, participants focus more often and for longer on the weapon compared to neutral objects in the hand of a perpetrator (e.g., Loftus, Loftus, & Messo, 1987). Many more laboratory studies have shown that weapon presence reduces identification accuracy (see meta-analysis by Steblay, 1992). Archival analyses and field studies have also investigated the effects of the presence of a weapon in real crimes on eyewitness identification accuracy (e.g., Mecklenburg, 2006; Tollestrup, Turtle, & Yuille 1994; Valentine et al., 2003). None of these studies and reports found a significant effect of the presence of a weapon on suspect identifications in show-ups, photographic lineups, live lineups, or person descriptions.

However, a meta-analysis conducted by Fawcett, Russell, Peace, and Christie (2013) included data from actual crimes, laboratory experiments, and simulated experiments, and found a moderate weapon focus effect on eyewitness identification accuracy and completeness of details in descriptions of the perpetrator. When effect sizes were calculated for each kind of study individually (e.g., actual crime, laboratory), a significant weapon focus effect still appeared, even in the studies that used real world data. This seemingly contradicts the studies reported above that did not find a weapon effect using real crime data. Fawcett et al. (2013) explained that there might have been an effect of the presence of weapons in most of the studies previously listed, but the effect was too small to detect in the context of a single study. Overall, the available data suggests that weapons focus does tend to impair identification accuracy as well as accuracy in descriptions of perpetrators and other details.

The role of the state of the witness

Although specific features of the environment may hijack attention, encoding may also be affected by the personal state of the witness. This can occur for several reasons, including overall chronic cognitive abilities or the acute cognitive state of the witness. Reflecting the latter, a few studies have investigated the effects of acute intoxication on eyewitness performance. Despite some inconsistencies between studies, results mostly show greater effects on false identifications than on failures of true identifications (see Davis & Loftus, 2018). By far, the greatest attention has been devoted to child witnesses, and the issue of how witness stress and arousal affects accuracy.

Child eyewitnesses

Substantial research has investigated effects of age on stranger identification, showing that older adults perform more poorly than young children, who also perform more poorly than young adults (Ericson, Lampinen, & Moore, 2015; Fitzgerald & Price, 2015). A meta-analysis of 91 studies containing over 20,000 participants found that for target-present lineups, young adults compared to children were more likely to correctly identify a target, but this difference decreased for older children (aged 9–13). Children (aged 4–17) were more likely than young adults to incorrectly reject a lineup or to misidentify a foil. For target-absent lineups, the odds of correctly rejecting the lineup were more than double for young adults compared to children (aged 4–17). When only comparing young adults to children aged 5–8, the odds of correctly rejecting the lineup were 2.75 times higher for young adults. Children and older adults were also more likely than young adults to make a choice from both types of lineups compared to younger adults, possibly explaining the large difference in correct lineup rejections for children compared to young adults (Fitzgerald & Price, 2015). In sum, young adults consistently perform better than children perform and make fewer mistakes. However, this difference decreases for older children, indicating that eyewitness identification accuracy improves throughout childhood.

Children might be more likely to incorrectly reject lineups or misidentify foils compared to young adults because children can be more susceptible to social pressures and suggestive procedures (Bruck & Ceci, 1999). Instructions that specifically warn the witness that the suspect may not be in the lineup reduce the misidentification rate among adults. But even with such instructions, children are less likely, compared to others, to reject a culprit-absent lineup (Keast, Brewer, & Wells, 2007). Children might not possess the cognitive skills necessary to recognize when they should reject a lineup and when to withhold inappropriate responses, with the result that target-absent lineups of strangers are particularly problematic for children (Fitzgerald & Price, 2015).

Stress and anxiety

The issue of witness emotion and stress has been of great interest for three reasons. First, criminal events commonly provoke extreme emotions such as fear and distress. Second, common sense seems to suggest that highly emotional or traumatic events will be better remembered, and therefore, witnesses to such events should be more likely to make accurate identifications. Third, psychological science has generally indicated that extreme emotion can result in a catastrophic drop-off in cognition, with the result that witness performance might also decline in such circumstances. Thus, the issue of effects of extreme emotion and stress is crucial to eyewitness situations, and there appears to be a contrast between commonsense understanding (and likely juror opinions) and what research on cognition might suggest (see Davis & Loftus, 2009; Deffenbacher, Bornstein, Penrod, & McGorty, 2004, for discussion of these issues).

Deffenbacher and colleagues (2004) conducted a meta-analysis of studies published through 1997. Analyses included 36 tests of the effects of stress on accuracy of witness descriptions of the perpetrator and other details (with 1,945 participants) and 27 laboratory tests (with 1,727 participants) investigating the effect of stress on identification accuracy. These included only studies in which the degree to which the witness was personally stressed was varied. Overall, stress impaired both forms of accuracy. More details were recalled correctly under low than high stress (64% vs. 52%). Perpetrators were more often correctly identified in perpetrator-present lineups under low stress (54% vs. 42%), and foils were misidentified less often (19% vs. 34%; see Morgan et al., 2004, for equivalent results). Unfortunately, only six experiments included perpetrator-absent lineups. Results were inconsistent between experiments, and overall, showed no effect of stress on false identifications. In sum, research on witness stress has shown negative effects on accuracy for both descriptions (e.g., Valentine & Mesout, 2009) and identifications (Deffenbacher et al., 2004). Yet, more research is needed that includes the crucial, forensically relevant, target-absent lineup condition.

What Happens Next? Post-Event Influences on Witness Memory

Immediately after a crime, witnesses are exposed to multiple influences with potential to change and distort their memories and accounts. This can begin immediately and extend through trial. In the following sections, we consider some of the most common post-event influences a witness is likely to experience, beginning with conversations with other witnesses.

Co-witnesses and memory conformity

Many crimes involve multiple victims and/or multiple witnesses. Indeed, a recent survey indicated that 77% of participants who had witnessed a crime knew one or more of the other witnesses. Eighty-six percent of these witnesses discussed their memory of the event with other witnesses *before* giving an official report to the police (Patterson & Kemp, 2006).

When witnesses discuss their memories of an event their accounts tend to become more similar, to incorporate misinformation acquired from one another, and to report more incorrect free-recall details (Allan & Gabbert, 2008; Gabbert, Memon, & Allan, 2003; Gabbert, Memon, Allan, & Wright, 2004; Hope, Ost, Gabbert, Healey, & Lenton, 2008). The greater agreement between witnesses creates an illusion of corroboration between witnesses that can affect police investigations, witnesses' confidence, and jurors' perceptions of eyewitness credibility.

An individual is most likely to be affected by another witness when there is reason to believe the other witness is correct, such as when the other seems more confident, had the opportunity to observe the event or perpetrator longer, or seemed more credible (see Davis & Loftus, 2007, for review). Of importance, given that so many witnesses are acquainted with one another, research has shown greater influence between witnesses the closer their relationship.

The influence is not always toward error, and it may not always lead to negative real world implications. Witnesses can become more accurate *if* they talk to witnesses who are correct (e.g., Allan & Gabbert, 2008; Shaw, Garven, & Wood, 1997). However, it is unlikely that another witness will be uniformly correct on other details, even if they are correct regarding the perpetrator. Moreover, because witnesses who have talked to others who agree with them not only become more confident, but also report more favorable witnessing conditions (such as opportunity to view, the amount of attention they paid to the perpetrator and others; Skagerberg, 2007), their credibility to jurors and others can be strongly affected. Thus, on balance, co-witness influences are risky and might best be avoided. In recognition of the many effects of co-witness discussions, Department of Justice Guidelines advise law enforcement to instruct witnesses not to discuss the case or their identifications with one another (Technical Working Group, 1999).

Initial reports to police

Describing the perpetrator

Whether one discusses a criminal event with other witnesses or not, witnesses must shortly describe the event and perpetrator to police who arrive on the scene. Strangely, the process of overwriting and distorting one's memory of a perpetrator can begin with this first effort to describe him. "Verbal overshadowing" refers, in effect, to overwriting (or interfering with) one's visual memory of a perpetrator with verbal attempts to describe him. Schooler and Engstler-Schooler (1990) first demonstrated this effect by showing a video of a bank robbery to participants. Half spent five minutes writing a description of what the perpetrator's face looked like, whereas the other half completed an unrelated filler task. Participants who first described the perpetrator were less able to identify him in an eight-person photo lineup compared to participants who did not describe him before the identification test. The authors hypothesized that verbal overshadowing occurs because the verbal description recodes the original memory to match the verbal description given, making the memory for the originally seen face less accurate. This effect has been established in a multisite registered replication (Alogna et al., 2014), which showed that the effect is stronger when there is a delay between the time the event is viewed and the verbal description of the perpetrator (Meissner & Brigham, 2001; Meissner, Sporer, & Susa, 2008).

Building a composite

Soon after the crime, the witness may be asked to help locate a suspect by assisting a police artist in creating a composite sketch of the perpetrator (or by using a computer program to do so). Like a verbal description, this forces witnesses to focus on individual features of the face, whereas facial recognition in everyday life is typically based on holistic representations of the *configuration* of features (e.g., Wells & Hasel, 2007). Witnesses must sift through many different variations of facial features to create a complete composite of a suspect, in the process distorting or overwriting their original visual representation of the perpetrator's face. Even exposure to composites constructed by another witness can cause memory distortion. Witnesses who create the composite are most impaired in subsequent identification attempts, followed by those who simply view the composite after exposure to the actual target. Those who had no form of exposure to a composite are most accurate (e.g., Topp-Mariquez, McQuiston, & Malpass, 2014).

Searching mugbooks and "unconscious transference"

Witnesses may be asked to engage in yet a third activity with potential to overwrite the original image of the perpetrator: that of looking through mugbooks in an attempt to locate him. An innocent person first seen in a mugbook may be misidentified as the perpetrator if he later appears in a lineup. This can be the result of a sense of familiarity created by the mugbook exposure combined with failure to correctly remember why the face is familiar. A meta-analysis of laboratory studies conducted by Deffenbacher, Bornstein, and Penrod (2006) examined 32 tests of mugshot exposure and identification accuracy that included 1,664 participants. They found that innocents in the lineup who were previously seen in mugbooks were more likely to be misidentified than those not previously seen.

This mugshot effect is one of a class of effects called "unconscious transference" (e.g., Deffenbacher et al., 2006; Loftus, 1976), whereby the witness falsely identifies an innocent person because he or she fails to recall the true circumstances in which the person was previously encountered, and mistakes the person for the perpetrator (i.e., "unconscious transference" of identities between the two). Transference effects can occur in many circumstances, such as when a suspect is an innocent person seen around the neighborhood or on social media (Davis & Loftus, 2012; Davis & Loftus, 2018), or when a witness views a composite sketch and then a similar looking person later appears in a lineup. For these reasons, witness memory researchers have advised strongly against repeated lineups where the suspect is the only member common to all (Steblay & Dysart, 2016).

Exposure to misinformation

The misinformation effect refers to a phenomenon whereby exposure to incorrect information after an event increases errors in recall reflecting that incorrect information (Loftus, Miller, & Burns, 1978). Many demonstrations of this effect have shown how easily participants' memories are altered through exposure to incorrect post-event information (see Davis & Loftus, 2007, for review).

In the context of identifying a person, misinformation may be visual: something that might overwrite or change the witness's internal image of the perpetrator (such as an image of the alleged perpetrator shown on television or in newspapers). Or, it might be information suggesting that a particular person is the perpetrator. This can consist of such things as misleading or mistaken "evidence" against the person. Either form of misinformation can be acquired from a number of sources, such as media publicity about the case, co-witnesses, suggestive police interviews, direct discussion of evidence with police, and even the witness's own attempts to investigate the case on social media or otherwise. These can change the semantic memory of the witness (the story he or she remembers of the event) by changing or solidifying beliefs about what happened.

Forgetting Over Time

We have discussed forces that can change and distort memory after an event is witnessed. These situations may or may not actually affect any given witness' memory or report, but there is one thing that does: the passage of time. Like memory for everything, memory for criminal events and perpetrators fades. A meta-analysis by Deffenbacher and colleagues (2008) reviewed 53 laboratory studies that varied the interval between the target event and attempts to identify the target or perpetrator. Their results suggested an initial upper limit of eyewitness accuracy at 67%, dropping to 50% after one week, and continuing to decline more slowly thereafter.

What Happens During the Official Identification? Do Police Procedures Matter?

Most central to post-event influences on identification performance are the procedures used to allow witnesses to attempt an identification. Though we cannot thoroughly review these procedures herein it is important to point out a few of the processes engaged by identification procedures that may vary in importance and impact between neurotypicals and atypicals.

Identification procedures can promote errors through their impact on perceptual difficulties, inference and decision processes, and social influence. For example, if a lineup is used, the choice of foils may create perceptual difficulties (such as when all members too closely resemble one another and the suspect), or may provide the basis of inference concerning which person *must be* the suspect (such as when one person is clearly the best fit to the description the witness had previously given of the suspect, looks more criminal, or stands out and draws attention for other reasons). Judgment and inference processes can also be affected by whether all persons are shown at once in a lineup (enabling more direct comparison processes, and the ability to pick the person closest to memory of the perpetrator) versus one at a time (making an absolute judgment of whether each person is or is not the perpetrator more likely). Social influence processes come into play if the lineup administrator does anything to explicitly suggest, hint, or inadvertently emit cues indicating that a specific lineup member is the suspect (or if other witnesses are present and able to convey such hints or suggestions). Even more basic is the likelihood that witnesses will infer that police believe the perpetrator is present in the lineup (Why else ask the witness to attempt an identification?). Such an inference may be even stronger if police offer a single suspect to a witness and ask if he is the perpetrator (i.e., a "show-up" or "cold show" procedure).

A large body of research has shown that these differences in procedure significantly affect witness accuracy, and has therefore formed the basis of a number of recommendations for procedures that will reduce error rates. This research and recommended procedures are discussed in the National Academy of Science's report, *Identifying the Culprit: Assessing Eyewitness Identification* (National Research Council, 2014); the National Institute of Justice's report, *Eyewitness Evidence: A Guide for Law Enforcement* (Technical Working Group, 1999); and Wells et al.'s (1998), *Eyewitness Identification Procedures: Recommendations for Lineups and Photospreads* (see also Davis & Loftus, 2018).

Conclusions

We began this chapter by highlighting one wrongfully convicted person, Brandon Burnside, who spent years in prison, in part, due to mistaken eyewitness identifications. He is only one of countless innocents who have been, and will in the future be, misidentified by eyewitnesses. Eyewitness researchers have made substantial progress in understanding why these errors are made and are investigating ways to minimize errors that are under some control of the justice system. By providing our review of the forces that shape witness perceptions, memories, and identification choices in neurotypical individuals, we hope to have also laid the foundation for consideration of the mechanisms through which individual differences, including autism, can influence eyewitness performance.

Take-Home Points

- Most studies identify mistaken eyewitness identifications as the largest contributor to wrongful convictions.
- Even under ideal circumstances, facial recognition of strangers is difficult and more inaccurate than widely assumed.

- Laboratory and archival studies find that roughly one third of identifications are misidentifications of innocent foils.
- Eyewitness science has identified numerous influences on eyewitness accuracy that may be translated to the study of eyewitness memory in autism.
- These include the conditions under which the witness was exposed to the perpetrator (e.g., lighting and distance) and witness characteristics (e.g., age and stress).
- They also include influences that can distort witness memory (e.g., talking with other witnesses, exposure to misinformation).
- Finally, they include procedures used to elicit witness perpetrator identifications.

References

Afraz, A., Vaziri-Pashkam, M., & Cavanagh, P. (2010). Spatial heterogeneity in the perception of face and form attributes. *Current Biology, 20*, 2112–2116. http://dx.doi.org/10.1016/j.cub.2010.11.017

Allan, K., & Gabbert, F. (2008). I still think it was a banana: Memorable "lies" and forgettable "truths." *Acta Psychologica, 127*, 299–308. doi:10.1016/j.actpsy.2007.06.001

Alogna, V. K., Attaya, M. K., Aucoin, P., Bahnik, S., Birch, S., Birt, A. R., ... Zwaan, R. A. (2014). Registered replication report: Schooler & Engstler-Schooler (1990). *Perspectives on Psychological Science, 9*, 556–578. doi:10.1177/1745691614545653

Badham, S. P., Wade, K. A., Watts, H. J. E., Woods, N. G., & Maylor, E. A. (2014). Replicating distinctive facial features in lineups: Identification performance in young versus older adults. *Psychonomic Bulletin & Review, 20*, 289–295. doi:10.3758/s13423-012-0339-2

Bar-Haim, Y., Ziv, T., Lamy, D., & Hodes, R. M. (2006). Nature and nurture in own-race face processing. *Psychological Science, 17*, 159–163.

Behrman, B. W., & Richards, R. E. (2005). Suspect/foil identification in actual crimes and in the laboratory: A reality monitoring analysis. *Law & Human Behavior, 29*, 279–301. doi:0.1007/s10979-005-3617-y

Bornstein, B. H., Deffenbacher, K. A., Penrod, S. D., & McGorty, E. K. (2012). Effects of exposure time and cognitive operations on facial identification accuracy: A meta-analysis of two variables associated with initial memory strength. *Psychology, Crime, & Law, 18*, 473–490. doi:10.1080/1068316X.2010.508458

Bothwell, R. K., Brigham, J. C., & Malpass, R. S. (1989). Cross-racial identification. *Personality & Social Psychology Bulletin, 15*, 19–25. doi:10.1177/0146167289151002

Brewer, N., Weber, N., & Semmler, C. (2005). Eyewitness identification. In N. Brewer & K. D. Williams (Eds.), *Psychology and law: An empirical perspective* (pp. 177–221). New York, NY: Guilford.

Brigham, J. C., Bennett, L. B., Meissner, C. A., & Mitchell, T. L. (2007). The influence of race on eyewitness memory. In R. C. L. Lindsay, D. F. Ross, J. D. Read, & M. P. Toglia (Eds.), *Handbook of eyewitness psychology: Memory for people* (Vol. *2*, pp. 257–282). Mahwah, NJ: Erlbaum.

Bruck, M., & Ceci, S. J. (1999). The suggestibility of children's memory. *Annual Review of Psychology, 50*, 419–439. http://dx.doi.org/10.1146/annurev.psych.50.1.419

Bureau of Justice Statistics (2005). *State Court Sentencing of Convicted Felons.* Washington, DC: U.S. Department of Justice.

Burton, A. M., & Jenkins, R. (2011). Unfamiliar face perception. In A. J. Calder, G. Rhodes, M. H. Johnson, & J. V. Haxby (Eds.), *Oxford handbook of face perception*. Oxford, England: Oxford University Press.

Carlson, C. A., & Carlson, M. A. (2012). A distinctiveness-driven reversal of the weapon focus effect. *Applied Psychology in Criminal Justice*, *8*, 36–53. Retrieved from http://dev.cjcenter.org/_files/apcj/apcjspring2012-tocarlson.pdf_1354815262.pdf

Carlson, C. A., & Carlson, M. A. (2014). An evaluation of lineup presentation, weapon presence, and a distinctive feature using ROC analysis. *Journal of Applied Research in Memory & Cognition*, *3*, 45–53. doi:10.1016/j.jarmac.2014.03.004

Charman, S. D., & Wells, G. L. (2006). Applied lineup theory. In R. C. L. Lindsay, D. F. Ross, J. D. Read, & M. P. Toglia (Eds.), *Handbook of eyewitness psychology: Memory for people* (pp. 219–254). Mahwah, NJ: Erlbaum.

Clark, S. E., Howell, R. T., & Davey, S. L. (2008). Regularities in eyewitness identification. *Law & Human Behavior*, *32*, 187–218. http://dx.doi.org/10.1007/s10979-006-9082-4

Davis, D., & Loftus, E. F. (2007). Internal and external sources of misinformation in adult witness memory. In M. P. Toglia, J. D. Read, D. F. Ross, & R. C. L. Lindsay (Eds.), *The handbook of eyewitness psychology: Vol. II: Memory for events* (pp. 195–237). Mahwah, NJ: Erlbaum.

Davis, D., & Loftus, E. F. (2009). Expectancies, emotion and memory reports of visual events. In J. R. Brockmole (Ed.), *The visual world in memory* (pp. 178–214). Hove, England, & New York, NY: Psychology Press.

Davis, D., & Loftus, E. F. (2012). The dangers of eyewitnesses for the innocent: Learning from the past and projecting into the age of social media. *New England Law Review*, *46*(4), 769–809. Retrieved from https://www.nesl.edu/students/law_review.cfm

Davis, D., & Loftus, E. F. (2018). 100 years of eyewitness science: What do we know, and where do we go from here? In E. Phelps & L. Davachi (Eds.), *Stevens' handbook of experimental psychology, Volume I: Learning and memory* (pp. 529–567). New York, NY: John Wiley.

Deffenbacher, K. A., Bornstein, B. H., & Penrod, S. D. (2006). Mugshot exposure effects: Retroactive interference, mugshot commitment, source confusion, and unconscious transference. *Law & Human Behavior*, *30*, 287–307. http://dx.doi.org/10.1007/s10979-006-9008-1

Deffenbacher, K. A., Bornstein, B. H., Penrod, S. D., & McGorty, E. K. (2004). A meta-analytic review of the effects of high stress on eyewitness memory. *Law & Human Behavior*, *28*, 687–706. doi:10.1007/s10979-004-0565-x

Deffenbacher, K. A., Bornstein, B. H., McGorty, E. K., & Penrod, S. D. (2008). Forgetting the once-seen face: Estimating the strength of an eyewitness's memory representation. *Journal of Experimental Psychology: Applied*, *14*, 139–150. doi:10.1037/1076-898X.14.2.139

Erickson, W. B., Lampinen, J. M., & Moore, K. N. (2015). Eyewitness identifications by older and younger adults: A meta-analysis and discussion. *Journal of Police & Criminal Psychology*. doi:10.1007/s1189 6-015-9176-3

Fawcett, J. M., Russell, E. J., Peace, K. A., & Christie, J. (2013). Of guns and geese: A meta-analytic review of the "weapon focus" literature, *Psychology, Crime & Law*, *19*, 35–66, doi:10.1080/1068316X.2011.599325

Fitzgerald, R. J., & Price, H. L. (2015). Eyewitness identification across the life span: A meta-analysis of age differences. *Psychological Bulletin*, *141*, 1228–1265. doi:10.1037/bul0000013

Garrett, B. F. (2011). *Convicting the innocent*. Cambridge, MA: Harvard University Press.

Goodman, G. S., Sayfan, L., Lee, J. S., Sandhei, M., Walle-Olsen, A., Magnussen, S., … Arredondo, P. (2007). The development of memory for own- and other-race faces. *Journal of Experimental Child Psychology*, *98*(4), 233–242. doi:10.1016/j.jeep.2007.08.004

Horry, R., Halford, P., Brewer, N., Milne, R., & Bull, R. (2014). Archival analyses of eyewitness identification test outcomes: What can they tell us about eyewitness memory? *Law & Human Behavior*, *38*, 94–108. doi:10.1037/lhb0000060

Keast, A., Brewer, N., & Wells, G. L. (2007). Children's metacognitive judgments in an eyewitness identification task. *Journal of Experimental Child Psychology, 97*, 286–314.

Lampinen, J. M., Erickson, W. B., Moore, K. N., & Hittson, A. (2014). Effects of distance on face recognition: Implications for eyewitness identification. *Psychonomic Bulletin & Review, 21*, 1489–1494. doi:10.3758/s13423-014-0641-2

Loftus, E. F. (1976). Unconscious transference in eyewitness identification. *Law & Psychology Review, 2*, 93–98. Retrieved from http://www.law.ua.edu/lawpsychology/

Loftus, E. F., Loftus, G. R., & Messo, J. (1987). Some facts about "weapon focus." *Law & Human Behavior, 11*, 55–62. doi:10.1007/BF01044839

Loftus, E. F., Miller, D. G., & Burns, H. J. (1978). Semantic integration of verbal information into a visual memory. *Journal of Experimental Psychology: Human Learning & Memory, 4*, 19–31. doi:http://dx.doi.org/10.1037/0278-7393.4.1.19

Loftus, G. R., & Harley, E. M. (2005). Why is it easier to identify someone close than far away? *Psychonomic Bulletin & Review, 12*, 43–65. doi:10.3758/BF03196348

Mecklenburg, S. H. (2006). *Report to the legislature of the State of Illinois: The Illinois pilot program on double-blind, sequential lineup procedures.* Springfield, IL: Illinois State Police.

Meissner, C. A., & Brigham, J. C. (2001). Thirty years of investigating the own-race bias in face memory for faces: A meta-analytic review. *Psychology, Public Policy, & Law, 7*, 1–35. http://dx.doi.org/10.1037//1076-8971.7.1.3

Meissner, C. A., Sporer, S. L., & Susa, K. J. (2008). A theoretical and meta-analytic review of the relationship between verbal descriptions and identification accuracy in memory for faces. *European Journal of Cognitive Psychology, 2*, 414–455. Retrieved from http://works.bepress.com/christian_meissner/32/

Memon, A., Havard, C., Clifford, B., Gabbert, F., & Watt, M. (2011). A field evaluation of the VIPER system: A new technique for eliciting eyewitness evidence. *Psychology, Crime & Law, 17*, 711–729. doi:10.1080/10683160903524333

Morgan, C.A., III, Hazlett, G. A., Doran, A., Garrett, S., Hoyt, G., Thomas, P., ... Southwick, S. M. (2004). Accuracy of eyewitness memory for persons encountered during exposure to highly intense stress. *International Journal of Law & Psychiatry, 27*, 265–279. doi:10.1016/j.ijlp.2004.03.004

National Research Council. (2014). *Identifying the culprit: Assessing eyewitness identification.* Washington, DC: The National Academies Press.

Ofshe, R. J., & Leo, R. A. (1997). The social psychology of police interrogation: The theory and classification of true and false confessions. *Studies in Law, Politics, & Society, 16*, 189–254. Retrieved from http://www.emeraldinsight.com/series/slps

Palmer, M. A., Brewer, N., & Horry, R. (2013). Understanding gender bias in face recognition: Effects of divided attention at encoding. *Acta Psychologica, 142*, 362–369. doi:10.1016/j.actpsy.2013.01.009

Patterson, H. M., & Kemp, R. I. (2006). Comparing methods of encountering post-event information: The power of co-witness suggestion. *Applied Cognitive Psychology, 20*, 1083–1099. doi:10.1002/acp.1261

Peterson, C., & Whalen, N. (2001). Five years later: Children's memory for medical emergencies. *Applied Cognitive Psychology, 15*, S7–S24. doi:10.1002/acp.832

Pezdek, K., Blandon-Gitlin, I., & Moore, C. (2003). Children's face recognition memory: More evidence for the cross-race effect. *Journal of Applied Psychology, 88*(4), 760. doi:10.1037/0021-9010.88.4.760

Rhodes, M. G., & Anastasi, J. S. (2012). The own-age bias in face recognition: A meta-analytic and theoretical review. *Psychological Bulletin, 138*, 146–174. doi:10.1037/a0025750

Scheck, B., Neufeld, P., & Dwyer, J. (2000). *Actual innocence.* New York, NY: Random House.

Schooler, J. W., & Engstler-Schooler, T. Y. (1990). Verbal overshadowing of visual memories: Some things are better left unsaid. *Cognitive Psychology*, *22*, 36–71. http://digitalcommons.utep.edu/cgi/viewcontent.cgi?article=1007&context=christian_meissner

Shaw, J. S., III, Garven, S., & Wood, J. M. (1997). Co-witness information can have immediate effects on eyewitness memory reports. *Law & Human Behavior*, *21*(5), 503–523.

Skagerberg, E. M. (2007). Co-witness feedback in line-ups. *Applied Cognitive Psychology*, *21*, 489–497.

Steblay, N. K. (1992). A meta-analytic review of the weapon focus effect. *Law & Human Behavior*, *16*, 413–424. doi:10.1007/BF02352267

Steblay, N. K., & Dysart, J. (2016). Repeated eyewitness identification procedures with the same suspect. *Journal of Applied Research in Memory & Cognition*, *5*, 284–289. http://dx.doi.org.unr.idm.oclc.org/10.1016/j.jarmac.2016.06.010

Steblay, N. K., Dysart, J., Fulero, S., & Lindsay, R. C. L. (2003). Eyewitness accuracy rates in police showup and lineup presentations: A meta-analytic comparison. *Law & Human Behavior*, *27*, 523–540. doi:10.1023/A:1025438223608

Steblay, N. K., Dysart, J. E., & Wells, G. L. (2011). Seventy-two tests of the sequential lineup superiority effect: A meta-analysis and policy discussion. *Psychology, Public Policy, & Law*, *17*, 99–139. http://dx.doi.org/10.1037/a0021650

Steidle, A., Werth, L., & Hanke, E. (2011). You can't see much in the dark: Darkness affects construal level and psychological distance. *Social Psychology*, *42*, 174–194. doi:10.1027/1864-9335/a000061

Technical Working Group for Eyewitness Evidence. (1999). *Eyewitness evidence: A guide for law enforcement.* Washington, DC: U.S. Department of Justice.

The Cases: DNA Exoneree Profiles. (2016, April 11). Retrieved from http://www.innocenceproject.org/cases-false-imprisonment

Tollestrup, P. A., Turtle, J. W., & Yuille, J. C. (1994). Actual victims and witnesses to robbery and fraud: An archival analysis. In D. F. Ross, J. D. Read, & M. P. Toglia (Eds.), *Adult eyewitness testimony: Current trends and developments* (pp. 144–162). Cambridge, England: Cambridge University Press.

Topp-Mariquez, L. D., McQuiston, D., & Malpass, R. S. (2014). Facial composites and the misinformation effect: How composites distort memory. *Legal & Criminological Psychology*, May, 1–18. doi:10.1111/lcrp.12054

Valentine, T., Pickering, A., & Darling, S. (2003). Characteristics of eyewitness identification that predict the outcome of real lineups. *Applied Cognitive Psychology*, *17*, 969–993. doi:10.1002/acp.939

Valentine, T., & Mesout, J. (2009). Eyewitness identification under stress in the London Dungeon. *Applied Cognitive Psychology*, *23*(2), 151–161. doi:10.1002/acp.1463

Wells, G. L., Charman, S. D., & Olson, E. A. (2005). Building face composites can harm lineup identification performance. *Journal of Experimental Psychology: Applied*, *11*, 147–156. doi:http://dx.doi.org/10.1037/1076-898X.11.3.147

Wells, G. L., & Hasel, L. E. (2007). Facial composite production by eyewitnesses. *Current Directions in Psychological Science*, *16*, 6–10. doi:10.1111/j.1467-8721.2007.00465.x

Wells, G. L., Memon, A., & Penrod, S. D. (2006). Eyewitness evidence: Improving its probative value. *Psychological Science in the Public Interest*, *7*(2), 45–75. doi:10.1111/j.1529-1006.2006.00027.x

Wells, G. L., Small, M., Penrod, S., Malpass, R. S., Fulero, S. M., & Brimacombe, C.A. E. (1998). Eyewitness identification procedures: Recommendations for lineups and photospreads. *Law & Human Behavior*, *22*, 603–647. Retrieved from http://www.jstor.org/stable/1394446

Wells, G. L., Steblay, N. K., & Dysart, J. E. (2011). An initial report of the AJS national eyewitness identification field studies. *American Judicature Society.* http://www.ajs.org/wc/pdfs/EWID_PrintFriendly.pdf

Wells, G. L., Steblay, N. K., & Dysart, J. E. (2014). Double-blind photo-lineups using actual eyewitnesses: An experimental test of a sequential versus simultaneous lineup procedure. *Law & Human Behavior*, *15*. doi:10.1037/lhb0000096

Wixted, J. T., Mickes, L., Clark, S. E., Gronlund, S. D., & Roediger, H. L. III. (2015). Initial eyewitness confidence reliably predicts eyewitness identification accuracy. *American Psychologist*, *70*, 515–526. doi:10.1037/a0039510

Wright, D. B., & Sladden, B. (2003). An own gender bias and the importance of hair in face recognition. *Acta Psychologica*, *114*, 101–114. doi:10.1016/S0001-6918(03)00052-0

Yarmey, A. D. (2004). Eyewitness recall and photo identification: A field experiment. *Psychology, Crime, & Law*, *10*, 53–68. doi:10.1080/10683160210000583

11

Eyewitness Memory in Children with Autism Spectrum Disorder

Michael Carlin

The ability of children with autism spectrum disorder (ASD) to recall details of past, witnessed events is complicated, relative to non-ASD peers and even adults with ASD, by many factors. Prior chapters in this volume focus on specific aspects of cognitive functioning and memory that differ across those with and without autism. Evidence for differences in memory profiles (Williams, Goldstein, & Minshew, 2006), executive functioning (e.g., Corbett, Constantine, Hendren, Rockey, & Ozonoff, 2009; Pennington & Ozonoff, 1996; Robinson, Goddard, Dritschel, Wisley, & Howlin, 2009), organization (e.g., Southwick et al., 2011), sense of self (Happé, 2003), self-referencing (Henderson et al., 2009), and source monitoring (e.g., Bowler, Gardiner, & Berthollier, 2004; Hala, Rasmussen, & Henderson, 2005; Russell & Jarrold, 1999) between those with and without ASD indicate likely differences in ability to remember and report past witnessed events. Remembering and describing past witnessed events well involves memory for complex scenes and the ability to structure a coherent narrative in which one is an actor in the context of the memory. Often, for forensic situations at least, knowledge of intentionality, temporal and action sequencing, and ability to differentiate one's own from others' actions is required. This form of recall therefore maps directly to most of the cited deficits, or differences, in cognition and memory functioning (e.g., Minshew & Goldstein, 2001) in those with ASD.

Unfortunately, few studies have used classic eyewitness testimony research methodologies and included children (less than 18 years of age) with ASD. In the recent review of eyewitness testimony research by Maras and Bowler (2014) only one study involving children (McCrory, Henry, & Happé, 2007) with ASD was cited. The present chapter focuses on those studies that have assessed memory for a witnessed and/or experienced event in children with ASD, with an eye toward identifying individual difference variables that can explain some of the variability between- and within-groups. The chapter also focuses on methodological issues and

The Wiley Handbook of Memory, Autism Spectrum Disorder, and the Law, First Edition.
Edited by Jonni L. Johnson, Gail S. Goodman, and Peter C. Mundy.

several areas of related research that should inform understanding of the accuracy of eyewitness reports provided by children with ASD.

Studies of eyewitness memory in children with ASD

One of the earliest studies performed on memory for an experienced event in those with ASD was that of Millward, Powell, Messer, and Jordan (2000). Millward et al. conducted a sophisticated study of memory for self-experienced and other-experienced events in children with and without ASD. Children with ASD ($n = 12$; 11 males; M CA ~ 13 years) were compared to children matched for verbal mental age ($n = 12$; 10 males; M CA ~ 6 years). The verbal mental ages (VMAs) were approximately 6 years, on average, in both groups. Each child participated in two walks with staged events along the way. The child was accompanied by just an experimenter in one condition. In the other condition, the child was accompanied by the experimenter and another child. In the latter condition, each child on the walk experienced different events. Thus, ability to remember self- and other-experienced events could be compared. Memory was assessed via both free recall and subsequent cued recall testing.

Results indicated that memory overall was poorer in those with ASD than in the comparison children. However, this group difference was present only for self-experienced events. There was no group difference for events involving the other child. Correlational tests showed no relationship between CA, VMA, and recall. Millward et al. (2000) hypothesized that this difficulty in memory for self-experienced events is due to a diminished sense of self in those with ASD. Notably, this study involved a comparison of groups differing in both CA and ASD diagnosis. Those in the ASD group were more than twice the age of those in the comparison group. Though CA was shown not to correlate with outcomes within-groups (though correlation values were not reported), the within-group variability was much lower than the between-group variability for CA. The ability to disentangle the effects of ASD and CA, therefore, is limited. This study also did not report statistical information necessary to compute effect sizes. Despite these limitations, however, Millward et al. is a good model for designing a study on eyewitness memory in those with ASD.

Cornett, Miora, Fass, and Dixon (2013) performed a straightforward study assessing whether children (ages 6–16 years; 40 males, 2 females) with autism differ in their abilities to recall personally experienced or witnessed events. Children were assigned to either the witnessed or experienced event conditions. Both events involved a parent briefly leaving a child alone and a stranger/confederate approaching the child while the parent was away. The personally experienced event occurred when the parent and child came to the office for the experiment. The parent was instructed to step away to take a phone call to provide the confederate an opportunity to speak with the child alone. The witnessed event was a videotaped event, watched by the participant, that involved a child and parent entering an office, the parent stepping away to answer a call, and a stranger approaching and speaking with the child. In each condition, the child approached by the stranger was asked several questions, including whether the child wanted to be driven home by the stranger. The 42 participants, equally divided into the two conditions, then were asked 11 recognition questions.

Results indicated that details of the witnessed event were better remembered than were details from the personally experienced event. The difference was not statistically significant due to low power (i.e., .36 for an effect size of $d = .50$), but the effect size (d) was 0.51, a degree typically considered significant. Results also showed that memory score was independent of age. This study supported the findings of Millward et al. (2000). Those with ASD had better memory for events experienced by others than for events experienced themselves, and recall was independent of CA.

The Cornett et al. (2013) study was limited in several respects, however. First, the study did not incorporate a comparison group of children without ASD. Second, no specific information regarding the level of intelligence or verbal skills of participants was provided. All participants were required to communicate verbally to complete the study, but no individual differences data were reported. These methodological limitations reduce the impact of the study. Despite these limitations, however, the study does appear to be adequately designed and the results support Millward et al. (2000) in that memory for personally experienced events is worse than memory for witnessed events in those with ASD.

In a more complete design, McCrory et al. (2007) assessed eyewitness memory for a live scene in children with and without Asperger syndrome. The groups were matched for verbal, performance, and full-scale IQ. The average ages of the groups were approximately 13 and the IQ averages were slightly above 100. The samples again were predominantly male (46 males, 5 females). This study was able to provide more information regarding eyewitness memory in those with ASD because the witnessed scene included two key events, one neutral (i.e., a broken tripod) and one socioemotional (i.e., one actor injured another's finger). The socioemotional event included a minor exchange between the two actors involving annoyance on the part of the injured person and remorse on the part of the other actor. This study also used multiple forms of questioning, including an initial free-recall phase and subsequent cued recall phases.

These elements of the design provided much more information in terms of results. Those without ASD recalled more information than those with ASD, though elements recalled were equally likely to be accurate. More important for understanding group differences, group interacted with event (neutral vs. socioemotional). Those with ASD were less likely to recall elements of the socioemotional event, but were more likely to recall elements of the neutral event than were those without ASD. This is consistent with the general belief that those with ASD are less attuned to emotional aspects of social interactions. A follow-up correlational analysis also showed that executive functioning ability was positively correlated with overall recall in the ASD group, but not the comparison group. A further qualification of the recall findings, however, emerged when the guided questioning data were reviewed. Group differences were not present in the guided memory phases of questioning. Thus, those with ASD may remember as much about past events, including socioemotional aspects of those events; they just do not report it spontaneously during free (i.e., unguided) recall. This pattern also commonly is reported in the literature on intelligence and eyewitness testimony (e.g., Ternes & Yuille, 2008).

McCrory et al. (2007) proposed that differences between those with and without ASD are due to weak central coherence in those with ASD, which leads to depressed gist memory. In terms of practical implications, McCrory et al. proposed that guided questioning may need to be emphasized when dealing with witnesses with ASD in order to elicit facts not produced during unguided recall. The methodological quality of this study was quite good, and could serve as a model for future research. One limiting factor was the inclusion of only people with average IQs. As noted, and generally in studies of cognitive processing in those with ASD, relatively few studies have investigated the correlation of IQ with performance of those with ASD. It appears that this study had a range of IQs, with SD ~ 15, but correlations between IQs and performance measures were not reported.

In a study focused primarily on autobiographical memory, Bruck, London, Landa, and Goodman (2007) tested memory for a staged magic show in children with and without ASD. Their sample included 30 children with autism (26 males, 4 females) with a mean age of 7.6 years and mean IQ of 96 (range 74–120). The comparison group of children without ASD (23 males, 15 females) averaged 7.4 years of age and an IQ of 105. Sex and IQ were not matched between groups in this study. Following multiple autobiographical memory assessments, children were asked to act as an assistant for a magician for a brief show. Within the magic show event, 20 key memory elements were embedded for future assessment. Memory for magic show events was tested multiple times in order to assess general memory for the show and to test for misinformation effects.

The initial free-recall assessment occurred about eight days after the magic show. This test occurred before any attempts to interject misinformation. Results showed that those without ASD recalled more information than did those with ASD. This is consistent with prior studies of eyewitness free recall involving those with ASD. Bruck et al. (2007) further assessed the accuracy of free reports across groups. Again, as commonly found in other studies the reports of those with and without ASD were equally accurate when considered as a percentage of their total reports. The groups of children with and without ASD were divided into younger and older groups via median split. No age differences or interactions involving age were found for free recall. Stronger evidence for the nature of the relationship would have been derived had age not been defined by median split, which causes most individual difference information to be lost. No data were presented regarding the relationship between IQ and recall of experienced events.

The final systematic study of eyewitness memory in children with ASD is that of Mattison, Dando, and Ormerod (2015). Mattison et al. assessed eyewitness memory accuracy and means for eliciting information from those with ASD. In their study, participants viewed a brief video of a crime. The video showed two people entering a store, and subsequently, running from the store being chased by the store's owner. Relatively large samples of 45 ASD children (M CA 14.5 years) and 45 children matched based on verbal mental age (M CA ~ 10 years) were compared. This study was unique because it employed three different recall conditions: sketch, mental reinstatement, and control (no special instruction). In the sketch condition, participants were asked to draw what happened in the video prior to being asked to explain it verbally. The mental-reinstatement condition involved cued recall of the child's day leading up to participation in the study, elements of the room in which the video was seen, who was present, and so on. The final element of the mental reinstatement involved the child thinking about the contents of the video itself. After a brief pause the formal request to report elements of the witnessed event commenced. The control condition involved just a request to recall as much of the video crime as possible. Overall, children without ASD recalled more elements of the video and were more accurate. The sketch condition, however, resulted in better memory performance for those with ASD and equivalent accuracy, overall, between groups. When considered by type of information recalled, those with ASD scored much lower for action elements than did those without ASD. This memory deficit for action elements in those with ASD held true even in the sketch condition.

Mattison et al. (2015) provided the best evidence to date for means to improve free reports of witnesses with ASD. Allowing those with ASD to draw what they remembered about the video led to better memory. During the drawing phase, however, the participants were asked to explain what they were drawing as they did it. This condition therefore involved greater focus on the elements of the video crime and opportunity to verbally rehearse responses prior to formal interviewing. That significant eyewitness accuracy improvements occurred has great practical importance. However, from an experimental viewpoint, it is only the first step toward understanding why this condition was effective. Additional comparison groups, for example, one involving additional opportunity for verbalizing what one remembers about a crime, are needed before definitive mechanisms for improvement can be specified. The mental-reinstatement condition involved some opportunity to report what they remembered about the crime, but only after a significant amount of time thinking about unrelated events (e.g., events prior to the video). The results though do demonstrate that free reports of those with ASD can be enhanced through use of evidence-based supports. This is particularly important for this population that has consistently been shown to underperform peers in free-recall conditions (e.g., Boucher, 1981).

Summary of results

Across these studies several general findings emerge. First, free recall of witnessed events is an area of deficit in those with ASD. Consistently across these studies, those with ASD recalled fewer elements of the events witnessed or experienced. Though it should be noted that accuracy of the information, in terms of percentage correct of total reported, did not differ between groups with and without ASD. Thus, the information recalled is as trustworthy as that of children without ASD.

The finding of limited total recall in those with ASD is not surprising given findings that event narratives of children with ASD differ systematically from those of children without ASD. For example, King, Dockrell, and Stuart (2013) had children with and without ASD recall past events from their lives. The children's reports were scored for elements such as mean length of utterance, total number of words, and number of references to mental states. The children with ASD had average IQs and vocabulary scores, and were compared to language- and CA-matched children. Results showed that narratives of those with ASD included fewer words, were less complex, and included fewer references to mental states than did narratives of matched controls. Similarly, Goldman (2008) reported that children with ASD, with average levels of intelligence, produced impoverished narratives relative to CA-matched comparisons. Goldman found specific deficits in those with ASD for elements such as coherence, action details, and resolution. Diehl, Bennetto, and Young (2006) similarly found that children with ASD provided narratives that were less temporally coherent and contained fewer causal linkages, though narrative length did not differ across groups with and without ASD. Diehl et al. hypothesized that the differences were due, at least in part, to diminished use of gist memory to structure memory-based narratives.

A second general finding in the literature on eyewitness memory in children with ASD is that recall deficiencies can be overcome via targeted questioning or other form of support. The studies of Millward et al. (2000) and McCrory et al. (2007) showed that total memory scores improved from free to cued recall formats. The latter study showed that large differences between groups for free reporting of event details were reduced to insignificance when guided questioning procedures were employed. For applied purposes, however, this greater reliance on directed remembering should be balanced against dangers of suggestion and misinformation effects.

Mattison et al. (2015) provided the first demonstration of use of a support to improve free reports in those with ASD. This is an important step toward defining group specific means for improving memory reports for experienced, or witnessed, events without the dangers of implanting false memories. The allowance of drawing what happened prior to and during recall enhanced free recall substantially. Though, as noted above, some questions remain about the mechanism(s) for this gain, additional pursuit of this and other methods for enhancing free recall for witnessed events in children with ASD seems warranted.

A third general finding from the literature so far is that memory for experienced events is worse than memory for witnessed events in children with ASD. The studies of Cornett et al. (2013) and Millward et al. (2000) both directly compared personally experienced to witnessed events and each study found the witnessed-events advantage in those with ASD. In Millward et al. the non-ASD participants showed the opposite, and typical, pattern of better memory for experienced than observed events. This is the standard finding, in accord with the classic self-reference effect (Rogers, Kuiper, & Kirker, 1977) and theories of the association between the self and autobiographical memory (Conway & Pleydall-Pearce, 2000). That this is consistently found not to be the case with children with ASD in these eyewitness situations seems to indicate that this is a distinct pattern in this population.

Finally, one of the goals of the review of the studies in eyewitness memory in children with ASD was to identify predictors of variability within- and between-groups. As the individual study descriptions indicate, little was done to directly assess such predictors thus far. Several of the studies have assessed the relationship between CA and memory performance, and all have found no relationship. Millward et al. (2000) assessed the relationship between VMA and memory, and found no significant correlation was present. The one instance of a significant correlate of event memory was that of executive functioning being positively correlated in the McCrory et al. (2007) study. This lack of specificity of correlates of eyewitness memory in children with ASD is addressed further in the discussion of methodology.

Summary of research methods

A brief overview of the methods employed in the five studies reviewed on eyewitness memory in children with ASD is shown in Table 11.1.

The first point to be made is that regarding sample sizes. As is true any time one is studying relatively small populations, obtaining a sufficient number of participants is challenging. The issue of statistical power therefore must be considered when interpreting results and designing studies. As is evident in Table 11.1, the majority of these studies had sample sizes below 25 in experimental groups. This low power necessitates

Table 11.1 Characteristics of Studies on Eyewitness Testimony in Children with ASD.

Study		*N (male: female)*	*CA (years)*	*VMA*	*IQ*	*Event*
Millward et al. (2000)	ASD	12 (11:1)	13.1	6.3	NA	Outdoor Walk
	TD	12 (10:2)	5.8	6.2	NA	
Bruck et al. (2007)	ASD	30 (26:4)	7.6	NA	96	Magic Show
	TD	38 (23:15)	7.4	NA	105	
McCrory et al. (2007)	ASD	24 (22:2)	13.02	NA	105	Classroom
	TD	27 (24:3)	12.55	NA	107	Presentation
Cornett et al. (2013)	ASD	42 (40:2)	10.8	NA	NA	Encounter with Stranger in Office
Mattison et al. (2015)	ASD	45 (NA)	14.6	NA	NA	Crime Video
	TD	45 (NA)	10.2	NA	NA	

reporting of effect sizes so meaningful summary of results can be undertaken. The risk of significant effect sizes being nonsignificant if using just the $p < .05$ criterion is quite high in these circumstances. Several of the studies did not report effect sizes or enough statistical information so they could be computed. This was particularly relevant when considering correlates of performances in these studies. First, sometimes correlations were simply stated as being nonsignificant without the values reported. Second, correlations would have to be quite large to be significant with the sample sizes employed in these studies.

A second issue regarding sampling is that of sex ratios. As is again apparent in Table 11.1, the majority of knowledge about eyewitness memory in children with ASD is based on performances of males. This is justified experimentally due to the actual sex distribution in the population of those with ASD, but it limits the applied value of the research. More attention to sex differences in memory and specifically, witnessed-event memory is needed.

A third sampling issue concerns distributions of intelligence in the studies of eyewitness memory. Studies have either included samples with low IQ (e.g., Millward et al., 2000) or samples with average IQ (e.g., McCrory et al., 2007). The ideal design would include a full range of intelligences so a better estimate of the relationship between intelligence and memory could be obtained. This same logic would apply to other correlates of interest, such as CA, executive functioning skill, and verbal, or narrative, ability. It even would apply to comparisons of children and adults with ASD. Studies to date have focused on one or the other group, which limits sample sizes and complicates correlational estimates due to range restriction.

In addition to expanding knowledge of the influences of intellectual level and age on eyewitness memory in those with ASD, attention to other qualifying variables is needed. The studies to date have sampled, and even directly compared, experienced, and witnessed events, which is a critical distinction for understanding (eyewitness) memory in children with ASD. Cornett et al. (2013) instituted an experienced stranger-danger scenario and a videotaped version. Millward et al. (2000) implemented two walks, within-subjects, to compare memory for personally experienced (accompanied and unaccompanied) events to memory for events occurring to another. Bruck et al. (2007) and McCrory et al. (2007) employed live events as opposed to videos of events (e.g., Mattison et al., 2015). This use of live events and focus on self- versus other-referencing is a strength of the literature to date. McCrory et al. (2007) also differentiated memory for socioemotional elements of the event, whereas Mattison et al. (2015) showed that those with ASD performed relatively more poorly for action elements within the crime video. Replication of these effects and focus on additional such variables will greatly advance knowledge of eyewitness testimony in children with ASD.

Related research

This section summarizes representative studies in areas of research that may inform research on eyewitness memory accuracy in children with ASD. As mentioned in the opening to this chapter, eyewitness memory is complicated and multifaceted, involving the interaction of many cognitive abilities. Given the relatively limited number of studies that directly assess eyewitness memory in this population, discussion of additional areas that may guide future studies seems warranted. The areas considered are temporal processing, schemas, false memory, and suggestibility. Per the goals of this chapter, studies involving children with ASD are the focus.

Temporal processing

The ability to understand event sequences and intentions of actors in context has been a focus of research on autism for many years (e.g., Bennetto, Pennington, & Rogers, 1996). Baron-Cohen, Leslie, and Frith (1986) compared participants with ASD to those with Down syndrome and no developmental disability. Participants had to complete four-frame pictured story sequences given just the first picture. The stories were categorized as depicting mechanical, behavioral, or intentional (i.e., involving knowledge of actor mental states) sequences. Results showed that those with ASD performed significantly more poorly in the intentional condition. Further, the narratives of the children with ASD did not include references to mental states, at least to the degree that the other two groups did so. This finding was replicated more recently by Goldstein et al. (2008) in the context of the Picture Arrangement task of the WAIS-III. This lack of attention to, and/or memory for, events involving intentionality has clear importance for eyewitness memory. In many applied eyewitness situations, the eyewitness is asked to report on the intentions of the people involved and the temporal sequencing of events. Deficits in these areas of cognitive processing and/or narration would impact eyewitness reports of those with ASD.

A focus on the roles of time perception and temporal processing deficits (e.g., Allman, 2011; Allman & Meck, 2012; Wallace & Happé, 2008) in understanding ASD has gained more attention in recent years. Boucher, Pons, Lind, and Williams (2007) compared the temporal processing abilities of children with ASD to those of children with learning disabilities (LDs). They specifically studied understanding of event sequencing, knowledge of temporal transformations, and the ability to synthesize events into a coherent whole. The work was modeled on that on "diachronic thinking" by Montangero (e.g., Maurice-Naville & Montangero, 1992; Montangero, Pons, & Cattin, 2000).

Participants in the Boucher et al. (2007) study were children with ASD aged 7–18 years and children with LDs aged 8–17 years. Groups were matched for IQ and vocabulary ability. Groups were assessed on three temporal processing parameters: tendency, transformation, and synthesis. Tendency involved describing changes over time during recall of a picture. Transformation involved representation of qualitative change in an object (i.e., a tree) over time. Synthesis involved providing a summary statement encompassing the events of a story. A series of general inference-making control tasks also was used to determine whether differences between groups were restricted to time-based inference making or more general. Results across two experiments showed that those with ASD performed significantly more poorly on the temporal processing tasks, but not the control tasks, relative to the children with LD. Boucher et al. also assessed correlations between task performance and IQ, CA, vocabulary skills, and theory of mind. None of the variables predicted performance on the temporal processing tasks. The lone significant predictor was group status (ASD < LD). It also was notable in this study that the general finding of low levels of free recall by those with ASD was replicated.

These studies on deficits in temporal processing in those with ASD raise concerns for eyewitness testimony from those with ASD. Differential processing of timing at very basic and higher-order levels (e.g., transformation and synthesis) would be expected to compromise eyewitness reports. This may relate to deficits in eyewitness reports of actions in context seen in the studies discussed above (e.g., Mattison et al., 2015).

Event schemas

Schemas are abstract mental representations of objects and events that likely occur in particular contexts. Schemas provide one form of top-down guidance for attention, and therefore, object and event memory. The role and use of schemas by those with ASD has been the focus of several studies performed by Loth and her colleagues in recent years. Loth, Gómez, and Happé (2008) assessed schema usage in narratives of children and young adults with ASD. Participants had to describe typical events occurring in a restaurant and at Christmas to a person unfamiliar with those situations or occasions. Narratives were scored generally for three components: causal-temporal ordering, hierarchical organization, and generality. Group comparisons were made between those with ASD who passed and did not pass theory of mind assessments, and between those with ASD and those with LD or who were typically developing. Results showed that those with ASD who failed theory of mind assessments did more poorly on the measure of causal-temporal ordering. There was no such difference for those with ASD who passed the theory of mind tests. Loth et al. speculated that narrative memory for events in those with ASD who do not pass theory of mind tests may differ qualitatively from that of those with ASD who score better on tests of theory of mind.

Loth, Gómez, and Happé (2011) provided more clarity regarding the relationship between ASD, schema integrity, and memory performance. Children (aged 8–16 years) with and without ASD were assessed for their memory of story-relevant pictures. Participants were read stories instantiating common scenarios (e.g., party). After being read the story a picture of a story-relevant scene (e.g., room with cake, balloons) was displayed for 30 seconds. Once the picture was removed from the screen, participants were asked to recall everything they could from the picture. Responses were coded as schema-relevant, schema-irrelevant, or neutral. Results showed that the groups of children with and without ASD did not differ in terms of total numbers of items recalled. However, when items were considered by category (schema-relevant, schema-irrelevant, neutral) group differences did emerge. The children with ASD recalled fewer schema-relevant items, but more neutral items than did the comparison children. The rates of recall for schema-irrelevant items were similar between groups. The children with ASD did not show the typical advantage for schema-relevant items over schema-irrelevant items. This classic difference was present in the group without ASD. Thus, children with ASD, and adults with ASD according to a follow-up study, do not use top-down guidance to differentially remember aspects of scenes. This certainly has direct relevance to most eyewitness situations in which the particular scene or aspects of the witnessed event are schema-consistent or inconsistent. Therefore, child witnesses with ASD may remember as much as other child witnesses, but what they remember may be qualitatively different.

False memory

As with other areas of focus in this chapter, the number of studies involving children with ASD is limited. In fact, no studies could be found specifically studying false memory in children with ASD. All of the published research (e.g., Beversdorf et al., 2000) involves samples of adults, at least based on average CAs reported. Thus, there is great need for studies involving children with ASD employing classic false memory paradigms such as the Deese-Roediger-McDermott (DRM) paradigm (Deese, 1959; Roediger & McDermott, 1995) or other event memory paradigms (e.g., Garry & Gerrie, 2005; Pezdek, Blandon-Gitlin, & Gabbay, 2006). Beversdorf et al. (2000) assessed true and false recognition in the DRM paradigm word-list paradigm in a sample of adults with ASD of average intelligence. Results indicated that those with ASD were less susceptible to critical item intrusions (i.e., false memories) than were CA-matched comparison participants. Beversdorf et al. attributed this to presence of restricted semantic networks in those with ASD.

An extension of this work to a predominantly adolescent sample was performed by Bellamy (2010) as part of her dissertation at the University of Edinburgh. Though the sample included just 13 individuals with ASD, 9 of the 13 were below 18 years of age. Results of this experiment were consistent with the published results of Beversdorf et al. in that those with ASD were less likely to report critical lures in the DRM paradigm. Bellamy concluded that the memory differences observed overall were consistent with a gist memory deficit in those with ASD. It should be noted, however, that this false memory paradigm is quite distinct from the types of memory intrusions or errors that are likely to occur in eyewitness contexts.

Suggestibility

Two studies have systematically assessed susceptibility to suggestion in children with ASD. Bruck et al. (2007), as part of the study described earlier in this chapter, included an interview during which true and false "reminders" were made. Four days after the reminders were given, another interview was conducted with each participant. This interview included both a free-recall phase and a recognition phase. In free recall, those without ASD provided more details about the event, but accuracy did not differ across the groups with and without ASD. This is a common finding when comparing children with and without ASD on free-recall test. The only other difference in free recall was that those with ASD produced more irrelevant statements that were not pertinent to the witnessed event.

In the recognition phase of the Bruck et al. (2007) study, both groups of children were quite susceptible to suggestion, with about twice as many falsely suggested items "recognized" as control items. However, the group with ASD was more likely to assent to false recognition items that had not been suggested during the prior interview.

Thus, children with ASD were more likely to report events during recognition that never occurred and never were suggested previously. Thus, these data are consistent with the interpretation that children with ASD are not more prone to suggestion via misinformation, but are more prone to report false events.

McCrory et al. (2007) included in their design, post-free recall, a questioning session that included 6 general questions to elicit more details than were provided in free recall, 10 specific questions, and 18 leading questions. Of the 18 leading questions, 9 dealt with social interactions and 9 concerned physical attributes. There were no differences between the groups with and without ASD with regard to responses to the leading questions. Both groups affirmed approximately half of the 18 "facts." No information regarding differences across the nine social and physical attributes questions were presented. Thus, again, those with and without ASD were equally prone to misinformation effects during questioning.

It is important to note that these two studies (i.e., Bruck et al., 2007; and McCrory et al., 2007) employed similar matching procedures for their groups with and without ASD. The groups in each study were matched for both CA and intelligence, with intelligence levels being average in all groups. Thus, these studies employed high-functioning individuals with autism. That groups were much more similar than different is not surprising given these factors. Individuals with ASD with lower levels of intelligence certainly could demonstrate quite different patterns of performance relative to CA-matched peers. This again highlights the need for additional research clarifying the role of factors such as age and intelligence on susceptibility to false memories, misinformation effects, and suggestion.

Summary

Remarkable progress in understanding cognition in those with ASD has been made in the past two decades. This has occurred despite significant methodological challenges, including recruitment of large numbers of participants and the great variability in the ASD population that makes identifying differences more difficult. The literature on eyewitness memory in children with ASD is somewhat limited at this time, but is developing. Despite this, however, confidence in some general findings is justified. First, several studies have shown that free reports of those with ASD are less complete than comparison children. This has held even when comparison groups are matched for verbal ability (Mattison, 2015; Millward et al., 2000) and intelligence (Bruck et al., 2007; McCrory et al., 2007). Second, memory for personally experienced events is an area of relative weakness in those with ASD. Both Cornett et al. (2013) and Millward et al. (2007) showed memory of those with ASD was better for events viewed happening to others than for events happening to themselves. These discrepancies between groups are diminished when guided questioning is used rather than free recall, but differences remain. Finally, several studies have shown that the types of details remembered by children with ASD may differ from age- and IQ-matched peers. McCrory et al. found that those with ASD were less likely to report socioemotional aspects of events, and Mattison found that memory for action elements of scenes was diminished in those with ASD relative to comparison children. Thus, the literature has been consistent in showing that eyewitness reports of children with ASD differ quantitatively and qualitatively from those of children without ASD.

The differences in eyewitness reports between children with and without ASD are not unexpected given the literature on more general aspects of cognitive and memory functioning in those with ASD. Many studies have identified aspects of executive functioning (e.g., use of gist and schemas, sense of self) and narrative organization and quality that differ between children with and without ASD. This consistency between the basic research described in other chapters and the more applied research on eyewitness testimony described in this chapter lends credibility to the findings and confidence that differences in eyewitness reports between these groups of children can be predicted with some accuracy. Though this certainly can be of some use in forensic contexts, some caution is still warranted. Much work still needs to be done to be able to predict how individual children will perform. Current knowledge provides some confidence in predicting group differences, but the research on individual differences variables still is lacking. Research focused on how individuals with ASD who differ in narrative ability, intelligence, age, and executive functioning perform in eyewitness situations is needed to inform public policy and forensic practice.

References

Allman, M. J. (2011). Deficits in temporal processing associated with autistic disorder. *Frontiers in Integrative Neuroscience, 5*(2).

Allman, M. J., & Meck, W. H. (2012). Pathophysiological distortions in time perception and timed performance. *Brain: A Journal of Neurology, 135*, 656–677.

Anderson, S. M., Carlson, C. A., Carlson, M. A., & Gronlund, S. D. (2014). Individual differences predict eyewitness identification performance. *Personality & Individual Differences, 60*, 36–40.

Baron-Cohen, S., Leslie, A. M., & Frith, U. (1986). Mechanical, behavioural, and intentional understanding of picture stories in autistic children. *British Journal of Developmental Psychology, 4*, 113–125.

Bellamy, K. J. (2010). *Cognitive neuroscience of false memory: The role of gist memory.* Unpublished dissertation.

Bennetto, L., Pennington, B. F., & Rogers, S. J. (1996). Intact and impaired memory functions in autism. *Child Development, 67*, 1816–1835.

Beversdorf, D. Q., Smith, B. W., Crucian, G. P., Anderson, J. M., Keillor, J. M., Barrett, A. M., Hughes, J. D., Felopulos, G. J., Bauman, M. L., Nadeau, S. E., & Heilman, K. M. (2000). Increased discrimination of "false memories" in autism spectrum disorder. *Proceedings of the National Academy of Sciences, 97*, 8734–8737.

Bordignon, S., Endres, R. G., Trentini, C. M., & Bosa, C. A. (2015). Memory in children and adolescents with autism spectrum disorder: A systematic literature review. *Psychology & Neuroscience, 8*, 211–245.

Boucher, J. (1981). Memory for recent events in autistic children. *Journal of Autism & Developmental Disorders, 11*, 293–301.

Boucher, J., Pons, F., Lind, S., & Williams, D. (2007). Temporal cognition in children with autistic spectrum disorders: Tests of diachronic thinking. *Journal of Autism & Developmental Disorders, 37*, 1413–1429.

Bowler, D. M., Gardiner, J. M., & Berthollier, N. (2004). Source memory in adolescents and adults with Asperger's syndrome. *Journal of Autism & Developmental Disorders, 34*, 535–542.

Bruck, M., London, K., Landa, R., & Goodman, J. (2007). Autobiographical memory and suggestibility in children with autism spectrum disorder. *Development & Psychopathology, 19*, 73–95.

Conway, M. A., & Pleydall-Pearce, C. W. (2000). The construction of autobiographical memories in the self-memory system. *Psychological Review*, *107*, 261–288.

Corbett, B. A., Constantine, L. J., Hendren, R., Rocke, D., & Ozonoff, S. (2009). Examining executive functioning in children with autism spectrum disorder, attention deficit hyperactivity disorder and typical development. *Psychiatry Research*, *166*, 210–222.

Cornett, K. A., Miora, D. S., Fass, T., & Dixon, D. (2013). Memory functioning for personally experienced and witnessed events in children with autism and the implications for educators, mental health professionals, and the law. *Journal of Applied Research on Children: Informing Policy for Children at Risk*, *4*(2).

Deese, J. (1959). On the prediction of occurrence of particular verbal intrusions in immediate recall. *Journal of Experimental Psychology*, *58*, 17–22.

Diehl, J. J., Bennetto, L., & Young, E. C. (2006). Story recall and narrative coherence of high-functioning children with autism spectrum disorders. *Journal of Abnormal Child Psychology*, *34*, 87–102.

Garry, M., & Gerrie, M. P. (2005). When photographs create false memories. *Current Directions in Psychological Science*, *14*, 321–325.

Goldman, S. (2008). Brief Report: Narratives of personal events in children with autism and developmental language disorders: Unshared memories. *Journal of Autism & Developmental Disorders*, *38*, 1982–1988.

Goldstein, G., Allen, D., Minshew, N. J., Williams, D. L., Volkmar, F., Klin, A., & Schultz, R. T. (2008). The structure of intelligence in children and adults with high functioning autism. *Neuropsychology*, *22*, 301–312.

Hala, S., Rasmussen, C, & Henderson, A. M. E. (2005). Three types of source monitoring by children with and without autism: The role of executive function. *Journal of Autism & Developmental Disorders*, *35*, 75–89.

Happé, F. (2003). Theory of mind and the self. *Annals of the New York Academy of Sciences*, *1001*, 134–144.

Henderson, H. A., Zahka, N. E., Kojkowski, N. M., Inge, A. P., Schwartz, C. B., Hileman, C. M., Coman, D. C., & Mundy, P. C. (2009). Self-referenced memory, social cognition, and symptom presentation in autism. *Journal of Child Psychology & Psychiatry*, *50*, 853–861.

King, D., Dockrell, J. E., & Stuart, M. (2013). Event narratives in 11–14 years olds with autistic spectrum disorder. *International Journal of Language & Communication Disorders*, *48*, 522–533.

Loth, E., Gómez, J. C., & Happé, F. (2008). Event schemas in autism spectrum disorders: The role of theory of mind and weak central coherence. *Journal of Autism & Developmental Disorders*, *38*, 449–463.

Loth, E., Gómez, J. C., & Happé, F. (2011). Do high-functioning people with autism spectrum disorder spontaneously use event knowledge to selectively attend to and remember context-relevant aspects in scenes? *Journal of Autism & Developmental Disorders*, *41*, 945–961.

Maras, K. L., & Bowler, D. M. (2014). Eyewitness testimony in autism spectrum disorder: A review. *Journal of Autism & Developmental Disorders*, *44*, 2682–2697.

Mattison, M. L. A., Dando, C. J., & Ormerod, T. C. (2015). Sketching to remember: Episodic free recall task support for child witnesses and victims with autism spectrum disorder. *Journal of Autism & Developmental Disorders*, *45*, 1751–1765.

Maurice-Naville, D., & Montangero, J. (1992). The development of diachronic thinking: 8–12-year-old Children's understanding of the evolution of forest disease. *British Journal of Developmental Psychology*, *10*, 365–383.

McCrory, E., Henry, L. A., & Happé, F. (2007). Eye-witness memory and suggestibility in children with Asperger syndrome. *Journal of Child Psychology & Psychiatry*, *48*, 482–489.

Millward, C., Powell, S., Messer, D., & Jordan, R. (2000). Recall for self and other in autism: Children's memory for events experienced by themselves and their peers. *Journal of Autism & Developmental Disorders*, *30*, 15–28.

Minshew, N. J., & Goldstein, G. (2001). The pattern of intact and impaired memory function in autism. *Journal of Child Psychology & Psychiatry*, *42*, 1095–1101.

Montangero, J., Pons, F., & Cattin, J.-P. (2000). The diachronic approach and solutions to interpersonal conflicts. *British Journal of Developmental Psychology*, *18*, 415–429.

Pennington, B. F., & Ozonoff, S. (1996). Executive functions and developmental psychopathology. *Journal of Child Psychology & Psychiatry*, *37*, 51–87.

Pezdek, K., Blandon-Gitlin, I., & Gabbay, P. (2006). Imagination and memory: Does imagining implausible events lead to false autobiographical memories? *Psychonomic Bulletin & Review*, *13*, 764–769.

Robinson, S., Goddard, L., Dritschel, B., Wisley, M., & Howlin, P. (2009). Executive functions in children with autism spectrum disorders. *Brain & Cognition*, *71*, 362–368.

Roediger, H.L., III., & McDermott, K. B. (1995). Creating false memories: Remembering words not presented in lists. *Journal of Experimental Psychology: Learning, Memory, & Cognition*, *21*, 803–814.

Rogers, T. B., Kuiper, N. A., & Kirker, W. S. (1977). Self-reference and the encoding of personal information. *Journal of Personality & Social Psychology*, *35*, 677–688.

Russell, J., & Jarrold, C. (1999). Memory for actions in children with autism: Self versus other. *Cognitive Neuropsychiatry*, *4*, 303–331.

Southwick, J. S., Bigler, E. D., Froehlich, A., DuBray, M. B., Alexander, A. L., Lange, N., & Lainhart, J. E. (2011). Memory functioning in children and adolescents with autism. *Neuropsychology*, *25*, 702–710.

Ternes, M., & Yuille, J. C. (2008). Eyewitness memory and eyewitness identification performances in adults with intellectual disabilities. *Journal of Applied Research in Developmental Disabilities*, *21*, 519–531.

Wallace, G. L., & Happé, F. (2008). Time perception in autism spectrum disorders. *Research in Autism Spectrum Disorders*, *2*, 447–455.

Williams, D. L., Goldstein, G., & Minshew, N. J. (2006). The profile of memory function in children with autism. *Neuropsychology*, *20*, 21–29.

Part III

Investigative Tools and Legal Application

12

Interactions of Individuals with Autism Spectrum Disorder with the Criminal Justice System: Influences on Involvement and Outcomes

Neil Brewer and Robyn L. Young

Adults and adolescents with autism spectrum disorder (ASD) sometimes come into contact with the criminal justice system. They may do so as witnesses, or perhaps, as suspects, offenders, or victims. Other chapters in this book closely examine the behavior of individuals with ASD in their role as a witness (whether as a nonvictim or victim), reporting on their memory of people and events to psychologists, social workers, or educators, or for police investigating a crime, or in response to questioning in the courts. In this chapter, we shift focus. Rather than concentrating on those characteristics of ASD, or more specifically of memory processing and reporting, that may affect the detail and accuracy of witnesses' or victims' reports, we focus on those characteristics that (a) may lead to an individual with ASD becoming involved with the criminal justice system as a suspect or perpetrator, and (b) may affect the trajectory and outcomes of the individual's subsequent interactions within the criminal justice system. Of course, as becomes apparent later in the chapter, it is likely that at least some of those characteristics that we discuss (especially with respect to subsequent engagement with the criminal justice system) may well affect how individuals with ASD are perceived and evaluated should they interact with the criminal justice system as victims or witnesses (e.g., providing testimony to police or the courts). Nevertheless, we constrain our discussion in this chapter to factors affecting outcomes for suspects and (known) perpetrators.

We believe that there are sociocognitive and behavioral characteristics associated with ASD that may contribute to individuals with ASD finding themselves at odds with the criminal justice system. We argue that these characteristics are linked to how individuals with ASD become involved in criminal activity, and to their sometimes apparent inability to extricate themselves from problematic situations. We also argue that these characteristics are linked to behaviors displayed when providing testimony

The Wiley Handbook of Memory, Autism Spectrum Disorder, and the Law, First Edition.
Edited by Jonni L. Johnson, Gail S. Goodman, and Peter C. Mundy.

during police interviews or interrogations or in the courtroom, behaviors that can steer those interactions in directions that ultimately will have negative consequences for them, particularly when they have been suspected of committing a crime. Crucially, however, we argue—as we have done elsewhere (Brewer & Young, 2015)—that these behavioral characteristics (which might prove to be risk factors for adverse interactions with the criminal justice system) will only prove to be influential given the presence of what might be called enabling or conducive (but, at the same time, unfavorable) situational conditions. Given that the likelihood of these conditions prevailing is almost certainly very low, we suggest that the likelihood that these behavioral characteristics will be translated into expressions of criminal behavior will also be low. In contrast, we believe the likelihood of negative interactions between suspects or perpetrators and police or courtroom interviewers is probably not so remote given the ways in which interviewing and interrogation in such contexts typically proceeds. As we suggest later in this chapter, many of the behavioral characteristics of individuals with ASD are likely to depart from what police, judges, and juries might consider to be normative, and hence, potentially compromise their evaluations of such individuals.

In this chapter, we briefly consider whether individuals with ASD are likely to be overrepresented in criminal activity or in particular types of criminal activity, and whether their involvement with the criminal justice system is necessarily linked to the presence of ASD. We then examine those social-cognitive and behavioral characteristics of ASD that we believe, given enabling environmental conditions, are potential risk factors for involvement in criminal activity. Further, we illustrate how some of these same characteristics may occasionally act as catalysts for negative interactions when individuals with ASD are being interviewed by police and lawyers or providing testimony in the courtroom. We show how these risk factors may, for example, contribute to an individual becoming involved in criminal activity or reduce their capacity to extricate themselves from situations that will likely culminate in criminal activity. And we show how these risk factors may become associated with self-incriminating or otherwise adverse interactions with police officers, contribute to lawyers and judges becoming antagonized, and shape behaviors that undermine the individual's credibility in the eyes of jurors.

The Involvement of Individuals with ASD Within the Justice System

For some time, researchers have taken a keen interest in the possibility that some characteristics of ASD may increase the likelihood of criminal activity, although there has not been a corresponding degree of interest in the nature of the ensuing interactions with the criminal justice system. We suspect that the interest in criminality and ASD is, in part, maintained by the occasional reporting of violent and high-profile crimes where the media has made a connection between ASD and the crime (e.g., Anders Breivik, Elliot Rodger, Jeffrey Dahmer), often regardless of the existence of any clear evidence supporting such a diagnosis. Just the nature of the crime and the known characteristics of the offender (e.g., a serial shooting by a young male who has always been known as a bit of a loner) can be sufficient to encourage speculation about the possibility the perpetrator may have ASD in the absence of a formal diagnosis, as appears to have been the case for Rodger, Breivik, and numerous others.

In the last couple of years or so, a number of researchers have focused quite intensely on possible links between ASD and involvement in criminal activity (e.g., Allely, Minnis, Thompson, Wilson, & Gillberg, 2014; Brewer & Young, 2015; King & Murphy, 2014; Maras, Mulcahy, & Crane, 2015), scrutinizing published evidence that has been obtained using a variety of methodologies. Some studies have, for example, examined the representation of adults with ASD in prison and psychiatric ward cohorts (e.g., Hare, Gould, Mills, & Wing, 1999; Scragg & Shah, 1994). Some studies have analyzed statistics gathered from different types of criminal justice system records (e.g., Siponmaa, Kristiansson, Jonson, Nydén, & Gillberg, 2001)—including analyses of particular types of crime (e.g., Mouridsen, Rich, Isager, & Nedergaard, 2008; Siponmaa et al., 2001). Other studies have investigated the offending rates of adults with ASD in community samples (e.g., Mouridsen et al., 2008). Interpretation of the findings of such studies is, however, severely compromised by an array of methodological issues, such as inadequate information on the basis (and hence, the integrity) of the diagnosis of ASD and on potentially significant co-morbid psychiatric conditions, biases operating at case referral or disposition by the criminal justice system, and with few exceptions (e.g., Lundström et al., 2014), completely inadequate sample sizes. Elsewhere, we have suggested that the strongest statement one can make based on such evidence is merely that it is possible that individuals with ASD are more likely to be involved in crime, and perhaps, even in some specific types of crime, than typically developing individuals (cf. Brewer & Young, 2015). But the available empirical evidence certainly cannot sustain the conclusion that there is some inexorable connection between an individual having an ASD and falling foul of the criminal justice system.

Commission of a crime by a person with ASD obviously does not mean there is a link between their disorder and the crime. The population of individuals with ASD is not protected from containing nasty people who may have co-morbid conditions known to be linked to crime or experiential histories that increase their vulnerability to the commission of crime. Although the literature on psychiatric co-morbidities with ASD is also littered with interpretative difficulties, there are several conditions (e.g., ADHD, affective disorders, and oppositional defiant, conduct, and personality disorders) that—either independently or when joined with alcohol or substance abuse—are associated with an elevated likelihood of criminal behavior (e.g., Copeland, Miller-Johnson, Keeler, Angold, & Costello, 2007; Eronen, Hakola, & Tiihonen, 1996; Lundström et al., 2014; Wareham & Boots, 2012). In other words, while the presence of ASD may provide a tempting candidate explanation for some crimes, there may often be a far more plausible candidate that only a careful forensic assessment will reveal (see Brewer & Young, 2015).

Despite ourselves and others (e.g., Brewer & Young, 2015; King & Murphy, 2014; Maras et al., 2015) arguing against some inexorable links among ASD, crime, and problematic interactions with the criminal justice system, in the remainder of this chapter we examine those sociocognitive and behavioral characteristics associated with ASD that could contribute to individuals with ASD finding themselves in conflict with the criminal justice system. We examine two different—yet, from the perspective of the contributing characteristics—clearly overlapping issues. First, we consider the characteristics that, given unfortunate environmental conditions, may lead to criminal activity. Second, we outline those characteristics that, once individuals are involved with the criminal judicial system, may make them vulnerable and compromise their right to being treated fairly.

ASD Characteristics as Risk Factors

As we indicated at the outset of this chapter, we believe that some specific characteristics of ASD may contribute to involvement in criminal activity, and subsequently, adverse interactions with police, lawyers, and judges. Yet, it is obvious, given the low prevalence of criminal activity involving individuals with ASD, that no single ASD-related deficit is sufficient to produce such outcomes. But, juxtapose specific deficits with unpropitious environmental conditions, and we suggest that problems may arise. Unfortunately, we cannot cite published empirical evidence that supports our position (although we do have some studies with promising findings in chain). There are, however, a number of case studies reported in clinical and forensic journals, and there are a number of clinical cases with which co-author Robyn Young has been closely involved that certainly appear consistent with our arguments (see, e.g., Brewer & Young, 2015).

Problems reading the intentions and reactions of others

Case studies of offenders with ASD typically highlight deficits in areas such as anticipating and interpreting the intentions and behaviors of people with whom problematic interactions have arisen, recognizing the potentially harmful impact that their behavior might have on other people or their property and empathizing accordingly, and maneuvering themselves out of problematic situations when they realize the wrongfulness of their impending actions. Such characteristics are generally considered to be illustrative of what have become known as theory of mind (ToM) deficits, which are considered to be independent of IQ. Broadly speaking, an intact or well-developed ToM allows individuals to decode the intentions, beliefs, and emotions of others, that is, to take the perspective of others or—as is sometimes argued—to read their minds. This, of course, also means that the individuals can read how other people are likely to react to their own social behavior. One can easily imagine how significant deficits in such domains might allow individuals to be almost unwittingly lured into criminal activity. Similarly, one can imagine how deficits in these areas might compromise the possibility of congenial interactions with police officers, attorneys, and judges. But more on that shortly.

First, we consider what is known—beyond a raft of clinical observations—about the nature and extent of ToM deficits in adults with ASD. A substantial proportion of the empirical work on ToM deficits and ASD has been conducted with samples of children (e.g., Baron-Cohen, Leslie, & Frith, 1985; Bowler, 1992; Happé, 1994; Wimmer & Perner, 1983). Research with adult samples is severely limited in terms of the number of studies and the size of the ASD samples, and these limitations compound the difficulties associated with disentangling ToM deficits from deficits that might arise from deficits in intellectual functioning. In addition, there are no standardized tests to assess ToM, likely due to factors such as the lack of a universally accepted operational definition of the construct and the difficulties in recruiting adequately large sample sizes. Measures of ToM that have been commonly used—such as the Strange Stories Test (Happé, 1994, 1999), the Frith-Happé animations (White, Coniston, Rogers, & Frith, 2011), The Reading the Mind in the Eyes Test (Baron-Cohen, Wheelwright, Hill, Raste, & Plumb, 2001), or items involving recognition of *faux pas* (cf. Baron-Cohen, O'Riordan, Stone, Jones, & Plaisted, 1999)—have not been subjected to close psychometric evaluation with adult samples. Moreover, the sample sizes reported in such studies are typically very small. For example, across seven different studies involving adults using various combinations of Happé's (1994) original Strange Stories items, only 139 participants with ASD were tested. By far, the largest-scale evaluation of a ToM measure with adults with ASD of which we are aware is provided by a recent study conducted by Brewer, Young, and Barnett (2017). The study provides extensive normative, reliability, and discriminant and concurrent validity data for an adult-theory of mind (the A-ToM) test, which involves examinees interpreting the meaning of social interactions depicted in digitally recorded scenarios immediately after they have finished viewing the scenario. The final version of the scale includes 12 items, 6 of which involve drawing inferences about the real or intended social, rather than the literal, meaning of verbal statements in interactions and 6 of which are control or physical interactions (i.e., no hidden social meaning). The social scenarios span items illustrating sarcasm, perspective taking or misunderstanding, *faux pas*, bluff or persuasion, and white lie. Of importance, the study includes 163 adults with ASD with IQs in the normal range of intelligence (i.e., >85) as well as a typically developing comparison group.

From the perspective of this chapter, there are two key findings reported in Brewer et al.'s (2017) study. First, at the group level, the adults with ASD performed significantly worse than controls (after controlling for IQ) on the items requiring social inferences, but not on the physical items. Second, the variability of performance on the social items was marked for the ASD sample. Scores ranged from just above floor to ceiling level, although extremely high scores were less prevalent than in the typically developing sample. In other words, from what appears to be the largest adult sample described in the literature, it is clear that adults with ASD are characterized by ToM deficits, although the extent of these is likely to vary considerably. We need to bear in mind, of course, that the A-ToM items sample a relatively limited range of sociocognitive inferences or behaviors. Thus, we do not know what the pattern of findings would look like if the items sampled a much broader domain. Given the supportive validity data reported by Brewer et al. (2017), we would expect to see both the overall group-level deficit and the between-individual variability in extent of deficit replicated. Elsewhere, we have argued that, just as individuals show differing patterns of abilities, or profiles, on tests of intelligence, it is also possible that ToM deficits vary in nature. In other words, we argue for deficits (or strengths) in general ToM juxtaposed with specific skills or weaknesses, analogous to Spearman's (1927) conceptualization of intelligence in terms of a general factor (*g*) and specific factors (*s*). For example, while most individuals are likely to show some degree of general deficit, some individuals may have particular difficulty with specific aspects of ToM such as recognizing sarcasm, metaphors, or figures of speech; others may be particularly poor at recognizing the emotions of others from their tone of voice during interactions, and so on (for more detail, see Brewer & Young, 2015).

The preceding section foreshadows that deficits in ToM might be manifested in a variety of ways. In this section, we try to capture the likely breadth of such deficits, and illustrate how they might contribute to involvement in criminal activity and create significant problems should the individual with ASD have to interact with police, lawyers, judges, and juries. Just as language abilities are often described in terms of receptive and expressive abilities and deficits, we find it convenient from a structural perspective to classify ToM strengths and weaknesses in a similar way.[1] We suggest

[1] Readers familiar with the diagnostic criteria for ASD will, of course, realize that it is not necessary to invoke the ToM construct to identify some of the likely deficit areas described in this section as they are clearly referenced in the diagnostic criteria. But we do so because it can be argued that this construct underpins ways of behaving that are identified as independent in some of the diagnostic criteria.

that the interaction of persons with ASD within the criminal judicial system is compromised by deficits in ToM, which are sometimes reflected in their inability to understand the intent of others and to express their own intent in socially normative ways.

Manifestations of expressive ToM deficits and their implications for interactions with the criminal justice system

Manifestations of expressive deficits include inappropriate or non-normative nonverbal behavior such as gaze aversion (or failure to make eye contact), nervous fidgeting or repetitive movements, lack of affect in facial expressions or spoken language, lengthy monologues, and frank but insensitive or tactless comments. Persons without ASD who are aware of the impact their behavior may have on others may be more calculating with respect to impression management, and thus, try to inhibit such behaviors.

It is widely recognized in the non-ASD literature that nonverbal behaviors such as failure to make eye contact and the presence of nervous shuffling, fidgeting, or personal grooming when interacting with others may lead to the perception that the individual is somehow less trustworthy or their communication less credible. Indeed, behavioral cues such as these are often considered to be likely markers of attempted deception or lying (Granhag & Vrij, 2005)—yet, coincidentally, such behaviors are also features of presentation in individuals with ASD. Similarly, a failure to demonstrate an appropriate degree of affect during interactions, or a display of inappropriate affect—whether it be captured in facial expressions or vocal expressions— has been found to undermine perceptions of the individual's credibility (e.g., Bollingmo, Wessel, Eilertsen, & Magnussen, 2008; Bollingmo, Wessel, Sandvold, Eilertsen, & Magnussen, 2009; Salekin, Ogloff, McFarland, & Rogers, 1995; Wessel, Drevland, Eilertsen, & Magnussen 2006). When describing their own actions (or even the actions of someone they have observed from their perspective as a victim or witness), an individual whose displays of affect, or perhaps of remorse, are not well calibrated with normative expectations regarding appropriate emotional displays may well be evaluated harshly. For example, a person arrested for killing his father appeared to rejoice inappropriately saying "my dad's dead, my dad's dead, my dad's dead" in a repetitive way, whereas it subsequently became clear that he was simply asking a question of police. Police investigators may be somewhat skeptical about the testimony of suspects behaving thus, judging them as callous and indifferent and likely pursuing the case against them more vigorously. Should such behavior characterize their courtroom testimony, we speculate that judges and jurors will be similarly skeptical about any testimony they might provide. As defendants in the courtroom, they might be perceived by judges and jurors as more blameworthy than otherwise might be the case. And while we are not aware of any empirical evidence on how lengthy tangential monologues or tactless remarks might undermine perceivers' evaluations of the trustworthiness of an individual's testimony, it seems reasonable to suggest that perceivers' judgments might align with our own expectations or intuitions, and with our own clinical observations in the courtroom. It is hard to imagine, for example, that jurors would be unaffected by a defendant tactlessly saying that a victim "smelled like crap" or that the neighbor's house that had burnt down was "just a dump."

As is clear from the preceding section, there is a paucity of empirical evidence on how individuals with ASD are perceived when providing testimony, regardless of whether the testimony is presented by a suspect or perpetrator or by a witness or victim. However, we are currently conducting studies that we hope will shed some light on these issues. In these studies, mock-jurors watched the video-recorded testimony of a number of individuals being interviewed about a rather gruesome crime they had purportedly witnessed. Some of the individuals had an ASD diagnosis and some were typically developing, and they were matched on age, gender, and IQ. We are examining the relation between (a) witness behavior, such as gaze aversion, repetitive motor movements, inappropriate facial emotional expressions, and displays of affect; and (b) mock-juror evaluations of the credibility of their testimony.

Manifestations of receptive ToM deficits and their implications for interactions with the criminal justice system

Manifestations of receptive deficits would, for example, include deficits in interpreting the intent or meaning of facial expressions, body gestures and poses, variations in vocal intonation, and nonliteral expressions such as sarcasm, metaphor, bluff, or deception (Brewer & Young, 2015; Happé, 1994; Jolliffe & Baron-Cohen, 1999) as well as placing a highly literal or pedantic construction on straightforward requests. Evidence for such deficits in association with ASD has been widely reported (e.g., Bachorowski & Owren, 1995; Banse & Scherer, 1996; Celani, Battacchi, & Arcidiacono, 1999; Giora, Gazal, Goldstein, Fein, & Stringaris, 2012; Gross, 2004; Kleinman, Marciano, & Ault, 2001; Martin & McDonald, 2004), with the exception of deficits in recognizing emotion on the basis of body postures. Indeed, recent evidence showed that children with ASD did just as well as typically developing controls at recognizing emotion from static body postures, although not from expressions conveyed by the eyes (Peterson, Slaughter, & Brownell, 2015). Nevertheless, emotion recognition did still correlate meaningfully with ToM in both groups. Whether these patterns would be replicated with more dynamic stimuli and more subtly expressed body postures is unknown.

The accurate interpretation of facial expressions may allow individuals to ascertain if, for example, a person with whom they are interacting is becoming bored, exasperated, frustrated, angry, and so on. Similar cues may be detected from a person's gestures or body positioning. Vocal intonation may provide invaluable information about how another individual is reacting to others' communication, and hence, convey important signals about how individuals might interpret the situation, and thus, adapt their behavior to meet the expectations of the person with whom they are interacting. The true meaning of what someone is saying is sometimes only deduced if a person can accurately interpret sarcastic remarks or grasp a metaphor or figure of speech. Realizing that another person is bluffing or attempting to deceive is often critical if an individual is to avoid conforming to some inappropriate suggestion or request.

In a similar vein, understanding that one doesn't have to apply the most pedantic interpretation possible of a remark or statement from another may help someone avoid responding in a way that just does not match the expectations of the person who made the remark. The following extract from an interview transcript provides an informative example. When a police officer commenced an interview with a woman regarding the sudden death of her mother by stating "The recorder has been activated at a quarter past four," the recently bereaved suspect responded "My watch says it's 4:14, yours is a minute fast." The police officer responded "Yes, it's 4:16 on mine," to which the suspect replied "Well, your watch is two minutes fast." This apparent lack of regard for the gravity of the situation may well raise alarm bells for the officer who was likely expecting a grief-stricken respondent rather than one who is debating the accuracy of her watch.

It is easy to extend the list of such examples by sketching out multiple scenarios in which, given certain environmental conditions, such deficits might contribute to individuals behaving in a manner that transgresses the law, increases the likelihood that they will become a victim, or creates a very negative impression when interacting with police interviewers or providing courtroom testimony (whether as defendants, victims, or independent witnesses).

Consider, for example, a young adult who has somehow become involved in an interaction with a group of other young people in a bar, individuals whose body language clearly suggests they are barely tolerating his involvement. Not only does he provide a long monologue about a special interest he has, but he is also less than tactful when another in the group interrupts him. He is unlikely to notice the nonverbal or vocal cues (e.g., rolling the eyes, raised eyebrows exchanged between other group members, increasingly terse tone of voice) indicating the exasperation or frustration of other group members at his behavior. Nor is he likely to pick up cues indicating that one of the group is starting to act quite aggressively toward him and that he could well become the victim of an assault. Alternatively, imagine in the same situation someone in the group producing a spray can of paint and suggesting (tongue in cheek and winking at the others in the group) that it would be good to graffiti the toilet walls (as after all, it will wash off easily). Or, take the case of an individual with an all-consuming interest in computers, an involvement in associated chatrooms and desperate for expressions of friendship. He might be "groomed" for months by someone apparently taking a keen interest in his well-being prior to being asked by the person to store some computer files for him, files that turn out to contain child pornography. His inability to anticipate the possible intent behind the protracted grooming process—coupled with his desire to accommodate someone apparently providing friendship—may increase the likelihood that he will comply with the request.

The inability to read the intent of others may not only have disastrous consequences in terms of becoming entwined in some criminal activity, but could also extend to further difficulties if involved in the criminal judicial system. An individual who finds herself a suspect in a police investigation may respond under questioning in ways that frustrate, and eventually, arouse the ire of investigating officers. For example, the co-tenant of an individual with ASD sees the police pull up outside their house and immediately asks his housemate if she can mind a box of cell phones for him. The police have a warrant to search the house, and they find the phones and take the innocent suspect to the police station for questioning. They place the phones in front of her and open their questioning with "Tell us all about these phones then." The suspect takes this request literally, and the police are then subjected to a very long monologue on the technical characteristics of the phones, and despite obvious nonverbal and verbal signs of escalating impatience from the police, she persists with the monologue, convincing the police that she is obstructing their inquiry. Similar types of behaviors may be exhibited, of course, when police question a victim or witness, with a likely consequence being that police start to doubt the individual's credibility and reliability as a witness. Numerous case study examples of behaviors such as these that may have an adverse impact on police perceptions of the suspect or witness are described in Brewer and Young (2015).

Likewise, an inability to read the intent of a lawyer's or judge's questioning in the courtroom may evoke extremely negative responses. In the questioning of a defendant in a recent case, we observed the prosecuting attorney draw the defendant's attention to a paragraph in the record of the police interview in order to verify that the defendant had made one particular statement. The attorney used the wording "Please read the paragraph beginning...." Taking the request literally, the defendant began working his way through the entire and lengthy paragraph, despite repeated attempts to focus him on the sentence in question. To the onlookers it was obvious that, when the judge interrupted, it was his intent to try to steer the defendant to the sentence in question, but the defendant was clearly oblivious to this intent. The judge's expectations of the defendant were also extremely obvious from his increasingly exasperated tone of voice, but again, the defendant did not pick up these cues. This resulted in the judge becoming angry and accusing him of deliberately trying to impede the conduct of the trial, with the defendant clearly extremely perplexed about what he was doing that was wrong. Similar reactions were elicited from the judge when the defendant was asked if there had been a meeting with his lawyers about his plea to one of the charges. It became apparent that many discussions between the two on the matter had occurred, but because they had not occurred in the context of a formal meeting in the lawyer's chambers, the defendant was adamant that there had not been any "meetings." He was then accused by the judge of being a liar.

Literal interpretations of questions, or other receptive ToM deficits, may lead to conversations (or miscommunications) that become incriminating for the suspect. For example, when a young man was asked why he did not offer a cup of tea to his flatmate who had collapsed and later died of dehydration, he responded, "He didn't drink tea." And when asked if he had called an ambulance he replied, "No." But it later emerged in a thorough cross-examination that he failed to add in response to the questions that he had, in fact, offered him water on several occasion, and that he had tried to call a doctor.

In sum, deficits in reading nonverbal and verbal cues in the communications of others—cues that for most people are instantly recognizable— may well have a significant effect on the tone, trajectory, and ultimate outcome of a wide variety of interactions that individuals with ASD may have in their encounters with the justice system.

Restricted and repetitive interests and behaviors and sensory sensitivities

The diagnostic criteria for ASD identify some other characteristics that we, and others, have argued may, given certain environmental conditions, not only contribute to individuals with ASD becoming involved in criminal acts, but could also contribute to their engagement in problematic interactions with the police. One of these characteristics is the pursuit of some narrow interest or preoccupation. For many individuals with ASD, this preoccupation is intense, all-consuming, and if interrupted, may cause considerable distress. Forensic case studies have been described in which individuals' criminal acts—often acts of aggression—appear to be related to the intense distress experienced when their engagement in this activity has been interrupted. That is, the individuals become quite distressed and lash out, apparently oblivious—as might be expected given the likely ToM deficits—to any adverse consequences that may be experienced by any third party involved. Elsewhere, we have outlined a number of examples from forensic cases that appear consistent with the operation of such a mechanism (Brewer & Young, 2015). However, we are not aware of empirical data from carefully controlled studies that support these case study observations, and such studies are, from an ethics perspective, obviously extremely tricky to do. We do, however, have research underway involving adults with ASD in which we first examine whether individuals' capacity to detect that interactions appear to be heading down a path toward some criminal act occurring is impeded by their being preoccupied by one of their own circumscribed interests, and then whether that apparently diminished capacity is exacerbated by the extent and nature of their ToM deficits. Whether the data from these studies support our hypothesis remains to be seen.

Quite similar patterns have been observed in forensic cases when individuals with ASD find their repetitive movements interrupted or their sensitivity to certain sensory stimuli highlighted. For example, we have reported cases where a police officer's attempt to interrupt repetitive pacing or compulsive checking of cell phones while the police were trying to question them about some activity or incident triggered an aggressive reaction toward the police officer that, not surprisingly, turned what might have been a straightforward informal questioning into a serious incident (Brewer & Young, 2015). Similar problematic responses from individuals with ASD have been noted when, for example, a police officer put a gentle hand on the shoulder of persons with ASD who had an extreme hypersensitivity to touch. Or, individuals with ASD may find themselves in difficulty with the law if their sensory seeking behavior leads them to touch another person inappropriately.

All of these examples depict what are probably quite low probability events. Yet, they are events that could have extremely unfortunate consequences. Police officers, judges, and jurors are unlikely to have an intimate understanding of how all-consuming these interests, routines, and sensitivities can be for the individual with ASD. Thus, they may have great difficulty grasping the possibility that the individual's behavior that has culminated in a criminal act, or in a problematic interaction with the police, could reflect an unfortunate amalgam of environmental conditions and some specific ASD-related behavior rather than intentionally unlawful or provocative behavior. Consequently, such behavioral reactions will likely be interpreted as the actions of a weird or perhaps aggressive and possibly quite dangerous individual.

An Emerging Issue: Interactions via the Internet

The incredible growth in the extent and variety of interactions conducted over the internet has obviously led to an enormous array of problems and incidents for many individuals. Whether these problems have been more prevalent for individuals with ASD is unknown. Nevertheless, we believe that a combination of several characteristics of ASD is likely to heighten the risks associated with internet interactions, although again, we emphasize we only have clinical observations to back up our views.

As already discussed, one diagnostic feature of ASD is the presence of some rather consuming and circumscribed interest. Interests in computers, computer technology, electronic gaming, and the internet turn out to be some of the dominant interests. Well over 50% of a sample of more than 150 adults with ASD who have recorded their special interests in a recent survey (conducted as part of another study we are conducting) nominated a dominant interest that involved some kind of interaction with the internet. In many cases, the interaction was specifically concerned with computers, gaming, and associated technology. However, even when the special interest related to quite separate topics such as gardening or cars, the internet provided the medium by which the interest was pursued. Pursuit of such interests over the internet provides opportunities for individuals to interact with others via chatrooms, social media, or other networking mechanisms. For individuals who have difficulty establishing and maintaining meaningful relationships, these networking sites provide hitherto unavailable but welcome opportunities. With these opportunities comes, of course, the possibility that individuals will be *groomed* by someone to eventually engage in some kind of undesirable and illegal activity (e.g., inadvertently downloading or distributing pornographic material). Individuals with ASD who are not skilled in recognizing the intent of others may be completely unsuspecting of what is going on as an internet relationship may be carefully and stealthily built up over a lengthy period of time. All they may realize is that they are very happily interacting with computers and at the same time developing what seems to be a meaningful relationship with another person. In other words, they don't see where the interaction is leading, and even when they do recognize warning signs, they may not have the interactive skills to extricate themselves from the situation before they have become enmeshed in some illegal activity (e.g., downloading and storing pornography). As we noted earlier, we have no data on the extent of this problem. Rather, we are totally reliant on observations gleaned from ongoing clinical cases. Nevertheless, there do seem to be some striking similarities in such cases that highlight the vulnerability of individuals characterized by ToM deficits, a lack of meaningful relationships, and consumed by some circumscribed interest that can be pursued in private with minimal protective screening from others.

Summary

Individuals with ASD can find themselves interacting with the criminal justice system for a variety of reasons. They may witness a crime, they may be victims, or they may be suspects or offenders. In this chapter, we have focused on whether specific characteristics of ASD could, under some circumstances, increase an individual's vulnerability both to involvement in crime and to adverse interactions when providing testimony to police or the courts.

We have argued that the answer to both queries is "yes." We have suggested that fundamental deficits in reading the intent or reactions of others may increase the likelihood of an individual becoming involved in some criminal act, perhaps initially quite unwittingly. We have also suggested that these deficits have the potential to cause major difficulties when the individual is being interrogated by the police or in the courtroom, thereby significantly increasing the likelihood that negative outcomes ensue from these interactions. Additionally, we have argued that the consequences of the deficits and difficulties that we have identified may, given an unfortunate alignment of environmental conditions, be exaggerated by the individual's repetitive interest or behavior, or by some sensory sensitivity.

Unfortunately, after reading this chapter, it is quite obvious that there are enormous gaps in the scientific knowledge. Much of our argument has been reliant on clinical observations and cases. Additional arguments for the likely impact of ASD have relied on extrapolating from research on how people interpret and react to certain types of behavior when displayed by typically developing individuals in different contexts. Moreover, if we reflect on exactly how we would go about filling those gaps, it will also be obvious that we will need to be very imaginative in developing novel paradigms to explore these issues in a rigorous manner while not violating important ethical principles. It is not a simple matter to demonstrate how some characteristic of ASD might compromise individuals' capacity to recognize that they may be about to commit a crime, to severely frustrate a police investigator, or to anger a judge in a courtroom.

It is probably also obvious that the key players in the criminal justice system—police officers, lawyers, judges, and jurors—are unlikely to be familiar with or appreciate the amalgam of factors that may shape the course of interactions in which the individual with ASD was involved. Moreover, we suspect that simply telling criminal justice personnel what the clinical observations suggest will not be sufficient. Rather, much more compelling arguments are likely to be made if there is a strong body of empirical evidence that has been acquired via research paradigms that appear to model the situations to which we are seeking to generalize in a reasonably convincing manner. Clearly, there is a lot of imaginative research that needs to be done.

Take-Home Points

- Under certain environmental conditions, some characteristics of ASD may contribute to involvement in crime and adverse interactions with criminal justice system professionals.
- An important contributor to such problems is a deficit in theory of mind, which limits the ability of individuals with ASD to interpret the intent and likely reactions of others as well as the impact of their own behavior on others.
- Such deficits may be reflected in a failure to decode (i.e., misread) the true meaning of another person's verbal or nonverbal communications, thereby contributing to subsequent maladaptive responses.
- A comprehensive psychometric evaluation of an Adult Theory of Mind (A-ToM) scale with large samples of adults with ASD and IQ-matched controls is described in Brewer, Young, and Barnett (2017).
- Currently, however, we rely heavily on clinical observations and case studies in understanding these issues, thus highlighting the need for novel paradigm development that will allow empirical research to advance.

References

Allely, C. S., Minnis, H., Thompson, L., Wilson, P., & Gillberg, C. (2014). Neurodevelopmental and psychosocial risk factors in serial killers and mass murderers. *Aggression & Violent Behavior, 19*, 288–301.

Bachorowski, J., & Owren, M. J. (1995). Vocal expressions of emotion: Acoustic properties of speech are associated with emotional intensity and content. *Psychological Science, 6*, 219–225.

Banse, R., & Scherer, K. R. (1996). Acoustic profiles in vocal emotion expression. *Journal of Personality & Social Psychology, 70*, 614–636.

Baron-Cohen, S., Leslie, A. M., & Frith, U. (1985). Does the autistic child have a "theory of mind"?' *Cognition, 21*, 37–46.

Baron-Cohen, S., O'Riordan, M., Stone, V., Jones, R., & Plaisted, K. (1999). Recognition of faux pas by normally developing children and children with Asperger syndrome or high-functioning autism. *Journal of Autism & Developmental Disabilities, 29*, 407–418.

Baron-Cohen, S., Wheelwright, S., Hill, J., Raste, Y., & Plumb, I. (2001). The "Reading the Mind in the Eyes" test revised version: A study with normal adults, and adults with Asperger syndrome or high-functioning autism. *Journal of Child Psychology & Psychiatry, 42*, 241–251.

Bollingmo, G., Wessel, E., Eilertsen, D. E., & Magnussen, S. (2008). Credibility of the emotional witness: A study of ratings by police investigators. *Psychology, Crime & Law, 14*, 29–40.

Bollingmo, G., Wessel, E., Sandvold, Y., Eilertsen, D. E., & Magnussen, S. (2009). The effect of biased and non-biased information on judgments of witness credibility. *Psychology, Crime & Law, 15*, 61–71.

Bowler, D. M. (1992). "Theory of mind" in Asperger's syndrome. *Journal of Child Psychology & Psychiatry, 33*, 877–893.

Brewer, N., & Young, R. L. (2015). *Crime and autism spectrum disorder: Myths and mechanisms.* London, England: Jessica Kingsley.

Brewer, N., Young, R. L., & Barnett, E. (2017). Measuring Theory of Mind in adults with Autism Spectrum Disorder. *Journal of Autism and Developmental Disorders, 47*, 1927–1941.

Celani, G., Battacchi, M. W., & Arcidiacono, L. (1999). The understanding of the emotional meaning of facial expressions in people with autism. *Journal of Autism & Developmental Disorders, 29*, 57–66.

Copeland, W. E., Miller-Johnson, S., Keeler, G., Angold, A., & Costello, E. J. (2007). Childhood psychiatric disorders and young adult crime: A prospective, population based study. *American Journal of Psychiatry, 164*, 1668–1675.

Eronen, M., Hakola, P., & Tiihonen, J. (1996). Mental disorders and homicidal behavior in Finland. *Archives of General Psychiatry, 53*, 497–501.

Giora, R., Gazal, O., Goldstein, I., Fein, O., & Stringaris, R. (2012). Salience and context: Interpretation of metaphorical and literal language by young adults diagnosed with Asperger's syndrome. *Metaphor & Symbol, 27*, 22–54.

Granhag, P. A., & Vrij, A. (2005). Deception detection. In N. Brewer & K. D. Williams (Eds), *Psychology and law: An empirical perspective* (pp. 43–92). New York, NY: Guilford.

Gross, T. F. (2004). The perception of four basic emotions in human and nonhuman faces by children with autism and other developmental disabilities. *Journal of Abnormal Child Psychology, 32*, 469–480.

Happé, F. G. E. (1994). An advanced test of theory of mind: Understanding of story characters' thoughts and feelings by able autistic, mentally handicapped, and normal children and adults. *Journal of Autism & Developmental Disorders, 24*, 129–154.

Happé, F. (May, 1999). *Instructions for theory of mind story task.* Unpublished document provided by F. Happé.

Hare, D. J., Gould, J., Mills, R., & Wing, L. (1999). *A preliminary study of individuals with autistic spectrum disorders in three special hospitals in England.* London, England: National Autistic Society.

Jolliffe, T., & Baron-Cohen, S. (1999). The strange stories test: A replication with high functioning adults with autism or Asperger syndrome. *Journal of Autism & Developmental Disorders, 29*, 395–406.

King, C., & Murphy, G. H. (2014). A systematic review of people with autism spectrum disorder and the criminal justice system. *Journal of Autism & Developmental Disabilities, 44*, 2717–2733.

Kleinman, J., Marciano, P. L., & Ault, R. L. (2001). Advanced theory of mind in high functioning adults with autism. *Journal of Autism & Developmental Disorders, 31*, 29–36.

Lundström, S., Forsman, M., Larsson, H., Kerekes, N., Serlachius, E., Långström, N., & Lichtenstein, P. (2014). Childhood neurodevelopmental disorders and violent criminality: A sibling control study. *Journal of Autism & Developmental Disorders, 44*, 2707–2716.

Maras, K., Mulcahy, S., & Crane, L. (2015). Is autism linked to criminality? *Autism, 19*, 515–516.

Martin, I., & McDonald, S. (2004). An exploration of causes of non-literal language problems in individuals with Asperger syndrome. *Journal of Autism & Developmental Disorders, 34*, 311–328.

Mouridsen, S. E., Rich, B., Isager, T., & Nedergaard, N. J. (2008). Pervasive developmental disorders and criminal behavior: A case control study. *International Journal of Offender Therapy & Comparative Criminology, 52*, 196–205.

Peterson, C. C., Slaughter, V., & Brownell, C. (2015). Children with autism spectrum disorder are skilled at reading emotion body language. *Journal of Experimental Child Psychology, 139*, 35–50.

Salekin, R. T., Ogloff, J. R. P., McFarland, C., & Rogers, R. (1995). Influencing jurors' perceptions of guilt: Expression of emotionality during testimony. *Behavioral Sciences & the Law, 13*, 293–305.

Scragg, P., & Shah, A. (1994). Prevalence of Asperger's syndrome in a secure hospital. *British Journal of Psychiatry, 165*, 679–682.

Siponmaa, L., Kristiansson, M., Jonson, C., Nydén, A., & Gillberg, C. (2001). Juvenile and young adult mentally disordered offenders: The role of child neuropsychiatric disorders. *Journal of the American Academy of Psychiatry & the Law, 29*, 420–426.

Spearman, C. (1927). *The abilities of man.* Oxford, England: Macmillan.

Wareham, J., & Boots, D. P. (2012). The link between mental health problems and youth violence in adolescence. *Criminal Justice & Behavior, 39*, 1003–1024.

Wessel, E., Drevland, G. C., Eilertsen, D. E., & Magnussen, S. (2006). Credibility of the emotional witness: A study of ratings by court judged. *Law & Human Behavior, 30*, 221–230.

White, S. J., Coniston, D., Rogers, R., & Frith, U. (2011). Developing the Frith-Happé animations: A quick and objective test of theory of mind for adults with autism. *Autism Research, 4*, 149–154.

Wimmer, H., & Perner, J. (1983). Beliefs about beliefs: Representation and constraining function of wrong beliefs in young children's understanding of deception. *Cognition, 13*, 103–128.

13

The Cognitive Interview and Its Use for People with Autism Spectrum Disorder: Can We Create an ASD Friendly Version?

Joanne Richards and Rebecca Milne

Within the Criminal Justice System (CJS), the collection of reliable and detailed information from witnesses is essential (Davis, McMahon, & Greenwood, 2005), initially providing investigators with the leads required to further their investigation (Kebbell & Milne, 1998), and subsequently, bringing potential evidence to court. Indeed, the perceived credibility of an eyewitness influences juror decision-making (O'Neill Shermer, Rose, & Hoffman, 2011), and mock jurors are impressed with witnesses who provide the greatest amount of detail (Bell & Loftus, 1988). The *goal* therefore of an interviewing officer is to gather information rich in both quantity and quality, providing the crucial details on what transpired and who was involved (Milne & Bull, 2006). Information is usually gathered during a face-to-face interview, where the witnesses[1] are required to recall events from their memory. However, human memory is known to be fragile, easily manipulated (Loftus & Palmer, 1974), constructed, incomplete (Bartlett, 1932), and influenced by schemas (Tuckey & Brewer, 2003). Moreover, encoding is selective. That is, certain details may be favored during the encoding stage at the expense of others. For example, those that are expected or familiar (see Milne & Bull, 1999) or related to goal-directed behavior (see Achtziger, Bayer, & Gollwitzer, 2012). Additionally, the phenomena *weapon focus* describes attention overly fixated on a weapon, reducing the possibility of encoding additional or peripheral details (Loftus, Loftus, & Messo, 1987). Thus, at its very worst, the delicate nature of human memory can result in unsafe testimonies culminating in miscarriages of justice (Poyser & Milne, 2011). The arduous task therefore of an interviewing officer is to protect memory against any negative effects of the interviewing process while preserving its integrity. A technique that has proven successful in increasing the quantity of a recalled memory without jeopardizing its accuracy is the cognitive interview (CI). This chapter first discusses the structure of the CI and its

1 The term *witness* is used to describe individuals who have witnessed or been a victim of an offense.

The Wiley Handbook of Memory, Autism Spectrum Disorder, and the Law, First Edition.
Edited by Jonni L. Johnson, Gail S. Goodman, and Peter C. Mundy.

tenets for eliciting detailed and accurate information from cooperative witnesses. The chapter then explores the protocol's effectiveness for application with individuals with autism spectrum disorder (ASD), considering modifications for use with a population group that has difficulties communicating personal experiences.

What is the Cognitive Interview (CI)?

In the 1970s, concern surfaced when research demonstrated how fragile, and consequently, unreliable, eyewitness memory is when exposed to misleading information (Loftus, 1975; Loftus & Palmer, 1974). Acknowledging that inappropriate interviewing practice can damage memorial recall, psychologists worked to develop techniques to safeguard memory against contamination. Applying theory concerning the retrieval of information from memory, namely, Tulving's encoding specificity principle (Tulving, 1983; Tulving & Thompson, 1973) and the multiple trace theory (Tulving, 1974), the CI was one such technique that was created (see Fisher & Geiselman, 1992; Milne & Bull, 1999). The original CI was comprised of four mnemonics; (a) report everything (RE), (b) mental reinstatement of context (MRC), (c) change temporal order (CTO), and (d) change perspective (CP).

The report-everything instruction gives witnesses the opportunity to provide an *uninterrupted* account of *everything* they remember about the witnessed event (see Milne & Bull, 1999). Thus, the RE defends memory against intrusion from the interviewer, such as the introduction of leading questions. The working principle of RE is that a witness must be encouraged not to edit their recall or leave out any details they believe are irrelevant or trivial. Indeed, the witness is encouraged to report on everything that "pops" into their mind (Griffiths & Milne, 2010). Furthermore, the witness is advised to report even partial memories. Due to feature overlap, incomplete memories can act as further retrieval cues (Paulo, Albuquerque, & Bull, 2013). As such, the RE instruction depends on cognitive and social communication skills. Police officers must communicate the ground rules, what they expect and what they require from the interviewee, whereas witnesses must communicate their own experiences in a way that is understandable to police officers (Fisher, 2010).

The MRC component emanates from Tulving's encoding specificity principle (Tulving, 1983; Tulving & Thompson, 1973), which recognizes that recall is enhanced when there is an overlap between the conditions present during encoding and those present during retrieval. For example, retrieval is increased when recall is situated in the environment or condition in which it was encoded (see Godden & Baddeley, 1975). However, in a real-life investigation, there may be several reasons why returning to the original, physical scene may be impractical and/or inappropriate. It could prove to be too traumatic for the witness, be too time consuming or costly, the scene may have become a secured forensic area, or the characteristics originally present may have changed, thus potentially contaminating witness memory. To accommodate these practical problems, the MRC instructs the witness to mentally reconnect with the event, reinstating both the physical and emotional entities that prevailed during encoding. To facilitate this, the interviewer must provide guidelines presented as a set of mini instructions, accompanied with deliberate pauses to allow the witness to cognitively connect with the directions. It is suggested that mental reinstatement can be effectively achieved using as few as 165 words (Dando & Milne, 2012). When delivering the instructions, it is recommended that the interviewer adopts a “slow, deliberate, quiet style” (Dando, Wilcock, Milne, & Henry, 2009, p. 702). To encourage the witness to concentrate, it is suggested the witness stares at the floor or a blank wall or simply close their eyes (Griffiths & Milne, 2010). Indeed, instructing witnesses to close their eyes during memorial retrieval has been found to have a positive effect (Perfect et al., 2008). Research suggests that visual environmental features distract eyewitnesses during their recall (Perfect, Andrade, & Syrett, 2012).

To provide an account of a past event, memory has to be reconstructed (Bartlett, 1932). Accessing memory requires a searching process whereby traces and links have to be identified and connected. The multiple trace theory (Tulving, 1974) is based on the understanding that all experiences and events create their own memory traces (Hintzman, 1988), and these traces are organized in memory as a complex system of neurons that contain coded information representing experiences and knowledge (Brown & Craik, 2000). As such, memory systems are likened to a vast network where memories are linked by connections referred to as associations (Anderson, 2009). The multiple trace theory recognizes that a memory can have more than one trace (Nadel, Samsonovich, Ryan, & Moscovitch, 2000), and to this effect, the CI provides several mnemonics to ignite memorial recall. If one retrieval method proves unsuccessful other methods can be called on (Gwyer & Clifford, 1997). Indeed, it is suggested that after utilizing one retrieval cue, if the next cue used is entirely “dissimilar” to the previous one, additional information may be elicited from witness memory (Gilbert & Fisher, 2006). To this effect, the CI provides additional tools, specifically CTO and CP, to stimulate memorial performance.

CTO requires witnesses to deliver their recall using a specifically directed sequential format. For example, an instruction may be given asking the witness to begin his or her recall with the last thing they remember about the event, and then work backward until they arrive at the start of the event. There is some suggestion that recalling information in reverse order may increase memory recall because starting with the final stages of the to-be-remembered event gives the impression that it occurred closer in time (Lam & Buehler, 2008). However, a key feature of the CTO mnemonic lies in its ability to break down schematic memory.

Knowledge of routine events is stored in long-term memory as a set of organized structures referred to as schemas (Neuschatz, Lampinen, Preston, Hawkins, & Toglia, 2002). A script is a type of schema. A script is a template for regular events providing stereotypical information related to the sequential details of routines (Schank & Abelson, 1977). Used in the reconstruction of memory, scripts aid retrieval by accessing previous experiences and generic knowledge (Anderson & Pichert, 1978). Scripts therefore provide a short-cut, which an individual can activate in order to quickly make sense of a situation while predicting what is going to happen next (Abelson, 1981).

Scripts are effective in reconstructing memory; however, the stereotypical information they yield can lead to errors in recall (Holst & Pezdek, 1992) and gaps in memory can be filled by script consistent information (Abelson, 1981). For example, if beef were ordered in a restaurant a script, inference could be that red wine was a compliment (Anderson & Pichert, 1978). A particular concern is that people can be in possession of scripts for events they have not directly personally experienced (Holst & Pezdek, 1992). In Holst and Pezdek's (1992) research, participants were asked to provide scripts for a burglary. Participants were able to produce detailed accounts even though the majority had never been involved in such an event. When asked later to recall details of written texts or photographic slides depicting a mock burglary, participants recalled information that was not part of the presented event, but was consistent with their own scripts (Holst & Pezdek, 1992). To deactivate script memory, the CI provides cognitively challenging tasks such as CTO.

The final technique CP emanates from Anderson and Pichert's (1978) research in which participants were asked to recall details of a narrative first from the perspective of a home buyer and second from that of a burglar (or vice versa). When the personal perspective was altered, additional information was delivered during recall. The CP mnemonic of the CI encourages the witness to recall details of the to-be-remembered event, concentrating on the perspective of a different person. For example, the witness could be asked to put a "spotlight" on a specific person in his or her memory and focus on his or her actions in the event (see Milne, 2015; Milne & Bull, 1999). Alternatively, if the witness was in an anxious state of mind, he or she might be asked to adopt the more *relaxed* perspective he or she had experienced prior to witnessing the event (Paulo, Albuquerque, & Bull, 2013). Geiselman and Fisher (2014) reported an incidence whereby a child victim of molestation was able to disclose information when the interviewing officers asked the child to take on the perspective of a stuffed toy that was sat on a shelf.

However, it is noted that special training and careful guidance is required when delivering this instruction, especially for use with vulnerable groups as damaging practice has been identified. For example, interviewers have erroneously asked witnesses to take on the perspective of a bird watching the incident from above (Griffiths & Milne, 2010). Additionally, witnesses must be informed to only report details they witnessed. Safeguards are required to discourage witnesses from activating their imagination, which could result in the reporting of false information (Milne & Bull, 1999). This highlights the importance of specific training in the CI carried out by experienced and knowledgeable individuals.

A few years after its initial inception, the CI was revised (see Fisher & Geiselman, 1992). The resultant enhanced CI (ECI) provided a structure to the interview process to account for the social interactions and communication dynamics that pervade during an encounter between a witness and an interviewer (Fisher, Milne, & Bull, 2011). The purpose of the revision was to create an environment that elevated the role of the interviewee, creating an equal partnership between the interviewer and the witness (see Milne & Bull, 1999).

To personalize the interview, the first phase requires the interviewer to establish rapport with the witness. The intention at this phase is to reduce the interviewee's anxiety. Adopted from the world of clinical therapy, rapport between a clinician and therapist is used to create a *harmonious* relationship (see Leach, 2005). Rapport during a forensic setting aims to introduce a discussion based on neutral topics to create an empathetic, sympathetic, and supportive environment (see Collins, Lincoln, & Frank, 2011). Additionally, the rapport phase can be viewed as a rehearsal period for the witness, who during this phase can gain experience of providing detailed accounts in response to open-ended questions. This is necessary because, in daily life, communication is perceived as a two-way process, and individuals are unaccustomed to giving, elaborate, uninterrupted narratives (Griffiths & Milne, 2010). The building of rapport is considered a vital component of an interview (Milne & Bull, 1999). Indeed, it has been found that an interview utilizing rapport-building strategies increases the amount of correct pieces of information collected from a witness (Collins, Lincoln, & Frank, 2002) and provides some inoculation against yielding to misinformation (Vallano & Compo, 2011).

The second phase of the ECI requires the interviewer to explain the purpose of the interview and establish the ground rules. This includes reminding the interviewee that during the process they will be required to concentrate and focus, report everything, and refrain from guessing or fabricating information (see Milne & Bull, 1999). A key feature of this phase is the transfer of control of the interview to the interviewee. The interviewer must establish that it is the witnesses who are in possession of information not known by the interviewing officer; thus, they are the ones who will be doing most of the talking. This technique further establishes communication rules and provides an opportunity to maximize the quantity of information.

The third phase initiates a free, uninterrupted recall applying the MRC as discussed earlier in this chapter and open-ended questions. Once this has been exhausted, the fourth phase, which involves the questioning of the interviewee, begins with the use of interviewee-compatible questioning. This concept recognizes that every witness will have his or her own *unique* record of an event, and the interviewer must pose questions in harmony with each individual's representation (Fisher, 2010). Thus, an interviewer must recognize the type of memory a witness is accessing, should pay attention to the order in which the witness presents the recalled events, and base questions on the events as they appear in the conscious recall of the witness (Fisher & Geiselman, 1992). Memory recall is most productive when the ordering of the questions mirrors the sequential format in which the witness presented their information (Milne & Bull, 1999). Additionally, the activation of mental imagery is applied to promote concentration and enhance memory access. A witness is asked to focus on the mental image of a particular aspect of the event, and this image is then probed using open-ended questions and prompts (Nori, Bensi, Gambetti, & Giusberti, 2014; Powell & Snow, 2007). Phase five introduces varied retrieval techniques, including CTO and CP. Once this is complete, phase six is implemented, which requires the interviewer to provide a summary of the account and cover topics of investigative interest that have not already arisen, for example, demographic and lifestyle details. The final phase requires the interviewer to *close* procedures and ensure that the witness leaves the process with any questions or concerns answered (see Milne & Bull, 1999, for an in-depth account of the phases of the ECI).

The CI has been tested in approximately 100 laboratory studies (Rivard, Fisher, Robertson, & Mueller, 2014), and has been researched in various countries, including the United States (Fisher & Geiselman, 1992), United Kingdom (Milne & Bull, 2002), Australia (Davis, McMahon, & Greenwood, 2005), Brazil (Stein & Memon, 2006), France (Ginet, Py, & Colomb, 2014), Portugal (Paulo, Albuquerque, Saraiva, & Bull, 2015), and Spain (Campos & Alonso-Quecuty, 2008). Indeed, the CI is considered to be one of the most successful products of applied memory research (Bekerian & Dennet, 1993). When compared with a structured interview (an interview that reflects good practice but contains none of the mnemonics and characteristics of the CI), the CI produces 25%–50% more detailed information from mock witnesses without jeopardizing accuracy (Fisher, Milne, & Bull, 2011, also see Köhnken, Milne, Memon, & Bull, 1999; Memon, Meissner, & Fraser, 2010, for meta-analytical studies).

Ultimately, the CI can result in less need for follow-up interviews (Kebbell, Milne, & Wagstaff, 1999), has been found to guard against attempts made to manipulate memory (Memon, Zaragoza, Clifford, & Kidd, 2010), and can protect children from the effects of suggestive questioning (Milne & Bull, 2003). Furthermore, the CI has no impact on the creation of false beliefs and false memories (Sharman & Powell, 2013). In test conditions, the CI is effective when eliciting memory of a live event from children (Saywitz, Geiselman, & Bornstein, 1992) after both a short and a long retention interval (Larsson, Granhag, & Spjut, 2003), and assists in the recollection of daily physical activities from as long ago as 35 years (Fisher, Falkner, Trevisan, & McCauley, 2000). The CI has been found to be effective for eliciting recall from witnesses to various types of crime, including violent crime and nonviolent crime such as fraud, road accidents, and robberies (Colomb, Ginet, Wright, Demarchi, & Sadler, 2013). It has also been seen to increase memorial recall for conversation, and is therefore potentially useful for use in crimes that involve verbal harassment (Campos & Alonso-Quecuty, 2008; Prescott, Mine, & Clarke, 2011). Furthermore, police officers report that the use of the CI increases the amount of person descriptions provided by witnesses (Brown, Lloyd-Jones, & Robinson, 2008). The CI also enhances the recollection of details for familiar events. As such, it can be an effective tool to assist recall from those who suffer prolonged and repeated victimization such as domestic violence or child abuse (Ginet et al., 2014). There is also suggestion that the use of the CI has therapeutic effects and promotes psychological well-being in victims (Fisher & Geiselman, 2010).

After lab studies found the CI to be a viable technique, research then had to explore its efficacy in an applied forensic context. Field studies were thus conducted to examine the effectiveness of the CI in the real world. Fisher, Geiselman, and Amador (1989) were the first who tested the skills of serving police officers from a Miami police department in the United States after receiving training in the CI. Clifford and George (1996) monitored the performance of police officers in the United Kingdom after being similarly trained in the CI. Both studies found that officers who had received CI training collected more information from their interviewees than those officers without training.

The success of the CI has resulted in it being adopted as one of the main interviewing methods used by police officers around the world, for example, in the United Kingdom, Norway, Australia, and New Zealand (Fisher, Milne, & Bull, 2011). However, in practice, it has been observed that police officers do not fully utilize all of its mnemonics and instructions (Clarke & Milne, 2001; Dando, Wilcock, & Milne, 2008; Griffith, Milne, & Cherryman, 2011). A failure to apply all of the components of the CI has been attributed to a number of factors, such as time constraints, inadequate training, the cognitive challenge of delivering instructions, and its inappropriateness for use with volume crime where police officers have less time to conduct lengthy interviews (see Dando, Wilcock, Behnkle, & Milne, 2011). Surveying novice police officers (Dando, Wilcock, & Milne, 2008), it was found that the components of the ECI perceived to be most regularly used, and thus, interpreted as most effective were as follows: develop rapport, provide an uninterrupted account, explain interview procedures, and the report everything instruction. Perceived to be used less frequently were MRC, witness-compatible questioning, a never-guess instruction, and the request to concentrate. The CTO and CP mnemonics were thought to be rarely used at all (Dando, Wilcock, & Milne, 2008).

As a result, researchers have attempted to create a more streamlined, time-efficient version to be useful in such circumstances as volume crime and to be more amenable for less experienced officers. Thus, the efficacy of a modified version of the CI where CTO and CP instructions were replaced with an additional recall was examined (Bensi, Nori, Gambetti, & Giusberti, 2011; Davis, McMahon, & Greenwood, 2005). Findings indicate that the omission of the two mnemonics had little impact on the quantity and quality of recall gained (Davis, McMahon, & Greenwood, 2005). In a study that compared three interview models, each comprised of only two recall stages: (a) free recall then free recall, (b) free recall then CTO, and (c) CTO then free recall, results indicated that the free recall then free recall model yielded the most amount of information and the greatest accuracy. Thus, a second free recall attempt was more effective than CTO (Dando, Ormerod, Wilcock, & Milne, 2011). Indeed, it was concluded that the CTO instruction actually damaged the ability to connect with a memory trace due to the disruption of the temporal ordering formed at the stage of encoding (see Dando, Ormerod, Wilcock, & Milne, 2011). As a result of this disruption, errors occurred in the form of confabulations (reporting details that were not present) and the quantity of memory recall was reduced in that many details were omitted (see Dando, Ormerod, Wilcock, & Milne, 2011). Nevertheless, other research has found the CTO mnemonic to be beneficial (see Milne & Bull, 2002).

What needs to be borne in mind is that the ECI provides interviewing officers with a framework on which to plan their interviews. A key factor of this model when used in the field is its versatility. The CI should be perceived as a set of *tools* from which officers can choose the most appropriate techniques. Adapting the interview to the needs of the individual witness is vital. Individual differences must be acknowledged. For example, very young children under the age of 5 may find the full ECI too demanding; therefore, a shortened version omitting the challenging mnemonics CTO and CP should be considered (Verkampt & Ginet, 2010).

As previously discussed, shortened versions omitting some of the mnemonics have proved efficacious. However, it is important to note that removing the MRC and RE instructions may not be advantageous as these are considered to be the most powerful and effective elements of the CI (Colomb & Ginet, 2012; Ginet et al., 2014; Paulo, Albuquerque, Saraiva, & Bull, 2015; Verkampt & Ginet, 2010). Some police officers find the MRC instruction cognitively demanding and too time-consuming to deliver (Clarke & Milne, 2001; Dando et al., 2008). To compensate for these, a modified version, referred to as the Sketch MRC, has yielded positive results. This method is discussed in greater detail later in this chapter.

The ECI can also be adapted to specific circumstances, for example, gathering information at the scene itself. A recent development of the CI is the self-administered interview (SAI) (Gabbert, Hope, & Fisher, 2009). Circumstances may arise where police are unable to immediately conduct interviews, for example, during street riots or terrorist attacks. A delay in interviewing can reduce the amount of information collected from eyewitnesses (see Hope, Gabbert, & Fisher, 2011). To counteract this effect, witnesses are provided with booklets to record their recall at the scene. The SAI incorporates elements of the CI to enable witnesses to self-generate their individual retrieval cues (Gabbert et al., 2009). The techniques also ask witnesses to provide a sketch of the to-be-remembered event (Gabbert et al., 2009). In test conditions, the use of the SAI has been found to increase recall (compared to a free-recall control) and to preserve recall (Gabbert, Hope, & Fisher, 2009). Indeed, the techniques have also yielded positive results in field trials (Hope et al., 2011).

In recent years, components of the CI have also been considered for use during an interview with a suspect of a crime. In particular, when there is a need to differentiate between the truth teller and the liar (Vrij et al., 2008). Based on the understanding that lying places a cognitive load on an individual, the objective of the interviewing officer is to increase this load. Consequently, to increase cognitive demands, the CTO retrieval cue has been used. Findings indicate that when asked to provide recall in reverse order, the liars produce accounts that are lacking in details and are littered with contradictions compared to the narrative delivered by truth tellers (see Vrij et al., 2012, for a comprehensive account). However, more research is needed in this area.

With encouraging results, the CI has also been studied for use with various populations: children (Milne & Bull, 2002), older witnesses (Holliday, Humphries, & Milne 2012; Prescott, Milne, & Clarke, 2011; Mello & Fisher, 1996; Wright & Holliday, 2007), people from developing countries (Stein & Memon, 2006), adults with intellectual disabilities (Brown & Geiselman, 1990; Clarke, Prescott, & Milne, 2013; Milne, Clare, & Bull, 1999), and children with intellectual disabilities (Milne, Sharman, Powell, & Mead, 2013). However, to date, only one study has examined the use of the CI with adults from the higher end of the autism spectrum, and this study found the CI to have a damaging effect on the memorial recall of people with ASD (Maras & Bowler, 2010). Before exploring this study in depth, it is useful to briefly consider some aspects of the memory profile of people with ASD.

The Memory Profile of People with ASD

Compared to typically developing individuals, people with ASD, when encoding or retrieving information from memory, employ different organization strategies. For example, performance during free-recall tasks is diminished when there is a need to create conceptual or semantic relations. Bowler, Matthews, and Gardiner (1997) presented adults with ASD with a list of related and unrelated words. They found that recall of unrelated words was unimpaired, but difficulties were encountered when recalling the categorized words. Rather than relying on semantic or relational properties, people with ASD organize their memory recall by focusing on more idiosyncratic features of the to-be-remembered item (Bowler, Limoges, & Mottron, 2009). For example, reliance on phonological properties of the spoken word, or visual-perceptual features of written text has been noted (Bowler, Gaigg, & Gardiner, 2008a). Subsequent research has supported findings, concluding that people with ASD are less likely to use subjective organization to assist recall (Bowler, Gaigg, & Gardiner, 2008b; Bowler, Limoges, & Mottron, 2009). This deficit therefore creates problems when complex organizational strategies are required to recall information (Bowler, Matthews, & Gardiner, 1997). As such, having to retrieve and organize information to provide recall of a witnessed event may prove difficult. Specific to CI instructions, following guidelines to mentally reinstate with an event, for example, placing oneself back in time, space, or place, involves complex strategies that some people with ASD may find problematic. This is discussed in greater detail later in this chapter.

Focusing on an investigative interview, a witness is required to extract information from autobiographical memory. This memory is comprised of episodic memories relating to personally experienced events and personal semantic memories that are concerned with information about one's self (Crane & Goddard, 2008). For people with ASD, it is generally accepted that they have intact semantic memory, demonstrating unimpaired rote memory and memory for facts (Ben-Shalom, 2003; Lind & Bowler, 2008), but have impaired episodic memory (Crane & Goddard, 2008; Gaigg, Bowler & Gardiner, 2014; Lind & Bowler, 2010).

A primary difference between these two memories is the type of consciousness each system employs during retrieval. Semantic memory provides information on facts and experiences about the world, and as such is rooted in familiarity and abstract knowledge (Gardiner & Richardson-Klavehn, 2000). Thus, this memory system is associated with noetic consciousness (Tulving, 1985). In contrast, episodic memory requires a conscious awareness of having experienced an event (Perner & Ruffman, 1995) and is related to a higher order of mental activity, requiring reflection, anticipation, and imagination skills (Wheeler, 2000). Episodic memory therefore is associated with autonoetic consciousness (Tulving, 1985). These different levels of awareness distinguish between "knowing" and "remembering." Research has found that adults with ASD are more geared to using noetic awareness (knowing) rather than autonoetic awareness (Bowler, Gardiner, & Grice, 2000). In a study by Bowler, Gardiner, & Grice (2000), adults with ASD were asked to recall words from a list, and were then invited to explain "how" they had remembered the words. This task was designed to explore if people with ASD *remembered* any specific experiences during encoding. For example, if participants were able to provide information regarding what they were thinking or picturing when they read the word, this would suggest autonoetic awareness. By contrast, if participants just simply *knew* that the word was on the list and did not recall any specific details about the time that they read the word, this would indicate noetic awareness. The study concluded that adults with ASD were more likely to give "know" responses rather than "remembering" (Bowler, Gardiner, & Grice, 2000).

Difficulties accessing autobiographical memory imply that a person with ASD will provide impoverished details when reporting a witnessed event. In a study conducted by Bruck, London, Landa, and Goodman (2007), children with ASD (age range 5–10 years) with an IQ >74 completed a questionnaire designed to measure autobiographical memory for key events. Compared to a control group, the memories of the ASD children, although accurate, were sparse for events in both their distant and recent past, and this included both personal episodic and personal semantic memories. A second facet to the Bruck et al. study (2007) required the children to take part in a staged event, a magic show. When asked to recall details, the free recall of children with ASD was less complete than that provided by children from the general population.

Similarly, in a study conducted by McCrory, Henry, and Happé (2007), children with ASD (mean age 13.02) were asked to use free recall to remember details of a scene involving a photography project acted out by two actors. The information children with ASD were provided was less detailed but no less accurate than the accounts provided by typically developing children, again implying problems with memorial recall rest in quantity rather than quality (McCrory, Henry, & Happé, 2007).

Of interest, it has been found that when appropriate cues are provided to assist recall performance in people with ASD, their recall is comparable to members of the general population. These findings have prompted the task support hypothesis (Bowler, Gaigg, & Gardiner, 2008b; Bowler, Gardiner, & Berthollier, 2004; Bowler, Matthews, & Gardiner, 1997). For example, it is suggested that people with ASD have problems in relational memory processes, meaning that difficulties arise when having to organize and integrate individual details (see Gaigg, Gardiner, & Bowler, 2008). However, in a study conducted by Gaigg, Gardiner, and Bowler (2008), which involved an orienting task, it was found that when cues were provided to assist in the categorization of words, performance of people with ASD improved. Thus, although relational processing was not spontaneously evoked in people with ASD, the presence of appropriate cues resulted in people with ASD performing comparably to members of the general population (Gaigg, Gardiner, & Bowler, 2008). It is interesting to note that these findings suggest that problems with memory function arise during retrieval strategies rather than difficulties during the encoding stage. This is important when considering the purpose of an investigative interview, implying that if the appropriate cues and support are implemented, people with ASD should be able to provide reliable information. As discussed earlier in this chapter, the CI has proved an efficacious tool for eliciting memorial recall for various population groups. It is now timely to explore the efficacy of the CI for use with adult witnesses with ASD.

The CI and Interviewees with ASD

Maras and Bowler (2010) conducted the first-ever study to explore the use of the CI with adult interviewees from the higher end of the autism spectrum (mean age 37.08 years). Participants in this study watched a film clip and were then asked to recall its details using either a structured interview (SI) or the CI. The SI was identical in structure to the CI (i.e., it followed the same phases) but omitted the use of the original mnemonics of the CI: (a) RE, (b) MRC, (c) CTO, and (d) CP (Maras & Bowler, 2010). The study found that, when interviewed with a SI (using free recall and questions), participants with ASD provided information that matched the quality and quantity of that elicited from members of the general population, an encouraging finding. However, during a subsequent experimental study (Maras & Bowler, 2011), participants with ASD were found to recall fewer correct details than members of the general population when using free recall. Thus, the effectiveness of unsupported free recall with people with ASD remains inconclusive.

Focusing on the use of the CI, specifically in the first study, the mnemonics failed to increase the quantity of information furnished by participants with ASD. Indeed, the technique was seen to have an unfavorable effect on accuracy (Maras & Bowler, 2010), and the MRC was identified as being particularly damaging (Maras & Bowler 2010). This is an interesting finding as generally the MRC is considered to be the most powerful tool for promoting memory performance (Davis, McMahon, & Greenwood, 2005; Gwyer & Clifford, 1997). In a follow-up study the self-administered interview (SAI) was used to assist recall from witnesses with ASD (Maras, Mulchay, Memon, Picariello, & Bowler, 2014). The SAI, as discussed earlier in this chapter, is a tool used to encourage witnesses to use a booklet to report their recall of a witnessed event (see Gabbert et al., 2009). The follow-up study considered that using a booklet to record events may be useful to people with ASD. This is because this method would reduce social interaction, something which people with ASD find difficult (Maras et al., 2014). However, the study concluded that the MRC instruction continued to remain problematic for people with ASD and was detrimental to their memorial recall (Maras et al., 2014). A study has also been conducted exploring the use of the MRC with children who have ASD. After watching a film clip of a nonviolent criminal event, children were interviewed using either a control interview (free recall), an MRC interview, or a sketch plan interview. Children with ASD in the MRC condition (mean age 14 years, 6 months) performed no better than those in the control interview (mean age 15 years, 1 month). Thus, the MRC instruction did not proffer any beneficial results. However, the children with ASD who were supported in the interview using a sketch plan (mean age 14 years, 1 month) performed better than their counterparts in both the control and MRC interviews (Mattison, Dando, & Ormerod, 2015). The use of a sketch plan will be discussed in greater detail later in this chapter.

These negative findings suggest that the CI may be problematic for interviewing people with ASD (Maras & Bowler, 2014). (Though see later in this chapter for a promising ASD friendly adapted version.) Nevertheless, subsequent research has found that actually returning to a physical environment and being given MRC instructions in the environment assists people with ASD to reconnect to a previous experience. Maras and Bowler (2012) explored the impact of the context reinstatement of a physical environment. Adults with ASD were asked to mentally reinstate and recall details from photographs either in the room in which encoding had taken place or a different location. The ASD participants who recalled their information in the room in which they had viewed the photograph produced memorial recall equivalent to those of the general population group. However, the study did conclude that people with ASD provided fewer details relating to both person descriptors and action compared to the typical population (Maras & Bowler, 2012). In light of the mixed results regarding the efficacy of the MRC instruction, it is useful to further explore the memory profile of people with ASD.

It is suggested that impaired episodic memory may have an impact on the effectiveness of the CI (Bekerian & Dennett, 1993). This is particularly pertinent to the MRC component, which encourages the use of autonoetic awareness in order to time travel back to an event to reconnect with contextual elements. Autonoetic consciousness is dependent on a person having a sense of self (Bowler & Gaigg, 2008). However, a lack of self-concept or self-awareness has been put forward as one explanation of impaired autobiographical memory in people with ASD (Crane, Goddard, & Pring, 2009). This deficit in self-awareness has been attributed to impairments in theory of mind (see Crane, Goddard, & Pring, 2011). Theory of mind (ToM) refers to the ability typically developing individuals have to attune themselves to the internal states of others, identifying their beliefs, thoughts, intentions, and needs (Frith & Happé, 1994). ToM activities are considered necessary for the development of social interaction skills, emotional understanding, and communication skills (Coull, Leekam, & Bennett, 2006). Consequently, impaired ToM accounts for the social and communication deficits which form part of the diagnosis for ASD (Hill & Frith, 2003). The relationship between ToM and self-awareness has been explored, concluding that poor performance on ToM tests results in diminished self-awareness (see Frith & Happé, 1999). To date, self-awareness in people with ASD is somewhat under-researched. However, in a study that required adults with ASD (mean age 28.25 years) to provide descriptors concerning their personalities and feelings, it was found that adults with ASD found it difficult to reflect on their mental states (Kristen, Rossmann, & Sodian, 2014). That is, compared to typically matched individuals, they provided fewer self-descriptors relating to life events (see Kristen, Rossmann, & Sodian, 2014). If people with ASD have limited self-awareness, a CI may not be useful. This is because the MRC instruction specifically requires a person to first recognize and then reinstate with their mental states. Thus, if people with ASD find self-reflection problematic, instruction to reconnect with inner feelings will be ineffective. Indeed, in the previously mentioned study where the MRC was used to interview children with ASD, the researchers concluded that the children had failed to apply the MRC instructions (Mattison, Dando, & Ormerod, 2015). That is, those children in the MRC condition performed no better than those in the control group. Thus, it was concluded that the MRC is both developmentally and intellectually unsuitable for children with ASD (Mattison, Dando, & Ormerod, 2015).

Source monitoring, whereby an individual can identify where, when, and how a memory was established, is considered to be impaired in people with ASD unless relevant support is supplied (Bowler, Gardiner, & Berthollier, 2004). For example, children with ASD (mean age 9.26 years, mean verbal mental age 6.66 years) have shown difficulties when asked to determine who had carried out a specific activity (i.e., naming a photograph; Lind & Bowler, 2009). Adults with ASD (mean age 41.11 years) have also demonstrated source errors reporting actions they had performed themselves as being performed by other people (Maras, Memon, Lambrechts, & Bowler, 2013). Related to source monitoring, people with ASD have been found to have problems binding experiences of events together in their memory (see Brock, Brown, Boucher, & Rippon, 2002). This manifests as difficulties collating information in order to develop causal links. A key function of the MRC is to create connections between a physical or emotional experience (contextual elements) and the actual witnessed event. Consequently, if elements are not bound together during encoding, any cues provided to reinstate will be of little use.

Furthermore, problems have been noted when using semantic information to recognize relationships between items (Gaigg, Gardiner, & Bowler, 2008). Thus, difficulties will arise when using organizational strategies that are dependent on initial formation of relational links. Hence, during an MRC instruction, the relation between an emotion and the to-be-remembered event may not be available to a person with ASD. It must, however, be remembered that item-specific information is not considered impaired in people with ASD (Gaigg, Gardiner, & Bowler, 2008). As such, individual details of an item may be recognized, but this information may not be stored in relation to spatial or temporal contextual details. Thus, in the course of a CI interview, people with ASD may respond effectively to the questioning phase when attention is directed to a specific item/event. Additionally, people with ASD may find the sketch plan a useful tool. As discussed in detail later in this chapter, the use of a sketch plan relies on event specific detail rather than a reliance on relational and contextual processes.

Appreciating findings from research and recognizing the memory profile of people with ASD, it is noted that there is a cause for reservation when applying the MRC to witnesses with ASD. However, before dismissing the mnemonic completely, it would prove useful to contemplate any adaptations that may help to create a more *ASD friendly* style of communicating the MRC instruction.

A Modified MRC for People with ASD

A study was conducted to explore the recall of adult participants with ASD (Richards, Milne, & Dando, in submission). After watching a film clip that depicted a nonviolent crime (the theft of personal belongings), participants were interviewed using: (a) a SI interview (free recall and questioning), (b) an MRC interview, and (c) a sketch plan interview (Richards, Milne, & Dando, in submission). This section concentrates on the MRC condition; other results are discussed later in this chapter. Concerning the MRC condition, attention was specifically given to: (a) reducing the complexity of the instructions given to mentally reinstate, (b) safeguarding against over- or under-stimulation from sensory stimuli, and (c) placing no limitations on the natural recall of the person with ASD. The study found that when such revisions were applied, high-functioning adults with ASD (mean age 25.73 years, mean verbal IQ 112.27) who had been assigned to the MRC condition provided overall 17% more correct pieces of information than those who had participated in a SI interview (i.e., free recall and questioning; Richards, Milne, & Dando, in submission). Additionally, those participants with ASD in the MRC condition provided more detailed person descriptions than their counterparts in the SI. That is information which described what a person looked like, including the person's physical features and information about what was worn. Unfortunately, though, this remained significantly lower than the person descriptions provided by the general population. However, the accuracy of the memorial recall *was not* jeopardized. Thus, the MRC was found to have no damaging effects, and instead, proved to be beneficial. To explain these results, it is useful to further explore the rationale behind the reasons for the adaptations.

In laboratory research, instructions to mentally reinstate participants with ASD have contained over 500 words, and the administration of this has lasted 10 minutes (Maras & Bowler, 2010). Instructions given have also required participants to perform a string of complex, mental gymnastics. For example, children with ASD (mean age 14 years, 6 months) were asked to initially focus on when they saw the video, and then jump to connect with events that happened some time before they entered the test condition. Children were then asked to reconnect with the environmental context that existed during the watching of the video, and then were directed to consider their prior expectations of the video. Several complex instructions were provided before they were asked to recall the actual to-be-remembered event (Mattison, Dando, & Ormerod, 2015).

However, people with ASD have problems processing complex and intricate information (Williams, Minshew, & Goldstein, 2008). Indeed, there is some suggestion that a problem with disambiguating complex information is one of the key definitions of ASD (Williams, Goldstein, & Minshew, 2006). These problems are thought to be associated with impaired brain connectivity (Minshew & Goldstein, 2001; Minshew, Goldstein, & Siegel, 1997; Minshew & Williams, 2007), supported by studies employing functional MRI scans (Just, Cherkassky, Keller, & Minshew, 2004). Whereas processing of simple information remains intact, when the integration of information and the use of organizational strategies are required, then difficulties occur (Minshew, Goldstein, & Siegel, 1995). Difficulties are thus potentially exacerbated when people with ASD are called on to decipher instructions involving complex language (Kleinhans, Akshoomoff, & Delis, 2005). To this effect, people with ASD benefit from instructions that are clear and succinct (Müller, Schuler, & Yates, 2008).

This therefore suggests that efforts are required to deliver MRC instructions that are easily accessible to people with ASD. Dando and Milne (2012) demonstrated how MRC directions can be delivered effectively to members of the general population using only 165 words. Incidentally, this format may also be welcomed by the interviewer. Police officers have complained that delivering the MRC is both "demanding" and "cumbersome" (Dando, Wilcock, Milne, & Henry, 2009). Richards, Milne, and Dando (in submission) used 162 words to mentally reinstate participants, and administration took 4 minutes.

To encourage individuals to mentally reinstate an environment, cues are posed to activate the senses (see Milne & Bull, 1999). For example, in test conditions, participants with ASD have been asked to concentrate on lights, noises, and colors (Maras & Bowler, 2010), or to activate olfactory senses (Mattison, Dando, & Ormerod, 2015). Currently, there is no research available to explore either the positive or negative effects of focusing on sensory stimuli during the reinstatement of context instruction with people with ASD. However, until there is conclusive evidence, there may be some need to adopt a cautionary approach. This is because people with ASD have sensory perceptions that differ from the general population (Bogdashina, 2003). People with ASD can be subjected to sensory overload, or conversely, may be understimulated (Hilton et al., 2010).

In a study exploring sensory processing, adults with ASD were reported to: (a) suffer discomfort when exposed to sensory stimuli; (b) respond slowly, or fail to notice sensory activity; or (c) carry out behaviors to actively avoid or reduce exposure (Crane Goddard, & Pring, 2009). Indeed, sensory interests and aversions now form part of a diagnosis of ASD (American Psychiatric Association, 2013). Some people with ASD have particular problems filtering out background stimuli, having heightened sensitivity to noises and flickering fluorescent lights (Ashburner, Bennett, Rodgers, & Ziviani, 2013). For the purpose of a forensic interview with a person with ASD, it might be useful to avoid instructions that may inadvertently heighten a focus or preoccupation with such stimuli. As a further cautionary note, sensory stimuli can also elicit associative memories (Bogdashina, 2003). This means that the cues may not effectively connect a person to the required event. Richards, Milne, and Dando (in submission) did not provide directions that would focus specifically on lights, noises, smells, or tastes.

In laboratory studies, participants with ASD have been asked to present their recall starting with events from the beginning of the film clip (Maras and Bowler, 2010; Mattison, Dando, & Ormerod, 2015). During tests for the temporal ordering of verbal information, people with ASD reported fewer details compared to members of the typical population (Bennetto, Pennington, & Rogers, 1996). Further, during free recall, individuals are most likely to recall the first few items presented in a list (the primacy effect) or the last few items mentioned (recency effect) (see Baddeley, 2009). There is some concern, however, that people with ASD demonstrate a diminished primacy effect compared to typically developing people (Bowler, Limoges, & Mottron, 2009). Indeed, it has been suggested that people with ASD show a preference toward latter stages and learn by "working backward" (Tochi & Kamio, 2003). Although research remains inconclusive regarding preference toward a primacy or recency effect, it may prove useful to resist placing demands on the sequential recall of people with ASD. Indeed, because episodic memory is reconstructed (see Bartlett, 1932) and recall may not by nature be veridical (Milne & Bull, 1999; Wilcock, Bull, &

Milne, 2008), a request to present recall in a strict chronological order may not be helpful. In adapting the MRC for people with ASD, Richards, Milne, and Dando (in submission) placed no restrictions on the order of episodic memorial recall, and thus, did not direct the participant to the start their recall from the beginning of the watched video recording. This allowed the person with ASD to reconstruct his or her memory in his or her own way.

The Sketch Plan MRC

It is noted that narratives do not have to be purely verbal; narratives can be constructed from written text, imagery, or sounds (Keats, 2009). The sketch plan MRC invites witnesses to construct a narrative by creating a picture, diagram, or sketch of the to-be-remembered event. Fisher and Geiselman (1992) suggested that drawing a sketch may be useful to help witnesses describe events that may be difficult to verbalize, and may be of particular use when recalling spatial information (Fisher & Geiselman, 2010). Research indicates that many officers utilize a form of the sketch plan in their everyday practice (Dando, Wilcock, & Milne, 2009b). One reason why the sketch plan MRC is popular among officers is because its application places few cognitive demands on the interviewer. The directions for the sketch plan involves asking witnesses to simply draw details about the event to be remembered while encouraging interviewees to describe aloud what they are drawing (Dando, Wilcock, Milne, & Henry, 2009). Such simplicity is welcomed, as it is noted that when officers are required to deliver the more complex instructions of the MRC, these instructions are often given in a vague or incomplete manner (Dando, Wilcock, Milne, & Henry, 2009).

A further advantage of the sketch plan MRC is that it encourages participants to generate their own contextual cues. During MRC directions, an interviewer may ask witnesses to reinstate with cues from the environment that stimulate the senses. However, these guided cues may not be pertinent or salient features of the witnesses' memory (Dando, Wilcock, & Milne, 2009a). The sketch plan MRC has been found to elicit detailed and accurate information from adult mock witnesses from the general population (Dando, Wilcock, & Milne, 2009a).

People with ASD respond well to visual information (Kunda & Goel, 2008). That is, the presentation of visual stimuli assists people with ASD in their processing of information (Bogdashina, 2003). Indeed, compared to members of the general population, people with ASD are thought to use visual imagery more readily to support their understanding (Kana, Keller, Cherkassky, Minshew, & Just, 2006). Thus, it follows that the use of the sketch plan MRC should be useful for people with ASD. However, less is known about people with ASD producing their *own* visual stimuli. Concerning visual perception, teenagers with ASD (mean age 19.41 years) are able to copy a picture of an object at the same speed and accuracy as members of the general population (Mottron, Belleville, & Ménard, 1999). However, it was noted that during the initial drawing stages, teenagers with ASD were more likely to favor local details rather than global information (Mottron, Belleville, & Ménard, 1999). Global detail was considered to be features defining the two-dimensional contour or outline of the object to be copied. Local detail was identified as internal details (see Mottron, Belleville, & Ménard, 1999).

There is limited information available regarding the ability of people with ASD to produce their own sketches from memory. Reports on people with ASD being assessed using the Rey-Osterrieth test have shown mixed results. The Rey-Osterrieth test is used to measure visual recall by asking a participant to draw a previously seen complex figure. Minshew and Goldstein (2001), when administering this measure to a group of adults with ASD (mean age 22.33 years), found they underperformed compared to members of the general population. Conversely, Gunter, Ghaziuddin, and Ellis (2002) found no significant differences between people with ASD and the general population when this test was administered. Thus, currently, there is little conclusive evidence to suggest how effectively people with ASD are able to draw a sketch depicting a remembered scene.

When considering the efficacy of the sketch plan MRC with people with ASD, a particular concern stems from the type of processing style people with ASD favor. The weak central coherence account of autism has proposed that people with ASD favor local details at the expense of global information, and thus, do not identify the gist of a situation (Frith & Happé, 1994). To this effect, people with ASD may produce drawings in a "piecemeal" fashion (Booth, Charlton, Hughes, & Happé, 2003). However, the weak coherence account of autism has developed into an understanding that, although local processing is superior, this is not accompanied by a deficit in global processing (Happé & Frith, 2006). Indeed, it has been established that when explicit directions are provided, people with ASD are able to focus on and process global information (see Happé & Frith, 2006). There is also concern that preservative behavior and a tendency to become "stuck in a groove" may impair interviewing procedures (Frith, 2008). That is, people with ASD may become overly preoccupied in creating a drawing that depicts an exact replica of the item or event they want to represent (Frith, 2008). On the positive side, it is understood that drawing abilities in people with ASD develop typically; indeed, a small subset show considerably advanced skills (see Ford & Rees, 2008). The sketch plan MRC may also prove useful with people who have ASD because it reduces the degree of interaction with the interviewer. Recognizing that people with ASD perform better on tasks that reduce the demands of social interaction (Robinson, Goddard, Dritschel, Wisely, & Howlin, 2009), this may be accommodating.

The use of the sketch plan MRC has been explored for use with children with ASD (Mattison, Dando, & Ormerod, 2015). When compared to a control and an MRC interview, it was found that the sketch plan MRC generated more accurate pieces of information. Of particular interest, it was noted that the sketch interview method resulted in more information related to person and action. This is a welcomed outcome as previous studies have found that people with ASD provide little detail relating to person information (Maras & Bowler, 2014). The success of the sketch plan MRC was attributed to its ability to encourage individuals to generate their own contextual retrieval cues: It focused on event specific information rather than relational and contextual detail, reducing instruction demands used to evoke the sketch plan (Mattison, Dando, & Ormerod, 2015).

Similarly, the sketch plan MRC has proven useful in encouraging recall from adults with ASD (Richards, Milne, & Dando, in submission). Compared to participants in an SI interview condition, those in the sketch plan MRC condition provided 27% more correct information, without jeopardizing accuracy. In particular, the sketch MRC encouraged more information relating to action details. That is, information regarding what people *did*. For example "the thief *ran* away" "the woman *fell over*." However, as with findings from the MRC interview, people with ASD continued to provide person descriptions (physical characteristics) significantly lower than members of the general population.

Overall, these findings are encouraging, and indicate that with the correct cues and support, people with ASD are able to provide accurate recall in response to an MRC interview and a sketch plan MRC interview. The search, however, must continue to discover ways of encouraging people with ASD to provide information rich in both quantity and quality. Specifically, methods are required to encourage people with ASD to provide information regarding person descriptors. After being interviewed with either an MRC interview, SI, or sketch plan MRC, Richards and Milne (in prep) provided participants with memory jogs to stimulate recall for item specific details. Participants were provided with *palettes* of colors, and were asked to focus on these and then report if they brought back any memories from the video clip they had watched. In all, 100% of the ASD participants were able to provide additional pieces of information (the interview conditions had no significant impact on results). Of particular interest, participants with ASD provided item-specific pieces of information relating to people description equal to that provided by the general population. For example, people with ASD described the clothing individuals in the film clip wore, their hairstyle and hair color, and also recalled names of key characters. None of these details had been provided in previous phases of the interview. These findings suggest that people with ASD are indeed capable of providing information about a person's description, and thus, the focus for future research is to further develop the cues and methods that will effectively elicit this information. In summary, it is recommended that the search for an effective interview method for people with ASD must be constructed in accordance with what is known about the strengths of people with ASD.

Take-Home Points

- The memory profile of people with ASD suggests that problems arise when people with ASD are called on to use complex strategies to encode or retrieve information.
- Research, however, has shown that when appropriate cues are used, the memory recall performance of people with ASD is comparable to members of the typical population.
- Consequently, during the course of a witness interview, if appropriate support is provided, this should encourage people with ASD to recall useful information from their memories.
- The CI has a proven track record of eliciting memory recall from various population groups. However, there has been concern expressed regarding its suitability for people with ASD.
- Research has demonstrated that a modified version of the MRC and the use of a sketch plan MRC, which both reduce the complexity of instruction to reinstate, can prove beneficial to people with ASD.
- A modified version of the MRC and the use of the sketch plan MRC help people with ASD to provide information that is comparable in accuracy to that of members of the typical population.

- However, the problem remains in finding techniques that can encourage people with ASD to recall details that match the quantity of that provided by members of the typical population. The use of memory jogs may prove beneficial in helping people with ASD increase the quantity of their recall. However, this is an area that requires further research.

References

Abelson, R. P. (1981). Psychological status of the script concept. *American Psychologist, 36*(7), 715–729.

Achtziger, A., Bayer, U. C., & Gollwitzer, P. M. (2012). Committing to implementation intentions: Attention and memory effects for selected situational cues. *Motivation & Emotion, 36*(3), 287—-300.

American Psychiatric Association. (2013). *Diagnostic and statistical manual of mental disorders, Fifth Edition* (DSM–5). Arlington, VA. American Psychiatric Publishing.

Anderson, M.C. (2009). Retrieval. In A. Baddeley, M. W. Eysenck, and M. C. Anderson (Eds.), *Memory* (pp. 163–189). Hove, England: Psychology Press.

Anderson, R. C., & Pichert, J. W. (1978). Recall of previously unrecallable information following a shift in perspective. *Journal of Verbal Learning & Verbal Behavior, 17*(1), 1–12.

Ashburner, J., Bennett, L., Rodger, S., & Ziviani, J. (2013). Understanding the sensory experiences of young people with autism spectrum disorder. A preliminary investigation. *Australian Occupational Therapy Journal, 60*, 171–180.

Baddeley, A. (2009). Short-term memory. In A. Baddeley, M. W. Eysenck, and M. C. Anderson (Eds.), *Memory* (pp. 19–68). Hove, England: Psychology Press.

Bartlett, F. C. (1932). *Remembering: An experimental and social study*. Cambridge, England: Cambridge University Press.

Bell, B. E., & Loftus, E. F. (1988). Degree of detail of eyewitness testimony and mock juror judgements. *Journal of Applied Social Psychology, 18*(14), 1171–1192.

Bekerian, D. A., & Dennett, J. L. (1993). The cognitive interview technique: Revising the issues. *Applied Cognitive Psychology, 7*, 275–297.

Ben-Shalom, D. (2003). Memory in autism: Review and synthesis. *Cortex, 39*, 1129–1138.

Bennetto, L., Pennington, B. F., & Rogers, S. (1996). Intact and impaired memory function in autism. *Child Development, 67*, 1816–1835.

Bensi, L., Nori, R., Gambetti, E., & Giusberti, F. (2011). The enhanced cognitive interview: A study on the efficacy of shortened variants and single techniques. *Journal of Cognitive Psychology, 23*(3), 311–321.

Bogdashina, O. (2003). *Sensory perceptual issues in autism and Asperger syndrome: Different sensory experiences. Different perceptual worlds.* London, England: Jessica Kingsley.

Booth, R., Charlton, R., Hughes, C., & Happé, F. (2003). Disentangling weak coherence and executive dysfunction: planning drawing in autism and attention-deficit/hyperactivity disorder. *Philosophical Transactions of the Royal Society B, 358*(1430), 387–392.

Bowler, D. M., & Gaigg, S. B. (2008). Memory in ASD: Enduring themes and future prospects. In J. Boucher & D. Bowler (Eds.), *Memory in autism*. (pp. 330–349). Cambridge, England: Cambridge University Press.

Bowler, D. M., Gaigg, S. B., & Gardiner, J. M. (2008a). Subjective organisation in the free recall learning of adults with Asperger's syndrome. *Journal of Autism & Developmental Disorders, 38*, 104–113.

Bowler, D. M., Gaigg, S., & Gardiner, J. M. (2008b). Effects of related and unrelated context on recall and recognition by adults with high functioning autism spectrum disorder. *Neuropsychologia*, *46*, 993–999.

Bowler, D. M., Gardiner, J. M., & Berthollier, N. (2004). Source memory in adolescents and adults with Asperger's syndrome. *Journal of Autism & Developmental Disorders*, *34*(5), 533–542.

Bowler, D. M., Gardiner, J. M., & Grice, S. J. (2000). Episodic memory and remembering in adults with Asperger syndrome. *Journal of Autism & Developmental Disorders*, *30*(4), 295–304.

Bowler, D. M., Limoges, E., & Mottron, L. (2009). Different verbal learning strategies in autism spectrum disorder: Evidence from the Rey auditory verbal learning test. *Journal of Autism & Developmental Disorders*, *39*, 910–915.

Bowler, D. M., Matthews, N. J., & Gardiner, J. M. (1997). Asperger's syndrome and memory: Similarity to autism but not amnesia. *Neuropsycholgia*, *35*(1), 65–70.

Brock, J., Brown, C., Boucher, J., & Rippon, G. (2002). The temporal binding deficit hypothesis of autism. *Development & Psychopathology*, *14*, 209–224.

Brown, S. C., & Craik, F. I. M. (2000). Encoding and retrieval of information. In E. Tulving & F. I. M Craik (Eds.), *The Oxford handbook of memory*. (pp. 93–107). Oxford, England: Oxford University Press.

Brown, C. L., & Geiselman, R. E. (1990). Eyewitness testimony of mentally retarded: Effect of the cognitive interview. *Journal of Police & Criminal Psychology*, *6*(2), 14–22.

Brown, C., Lloyd-Jones, T. J., & Robinson, M. (2008). Eliciting person descriptions from eyewitnesses: A survey of police perceptions of eyewitness performance and reported use of interview techniques. *European Journal of Cognitive Psychology*, *20*(3), 529–560.

Bruck, M., London, K., Landa, R., & Goodman, J. (2007). Autobiographical memory and suggestibility in children with autism spectrum disorder. *Development & Psychopathology*, *19*, 73–95.

Campos, L., & Alonso-Quecuty. M. L. (2008). Language crimes and the cognitive interview: Testing its efficacy in retrieving a conversational event. *Applied Cognitive Psychology*, *22*, 1211–1227.

Clarke, C., & Milne, R. (2001). *National evaluation of the PEACE Investigative Interviewing Course. Police Award Scheme*. London, England: Home Office.

Clarke, J., Prescott, K., & Milne, R. (2013). How effective is the cognitive interview when used with adults with intellectual disabilities specifically with conversation recall? *Journal of Applied Research in Intellectual Disabilities*, *26*, 546–556.

Clifford, B. R., & George, R. (1996). A field evaluation in three methods of witness/victim investigative interviewing. *Psychology, Crime & Law*, *2*(3), 231–248.

Collins, R., Lincoln, R., & Frank, M. G. (2011). The effect of rapport in forensic interviewing. *Psychiatry, Psychology & Law*, *9*(1), 69–78.

Colomb, C., & Ginet, M. (2012). The cognitive interview for use with adults: An empirical test of an alternative mnemonic and of a partial protocol. *Applied Cognitive Psychology*, *26*, 35–47.

Colomb, C., Ginet, M., Wright, D., Demarchi, S., & Sadler, C. (2013). Back to the real: Efficacy and perception of a modified cognitive interview in the field. *Applied Cognitive Psychology*, *27*, 574–583.

Coull, G. J., Leekam, S. R., & Bennett, M. (2006). Simplifying second-order belief attribution: What facilitates children's performance on measures of conceptual understanding? *Social Development*, *15*(3), 548–563.

Crane, L., & Goddard, L. (2008). Episodic and semantic autobiographical memory in adults with autism spectrum disorders. *Journal of Autism & Developmental Disorders*, *38*, 498–506.

Crane, L., Goddard, L., & Pring, L. (2009). Sensory processing in adults with autism spectrum disorders. *Autism*, *13*(3), 215–228.

Crane, L., Goddard, L., & Pring, L. (2011). Autobiographical memory in adults with autism spectrum disorder: The role of depressed mood, rumination, working memory and theory of mind. *Autism, 17*(2), 205–219.

Dando, C., & Milne, R. (2012). The cognitive interview. Retrieved from CIp.praguesummerschools.org/files/clp/2012.2.pdf

Dando, C. J., Ormerod, T. C., Wilcock, R., & Milne, R. (2011). When help becomes a hindrance: Unexpected errors of omission and commission in eyewitness memory resulting from change temporal order at retrieval. *Cognition, 121*(3), 416–421.

Dando, C. J., Wilcock, R., Behnkle, C., & Milne, R. (2011). Modifying the cognitive interview: countenancing forensic application by enhancing practicability. *Psychology, Crime & Law, 17*(6), 491–511.

Dando, C., Wilcock. R., & Milne, R. (2008). The cognitive interview: Inexperienced police officers' perceptions of their witness/victim interviewing behavior. *Legal & Criminological Psychology, 13*, 59–70.

Dando, C., Wilcock, R., & Milne, R. (2009a). The cognitive interview. The efficacy of a modified mental reinstatement of context procedure for frontline police investigators. *Applied Cognitive Psychology, 23*, 138–147.

Dando, C., Wilcock, R., & Milne, R. (2009b). The cognitive interview: novice police officers' witness/victim interviewing practices. *Psychology, Crime & Law, 15*(8), 679–696.

Dando, C., Wilcock, R., Milne, R., & Henry, L. (2009) A modified cognitive interview procedure for frontline police investigators. *Applied Cognitive Psychology, 23*, 698–716.

Davis, M. R., McMahon, M., & Greenwood, K. M. (2005). The efficacy of mnemonic components of the cognitive interview: Towards a shortened variant for time-critical investigations. *Applied Cognitive Psychology, 19*, 75–93.

Fisher, R. P. (2010) Interviewing cooperative witnesses. *Legal & Criminological Psychology, 15*, 25–38.

Fisher, R. P., Falkner, K. L., Trevisan, M., & McCauley, M. R. (2000). Adapting the cognitive interview to enhance long-term (35 years) recall of physical activities. *Journal of Applied Psychology, 85*(2), 180–189.

Fisher, R. P., & Geiselman, R. E. (1992). *Memory enhancing techniques for investigative interviewing. The cognitive interview*. Springfield, IL: Charles C. Thomas Publishers.

Fisher, R. P., & Geiselman, R. E. (2010). The cognitive interview method of conducting police interviews: Eliciting extensive information and promoting therapeutic jurisprudence. *International Journal of Law & Psychiatry, 33*, 321–328.

Fisher, R. P., Geiselman, R. E., & Amador, M. (1989). Field test of the cognitive interview. Enhancing the recollection of actual victims and witnesses of crime. *Journal of Applied Psychology, 74*(5), 722–727.

Fisher, R. P., Milne, R., & Bull, R. (2011). Interviewing cooperative witnesses. *Current Directions in Psychology, 20*(1), 16–19.

Ford, R. M., & Rees, E. L. (2008). Representational drawing and the transition from intellectual to visual realism in children with autism. *British Journal of Developmental Psychology, 26*, 197–219.

Frith, U. (2008), *Autism: A very short introduction.* Oxford, London: Oxford University Press.

Frith, U., & Happé, F. (1994). Autism: Beyond "theory of mind." *Cognition, 50*, 115–132.

Frith, U., & Happé, F. (1999). Theory of mind and self-consciousness. What is it like to be autistic? *Mind & Language, 14*(1), 1–22.

Gabbert, F., Hope, L., & Fisher, R. P. (2009). Protecting eyewitness evidence: Examining the efficacy of a self-administered interview tool. *Law & Human Behavior, 33*(4), 298–307.

Gaigg, S. B., Bowler, D. M., & Gardiner, J. M. (2014). Episodic but not semantic order memory difficulties in autism spectrum disorder: Evidence from the historical figure task. *Memory, 22*(6), 669–678.

Gaigg, S. B., Gardiner, J. M., & Bowler, D. M. (2008). Free recall in autism spectrum disorder: The role of relational and item specific encoding. *Neuropsychologia, 46*(4), 983–992.

Gardiner, J. M., & Richardson-Klavehn, A. (2000). Remembering and knowing. In E. Tulving & F. I. M. Craik (Eds.), *The Oxford handbook of memory* (pp. 229–244). Oxford, England: Oxford University Press.

Geiselman, R. E., & Fisher, R. P. (2014). Interviewing witnesses and victims. Retrieved from http://www.psych.ucla.edu/sites/.../files/.../current_Research.d

Gilbert, J. A. E., & Fisher, R. P. (2006). The effects of varied retrieval cues on reminiscence in eye witness memory. *Applied Cognitive Psychology, 20*(6), 723–739.

Ginet, M., Py, J., & Colomb, C. (2014). The differential effectiveness of the cognitive interview instructions for enhancing witnesses' memory of a familiar event. *Swiss Journal of Psychology, 73*(1), 25–34.

Godden, D. R., & Baddeley, A. D. (1975). Context dependent memory in two natural environments: On land and underwater. *British Journal of Psychology, 66*(3), 325–331.

Griffith, A., & Milne, R. (2010). The application of the cognitive interview techniques as part of an investigation. In C. A. Ireland & M. J. Fisher (Eds.), *Consultancy and advising in forensic practice: Empirical and practical guidelines* (pp. 71–90). Chichester, England: Wiley.

Griffith, A., Milne, R., and Cherryman, J. (2011). A question of control? The formulation of suspect and witness interview question strategies by advanced interviewers. *International Journal of Police Science & Management, 13*(3), 255–267.

Gunter, H. L., Ghaziuddin, M., & Ellis, H. D. (2002). Asperger syndrome: Tests of right hemisphere functioning and interhemispheric communication. *Journal of Autism & Developmental Disorders, 32*(4), 263–281.

Gwyer, P., & Clifford, B. R. (1997). The Effects of the cognitive interview on recall, identification, confidence and the confidence/accuracy relationship. *Applied Cognitive Psychology, 11*, 121–145.

Happé, F., & Frith, U. (2006). The weak coherence account. Detail—focused cognitive style in autism spectrum disorders. *Journal of Autism & Developmental Disorders, 36*(1), 5–25.

Hill, E. L., & Frith, U. (2003) Understanding autism: Insights from mind and brain. *Philosophical Transactions of the Royal Society, 358*, 281–289.

Hilton, C., Harper, J., Holmes Kueker, R., Runzi Lang, A., Abbacchi, A., Todorov, A., & LaVesser, P. (2010). Sensory Responsiveness as a predictor of social severity in children with high functioning autism spectrum disorders. *Journal of Autism & Developmental Disorders, 40*, 937–945.

Hintzman, D. L. (1988). Judgments of frequency and recognition memory in a multiple-trace memory model. *Psychological Review, 95*(4), 528–551.

Holliday, R. E., Humphries, J. E., & Milne, R. (2012). Reducing misinformation effects in older adults with cognitive interview mnemonics. *Psychology & Aging, 27*(4), 1191–1203.

Holst, V. F., & Pezdek, K. (1992). Scripts for typical crimes and their effects on memory for eyewitness testimony. *Applied Cognitive Psychology, 6*, 573–587.

Hope, L., Gabbert, F., & Fisher, R. P. (2011). From laboratory to the street: Capturing witness memory using the self-administered interview. *Legal & Criminological Psychology, 16*, 211–226.

Just, M. A., Cherkassky, V. L., Keller, T. A., & Minshew, N. J. (2004). Cortical activation and synchronization during sentence comprehension in high-functioning autism: Evidence of underconnectivity. *Brain, 127*, 1811–1821.

Kana, R. K., Keller, T., Cherkassky, V., Minshew, N., & Just, M. (2006). Sentence comprehension in autism: Thinking in pictures with decreased functional connectivity. *Brain, 129*, 2484–2493.

Keats, P. A. (2009). Multiple text analysis in narrative research: Visual, written and spoken stories of experience. *Qualitative Research, 9*, 181–195.

Kebbell, M. R., & Milne, R. (1998). Police officers' perceptions of eyewitness performance in forensic investigations. *Journal of Social Psychology, 138*(3), 323–330.

Kebbell, M. R., Milne, R., & Wagstaff, G. F. (1999). The cognitive interview: A survey of its forensic effectiveness. *Psychology, Crime & Law, 5*, 101–115.

Kleinhans, N., Akshoomoff, N., & Delis, D. C. (2005). Executive functions in autism and Asperger's disorder: Flexibility, fluency, and inhibition. *Developmental Neuropsychology, 27*(3), 379–401.

Köhnken, G., Milne, R., Memon, A., & Bull, R. (1999). The cognitive interview: A meta-analysis. *Psychology, Crime & Law, 5*(1–2), 3–27.

Kristen, S., Rossmann, F., & Sodian, B. (2014). Theory of mind and autobiographical memory in adults with ASD. *Research in Autism Spectrum Disorders, 8*(7), 827–837.

Kunda, M., & Goel, A. K. (2008). Thinking in pictures: A fresh look at cognition in autism. Retrieved on 8 November 2009 from http://csjarchives.cogsci.rpi.edu/Proceeding/2008/pdfs/p321.pdf

Lam, K. C. H., & Buehler, R. (2009). Trips down memory lane: Recall direction affects the subjective distance of past events. *Personality & Social Psychology Bulletin, 35*, 230–242.

Larsson, A. S., Granhag, P. A., & Spjut, E. (2003). Children's recall and the cognitive interview. Do the positive effects hold over time? *Applied Cognitive Psychology, 17*, 203–214.

Leach, M. J. (2005). Rapport: A key to treatment success. *Complementary Therapies in Clinical Practice, 11*, 262–265.

Lind, S., & Bowler, D. (2008). Episodic memory and autonoetic consciousness in autistic spectrum disorders: The role of self-awareness, representational abilities and temporal cognition. In J. Boucher & D. Bowler (Eds.), *Memory in autism: Theory and evidence* (pp. 166–187). Cambridge, England: Cambridge University Press.

Lind, S. E., & Bowler, D. M. (2009). Recognition memory, self-other source memory, and theory-of-mind in children with autism spectrum disorder. *Journal of Autism & Developmental Disorders, 39*(9), 1231–1239.

Lind, S. E., & Bowler, D. M. (2010). Episodic memory and episodic future thinking in adults with autism. *Journal of Abnormal Psychology, 119*(4), 896–905.

Loftus, E. F. (1975). Leading questions and the eyewitness report. *Cognitive Psychology, 7*, 550–572.

Loftus, E. F., Loftus, G. R., & Messo, J. (1987). Some facts about "weapon focus." *Law & Human Behavior, 11*(1), 55–62.

Loftus, E. F., & Palmer, J. C. (1974). Reconstruction of automobile destruction: An example of the interaction between language and memory. *Journal of Verbal Learning & Verbal Behavior, 13*, 585–589.

Maras, K. L., & Bowler, D. M. (2010). The cognitive interview for eyewitnesses with autism spectrum disorder. *Journal of Autism & Development Disorders, 40*, 1350–1360.

Maras, K. L., & Bowler, D. M. (2011). Brief report: Schema consistent misinformation effects in eyewitnesses with autism spectrum disorder. *Journal of Autism & Developmental Disorders, 41*, 815–820.

Maras, K. L., & Bowler, D. M. (2012). Context reinstatement effects on eyewitness memory in autism spectrum disorder. *British Journal of Psychology, 103*, 330–342.

Maras, K. L., & Bowler, D. M. (2014). Eyewitness testimony in autism spectrum disorder: A review. *Journal of Autism & Developmental Disorders, 44*(11), 2682–2697.

Maras, K. L., Memon, A., Lambrechts, A., & Bowler, D. M. (2013). Recall of a live and personally experienced eyewitness event by adults with autism spectrum disorder. *Journal of Autism & Developmental Disorders. doi:*10.1007/s10803-012-1729-z

Maras, K. L., Mulchay, S., Memon, A., Picariello, F., & Bowler, D. M. (2014). Evaluating the effectiveness of the self-administered interview for witnesses with autism spectrum disorder. *Applied Cognitive Psychology, 28*(5), 693–701.

Mattison, M. L. A., Dando, C. J., & Ormerod, T. C. (2015). Sketching to remember: Episodic free recall task support for child witnesses and victims with autism spectrum disorder. *Journal of Autism & Developmental Disorders*, *45*, 1751–1765. doi:10.1007/s10803-014-2335-z

McCrory, E., Henry, L. A., & Happé, F. (2007). Eye-witness memory and suggestibility in children with Asperger syndrome. *Journal of Child Psychology & Psychiatry*, *48*(5), 482–489.

Mello, E. W., & Fisher, R. P. (1996). Enhancing older adult eyewitness memory with the cognitive interview. *Applied Cognitive Psychology*, *10*, 403–417.

Memon, A., Meissner, C. A., & Fraser, J. (2010). The cognitive interview: A meta-analytic review and study space analysis of the past 25 years. *Psychology, Public Policy & Law*, *16*(4), 340–372.

Memon, A., Zaragoza, M., & Clifford, B. R. (2010). Inoculation or antidote? The effects of cognitive interview timing on false memory for forcibly fabricated events. *Law & Human Behavior*, *34*,105–117.

Milne, R. (2015). *The cognitive interview-a step-by-step guide*. Unpublished training manual.

Milne, R., & Bull, R. (1999). *Investigative interviewing: Psychology and practice*. Chichester, England: John Wiley & Sons Ltd.

Milne, R., & Bull, R. (2002). Back to basics: A componential analysis of the original cognitive interview mnemonics with three age groups. *Applied Cognitive Psychology*, *16*, 743–753.

Milne, R., & Bull, R. (2003). Does the cognitive interview help children to resist the effects of suggestive questioning? *Legal & Criminological Psychology*, *8*, 21–38.

Milne, R., & Bull, R. (2006). Interviewing victims of crime, including children and people with intellectual difficulties. In M. R. Kebbell & G. M. Davies (Eds.), *Practical psychology for forensic investigations* (pp. 7–23). Chichester, England: Wiley.

Milne, R., Clare, I. C. H., & Bull, R. (1999).Using the cognitive interview with adults with mild learning disabilities. *Psychology, Crime & Law*, *5*(1), 81–99.

Milne, R., Sharman, S. J., Powell, M. B., & Mead, S. (2013). Assessing the effectiveness of the cognitive interview for children with severe intellectual disabilities. *International Journal of Disability, Development & Education*, *60*(1), 18–29.

Minshew, N. J., & Goldstein, G. (2001). The pattern of intact and impaired memory functions in autism. *Journal of Child Psychology & Psychiatry*, *42*(8), 1095–1101.

Minshew, N. J., Goldstein, G., & Siegel, D. (1995). Speech and language in high-functioning autistic individuals. *Neuropsychology*, *9*(2), 255–261.

Minshew, N. J., Goldstein, G., & Siegel, D. J. (1997). Neuropsychological functioning in autism: Profile of a complex information processing disorder. *Journal of International Neuropsychologcal Society*, *3*(4), 303–316.

Minshew, N. J., & Williams, D. L. (2007). The new neurobiology of autism context, connectivity and neuronal organisation. *Archives of Neurology*, *64*(7), 945–950.

Mottron, L., Belleville, S., & Ménard, E. (1999). Local bias in autistic subjects as evidenced by graphic tasks: Perceptual hierarchization or working memory deficit? *Journal of Child Psychology & Psychiatry*, *40*(5), 743–755.

Müller, E., Schuler, A., & Yates, G. B. (2008). Social challenges and supports from the perspective of individuals with Asperger syndrome and other autism spectrum disabilities. *Autism*, *12*(2), 173–190.

Nadel, L., Samsonovich, A., Ryan, L., & Moscovitch, M. (2000). Multiple trace theory of human memory: Computational, neuroimaging and neuropsychological results. *Hippocampus*, *10*, 352–368.

Neuschatz, J. S., Lampinen, J. M., Preston, E. L., Hawkins, E. R., & Toglia, M. P (2002). The effect of memory schemata on memory and the phenomenological experience of naturalistic situations. *Applied Cognitive Psychology*, *16*(6), 687–708.

Nori, R., Bensi, L., Gambetti, E., & Giusberti, F. (2014). Individual differences in the enhanced cognitive interview: The role of imagery. *Psychology, Crime & Law*, *20*(9), 833–851.

O'Neill Shermer, L., Rose, K. C., & Hoffman, A. (2011). Perception and credibility: Understanding the nuances of eyewitness testimony. *Journal of Contemporary Criminal Justice*, *27*(2), 183–203.

Paulo, R. M., Albuquerque, P. B., & Bull, R. (2013). The enhanced cognitive interview: Towards a better use and understanding of this procedure. *International Journal of Police Science & Management*, *15*(3), 190–199.

Paulo, R. M., Albuquerque, P. B., Saraiva, M., & Bull, R. (2015). The enhanced cognitive interview: Testing appropriateness perception, memory capacity and error estimate relation with report quality. *Applied Cognitive Psychology*, *29*, 536–543.

Perfect, T. J., Andrade, J., & Syrett, L. (2012). Environmental distractions during retrieval affects the quality not the quantity of eyewitness recall. *Applied Cognitive Psychology*, *26*, 296–300.

Perfect, T. J., Wagstaff, G. F., Moore, D., Andrews, B., Cleveland, V., Newcombe, S., Brisbane, K., & Brown, L. (2008). How can we help witnesses to remember more? It's an (eyes) open and shut case. *Law & Human Behavior*, *32*(4), 314–324.

Perner, J., & Ruffman, T. (1995). Episodic memory and autonoetic consciousness: Developmental evidence and a theory of childhood amnesia. *Journal of Experimental Child Psychology*, *59*, 516–548.

Powell, M. B., & Snow, P. C. (2007). Guide to questioning children during the free-narrative phase of an investigative interview. *Australian Psychologist*, *42*(1), 57–65.

Poyser, S., & Milne, R. (2011). Miscarriages of justice: A call for continued research focusing on reforming the investigative process. *British Journal of Forensic Practice*, *13*, 61–71.

Prescott, K., Milne, R., & Clarke, J. (2011). How effective is the enhanced cognitive interview when aiding recall retrieval of older adults including memory for conversation? *Journal of Investigative Psychology & Offender Profiling*, *8*, 257–270.

Richards, J., & Milne, R. (in prep). Using memory jogs to encourage item specific details from witnesses with autism spectrum disorder.

Richards, J., Milne, R., & Dando, C. (in submission). Exploring the use of context (mental and sketch plan) to elicit memorial recall in people with autism spectrum disorder.

Rivard, J. R., Fisher, R. P., Robertson, B., & Mueller, D. H. (2014). Testing the cognitive interview with professional interviewers: Enhancing recall of specific details of recurring events. *Applied Cognitive Psychology*, *28*, 917–925.

Robinson, S., Goddard, L., Dritschel, B., Wisely, M., & Howlin, P. (2009). Executive functions in children with autism spectrum disorders. *Brain & Cognition*, *71*, 362–368.

Saywitz, K. J., Geiselman, R. E., & Bornstein, G. K. (1992). Effects of cognitive interviewing and practice on children's recall performance. *Journal of Applied Psychology*, *77*, 744–756.

Schank, R. C., & Abelson, R. P. (1977). *Scripts, plans, goals and understanding: An inquiry into human knowledge structures.* Hillsdale, NJ: Lawrence Erlbaum Associates.

Sharman, S. J., & Powell, M. B. (2013). Do cognitive interview instructions contribute to false belief memories? *Journal of Investigative Psychology & Offender Profiling*, *10*, 114–124.

Stein, L. M., & Memon, A. (2006). Testing the efficacy of the cognitive interview in a developing country. *Applied Cognitive Psychology*, *20*, 597–605.

Toichi, M., & Kamio, Y. (2003). Long-term memory in high-functioning autism; Controversy on episodic memory in autism reconsidered. *Journal of Autism & Developmental Disorders*, *33*(2), 151–161.

Tuckey, M. R., & Brewer, N. (2003). The influence of schemas, stimulus ambiguity and interview schedule on eyewitness memory over time. *Journal of Experimental Psychology*, *9*(2), 101–118.

Tulving, E. (1974). Cue-dependent forgetting. *American Scientist*, *62*(1), 74–82.

Tulving, E. (1983). *Elements of episodic memory.* Oxford, England: Open University Press.

Tulving, E. (1985). Memory and consciousness. *Canadian Psychology*, *26*, 1–12.

Tulving, E., & Thompson, D. (1973). Encoding specificity and retrieval processes in episodic memory. *Psychological Review*, *80*(5), 352–373.

Vallano, J. P., & Compo, N. S. (2011). A comfortable witness is a good witness: Rapport-building and susceptibility to misinformation in an investigative mock-crime interview. *Applied Cognitive Psychology*, *25*, 960–970.

Verkampt, F., & Ginet, M. (2010). Variations of the cognitive interview. Which one is the most effective in enhancing children's testimonies? *Applied Cognitive Psychology*, *24*, 1279–1296.

Vrij, A., Leal, S., Mann, S., & Fisher, R. (2012). Imposing cognitive load to elicit cues to deceit: Including the reverse order technique naturally. *Psychology, Crime & Law*, *18*(6), 579–594.

Vrij, A., Mann, S. A., Fisher, R. P., Leal, S., Milne, R., & Bull, R. (2008). Increasing cognitive load to facilitate lie detection: The benefit of recalling an event in reverse order. *Law & Human Behavior*, *32*(3), 253–265.

Wheeler, M. A. (2000). Episodic memory and autonoetic awareness. In E. Tulving & F. I. M. Craik (Eds.), *The Oxford handbook of memory* (pp. 597–608). Oxford, England: Oxford University Press.

Wilcock, R., Bull, R., & Milne, R. (2008). *Witness identification in criminal cases.* Oxford, England: Oxford University Press.

Williams, D. L., Goldstein, G., & Minshew, N. J. (2006). The profile of memory function in children with autism. *Neuropsychology*, *20*(1), 21–29.

Williams, D. L., Minshew, N. J., & Goldstein, G. (2008). Memory within a complex information processing model of autism. In J. Boucher & D. Bowler (Eds.), *Memory in autism* (pp. 125–142). Cambridge, England: Cambridge University Press.

Wright, A. M., & Holliday, R. E. (2007). Interviewing cognitively impaired older adults: How useful is a cognitive interview? Retrieved on 10 February 2008 From http://www.informaworld.com/smpp/section?content=a769973005&fulltext=7132409 (pp. 1–16).

14

Narrative Elaboration Technique

Lorinda B. Camparo, Ambar Guzman, and Karen J. Saywitz

Providing eyewitness testimony is not easy. At the very least, it involves recalling emotionally charged memories and perceptions—often encoded only incidentally at the time—and then providing a comprehensive and accurate verbal report of those memories and perceptions in response to verbally posed questions by an unfamiliar authority figure in an unfamiliar context. It requires skills and competencies that even typically developing (TD) children may not have acquired: the ability to mentally travel in time, attend selectively, monitor and remember the source of information, produce and comprehend spoken language, take another's perspective, understand that others may have different intentions and beliefs than one's own, and resist suggestion as well as a developed sense of self and emotional maturity. Yet, many of these competencies develop only gradually as children's brains mature, and deficits in nearly all of these competencies is precisely what characterizes autism spectrum disorder (ASD). Unfortunately, deficits in these competencies may also put children with ASD at higher risk for becoming a victim or witness to a crime (e.g., Petersilia, 2001). Without accommodation to a child's unique developmental and clinical capabilities and limitations, the demands of the forensic interview can quickly lead to miscommunication, misinterpretation, and potentially, even false reports.

The developmental narrative elaboration (DNE) interview (see Saywitz & Camparo, 2014, for a full description) was designed to address the specific mismatches between the demands of the forensic context and the capabilities of young children by providing the scaffolding, structure, task support, and guidance necessary for optimal performance by children—whether typically or atypically developing. This is accomplished with a template and a set of memory and communication strategies that equip children with the support and knowledge necessary to understand the unfamiliar context and task demands of the forensic interview, provide children with unbiased retrieval cues to help them organize their memory search, and offer children optional instructions and preparation to enhance memory and reduce the potential for miscommunication and suggestibility.

In the following section, we describe the DNE with particular focus on the core template of the DNE: the narrative elaboration (NE) protocol. We then discuss specific ways in which the DNE addresses immaturities and impairments in TD and ASD

The Wiley Handbook of Memory, Autism Spectrum Disorder, and the Law, First Edition.
Edited by Jonni L. Johnson, Gail S. Goodman, and Peter C. Mundy.

children's memory, language and narrative competence, cognition, and resistance to suggestion. Finally, we present the research from which the DNE was derived, and in the final section, we discuss the potential application of the NE and DNE to interviewing children with ASD.

What are the DNE and NE?

The full DNE is a semi-structured "tool kit" of instructions and techniques designed for interviewing 4- to-12-year-old children in a forensic context. The goal is to help children tell as much as they can about their experiences and perceptions in their own words without tainting their reports. The full DNE consists of three principal phases, with the NE comprising the second, core phase (see Saywitz & Camparo, 2014, for the full template and instructions).

Phase I

Phase I is a preliminary phase that includes introductions, rapport development, instructions, and ground rules, plus optional practice in the use of strategies for enhancing memory reports, improving comprehension monitoring, and reducing suggestion. These two latter techniques, which comprise the more comprehensive DNE, can be embedded into the NE core template (Phase II) at the interviewer's discretion as cases unfold.

Phase II

Phase II, the "Core NE Template," consists of three steps: Free Recall, Cued Elaboration, and Short Answer Follow-up Questions. Each step lays a foundation for the step that follows and builds on the step that precedes it.

Step 1: Free Recall
In the first step of the Core NE Template, the interviewer creates an opportunity for the child to give a spontaneous or minimally prompted narrative of a potential forensically relevant incident (e.g., "What happened?") followed by one or two open-ended prompts (e.g., "Tell me more" or "What happened next?").

Step 2: Cued Elaboration
It is the second step of the Core NE Template, Cued Elaboration, that distinguishes the NE from all other interview formats. During Cued Elaboration, the interviewer provides the child with either visual or verbal cues designed to prompt the child to provide additional detail about four empirically derived categories of information: (a) participants, (b) location, (c) actions, and (d) conversations/affective states.

The *visual cues* include four "Reminder Cards," each with a simple, generic, line drawing representing the participants, location, actions, or conversations/affective states (see Saywitz & Camparo, 2014, Appendix A for visual cues for school-aged children, and Appendix B for visual cues for preschoolers). If the interviewer intends to use the visual cues, the cards must first be introduced to the child during the Preliminary Phase I as "a good way to tell about things that happen to you," and the children must be given practice in their use (Saywitz & Camparo, 2014). After the child has demonstrated an understanding of the cards' use during the Preliminary Phase I and the child has disclosed a spontaneous narrative of a forensically relevant event during the Free Recall step of Phase II, the interviewer presents each card individually to the child during the Cued-Elaboration step, and asks the child if the card reminds the child to tell anything more about each of the four categories of information (Saywitz & Camparo, 2014).

If the interviewer decides not to use the visual cues, simple *verbal cues* may be used instead, without introduction during the Preliminary Phase I or practice. The *verbal cues* include four questions presented individually during the Cued-Elaboration step: "Tell me more about the people who were there and how the people looked"; "Tell me more about where it was and how the place looked"; "Tell me more about what happened, and what all the people did"; "Tell me more about what all of the people said and how they felt" (see Saywitz & Camparo, 2014, for different language options for verbal cues).

The NE inserts this step between Free Recall and Short-Answer Follow-up Questions to provide children with a chance to elaborate on their initial narratives in their own words. It does so by helping children structure and organize their memory search through the use of generic, nonsuggestive verbal and/or visual cues. As is discussed later, the additional detail elicited during this step has ranged from over two to eight times more information as elicited in standard interviews, without concomitant increases in error. Thus, this step provides interviewers with a larger data set of information from which to craft better-informed, and potentially, less-biased, follow-up questions in Step 3 than would otherwise be possible.

Step 3: Short-Answer Follow-up Questions

In the third step, the interviewer employs specific follow-up questions to double back and explore important, vague, or inconsistent information mentioned by the child during Free Recall or Cued Elaboration. These questions are informed by the additional information provided by the child during Cued Elaboration, and are formulated according to guidelines in the DNE for generating developmentally appropriate and nonleading questions.

Phase III

Phase III provides an opportunity for closure. It consists of guidelines for soliciting and addressing children's questions, educating them about next steps, helping them regain their composure if upset, identifying potential stressors, and generating anticipatory coping strategies (see Saywitz & Camparo, 2014, for full description of all phases).

How Does the DNE Address Children's Limitations?

Addressing limitations in memory

Young TD children exhibit many strengths, as well as limitations, in the domain of memory. For example, they are often remarkably adept at noticing subtle, unexpected events (Gopnik, 2009). They are also able to recall a notable amount of information about past autobiographical events, especially highly salient, unique, emotionally engaging, and meaningful (to them) events (Bauer, 2007; Nelson & Fivush, 2004), and these are precisely the types of events most likely to be relevant in the forensic context. However, the completeness and accuracy of young children's recall is highly dependent on the way they are questioned (Larsson & Lamb, 2009). The information children report in response to free-recall questions (e.g., responses to "What happened?") is generally accurate, but it is also typically incomplete and not necessarily relevant to the questioner's interests. Eliciting details relevant to the questioner's interests often requires additional questions; however, if these follow-up questions are misleading, they can distort children's reports.

Similar to TD children, high-functioning individuals diagnosed with ASD also tend to notice small details (Maras & Bowler, 2014, for a review), and the information they report in response to free-recall questions also tends to be highly accurate, although even less complete than non-ASD control groups, particularly, in regard to gist and socially salient information (McCrory, Henry, & Happé, 2007). Indeed, research has now established that ASD individuals exhibit "a unique memory profile" (Maras & Bowler, 2014, p. 2683), performing at the level of their non-ASD peers in some areas and exhibiting potentially serious deficits in others. For example, whereas memory for facts, recall of events that happened to others, and performance on cued-recall and recognition tasks by high-functioning ASD individuals do not differ from non-ASD control groups, episodic memory, recall of events that happened to themselves, and source monitoring are impaired in ASD groups (Boucher, Mayes, & Bigham, 2012; Bruck, London, Landa, & Goodman, 2007; Goddard, Dritschel, Robinson, & Howlin, 2014; see Maras & Bowler, 2014, for a brief review; Millward, Powell, Messer, & Jordan, 2000). In one study specifically examining autobiographical memory, researchers found that 5- to 10-year-old children with mild to moderate ASD exhibited poorer autobiographical memory and provided significantly fewer details for personally experienced events, including a staged event, than did non-ASD age mates (Bruck et al., 2007). Consistent with their "sparseness of true memories" (p. 89), most errors in ASD children's autobiographical-memory reports were errors of omission rather than errors of commission (Bruck et al., 2007).

For young TD children, part of the difficulty in autobiographical memory reports is that their awareness of how their own memory works tends to be restricted and faulty. Additionally, they have more difficulty retrieving information from memory than do older children and adults who use more complex and successful retrieval strategies to increase the amount of information they retrieve independently (Ornstein, Naus, & Liberty, 1975; Schneider & Pressley, 1989). Nevertheless, research has demonstrated that even young TD children can benefit from learning new memory-enhancing and cueing strategies they could not have generated without adult guidance (Elischberger & Roebers, 2001; Schneider & Pressley, 1989). Similarly, adolescents and adults with ASD have been found to benefit from "task support" (Bowler, Gardiner, & Berthollier, 2004), especially supportive cues related to location of information (Bowler et al., 2015; Maras & Bowler, 2014), leading researchers to speculate that deficits in recall in individuals diagnosed with ASD are more a function of retrieval than encoding (Maras & Bowler, 2014).

Thus, the core NE template was designed to take full advantage of the fact that TD children's initial free-recall narratives are most accurate and compensate for difficulty in retrieving details independently through the use of four event-category cues that structure recall efforts without the use of specific or potentially leading questions.

Addressing limitations in communicative and narrative competence

Addressing limitations in communicative competence is one of the greatest challenges when interviewing young TD children, and this challenge is likely to be exacerbated when interviewing ASD children who often experience speech and language disorders (see Boucher, 2012, for review; Lord & Paul, 1997) and for whom "persistent impairment in social communication and social interaction" is one of the essential features (American Psychiatric Association, 2013). TD preschoolers' and ASD individuals' conversations are often replete with irrelevant or idiosyncratic responses (Tager-Flusberg, 2000), and most young TD children and ASD individuals have not mastered the grammar required to add the prepositional phrases, adverbs, adjectives, and embedded clauses that provide the type of detail needed in forensic investigations (Boucher, 2012; Owens, 2012). For most TD children, comprehension of adult grammar, vocabulary, and discourse rules continues to develop into late childhood (Owens, 2012); however, it is not uncommon for much younger witnesses and even some witnesses with intellectual difficulties to be asked questions using grammar that is too complex and vocabulary that is too sophisticated for them to comprehend (e.g., Brennan & Brennan, 1988; Evans, Lee, & Lyon, 2009; Kebbell, Hatton, & Johnson, 2014; Perry et al., 1995).

Compounding the problem, young TD children often have difficulty monitoring whether or not they fully understand adult language and "almost invariably" attempt to answer even bizarre, nonsensical questions (Hughes & Grieve, 1980, p. 149), resulting in confusion and apparent inconsistency (e.g., Carter, Bottoms, & Levine, 1996; Markman, 1981; Saywitz, Snyder, & Nathanson, 1999). Metalinguistic awareness and comprehension-monitoring skills develop gradually; consequently, many children enter elementary school demonstrating difficulties in these areas (Saywitz & Wilkinson, 1982).

Adding to these linguistic challenges, TD children's narrative skills also develop slowly over time (Berman, 1997; Hudson & Shapiro, 1991), with most TD children not achieving narrative competence until 9 years of age (Karmiloff-Smith, 1985). Researchers have recently begun to distinguish between two types of event narratives: general event narratives, which, like scripts, are based on general, semantic memory; and specific event narratives, which, like autobiographical memory, are based on episodic memory for personally experienced events (King et al., 2013; Nelson, 2003). Competency in specific event narratives is most relevant to the forensic context; however, research with TD children suggests that competency in specific event narratives develops later than competency in general event narratives (Gruendel & Nelson, 1986). Moreover, well-established deficits in episodic memory in individuals with ASD (Millward, Powell, Messer, & Jordan, 2000) may be expected to result in even more impoverished specific-event narratives compared to general-event narratives for ASD individuals.

Given the obvious relevance of narrative ability to the forensic context, research has examined general and specific event narratives for TD children (e.g., Brubacker, Roberts, & Powell, 2011; Farrar & Goodman, 1990; Gruendel & Nelson, 1986; Nelson, 2003; Schneider, Price, Roberts, & Hedrick, 2011) and ASD children

(King et al., 2013). King et al. assessed the *structure* and *use of evaluative devices* in general-event narratives (e.g., the prompt asked "What usually happens when someone goes on holiday?") and specific-event narratives (e.g., the prompt asked "Can you tell me about a time when you went on holiday?"). *Structure* of the narratives was operationalized as length of narratives (number of main body words), mean length of utterances, number of different root words, and fluency (number of repetitions, revisions, false starts, and filled pauses; lower numbers indicated greater fluency). Use of evaluative devices was operationalized as number of references to mental states, causal statements, negative comments, emphatic markers, character speech, and use of terms such as *sometimes*, *perhaps*, *probably*, and *might* to distance the speaker. Participants included 11- to 14-year-old high-functioning ASD children, 11- to 14-year-old TD children matched with the ASD group on nonverbal ability and chronological age (CAM group), and 5- to 15-year-old TD children matched with the ASD group on nonverbal ability and expressive-language ability (LM group).

As would be expected, ASD children produced shorter, less descriptive, and less grammatically complex event narratives of both types than did children in the CAM and LM groups. Nevertheless, both types of narratives for the ASD group were more fluent than the narratives for the other two groups. With regard to the use of evaluative devices, the ASD group provided the same proportion as the LM group, but a significantly lower proportion than the CAM group in their specific event narratives, and they provided a significantly lower proportion than both groups in their general event narratives. Finally, although ASD children's impaired episodic memory may have suggested that their specific event narratives would be more impoverished across all measures than their general event narratives, there were no differences for the ASD group in the proportion of evaluative devices they used in their general or specific event narratives (King et al., 2013).

To address limitations in TD and ASD children's grammar and vocabulary, the NE offers guidelines for phrasing questions in simple grammar and vocabulary that young TD children and higher-functioning ASD children are likely to comprehend. Additionally, an optional DNE technique provides instructions and strategies to help children notice when they fail to comprehend, to indicate lack of comprehension to the interviewer, and to elicit rephrasing rather than guess at an answer (Cordón, Saetermoe, & Goodman, 2005; Lamb & Brown, 2006; Peters & Nunez, 1999; Saywitz et al., 1999). Finally, studies of TD children's general-event knowledge (e.g., generalized scripts for common events) suggest that event recall is guided by psychologically salient constructs that include the categories of participants, setting, actions, and conversations/affective states (Mandler & Johnson, 1977; Stein & Glenn, 1978)—the same categories used during the Cued-Elaboration step in Phase II of the core NE template. Thus, the Cued Elaboration provides the TD (and potentially, the ASD) child with the necessary structure to guide event recall as well as an additional opportunity to add to the structural or evaluative content of the narrative without the use of potentially leading or suggestive questioning.

Addressing limitations in children's cognitive abilities

Studies are clear that TD children under 8 years of age and ASD individuals of all ages have limited perspective-taking skills (Dickson, 1981; Maras & Bowler, 2010; Piaget, 1926; Shantz, 1975); have difficulty drawing inferences about others, including the listener's intentions; and possess limited referential-communication skills (i.e., "ability to speak so that others will understand and to listen so that you will understand others or know when you have not"; Sonnenschein & Whitehurst, 1984, p. 1936), all of which contribute to a failure to orient the listener fully to person, place, context, and timing (Flavell, Botkin, Fry, Wright, & Jarvis, 1968; Goldman, 2008; Robinson & Robinson, 1978; Tager-Flusberg, 2000). Additionally, young TD and ASD children have a limited understanding of causality and abstract hypothetical-deductive reasoning (Bruner, 1957; Flavell, 1985; Piaget, 1930), and ASD children exhibit difficulties in relational-processing (Gaigg, Gardiner, & Bowler, 2008; see King et al., 2013 for a brief review) and emotional-processing domains (e.g., Dawson, Hill, Spencer, & Galpert, 1990, Yimiya, Sigman, Kasari, & Mundy, 1992,). TD children's metacognitive skills develop rapidly between 7 and 9 years of age (Flavell, 1981), but before they are fully developed, TD children have difficulty analyzing and evaluating their own thoughts as independent objects, and as a result, they often do not know what they do not know (Wellman & Somerville, 1982).

Younger TD and likely many ASD children also have difficulty reasoning about such abstract concepts as justice and society, and have limited and flawed knowledge of the legal or social-service systems (Flin, Stevenson, & Davies, 1989; Saywitz, 1989; Warren-Leubecker, Tate, Hinton, & Ozbek, 1989). This can lead to incomplete reports and unrealistic fears (Sas, Austin, Wolfe, & Hurley, 1991; Saywitz, Nathanson, Snyder, & Lamphear, 1993, Experiment 7). Researchers have shown that young TD children can learn basic facts about the legal system when presented at their developmental level, and in fact, that greater knowledge may be associated with less stress (lowered heart rate while answering questions) and greater recall (Nathanson & Saywitz, 2003).

In an effort to address some of the limitations on TD children's cognitive abilities, the NE (a) offers guidelines for creating a child-friendly atmosphere that minimizes visual and auditory distractions (which would also be important for ASD populations); (b) provides instructions for children to pay attention and listen carefully as well as interviewer guidelines for redirecting them to the task at hand; (c) provides optional use of visual reminder cues that help some children focus on the task at hand and may serve as "task support" for ASD children (Bowler et al., 2004); (d) makes an effort to demystify the legal process and the interviewer's intentions by providing children with clear, concrete explanations of the interview purpose, child's and interviewer's roles, and aspects of the legal process as it pertains to the information-gathering phase of the investigation in language and concepts children can understand; and (e) provides guidelines for avoiding questions that require abstract concepts and reasoning skills that are likely to be beyond a child's phase of cognitive development.

Addressing children's suggestibility

Another weakness of young TD children's reports is their vulnerability to misleading, suggestive, or option-posing questions from adults (e.g., Bruck, Ceci, Francoeur, & Barr, 1995; Leichtman & Ceci, 1995; Lepore & Sesco, 1994). During the preschool years, TD children are still in the process of understanding how knowledge and beliefs are acquired (Flavell & Miller, 1998), that some beliefs are true and some are false, or that one can hold a belief with more or less certainty (e.g., Moore & Furrow, 1991). Hence, young TD children may not understand that suggestions embedded in leading questions are often unintentional attempts to elicit vital details born out of frustration rather than commands to say what they believe interviewers want to hear.

Adding to the problem is TD children's tendency to defer to adults as authority figures (Ceci, Ross, & Toglia, 1987). This tendency may be due, at least in part, to young children's tendency to trust adult knowledge (Taylor, Cartwright, & Bowden, 1991) and their assumptions that adult interviewers, like their teachers and parents, already know the answers to their own questions (Saywitz & Nathanson, 1993). Yet, research has found that these suggestibility effects can be mitigated in TD preschoolers through source-monitoring instructions (e.g., Bright-Paul, Jarrold, & Wright, 2005; Thierry & Spence, 2002) and if adults explicitly state they had no special knowledge of what happened (Toglia, Ross, Ceci, & Hembrooke, 1992).

There is also an expanding body of research on suggestibility in high-functioning ASD individuals, which indicates that they are no more or less suggestible than non-ASD control groups (Bruck et al., 2007; Maras & Bowler, 2011; McCrory et al., 2007). Nevertheless, McCrory et al. cautioned against generalizing findings on ASD children's *suggestibility*, which, they noted, "implies personal acceptance of the information provided" (p. 370) to *compliance*, which, they noted, "refers to the tendency of an individual to go along with propositions, requests or instructions while not necessarily accepting that they are true or right" (Gudjonsson, 2003, p. 370). They further argued that given deficits in theory of mind and an increased propensity for anxiety in individuals with ASD, such individuals may also be expected to exhibit an increased propensity toward compliance (McCrory et al., 2007).

Relevant to this concern, Bruck et al. (2007) found that their ASD group (aged 5- to 10-years old) assented to more yes/no questions about "silly events" (e.g., "Have you ever helped a lady find a monkey in the park?") than the non-ASD control group did, although the effect was small. However, the ASD group did not assent to more yes/no questions about "plausible events" (e.g., "Have you ever been on an airplane?") than the non-ASD control group did, even though some of these items were true. Together, these findings led Bruck et al. (2007) to speculate that the ASD group's higher rate of agreement with the silly questions "do[es] not reflect a pattern of yea-saying (or compliance)" (p. 90) given that the ASD group did not consistently assent to other, more plausible questions, including some true statements. Rather, they argued that, whereas TD children will use their complete lack of familiarity with never-before-heard "silly" items to reject them, children with ASD don't, leaving them as vulnerable to suggestion about "silly" or "unfamiliar" events as they are to "plausible" events. Based on these findings, Maras and Bowler (2014) speculated that children with ASD may be more likely than TD children to acquiesce to a biased forensic interviewer's line of questioning about an event that differs significantly from the version reported by the child.

The NE is designed to minimize suggestibility by including (a) optional DNE instructions informing children that the child, not the interviewer, is the expert on what happened at the event because the interviewer was not present; (b) optional DNE instructions informing children that interviewers might put their guess into a question and that children should correct the interviewer when necessary as well as optional DNE practice recognizing such questions and correcting the interviewer; (c) guidelines for interviewers on avoiding suggestive-questions when follow-up questions are necessary, relying instead on questions that require multi-word responses;

and finally, (d) an interim step of Cued Elaboration as an additional opportunity for the child to elaborate on initial narratives prior to follow-up questions, thereby reducing the need for specific and potentially leading questions.

Research on the Efficacy of the Narrative Elaboration Technique

The narrative elaboration procedure is the heart of the DNE. This method has been studied with over 1,000 children. It has been tested with preschoolers of varied levels of socioeconomic status (Bowen & Howie, 2002; Dorado & Saywitz, 2001) and children in elementary school (Brown & Pipe, 2003a; Brown & Pipe, 2003b; Camparo, Wagner, & Saywitz, 2001; Saywitz & Snyder, 1996; Saywitz, Snyder, & Lamphear, 1996) over retention intervals ranging from two weeks to nine months (Brown & Pipe, 2003b), regarding memory for staged classroom events (Bowen & Howie, 2002; Saywitz & Snyder, 1996), field trips, highly stressful, naturally occurring events like injuries requiring emergency-room treatment (Peterson, Warren, & Hayes, 2012), and fictitious events to test suggestibility effects (Camparo et al., 2001). Most relevant to this chapter, it has been studied in children with learning disabilities (Nathanson, Crank, Saywitz, & Ruegg, 2007) and varied levels of intelligence (Brown & Pipe, 2003a). Studies have been conducted in our own laboratories in southern California and extended to other laboratories in the United States, Australia, New Zealand, and Canada. In the sections that follow, we highlight the findings of these studies and the evolution of the NE interview (see Saywitz & Camparo, 2014, for review).

Evolution of the NE

The NE procedure was originally developed by Saywitz and Snyder (1996) for use with 7- to 11-year-old children and revised in a follow-up replication study by Saywitz et al. (1996) designed to isolate some of the active ingredients responsible for the outcome. In both studies, children participated in a staged and videotaped classroom event, and two weeks later, children were randomly assigned to participate in either NE or control activities prior to an interview that tested their recall for the classroom event. Findings from these studies indicated that the children in the NE group demonstrated a significant increase in accurate information over the children in the control groups, and that the additional information reported as a result of the NE protocol was enhanced in both complexity (main ideas) and richness (details). Perhaps most noteworthy, findings indicated that gains in the amount of accurate information in the NE condition were not offset by any increase in inaccurate information in the NE condition (Saywitz & Snyder, 1996; Saywitz et al., 1996).

Additionally, Saywitz and Snyder (1996) found that although the older children in their study generally recalled a significantly greater amount of accurate information and made significantly fewer errors during Cued Elaboration and probed recall than the younger children did, the effects of the NE intervention were equivalently beneficial for both the younger and older children. In fact, younger children using the NE procedure demonstrated recall comparable to older children in the control group.

This finding is particularly important because younger children are most likely to produce skeletal narratives requiring follow-up questions for clarification, yet they are also least able to resist when follow-up questions are suggestive. Hence, they may benefit most from help in providing a larger store of reliable information in their own words on which to base follow-up questions.

Extending these original studies, which tested the efficacy of the NE after only a two-week delay, Brown and Pipe (2003b) examined the efficacy of NE in 6- to 8-year-old children over a two-week and a nine-month delay. After the two-week delay, children in the NE condition reported approximately twice as much accurate information as did children in the control condition, and after the nine-month delay, children in the NE condition reported 55% more information overall than did controls—and the additional details were reported during the Cued-Elaboration phase of the interview. Consistent with previous research, there were no group differences in overall amount of errors (Brown & Pipe, 2003b).

Adapting the NE for preschoolers

The NE protocol was adapted for preschoolers by two research teams. First, Dorado and Saywitz (2001) conducted a preliminary study of 40 4- to 5-year-olds and then a more extensive study of an additional 99 4- to 5-year-olds. Modifications involved simplifying the reminder card drawings to reduce stimulus-bound responses (see Saywitz & Camparo, 2014, Appendix B) as well as modifying the rationale and the way the cards were introduced. Then, Bowen and Howie (2002) tested a briefer NE procedure with 72 4- to 6-year-olds. Consistent with the research on school-aged children, results from both research teams indicated that preschoolers in the NE training groups reported a significantly greater amount of accurate, but not inaccurate, information, than children in the control groups. On average, preschoolers using the NE approach produced more than twice as much accurate information as did preschoolers in the control group. Remarkably, the preschoolers produced very little inaccurate information; however, although preschoolers did make quite a few off-task remarks, children in the NE group did not produce significantly more irrelevant or vague remarks than did those in the control group. When off-task or irrelevant comments were made, it was not difficult for interviewers to identify them and redirect preschoolers back to the task at hand.

Since these two studies were published, other researchers have included preschoolers in their sample with positive effects (e.g., Peterson et al., 2012). Hence, interviewers will find a variation for preschoolers and a variation for elementary school-aged children as well as tips for using the NE with preschoolers derived from this research (see Saywitz & Camparo, 2014).

Streamlining the narrative elaboration protocol

Although quite effective, the original NE protocol included several elements that made it cumbersome to use in the field. Therefore, a number of research teams have tested streamlined versions of the procedure (Bowen & Howie, 2002; Brown & Pipe, 2003a; Camparo et al., 2001).

Consistent with the results of the original studies, all three studies of a shortened version found significant increases in the amount of accurate information—but not the amount of inaccurate information—over standard protocols or control conditions, and the effects were quite robust despite considerable variation in the procedure across studies. These findings suggest that perhaps the most important component of the NE protocol is the extra opportunity for category Cued Elaboration, whether visual or verbal, inserted after Free Recall and prior to Follow-up Questioning. In all of the studies reviewed thus far, information children provided prior to specific follow-up questions (Free Recall plus Cued Elaboration) was expanded significantly, creating a larger base of reliable information from which interviewers can construct follow-up questions, thereby reducing the potential for leading questions and contamination.

Does the NE lead to false reports?

Ironically, the finding that the NE significantly enhances the amount of information children report raised a very serious concern: Does the NE also lead children to report more information about an event that we know did *not* happen? To address this concern, Camparo et al. (2001) asked children to report about both a staged field-trip event and a fictitious field trip to the desert. Results indicated there were no group differences in the amount of false information reported about the fictitious event. Nevertheless, similar to previous research with the NE, standard deviations for children in the NE and one of the control groups were quite large. Post-hoc analyses revealed two outliers: One child provided no information in response to either the Free-Recall or Cued-Elaboration prompts, but when the interviewer continued to ask a series of follow-up questions about the fictitious event, he provided 906 pieces of (inaccurate) information in response to the standardized Follow-up Questions about the fictitious event. The second child repeatedly denied experiencing the fictitious event during all three free-recall prompts; however, when the interviewer proceeded to question the child about the field trip anyway, the child responded to the Cued-Elaboration cards with the question, "You mean, even if I didn't go?" When the interviewer did not answer, the child proceeded to provide 520 pieces of (inaccurate) information about the fictitious event over the remainder of the interview. These two children highlight the rare but serious danger of ignoring children's denials or implying, through repeated prompting or silence, that they should answer questions about events they deny occurred.

Does the NE enhance children's narratives of emotionally charged real-life events?

Another concern raised by methodological limitations of the research testing the efficacy of the NE was that the NE may only be useful for enhancing children's recall of "child-friendly" staged events. To address this limitation, Peterson et al. (2012) used a streamlined version of the NE to examine the efficacy of the NE for eliciting 3- to 7-year-old children's autobiographical reports of a recent injury sustained by the child that was serious enough to require emergency-room medical treatment. Because previous findings have indicated that children's recall for highly salient, emotionally charged, and unique events—properties that characterize many forensic events—is already quite accurate and fairly complete (e.g., Peterson & Warren, 2009), use of such a target event provides invaluable information regarding the efficacy of the NE protocol under such real-world circumstances. Moreover, unlike most real-world cases of sexual or physical abuse, facts surrounding an injury that requires medical treatment can often be verified. Thus, both the accuracy and completeness of the children's reports may be determined.

Consistent with previous research, results indicated that children in the NE group provided a significantly greater amount of correct information (59% improvement) in response to open-ended recall (Free Recall + Cued Elaboration) questions than did the children in the control group (Free-Recall questions only). Moreover, there was no significant difference in errors provided by each group. It is worth noting, however, that the benefits did not extend to the 3-year-olds; hence, we recommend that NE is most effective with children 4 years of age and older.

Does the NE improve the quality of information from children?

Although the amount of information has obvious benefits for the investigative phase of any criminal case, the descriptive detail, coherence (i.e., use of appropriate conjunctions, disjunctions, and other connectors within sentences), and references to locations in the child's report has a profound impact on perceptions of the child's credibility (Bell & Loftus, 2006; Peterson et al., 2012). Moreover, researchers have found that children who provided more descriptive reports about a staged event were also more resistant to suggestive questioning about that same staged event and that narrative quality superseded age as a predictor of such resistance (Kulkofsky & Klemfuss, 2008).

To explore differences in the quality of children's narratives when using the NE versus a standard interview protocol, researchers examined several qualities of children's narrative reports about a staged event (Camparo & Camparo, 2011), a fictitious event (Normand, Camparo, & Almeria, 2012), and a serious injury (Peterson et al., 2012) when interviewed with either the NE or a standard protocol. Camparo and Camparo (2011) and Normand et al. (2012) focused on the descriptive quality of the narratives of 4- to 6-, 7- to 9-, and 10- to 12-year-olds, and Peterson et al. (2012) focused on causal connectives (e.g., "because," "if," "so"), temporal connectives ("first," "next," "later," "before," "after"), and contextual embedding (specification of location) of 3- to 7-year-olds.

As predicted, children interviewed with the NE provided more accurate descriptors about the staged event than did children interviewed with the standard protocol (Camparo & Camparo, 2011) without an increase in the number of (inaccurate) descriptors about a fictitious event (Normand et al., 2012). Similarly, Peterson et al. (2012) found that the NE elicited significantly more coherent sentences (use of conjunctions, disjunctions, and other connectors) and more references to locations in response to open-ended questions than did the standard protocol; however, there were no significant differences for causal (e.g., "because") or temporal (e.g., "then") connectives. Given that narrative quality may be more strongly associated with resistance to suggestive questioning about the same event than age, and that it is associated with perceptions of greater credibility, these findings are particularly compelling.

Special Population Research

NE enhances narratives of children from middle- and low-SES levels

Dorado and Saywitz (2001) compared reports from low-SES ethnic-minority children to the reports of middle-SES children. Analyses demonstrated that the benefits of NE training were significant for both middle- and low-SES children. Low-SES preschoolers in the NE group produced nearly 2½ times more accurate information than did low-SES children in the control group. Dorado and Saywitz's (2001) findings are particularly noteworthy because they allow us to extend the benefits of NE to children from low-SES communities who were predominately from ethnic-minority backgrounds.

NE enhances narratives of children with learning disabilities and lower IQ scores

Children with disabilities are at higher risk for victimization than are their nondisabled peers (Hershkowitz, Lamb, & Horowitz, 2007; Sullivan & Knutson, 2000; Westcott, 1991; Westcott & Jones, 1999); yet, a number of studies have indicated that oral narration is more difficult for children with learning disabilities when compared to their nondisabled peers (e.g., Scott & Windsor, 2000). According to one theory, these children do not lack the ability to give full narrative accounts, rather, they lack the strategies for organizing and delivering narratives (Deshler & Schumaker, 1993), and this account is consistent with previously cited research on ASD individuals. Nathanson et al. (2007) tested the efficacy of NE with 7- to 12-year-olds identified as learning disabled by their school districts. Similar to other studies of NE, children with learning disabilities in the NE condition reported a significantly greater amount of accurate information than did children with learning disabilities in the control group. Although the free recall of the two groups did not differ significantly, the results of the Cued-Elaboration task were particularly notable: Children with learning disabilities in the NE condition reported almost eight times more accurate information during the Cued-Elaboration stage than did children with learning disabilities in the control group without any difference in the amount of inaccurate information reported.

In addition, studies have found that the NE procedure is especially helpful to children who score lower on standard tests of intelligence. Brown and Pipe (2003a) found that performance on a standard interview protocol was predicted by children's IQ score—children with higher IQ scores (over the mean of 100 on the Wechsler Intelligence Test of Children) reported more correct information than did children with lower IQ scores (less than 100). However, there were no such differences when the NE procedure was employed. Both the NE visual-cue option and the NE verbal-cue option were effective for children of lower IQ scores.

Can the NE Serve Children with ASD? Speculation and Call for Future Research

Although the effectiveness of the NE has not been tested with ASD individuals, as noted earlier, there is now a growing body of research with such individuals examining limitations in autobiographical memory (Bruck et al., 2007; Diehl et al., 2006;

Goddard et al., 2014; Millward et al., 2000), narrative competence (Diehl et al., 2006; Goldman, 2008; King et al., 2013), source monitoring, suggestibility, and eyewitness skills (Bruck et al., 2007; Maras & Bowler, 2014; McCrory et al., 2007) that can serve to inform predictions for future research with the NE. Some of the impairments and deficits characteristic of ASD are similar to those exhibited by young TD children, and we have already discussed in earlier sections how the NE was designed to compensate for these specific limitations. However, research demonstrating the success of the NE for increasing the amount of accurate information and the quality and cohesion of event narratives without increasing error, and especially, the research demonstrating the success of the NE with preschool children and children with learning disabilities and lower IQ scores may also provide preliminary support for speculating that some children with ASD—particularly those who are high-functioning—may benefit from the structure and support provided by the NE.

Based on the literature examining the efficacy of the NE, it is now well established that the Cued-Elaboration component of the NE significantly increases the amount of accurate information provided by TD 4- to 12-year-old children, low-income, and lower-IQ children who would otherwise produce accurate, but highly abridged free-recall narratives. Given that ASD children also tend to produce accurate, but even less complete free-recall narratives than TD children do, we could speculate that ASD children would also benefit from the Cued-Elaboration component of the NE. Thus, the Cued-Elaboration component of the NE may hold real promise for providing ASD individuals with the support they need to structure and organize their memory search in autobiographical-memory tasks, particularly because deficits in recall in ASD individuals appear to be more a function of retrieval (e.g., impaired ability to spontaneously organize information or use categorical relations among items to aid recall) than encoding (Bowler et al., 2004; Minshew & Goldstein, 2001), and because research has demonstrated that ASD individuals can benefit significantly from "task support" (Bowler et al., 2004) and additional prompting (Goddard et al., 2014). In fact, research has shown that having a visual cue, such as a picture book, helps reduce the cognitive load for TD children and children with language disorders, which in turn, allows them to provide a lengthier, more complex (see Diehl et al., 2006), and perhaps, more coherent narrative (Peterson et al., 2012). Based on these findings, King et al. (2013) paired generic pictures with their general- and specific-event narrative prompts for the ASD group only, stating that "piloting…showed that the children with ASD were more able to complete the task when pictures were presented alongside the question therefore pictures illustrating the prompt question (e.g., someone going on holiday) were presented at the same time as the prompt question" (p. 526).

Besides helping the child organize information for retrieval purposes, the four visual and verbal cues used during Cued Elaboration may also help the child focus on information the interviewer needs to know: the participants, setting/location, actions, and conversations/affective states relevant to the event. Given research indicating that ASD individuals show deficits in understanding what others need to know (e.g., Tager-Flusberg, 2000), we could speculate that use of these categorical cues might result in an increased amount of forensically relevant information reported by ASD individuals.

Finally, in their study of memory for a classroom event and suggestibility in children with Asperger syndrome (AS), McCrory et al. (2007) concluded that, "children with AS can act as reliable witnesses, but they may be more reliant on questioning to facilitate recall" (p. 482). However, they also cautioned that "…any use of directive questioning needs to be balanced against a likely increase in error rate, relative to free recall" (p. 488). The Cued-Elaboration component of the NE provides interviewers with four generic, open-ended follow-up questions and children with four additional opportunities to elaborate on their own free-recall using their own words—without the use of potentially biased or suggestive follow-up questions crafted by the interviewer. Consequently, Cued Elaboration provides interviewers with a much larger, more detailed, more coherent, and predominantly accurate "data set" of information from which they can craft follow-up questions during the third stage of the NE. And if interviewers have a larger and more detailed and accurate data set, they may be less likely to inadvertently question children about a completely different version of the event (Maras & Bowler, 2014), thereby reducing suggestibility and the potential for compliance or acquiescence.

Despite recent increases in rates of ASD (American Psychiatric Association, 2013) and researchers' growing concern that the deficits that accompany the disorder may actually lead to an overrepresentation of ASD individuals as victims, witnesses, and even (unwitting) perpetrators in the criminal system (Maras & Bowler, 2014), there is still no single interviewing technique that has been empirically established as effective for witnesses with ASD (Maras & Bowler, 2014). Clearly, the next step is a series of experimental studies in which high- and low-functioning ASD children and appropriate control groups participate in a staged event and are interviewed about the staged event and a fictitious event using either the NE or a standard protocol. As described earlier, the NE (Saywitz & Camparo, 2014) consists of a relatively simple three-step process that can be implemented with minimal training. Moreover, it does not involve the use of any techniques that would be expected to pose specific challenges to ASD individuals, as some other interview techniques do (Maras & Bowler, 2010). Rather, the Cued-Elaboration component may be expected to provide the same type of "task support" as that used by Bowler et al. (2015).

Analog research with over 1,000 children is now clear that the structure of the NE provides the building blocks to a solid autobiographical memory narrative by TD preschool and school-aged children as well as low-SES and lower-IQ children. The interviewer takes charge of helping children piece together the narrative *in the children's own words* through a simple, easy-to-implement, three-step process that provides children with an opportunity to (a) freely recall the event; (b) elaborate on their own Free-Recall narrative in response to nonleading Cued-Elaboration prompts relevant to forensic interviews; and (c) provide additional details in response to follow-up questions crafted by the interviewer based on a larger and more coherent set of data from the child. This body of research is also clear that the NE does not lead to increased error or false reports of fictitious events. Given the success of the NE with these varied populations, we believe it is now time to test its efficacy with children diagnosed with ASD.

Take-Home Points

- Children with ASD are at high risk for involvement in the legal system.
- Children with ASD present limitations in many skills and competencies required for providing testimony in court.

- Many limitations in skills and competencies presented by children with ASD are similar to those presented by typically developing young children.
- The narrative elaboration protocol compensates for limitations presented by typically developing preschool and school-aged children with a template that provides them with an extra opportunity to elaborate on their own free recall in their own words in response to four generic open-ended questions.
- Research with preschool and school-aged typically developing and learning-disabled, average- and lower-intelligence children from middle- and low-SES communities indicates that the narrative elaboration protocol increases the amount of accurate, but not inaccurate information, as well as the quality of children's autobiographical narratives.
- Research is needed to examine the efficacy of the narrative elaboration protocol with children with ASD.

References

American Psychiatric Association. (2013). Neurodevelopmental disorders. In *Diagnostic and statistical manual of mental disorders* (5th Ed.), Washington, D.C.: American Psychiatric Publishing. doi:10.1176/appi.books.9780890425596.dms01

Bauer, P. J. (2007). *Remembering the times of our lives: Memory in infancy and beyond: The developing mind series.* Mahwah, NJ: Lawrence Erlbaum Associates Publishers.

Bell, B. E., & Loftus, E. F. (2006). Degree of detail of eyewitness testimony and mock juror judgments. *Journal of Applied Social Psychology, 18*(14), 1171–1192. doi:10.1111/j.1559—1816.19888.tb01200.x

Berman, R. A., 1997. Preschool knowledge of language: What five-year-olds know about language structure and language use. In C. Pontecorvo (Ed.), *Writing development: An interdisciplinary view.* Amsterdam, The Netherlands: John Bengamins Publishing Company.

Boccia, M., & Campos, J. (1989). Maternal emotional signals, social referencing, and infants' reactions to strangers. *New Directions for Child & Adolescent Development, 44,* 25–49. doi:10.1002/cd.23219894404

Bottoms, B. L., Quas, J. A., & Davis, S. L. (2007). The influence of the interviewer-provided social support on children's suggestibility, memory, and disclosures. In M.-E. Pipe, M. E. Lamb, Y. Orbach, & A.-C. Cederborg (Eds.), *Child sexual abuse: Disclosure, delay, and denial* (pp. 135–153). Mahwah, NJ: Lawrence Erlbaum Associates, Publishers.

Boucher, J. (2012). Research review: Structural language in autistic spectrum disorder— characteristics and causes. *Journal of Child Psychology & Psychiatry, 53,* 219–233. doi:10.1111/j.1469-7610.2011.02508.x

Boucher, J., Mayes, A., & Bigham, S. (2012). Memory in autistic spectrum disorder. *Psychological Bulletin, 138,* 458–496. doi:10.1037/a0026869

Bowen, C. J., & Howie, P. M. (2002). Context and cue cards in young children's testimony: A comparison of brief narrative elaboration and context reinstatement. *Journal of Applied Psychology, 87,* 1077–1085. doi:10.1037//0021-9010.87.6.1077

Bowler, D. M., Gaigg, S. B., & Gardiner, J. M. (2015). Brief report: The role of task support in the spatial and temporal source memory of adults with autism spectrum disorder. *Journal of Autism & Developmental Disorders, 45,* 2613–2617. doi:10.1007/s10803-015-2378-9

Bowler, D. M., Gardiner, J. M., & Berthollier, N. (2004). Source memory in adolescents and adults with Asperger's syndrome. *Journal of Autism & Developmental Disorders, 34,* 533–542.

Brennan, M., & Brennan, R. (1988). *Strange language: Child victims under cross examination.* Riverina, Australia: Charles Stuart University.

Bright-Paul, A., Jarrold, C., & Wright, D. B. (2005). Age-appropriate cues facilitate source-monitoring and reduce suggestibility in 3- to 7-year-olds. *Cognitive Development, 20,* 1–18. doi:10.1016/j.cogdev.2004.06.001

Brown, D., & Pipe, M.-E. (2003a). Individual differences in children's event memory reports and the Narrative Elaboration technique. *Journal of Applied Psychology, 88,* 195–206.

Brown, D., & Pipe, M.-E. (2003b). Variations on a technique: Enhancing children's recall using narrative elaboration training. *Applied Cognitive Psychology, 17,* 377–399.

Brubacher, S. P., Roberts, K. P., & Powell, M. (2011). Effects of practicing episodic versus scripted recall on children's subsequent narratives of a repeated event. *Psychology, Public Policy, & Law, 17,* 286–314. doi:10.1037/a0022793

Bruck, M., Ceci, S. J., Francoeur, E., & Barr, R. (1995). "I hardly cried when I got my shot!" Influencing children's reports about a visit to their pediatrician. *Child Development, 66,* 193–208. doi:10.1111/j.1467-8624.1995.tb00865.x

Bruck, M., Ceci, S. J., & Hembrooke, H. (1998). Reliability and credibility of young children's reports: From research to policy and practice. *American Psychologist, 53,* 136–151.

Bruck, M., London, K., Landa, R., & Goodman, J. (2007). Autobiographical memory and suggestibility in children with autism spectrum disorder. *Development & Psychopathology, 19,* 73–95. doi:10.1017/S0954507070058

Bruner, J. S. (1957). On perceptual readiness. *Psychological Review, 64*(2), 123–152. doi:10.1037/h0043805

Camparo, L. B., & Camparo, J. C. (March, 2011). *Developmental differences in children's event memories: Enhancing narrative quality with the narrative elaboration and the verbal labels procedures.* Presented at the Biennial Meeting for the Society for Research on Child Development, Montreal, Canada.

Camparo, L. B., Wagner, J. T., & Saywitz, K. J. (2001). Interviewing children about real and fictitious events: Revisiting the narrative elaboration procedure. *Law & Human Behavior, 25,* 63–80.

Carter, C. A., Bottoms, B. L., & Levine, M. (1996). Linguistic and socioemotional influences on the accuracy of children's reports. *Law & Human Behavior, 20,* 335–358.

Ceci, S. J., Ross, D. F., & Toglia, M. P. (1987). Suggestibility of children's memory: Psycholegal implications. *Journal of Experimental Psychology: General, 116,* 38–49.

Cordón, I. M., Saetermoe, C. L., & Goodman, G. S. (2005). Facilitating children's accurate responses: Conversation rules and interview style. *Applied Cognitive Psychology, 19,* 249–266.

Cramer, P. (1981). *Development of defense mechanisms: Theory, research, and assessment.* New York, NY: Springer-Verlag Publishing.

Davies, G. M., Westcott, H. L., & Horan, N. (2000). The impact of questioning style on the content of investigative interviews with suspected child sexual abuse victims. *Psychology, Crime, & Law, 6,* 81–97.

Dawson, G., Hill, D., Spencer, A., Galpert, L., & Watson, L. (1990). Affective exchanges between young autistic children and their mothers. *Journal of Abnormal Child Psychology, 18,* 335–345.

Deshler, D. D., & Schumaker, J. B. (1993). Strategy mastery by at-risk students: Not a simple matter. *The Elementary School Journal, 94,* 153–167.

Dickson, W. (Ed.) (1981). *Children's oral communication skills.* New York, NY: Academic Press.

Diehl, J. J., Bennetto, L., & Carter Young, E. (2006). Story recall and narrative coherence of high-functioning children with autism spectrum disorders. *Journal of Abnormal Child Psychology, 34,* 87–102. doi:10.10007/s10802-005-9003-x

Dorado, J. S., & Saywitz, K. J. (2001). Interviewing preschoolers from low- and middle-SES communities: A test of the narrative elaboration recall improvement technique. *Journal of Clinical Child Psychology, 30,* 568–580.

Elischberer, H. B. & Roebers, C. M. (2001). Improving young children's free narratives about an observed event: The effects of nonspecific verbal prompts. *International Journal of Behavioral Development*, *25*(2), 160–166.

Evans, A. D., Lee, K., & Lyon, T. D. (2009). Complex questions asked by defense lawyers but not prosecutors predicts convictions in child abuse trials. *Law & Human Behavior*, *33*, 258–264.

Farrar, M. J., & Goodman, G. S. (1990). Developmental differences in the relation between scripts and episodic memory: Do they exist? In R. Fivush, & J. A. Hudson (Eds.), *Knowing and remembering in young children* (pp. 30–64). Cambridge, England: Cambridge University Press.

Flavell, J. H. (1981). Cognitive monitoring. In W. P. Dickson (Ed.), *Children's oral communication skills* (pp. 35–60). New York, NY: Academic Press.

Flavell, J. H. (1985). *Cognitive development* (Rev. ed.). Englewood Cliffs, NJ: Prentice-Hall.

Flavell, J. H., Botkin, P. T., Fry, C. L., Wright, J. W., & Jarvis, P. E. (1968). *The development of role taking and communication skills in children*. New York, NY: Wiley.

Flavell, J. H., & Miller, P. H. (1998). Social cognition. In W. Damon (Ed.), *Handbook of child psychology: Volume 2: Cognition, perception, and language* (pp. 851–898). Hoboken, NJ: John Wiley & Sons Inc.

Flin, R. H., Stevenson, Y., & Davies, G. M. (1989). Children's knowledge of court proceedings. *British Journal of Psychology*, *80*, 285–297.

Gaigg, S. B., Gardiner, J. M., & Bowler, D. M. (2008). Free recall in autism spectrum disorder: The role of relational and item-specific encoding. *Neuropsychologia*, *46*, 983–992. doi:10.1016/j.neuropsychologia.2007.11.011

Garven, S., Wood, J. M., & Malpass, R. S. (2000). Allegations of wrongdoing: The effects of reinforcement on children's mundane and fantastic claims. *Journal of Applied Psychology*, *85*, 38–49.

Goddard, L., Dritschel, B., Robinson, S., & Howlin, P. (2014). Development of autobiographical memory in children with autism spectrum disorders: Deficits, gains, and predictors of performance. *Development & Psychopathology*, *26*, 215–228. doi:10.1017/S0954579413000904

Goldman, S. (2008). Brief report: Narratives of personal events in children with autism and developmental language disorders: Unshared memories. *Journal of Autism & Developmental Disorders*, *38*, 1982–1988. doi:10.1007/s10803-008-0588-0

Gopnik, A. (2009). *The philosophical baby*. New York, NY: Farrar, Straus & Giroux.

Gruendel, J., & Nelson, K. (1986). *Event knowledge, structure, and function in development*. Hillsdale, NJ: Lawrence Erlbaum.

Gudjonsson, G. H. (2003). *The psychology of interrogations and confessions: A handbook*. Chichester, England: John Wiley & Sons, Ltd.

Harari, H., & McDavid, J. W. (1969). Situational influences on moral justice: A study of "finking." *Journal of Personality & Social Psychology*, *11*, 240–244.

Hershkowitz, I. (2009). Socioemotional factors in child abuse investigations. *Child Maltreatment*, *12*(2), 172–181.

Hershkowitz, I. (2011). Rapport building in investigative interviews of children. In M. E. Lamb, D. J. LaRooy, L. C. Malloy, & C. Katz. (Eds.), *Children's testimony: A handbook of psychological research and forensic practice* (pp. 109–128). Malden, MA: Wiley-Blackwell.

Hershkowitz, I., Lamb, M. E., & Horowitz, D. (2007). Victimization of children with disabilities. *American Journal of Orthopsychiatry*, *77*, 629–635. doi:10.1037/0002-9432.77.4.629

Hudson, J., & Shapiro, R. (1991). From knowing to telling: The development of children's scripts, stories, and personal narratives. In A. McCabe & C. Peterson (Eds.), *Developing narrative structure* (pp. 89–135). Hillsdale, NJ: Lawrence Erlbaum Associates.

Hughes, M., & Grieve, R. (1980). On asking children bizarre questions. *First Language*, *1*, 149–160.

Karmiloff-Smith, A. (1985). Language and cognitive processes from a developmental perspective. *Language & Cognitive Processes, 1*, 61–85.

Kebbell, M. R., Hatton, C., & Johnson, S. D. (2004). Witnesses with intellectual disabilities in court: What questions are asked and what influence do they have? *Legal & Criminological Psychology, 9*, 23–35.

King, D., Dockrell, J. E., & Stuart, M. (2013). Event narratives in 11–14 year olds with autistic spectrum disorder. *International Journal of Language & Communication Disorders, 48*, 522–533. doi:10.1111/1460-6984.12025

Krakow, E. (2010). Narratives distinguish experienced from imagined childhood events. *American Journal of Psychology, 123*(1), 71–80.

Kulkofsky, S., & Klemfuss, J. Z. (2008). What the stories children tell can tell about their memory: Narrative skill and young children's suggestibility. *Developmental Psychology, 44*, 1442–1456. doi:10.1037/a0012849.

Kulkofsky, S., Wang, Q., & Ceci, S. J. (2008). Do better stories make better memories? Narrative quality and memory accuracy in preschool children. *Applied Cognitive Psychology, 22*, 21–38. doi:10.1002/acp.1326

Lamb, M. E., & Brown, D. A. (2006). Conversational apprentices: Helping children become competent informants about their own experiences. *British Journal of Developmental Psychology, 24*, 215–234.

Larsson, A. S., & Lamb, M. E. (2009). Making the most of information-gathering interviews with children. *Infant & Child Development, 18*, 1–16. doi:10.1002/ICD.573

Leichtman, M. D., & Ceci, S. J. (1995). The effects of stereotypes and suggestions on preschoolers' reports. *Developmental Psychology, 31*, 568–578.

Lepore, S. J., & Sesco, B. (1994). Distorting children's reports and interpretations of events through suggestion. *Journal of Applied Psychology, 79*, 108–120.

Lord, C., & Paul, R. (1997). Language and communication in autism. In D. J. Cohen & F. R. Volkmar (Eds.), *Handbook of autism and pervasive developmental disorders* (2nd ed., pp. 195–225). New York, NY: Wiley.

Lyon, T. D., Malloy, L. C., Quas, J. A., & Talwar, V. (2008). Coaching, truth induction, and young maltreated children's false allegations and false denials. *Child Development, 79*, 914–929.

Mandler, J. M., & Johnson, N. S. (1977). Remembrance of things parsed: Story structure and recall. *Cognitive Psychology, 9*, 111–151.

Maras, K. L., & Bowler, D. M. (2010). The cognitive interview for eyewitnesses with autism spectrum disorder. *Journal of Autism & Developmental Disorders, 40*, 1350–1360. doi:10.1007/s10803-010-0997-8

Maras, K. L., & Bowler, D. M. (2011). Brief report: Schema consistent misinformation effects in eyewitnesses with austism spectrum disorder. *Journal of Autism & Developmental Disorders, 41*, 815–820. doi:10.1007/s10803-010-1089-5

Maras, K. L., & Bowler, D. M. (2014). Eyewitness testimony in autism spectrum disorder: A review. *Journal of Autism & Developmental Disorders, 44*, 2682–2697. doi:10.1007/s10803-012-1502-3

Markman, E. M. (1981). Comprehension monitoring. In W. P. Dickson (Ed.), *Children's oral and communication skills* (pp. 61–84). New York, NY: Academic Press.

McCrory, E., Henry, L. A., & Happé, F. (2007). Eye-witness memory and suggestibility in children with Asperger syndrome. *Journal of Child Psychology & Psychiatry, 48*, 482–489. doi:10.1111.j.1469-7610.2006.01715.x

Millward, C., Powell, S., Messer, D., & Jordan, R. (2000). Recall for self and other in autism: Children's memory for events experienced by themselves and their peers. *Journal of Autism & Developmental Disorders, 30*, 15–28. doi:10.1023/A:1005455926727

Minshew, N. J., & Goldstein, G. (2001). The pattern of intact and impaired memory functions in autism. *Journal of Child Psychology & Psychiatry, 42*, 1095–1101.

Moore, C., & Furrow, D. (1991). The development of the language of belief. In D. Frye & C. Moore (Eds.), *Children's theories of mind: Mental states and social understanding* (pp. 173–194). Hillsdale, NJ: Lawrence Erlbaum Associates, Inc.

Nathanson, R., Crank, J. N., Saywitz, K. J., & Ruegg, E. (2007). Enhancing the oral narratives of children with learning disabilities. *Reading & Writing Quarterly, 23*, 315–331.

Nathanson, R., & Saywitz, K. J. (2003). The effects of the courtroom context on children's memory and anxiety. *Journal of Psychiatry & Law, 31*, 67–98.

Nelson, K. (1986). *Event knowledge: Structure and function in development.* Hillsdale, NJ: Lawrence Elrbaum.

Nelson, K. (2003). Self and social functions: Individual autobiographical memory and collective narrative. *Memory, 11*, 125–136. doi:10.1080/09658210244000315

Nelson, K., & Fivush, R. (2004). The emergence of autobiographical memory: A social cultural developmental theory. *Psychological Review, 111*, 486–511.

Normand, K. E., Camparo, L. B., & Almeria, H. (2012, April). Descriptive quality of children's narratives about real and fictitious events: A comparison of three interview protocols. *Convention for the Western Psychological Association*, San Francisco, CA.

Ornstein, P. A., Naus, M. J., & Liberty, C. (1975). Rehearsal and organizational processes in children's memory. *Child Development, 46*, 818–830.

Owens, R. E. (2012). *Language development: An introduction* (8th ed.). Boston, MA: Allyn & Bacon.

Perry, N. W., McAuliff, B. D., Tam, P., Claycomb, L., Dostal, C., & Flanagan, C. (1995). When lawyers question children: Is justice served? *Law & Human Behavior, 19*, 609–629.

Peters, W. W. & Nunez, N. (1999). Complex language and comprehension monitoring: Teaching child witnesses to recognize linguistic confusion. *Journal of Applied Psychology, 84*, 661–669.

Petersilia, J. R. (2001). Crime victims with developmental disabilities—A review essay. *Criminal Justice & Behavior, 28*, 655–694.

Peterson, C. (1990). The who, when, where of early narratives. *Journal of Child Language, 17*(2), 43–455.

Peterson, C., & Warren, L. K. (2009). Injuries, emergency rooms, and children's memory: Factors contributing to individual differences. In J. A. Quas & R. Fivush (Eds.), *Emotion and memory in development: Biological, cognitive, and social considerations* (pp. 60–85). New York, NY: Oxford University Press.

Peterson, C., Warren, K. L., & Hayes, A. H. (2012). Revisiting the narrative elaboration training an ecologically relevant event. *Journal of Cognition & Development.* doi:10.1080/15248372.2011.638688

Piaget, J. (1926). *The language and thought of the child.* New York, NY: Harcourt, Brace & Company, Inc.

Piaget, J. (1930). *The child's conception of physical causality.* London, England: Kegan Paul (Republished: Totowa, NJ: Littlefield, Adams, 1967).

Quas, J. A., Malloy, L. C., Melinder, A., Goodman, G. S., D'Mello, M., & Schaaf, J. (2007). Developmental differences in the effects of repeated interviews and interviewer bias on young children's event memory and false reports. *Developmental Psychology, 43*, 823–837.

Quas, J. A., & Sumaroka, M. (2011). Consequences of legal involvement on child victims of maltreatment. In M. E. Lamb, D. J. La Rooy, L. C. Malloy, & C. Katz (Eds.), *Children's testimony: A handbook of psychological research and forensic practice* (pp. 323–350). Malden, MA: Wiley-Blackwell.

Robinson, E. J., & Robinson, W. P. (1978). Explanations of communication failure and ability to give bad messages. *British Journal of Social & Clinical Psychology, 17*, 219–225.

Sas, L., Austin, G., Wolfe, D., & Hurley, P. (1991). *Reducing the system-induced trauma for child sexual abuse victims through court preparation, assessment and follow up* (Final Report for project #4555-1-125). Canada: Health and Welfare, Canada, National Welfare Grants Division.

Saywitz, K. J. (1989). Children's conception of the legal system: Court is a place to play basketball. In S. Ceci, D. Ross, & M. Toglia (Eds.), *Perspectives on children's testimony* (pp. 131–157). New York, NY: Springer-Verlag.

Saywitz, K. J., & Camparo, L. B. (2014). *Evidence-based child forensic interviewing: The developmental narrative elaboration interview*. New York, NY: Oxford University Press.

Saywitz, K., Jaenicke, C., & Camparo, L. (1990). Children's knowledge of legal terminology. *Law & Human Behavior, 14*, 523–535.

Saywitz, K. J., & Nathanson, R. (1993). Children's testimony and their perceptions of stress in and out of the courtroom. *Child Abuse & Neglect, 17*, 613–622.

Saywitz, K. J., Nathanson, R., Snyder, L., & Lamphear, V. (1993). *Preparing children for the investigative and judicial process: Improving communication, memory and emotional resiliency* (Final Report to the National Center on Child Abuse and Neglect, Grant No. 90-CA-1179). Los Angeles: University of California.

Saywitz, K. J., & Snyder, L. (1996). Narrative elaboration: Test of a new procedure for interviewing children. *Journal of Consulting & Clinical Psychology, 64*, 1347–1357.

Saywitz, K. J., Snyder, L., & Lamphear, V. (1996). Helping children tell what happened: A follow-up study of the narrative elaboration procedure. *Child Maltreatment, 1*, 200–212.

Saywitz, K. J., Snyder, L., & Nathanson, R. (1999). Facilitating the communicative competence of the child witness. *Applied Developmental Science, 3*, 58–68.

Saywitz, K. J., & Wilkinson, L. (1982). Age-related differences in meta-linguistic awareness. In S. Kuczaj (Ed.), *Language development: Vol. 2. Language, thought and culture* (pp. 229–250). Hillsdale, N.J.: Erlbaum.

Schneider, L., Price, H. L., Roberts, K. P., & Hedrick, A. M. (2011). Children's episodic and generic reports of alleged abuse. *Applied Cognitive Psychology, 25*, 862–870. doi:10.1002/acp.1759

Schneider, W., & Pressley, M. (1989). *Memory development between 2 and 20: Springer series on cognitive development*. New York, NY: Springer-Verlag Publishing.

Scott, C. M., & Windsor, J. (2000). General language performance measures in spoken and written narrative and expository discourse of school-age children with language learning disabilities. *Journal of Speech, Language, & Hearing Research, 43*, 324–339.

Shantz, C. (1975). *The development of social cognition*. Chicago, IL: University of Chicago Press.

Sonnenschein, S., & Whitehurst, G. J. (1984). Developing referential communication: A hierarchy of skills. *Child Development, 55*, 1936–1945.

Stein, N. L. & Glenn, C. G. (1978). An analysis of story comprehension in elementary school children. In R. O. Freedle (Ed.), *Multidisciplinary perspectives in discourse comprehension*. Hillsdale, NJ: Ablex, Inc.

Sullivan, P. M., & Knutson, J. F. (2000). Maltreatment and disabilities: A population-based epidemiological study. *Child Abuse & Neglect, 24*, 1257–1273. doi:10.1016/s0145-2134(00)00190-3

Tager-Flusberg, H. (2000). Understanding the language and communicative impairments in autism. *International Review of Research in Mental Retardation, 23*, 185–205.

Taylor, M., Cartwright, B. S., & Bowden, T. (1991). Perspective taking and theory of mind: Do children predict interpretive diversity as a function of differences in observers' knowledge? *Child Development, 62*, 1334–1351. doi:10.1111/j.1467-8624.1991.tb01609.x

Thierry, K. L., & Spence, M. J. (2002). Source-monitoring training facilitates preschoolers' eyewitness memory performance. *Developmental Psychology, 38*, 428–437. doi:10.1037//0012-1649.38.3.428

Toglia, M. P., Ross, D. F., Ceci, S. J., & Hembrooke, H. (1992). The suggestibility of children's memory: A social psychological and cognitive interpretation. In M. L. Howe, C. J. Brainerd, & V. R. Reyna (Eds.), *Development of long-term retention*. New York, NY: Springer-Verlag.

Wandrey, L., Lyon, T. D., Quas, J. A., & Friedman, W. J. (2011). Maltreated children's ability to estimate temporal location and numerosity of placement changes and court visits. *Psychology, Public Policy & the Law, 18*(1), 79–104.

Warren-Leubecker, A., Tate, C., Hinton, I., & Ozbek, N. (1989). What do children know about the legal system and when do they know it? In S. J. Ceci, D. F. Ross, & M. P. Toglia (Eds.), *Perspectives on children's testimony* (pp. 131–157). New York, NY: Springer-Verlag.

Wellman, H. M., & Somerville, S. C. (1982). The development of human search ability. In M. E. Lamb & A. L. Brown (Eds.), *Advances in developmental psychology: Volume 2.* Hillsdale, NJ: Lawrence Erlbaum Associates, Inc.

Westcott, H. (1991). The abuse of disabled children: A review of the literature. *Child: Care, Health & Development, 17,* 243–258.

Westcott, H. L., & Jones, D. P. H. (1999). Annotation: The abuse of disabled children. *Journal of Child Psychology & Psychiatry, 40,* 497–506. doi:10.1017/s0021963099003893

White, T. L., Leichtman, M. D., & Ceci, S. J. (1997). The good, the bad, and the ugly: Accuracy, inaccuracy, and elaboration in preschoolers' reports about past events. *Applied Cognitive Psychology, 11,* S37–S54.

Yirmiya, N., Sigman, M. D., Kasari, C., & Mundy, P. (1992). Empathy and cognition in high-functioning children with autism. *Child Development, 63,* 150–160.

15

Interviewing Children with Autistic Spectrum Disorder: The NICHD Protocol and Ten-Step Investigative Interview

Lindsay C. Malloy, Allison P. Mugno, and Andrea Arndorfer

Adults ask children questions about past events on a daily basis. These questions range from the mundane (e.g., What happened at school today?) in family and school contexts to the consequential (e.g., Who fired the gun?) in legal contexts. For decades, research has examined typically developing (TD) children's event memory and suggestibility with a focus on the implications of memory development for children's eyewitness testimony. This research has advanced our understanding of reconstructive memory processes, enhanced theories of cognitive development, and allowed researchers to develop empirically based interviewing protocols for obtaining information from children, including those who have been abused, whose testimony may be crucial. Recent reviews highlight the need to expand research on children's memory and suggestibility to children with specific characteristics, disabilities, and disorders so that investigative interviews can meet all children's needs (Henry, Bettenay, & Carney, 2011).

Children with disabilities are at increased risk of victimization and neglect (e.g., Hershkowitz, Lamb, & Horowitz, 2007; Sullivan & Knutson, 2000), yet may be less likely than TD children to report maltreatment and to have those complaints investigated (Reiter, Bryen, & Shachar, 2007). Despite the concomitant need for many children with disabilities to be interviewed about their experiences, little research has been devoted to understanding the eyewitness capabilities of children with disabilities. Most of the relatively limited research has focused on the testimonial capacities of children with "intellectual disabilities" (ID), a diverse group of children who may have different diagnoses. Many children with autistic spectrum disorder (ASD), the focus of the current chapter, have co-morbid ID (Henry et al., 2011). Very few studies have concentrated on the event memory of children with ASD specifically (but see Bruck, London, Landa, & Goodman, 2007), despite the fact that their unique characteristics (e.g., deficits in social communication and theory of mind) may make them particularly challenging to interview.

The Wiley Handbook of Memory, Autism Spectrum Disorder, and the Law, First Edition.
Edited by Jonni L. Johnson, Gail S. Goodman, and Peter C. Mundy.

Although our understanding of ASD has increased considerably over the past few decades, it has been difficult to obtain a clear understanding of the cognitive abilities of individuals with ASD, in part, because (a) there is enormous individual variability, and (b) researchers have focused on a restricted number of characteristics. Event memory and suggestibility are areas that have received relatively little empirical attention concerning children with ASD, and yet, are crucial for understanding how best to interview these children about their personal experiences, a goal that becomes critical in the context of potential child maltreatment.

In this chapter we first describe two protocols for interviewing children about experienced and witnessed events with a focus on maltreatment allegations—the National Institute of Child Health and Human Development (NICHD) Investigative Interview Protocol and the Ten-Step Investigative Interview, hereafter referred to as the NICHD Protocol and the Ten Step, respectively. We review evidence concerning these protocols' effectiveness for interviewing TD children. Because research has not directly addressed whether these protocols work for children with ASD, we review research concerning interviewing atypically developing children generally. Finally, we speculate about how these protocols may work (and not work) for children with ASD, and suggest potential modifications to the protocols.

NICHD Protocol

Following numerous studies indicating that forensic interviewers often have difficulties maintaining standards of best practice (e.g., Aldridge & Cameron, 1999; Sternberg, Lamb, Davies, & Westcott, 2001a; Warren et al., 1999), researchers concluded that a more structured interviewing protocol was necessary. The NICHD Protocol was thus developed to enhance the quantity and quality of information elicited from suspected child victims of maltreatment (see Lamb, Hershkowitz, Orbach, & Esplin, 2008; Lamb, La Rooy, Malloy, & Katz, 2011, for reviews). The NICHD Protocol is comprised of two phases: a phase leading up to the discussion of the target event (the *pre-substantive phase*), and a phase designed to elicit detailed information about the target event (the *substantive phase*) with a brief transition between the two phases.

Pre-substantive phase

The aim of the pre-substantive phase is threefold. The interviewer must do the following: (a) relay the ground rules of the interview, (b) build rapport, and (c) provide the child with an opportunity to practice providing a detailed narrative.

Introduction and ground rules

Interviewers begin by introducing themselves. To ensure children can discern between "truth" and "lies," a requirement in some jurisdictions, interviewers also conduct a truth-lie ceremony. The interviewer may ask questions such as, "If I say that my shoes are red, is that true or not true?" Once children have demonstrated adequate truth-lie understanding, interviewers relay and practice the following ground rules with children: (a) children should say "don't know" when they are unsure of the answer to a question (e.g., "If I ask you 'What is my dog's name?', what would you say?"); (b) children should indicate when they do not understand a question (i.e., "If I ask a question that you don't understand, just say, 'I don't understand.'"); (c) children should tell and/or correct the interviewer if the interviewer makes a mistake (e.g., "If I say things that are wrong, you should tell me. So if I said that you are a 2-year-old girl [when interviewing a 5-year-old boy], what would you say?").

Rapport building

Interviewers then engage in rapport-building exercises to make children feel relaxed and comfortable potentially disclosing traumatic or sensitive information. The NICHD Protocol recommends interviewers build rapport by asking children to describe activities they enjoy (e.g., "Tell me about things you like to do").

Practice narrative

During the final portion of the pre-substantive phase, interviewers allow children to practice providing a detailed narrative about a recent neutral event (e.g., holiday celebration, birthday party). Children are typically unaccustomed to providing the rich, exhaustive narratives required in forensic interviews. This exercise allows children to practice these narrative skills and learn the level of detail interviewers will expect of them during the substantive phase. Because this technique allows children to practice recalling *specific* memory episodes, it may be especially useful in cases involving allegations of repeated abuse.

Transition to the substantive phase

Before moving to the substantive phase, children must identify the target event. Interviewers use open-ended prompts to encourage disclosure (e.g., "Tell me why you are here talking to me today"), thereby exerting minimal influence on children's initial allegations. If children fail to disclose, interviewers can use additional prompts (e.g., "I heard that you talked to a social worker. Tell me what you talked about").

Substantive phase

The substantive phase conforms to a funnel-based approach whereby interviewers begin by using open-ended prompts followed by more specific questioning later in the interview if necessary. Children should be well acquainted with this approach because it follows the same structure as the practice narrative. Due to the robust literature demonstrating that children, like adults, tend to provide the most accurate information in free recall (e.g., Dent & Stephenson, 1979; Oates & Shrimpton, 1991), the NICHD Protocol recommends that interviewers elicit detailed accounts from children by primarily relying on invitation prompts (e.g., "Tell me everything about that. Then what happened?"). These prompts are free of interviewer input and biases, and tap into children's free-recall memory. However, children, especially preschool children, typically provide relatively sparse accounts in response to invitation prompts that may lead interviewers to launch into more focused or specific questions (see Lamb, Orbach, Hershkowitz, Horowitz, & Abbott, 2007a, for a review).

The NICHD Protocol, however, recommends that interviewers elicit additional details by following up on information previously mentioned by the child with cued invitations (e.g., "You mentioned X. Tell me more about X"). For example, interviewers may prompt, "Earlier, you said that your teacher touched you. Tell me more about him touching you." Interviewers should refrain from asking directive questions (e.g., "You said that someone saw your teacher touch you. Who else was there?") until after children's free recall has been exhausted with invitations and cued invitations. Option-posing questions (e.g., "Did he touch you over or under your clothes?") should be used sparingly and only in circumstances in which critical details are missing from children's reports and cannot be obtained using other prompt types. The NICHD Protocol strongly advises against the use of suggestive or leading questions such as those that introduce new information (e.g., "Where did he touch you?" [when the child has not mentioned touch]) or suggest the child's expected response (e.g., "He hurt you, didn't he?").

Although the NICHD Protocol has been shown to improve interviewer adherence to best practice (e.g., using more open-ended invitation prompts; Lamb et al., 2007b) when interviewing child victims and witnesses, interviewers may be intimidated by its length. Its use requires extensive training to ensure interviewers feel comfortable with the different phases and its many conditional aspects (e.g., if the child responds with [X], ask [Y]). Also, continued peer review and refresher trainings appear necessary for interviewers to maintain the improvements that result from initial training, which requires additional resources. Consequently, interviewers and the agencies that employ them may be hesitant to learn or implement the NICHD Protocol, but may be open to using a modification of it—the Ten Step (Lyon, 2005).

The Ten Step

The Ten Step includes many of the same components as the NICHD Protocol. In the first five steps, interviewers review the ground rules. Although the Ten Step incorporates most of the ground rules established in the NICHD Protocol, it does not involve a truth-lie discussion, and instead, includes a child-friendly version of "the oath." Also, in the Ten Step, interviewers inform children of their ignorance regarding the events under investigation. The Ten Step suggests that interviewers move through the following nine steps, with the tenth step focused on how to proceed when children allege multiple incidents of abuse:

1 Don't Know: Children should say they "don't know" if they are unsure of the answer to a question, but should indicate they *do know* and provide a response if they are sure of the answer. To allow children to practice this request, interviewers ask children an unanswerable question that should elicit a "don't know" response (e.g., "What is my dog's name?"), and one that should be answerable. Interviewers give children feedback on their responses.
2 Don't Understand: Children should indicate when questions are unclear by simply stating, "I don't know what you mean." To practice, interviewers might ask, "What is your gender?" to which children will likely indicate that they do not understand because "gender" is not part of their vocabulary. Then, interviewers can ask, "Are you a boy or a girl?", demonstrating to children that questions can be rephrased to make them easier to comprehend.
3 You're Wrong: Interviewers should tell children that they sometimes make mistakes, and invite children to correct them. To familiarize children with this concept, interviewers may ask, "If I say you are 30 years old, what do you say?" When the children state that they are not 30 years old, interviewers can ask, "Okay, so how old are you?"

4 Ignorant Interviewer: Interviewers must convey that children should lead the interview (e.g., "I don't know what's happened to you and won't be able to tell you the answer to my questions"). This instruction reminds children that they have information of value to interviewers.
5 Promise to Tell the Truth: Interviewers should request that children promise to tell the truth, a step that is not part of the NICHD Protocol. The Ten Step recommends that interviewers ask, "Do you promise to tell the truth? Will you tell me any lies?" Asking questions that require both "yes" and "no" responses should avoid claims that children's potential yay- or nay-saying biases explain their willingness to take this oath.
6 Practice Narratives: Like the rapport-building and practice narrative components of the NICHD Protocol, interviewers should have children practice freely recalling neutral events before discussing any allegations. Using open-ended prompts, interviewers ask children about what they like to do, what they do not like to do, and about what happened on their last birthday.
7 Allegation Question: If children have not yet mentioned the alleged incident(s) of abuse, interviewers should inquire about why the children have come to talk to them. This is equivalent to the transition to the substantive phase of the NICHD Protocol. For example, interviewers might say, "Tell me why I came to talk to you. It's really important for me to know why I came to talk to you." However, at times, interviewers may need to be more specific (e.g., "I heard that someone might have bothered you. Tell me everything about that").
8 Allegation Follow-up: Following children's initial abuse disclosure, interviewers request a detailed narrative with an open-ended prompt (e.g., "You said that [repeat allegation]. Tell me everything that happened").
9 Additional Follow-up: As children engage in free recall, interviewers probe the incident(s) further with open-ended prompts (e.g., "Tell me more about [event detail]. What happened next?"). Interviewers should avoid option posing and yes-no questions.
10 Multiple Incidents: Interviewers should try to gather incident-specific details when children allege multiple incidents of abuse. However, it is difficult for children to recall temporal information (e.g., how many times an event occurred; Wandrey, Lyon, Quas, & Friedman, 2012). Interviewers can ask questions such as, "Did [name allegation] happen one time or more than one time?" and "Tell me everything that happened the first time."

The Ten Step is quite similar to the NICHD Protocol, but it can be provided to interviewers as a simplified, one-page document. Although no empirical studies have examined the Ten Step in its entirety, various components of this protocol are supported by scientific research (e.g., practice narratives, promise to tell the truth; Lyon, 2011; Roberts, Brubacher, Powell, & Price, 2011). Next, we briefly review field and laboratory studies testing the effectiveness of the NICHD Protocol and the Ten Step or their various components in interviews with TD children.

Interviewing Typically Developing Children

A number of field studies in several countries (e.g., United States, United Kingdom, Israel, South Korea) have compared the effectiveness of the NICHD Protocol to a "standard" investigative interview. These studies have typically involved alleged victims between the ages of 4 and 12 years old. Examining real-world cases of suspected child maltreatment, these field studies have reliably found that the NICHD Protocol improves both the quality of the investigative interviews (i.e., types of questions asked by interviewers) and the amount of information that children recall, especially in response to vague open-ended prompts (see La Rooy et al., 2015; Lamb et al., 2007, for reviews). Regarding interview quality, training interviewers to use the NICHD Protocol increased the number of open-ended prompts (prompts that tend to elicit the most accurate information; Dent & Stephenson, 1979; Oates & Shrimpton, 1991) used by interviewers in comparison to nonprotocol interviews, and decreased the number of option-posing and suggestive questions asked. Also, option-posing and suggestive questions were usually asked later in the interviews, thus giving children the opportunity to freely recall most information without any input from the interviewers (Benia, Hauck-Filho, Dillenburg, & Stein, 2015; Lamb, Orbach, Hershkowitz, Esplin, & Horowitz, 2007b).

Regarding children's recall, children reported more details, including more central or forensically relevant details, in response to invitations when the NICHD Protocol was used than when a nonprotocol interview was used (Lamb et al., 2007b; Orbach, Hershkowitz, Lamb, Esplin, & Horowitz, 2000; Sternberg, Lamb, Orbach, Esplin, & Mitchell, 2001b). Furthermore, substantially more children initially disclosed abuse to open-ended prompts in the NICHD Protocol versus a nonprotocol interview (Lamb et al., 2007b; Sternberg et al., 2001b). This is crucial for children's credibility; if allegations are made, they should be free of interviewer input. Although the NICHD Protocol seems to improve the quantity (and potentially the quality via the increase in details elicited in response to open-ended prompts) of children's recall, approximately 25% of details reported by children in these studies were in response to option-posing and suggestive questions. Thus, there is a continued need for improving interviewer training and practice (Lamb et al., 2007b).

Although field studies are certainly informative, they cannot determine whether the NICHD Protocol improves children's accuracy, a crucial question in legal contexts. With real-world cases, there are typically no objective records with which to compare children's accounts of abuse. It is imperative to conduct experimental studies that test the accuracy of children's reports when interviewed with the NICHD Protocol, but surprisingly few such studies exist. In one study, Brown et al. (2013) used the NICHD Protocol to test 5- to 7-year-olds' memory for a staged event following a four- to six-week delay. Invitations elicited more accurate information than all other prompt types (cued invitations, directives, suggestive). Whereas cued invitations resulted in more correct central and peripheral details than all other prompt types, they also elicited more erroneous central and peripheral details than other prompt types. Although Brown et al. (2013) did not compare the NICHD Protocol to another interview method, this study demonstrates that young children can manage the length and style of the NICHD Protocol and that their reporting is generally improved by relying on the prompts emphasized by the protocol.

Because the Ten Step has adopted most of the components of the NICHD Protocol, it is possible that similar results would emerge if it were tested empirically. Future research should examine how interviewers and children respond to the Ten Step in its entirety. As we discuss next, many studies have investigated the components that comprise the NICHD Protocol and Ten Step rather than the protocols as a whole.

Ground rules

Based on the fairly small body of research on investigative interview ground rules, it is difficult to draw definitive conclusions about the rules' effectiveness because studies have examined variations of the rules, the rules have not been studied in isolation, and/or different methodologies been used to study the same rule (see Brubacher, Poole, & Dickinson, 2015, for a review). Of the ground rules, the "don't know" instruction has received the most empirical attention, whereas few studies have investigated the "don't understand" and "correct the interviewer" instructions. Generally, the ground rules appear to be at least somewhat effective, especially when children have the opportunity to practice applying them. However, children may require more training than is currently incorporated into the structured protocols, and additional research on the ground rules is sorely needed (Brubacher et al., 2015).

Research suggests that the truth-lie ceremony, a component of the NICHD Protocol, may be unnecessary. Generally, truth-lie discussions do not encourage truth-telling (e.g., Evans & Lee, 2010; Talwar, Lee, Bala, & Lindsay, 2002, 2004), particularly in the brief form that they have been incorporated into the NICHD Protocol. Also, if children do not perform well during a truth-lie ceremony, they may be considered incompetent to testify (Lyon, 2011). A "child-friendly oath" may be an appropriate alternative to the truth-lie discussion and is part of the Ten Step. Eliciting a promise to tell the truth from children has been shown to increase their true disclosures of wrongdoing (Evans & Lee, 2010; Lyon & Dorado, 2008; Talwar et al., 2002).

Rapport building

Children may be reluctant to disclose abuse (see Pipe, Lamb, Orbach, & Cederborg, 2007, for a review). To encourage children to feel comfortable revealing potentially traumatic experiences, rapport building is part of both protocols. Furthermore, rapport building is intended to improve the amount and accuracy of information that children report by allowing children to devote more cognitive resources to memory retrieval and narration rather than coping with stress. However, it has been difficult to draw precise conclusions about the effectiveness of rapport building, in part, because rapport has been defined in various ways and few studies have examined rapport in isolation (see Saywitz, Larson, Hobbs, & Wells, 2015, for a review).

Field studies have revealed that rapport is associated with less reluctance to disclose abuse among children (Hershkowitz, Lamb, & Katz, 2014; Hershkowitz, Lamb, Katz, & Malloy, 2015). Regarding the quantity and quality of children's reports once they have disclosed, rapport building is associated with more detailed responses from children (see Hershkowitz, 2011, for a review). Also, in some laboratory studies, rapport has improved the accuracy of children's reports (e.g., Roberts, Lamb, & Sternberg, 2004).

Practice narratives

Open-ended narrative practice is associated with children providing more detailed responses in the substantive phase of the interview, especially in response to open-ended prompts (Price, Roberts, & Collins, 2013). Furthermore, both observational and experimental studies have revealed that having children practice recalling repeated events facilitates their episodic recall in the substantive phase (Brubacher, Powell, & Roberts, 2014).

Although many of the studies conducted on components of the NICHD Protocol and Ten Step highlight their benefits when interviewing TD children, the complete protocols and their various components in isolation warrant further empirical attention, particularly in determining whether they improve children' accuracy when questioned about past events. Thus far, our discussion has focused on interviewing TD children, but it is important to consider whether these protocols and their components are appropriate for atypically developing children as well.

Interviewing Atypically Developing Children

Research on conducting investigative interviews with atypically developing populations is limited. Extant studies have primarily examined the testimonial capabilities of children broadly defined as having ID. Generally, this research has revealed that TD children provide more information than children with intellectual disabilities (CWID) in response to open-ended invitations. However, the information elicited from both TD children and CWID tends to be quite accurate (Henry et al., 2011; Milne, Sharman, Powell, & Mead, 2013).

Only two published studies (Brown, Lewis, & Lamb, 2015; Brown, Lewis, Lamb, & Stephens, 2012) have examined CWID's recall when interviewed with the NICHD Protocol. These studies tested children across a wide age range who had mild (IQ = 55–78) or moderate (IQ = 44–53) ID. Furthermore, the researchers examined children's memory for personally experienced events, as opposed to observed events, which makes the methodologies more generalizable to experiences of victimization about which children may testify. In both studies, children participated in an interactive safety event and were later interviewed by a research assistant using the NICHD Protocol, which was modified to include suggestive questions.

Brown et al. (2012) compared the event memories of CWID (mild and moderately impaired) and TD children (chronological age-matched [CA] and mental age-matched [MA] controls) after either a short (one-week) or long (six-month) delay. Children with mild ID performed as well or better than MA-matched children, even when asked suggestive questions. Children with moderate ID provided reliable responses, but were less accurate and more suggestible than children with mild ID. CA-matched children provided more detailed and accurate information than all other groups. Brown et al. (2015) compared the recall of CWID and TD children in repeated interviews. Children were interviewed once (six months after participating in the staged event) or twice (one week and six months after participating in the staged event). Children with mild ID did not significantly differ from their MA-matches in amount of information recalled, and they performed similarly to CA-matches in terms of accuracy. Children with moderate ID were comparable to MA-matches in terms of accuracy but recalled less information. From these studies, two key lessons emerge: (1) children with mild and moderate ID are capable of providing accurate event reports, and (2) children with mild and moderate ID can respond appropriately to the NICHD Protocol.

Overall, this research underscores that children of varying intellectual abilities can provide meaningful and reliable information when interviewed in a developmentally appropriate manner, a notable finding given that CWID are routinely interviewed in legal contexts, including with the NICHD Protocol (Hershkowitz et al., 2007). Although studies of CWID have involved children with mild and moderate impairments, additional research is needed examining children with more severe ID and on specific disorders such as ASD.

Interviewing Children with ASD

Despite popular references to the prodigious memories of individuals with ASD (*Rain Man*, *The Curious Incident of the Dog in the Night*), there is much yet to be learned about how well children with ASD remember and communicate about personal experiences, including potentially traumatic ones, and individual differences are substantial. It has been difficult to develop a complete "memory profile" of children with ASD, though such a profile would benefit those who design interviewing protocols. The limited research on the memory of individuals with ASD has largely focused on memory for specific information (e.g., word lists, faces) rather than personal experiences (e.g., Boucher & Lewis, 1989). A few studies have inquired about autobiographical memories for which accuracy cannot be assessed (Bruck et al., 2007; Goldman, 2008). It is unclear how much the memory of children with ASD is affected by suggestion, delay, and repetition. Also, research has not determined how children with ASD respond to specific interview components (e.g., rapport building, ground rules).

Clearly, the extant studies have left many questions unanswered about the capacities and limitations of children with ASD when questioned about personally meaningful events. Filling these gaps in the literature would have considerable implications for forensic interview contexts. However, as we review next, knowledge concerning the characteristics of children with ASD has implications for how the interview protocols reviewed in this chapter may be applicable (or inapplicable) to children with ASD. For example, given the deficits of children with ASD in social communication and tendency to experience social anxiety (MacNeil, Lopes, & Minnes, 2009), interviewers' attempts at building rapport may be unsuccessful with children with ASD. Our review is not exhaustive; rather, we focus on several key areas where research on ASD has implications for interview protocols. Some children with ASD will be incapable of communicating verbally; in this chapter, we focus on obtaining information from children with ASD who are verbal. We make suggestions for potential modifications to these existing interview protocols that can be tested in future research.

Quantity and accuracy of free-recall narratives

Best-practice interviewing guidelines such as Achieving Best Evidence (Home Office, 2011) recommend first accessing individuals' free-recall memory by obtaining a narrative account. At their core, the NICHD Protocol and Ten Step are methods of assisting interviewers with eliciting narratives from children while minimizing input from interviewers. However, as described next, children with ASD have difficulty with free recall, and their narratives are quantitatively and qualitatively different from those of TD children.

Children with ASD may provide fewer event details than their TD peers. For example, Bruck et al. (2007) found that high-functioning 5- to 10-year-olds with ASD reported fewer correct details about a staged magic show event than TD children of the same age. McCrory, Henry, and Happé (2007) revealed that 11- to 14-year-olds diagnosed with Asperger syndrome reported significantly less information than TD youth when asked to freely recall a live classroom event involving a scripted visit from two individuals. Millward, Powell, Messer, and Jordan (2000) took 12- to 16-year-olds with ASD and moderately severe language delays on two walks that involved scripted comments and interactions. Children with ASD reported fewer personally experienced events than did 5- to 6-year-old control participants who were matched on language ability. Mattison, Dando, and Ormerod (2015) also found that free-recall performance was diminished among children with ASD (*M* age = 14 years, 6 months) in comparison to TD peers (*M* age = 10 years, 2 months) who were matched on verbal mental age. In their study, TD children recalled significantly more correct information than children with ASD about a brief crime video following a one-hour delay.

It is unclear whether the group differences evident in free-recall narrative length stem from differences in ability, motivation, or some other facet of interviewing. Determining the mechanisms underlying these differences will allow for the development of strategies designed to increase the number of details provided by children with ASD in the critical free-recall portion of investigative interviews. Interestingly, although children with ASD may say less than TD children in free recall, their accounts appear as accurate as those of TD children, as described next. For example, in Bruck et al.'s study (2007) examining children's memory for a magic show, no differences emerged between children with ASD and TD children in terms of the number of incorrect utterances in free recall. Similarly, McCrory et al. (2007) found that details provided in free recall about a staged event were highly accurate (on average, 97%) among both TD children and children with ASD with accuracy defined as the number of correct pieces of information recalled in response to free recall, general, and specific questions out of the total number of pieces of information recalled about a live classroom event. However, Mattison et al. (2015) revealed significantly lower accuracy rates (i.e., the total number of correct items recalled from a catalog of potential details out of the total overall number of items recalled about a video clip) among children with ASD in comparison to TD children.

Although more research is undoubtedly needed, the findings reviewed thus far suggest that children with ASD may need additional support to enhance the amount and accuracy of information that they provide in free recall. Of importance, despite their challenges with providing free-recall narratives relative to TD children, we do not recommend eliminating or reducing the free-recall portion of investigative interviews for children with ASD. They should be invited to narrate about the target event—a central tenet of both the NICHD Protocol and Ten Step. However, interviewers should be aware of the free-recall deficits common among children with ASD so they can adjust their expectations accordingly and avoid becoming coercive when interviewing affected children. Children with ASD may benefit from additional "scaffolding" and prompting. Cued invitations (known as the suggested "follow-up" prompts in the Ten Step) may be particularly important for children with ASD, a question worthy of further research.

One promising technique that could be developed further and potentially incorporated into the NICHD Protocol or Ten Step is sketching. Noting the Task Support Hypothesis (Bowler, Matthews, & Gardiner, 1997), or the idea that individuals with ASD can exhibit memory performance comparable to their TD peers through appropriate support at retrieval, Mattison et al. (2015) tested the effects of sketching and mental context reinstatement, the latter of which is sometimes used in NICHD Protocol interviews, on youths' event reports. Results revealed that, despite being matched on verbal mental age, youth with ASD (*M* age = 14 years, 6 months) were less accurate overall than their TD counterparts (*M* age = 10 years, 2 months). However, youth with ASD in the sketching condition (*M* age = 14 years, 1 month) were as accurate as the TD comparison youth. Mental context reinstatement was ineffective with both groups of children. Additional research is needed on methods like sketching, which can be relatively easily incorporated into existing protocols and which may "boost" children with ASD's memory performance in interviews.

Content of free-recall narratives

Not only might the narratives of children with ASD differ from those of TD children in quantity and accuracy, but they may vary in content as well. Children with ASD often focus on peripheral event details and have difficulty extracting the greater meaning or gist (McCrory et al., 2007; see Happé & Frith, 2006, for a review). Therefore, they may be more prone to reporting peripheral information (e.g., description of a bystander) and leaving out central details (e.g., description of the perpetrator) that may be critically important to investigators.

In general, the narratives of children with ASD tend to lack coherence, organization around central themes, evaluative devices (e.g., character dialog), and causal and mental state information (e.g., Capps, Losh, & Thurber, 2000; Diehl, Bennetto, & Young, 2006). Also, their narratives are likely to include bizarre or inappropriate information (Loveland, McEvoy, & Tunali, 1990). Unfortunately, most research on the narrative coherence of children with ASD has involved storybook narratives rather than descriptions of personally meaningful events, including objectively verifiable events that allow for accuracy to be measured. In a study investigating children's memory for an objectively verifiable event, Bruck et al. (2007) found that children with ASD provided more "off topic" utterances than TD children. Overall, this research suggests that the narratives of children with ASD may be perceived as more confusing and less rich than TD children's narratives, which may impact their credibility with jurors and other fact finders. Again, interviewers may need to provide more scaffolding for children with ASD by emphasizing cued invitations. Also, interviewers trained in the NICHD Protocol may use time segmentation prompts to inquire about events previously mentioned by the child (e.g., "Think back to that day and tell me everything that happened from the time you left school until the time your friend came over") to help children with ASD produce coherent, logical narratives.

Because of their deficits in communication and social cognition, children with ASD may supply narratives that are less social in nature than those of TD children by, for example, leaving out details about emotions, social relationships, and conversations with others, focusing on factual information instead. In fact, research indicates that adults with ASD have more difficulty recalling correct event details about people and actions than adults without ASD (Maras & Bowler, 2010). Interviewers may be able to address these challenges in various ways. For example, Mattison et al. (2015) found that children with ASD who sketched while narrating were more accurate when reporting about "person" information and reported more correct "action" details—at least compared to other children with ASD in the control and mental context reinstatement conditions. These results suggest that sketching may enhance the performance of children with ASD about information that could be considered more "social." However, the potential benefits of sketching depend on whether social information is encoded in the first place. Future studies need to determine the extent to which children with ASD have difficulty encoding social information, and thus, may need support orienting their attention to social aspects of an event as it occurs versus the extent to which they have difficulty retrieving or communicating social details, and thus, may benefit from a tool like sketching.

Interviewers may need to prompt specifically for social information, such as what was said, felt, or thought during an event. Jurors and other fact finders may consider children's emotional or subjective reactions to abuse when assessing their credibility as victims/witnesses (e.g., Myers, Redlich, Goodman, Prizmich, & Imwinkelreid, 1999). However, field research indicates that even TD children rarely include their subjective feelings in forensic interviews about suspected maltreatment (Westcott & Kynan, 2004). Examining transcripts of courtroom testimony and forensic interviews about child sexual abuse, Lyon, Scurich, Choi, Handmaker, and Blank (2012) revealed that asking children "How did you feel?" increased the amount of the evaluative information (emotional, cognitive, and physical reactions to alleged abuse) that children reported. Future research should test how children with ASD respond to prompts intended to elicit social or evaluative information (e.g., "How did you feel? What did you talk about?"). If children with ASD struggle with retrieving this information or fail to report it because they do not consider it important, then such prompts may enhance these children's testimony. However, if they do not report social or evaluative information because they failed to encode it, then such prompts will likely be ineffective in eliciting this content.

Suggestibility

Children's suggestibility has been a major concern among researchers and practitioners for decades (see Ceci & Bruck, 1995, for a review). Bruck et al. (2007) outlined the reasons why children with ASD may be more or less suggestible than their TD peers. On the one hand, they may be less suggestible because their social deficits allow them to resist or even fail to notice the social cues embedded in suggestive questions (e.g., "That hurt, didn't it?"). Also, they may lack the desire to please the interviewer, and thus, be less compliant with interviewer suggestions or comments (e.g., "All the other kids told"). On the other hand, they may be more suggestible due to cognitive deficits that limit their source monitoring abilities and memory trace strength.

The limited extant research demonstrates that children with ASD show suggestibility effects but no more so than their TD peers. For example, McCrory et al. (2007) found that 11- to 14-year-old youths with ASD were not more suggestible than TD comparison youth when answering "leading" questions (e.g., "What color was the man's scarf?" when he was not wearing a scarf) about a live classroom event. Likewise, Bruck et al. (2007) revealed that 5- to 10-year-old children with ASD did not differ significantly from 5- to 10-year-old TD children when responding to misleading questions about a magic show event following a one-week delay. It is worth noting that these two studies involved relatively high-functioning samples of youth with ASD. Significant differences may emerge between children with ASD and TD children if children with ASD have more moderate or severe impairments in IQ or language. Furthermore, these studies assessed children's responses to leading or misleading questions as measures of suggestibility. However, suggestion in investigative interviews can come in various forms (e.g., biased interviewer instructions, repeated questions; Ceci & Bruck, 1995) and from various individuals (e.g., interviewers, peers, parents; Malloy & Mugno, 2016; Principe, Kanaya, Ceci, & Singh, 2006). Therefore, conclusions about suggestibility among children with ASD are premature, and future research should take into account the various sources of potential contamination on children's reports.

Given concerns about children's suggestibility irrespective of ASD diagnosis, we recommend that interviewers follow the NICHD Protocol and Ten Step approaches for avoiding suggestive questions and comments with *all* children. That is, interviewers should use open-ended prompts as much as possible. Based on the current, albeit limited, literature, it does not appear that interviewers should be *more* concerned about suggestibility when interviewing children with ASD. Nevertheless, children with ASD appear to be as suggestible as their TD peers, and thus, current best-practice precautions are likely appropriate and necessary.

Identifying the target event

ASD is associated with major difficulties in understanding others' minds (Baron-Cohen, 2000), or representing and attributing the mental states of others. In fact, 8- to 10-year-olds with ASD often fail false belief tasks designed to measure theory of mind that 4-year-old TD children pass (e.g., Peterson, Wellman, & Liu, 2005). Well-documented deficits in theory of mind of children with ASD have implications for investigative interviews in terms of their knowledge and awareness concerning what to report about past events. Children with ASD may not grasp the significance of abusive incidents. This may make them less reluctant to disclose abuse than TD children, but also less aware that they have information worth reporting in a forensic interview, possibilities that have yet to be tested empirically. The success of forensic interviews depends, in part, on interviewees' understanding that they have unique information about their experiences. This may mean that children with ASD have difficulty identifying the target event in response to open-ended prompts as recommended by both the NICHD Protocol and Ten Step. Likewise, if children with ASD identify the target event, they may not fully understand that interviewers lack knowledge of what happened. Thus, the "ignorant interviewer" instruction of the Ten Step may be particularly important to emphasize when interviewing children with ASD. Currently, however, there is no research investigating whether this instruction improves children with ASD's reports in light of their problems with perspective taking.

Engaging in deception

Theory of mind development also has implications for children's deceptive abilities because lying involves intentionally manipulating another's mental state by attempting to instill a false belief (see Talwar & Crossman, 2012). Investigators and other fact finders assess whether they believe that victims and witnesses are telling the truth. Also, children may be asked to demonstrate that they understand the difference between "truths" and "lies" (NICHD Protocol) or promise to tell the truth (Ten Step) before being interviewed.

Deception appears to be difficult for at least some children with ASD. For example, children and adolescents with ASD are worse at engaging in strategic deception (e.g., deceiving a competitor) than TD children (e.g., Baron-Cohen, 1992; Sodian & Frith, 1992). However, these studies examined children's deception in game contexts rather than spontaneous deception in interviews. Talwar et al. (2012) examined children's spontaneous antisocial lies to conceal transgressions among 4- to 11-year-old children with ASD and TD children who were matched on verbal age. Results revealed that not only were children with ASD significantly less likely to lie in a temptation resistance paradigm than TD children, but children with ASD were less successful in maintaining their lies as well. That is, children with ASD were less likely to feign ignorance about the identity of a toy or guess another toy, strategies that represent "semantic leakage control" by concealing knowledge that reveals one's lie. Li, Kelley, Evans, and Lee (2011) also found that children with ASD were worse at maintaining lies to conceal a transgression than TD children who were matched on verbal mental age. However, in their study, children with ASD were as likely as TD children to tell lies to conceal a transgression and "white" lies for politeness purposes.

It appears as though children with ASD are less able or willing to lie convincingly, a difference that is at least partially rooted in their theory of mind deficits. This may be useful information for interviewers and fact finders as they evaluate the veracity of children's allegations, especially if there are claims that the child is making up the allegations or has been coached to lie. Findings have been somewhat inconsistent, however, and the truth-telling tendencies of children with ASD relative to TD children in experimental paradigms do not mean that reports from children with ASD in forensic interviews are necessarily accurate or truthful.

Understanding deception

Children with ASD may never have the opportunity to testify, however, if they fail truth-lie competency tasks that are part of the NICHD Protocol and are required in some jurisdictions (Lyon, 2011). Research suggests that children with ASD may have difficulty distinguishing truths from lies. Even adults with ASD demonstrate problems with understanding and explaining nonliteral speech such as lies, jokes, and sarcasm (Happé, 1994). Leekam and Prior (1994) demonstrated that second-order false belief understanding ("He thinks that she thinks X") was important for 4- to 5-year-old TD children and 7- to 17-year-old youths with ASD (verbal mental age of 5 years, 3 months, to 16 years, 5 months) to accurately distinguish between antisocial lies and jokes. Furthermore, the truth-lie questions in the NICHD Protocol involve hypothetical reasoning which may be difficult for children with ASD because children must imagine what might be from another's perspective (e.g., "If I said that my shoes were red, would that be true or not true?).

Conclusions and Future Directions

Memory reports are often necessary if we are to know when children have been victimized, and children with disabilities (e.g., ID, ASD) are at greater risk of experiencing victimization. Thus, it is imperative to understand the eyewitness capabilities of these children and how best to facilitate their recall and disclosure of potentially traumatic experiences.

In the current chapter, we reviewed two protocols for interviewing children about past events, primarily suspected child maltreatment. The NICHD Protocol is a developmentally appropriate method designed to optimize retrieval. It has been studied extensively in the field, and although it has not been tested among children with ASD specifically, it has shown promise when used with children with mild and moderate ID. There has been little laboratory analog research on the NICHD Protocol, however, and such studies are crucial for determining whether this protocol results in particularly accurate information from both TD and atypically developing children. The Ten Step is a brief modification of the NICHD Protocol. Although the Ten Step has not been subject to empirical examination as a whole, its various steps are supported by scientific research. Future research may result in modifications to these structured interviewing approaches for both TD and atypically developing children. However, it is evident that these protocols are much-needed improvements over standard interviews.

As we reviewed, children with ASD differ from TD children and those with other IDs in ways that appear to produce quantitative and qualitative differences in their event reports, especially their free-recall narratives. However, little research has focused on the episodic memories of children with ASD. Most studies on interviewing atypically developing youth include heterogeneous groups of children with ASD, ID, and/or "mental retardation" (e.g., Dent, 1986; McCrory et al., 2007; Michel, Gordon, Ornstein, & Simpson, 2000; Milne & Bull, 1996). Studies of children with ASD have tended to include relatively small samples of children with mild intellectual impairments (Bruck et al., 2007; McCrory et al., 2007).

Future research with children with ASD should take into account both methodological and practical concerns. Studies should test components of the interview protocols and potential protocol modifications with large, clearly defined samples of children with ASD who have a wide range of intellectual and language abilities. Also, studies should consider more ecologically valid designs such as interviewing children about complex, experienced events that involve others' wrongdoing following longer delays. Furthermore, researchers should investigate jurors' perceptions of children with ASD in forensic interviews. These studies can help investigators and other fact finders develop realistic expectations concerning the testimonial capacities and limitations of children with ASD and determine whether, for example, expert witness testimony is needed to correct potential misperceptions about the memory reports of these children. Overall, future research will enhance our understanding of the capabilities of children with ASD and help researchers design effective means for communicating with these children.

References

Aldridge, J., & Cameron, S. (1999). Interviewing child witnesses: Questioning techniques and the role of training. *Applied Developmental Science*, *3*, 136–147. doi:10.1207/s1532480xads0302_7

Baron-Cohen, S. (1992). Out of sight or out of mind? Another look at deception in autism. *Child Psychology & Psychiatry & Allied Disciplines*, *33*, 1141–1155. doi:10.1111/j.1469-7610.1992.tb00934.x

Baron-Cohen, S. (2000). Theory of mind and autism: A fifteen year review. In S. Baron-Cohen, H. Tager-Flusberg, & D. Cohen (Eds.), *Understanding other minds: Perspectives from developmental cognitive neuroscience, 2nd ed.* (pp. 3–20). New York, NY: Oxford University Press.

Benia, L. R., Hauck-Filho, N., Dillenburg, M., & Stein, L. M. (2015). The NICHD investigative interview protocol: A meta-analytic review. *Journal of Child Sexual Abuse: Research, Treatment, & Program Innovations for Victims, Survivors, & Offenders, 24*, 259–279. doi:10.1080/10538712.2015.1006749

Boucher, J., & Lewis, V. (1989). Memory impairments and communication in relatively able autistic children. *Child Psychology & Psychiatry & Allied Disciplines, 30*, 99–122. doi:10.1111/j.1469-7610.1989.tb00771.x

Bowler, D. M., Matthews, N. J., & Gardiner, J. M. (1997). Asperger's syndrome and memory: Similarity to autism but not amnesia. *Neuropsychologia, 35*, 65–70. doi:10.1016/s0028-3932(96)00054-1

Brown, D. A., Lamb, M. E., Lewis, C., Pipe, M., Orbach, Y., & Wolfman, M. (2013). The NICHD investigative interview protocol: An analogue study. *Journal of Experimental Psychology: Applied, 19*, 367–382. doi:10.1037/a0035143

Brown, D. A., Lewis, C. N., & Lamb, M. E. (2015). Preserving the past: An early interview improves delayed event memory in children with intellectual disabilities. *Child Development, 86*, 1031–1047. doi:10.1111/cdev.12364

Brown, D. A., Lewis, C. N., Lamb, M. E., & Stephens, E. (2012). The influences of delay and severity of intellectual disability on event memory in children. *Journal of Consulting & Clinical Psychology, 80*, 829–841. doi:10.1037/a0029388

Brubacher, S. P., Poole, D. A., & Dickinson, J. J. (2015). The use of ground rules in investigative interviews with children: A synthesis and call for research. *Developmental Review, 36*, 15–33. doi:10.1016/j.dr.2015.01.001

Brubacher, S. P., Powell, M. B., & Roberts, K. P. (2014). Recommendations for interviewing children about repeated experiences. *Psychology, Public Policy, & Law, 20*, 325–335. doi:10.1037/law0000011

Bruck, M., London, K., Landa, R., & Goodman, J. (2007). Autobiographical memory and suggestibility in children with autism spectrum disorder. *Development & Psychopathology, 19*, 73–95. doi:10.1017/S0954579407070058

Capps, L., Losh, M., & Thurber, C. (2000). "The frog ate the bug and made his mouth sad": Narrative competence in children with autism. *Journal of Abnormal Child Psychology, 28*, 193–204. doi:10.1023/A:1005126915631

Ceci, S. J., & Bruck, M. (1995). *Jeopardy in the courtroom: A scientific analysis of children's testimony.* Washington, DC: American Psychological Association.

Dent, H. R. (1986). An experimental study of the effectiveness of different techniques of questioning mentally handicapped child witnesses. *British Journal of Clinical Psychology, 25*, 13–17. doi:10.1111/j.2044-8260.1986.tb00666.x

Dent, H. R., & Stephenson, G. M. (1979). An experimental study of the effectiveness of different techniques of questioning child witnesses. *British Journal of Social & Clinical Psychology, 18*, 41–51. doi:10.1111/j.2044-8260.1979.tb00302.x

Diehl, J. J., Bennetto, L., & Young, E. C. (2006). Story recall and narrative coherence of high-functioning children with autism spectrum disorders. *Journal of Abnormal Child Psychology, 34*, 87–102. doi:10.1007/s10802-005-9003-x

Evans, A. D., & Lee, K. (2010). Promising to tell the truth makes 8- to 16-year-olds more honest. *Behavioral Sciences & the Law, 28*, 801–811. doi:10.1002/bsl.960

Goldman, S. (2008). Brief report: Narratives of personal events in children with autism and developmental language disorders: Unshared memories. *Journal of Autism & Developmental Disorders, 38*, 1982–1988. doi:10.1007/s10803-008-0588-0

Happé, F., & Frith, U. (2006). The weak coherence account: Detail-focused cognitive style in autism spectrum disorders. *Journal of Autism & Developmental Disorders*, *36*, 5–25. doi:10.1007/s10803-005-0039-0

Henry, L. A., Bettenay, C., & Carney, D. P. (2011). Children with intellectual disabilities and developmental disorders. In M. E. Lamb, D. J. La Rooy, L. C. Malloy, & C. Katz (Eds.), *Children's testimony: A handbook of psychological research and forensic practice* (pp. 251–283). West Sussex, England: Wiley-Blackwell.

Hershkowitz, I. (2011). The effects of abuse history on sexually intrusive behavior by children: An analysis of child justice records. *Child Abuse & Neglect*, *35*, 40–49. doi:10.1016/j.chiabu.2010.09.002

Hershkowitz, I., Lamb, M. E., & Horowitz, D. (2007). Victimization of children with disabilities. *American Journal of Orthopsychiatry*, *77*, 629–635. doi:10.1037/0002-9432.77.4.629

Hershkowitz, I., Lamb, M. E., & Katz, C. (2014). Allegation rates in forensic child abuse investigations: Comparing the revised and standard NICHD protocols. *Psychology, Public Policy, & Law*, *20*, 336–344. doi:10.1037/a0037391

Hershkowitz, I., Lamb, M. E., Katz, C., & Malloy, L. C. (2015). Does enhanced rapport-building alter the dynamics of investigative interviews with suspected victims of intra-familial abuse? *Journal of Police & Criminal Psychology*, *30*, 6–14. doi:10.1007/s11896-013-9136-8

Home Office. (2011). *Achieving best evidence in criminal proceedings: Guidance on interviewing victims and witnesses, and using special measures.* London, England: Author.

La Rooy, D., Brubacher, S. P., Aromaki-Stratos, A., Cyr, M., Hershkowitz, I., Korkman, J., Myklebust, T., Naka, M., Peixoto, C., Roberts, K. P., Stewart, H., & Lamb, M. E. (2015). The NICHD Protocol: A review of an internationally-used evidence-based tool for training child forensic interviewers. *Journal of Criminological Research, Policy, & Practice*, *1*, 76–89. doi:10.1108/JCRPP-01-2015-0001

Lamb, M. E., Hershkowitz, I., Orbach, Y., & Esplin, P. W. (2008). *Tell me what happened: Structured investigative interviews of child victims and witnesses.* Hoboken, NJ: John Wiley & Sons Inc.

Lamb, M. E., La Rooy, D. J., Malloy, L. C., & Katz, C. (Eds.). (2011). *Children's testimony: A handbook of psychological research and forensic practice.* West Sussex, England: Wiley-Blackwell.

Lamb, M. E., Orbach, Y., Hershkowitz, I., Horowitz, D., & Abbott, C. B. (2007a). Does the type of prompt affect the accuracy of information provided by alleged victims of abuse in forensic interviews? *Applied Cognitive Psychology*, *21*, 1117–1130. doi:10.1002/acp.1318

Lamb, M. E., Orbach, Y., Hershkowitz, I., Esplin, P. W., & Horowitz, D. (2007b). Structured forensic interview protocols improve the quality and informativeness of investigative interviews with children: A review of research using the NICHD Investigative Interview Protocol. *Child Abuse & Neglect*, *31*, 1201–1231. doi:10.1016/j.chiabu.2007.03.021

Leekam, S. R., & Prior, M. (1994). Can autistic children distinguish lies from jokes? A second look at second-order belief attribution. *Journal of Child Psychology & Psychiatry*, *35*, 901–915. doi:10.1111/j.1469-7610.1994.tb02301.x

Li, A. S., Kelley, E. A., Evans, A. D., & Lee, K. (2011). Exploring the ability to deceive in children with autism spectrum disorders. *Journal of Autism & Developmental Disorders*, *41*, 185–195. doi:10.1007/s10803-010-1045-4

Loveland, K. A., McEvoy, R. E., & Tunali, B. (1990). Narrative story telling in autism and Down's syndrome. *British Journal of Developmental Psychology*, *8*, 9–23. doi:10.1111/j.2044-835x.1990.tb00818.x

Lyon, T. D. (2005). *Ten step investigative interview.* Los Angeles, CA: T. D. Lyon. Retrieved from http://works.bepress.com/thomaslyon/5/

Lyon, T. D. (2011). Assessing the competency of child witnesses: Best practice informed by psychology and law. In M. E. Lamb, D. J. La Rooy, L. C. Malloy, & C. Katz (Eds.), *Children's testimony: A handbook of psychological research and forensic practice* (pp. 69–85). Oxford, England: Wiley-Blackwell.

Lyon, T. D., & Dorado, J. S. (2008). Truth induction in young maltreated children: The effects of oath-taking and reassurance on true and false disclosures. *Child Abuse & Neglect*, *32*, 738–748. doi:10.1016/j.chiabu.2007.08.008

Lyon, T. D., Scurich, N., Choi, K., Handmaker, S., & Blank, R. (2012). "How did you feel?": Increasing child sexual abuse witnesses' production of evaluative information. *Law & Human Behavior*, *36*, 448–457. doi:10.1037/h0093986

MacNeil, B. M., Lopes, V. A., & Minnes, P. M. (2009). Anxiety in children and adolescents with autism spectrum disorders. *Research in Autism Spectrum Disorders*, *3*, 1–21. doi:10.1016/j.rasd.2008.06.001

Malloy, L. C., & Mugno, A. P. (2016). Children's recantation of adult wrongdoing: An experimental investigation. *Journal of Experimental Child Psychology*, *145*, 11–21. doi:10.1016/j.jecp.2015.12.003

Maras, K. L., & Bowler, D. M. (2010). The cognitive interview for eyewitnesses with autism spectrum disorder. *Journal of Autism & Developmental Disorders*, *40*, 1350–1360. doi:10.1007/s10803-010-0997-8

Mattison, M. L. A., Dando, C. J., & Ormerod, T. C. (2015). Sketching to remember: Episodic free recall task support for child witnesses and victims with autism spectrum disorder. *Journal of Autism & Developmental Disorders*, *45*, 1751–1765. doi:10.1007/s10803-014-2335-z

McCrory, E., Henry, L. A., & Happé, F. (2007). Eye-witness memory and suggestibility in children with Asperger syndrome. *Journal of Child Psychology & Psychiatry*, *48*, 482–489. doi:10.1111/j.1469-7610.2006.01715.x

Michel, M. K., Gordon, B. N., Ornstein, P. A., & Simpson, M. A. (2000). The abilities of children with mental retardation to remember personal experiences: Implications for testimony. *Journal of Clinical Child Psychology*, *29*, 453–463. doi:10.1207/s15374424jccp2903_16

Millward, C., Powell, S., Messer, D., & Jordan, R. (2000). Recall for self and other in autism: Children's memory for events experienced by themselves and their peers. *Journal of Autism & Developmental Disorders*, *30*, 15–28. doi:10.1023/A:1005455926727

Milne, R., & Bull, R. (1996). Interviewing children with mild learning disability with the cognitive interview. *Issues in Criminological & Legal Psychology*, *26*, 44–51.

Milne, R., Sharman, S. J., Powell, M. B., & Mead, S. (2013). Assessing the effectiveness of the cognitive interview for children with severe intellectual disabilities. *International Journal of Disability, Development & Education*, *60*, 18–29. doi:10.1080/1034912X.2013.757137

Myers, J. E. B., Redlich, A. D., Goodman, G. S., Prizmich, L. P., & Imwinkelried, E. (1999). Jurors' perceptions of hearsay in child sexual abuse cases. *Psychology, Public Policy, & Law*, *5*, 388–419. doi:10.1037/1076-8971.5.2.388

Oates, K. & Shrimpton, S. (1991). Children's memories for stressful and non-stressful events. *Medicine, Science & the Law*, *31*, 4–10.

Orbach, Y., Hershkowitz, I., Lamb, M. E., Esplin, P. W., & Horowitz, D. (2000). Assessing the value of structured protocols for forensic interviews of alleged child abuse victims. *Child Abuse & Neglect*, *24*, 733–752. doi:10.1016/S0145-2134(00)00137-X

Peterson, C. C., Wellman, H. M., & Liu, D. (2005). Steps in theory-of-mind development for children with deafness or autism. *Child Development*, *76*, 502–517. doi:10.1111/j.1467-8624.2005.00859.x

Pipe, M. E., Lamb, M. E., Orbach, Y., & Cederborg, A.-C. (2007). *Child sexual abuse: Disclosure, delay and denial*. Mahwah, NJ: Lawrence Erlbaum Associates.

Price, H. L., Roberts, K. P., & Collins, A. (2013). The quality of children's allegations of abuse in investigative interviews containing practice narratives. *Journal of Applied Research in Memory & Cognition*, *2*, 1–6. doi:10.1016/j.jarmac.2012.03.001

Principe, G. F., Kanaya, T., Ceci, S. J., & Singh, M. (2006). Believing is seeing: How rumors can engender false memories in preschoolers. *Psychological Science*, *17*, 243–248. doi:10.1111/j.1467-9280.2006.01692.x

Reiter, S., Bryen, D. N., & Shachar, I. (2007). Adolescents with intellectual disabilities as victims of abuse. *Journal of Intellectual Disabilities, 11*, 371–387. doi:10.1177/1744629507084602

Roberts, K. P., Lamb, M. E., & Sternberg, K. J. (2004). The effects of rapport-building style on children's reports of a staged event. *Applied Cognitive Psychology, 18*, 189–202. doi:10.1002/acp.957

Roberts, K. P., Brubacher, S. P., Powell, M. B., & Price, H. L. (2011). Practice narratives. In M. E. Lamb, D. J. La Rooy, L. C. Malloy, & C. Katz (Eds.), *Children's testimony: A handbook of psychological research and forensic practice* (pp. 129–145). Oxford, England: Wiley-Blackwell. doi:10.1002/9781119998495.ch7

Saywitz, K. J., Larson, R. P., Hobbs, S. D., & Wells, C. R. (2015). Developing rapport with children in forensic interviews: Systematic review of experimental research. *Behavioral Sciences & the Law, 33*, 372–389. doi:10.1002/bsl.2186

Sodian, B., & Frith, U. (1992). Deception and sabotage in autistic, retarded and normal children. *Child Psychology & Psychiatry & Allied Disciplines, 33*, 591–605. doi:10.1111/j.1469-7610.1992.tb00893.x

Sternberg, K. J., Lamb, M. E., Davies, G. M., & Westcott, H. L. (2001a). The Memorandum of Good Practice: Theory versus application. *Child Abuse & Neglect, 25*, 669–681. doi:10.1016/s0145-2134(01)00232-0

Sternberg, K. J., Lamb, M. E., Orbach, Y., Esplin, P. W., & Mitchell, S. (2001b). Use of a structured investigative protocol enhances young children's responses to free-recall prompts in the course of forensic interviews. *Journal of Applied Psychology, 86*, 997–1005. doi:10.1037/0021-9010.86.5.997

Sullivan, P. M., & Knutson, J. F. (2000). Maltreatment and disabilities: A population-based epidemiological study. *Child Abuse & Neglect, 24*, 1257–1273. doi:10.1016/S0145-2134(00)00190-3

Talwar, V., & Crossman, A. M. (2012). Children's lies and their detection: Implications for child witness testimony. *Developmental Review, 32*, 337–359. doi:10.1016/j.dr.2012.06.004

Talwar, V., Lee, K., Bala, N., & Lindsay, R. C. L. (2002). Children's conceptual knowledge of lying and its relation to their actual behaviors: Implications for court competence examinations. *Law & Human Behavior, 26*, 395–415. doi:10.1023/A:1016379104959

Talwar, V., Lee, K., Bala, N., & Lindsay, R. C. L. (2004). Children's lie-telling to conceal a parent's transgression: Legal implications. *Law & Human Behavior, 28*, 411–435. doi:10.1023/B:LAHU.0000039333.51399.f6

Talwar, V., Zwaigenbaum, L., Goulden, K. J., Manji, S., Loomes, C., & Rasmussen, C. (2012). Lie-telling behavior in children with autism and its relation to false-belief understanding. *Focus on Autism & Other Developmental Disabilities, 27*, 122–129. doi:10.1177/1088357612441828

Wandrey, L., Lyon, T. D., Quas, J. A., & Friedman, W. J. (2012). Maltreated children's ability to estimate temporal location and numerosity of placement changes and court visits. *Psychology, Public Policy, & Law, 18*, 79–104. doi:10.1037/a0024812

Warren, A. R., Woodall, C. E., Thomas, M., Nunno, M., Keeney, J. M., Larson, S. M., & Stadfeld, J. A. (1999). Assessing the effectiveness of a training program for interviewing child witnesses. *Applied Developmental Science, 3*, 128–135. doi:10.1207/s1532480xads0302_6

Westcott, H. L., & Kynan, S. (2004). The application of a "story-telling" framework to investigative interviews for suspected child sexual abuse. *Legal & Criminological Psychology, 9*, 37–56. doi:10.1348/135532504322776843

16

Clinical and Forensic Interviewing of Children and Adults with Autism Spectrum Disorder: Strategies for Improving Eyewitness Memory Reports

Elisa Krackow

Professionals who treat and educate youth with autism spectrum disorder (ASD) are frequently mandated reporters of suspected maltreatment. Child abuse reporting laws are enacted by states. Some states such as California also mandate reporting of adult disclosure of childhood maltreatment when minors may be endangered due to contact with the alleged perpetrator (Rady Children's Hospital San Diego, 2012). Therefore, professionals in some states may encounter youth with ASD and be required to report their alleged childhood maltreatment. Moreover, states vary tremendously in the length of time allowed by the statute of limitations for criminal prosecution of child abuse. Many states have lengthy or no statute of limitations, rendering allegations of maltreatment plausible well into adulthood for adults with and without ASD, thereby significantly taxing eyewitness memory abilities.

ASD, defined as a developmental disorder with social/communication deficits and restricted interests/repetitive behaviors, affects functioning in cognitive, social, and emotional domains (American Psychiatric Association, 2013). As such, adaptations to clinical/forensic interviews are necessary to obtain the most accurate memory reports from individuals with ASD.

This chapter provides a brief overview of symptoms associated with ASD, discusses the role of clinical versus forensic interviewers, and provides guidance as to critical background information to be obtained during clinical/forensic interviews. The chapter reviews research on autobiographical memory and suggestibility in children and adults with ASD. Next, the chapter provides recommendations for modifications to the clinical/forensic interview in the areas of rapport development, managing emotion regulation deficits, and establishing interview expectations. The chapter provides empirically based interviewing recommendations grounded in the literatures on ASD, cognitive development, eyewitness memory, and forensic interviewing. Specifically,

The Wiley Handbook of Memory, Autism Spectrum Disorder, and the Law, First Edition.
Edited by Jonni L. Johnson, Gail S. Goodman, and Peter C. Mundy.

the chapter discusses how to elicit more elaborate memory reports and how to minimize suggestibility as well as provides recommendations regarding the use of photo lineup identifications (e.g., selecting alleged perpetrators from an array of photos), source monitoring questions that ask the interviewee to provide information regarding the avenue by which the interviewee acquired knowledge (e.g., Did the event in question actually occur or did the interviewer present the event detail within a question?), and questions about emotions. Possible implications of co-morbid ASD and intellectual deficiency are discussed. Next the chapter discusses and provides recommendations regarding the use of "child-friendly" non-empirically supported interviewing techniques followed by empirically supported interviewing techniques. The chapter closes with a discussion of cultural considerations in interviewing and a summary of take-home points. Based on the scientific literature, the author's clinical experience and/or experience as an expert witness, the author provides a number of recommendations throughout. Consistent with the *Diagnostic and Statistical Manual, 5th edition* (DSM-5), this author does not distinguish among autistic disorder, Asperger syndrome, and pervasive developmental disorder, not otherwise specified (PDD-NOS), although the research reports cited herein typically classify participant samples into these more specific disorders. Throughout the chapter, the author differentiates recommendations applicable to clinical (i.e., interviews by mental health professionals) versus forensic interviewers. Use of the term *clinical/forensic* designates application to both clinical and forensic interviewers. The information on clinical interviewing is specific to the United States and is based on Krackow (2015).

Clinical Interviewing in Suspected Maltreatment Cases

It is important to remember that the role of professionals in assessing maltreatment varies depending on the specific circumstances. In the case where a child or adult discloses what might be maltreatment to a mandated reporter, the person has an obligation to interview the child or adult to obtain just enough specifics, including who, what, when, and how, and enough contextual information to determine whether the child or adult is describing maltreatment. If the clinician deems the account to be describing maltreatment, she is legally obligated to follow the laws of the state in which she is conducting the clinical interview or in which the minor resides regarding mandated reporting, which typically require phoning child protective services within an allotted time frame. It is important to note that it is beyond the expertise of the clinician to conduct a full forensic interview; this should be left to forensic interviewers. In addition, the reporting professional is often asked to provide a written account of the disclosure. It is critical that the clinician obtain the purest account possible without suggesting event details to the interviewee given that suggested details can become infused into memory reports with the potential for the infusions to endure over time (Leichtman & Ceci, 1995). It is recommended that the clinical interview be audio-recorded given that this may be the alleged victim's first report of maltreatment.

In the case where a potential victim has not disclosed abuse, clinicians need to be careful regarding interviewing based on suspicions of maltreatment. It is a myth that a clinician can examine a profile of psychological symptoms, and therefore, conclude with certainty that a child or adult has been maltreated (Kendall-Tackett, Williams, & Finkelhor, 1993; see Lynn, Krackow, Loftus, Lock, & Lilienfeld, 2015, for review). Loftus (1994) referred to the tendency for some clinicians to conclude that an individual was maltreated based on psychological symptoms as "symptom interpretation." Clinicians who engage in such symptom interpretation may proceed to use memory recovery techniques that have been shown by a large body of research to result in false event reports and false memories, and in some cases, additional psychological symptoms emerge (Loftus, 1997; Lynn et al., 2015, Ost, Wright, Easton, Hope, & French, 2013). Loftus documented the negative effects of memory recovery therapy in adults (Loftus, 1997).

Some, but not all, individuals with a history of maltreatment experience psychological symptoms, and therefore, may benefit from psychotherapy (Kendall-Tackett et al., 1993; Mannarino, Cohen, Deblinger, Runyan, & Steer, 2012). If symptomatic, common psychological symptoms that present in maltreated children include depression, anxiety, disruptive behavior disorders, posttraumatic stress disorder, and developmental trauma disorder (Browne & Finkelhor, 1987; Finkelhor, 1990). Among youth with reactive attachment disorder, maltreatment is often a precipitating event; however, reactive attachment disorder is rare, even in children with maltreatment histories, and this disorder is often diagnosed incorrectly in place of disruptive behavior disorders (Hanson & Spratt, 2000). Adults with maltreatment histories may develop eating disorders, substance dependence, and borderline personality disorder along with the symptoms noted above that commonly present in children (Polusny & Follette, 1995). Despite popular belief that dissociative identity disorder develops as a way of coping with a maltreatment history, an alternative etiological conceptualization suggests that dissociative identity disorder is a culturally constructed phenomenon that emerges as a result of cultural scripts, media coverage, and psychotherapists' use of memory recovery techniques and reinforcement (Lilienfeld & Lynn, 2015). In summary, it would be erroneous reasoning to conclude that a person has been maltreated due to the presentation of a specific psychological symptom profile.

If it is necessary to report alleged maltreatment to child or adult protective services, and these agencies deem the report to warrant a forensic interview, the stakes become heightened given the ramifications for the alleged victim, family, and alleged perpetrator. Further, the quality of the forensic interview can be used by judges and expert witnesses to lend credibility to or discredit the child or adult's testimony, which can ultimately influence legal decision-making.

Overview of Social, Cognitive, and Emotional Excesses and Deficits in ASD

ASD can be conceptualized in terms of "excesses" and "deficits" (El-Ghoroury & Krackow, 2011, p. 11). According to the American Psychiatric Association (APA) (2013), ASD is defined by the following excesses and deficits: Social/communication problems include, but are not limited to, disinterest in interpersonal relations, poor eye contact, lack of joint attention engagement, and inability to match social behaviors. Language and conversational characteristics can include deficits in expressive language (i.e., language generation), lack of reciprocal conversation (i.e., back and forth conversation), pronoun reversal (e.g., confusion of "you" vs. "I"), echolalia (i.e., repeating words, parts of words, or word sounds), literal/concrete interpretations of language (i.e., verbatim interpretation of the meaning of words or statements), and abnormal prosody (i.e., rhythm, sound emphasis, and intonation). Other cognitive characteristics include intellectual deficits, the inability to imagine including lack of pretend play, perspective-taking difficulty, and attention deficits. Emotion-based deficits include emotion processing, understanding, and recognition difficulties as well as emotion regulation problems. Restricted or fixed interests/repetitive behaviors can manifest themselves with regard to specific subjects or parts of objects. All of the preceding mentioned defining or associated features of ASD could impede a person's ability to accurately report maltreatment or other experienced/witnessed crimes. Given that interviewing strategies can influence the accuracy of memory reports (Krackow & Lynn, 2003, 2010), adaptations in interviewing strategies may be required by mental health and other professionals who perform clinical/forensic interviews with people on the autism spectrum. In addition, there are frequent co-occurring associated features and co-morbid disorders with ASD, including but not limited to, disruptive behavior and anxiety that are not part of the diagnostic criteria (APA, 2013). These, too, may require specialized knowledge on the part of mental health, forensic, and other professionals who interact with individuals with ASD.

Critical Background Information Necessary to Guide Clinical/Forensic Interviews

It is imperative that a range of background information be obtained by interviewing the alleged victim's non-offending primary caregiver prior to a scheduled interview about maltreatment. Ideally, the former interview would be conducted in the days prior to the forensic interview. In cases where an unanticipated disclosure occurs in a clinical context, the clinical interviewer may be privy to some or all of the about-to-be discussed information. Otherwise, it may not be possible to obtain the information.

The presence or absence of intellectual deficits is noted only after a diagnosis of ASD is determined, as opposed to being incorporated into the diagnostic criteria for ASD, thereby functionally allowing the clinician to estimate the level of intelligence as opposed to determining intelligence via formal psychological assessment (APA, 2013). However, it is necessary that forensic interviewers who interact with clients obtain reliable and recent data about the alleged victim's intelligence level. The forensic interviewer should request that the caregiver provide records of the child's or adult's psychological assessments, including intelligence/cognitive testing. If prior test results are obtained, it is recommended that a clinician trained in psychological testing carefully review the results of the intelligence tests and any other measures of cognitive functioning administered. If cognitive testing results are not available, it is recommended that the interviewee be assessed. Forensic interviews often contain complex questions that can degrade the accuracy of interviewees' responses (Carter, Bottoms, & Levine, 1996; Krackow & Lynn, 2003, 2010). Therefore, this author recommends that cognitive testing results be used, in part, to judge the complexity of questioning that an individual can comprehend; question complexity should be reduced, especially when intelligence is lower.

It is not uncommon to find that a child or adult with low verbal intelligence may not be able to answer basic questions typically asked at the beginning of the forensic interview regarding name, address, current school, persons residing in the home, and so forth. Furthermore, the interviewee may not have a basic understanding of temporal terms such as yesterday or last week, or may not be able to specify dates, which are commonly inquired about in forensic interviews (Friedman, Cederborg, Hultman, Anghagen, & Magnusson, 2010). For example, in one study, the majority of a sample of typically developing children ages 4, 5.5, and 7.5 demonstrated a basic understanding of *yesterday*, but children had significantly more trouble comprehending the present representation of *today* and the future representation of *tomorrow* (Benson, Grossman, & Hanebuth, 1993, as cited in Benson, 1997). In another study, maltreated children, ages 6 to 10, were by and large unable to provide accurate specifics about foster care residences including age (42% accurate) or time of year (month 7%, season 26% accurate) regarding their initial foster placement (Wandrey, Lyon, Quas, & Friedman, 2012). Percentages were similar for their current foster placement. These data demonstrate children's substantial difficulties with temporal terms and highlight the need for interviewers to formulate appropriate developmental expectations about the types of questions children can answer.

Unfortunately, research demonstrates that legal professionals do not adapt their interview styles for adult clients with intellectual disabilities (Kebbell, Hatton, & Johnson, 2004). In one study, the researchers analyzed transcripts of adults testifying during court proceedings. The samples included adults with a broad range of intellectual disabilities and a demographically matched comparison sample (Kebbell et al., 2004; M. R. Kebbell, personal communication, December 12, 2016). This analysis revealed that legal personnel asked all adults a constellation of linguistically complex questions. Presumably, these questions would be difficult for the adults with intellectual disabilities to comprehend, thereby revealing a failure of legal personnel to revise the questions to be congruent with the cognitive abilities of the witness. Included were questions with a double negative construction, questions that were repeated, and questions that were presented in sequence before the witness was given an opportunity to answer (as opposed to presenting questions one at a time). Even more striking are findings that indicate that judges do not intervene to help improve attorney-witness communication when witnesses have an intellectual disability (O'Kelly, Kebbell, Hatton, & Johnson, 2003). These data imply that adaptations to communication within forensic contexts may not naturally occur, but are necessary and important, especially given that ASD is often co-morbid with intellectual deficits (APA, 2013).

In addition, it is critical that the clinician speak with a non-offending primary caregiver to obtain information about the specific diagnostic features of autism displayed by that individual so that the interviewer has the appropriate context to interpret, and if necessary, manage behavior during the interview. For example, is the person likely to echo the interviewer by repeating words or phrases? If so, the repetition of the interviewer's words might be taken as erroneously affirming the interviewer. What is the interviewee's estimated attention span? How long can you talk to the interviewee without providing a break? Are there certain ways to bring the interviewee back to attending that the caregiver has found to be effective? Does the interviewee speak only when spoken to? Does the interviewee engage in pronoun reversal, and if so, which pronouns, and how frequently? Does the interviewee have certain topics that are repeatedly discussed (i.e., restricted interests)? The interviewer may need to modify the interview to take this information into account by not over interpreting echoed words or phrases, by interspersing behavior management techniques using behavior principles within the interview to keep the interviewee's attention, by taking more frequent breaks than in interviews with individuals without ASD, and by engaging in critical reasoning skills that are necessary to formulate follow-up questions if it appears that the interviewee is infusing restricted interests into the interview.

Autobiographical Memory in Children and Adults with ASD

Before providing recommendations regarding how to elicit complete memory reports, this chapter now reviews the literature on autobiographical memory in children and adults with ASD. To date, few studies on autobiographical memory in children with ASD exist. One study with children showed that youth with ASD (ages 11.8–15.8 years) recalled significantly less than a typically developing comparison group matched for mental age (ages 5.1–6.3 years) about activities experienced near the school grounds (Millward, Powell, Messer, & Jordan, 2000). Some of the activities were experienced by the self and some by another child. The findings demonstrated that children with ASD had significantly better recall for activities performed by other children than themselves, whereas the opposite pattern regarding the effects of participation emerged for typically developing youth. These findings replicated in a second study in which the comparison group had moderate learning disabilities, thereby reducing the likelihood that cognitive functioning accounted for the results.

A second study of children with ASD, ages 6 to 14, examined autobiographical memory reports of positive memories, negative memories, and earliest memories (Brown, Morris, Nida, & Baker-Ward, 2012). Results revealed no significant differences in length of memory reports for children with ASD versus comparison participants. However, the memory accounts of youth with ASD included a lower percentage of emotion (e.g., sad, angry), cognitive (e.g., thought, believed), and perceptual words (e.g., saw, heard). According to the authors, youth with ASD may not recognize the importance of including emotion, cognitive, and perceptual information in memory reports.

In another study, researchers analyzed data on a variety of autobiographical memories of children 5 to 10 years old (Bruck, London, Landa, & Goodman, 2007). Compared to children without ASD, 5- to 10-year-old children with ASD exhibited less correct autobiographical recall relevant to current life circumstances (e.g., teacher's name). Significant differences in recall of past autobiographical events were limited to younger children (ages 5.0–8.25 years). Also, younger children with ASD exhibited fewer responses to yes-no questions that were congruent with parental report about autobiographical events (e.g., getting lost on a trip). Children with ASD also exhibited higher error rates to improbable autobiographical event questions. When asked for their open-ended recall of several distant autobiographical events confirmed by a parent and one specific event (going to the hospital) confirmed by a parent, children with ASD recalled less confirmed information than children without ASD. A larger percentage of children with ASD (44%) were unable to recall a time when they had to go to the hospital (presumably an emotional event) compared to children without ASD (4%). There were no significant differences in incorrect recall or recall that could not be confirmed as correct or incorrect by the parent.

This same study also contained a staged event (a magic show) with two subsequent interviews 8 and 12 days following the event. Comparison children reported more correct information about the magic show in open-ended recall than children with ASD. The comparison (vs. ASD) children also responded correctly to more questions in a yes-no format about event components that actually occurred. There was no significant difference in the proportion of incorrect recall when the analyses were limited to nonsuggested event components.

Maras and colleagues examined memory for a staged lab event in adults with ASD (Maras, Memon, Lambrechts, & Bowler, 2013). Dyads, consisting of a research assistant and an adult with or without ASD, performed certain actions on a manikin that was supposedly injured during a car crash (e.g., placed bandages on injury sites). One hour later, participants were interviewed. During the interview, they were asked for their open-ended recall of the event and were asked to identify whether the participant or experimenter performed each action (i.e., a source monitoring task). Participants with and without ASD recalled the equivalent number of details in open-ended recall. However, participants with ASD made more reconstructive errors (i.e., changes in memory for actually occurring event details), but they did not confabulate event details that never occurred. Regardless of the presence or absence of ASD, participants demonstrated superior recall for participant-performed actions compared to experimenter-performed actions in open-ended recall. However, when specifically asked to identify who (participant vs. experimenter) performed each action (i.e., source monitoring questions), participants with ASD made more errors. This increase in errors occurred only in response to the source monitoring questions. When participants included descriptions of actions during open-ended recall, they correctly indicated which person (participant vs. experimenter) performed the action.

A series of two studies that did not involve recall of autobiographical events but is relevant to reports of maltreatment, given that maltreatment is generally considered to be an emotional event, compared the recall of adults with and without ASD for emotionally laden stimuli (Maras, Gaigg, & Bowler, 2012). In Study 1, adults with and without ASD viewed either an emotional or neutral version of a slide show with accompanying verbal audio. The emotional version included several slides with accompanying verbal audio that differed from the neutral version. Both groups of participants recalled the emotional version better than the neutral version. The authors completed further analyses of memories of the emotional version in which they examined the accuracy of recall pertaining to the emotional portion of the slide show versus the non-emotional portions of the slide show. The group with ASD had a nonsignificant tendency to make more errors on recall that pertained to the emotional portion of the slide show than the comparison group, but the effect size was large ($d = 1.00$). Recall was equivalent across groups for the non-emotional portions of the slide show. In Study 2, participants viewed either an emotional or neutral version of a video. Only a small portion in the video differed across conditions. Recall was tested immediately, one hour, and one day after viewing the video. Participants with ASD had a nonsignificant tendency ($p = .06$) to recall less than comparison participants at the one-hour delay; the effect size was in the medium range ($d = .55$). Recall was statistically equivalent at the immediate and one-day interview delays. Participants with ASD made more recall errors during the immediate interview, but not in the two subsequent interviews.

In summary, the previously discussed studies on autobiographical memory in ASD demonstrate that the memory reports of children and adults are generally more impoverished than those of comparison participants. On a rare occasion, group differences are detected by the presence of medium effect sizes when *p* values do not reach significance. In addition, there are a greater number of inaccuracies in the memory reports of participants with ASD, sometimes revealed by effect sizes only, although this finding does not hold on all measures of memory. In some cases, the errors represent reconstructive processes of extant details as opposed to confabulations of nonexistent details. In some investigations, the recall errors do not endure across multiple interviews. However, regardless of whether differences between participants with and without ASD emerge in studies, it is important to note that striving for the most complete recall is desirable because the interviewee cannot determine which aspects of recall might be critical to a case (Fisher & Geiselman, 1992), and any error might be quite problematic in forensic investigations.

Suggestibility in Children and Adults with ASD

The previously discussed study by Bruck and colleagues also examined suggestibility in children ages 5 to 10 with ASD (Bruck et al., 2007). In the first interview about a magic show experienced by children approximately eight days earlier, researchers attempted to infuse suggestive information into the event representations of the children via providing statements about non-occurring event components, followed by asking option-posing questions about the non-occurring event components. These suggestive interviewing techniques were accompanied by interviewer pressure to select a response if the children did not reply. If the child selected a non-occurring event option, the research assistant restated the option (i.e., "You told me that…," Bruck et al., 2007, p. 86). Children were complimented during the course of the interview, but the compliments were not necessarily tied to selecting non-occurring event options. Children with ASD and comparison children did not significantly differ in the likelihood of selecting one of the two non-occurring event components, 67% and 55%, respectively. Approximately four days later, children were interviewed a second time to measure the incorporation of false information presented within Interview 1 into children's event representations. Incorporation of false information was measured in children's open-ended recall and their responses to yes-no questions. There were no significant differences in children's incorporation of false information into open-ended recall (20% ASD children vs. 17% comparison children). However, children with ASD were more suggestible to misleading questions asked in a yes-no format about the previously suggested non-occurring event components, only if the misleading question contained information that was restated by the research assistant. These results imply that children with ASD may only be more suggestible than youth without ASD when certain highly coercive interviewing techniques are used. Further research is needed that continues to examine the issue of suggestibility in children with ASD.

Two studies examining suggestibility in adults with ASD used the Gudjonnson Suggestibility Scales, a measure of suggestibility that includes two scales, one measuring the tendency to acquiesce to the interviewer's suggestions contained in questions about a previously heard story (yield), and the other measuring the tendency to change responses to questions when provided with negative feedback about previous responses (shift) (Gudjonsson, 1997; North, Russell,

& Gudjonsson, 2008). No significant differences in suggestibility between the ASD group and the comparison group emerged. Although these two studies do not show differences in suggestibility, further research using additional methodologies other than the Gudjonsson Suggestibility Scales is needed before firm conclusions can be drawn that no significant differences exist in suggestibility in adults with and without ASD.

Recommendations for Modifications to the Clinical/Forensic Interview

Establishing rapport, managing emotion regulation deficits, and interview expectations

Rapport establishment is typically not an issue in clinical contexts given that traditionally the clinical interviewer has developed rapport with the child or adult client by the time the person makes a disclosure. Although traditional rapport establishment can be attempted with individuals with ASD within forensic interviews, establishing rapport with an interviewee with ASD might be challenging given the higher than average likelihood of diminished interest in social interaction. Rapport establishment may consequently be less important than suggested by prior research with typically developing children (Davis & Bottoms, 2002). Therefore, the interviewer ought to exercise enough flexibility to revise typical expectations regarding the interview including with regard to rapport development. As such, the interviewer is best off resisting the temptation to repeatedly prompt the interviewee to make eye contact, but instead is advised to attempt to keep the interviewee's face in sight in order to facilitate the ability to see the mouth and hear the words being spoken given the likelihood of language/communication deficits. In addition, the interviewer should be careful not to interpret social deficits such as lack of eye contact in the interview as signs of fear or embarrassment in response to questions.

Moreover, emotion regulation abilities, including the ability to regulate responses to sensory stimuli, are often impaired in individuals with ASD (Samson, Huber, & Gross, 2012). Emotion regulation may be related to the ease with which individuals with ASD become overstimulated. Within both clinical/forensic interviews, this can manifest itself in the interviewee becoming overwhelmed by negative emotion or positive emotion (often unrelated to the interview conversation content), which can be expressed, for example, by the interviewee displaying signs of distress, including anger, inattention, or over excitement during the interview. Given this possibility, monitoring the interviewee (via reading the interviewee's cues) is an important task of the interviewer. Consideration should be given to when to engage the interviewee in emotion regulation strategies, such as diaphragmatic breathing or taking a short break, while weighing the pros and cons of doing so, including the timing of disrupting the flow of the interview. If possible, it is best to arrange the interviewing environment, including the décor, to minimize the likelihood of overstimulation.

Due to the difficulty people with ASD experience making transitions, one task of the forensic interviewer is to inform the interviewee as to what to expect during the interview, and if possible, to avoid unplanned occurrences. For example, in forensic interviews, it is not uncommon for the interviewer to leave the room to seek the consultation of other professionals observing the interview (e.g., Brown et al., 2013). If this might occur, preparation of the interviewee is necessary. The interviewer should inform the person from the outset that this is typical, collaboratively figure out what activities the interviewee can engage in while waiting, and if possible, assign a designated professional to engage in these activities with the interviewee, introduce the interviewee to the person who will be that designee, and assure the interviewee that you will return to continue talking with them. Furthermore, the designated professional is advised to prepare the interviewee for the interviewer's return and to help the interviewee transition from the presumably more pleasurable activities that they were engaged in to decrease the chance of protests or temper tantrums. Providing the interviewee with expectations about the interview is typically not needed in clinical interviews, given that disclosure of maltreatment usually occurs within the context of an ongoing therapy session in which natural conversational rules (e.g., asking follow-up questions) would apply following a disclosure.

Eliciting complete memory reports

The potential for incomplete, sparse event reports is of major concern in forensic interviews for typically developing children (e.g., Orbach, Hershkowitz, Lamb, Esplin, & Horowitz, 2000; Saywitz, Geiselman, & Bornstein, 1992). Memory reports may be even more impoverished for youth and adults with ASD given the language deficits/communication deficits apparent in ASD and the lack of spontaneous, reciprocal conversation that can result in truncated responses that lack elaboration. Therefore, the forensic interview may resemble a one question, one sentence exchange. The forensic interviewer may need to use additional prompts to promote further elaboration. The forensic interviewer is advised to take the time to obtain a full event report and to attend to the specific prompts used that appear to be effective in eliciting additional information. After exhausting open-ended recall, instead of asking specific questions that provide detail to the interviewee, the interviewer should use open-ended prompts that inquire about previous statements made by the interviewee (Krackow, 2015; Orbach et al., 2000). Based on the previously reviewed literature, if possible, it is advisable that one or more professionals be designated to observe the interview from a one-way mirror to monitor the complexity of questions and the level of suggestive questioning. Ideally, the forensic interviewer would wear a bug-in-the-ear device to enable the professionals to prompt the interviewer to rephrase a question as well as to suggest additional questions that need to be asked to obtain a complete account of events. The clinical interviewer is advised to use the same questioning techniques as previously noted, but should obtain a more limited account, as previously mentioned, if a forensic interview might follow.

The clinical/forensic interviewer should be attuned to the possibilities of pronoun reversal (e.g., you vs. me) and other language referent deficits such as using contextual words without explaining the context, which can occur even in children and adolescents with high-functioning autism (e.g., "Put it down over there") (Jordon, 1989; Noens & Berckelaer-Onnes, 2005). Jordan (1989) found that youth ages 6.8–16.5 years with ASD regularly confused whether the experimenter or child was the recipient of an experimenter-induced action. This kind of confusion may extend to temporal terms (Noens & Berckelaer-Onnes, 2005). Other research demonstrated that adults with high-functioning ASD/Asperger syndrome more frequently used pronouns that could refer to multiple characters when asked to narrate the events in a storybook (Colle, Baron-Cohen, Wheelwright, & van der Lely, 2008). Therefore, in response to an interviewee's statements, it is necessary for the clinical/forensic interviewer to clarify the specifics of the people involved while remaining attuned to the possibility that continued pronoun reversal may occur. When asking questions about people, this author advises that the clinical/forensic interviewer regularly use the names of individuals in the questions, including the name of the interviewee, as opposed to substituting pronouns for names. Also, given that people with ASD are more susceptible to using neologisms (i.e., generating nonwords) (Jordon, 1989; Noens & Berckelaer-Onnes, 2005), clarifying any unfamiliar terms used by the interviewee may be necessary.

Additional deficits in narrative ability may require the clinical/forensic interviewer to ask follow-up questions to clarify information, although as previously discussed, clinical interviewers need not conduct interviews that are as in-depth as forensic interviewers. Deficits in narrative ability may result, in part, from the interviewee's inability to take the naïve perspective of the interviewer with respect to the determining the information she needs to relay in order for her message to be comprehensible (Krackow & Lynn, 2010; McCabe & Peterson, 1991). Previous research has documented the occurrence of perspective-taking deficits in narratives of typically developing preschool children (Krackow & Lynn, 2010; McCabe & Peterson, 1991). For example, this author reported that preschoolers would recount their memory reports of a game played with a research assistant by saying, "We did Shapes" without describing the game of Shapes (Krackow & Lynn, 2010). Due to deficits in perspective-taking/theory of mind, children and adults with ASD may be particularly susceptible to providing egocentric narratives that lack critical details necessary for understanding the communication (Baron-Cohen, 1990). For example, one study included a task that required perspective-taking ability in order for the adolescent participant to accomplish a goal—receiving an offer of hire by a neighbor to do household tasks (Scheeren, Banerjee, Koot, & Begeer, 2016). The authors documented that adolescents (ages 12–19) with ASD who were questioned using an open-ended prompt, "Can you tell me something about yourself?" for the purpose of convincing an unfamiliar neighbor to hire the adolescent to do household tasks produced fewer positive statements than typically developing peers (Scheeren et al., 2016, p. 651). This may have reflected ASD adolescents' lack of perspective-taking ability regarding the understanding that the hiring neighbor was in search of an employee with particular characteristics.

Consistent with this view of perspective-taking deficits, when adults with ASD were asked to write narrative accounts of a television show, they often provided specific detail about the actors, physical setting, and the resolution, but more often omitted important contextual information compared to participants without ASD (Barnes & Baron-Cohen, 2012). These omissions did not include information related to the main action depicted in the video (i.e., conflict). In another study, adults with ASD produced more impoverished written narratives about a film than comparison adults (Barnes, Lombardo, Wheelwright, & Baron-Cohen, 2009). Unfortunately, the details of what accounts for differences in narrative length are unclear from the coding system. The authors did indicate that there were no significant differences between comparison adults and adults with ASD in references to objects, but adults with ASD used fewer mental state references related to the film actors. Furthermore, adults with ASD used fewer temporal references within their narratives (Barnes et al., 2009; Colle et al., 2008). Based on these patterns of narration, the interviewer may need to put forth additional effort to inquire about and clarify the temporal sequence of events, including simultaneous and successive events. In addition to perspective-taking deficits in narrative contexts, deficits in visual perspective-taking ability, in which a person is asked to intentionally take the perspective of another individual, have been documented in adults with ASD (Conson et al., 2015; Schwarzkopf, Schilbach, Vogeley, & Timmermans, 2014).

Although the numerous cognitive deficits associated with ASD may impact encoding, retrieval, and the reporting of memories, deficits related to the self may be an additional obstacle to the formation of autobiographical memories in persons with ASD (Millward et al., 2000). Research shows important differences in autobiographical memory reports of adults with autism compared to comparison participants without ASD. First, the length of time to retrieve memories is longer in adults with ASD (Crane, Pring, Jukes, & Goddard, 2012), implying that the clinical/forensic interviewer may need to be patient after asking questions, thereby allotting ample time for the interviewee to respond. Second, when asked to provide memories of recently experienced events and those from earlier in life, adults with ASD provide equally well-developed memories of similar lengths, but they are more likely to recount generalized event representations as opposed to specific episodic memories (Crane & Goddard, 2008; Crane, Goddard, & Pring, 2009, 2010). This generalized style of narrating events is problematic in abuse investigations when accounts of specific instances of maltreatment need to be provided.

Therefore, it is necessary to attempt to train individuals with ASD to provide reports of specific episodes of maltreatment (Orbach et al., 2000). This training can be accomplished via education regarding what constitutes a single event episode and practice separating event episodes (Orbach et al., 2000). Research documents that education is necessary but not sufficient to accomplish this goal; practice seems to be particularly important (Crane et al., 2009). Crane et al. provided exemplars of episodic versus repeated events at the beginning of their memory task, but this was not sufficient to obtain reports of episodic events; instead, the adult participants described repeated events. It is important to note two phenomena related to memory recall of repeated events: (a) although interviewers can attempt to obtain specific event instances, some details of one episode may be interjected into another episode; and (b) after events are repeated, specific episodes of events become more difficult to recall; instead, schemata (i.e., representations of what typically happens in an event) form regarding what typically happens in a situation (Hudson, 1990; Hudson, Fivush, & Kuebli, 1992; Hudson & Nelson, 1986).

Minimizing suggestibility

The Bruck et al. (2007) findings documenting increased levels of suggestibility in 5- to 10-year-old children with ASD support the need for this author's already stated recommendations in this chapter, namely, that (a) it is important for interviewers to avoid leading questions when possible, which can be difficult to do, even for experienced interviewers (Warren et al., 1999); and (b) a team approach to the identification of suggestive questions may be helpful. However, the best way for clinical/forensic interviewers to avoid suggestive questions is to obtain the necessary information via nonsuggestive methods of questioning. This can be accomplished, in part, by following a temporally based sequence of questioning in which the interviewer employs a sequence of open-ended questions followed by neutral prompts to elicit an initial account, and use of open-ended questions that inquire about interviewee-provided details (Krackow, 2015; Orbach et al., 2000). Additionally, the Bruck et al. (2007) results imply the need to avoid option-posing questions, or to include a "neither" option, if such questions are absolutely necessary (Krackow, 2015).

Photo lineup identifications

Photo lineup identifications are common in forensic interviews. However, it is recommended that forensic interviewers avoid the use of photo lineups with individuals with ASD until further research is conducted. A large body of research shows that there are impairments in face processing in autistic individuals compared to individuals without ASD (e.g., Dawson, Webb, & McPartland, 2005; Dalton et al., 2005; McPartland, Dawson, Webb, Panagiotides, & Carver, 2004; Monk et al., 2010, 2005; Sterling et al., 2008). More specifically, youth and adults with autism (vs. without ASD) focus less on the eyes, and attend less to the entire face and more to individual facial features in the lower region of the face such as the mouth (Dalton et al., 2005; Dawson et al., 2005; McPartland et al., 2004; Monk et al., 2010, Sterling et al., 2008). As a result of differential face processing, youth with ASD show better inverted face identification, presumably because they attend more to features on the lower half of the face (Dawson et al., 2005). These face recognition deficits are so pronounced that when presented with photos, event-related potential patterns of preschool children with ASD indicated that they can recognize their favorite toy, but they fail to recognize a primary caregiver (mother) (Dawson et al., 2002). Although a complete literature review is beyond the scope of this chapter, suffice to say that brain functioning has been identified in the etiology of face processing disturbances with studies using event-related potential measures showing longer N170 and/or N300 latency in adolescents and adults with ASD and increased activation of the amygdala and fusiform gyrus, implying heightened emotional responding during face processing and bilateral as opposed to unilateral right-brain processing (Dalton et al., 2005; McPartland, et al., 2004; Monk et al., 2010). Furthermore, data imply that perceptual deficits play a role in differential face processing (Bermann, Thomas, & Humphries, 2006). Sasson (2006) suggested that infancy serves as a critical developmental period in which bi-directional influences between social and neurological factors support face recognition skills. Avoidance of faces provides the infant with ASD less experience processing faces, which serves to weaken the neural pathways critical to face processing.

These data may have important implications for the identification of suspects in photo and live lineups, implying that youth and adults with ASD would perform below the level of comparison participants without ASD. It may be possible to improve face identification through training adults with ASD to engage in wholistic face processing, which includes attending to the space between facial features (i.e., configural processing) (Faja et al., 2012). Two studies demonstrate that adolescents and adults can be successfully trained to engage in wholistic face processing (Faja et al., 2012; Faja, Aylward, Bernier, & Dawson, 2008). Unfortunately, only very preliminary data with a small sample of adult participants ($n = 6$ per condition) exist to support the notion that this type of training can improve face identification using a photo lineup array in an eyewitness analog task (Faja et al., 2012). Following training, a small number of participants with ASD ($n = 4$) accurately identified an adult who entered the room during their research session from a photo lineup array compared to ($n = 1$) untrained control participants with ASD, although this difference did not reach statistical significance (Faja et al., 2012).

Source-monitoring questions

Source monitoring, the ability to distinguish how information was acquired (e.g., "Did my mother tell me about that news event or did I read it online?") is important in eyewitness memory cases (Johnson, Hashtroudi, & Lindsay, 1993). A few studies that include adults with ASD have examined source monitoring with discrepant results. In one study, researchers asked participants to distinguish whether the cues were self- or researcher-read, and if a word was (a) seen on the screen, (b) never presented but was imagined via the participant being asked to mentally generate the word, or (c) never presented (Cooper, Plaisted-Grant, Baron-Cohen, & Simons, 2016). Adults with ASD were less accurate on the source-monitoring task regardless of whether the cues were self- or researcher-generated, or seen or imagined.

In another study, adults with ASD identified self- versus research-assistant–performed actions at equivalent levels of accuracy (Zalla et al., 2010). In contrast, Maras and colleagues found that adults with ASD over-attributed performed actions to themselves in free recall (Maras et al., 2013). This did not occur during the more structured phase of the interview. Given the disturbances of sense of self in ASD and difficulties with pronoun reversal, this is not surprising. Therefore, within the context of the clinical/forensic interview, clinical/forensic interviewers should be sure to clarify who completed which actions being described. This should be done in part by asking questions that use proper names instead of pronouns, and in part, by the interviewer engaging in critical thinking about whether descriptions of which person completed which action make conceptual sense. Clinical/forensic interviewers should recognize that errors in source monitoring may remain even after these steps are taken.

Emotion questions

In addition to cognitive and communication deficits, individuals with ASD have deficits in understanding or recognizing emotions (Ashwin, Chapman, Colle, & Baron-Cohen, 2006). These may result in difficulty accurately appraising situations that elicit emotions, which are particularly important in forensic interviews given that following a report of possible maltreatment, interviewers often ask questions about the emotions evoked by the actions of the alleged perpetrator (e.g., "Was a perpetrator angry? Did you feel scared?"). For example, in one study, youth ages 7 to 13 with ASD had difficulty providing exemplars of situations that elicited emotions such as happy, sad, proud, or embarrassed, and a substantial percentage of youth with ASD when asked about positive emotions (e.g., happy, proud) described an event with a happy bent and when asked about negative emotions (e.g., sad, embarrassed) described an event with a sad or angry bent (Losh & Capps, 2006).

Losh and Capps (2006) reported the response of one 12-year-old (male) child with ASD and average verbal intelligence who was asked about a time when he was embarrassed. The following excerpts are verbatim from the evaluator's interview (Losh & Capps, 2006, p. 814). (The evaluator's responses were deemed to be non-substantive, and therefore, were omitted.) After presenting these excerpts, the author provides a critical examination of the child's responses.

EVALUATOR: Can you tell me about a time when you felt embarrassed?

CHILD: When I wore my camouflage to school. I like it [my camouflage] 'cause it's comfortable, but everybody was looking and going "Ha-ha ha-ha! There's camel boy! Camel boy's gonna cry?" They gave me like all these weird nicknames about that.

CHILD: Like when I wore my Navy suit to school, which I really really like because it was a really cold day...when it was about...well, let's put it as, the puddles were frozen.

CHILD: We could ice skate on them at recess.

CHILD: And I wore my wool Navy suit and I had my color bars on it and my um Annapolis pins and like the collar, and my, and everybody...and it's made of wool, and it looked really, really warm'cause it was really really cold.

CHILD: And everybody started making fun of me.

A critical examination of the child's response (made by this author), such as what follows in the next paragraph, is necessary in order to prevent errors in the comprehension of the child's event report. Such an analysis would also reduce the number of missed opportunities to ask additional critical questions in order to gather the necessary contextual information to be able to understand the reported event.

Although the child's response indicated that other children made fun of him for wearing a camouflage outfit to school, he abandoned discussion of the first instance of embarrassment in subsequent exchanges in this conversation, but continued the theme of clothing and added a theme about being cold. However, it was unclear whether these subsequent instances were additional instances similar to the first in which he was ridiculed by children at school, and therefore, felt embarrassed, or instead, whether he was perseverating on the theme of clothing. Although he closed with a statement regarding being ridiculed, it would be erroneous for an interviewer to conclude that the second instance describing wearing a Navy suit reflected an example of being embarrassed due to verbal taunting. If so, additional clarification is needed as to whether the third instance regarding wearing the Navy wool suit with pins described in the conversation reflects the same instance as the second instance or is actually a third instance. Further clarification initiated by an interviewer would be required to make these determinations. It is noteworthy that his response lacked narrative coherence, including the lack of a temporal structure, omitted character names, and included what appears to be extraneous information. It would be important for the interviewer to formulate questions in order to obtain information pertaining to these narrative omissions.

Further examples of emotion processing difficulty can be found in a study by Golan and colleagues, who documented that children with ASD are often unable to select the correct emotion of the actor at the end of a film scene (Golan, Baron-Cohen, & Golan, 2008). Children (ages 8.3–11.8 years) with ASD appeared to have difficulty integrating information to correctly appraise the situation, as depicting deception, for example. The authors point out that youth with ASD had difficulty integrating information from various modalities throughout the entire scene and relied most on recently presented information to make their appraisals. However, an unexplored alternative explanation is a sole preference for recent information exclusive of modality.

Given the emotion processing deficits associated with ASD, the author advises clinical/forensic interviewers to avoid asking about emotions associated with the content of the maltreatment disclosure, regardless of whether the question is asked in a yes-no or option-posing format. That is, interviewers should avoid asking if the alleged defendant's actions scared them, hurt them, or made them feel sad. In addition, youth with ASD have trouble producing emotion words (Moseley et al., 2015), which may impede their ability to respond to open-ended questions about emotion. Therefore, in addition to avoiding yes-no and option-posing questions about emotions, open-ended questions about emotion should be avoided also. Furthermore, these questions are likely irrelevant to forensic interviews regarding child sexual and physical maltreatment given that the act of engaging in child sexual abuse is considered maltreatment regardless of how it felt to the child, and definitions of physical maltreatment are typically based on the appearance of marks on the body. In some instances, child sexual abuse is reported to feel pleasurable at the time. Therefore, obtaining information about actions in order to ascertain the specifics of the alleged event(s) should be the focus of interview. This author advises that the interviewer ask questions in order to clarify the interviewee's intended meaning of each event component (i.e., action).

The interviewer must consider the entire content of the event being described, evaluate what does and does not make sense, and be sure to ask the obvious questions. For example, a child with ASD might report that she was slapped on the face when, in fact, a caregiver brushed the side of her face to get something off of it. Alternatively, family dynamics (e.g., highly conflictual divorce) may have resulted in a coached report of alleged maltreatment.

Possible modifications for individuals with co-morbid ASD and intellectual deficiency

Research has also shown that children with low intelligence are likely to provide less developed memory reports than their peers with average intelligence. For example, in one study, youth (mean age 11 years, approximate range 9–14) diagnosed with intellectual deficiency recalled less information in open-ended recall about a visit to the pediatrician compared to similar-aged children without intellectual deficiency, although their recall was not less accurate (Michel, Gordon, Ornstein, & Simpson, 2000). In a second study, typically developing youth, ages 8- to 11-years-old recalled significantly more correct information in open-ended recall and significantly less incorrect information than same-aged youth with intellectual deficiency (Milne, Sharman, Powell, & Mead, 2013). Although the authors reported that the youth with intellectual deficiency were recruited from a special school serving children with severe intellectual deficiency, the samples of youth were difficult to evaluate given that limited information was gathered by the researchers regarding the intelligence level of both groups. Furthermore, the limited information that was provided implies that some of the typically developing children were of below average intelligence on the only subscale of the intelligence test gathered by the researchers to assess intelligence. Similar findings emerged in adults, namely, that the group with intellectual deficiency recalled less correct information compared to the group without intellectual deficiency, although the amount of incorrect recall was equivalent between groups (Brown & Geiselman, 1990).

Some research examines suggestibility in children and adults with intellectual deficiency. Children (mean age 11 years, approximate range 9–14) with an existing diagnosis of intellectual deficiency demonstrated higher levels of suggestibility to leading questions and elaborated more in open-ended recall in response to suggestive questions than did similar aged-peers with receptive vocabulary scores in the average range (Michel et al., 2000). In a second study, use of an adapted version of the Gudjonnson Suggestibility Scale revealed that adult participants with mild intellectual deficiency were more suggestible in response to misleading questions than those without intellectual disabilities (Milne, Clare, & Bull, 2002). Participants with stronger memories for the video were less suggestible. However, the shift measure of suggestibility revealed that participants with intellectual disabilities did not change responses more often when provided with negative feedback. In a third study, typically developing youth ages 8 to 11 responded more accurately to misleading questions than did children with intellectual deficiency in the same age range (Milne et al., 2013). This is particularly noteworthy in light of the fact that the group with intellectual deficiency responded significantly more often with a "don't know" response, which presumably decreased their error rates to misleading questions.

The previously reviewed studies show that individuals with intellectual deficiency may provide sparser memory reports, sometimes with increases in incorrect recall, and may demonstrate higher levels of suggestibility, leaving open the possibility that co-morbid ASD/intellectual deficiency could compromise memory and increase susceptibility to suggestion more than ASD alone. However, studies are needed to determine whether this is the case, and if so, to elucidate the precise patterns of impact of co-morbid ASD/intellectual deficiency on eyewitness reports. Until such research exists, the recommendations contained herein can be used with caution. However, it is important not to surmise that a specific memory intervention can be transported from populations with intellectual disability to populations with ASD/intellectual deficiency.

Non-empirically supported "child-friendly" interviewing techniques

In this section, the author discusses interviewing techniques that were developed for children with the best of intentions given children's developmental limitations. However, these have not been determined in the research studies to improve children's eyewitness reports. The first such technique is facilitated communication. Given the pronounced verbal expressive deficits associated with ASD, facilitated communication was originally developed with the intention of elevating autistic youth's communication competence (Howlin & Jones, 1996). In facilitated communication, a professional facilitator assists the youth with autistic disorder by physically typing on the youth's behalf (Howlin & Jones, 1996). However, facilitated communication must be avoided in clinical/forensic contexts due to its lack of empirical support and tendency to elicit false allegations. A review of the literature that serves as the basis for this author's recommendation is next discussed.

Siegel (1995) used facilitated communication with two adolescents ages 14 and 15 with ASD with severe intellectual deficiencies to determine whether facilitated communication could be used to elicit accurate information regarding verifiable facts (family composition, composition of household). Siegel concluded that facilitated communication was not effective in eliciting accurate responses to factual questions for either child. Both of these children had a history of making allegations of maltreatment against a parent, and for both children, the allegations made via the use of facilitated communication resulted in removal from the home.

A procedure accepted by an Indiana state court to determine whether a 10-year-old child's sexual abuse allegations were credible provides another example of questionable use of facilitated communication (Bligh & Kupperman, 1993). As part of the procedure, the court allowed facilitated communication between each child and a teacher to be video recorded and analyzed. During the facilitated communication, the child made allegations against the mother's fiancé. Bligh and Kupperman's analysis of the communications revealed that the content of the allegations was unlikely to have originated from the child given indicators that included, but were not limited to, the use of language, semantics, and syntax beyond the level of the child, knowledge beyond the level of the child, and the child's inability to respond to basic factual questions.

It is noteworthy that other authors have used similar observations to document whether a child's communications during facilitated communication are congruent with their developmental skills and abilities (Howlin & Jones, 1996). However, Howlin and Jones used a second evaluative tool in this same case to examine the credibility of a child's statements (mid-adolescent age range). The second tool examined this same child's suggestibility by having the child place cards in piles in response to evaluative judgments ("Nice, Bad/Nasty, Just OK") regarding family members and other objects (e.g., animals) (Howlin & Jones, 1996, p. 106). The child was asked to re-sort the cards into a "yes" versus "no" stack a second time based on whether the responses to the questions were "true" or "false." During the second sorting, an adult was present in order to emit nonverbal cues (e.g., head shake) or verbal feedback (e.g., questioning whether the child was certain of his or her sort). It was then determined whether the child responded in accordance with the adult's cues. The child being evaluated did prove to be sensitive to the cues provided by the adult as indicated by changes in sorting behavior. Based on all of the evidence, the authors concluded that the child they were assessing was unlikely to have experienced the events described in the maltreatment allegations.

Clinical/forensic interviewers might be tempted to use anatomical dolls given the limited verbal capacity of many youth with ASD. In a review of the literature, Krackow (2015) recommended against the use of anatomical or regular dolls for typically developing children ages 5 and under due to research showing high error rates with regard to bodily touch almost immediately after the event, play with the dolls that might be interpreted as sexualized, and difficulty representing the doll as oneself (Bruck, Ceci, & Francouer, 2000; Bruck, Ceci, Francouer, & Renick, 1995; Deloache & Marzolf, 1995; Gordon et al., 1993; see also Lytle, London, & Bruck, 2015, for convergent findings). The author's recommendation applies to the use of dolls whether used before or after a verbal interview given that dolls are not likely to enhance the memory reports of preschool children above and beyond a verbal interview (Bruck et al., 1995, 2000). It should be noted that this author is aware of clinicians who use dolls as part of treatment for youth in which abuse has been founded. This practice could be considered dangerous given the previously mentioned negative impacts to event reporting, including the potential to alter memories for the actually experienced maltreatment.

Convergent evidence across studies suggests that anatomical dolls may assist older children in reporting genital touch that actually occurred (within medical procedures) (Goodman, Quas, Batterman-Faunce, Riddlesburg, & Kuhn 1997; Saywitz, Goodman, Nicholas, & Moan, 1996). It was not until the 7- to 10-year-old age range (vs. 3- to 6-year-old age range) that children more frequently reported genital touch using anatomical dolls (75% compared to 25% when interviewed verbally), *and* anatomical dolls increased correct recall above and beyond a verbal interview with little trade-off for increased incorrect information (92.5%) (Goodman et al., 1997). In another study, the benefits of anatomical dolls extended downward to younger children; anatomical dolls helped 5- and 7-year-old children (girls) accurately report genital touch (86% reported accuracy vs. 22% verbal report only, 2.86% false positive with doll) that occurred within a medical examination (Saywitz et al., 1996).

Additional interview methods designed for use with children are not recommended for use with children with or without ASD. Krackow (2015) recommended against the use of human figure drawings based on findings documented by Bruck (2009) (see also Lytle et al., 2015, for convergent findings). This author (Krackow, 2015) has recommended against clinical/forensic interviewers asking children to draw about traumatic events that might require accurate reporting in legal contexts because it is difficult if not impossible to use drawing without accompanying suggestion as the interview's suggestions might become incorporated into the child's memory reports (Bruck, Melnyk, & Ceci, 2000). This author does not recommend that clinical/forensic interviewers use dolls or human figure drawings with children with ASD, regardless of their age, given the above cited concerns, along with the poor perspective-taking abilities of youth with ASD.

Avoiding sign language in forensic interviews is also recommended. Research shows that fluency in sign language is rare in youth with ASD. Although children with ASD can be taught to make basic requests via the use of sign language, a large body of research indicates that acquisition of sign language to the level of full conversation as opposed to single-word representations is not likely for the majority of youth with ASD (Tincani, 2004). In one study, for example, three children approximately aged 15 required 69, 33, and 53 sessions, respectively, to acquire a total of 20 signs in basic semantic categories (foods, clothes), although rate of learning novel signs did increase substantially over time (Carr, Binkoff, Kologinsky, & Eddy, 1978). In the rare event that a child with ASD is fluent in sign language, it is advised that the forensic interview be conducted in sign language as opposed to including an interpreter. It is currently unclear how the use of interpreters influences the quantity and accuracy of eyewitness accounts.

Empirically supported interviews

The revised cognitive interview (Fisher & Geiselman, 1992) is used with adults and children nationally and internationally, and is among the most empirically supported forensic interviews. It includes the memory components of mentally or physically reinstating the context of the crime prior to reporting everything that the individual recalls without censoring information, forward recall, reverse-order recall, and recalling the event from the perspective of other people present at the crime scene. However, the perspective-taking deficits associated with ASD (Conson et al., 2015; Schwarzkopf et al., 2014) as well as the inability to use mental imagery (Maras, Wimmer, Robinson,

& Bowler, 2014) may reduce the effectiveness of the context reinstatement backdrop and perspective-taking components of the revised cognitive interview. Deficits in executive functioning in ASD (White, 2013) may present difficulties with reverse-order recall. The revised cognitive interview is hypothesized to interact too heavily with the deficits associated with ASD regardless of whether the DSM-4 or DSM-5 criteria are used as a basis for diagnosis. Therefore, it is not surprising that the limited extant research shows that the revised cognitive interview did not improve the memory reports of adult participants with ASD (Maras & Bowler, 2010). In fact, not only did the revised cognitive interview fail to increase accurate recall, but its use increased inaccurate recall in adults with ASD (Maras & Bowler, 2010). Therefore, at the current time, this author does not recommend that the revised cognitive interview be used with people with ASD. Future research should explore whether this tool is effective for subsets of people with ASD (i.e., Asperger syndrome) in which language skills and intelligence are typically at least in the average range.

One study examined use of context reinstatement, a component of the revised cognitive interview, in adults with ASD (Maras & Bowler, 2012). The study showed a nonsignificant trend ($p = .07$) for a combination of mental and physical context reinstatement (i.e., returning to the room in which the to-be-remembered event was experienced) to improve memory reports for a group with ASD as opposed to mental context reinstatement alone. However, these data are difficult to interpret without the inclusion of no-context reinstatement comparison groups with and without ASD.

Developmental narrative elaboration (formally narrative elaboration) teaches children as young as age 3 to recall events using reminders to include the people, actions, event setting, conversation, and emotion via the use of cue cards or verbal means, and it includes an optional component designed to diminish suggestibility (Saywitz & Camparo, 2014; Saywitz & Snyder, 1996). To date, narrative elaboration is the most promising interview producing large increases in correct information without trade-off of increases in incorrect information (see Krackow, 2015, for a review). To this author's knowledge, developmental narrative elaboration/narrative elaboration has not been tested with children with ASD. However, future research should examine the efficacy of developmental narrative elaboration with ASD. In the interim, based on the emotion deficits associated with ASD, this author recommends that interviewers using developmental narrative elaboration eliminate the emotion component, although future research should test its use empirically and should include analyses of total correct and incorrect information, and an analysis that dismantles recall by specific event detail categories (i.e., people, actions, event setting, conversation, and emotion).

The National Institute of Child Health and Human Development (NICHD) investigative protocol (Orbach et al., 2000) begins with rapport establishment, followed by education and practice separating event episodes, free recall followed by questions designed to build on the child's responses, and when necessary, allows for the use of option-posing questions, although elsewhere this author has recommended that a "neither" option be provided (Krackow, 2015). Although this interview is empirically based, its effectiveness has been evaluated primarily in field studies of actual child sexual abuse investigations as opposed to first being evaluated in laboratory studies before disseminating the interview to the field. A number of the interviewing recommendations contained within this chapter are consistent with this protocol, although no published data speak to its effectiveness with youth with ASD.

This author recommends that the NICHD protocol be evaluated in youth with ASD using laboratory designs that will enable researchers to determine how the interview impacts correct and incorrect recall. Until that point, it is not recommended that forensic interviews use the NICHD protocol with youth with ASD.

Cultural Considerations

Culture may influence the perception and reporting of maltreatment in numerous ways. Definitions of maltreatment, parenting practices related to maltreatment, degree of family acculturation, and perceptions of disabilities may all show cultural variation (Blacher & McIntyre, 2006; Chang, Rhee, & Weaver, 2006; Rhee, Chang, Weaver, & Wong, 2008). It is important to be cognizant of the fact that cultural considerations play a role in high-quality assessment of maltreatment and in the assistance that families might need if maltreatment allegations are supported. First, we must consider that the implications of founded maltreatment might differentially impact families from different cultures. In cases in which abuse is alleged against a family member living in the household, families in some cultural circumstances may be plagued by greater uncertainty and stress than other families. If so, the child's uncertainty about whether to disclose maltreatment may be heightened, which could lead to less consistency in reporting maltreatment, including retractions, which could spill over to the forensic interview. The family's current perceptions of mental health and related professionals may be impacted by the previously experienced autism diagnostic process. Previous literature shows cultural disparities with regard to the ASD diagnostic process (Mandell, Ittenbach, Levy, & Pinto-Martin, 2007; Mandell et al., 2009). Additionally, lack of trust in mental health professionals is often heightened in non-Caucasian families, thereby serving as a barrier to relationship development, which is a major determinant of child welfare decision-making (Azar & Goff, 2007).

El-Ghoroury and Krackow (2012) previously reviewed the literature on racial and ethnic disparities in the diagnosis of ASD and proposed a model of culturally sensitive assessment. Given that non-Caucasian youth tend to be diagnosed with ASD at a later age, and therefore, are more likely than Caucasian children to miss the critical intervention period, youth with ASD who are from diverse cultural backgrounds might be lower functioning than those from mainstream groups (El-Ghoroury & Krackow, 2012), thereby making forensic interviewing more challenging. Nevertheless, it is necessary for the interviewer to strive to understand the context of the child's statements, and perhaps, discuss with the forensic interviewing team their interpretations during the interviews so that bias does not ensue and the necessary questions are asked. Azar and Goff (2007) highlighted the role of implicit cognitive biases in interactions and decision-making, such as attributing the situation to an individual's characteristics versus a situational context. It is through these biased lenses that a forensic interviewer might fail to consider important contextual information about a situation and be more likely to find that an individual maltreated a child or alternatively might neglect to appraise a situation as maltreatment. An interviewer's cognitive biases may be more likely to emerge under stressful circumstances, such as in a forensic interviewing situation, thereby rendering information processing more difficult (Azar & Goff, 2007). The literature on the intersection of cultural biases and social information processing combined with the literature on interviewers' inability to record and accurately recollect whether they asked leading questions (Lamb, Orbach, Sternberg, Hershkowitz, & Horowitz, 2000) argues for the team approach to forensic interviewing. This approach is often used in child advocacy centers in which a team of observers can discuss the interview behind a one-way mirror as it is unfolding.

Closing Remarks

In closing, it is incumbent on mental health professionals, other mandated reporters, and forensic interviewers to rise to the challenge of using interviewing procedures that serve to balance the protection of children and adults from further maltreatment, if, in fact, maltreatment has occurred, and the protection of families and society from the negative ramifications that can ensue from obtaining false reports of maltreatment. The former can include inadequate physical and emotional protection of a child who has been maltreated as well as potential risk to other children in or outside of the home. The latter can include the possible break-up of families that might result in out-of-home placement of children, disruptions in the child's significant relationships, loss of freedom for adults, and the possible harmful effects associated with false memories of maltreatment.

Take-Home Points

- Overall, autobiographical memory reports are less elaborate in children and adults with ASD.
- Limited existing research shows that coercive interviewing techniques can have an equivalent negative impact on children with and without ASD (Bruck et al., 2007). However, interviewer review of non-occurring events (i.e., telling children that they said X happened when the child had not said so) resulted in greater suggestibility in children with ASD (Bruck et al., 2007). To date, studies (albeit limited in number) show equivalent levels of suggestibility in adults with and without ASD (Maras & Bowler, 2012; North, Russell, & Gudjonsson, 2008).
- The cognitive, social, and emotional deficits associated with ASD require that clinical and forensic interviewers modify their interview approaches when interviewing children and adults with ASD.
- These modifications include obtaining additional background information on the interviewee's specific profile of ASD symptoms, and obtaining previous reports of or assessing current intellectual/cognitive functioning.
- Questions should be asked in a developmentally appropriate manner while taking into account the interviewee's level of cognitive functioning. Use of pronouns within questions should be minimized. Instead, questions should substitute proper names for pronouns. Questions about emotions should be avoided.
- Interviewers are advised to use critical thinking skills to assess the context of the alleged maltreatment. Doing so will often lead the interviewer to ask additional questions. Tracking the conversation between interviewer and interviewee and entertaining alternative explanations of the meaning of the interviewee's statements will help to maximize the interviewer's understanding of the interviewee's report.

- Anatomical and regular dolls, human figure drawings, regular drawings, facilitated communication, and sign language should be avoided. Instead, use of open-ended questions with open-ended follow-up questions that build on the individual's previous statements should be used.

Empirically supported interviews shown to be effective for typically developing children/adults and children/adults with intellectual deficiency should not be used with children with ASD until empirically validated with this population.

Author Note

Thank you to Nabil Hassan El-Ghoroury for suggesting inclusion of a section on facilitated communication.

References

American Psychiatric Association. (2013). *Diagnostic and Statistical Manual of Mental Disorders* (Fifth ed.). Arlington, VA: American Psychiatric Association.

Ashwin, C., Chapman, E., Colle, L., & Baron-Cohen, S. (2006). Impaired recognition of negative basic emotions in autism: A test of the amygdala theory. *Social Neuroscience*, *1*(3–4), 349–363. doi:10.1080/17470910601040772

Azar, S. T., & Goff, P. E. (2007). Can science help Solomon? Child maltreatment cases and the potential for racial and ethnic bias in decision making. *St. John's Law Review*, 533–573.

Barnes, J. L., & Baron-Cohen, S. (2012). The big picture: Storytelling ability in adults with autism spectrum conditions. *Journal of Autism & Developmental Disorders*, *42*(8), 1557–1565. doi:10.1007/s10803-011-1388-5

Barnes, J. L., Lombardo, M. V., Wheelwright, S., & Baron-Cohen, S. (2009). Moral dilemmas film task: A study of spontaneous narratives by individuals with autism spectrum conditions. *Autism Research*, *2*(3), 148–156. doi:10.1002/aur.79

Baron-Cohen, S. (1990). Autism: A specific cognitive disorder of "mind-blindness." *International Review of Psychiatry*, *2*(1), 81–90. doi:10.3109/09540269009028274

Behrmann, M., Thomas, C., & Humphreys, K. (2006). Seeing it differently: Visual processing in autism. *Trends in Cognitive Sciences*, *10*(6), 258–264. doi:10.1016/j.tics.2006.05.001

Benson, J. B. (1997). The development of planning: It' about time. In S. L. Friedman, E. K. Scholnick (Eds.), *The developmental psychology of planning: Why, how, and when do we plan?* (pp. 43–75). Mahwah, NJ: Lawrence Erlbaum Associates Publishers.

Blacher, J., & McIntyre, L. L. (2006). Syndrome Specificity and behavioural disorder in young adults with intellectual disability: Cultural differences in family impact. *Journal of Intellectual Disability Research*, *50*(3), 184–198. doi:10.1111/j.1365-2788.2005.00768.x

Bligh, S., & Kupperman, P. (1993). Facilitated communication evaluation procedure accepted in a court case. *Journal of Autism & Developmental Disorders*, *23*(3), 553–557.

Brown, C. L., & Geiselman, E. R. (1990). Eyewitness testimony of mentally retarded: Effect of the cognitive interview. *Journal of Police & Criminal Psychology*, *6*(2), 14–22.

Brown, B. T., Morris, G., Nida, R. E., & Baker-Ward, L. (2012). Making experience personal: Internal states language in the memory narratives of children with and without Asperger's disorder. *Journal of Autism & Developmental Disorders*, *42*(3), 441–446. doi:10.1007/s10803-011-1246-5

Brown, D. A., Lamb, M. E., Lewis, C. N., Pipe, M.-E., Orbach, Y., & Wolfman, M. (2013). Evaluating the NICHD Investigative Interview Protocol: A laboratory study. *Journal of Experimental Psychology: Applied, 19*, 367–382.

Browne, A., & Finkelhor, D. (1987). Impact of child sexual abuse: A review of the research. *Annual Progress in Child Psychiatry & Child Development, 55*(4), 555–584.

Bruck, M. (2009). Human figure drawings and children's recall of touching. *Journal of Experimental Psychology: Applied, 15*(4), 361–374. doi:10.1037/a0017120

Bruck, M., Ceci, S. J., & Francoeur, E. (2000). Children's use of anatomically detailed dolls to report genital touching in a medical examination: Developmental and gender comparisons. *Journal of Experimental Psychology: Applied, 6*(1), 74–83. doi:10.1037/1076-898X.6.1.74

Bruck, M., Ceci, S. J., Francouer, E., & Renick. A. (1995). Anatomically detailed dolls do not facilitate preschoolers' reports of a pediatric examination involving genital touching. *Journal of Experimental Psychology: Applied, 1*(2), 95–109.

Bruck, M., London, K., Landa, R., & Goodman, J. (2007). Autobiographical memory and suggestibility in children with ASD. *Development & Psychopathology, 19*(1), 73–95. doi:10.1017/S0954579407070058

Bruck, M., Melnyk, L., & Ceci, S. J. (2000). Draw it again Sam: The effect of drawing on children's suggestibility and source monitoring ability. *Journal of Experimental Child Psychology, 77*(3), 169–196. doi:10.1006/jecp.1999.2560

Carr, E. G., Binkoff, J. A., Kologinsky, E., & Eddy, M. (1978). Acquisition of sign language by autistic children: I. Expressive labelling. *Journal of Applied Behavior Analysis, 11*(4), 489–501. doi:10.1901/jaba.1978.11-489

Carter, C. A., Bottoms, B. L., & Levine, M. (1996). Linguistic and socioemotional influences on the accuracy of children's reports. *Law & Human Behavior, 20*(3), 335–358. doi:10.1007/BF01499027

Chang, J., Rhee, S., & Weaver, D. (2006). Characteristics of child abuse in immigrant Korean families and correlates of placement decisions. *Child Abuse & Neglect, 30*(8), 881–891. doi:10.1016/j.chiabu.2006.03.002

Colle, L., Baron-Cohen, S., Wheelwright, S., & van der Lely, H. J. (2008). Narrative discourse in adults with high-functioning autism or Asperger syndrome. *Journal of Autism & Developmental Disorders, 38*(1), 28–40. doi:10.1007/s10803-007-0357-5

Conson, M., Mazzarella, E., Esposito, D., Grossi, D., Marino, N., Massagli, A., & Frolli, A. (2015). "Put myself into your place": Embodied simulation and perspective taking in ASDs. *Autism Research, 8*(4), 454–466. doi:10.1002/aur.1460

Cooper, R. A., Plaisted-Grant, K. C., Baron-Cohen, S., & Simons, J. S. (2016). Reality monitoring and metamemory in adults with autism spectrum conditions. *Journal of Autism & Developmental Disorders, 46*(6), 2186–2198. doi:10.1007/s10803-016-2749-x

Crane, L., & Goddard, L. (2008). Episodic and semantic autobiographical memory in adults with ASDs. *Journal of Autism & Developmental Disorders, 38*(3), 498–506. doi:10.1007/s10803-007-0420-2

Crane, L., Goddard, L., & Pring, L. (2009). Specific and general autobiographical knowledge in adults with ASDs: The role of personal goals. *Memory, 17*(5), 557–576. doi:10.1080/09658210902960211

Crane, L., Goddard, L., & Pring, L. (2010). Self-defining and everyday autobiographical memories in adults with ASDs. *Journal of Autism & Developmental Disorders, 40*(3), 383–391. doi:10.1007/s10803-009-0875-4

Crane, L., Pring, L., Jukes, K., & Goddard, L. (2012). Patterns of autobiographical memory in adults with ASD. *Journal of Autism & Developmental Disorders, 42*(10), 2100–2112. doi:10.1007/s10803-012-1459-2

Dalton, K. M., Nacewicz, B. M., Johnstone, T., Schaefer, H. S., Gernsbacher, M. A., Goldsmith, H. H., ... Davidson, R. J. (2005). Gaze fixation and the neural circuitry of face processing in autism. *Nature Neuroscience, 8*(4), 519–526.

Davis, S. L., & Bottoms, B. L. (2002). Effects of social support on children's eyewitness reports: A test of the underlying mechanism. *Law & Human Behavior*, *26*(2), 185–215. doi:10.1023/A:1014692009941

Dawson, G., Carver, L., Meltzoff, A. N., Panagiotides, H., McPartland, J., & Webb, S. J. (2002). Neural correlates of face and object recognition in young children with ASD, developmental delay and typical development. *Child Development*, *73*(3), 700–717. doi:10.1111/1467-8624.00433

Dawson, G., Webb, S. J., & McPartland, J. (2005). Understanding the nature of face processing impairment in Autism: Insights from behavioral and electrophysiological studies. *Developmental Neuropsychology*, *27*(3), 403–424. doi:10.1207/s15326942dn2703_6

DeLoache, J. S., & Marzolf, D. P. (1995). The use of dolls to interview young children: Issues of symbolic representation. *Journal of Experimental Child Psychology*, *60*(1), 155–173. doi:10.1006/jecp.1995.1036

El-Ghoroury, N. H., & Krackow, E. (2011). A developmental-behavioral approach to outpatient psychotherapy with children with autism spectrum disorders. *Journal of Contemporary Psychotherapy*, *41*(1), 11–17. doi:10.1007/s10879-010-9155-z

El-Ghoroury, N. H., & Krackow, E. (2012). Enhancing the identification of ASDs via a model of culturally sensitive childhood assessment. *Professional Psychology: Research and Practice*, *43*(3), 249–255. doi:10.1037/a0027354

Faja, S., Aylward, E., Bernier, R., & Dawson, G. (2008). Becoming a face expert: A computerized face-training program for high-functioning individuals with Autism spectrum disorders. *Developmental Neuropsychology*, *33*(1), 1–24. doi:10.1080/87565640701729573

Faja, S., Webb, S. J., Jones, E., Merkle, K., Kamara, D., Bavaro, J., ... Dawson, G. (2012). The effects of face expertise training on the behavioral performance and brain activity of adults with high functioning ASDs. *Journal of Autism & Developmental Disorders*, *42*(2), 278–293. doi:10.1007/s10803-011-1243-8

Finkelhor, D. (1990). Early and long-term effects of child sexual abuse: An update. *Professional Psychology: Research & Practice*, *21*(5), 325–330. doi:10.1037/0735-7028.21.5.325

Fisher, R. P., & Geiselman, R. E. (1992). *Memory-enhancing techniques for investigative interviewing: The cognitive interview*. Springfield, IL: Charles C. Thomas, Publisher.

Friedman, W. J., Cederborg, A., Hultman, E., Änghagen, O., & Magnusson, K. F. (2010). Children's memory for the duration of a paediatric consultation. *Applied Cognitive Psychology*, *24*(4), 545–556.

Golan, O., Baron-Cohen, S., & Golan, Y. (2008). The "Reading the Mind in Films" Task [Child version]: Complex emotion and mental state recognition in children with and without autism spectrum conditions. *Journal of Autism & Developmental Disorders*, *38*(8), 1534–1541. doi:10.1007/s10803-007-0533-7

Goodman, G. S., Quas, J. A., Batterman-Faunce, J. M., Riddlesberger, M. M., & Kuhn, J. (1997). Children's reactions to and memory for a stressful event: Influences of age, anatomical dolls, knowledge, and parental attachment. *Applied Developmental Science*, *1*(2), 54–75. doi:10.1207/s1532480xads0102_1

Gordon, B. N., Ornstein, P. A., Nida, R. E., Follmer, A., Crenshaw, M. C., & Albert, G. (1993). Does the use of dolls facilitate children's memory of visits to the doctor? *Applied Cognitive Psychology*, *7*(6), 459–474. doi:10.1002/acp.2350070602

Gudjonsson, G. H. (1997). *The Gudjonsson Suggestibility Scales manual*. Hove, England. Psychology Press.

Hanson, R. F., & Spratt, E. G. (2000). Reactive attachment disorder: What we know about the disorder and implications for treatment. *Child Maltreatment*, *5*(2), 137–145. doi:1177/1077559500005002005

Howlin, P., & Jones, D. H. (1996). An assessment approach to abuse allegations made through facilitated communication. *Child Abuse & Neglect*, *20*(2), 103–110. doi:10.1016/0145-2134(95)00121-2

Hudson, J. A. (1990). Constructive processing in children's event memory. *Developmental Psychology*, *26*(2), 180–187. doi:10.1037/0012-1649.26.2.180

Hudson, J. A., Fivush, R., & Kuebli, J. (1992). Scripts and episodes: The development of event memory. *Applied Cognitive Psychology*, *6*(6), 483–505. doi:10.1002/acp.2350060604

Hudson, J., & Nelson, K. (1986). Repeated encounters of a similar kind: Effects of familiarity on children's autobiographic memory. *Cognitive Development*, *1*(3), 253–271. doi:10.1016/S0885-2014(86)80004-1

Johnson, M. K., Hashtroudi, S., & Lindsay, D. S. (1993). Source monitoring. *Psychological Bulletin*, *114*(1), 3–28. doi:10.1037/0033-2909.114.1.3

Jordan, R. R. (1989). An experimental comparison of the understanding and use of speaker-addressee personal pronouns in autistic children. *British Journal of Disorders of Communication*, *24*(2), 169–179. doi:10.3109/13682828909011954

Kebbell, M. R., Hatton, C., & Johnson, S. D. (2004). Witnesses with intellectual disabilities in court: What questions are asked and what influence do they have? *Legal & Criminological Psychology*, *9*(1), 23–35. doi:10.1348/135532504322776834

Kendall-Tackett, K. A., Williams, L. M., & Finkelhor, D. (1993). Impact of sexual abuse on children: A review and synthesis of recent empirical studies. *Psychological Bulletin*, *113*(1), 164–180. doi:10.1037/0033-2909.113.1.164

Krackow, E. (2015). Clinical interviewing in child sexual abuse cases. In R. Cautin & S. O. Lilienfeld (Eds.), *The encyclopedia of clinical psychology* (pp. 588–594). New York, NY: Wiley-Blackwell. doi:10.1002/9781118625392.wbecp395

Krackow, E., & Lynn, S. J. (2003). Is there touch in the game of Twister®? The effects of innocuous touch and suggestive questions on children's eyewitness memory. *Law & Human Behavior*, *27*(6), 589–604. doi:10.1023/B:LAHU.0000004888.52210.35

Krackow, E., & Lynn, S. J. (2010). Event report training: An examination of the efficacy of a new intervention to improve children's eyewitness reports. *Applied Cognitive Psychology*, *24*(6), 868–884. doi:10.1002/acp.1594

Lamb, M. E., Orbach, Y., Sternberg, K. J., Hershkowitz, I., & Horowitz, D. (2000). Accuracy of investigators' verbatim notes of their forensic interviews with alleged child abuse victims. *Law & Human Behavior*, *24*(6), 699–708. doi:10.1023/A:1005556404636

Leichtman, M. D., & Ceci, S. J. (1995). The effects of stereotypes and suggestions on preschoolers' reports. *Developmental Psychology*, *31*(4), 568–578. doi:10.1037/0012-1649.31.4.568

Lilienfeld, S. O., & Lynn, S. J. (2015). Dissociative identity disorder: A contemporary scientific perspective. In S. O. Lilienfeld, S. J. Lynn, & J. M. Lohr (Eds.), *Science and pseudoscience in clinical psychology* (2nd Ed.) (pp. 113–152). New York, NY: Guilford Press.

Loftus, E. F. (1994). The repressed memory controversy. *American Psychologist*, *49*(5), 443–445. doi:10.1037/0003-066X.49.5.443.b

Loftus, E. F. (1997). Repressed memory accusations: Devastated families and devastated patients. *Applied Cognitive Psychology*, *11*(1), 25–30. doi:10.1002/(SICI)1099-0720(199702)11:1<25::AID-ACP452>3.0.CO;2-J

Losh, M., & Capps, L. (2006). Understanding of emotional experience in autism: Insights from the personal accounts of high-functioning children with autism. *Developmental Psychology*, *42*(5), 809–18.

Lynn, S. J., Krackow, E., Loftus, E. F., Locke, T. G., & Lilienfeld, S. O. (2015). Constructing the past: Problematic memory recovery techniques in psychotherapy. In S. O. Lilienfeld, S. J. Lynn, & J. M. Lohr (Eds.), *Science and pseudoscience in clinical psychology* (2nd ed., pp. 210–244). New York, NY: Guilford Press.

Lytle, N., London, K., & Bruck, M. (2015). Young children's ability to use two-dimensional and three-dimensional symbols to show placements of body touches and hidden objects. *Journal of Experimental Child Psychology*, *134*, 30–42. doi:10.1016/j.jecp.2015.01.010

McCabe, A., & Peterson, C. (1991). *Developing narrative structure.* Hillsdale, NJ, England: Lawrence Erlbaum Associates, Inc.

McPartland, J., Dawson, G., Webb, S. J., Panagiotides, H., & Carver, L. J. (2004). Event-related brain potentials reveal anomalies in temporal processing of faces in ASD. *Journal of Child Psychology & Psychiatry, 45*(7), 1235–1245. doi:10.1111/j.1469-7610.2004.00318.x

Mandell, D. S., Ittenbach, R. F., Levy, S. E., & Pinto-Martin, J. A. (2007). Disparities in diagnoses received prior to a diagnosis of autism spectrum disorder. *Journal of Autism & Developmental Disorders, 37*(9), 1795–1802. doi:10.1007/s10803-006-0314-8

Mandell, D. S., Wiggins, L. D., Carpenter, L. A., Daniels, J., DiGuiseppi, C., Durkin, M. S., … Kirby, R. S. (2009). Racial/ethnic disparities in the identification of children with autism spectrum disorders. *American Journal of Public Health, 99*(3), 493–498. doi:10.2105/AJPH.2007.131243

Mannarino, A. P., Cohen, J. A., Deblinger, E., Runyon, M. K., & Steer, R. A. (2012). Trauma-focused Cognitive-Behavioral Therapy for children: Sustained impact of treatment 6 and 12 months later. *Child Maltreatment, 17*(3), 231–241. doi:10.1177/107755951245178

Maras, K. L., & Bowler, D. M. (2010). The cognitive interview for eyewitnesses with ASD. *Journal of Autism & Developmental Disorders, 40*(11), 1350–1360. doi:10.1007/s10803-010-0997-8

Maras, K. L., & Bowler, D. M. (2012). Context reinstatement effects on eyewitness memory in ASD. *British Journal of Psychology, 103*(3), 330–342. doi:10.1111/j.2044-8295.2011.02077.x

Maras, K. L., Gaigg, S. B., & Bowler, D. M. (2012). Memory for emotionally arousing events over time in ASD. *Emotion, 12*(5), 1118–1128. doi:10.1037/a002667

Maras, K. L., Memon, A., Lambrechts, A., & Bowler, D. M. (2013). Recall of a live and personally experienced eyewitness event by adults with ASD. *Journal of Autism & Developmental Disorders, 43*(8), 1798–1810. doi:10.1007/s10803-012-1729-z

Maras, K. L., Wimmer, M. C., Robinson, E. J., & Bowler, D. M. (2014). Mental imagery scanning in autism spectrum disorder. *Research in Autism Spectrum Disorders, 8*(10), 1416–1423. doi:10.1016/j.rasd.2014.07.003

Michel, M. K., Gordon, B. N., Ornstein, P. A., & Simpson, M. A. (2000). The abilities of children with mental retardation to remember personal experiences: Implications for testimony. *Journal of Clinical Child Psychology, 29*(3), 453–463. doi:10.1207/S15374424JCCP2903_16

Millward, C., Powell, S., Messer, D., & Jordan, R. (2000). Recall for self and other in autism: Children's memory for events experienced by themselves and their peers. *Journal of Autism & Developmental Disorders, 30*(1), 15–28. doi:10.1023/A:1005455926727

Milne, R., Clare, I. H., & Bull, R. (2002). Interrogative suggestibility among witnesses with mild intellectual disabilities: The use of an adaptation of the GSS. *Journal of Applied Research in Intellectual Disabilities, 15*(1), 8–17. doi:10.1046/j.1360 2322.2001.00096.x

Milne, R., Sharman, S. J., Powell, M. B., & Mead, S. (2013). Assessing the effectiveness of the cognitive interview for children with severe intellectual disabilities. *International Journal of Disability, Development & Education, 60*(1), 18–29. doi:10.1080/1034912X.2013.757137

Monk, C. S., Weng, S., Wiggins, J. L., Kurapati, N., Louro, H. C., Carrasco, M., … Lord, C. (2010). Neural circuitry of emotional face processing in autism spectrum disorders. *Journal of Psychiatry & Neuroscience, 35*(2), 105–114. doi:10.1503/jpn.090085

Moseley, R. L., Shtyrov, Y., Mohr, B., Lombardo, M. V., Baron-Cohen, S., & Pulvermüller, F. (2015). Lost for emotion words: What motor and limbic brain activity reveals about autism and semantic theory. *Neuroimage, 104*, 413–422. doi:10.1016/j.neuroimage.2014.09.046

Noens, I. J., & van Berckelaer-Onnes, I. A. (2005). Captured by details: Sense-making, language and communication in autism. *Journal of Communication Disorders, 38*(2), 123–141. doi:10.1016/j.jcomdis.2004.06.002

North, A. S., Russell, A. J., & Gudjonsson, G. H. (2008). High functioning ASDs: An investigation of psychological vulnerabilities during interrogative interview. *Journal of Forensic Psychiatry & Psychology, 19*(3), 323–334. doi:10.1080/14789940701871621

O'Kelly C., Kebbell, M., Hatton C., & Johnson S. (2003). Judicial intervention in court cases involving witnesses with and without learning disabilities. *Legal & Criminological Psychology*, *8*(2), 229–240.

Orbach, Y., Hershkowitz, I., Lamb, M. E., Esplin, P. W., & Horowitz, D. (2000). Assessing the value of structured protocols for forensic interviews of alleged child abuse victims. *Child Abuse & Neglect*, *24*(6), 733–752. doi:10.1016/S0145-2134(00)00137-X

Ost, J., Wright, D. B., Easton, S., Hope, L., & French, C. C. (2013). Recovered memories, satanic abuse, dissociative identity disorder and false memories in the UK: A survey of clinical psychologists and hypnotherapists. *Psychology, Crime & Law*, *19*(1), 1–19. doi:10.1080/1068316X.2011.598157

Polusny, M. A., & Follette, V. M. (1995). Long-term correlates of child sexual abuse: Theory and review of the empirical literature. *Applied & Preventive Psychology*, *4*(3), 143–166. doi:10.1016/S0962-1849(05)80055-1

Rady Children's Hospital San Diego. (2012). *The California Child Abuse & Neglect Reporting Law*. Retrieved from: http://mandatedreporterca.com/images/pub132.pdf

Rhee, S., Chang, J., Weaver, D., & Wong, D. (2008). Child maltreatment among immigrant Chinese families: Characteristics and patterns of placement. *Child Maltreatment*, *13*(3), 269–279. doi:10.1177/1077559507313461

Samson, A. C., Huber, O., & Gross, J. J. (2012). Emotion regulation in Asperger's syndrome and high-functioning autism. *Emotion*, *12*(4), 659–665. doi:10.1037/a0027975

Sasson, N. J. (2006). The development of face processing in autism. *Journal of Autism & Developmental Disorders*, *36*(3), 381–394. doi:10.1007/s10803-006-0076-3

Saywitz, K. J., & Camparo, L. B. (2014). *Evidence-based child forensic interviewing: The developmental narrative elaboration interview: Interviewer guide*. New York, NY: Oxford University Press.

Saywitz, K. J., Geiselman, R. E., & Bornstein, G. K. (1992). Effects of cognitive interviewing and practice on children's recall performance. *Journal of Applied Psychology*, *77*(5), 744–756. doi:10.1037/0021-9010.77.5.744

Saywitz, K. J., Goodman, G. S., Nicholas, E., & Moan, S. F. (1991). Children's memories of a physical examination involving genital touch: Implications for reports of child sexual abuse. *Journal of Consulting & Clinical Psychology*, *59*(5), 682–691. doi:10.1037/0022-006X.59.5.682

Saywitz, K. J., & Snyder, L. (1996). Narrative elaboration: Test of a new procedure for interviewing children. *Journal of Consulting & Clinical Psychology*, *64*(6), 1347–1357. doi:10.1037/0022-006X.64.6.1347

Scheeren, A. M., Banerjee, R., Koot, H. M., & Begeer, S. (2016). Self-presentation and the role of perspective taking and social motivation in autism spectrum disorder. *Journal of Autism & Developmental Disorders*, *46*(2), 649–657. doi:10.1007/s10803-015-2610-7

Schwarzkopf, S., Schilbach, L., Vogeley, K., & Timmermans, B. (2014). "Making it explicit" makes a difference: Evidence for a dissociation of spontaneous and intentional level 1 perspective taking in high-functioning autism. *Cognition*, *131*(3), 345–354. doi:10.1016/j.cognition.2014.02.003

Siegel, B. (1995). Assessing allegations of sexual molestation made through facilitated communication. *Journal of Autism & Developmental Disorders*, *25*(3), 319–326. doi:10.1007/BF02179293

Sterling, L., Dawson, G., Webb, S., Murias, M., Munson, J., Panagiotides, H., & Aylward, E. (2008). The role of face familiarity in eye tracking of faces by individuals with ASDs. *Journal of Autism & Developmental Disorders*, *38*(9), 1666–1675. doi:10.1007/s10803-008-0550-1

Tincani, M. (2004). Comparing the Picture Exchange Communication System and sign language training for children with autism. *Focus on Autism & Other Developmental Disabilities*, *19*(3), 152–163. doi:10.1177/10883576040190030301

Wandrey, L., Lyon, T. D., Quas, J. A., & Friedman, W. J. (2012). Maltreated children's ability to estimate temporal location and numerosity of placement changes and court visits. *Psychology, Public Policy, & Law*, *18*(1), 79–104. doi:10.1037/a0024812

Warren, A. R., Woodall, C. E., Thomas, M., Nunno, M., Keeney, J. M., Larson, S. M., & Stadfeld, J. A. (1999). Assessing the effectiveness of a training program for interviewing child witnesses. *Applied Developmental Science*, *3*(2), 128–135. doi:10.1207/s1532480xads0302_6

White, S. J. (2013). The Triple I hypothesis: Taking another('s) perspective on executive dysfunction in autism. *Journal of Autism & Developmental Disorders*, *43*(1), 114–121. doi:10.1007/s10803-012-1550-8

Zalla, T., Daprati, E., Sav, A., Chaste, P., Nico, D., & Leboyer, M. (2010). Memory for self-performed actions in individuals with Asperger syndrome. *Plos ONE*, *5*(10), doi:10.1371/journal.pone.0013370

17

Children with Autism Spectrum Disorder in the Courtroom: How Courts Handle Testimony Today and What We Can Do in the Future

Deborah Goldfarb and Alejandra Gonzalez

Hardly anybody wants to go to court. The courtroom is an intimidating place, particularly for witnesses who are asked to recall highly personal or traumatic events that may have occurred a long time prior. Legal proceedings involve unfamiliar settings and procedural nuances that can come across to nonlawyers as formalistic (at best). Witnesses' distress may be further compounded when witnesses are subjected to difficult questions and sometimes aggressive cross-examination, often by individuals who are complete strangers. For children with autism spectrum disorder (ASD), who, as the other chapters have detailed, may have sensory processing, communication, or socioemotional differences, these factors may render the courtroom untenable.

This lack of fit between the mechanics of the courtroom and the particular needs of children with ASD is not without effect. Children with disabilities, including those with ASD, disproportionately experience childhood victimization (Sullivan & Knutson, 2000; Wissink, van Vugt, Moonen, Stams, & Hendriks, 2015). And, even outside of criminal settings, children have a number of venues in which they must or may testify, including educational proceedings or custody decisions (Goldfarb, Goodman, & Lawler, 2015). As courts become more receptive to hearing children's testimony, so, too, must courtroom settings and procedures adapt to provide an environment that ensures the accuracy of the testimony, protects the rights of the defendants, and avoids retraumatizing children. This, however, requires that the courts not only understand child development generally, but also the individual needs of the child testifying, including how developmental disorders may further impinge on the ability to provide testimony.

The Wiley Handbook of Memory, Autism Spectrum Disorder, and the Law, First Edition.
Edited by Jonni L. Johnson, Gail S. Goodman, and Peter C. Mundy.

The judicial system is slowly evolving in its responsiveness to children's individualized needs. The past few decades have seen numerous changes in both the law and relevant research on children with ASD testifying in the courtroom, including the increasing admission of testimony from children with ASD. Even with that progress, we are still far from where we need to be. Given the incredible breadth of potential legal issues and areas for amelioration, there are numerous topics, each of them of their own import, on which this chapter could focus. Here, we concentrate on children with ASD as witnesses in the courtroom to either their own victimization or having witnessed the alleged victimization of others. As many of the issues below are also applicable to adults with ASD, particularly if there are other co-occurring developmental or cognitive delays, we raise relevant case law where possible. We primarily focus on children, however, given that research thus far has primarily focused on adults or children, and not the potential overlap between these two populations. Specifically, we describe how courts have responded to children with ASD testifying in the courtroom as eyewitnesses. Next, we consider the effects of such testimony and how the courtroom can be accommodated to better meet the needs of these children. Finally, we look at research on how legal actors perceive child eyewitnesses with ASD and consider how legal actors could help diminish pre-existing biases.

Children with ASD as Eyewitnesses in the Courtroom

Prior to admitting testimony into evidence, courts in the United States require that all witnesses (including children) are competent to testify (though some states presume competence unless a challenge is heard; see Cal. Evid. Code § 700. One factor included in competency determinations is whether a witness understands the obligation to tell the truth. Although courts vary in how they judge the veracity aspect of competency, courts in the United States consider whether children understand the difference between a truth and a lie, and that they can affirm that they will tell the truth (Lyon, 2011). Courts have queried whether children with ASD are able to tell the truth, and, in some cases (after engaging in a series of questions with the child witness), found that they can (see *People v. Price*, 2014). In studies involving children without ASD, promises to tell the truth appear to have a beneficial effect. Specifically, having children promise to tell the truth and not lie can decrease rates of lying (Evans & Lee, 2010), and when worded in a developmentally appropriate manner, children as young as 3 years old understand promises of future behavior (e.g., "I will not lie"; Lyon & Evans, 2014). Less work, however, has examined the effects of these conditional promises and guarantees of future behavior in children with ASD. As this is the first hurdle children must cross to have their testimony heard, this issue is worthy of further consideration.

Courts have also considered whether children with ASD can competently and capably express themselves at a level such that their testimony is admissible. Although each case requires its own review of the child's individual needs, courts have found children with ASD as competent witnesses for a number of years (*Carter v. State of Indiana*, 2001; *Spraggins v. Minnesota*, 2015). Indeed, when admissibility has been directly challenged, many courts have denied claims that an ASD diagnosis alone affects the reliability of children's statements without direct evidence establishing the connection between the two (*Washington v. Tanner*, 2015). In fact, the child in the *Spraggins* matter was diagnosed with (what was then labelled) "autism spectrum disorder, attention deficit/hyperactivity disorder, and several learning disabilities as well as a history of behavioral problems," but the trial court permitted him to testify and the issue was not raised on appeal.

This is not to say that courts do not impose admissibility limitations arising from the children's diagnoses; courts have found that communication disabilities can render children incompetent to testify (*State v. Sarich*, 2012). For example, the court in *State v. Sarich* considered the admissibility of Z's testimony (his name has been abbreviated for confidentiality) in light of the fact that he was diagnosed with ASD as a child. Z, who was 19 at the time of trial, was alleged to have witnessed his mother murder his caregiver Bill three years prior, when Z was still an adolescent. A psychologist specializing in ASD testified that Z could only answer questions "identifying something rather than a traditional who, what, why, when, where type of question…." The court thus engaged in a series of questions with Z attempting to ascertain the limits of his communication abilities. Although Z successfully answered questions such as "Is this a book" and "Is this a banana?", Z was unable to respond to question such as "Are we in water right now?", "Are we indoors now or outdoors?", and "Do you see a tree in this room?". Z's testimony was thus excluded on the basis of his inability to competently testify.

On appeal, the Oregon Supreme Court upheld the trial court's decision excluding Z's testimony (*State v. Sarich*, 2012). The court differentiated this case from one where individuals are not permitted to testify because of their inability to speak English (or presumably, other communication limitations). In those cases, the inability can be remedied via an interpreter or other methods, and the witnesses still retain the ability to communicate their perceptions to others. Here, the appellate court upheld the trial court's finding that Z was "incapable of testifying in a way that would be useful at trial" and the charges were later dropped (Odegard, 2012).

When children with ASD are questioned in a suggestive manner outside of the courtroom, courts are also reluctant to admit the interviews into evidence. For example, the appellate court in *State v. Sarich* (2012) also upheld the exclusion of a video that showed Z directing police officers to the site of the victims' remains. Both the appellate court and the Oregon Supreme Court noted that the police officers repeatedly led Z with suggestive questions, and when Z incorrectly chose which direction to go, the officers went back to the previous intersection and allowed him to guess again. Eventually, the detectives stopped asking Z questions, directed themselves to the location, and informed Z that the correct location will be in "3.9, almost 4 miles" and will be "coming up close." The court found that the unfair prejudice of the video outweighed its probative value given the many improprieties with the interviewing techniques used by the officers. Thus, courts are receptive to testimony by children with ASD, but there are limitations to the level of competency and interview techniques that courts find acceptable.

Despite courts' willingness to accept testimony of children with ASD, judges sometimes reveal difficulty understanding the ways in which children with learning disabilities or other intellectual/communicative limitations can testify in court. Cederborg and Lamb (2006) analyzed 39 Swedish cases where children with such diagnoses testified. The researchers analyzed how the courts referenced the victims' behavior and testimony when discussing their credibility. In 22 of the 39 cases, the judges' credibility criteria for these victims was identical to that which they would use where the alleged victims were typically developing. In these cases, the veracity of the children's statements was questioned by the judge due to a failure to provide a coherent, clear, and detailed account. Furthermore, some cases failed to mention the children's mental age or their developmental delays, which might have affected the children's ability to provide a coherent and detailed report. Thus, judges may benefit from additional training so that they can ensure that the relevant evidence is admitted into the record, allowing them to render full-informed decisions.

In addition to the capacity to testify, courts also consider the potential harm of testifying to the children; where testifying would be traumatic to children with ASD, courts have considered children unavailable to testify (thus, permitting hearsay evidence regarding the testimony, including the children's own prior testimony) (*People v. Christensen*, 2014). In *People v. Christensen*, Joshua, the alleged victim, had been diagnosed with Asperger syndrome. After testifying in the first trial, which ended in mistrial, Joshua suffered "significant emotional trauma," including angry outbursts, bouts of crying, and regressive behaviors, such as sleeping in his parents' room, nightmares, and fears for his safety. The court found that, based on the expert testimony offered, the child was unable to testify a second time. In so ruling, the court rejected the defendant's argument that Asperger syndrome was not a sufficient diagnosis to excuse the witness from testifying in this case (to qualify for an exception to the hearsay rule) as a "callous and myopic characterization of the evidence." Indeed, the court stated that the Asperger's diagnosis did not drive the decision, but instead, that the decision was driven by the severity of the child's emotional condition from testifying. Thus, courts not only consider children with ASD as potentially competent witnesses; the courts have also shown, under certain circumstances, the ability to understand how testifying would undermine these children's emotional stability.

Expert testimony regarding the veracity of testimony by children with ASD

Experts are frequently called to testify regarding ASD, including as to its repercussions on eyewitness memory, testimonial capacity generally, and a specific child's ability to testify (*Carter v. State*, 2011; *State v. Sarich*, 2012). Courts have also upheld the admission of evidence regarding ASD's effects on an individual's behavior while testifying in cases where the defendant was diagnosed with ASD. Specifically, an appellate court found that it was reversible error (grounds for overturning a criminal conviction) that the trial court refused to admit expert testimony explaining defendant's "odd demeanor and mannerisms, as well as his difficulty with interpersonal dealings" (*State v. Burr*, 2008). Such expert testimony could similarly benefit child witnesses with ASD. It would not only aid jurors in understanding certain behavioral manifestations, but it also could inform the court both as to the child's limitations in testifying and how to meet the child's particular needs. Psychologists with clinical expertise can also identify possible source of errors and why a child with ASD may have cognitive, social, and emotional difficulty providing testimony (Cederborg & Lamb, 2006).

Judges, however, do not always utilize or have available to them the expert testimony often necessary to understand the needs of children with developmental or communicative disorders. In Cederborg and Lamb's (2006) analysis of legal proceedings in which children with developmental disorders testified, expert guidance was not available in 18 of the 39 cases; thus, these judges were deprived of a source who could aid their understanding of the specific disorders and the testimonial implications for the child witnesses. Even when assessment was available, the courts varied in their utilization of the information depending on the information the clinician included in the report. For instance, Cederborg and Lamb (2006) highlighted a case where the court's failure to connect an ASD diagnosis and the potential communicative limitations had harmful results. The police interviewed an alleged child victim who was described as having "developmental disabilities with autistic features." The interview was described as "not coherent" and "poorly structured," yet there was no discussion in the police report of how the child's diagnoses could have affected their ability to describe what had occurred. As the victim was unable to answer questions and avoidant when the interviewer broached the alleged physical abuse, the court ruled the report unreliable. A clinical assessment could have allowed the police to structure the interview to the child's needs as well as educated the court on what could have been expected from the child.

Even when expert evaluations are provided, there are often problems with the reports (Cederborg & Lamb, 2006). Reports may have been previously written for other purposes, such as educational or social welfare matters, and may have involved assessments conducted anywhere from two to five years before the legal case. Additionally, such delays may make it impossible to draw accurate conclusions about the developmental status of the child. Assessments also can consist solely of a general written description of the child's diagnosis and lack any details as to what this implies for the child's general functioning. There is little work, however, on how judges treat cases involving children with developmental disorders and a current systematic review is needed to understand how, on average, legal officers consider expert testimony on children's diagnoses, and subsequently, adapt interviews and courtroom proceedings to the child's specific needs. Further, additional consistency in screenings and evaluations would ensure that courts and other legal actors receive the details necessary for them to properly respond to the case at hand.

Some courts have also permitted expert testimony regarding the general veracity of children with ASD. In *Carter v. State of Indiana* (2012), an expert testified that children with ASD have difficulty lying, but did not comment on the statements by the child at issue. The court upheld the admission of this evidence on appeal noting that the expert qualified her statements in that it was a general statement about children with ASD. She did not testify specifically about the child at issue, and thus, the jury could still draw its own conclusion about the credibility of the witness. *In re PD and AD* (2012), the state also offered expert testimony in support of its termination of the defendant's parental rights. The expert there opined that children with ASD "cannot lie" as they lack the imagination, creativity, or foresight necessary to formulate a lie. The court rejected with the argument that the expert did not have the background necessary to proffer such an opinion. Thus, courts appear willing to admit evidence that children with ASD have more difficulty telling a lie, and will sometimes allow them to go as far as saying that children with ASD "cannot lie."

Testimony that children with ASD cannot lie is a stretch of the current research. Children with ASD do lie at a lower rate that children without ASD and have more difficult maintaining a lie when asked additional questions (Talwar et al., 2012). That said, it is not that children with ASD simply cannot or do not lie. In Talwar and colleagues' (2012) study, more children in the non-ASD group (96%) lied about having peaked at a toy than children with ASD, but 72% of the children with ASD did still lie about the transgression. Thus, any statements that children with ASD "cannot lie" are unsupported by the evidence. Expert testimony regarding children with ASD and their ability to lie should be constrained to accurately reflect the research (Faigman, Monahan, & Slobogin, 2014).

Effects of Testifying for Children with ASD

Little is known about the effects of testifying on children with ASD. Thus, our review focuses primarily on research with child victims and witnesses without known ASD. Where possible, we talk about how the research may apply to children with ASD and what further research is needed.

As might be predicted, children who testify in criminal cases report that it can be a stressful and anxiety-inducing experience (Goodman et al., 1992). In particular, children indicate that seeing the defendant is one of the most frightening parts of being in the courtroom in criminal cases (Goodman et al., 1992; Hobbs et al., 2014). Increased anxiety levels may also result from children's limited understanding of how the court works and of the legal terminology (Quas et al., 2009; Saywitz, 1992). This distress can have a negative effect on the quality of children's testimony; children with higher levels of anxiety and negativity also have the most difficulty answering questions on the stand (Goodman et al., 1992). Laboratory work on the effect of distress on mock-courtroom testimony substantiates this finding and shows that children who reported being more distressed in a courtroom for a mock trial had lower rates of accurate free recall (Saywitz & Nathanson, 1993). The stress of testifying appears to be compounded when the abuse was severe and children testified numerous times. These children reveal long-term emotional consequences even when interviewed years later (Quas et al., 2005).

In addition to their fears of seeing the defendant, child victims also fear cross-examination by the defense attorney (and even sometimes questions by the prosecution; Andrews, Lamb, & Lyon, 2015; Stolzenberg & Lyon, 2014). Cross-examination has consistently been shown to be harmful to the accuracy of children's testimony where prior testimony was indeed correct (Zajac & Hayne, 2003; Zajac & Hayne, 2006). Although cross-examination can reveal more truthful testimony when a child was previously lying (Fogliati & Bussey, 2015; Zajac, Irvine, Ingram, & Jack, 2016), there is typically no way to determine in actual legal cases (at least from the child changing his/her testimony) whether the original testimony was incorrect (Zajac, Irvine, Ingram, & Jack, 2016). Thus, cross-examination has been shown to be deleterious to children's testimony, and when changes occur, not diagnostic as to the veracity of the original statements. It is unclear, however, whether these same results would hold for children with ASD as no study thus far has considered this issue.

Testifying's negative outcomes can also be seen in behavioral maladjustments. Goodman et al. (1992) compared behavior problems, measured by parent report on the Child Behavior Checklist (CBCL) and teacher report on the Teacher Report Form (TRF), of child victims who did or did not testify in sexual abuse prosecutions. The testifiers' behavior problems did not improve seven months after testifying, whereas the nontestifiers' behavior problems significantly decreased over time. A follow-up study of the same children, conducted by Quas and colleagues (2005), found that those victims who had testified repeatedly as children reported increased internalization and behavioral problems even 12 years later. Other studies similarly find increased negative outcomes, such as lower self-control and an increase in both internalizing and externalizing symptoms, when comparing testifiers relative to nontestifiers (Bill, 1995; Oates & Tong, 1987; Quas & Goodman, 2012; Quas & McAuliff, 2009).

The links between testifying and mental health problems often depend on additional factors. Children who testified repeatedly, lacked corroborative evidence for their claims, lacked maternal support, or experienced severe sexual abuse are at the greatest risk for developing adverse mental health outcomes (Goodman et al., 1992; Quas et al., 2005). A lack of corroborative evidence often centers the case on the children's reports, which in turn, could increase their anxiety level as well as the pressures to take the stand. Severe abuse cases may involve a closely related perpetrator or abuse that persisted over a long period of time. Pressures from the perpetrator or family members and conflictual feelings about the perpetrator are likely greatest in these circumstances, making it especially challenging for children to face the perpetrator repeatedly while being cross-examined on the stand about their experiences (Quas & Goodman, 2012).

In addition to fears of testifying due to the courtroom or the parties in the case, children may face a number of other emotional factors that increase the traumatization of testifying (Goldfarb, Goodman, Chong, & Goodman-Shaver, 2014). For instance, relatives may be unsupportive or try to persuade child victims to drop the claims that the abuse occurred (particularly in cases of familial abuse) (Malloy, Lyon, & Quas, 2007). Without caregiver support, the stress of testifying may overwhelm children's coping resources (Malloy & Lyon, 2006; Sas, 1993). Providing support to the children may buffer some of the negative effects, and one might even deem testifying as beneficial to children in providing them with an opportunity to voice what happened. Future work should consider, as discussed more later, potential support systems for children with ASD and ways to buffer the negative effects of testifying based on their individual diagnoses.

Indeed, although testifying can be a highly emotional event for child witnesses, there are also potential positive outcomes, particularly when testifying occurs in a supportive and developmentally appropriate setting. Research supports that children who testify in criminal cases have increased positivity both about the legal system generally and the case specifically when the defendant's sentence is severe (e.g., Goodman et al., 1992; Sas, 1997). Similarly, foster youth have more positive perceptions of the dependency court system when they have high quality communications and representation by their attorneys (Goldfarb et al., 2018). Adverse mental health outcomes have also been shown to occur in children who experienced less severe abuse, but did not testify, particularly when the perpetrator was found not guilty or received a lenient sentence (Quas et al., 2005). Testifying provides children with an opportunity to speak and have their voices heard. This opportunity may be particularly important when children have experienced crimes that demean their sense of self and worth.

No research thus far, however, has considered whether these same effects occur in children with ASD in the courtroom. Popular press on children with ASD often paints them as having decreased or depressed emotional or social responses. Thus, one might assume that some of the stress of testifying would be lessened. However, children with ASD are similarly stressed by having to speak in front of others, and as such, testifying in criminal court may have the same deleterious (and sometimes, as previously discussed, beneficial, for purposes of voice) effects as it does for typically developing children.

Accommodating the Courtroom

There are a number of potential accommodations that courts can make to enable children with ASD to testify in a manner that is likely not (or at least less) harmful to their emotional well-being. Here, rather than an exhaustive review of such accommodations, we suggest a few major techniques that have been used when children with and without ASD testify.

Assistive technologies

Accommodations to state courtrooms are mandated pursuant to the Americans with Disabilities Act (ADA).[1] Under the ADA, the court must consider both architectural and communication barriers that may prohibit or impair testimony (Blanck, Wilichowski, & Schmeling, 2003). Indeed, assistive technologies can be required, such as accommodations to help individuals see and process the evidence presented. At the same time, technology should be used carefully to ensure that children with ASD are not negatively impacted by their inclusion. Children with ASD may have sensory processing difficulties that render certain adjustments to courtroom presentations (including increasing the volume of presentations or large pictures of evidence) overwhelming. By taking the individualized approach mandated by the ADA and working to accommodate children's specific needs, such as being cognizant of a child's sensitivity to sights and sounds, courts help may the courtroom better fit the children's needs.

Facilitated communication

One accommodation that was previously used for children with ASD that has come under scrutiny is facilitated communication. Facilitated communication is a technique developed in the 1990s whereby individuals with communication limitations, including children with ASD, would "communicate" with the aid of a facilitator (APA, 2003). Facilitators would enable the individual to "communicate" by guiding the individual with ASD to use a keyboard or a similar device. The argument went that this dyadic interaction removed any communication or motor skills barriers that were otherwise masking disabled individuals' abilities to speak with others.

The use of facilitated communication came under criticism shortly after its introduction. In 1994, the American Psychological Association adopted a resolution stating that the purported communication "attributed to the clients was directed or systematically determined by the paraprofessional/professional therapists who provided facilitated assistance" (APA, 1994). Subsequent meta-analyses have empirically supported this resolution; studies that analyze facilitated communication's effectiveness using a control group (e.g., comparing accuracy in story reporting of facilitators who are informed of the story to naïve facilitators who do not know any story details) find that the technique is problematic or simply does not work (Mostert, 2001).

[1] The federal courts are mandated to meet communication disabilities pursuant to the Guide to Judiciary Policy (2016).

Specifically, control facilitators are unable to accurately recount information from the individual purportedly communicating with the facilitator.

Courts have grown increasingly aware of the limitations and lack of empirical support for facilitated communication. Indeed, in 2013, two parents sued various governmental entities arguing that they were the subject of malicious prosecution. Specifically, their child, who was diagnosed with autism and is nonverbal, was removed from their home after she purportedly alleged via facilitated communication that her parents sexually abused her. In reviewing the motion in front of them, the Sixth Circuit noted that facilitated communication had "caused numerous instances of false allegations of sexual abuse" and that numerous organizations had cautioned against using it to confirm abuse allegations (*Wendrow v. Michigan Department of Human Services*, 2013).

One court has gone so far as to note that if facilitated communication was the sole basis for children's removal from their parents' home that "it would categorically hold that [the parents'] First, Fourth, Fifth, and Fourteenth Amendment rights to custody of their child would have been violated" (*Covell v. Johnson*, 2001). Indeed, the court in *Covell v. Johnson* categorized statements derived using facilitated communication as "constitutionally infirm." That said, the court declined to find a constitutional violation in this case as the defendants had other evidence to support the removal of the children from the home.

Despite this increased scrutiny, facilitated communication or similar forms of communication aids continue to be used (Elliott, 2016). Supporters of these techniques vociferously argue that they aid individuals to communicate with someone who would otherwise be deprived of their voice. When there are questions as to whether a child, who is otherwise uncommunicative, is being harmed, it is easy to understand why such techniques would be appealing as they could unlock victimization that would otherwise remain undiscovered. The empirical work thus far, however, would seem to support the skeptical approach taken by the courts.

Preparatory programs for child witnesses

Children's distress regarding testifying in court has been found to be reduced via participation in preparatory programs. In these programs, children undergo a number of different activities to help them understand what will occur in the courtroom, such as giving children a tour of the courtroom or having a mock trial (including answering questions and having adults yell out objections) prior to the appearance, and ways to manage stress (Rainville, 2013). For children with ASD who may be upset by an unfamiliar and rigid environment, training may be especially beneficial. For example, familiarity with an interviewer improves children with ASD's performance on cognitive and verbal tasks (Szarko, Brown, & Watkins, 2013). Thus, prior preparations with courtroom actors, including the attorneys and judicial officers, may help these children with their later performance.

In addition to informal case preparation, a number of formal preparatory programs have been shown to be helpful in reducing children's stress levels that may similarly be helpful for children with ASD. For example, victims of childhood sexual abuse who took part in a court preparation program that implemented stress-reduction techniques did not show adverse mental health outcomes after testifying compared to children who were not in the program (Sas, 1991; Sas, 1993). This lack of relation held even three years later, indicating that intervention programs might successfully reduce adverse mental health outcomes in children related to testifying. Similarly, Dr. Rebecca Nathanson's Kids' Court School educates children on courtroom procedures, allows them to take part in a mock trial, and trains them on how to handle the stress of testifying (Nathanson & Saywitz, 2015). Program attendance decreases children's anxiety about testifying. Children with ASD have shown similar stress decreases after participating in theater camps that help with behavioral and theatrical strategies (Corbett et al., 2014). Given these findings, court preparatory programs may have similarly beneficial effects for children with ASD, particularly when programs are designed to meet the children's communication and preparation needs.

Victim witness advocates

Victim witness advocates can provide invaluable support to child witnesses as children both prepare to and actually testify on the stand. Although victim witness advocates perform a wide variety of services, their primary function in the United States is to provide children with emotional and informational support during legal proceedings, especially criminal trials (McAuliff, Nicholson, Amarillo, & Ravanshenas, 2008). Normally, victim witness advocates are appointed by the district attorney's office or the court to help children throughout the pendency of the proceedings. The goal is to help reduce the children's anxiety and to lower trauma that may result from testifying. As children greatly benefit from having supportive adults present in the courtroom (Goodman et al., 1992; Sas, Wolfe, & Gowdey, 1996), having a victim advocate may provide children with emotional support, even if the children's non-offending caregivers are excluded. As with the support programs previously discussed, this may be particularly helpful for children with ASD as a method for them to gain familiarity with another person in the courtroom (Szarko et al., 2013).

Unfortunately, research reveals that victim witness advocates may have a negative effect on jurors' perceived credibility of child victims; jurors on average rate children who are accompanied by a support person as less trustworthy than children who appear alone (Nefas, Neal, Maurice, & McAuliff, 2008). This potential harm may be ameliorated by appropriate instructions or education from the judge. No research thus far has considered this effect on children or witnesses with ASD. It may be that having an advocate present would draw attention to any developmental/communication limitations or cause jurors to assume limitations where none are present. Alternatively, it may be that putative jurors would be more understanding of the presence of an advocate for a child with ASD. Further research may clarify how to provide all children and children with ASD in particular with the necessary supports without incurring unwarranted bias.

Therapy

In addition to victim witness advocates, therapeutic professionals (such as psychologists or counselors) can play a vital role in helping children through the difficult experience of a pending litigation. Therapy may be especially beneficial for children with ASD given the co-occurrence of ASD not only with a variety of medical disorders, such as Fragile X syndrome, tuberous sclerosis, seizure disorders, and hearing and visual impairments as well as developmental delays (LoVullo & Matson, 2009;

Gillberg & Billstedt, 2000; Matson & Boisjoli, 2007), but also with psychopathology (Matson & Nebel-Schwalm, 2007). For instance, Russell and colleagues (2005) found that 1 in 4 adults diagnosed with high-functioning autism (what was previously termed Asperger's) also met the criteria for obsessive compulsive disorder (OCD). There is also sufficient evidence that ASD co-occurs with depression (Ghaziuddin, Ghaziuddin, & Greden, 2002; Stewart, Barnard, Pearson, Hasan, & O'Brien, 2006) and anxiety disorders (LoVullo & Matson, 2009; Bellini, 2004; Gillott, Furniss, & Walter, 2001; Kim, Szatmari, Bryson, Streiner, & Wilson, 2000).

There are a growing number of reports that children with ASD present with more psychiatric symptoms or disorders than other children (Gadow, DeVincent, Pomeroy, & Azizian, 2004; Gillberg & Billstedt, 2000). These disorders include mood disorders (Bradley, Summers, Wood, & Bryson, 2004; Ghaziuddin, Ghaziuddin, & Greden, 2002), high anxiety or fears (Gillot, Furniss, & Walter, 2001; Kim, Szatmari, Bryson, Streiner, & Wilson, 2000), and ADHD symptoms, such as inattention, impulsivity, hyperactivity, and temper outbursts (Goldstein & Schwebach, 2004; Kim, Szatmari, Bryson, Streiner, & Wilson, 2000). Cognitive and perceptual disturbances caused by ASD may also lead to increased mental health problems because of the stress experienced by these children in their interactions with others and the consequently disturbed responses of others toward them (Brereton, Tonge, & Einfeld, 2006). One study also shows that children with ASD commonly meet criteria for not just one, but several, co-morbid psychiatric disorders (Leyfer et al., 2006).

Given this level of co-morbidity, attention by legal professionals to therapeutic interventions during the pendency of legal proceedings is of the utmost importance. Ultimately, psychologists and legal professionals should work together to avoid the retraumatization of children during legal cases. With adequate support and preparation, adverse mental health outcomes can be reduced (if not avoided all together) (Sas, 1991; Sas, 1993). Further, therapy may help children process their feelings regarding the alleged criminal acts and decrease outbursts while testifying on the witness stand. Helping children process to the point where they are neutral in their expressions may, however, have a downside. Mock jurors expect children without ASD to display negative emotions (crying) while they testify and rate as less credible children who are stoic in their testimony (Cooper, Quas, & Cleveland, 2014; Golding, Fryman, Marsil, & Yozwiak, 2003; Regan & Baker, 1998). Additional research on the downstream effects on therapy on the children's welfare, including mental health, and case outcomes is thus worthy of further consideration.

Closed-circuit television

When testifying in the open courtroom presents sensory challenges for children with ASD or when seeing the defendant is too emotionally traumatizing, courts may permit children to testify via closed-circuit television (CCTV). CCTV allows for child witnesses to testify outside of the direct gaze of the defendants, which can be highly intimidating to children, but still allows for defendants to observe the children's testimony. The Supreme Court has upheld CCTV as a permissible accommodation that does not per se violate the Sixth Amendment's confrontation requirements, and instead, may be used after an individualized case assessment (*Maryland v. Craig*, 1990). CCTV is generally found to decrease both children's anxiety regarding testifying and suggestibility in young children (Goodman et al., 1998). Further, jurors are just as accurate in detecting the veracity of children's testimony when children testify via CCTV as compared to testifying in open court (Orcutt, Goodman, Tobey, Batterman-Faunce, & Thomas, 2001).

Of note, in the *State v. Sarich* (2012) case, after the child witness (Z) failed to correctly respond to the prosecutor's competency questions, the prosecutor noted that he did not think Z could

> ...continue with having direct eye contact with his mother. And that his mother obviously had a constitutional right to have direct eye contact. So I don't have any further questions.

These statements fairly raise the question of whether CCTV would have enabled Z's testimony. Unfortunately, no studies thus far have considered whether CCTV shows similar positive results for children with ASD as it does with typically developing children.

CCTV is also not without limitations; children who testify via CCTV are viewed as less confident and consistent by putative jurors than children who testify in open court (Goodman et al., 1998). As research has not examined use of CCTV with children with ASD or jurors' views of children with ASD testifying via CCTV, it is unclear whether there would be positive effects for these children and negative effects on jurors' perceptions.

Views of Children with ASD by Legal Actors

Although there is a growing literature on judges' views of individuals with ASD as criminal offenders (Berryessa, 2014a; Berryessa, 2014b; Foster, 2015), there is less work on views of such individuals as victims. Studies find that witnesses with ASD are viewed as less credible than (but equally confident as) witnesses without this diagnosis (Maras & Memon, 2014). Mock jurors who were informed of the witnesses' ASD diagnoses were less likely to report such differences. Courts have noted that expert testimony about ASD may be necessary for the jury to understand a defendant's particular behavior or actions while testifying at trial (*State v. Burr*, 2008). Thus, courts have already implicitly recognized that jurors may need further education on ASD in order to be able to understand why individuals with ASD may display certain behaviors. Less is understood as to whether this testimony actually aids the jurors versus a judicial instruction or other admonition.

Despite the lack of literature on jurors' views of child victims with ASD, there is a growing body of research on mock jurors' views of victims with varying intellectual disabilities (Bottoms, Nysse-Carris, Harris, & Tyda, 2003). Victims described as "mildly mentally retarded" are perceived as more credible, honest, and less likely to fabricate than victims described as having "average intelligence." These same victims are, however, also described as being less cognitively competent and less accurate in responding to suggestive questions (Brown & Lewis, 2013). Other studies using transcripts of court cases found that participants viewed individuals with an intellectual disability as less credible, due, in part, to the fact that they provided fewer details, than typically developing witnesses (Henry, Ridley, Perry, & Crane, 2011).

There is also little work on judges' or prosecutors' (as opposed to jurors') perceptions of individuals with ASD specifically and intellectual disabilities more generally. Research has shown that prosecutors are less likely to believe the eyewitness testimony (the accuracy of recall and resistance to false suggestion) of children with disabilities than those without, and prosecutors also viewed children with disability as less sincere (Nathanson & Platt, 2005). The prosecutors believed that jurors would likely feel the same way (Nathanson & Platt, 2005).

Thus, although some preliminary work considered the relation between ASD and judges' and jurors' views of eyewitnesses with ASD, there is still plenty of room for additional research and analyses. Given the judge's vital role in deciding what accommodations are necessary for a child to testify, prosecutors in deciding which cases ought to be pursued, and the jurors' role in the ultimate decision in the case, this would be a fruitful and impactful area for future research.

Take-Home Points

As we have detailed throughout this chapter, there are many issues yet to resolve when it comes to children with ASD testifying as victims or witnesses in the courtroom. Specifically, we have noted that:

- Courts can and do admit the eyewitness testimony of children with ASD. Although judges show an awareness of some of the emotional effects of testifying and potential developmental limitations, experts and academics could continue to aid courts in their comprehension of developmental disorders and how they affect testifying. This includes work into the effectiveness of oaths or promises to tell the truth on accurate testimonies by children with ASD. Indeed, empirically supported educational programs and tools from researchers could aid courts and legal advocates in the difficult job that they do every day.
- Expert testimony can aid courts in understanding the contours of a child's diagnosis and ensure that the child testifies in a manner that is fair and beneficial to all parties. Although courts could further utilize experts (particularly in understanding the implications of ASD on testimony), experts do testify (and courts permit testimony on) issues that are not fully upheld by the current research. Thus, in addition to opening the doors to additional expert testimony, courts should continue to utilize their gate keeping role.
- There are a number of potential ways that courts can limit the retraumatization of child witnesses, including courtroom preparation programs and victims' advocates. However, little is known both as to the effects of testifying on children with ASD and the benefits and limitations of these interventions. Further research is necessary to understand the particular needs of children with ASD in decreasing the stress of testifying, particularly regarding emotional matters.
- Children with ASD experience a number of co-morbid disorders, including mental health problems, and courts must competently respond to those issues. This may include encouraging children to attend therapy while their legal proceeding is ongoing. Given the complexity of symptomology that co-occurs in children with ASD, researchers would be wise to include such potential covariates

in their analyses so that courts can better extrapolate findings to the individual child testifying in front of them.

- Little is known about how jurors and judges perceive children with ASD and whether jury instructions or expert testimony could further influence the way these child witnesses are viewed. Empirical studies on jurors' reactions to children with ASD, particularly the efficacy of pattern jury instructions that can educate jurors on potential behavioral differences while testifying, would greatly benefit courts by ensuring that jurors are educated and unbiased (to the extent possible) in their evaluation of the testimony.

Thus, although some research exists on the issues facing children with ASD inside and outside of the courtroom, there is still much to be understood and studied. As social science struggles to determine the best ways to respond to child eyewitnesses with ASD, these children come into the courtroom every day. Every day that goes by thus leaves another child subject to questioning that simply may not be in the best interests of the parties involved. For that reason, we simply must make further efforts to ensure that we understand how children (indeed, people) with ASD can and should testify in the courtroom.

References

American Psychological Association (2013). Facilitated communication: Sifting the psychological wheat from the chaff. November 20, 2003. http://www.apa.org/research/action/facilitated.aspx.

Andrews, S. J., Lamb, M. E., & Lyon, T. D. (2015). Question types, responsiveness and self-contradictions when prosecutors and defense attorneys question alleged victims of child sexual abuse. *Applied Cognitive Psychology*, *29*(2), 253–261.

Bellini, S. (2004). Social skill deficits and anxiety in high-functioning adolescents with autism spectrum disorders. *Focus on Autism & Other Developmental Disabilities*, *19*(2), 78–86.

Bill, D. F. (1995). The effect of testifying in court on children who have been sexually abused. Unpublished doctoral dissertation. The Fielding Institute.

Billstedt, E. (2000). Autism and Asperger syndrome: coexistence with other clinical disorders. *Acta Psychiatrica Scandinavica*, *102*(5), 321–330.

Berryessa, C. M. (2014). Judicial perceptions of media portrayals of offenders with high functioning autistic spectrum disorders. *International Journal of Criminology & Sociology*, *3*, 46.

Berryessa, C. M. (2014). Judiciary views on criminal behaviour and intention of offenders with high-functioning autism. *Journal of Intellectual Disabilities & Offending Behaviour*, *5*(2), 97–106.

Blanck, P., Hill, E., Siegal, C., & Waterstone, M. (2004). Disability civil rights law and policy. *St. Paul, Thomson/West.*

Bradley, E. A., Summers, J. A., Wood, H. L., & Bryson, S. E. (2004). Comparing rates of psychiatric and behavior disorders in adolescents and young adults with severe intellectual disability with and without autism. *Journal of Autism & Developmental Disorders*, *34*(2), 151–161.

Brereton, A. V., Tonge, B. J., & Einfeld, S. L. (2006). Psychopathology in children and adolescents with autism compared to young people with intellectual disability. *Journal of Autism & Developmental Disorders*, *36*(7), 863–870.

Brown, D. A., & Lewis, C. N. (2013). Competence is in the Eye of the Beholder: Perceptions of intellectually disabled child witnesses. *International Journal of Disability, Development & Education*, *60*(1), 3–17.

Carter v. State, 754 N.E.2d 877 (Ind. 2001).

Cederborg, A. C., & Lamb, M. E. (2006). How does the legal system respond when children with learning difficulties are victimized? *Child Abuse & Neglect*, *30*(5), 537–547.

Cooper, A., Quas, J. A., & Cleveland, K. C. (2014). The emotional child witness: Effects on juror decision making. *Behavioral Sciences & the Law*, *32*, 813–828. doi:10.1002/bsl.2153

Corbett, B. A., Swain, D. M., Coke, C., Simon, D., Newsom, C., Houchins-Juarez, N.,... Song, Y. (2014). Improvement in social deficits in autism spectrum disorders using a theatre-based, peer-mediated intervention. *Autism Research*, *7*(1), 4–16.

Covell ex rel. Johnson v. County of Oswego, 165 F. Supp. 2d 241 (N.D.N.Y. 2001).

Elliott, J. (2016, July 20). The battle over a controversial method for Autism communication. *The Atlantic*. Retrieved from http://www.theatlantic.com/education/archive/2016/07/a-controversial-method-for-autism-communication/491810/

Evans, A. D., & Lee, K. (2010). Promising to tell the truth makes 8- to 16-year-olds more honest. *Behavioral Sciences & the Law*, *28*(6), 801–811.

Evans, A. D., & Lyon, T. D. (2012). Assessing children's competency to take the oath in court: The influence of question type on children's accuracy. *Law & Human Behavior*, *36*(3), 195.

Faigman, D. L., Monahan, J., & Slobogin, C. (2014). Group to individual (G2i) inference in scientific expert testimony. *The University of Chicago Law Review*, 417–480.

Fogliati, R., & Bussey, K. (2015). The effects of cross-examination on children's coached reports. *Psychology, Public Policy, & Law*, *21*(1), 10–23. doi:10.1037/law0000036

Foster, S. (2015). Autism is not a tragedy-ignorance is: Suppressing evidence of Asperger's syndrome and high-functioning autism in capital trials prejudices defendants for a death sentence. *Lincoln Memorial University Law Review*, *2*(9).

Gadow, K. D., DeVincent, C. J., Pomeroy, J., & Azizian, A. (2004). Psychiatric symptoms in preschool children with PDD and clinic and comparison samples. *Journal of Autism & Developmental Disorders*, *34*(4), 379–393.

Gillberg, C., & Billstedt, E. (2000). Autism and Asperger syndrome: Coexistence with other clinical disorders. *Acta Psychiatrica Scandinavica*, *102*(5), 321–330.

Gillott, A., Furniss, F., & Walter, A. (2001). Anxiety in high-functioning children with Autism. *Autism*, *5*(3), 277–286.

Ghaziuddin, M., Ghaziuddin, N., & Greden, J. (2002). Depression in persons with autism: Implications for research and clinical care. *Journal of Autism & Developmental Disorders*, *32*(4), 299–306.

Goldfarb, D. A., Goodman, G. S., & Lawler, M. J. (2015). Children's evidence and the convention on the rights of the child: Improving the legal system for children. In *Child-friendly Justice* (pp. 85–109). Leiden, The Netherlands: Brill.

Goldfarb, D., Tashjian, S., Goodman, G. S., Bederian-Gardner, D., Hobbs, S., Ogle, C., Bakanosky, S., Narr, R. K., Chae, Y., & NYTD/CYTD Research Group (2018). Legal socialization theory: The importance of voice in dependency court. Manuscript in progress.

Golding, J. M., Fryman, H. M., Marsil, D. F., & Yozwiak, J. A. (2003). Big girls don't cry: The effect of child witness demeanor on juror decisions in a child sexual abuse trial. *Child Abuse & Neglect*, *27*, 1311–1321. doi:10.1016/j.chiabu.2003.03.001

Goldstein, S., & Schwebach, A. J. (2004). The comorbidity of pervasive developmental disorder and attention deficit hyperactivity disorder: Results of a retrospective chart review. *Journal of Autism & Developmental Disorders*, *34*(3), 329–339.

Goodman, G. S., Goldfarb, D. A., Chong, J. Y., & Goodman-Shaver, L. (2014). Children's eyewitness memory: The influence of cognitive and socio-emotional factors. *Roger Williams University Law Review*, *19*, 476.

Goodman, G. S., Taub, E. P., Jones, D. P., England, P., Port, L. K., Rudy, L., … Melton, G. B. (1992). Testifying in criminal court: Emotional effects on child sexual assault victims. *Monographs of the Society for Research in Child Development*, i–159.

Goodman, G. S., Tobey, A. E., Batterman-Faunce, J. M., Orcutt, H., Thomas, S., Shapiro, C., & Sachsenmaier, T. (1998). Face-to-face confrontation: Effects of closed-circuit technology on children's eyewitness testimony and jurors' decisions. *Law & Human Behavior*, *22*(2), 165.

Guide to Judiciary Policy. (2016). Vol. 5, Ch. 2.

Henry, L., Ridley, A., Perry, J. and Crane, L. (2011), Perceived credibility and eyewitness testimony of children with intellectual disabilities. *Journal of Intellectual Disability Research*, *55*, 385–391. doi:10.1111/j.1365-2788.2011.01383.x

Hobbs, S. D., Goodman, G. S., Block, S. D., Oran, D., Quas, J. A., Park, A., … Baumrind, N. (2014). Child maltreatment victims' attitudes about appearing in dependency and criminal courts. *Children & Youth Services Review*, *44*, 407–416.

In re PD and AD. (2012). No. 11-0979 (Supreme Court of Appeals of West Virginia).

Kim, J. A., Szatmari, P., Bryson, S. E., Streiner, D. L., & Wilson, F. J. (2000). The prevalence of anxiety and mood problems among children with autism and Asperger syndrome. *Autism*, *4*(2), 117–132.

Leyfer, O. T., Folstein, S. E., Bacalman, S., Davis, N. O., Dinh, E., Morgan, J., … Lainhart, J. E. (2006). Comorbid psychiatric disorders in children with Autism: Interview development and rates of disorders. *Journal of Autism & Developmental Disorders*, *36*(7), 849–861.

Lyon, T.D. (2011). Assessing the competency of child witnesses: Best practice informed by psychology and law. In M. E. Lamb, D. La Rooy, L. C. Malloy, & C. Katz (Eds.), *Children's testimony: A handbook of psychological research and forensic practice* (pp. 69–85). Sussex, England: Wiley-Blackwell.

LoVullo, S. V., & Matson, J. L. (2009). Comorbid psychopathology in adults with Autism Spectrum Disorders and intellectual disabilities. *Research in Developmental Disabilities*, *30*(6), 1288–1296.

Malloy, L. C., Lyon, T. D., & Quas, J. A. (2007). Filial dependency and recantation of child sexual abuse allegations. *Journal of the American Academy of Child & Adolescent Psychiatry*, *46*(2), 162–170.

Matson, J. L., & Boisjoli, J. A. (2007). Differential diagnosis of PDDNOS in children. *Research in Autism Spectrum Disorders*, *1*(1), 75–84.

Matson, J. L., & Nebel-Schwalm, M. S. (2007). Comorbid psychopathology with autism spectrum disorder in children: An overview. *Research in Developmental Disabilities*, *28*(4), 341–352.

Maras, K. L. and Memon, A., (2014, 14 May and 21 June). Perceived credibility of witnesses with autism spectrum disorder: Do behavioural manifestations influence mock juror perceptions? In *International Meeting for Autism Research*, USA.

Maryland v. Craig, 497 U.S. 836, 110 S. Ct. 3157, 111 L. Ed. 2d 666 (1990).

Mostert, M. P. (2001). Facilitated communication since 1995: A review of published studies. *Journal of Autism & Developmental Disorders*, *31*(3), 287–313.

Nathanson, R., & Platt, M. D. (2005). Attorneys' perceptions of child witnesses with mental retardation. *Journal of Psychiatry & Law*, *33*(1), 5–42.

Nathanson, R., & Saywitz, K. J. (2015). Preparing children for court: Effects of a model court education program on children's anticipatory anxiety. *Behavioral Sciences & the Law*, *33*(4), 459–475.

Nefas, C., Neal, E., Maurice, K., & McAuliff, B. D. (2008, March). Support person use and child victim testimony: Believe it or not. Paper presented at the Annual meeting of the American Psychology-Law Society, Jacksonville, FL.

Oates, R. K., & Tong, L. (1987). Sexual abuse of children: An area with room for professional reforms. *The Medical Journal of Australia, 147*, 544–548.

Odegard, K. (2012). Witness blocked, so murder charge dropped. *Corvallis Gazette-Times.* Retrieved from: http://www.gazettetimes.com/news/local/crime-and-courts/witness-blocked-so-murder-charge-dropped/article_6f86020e-4120-11e2-a3dd-0019bb2963f4.html

Orcutt, H. K., Goodman, G. S., Tobey, A. E., Batterman-Faunce, J. M., & Thomas, S. F. (2001). Detecting deception in children's testimony: Factfinders' abilities to reach the truth in open court and closed-circuit trials. *Law & Human Behavior, 25*, 339–372. doi:10.1023/A:1010603618330

People v. Christensen, 229 Cal. App. 4th 781, 177 Cal. Rptr. 3d 712 (Ct. App. 2014).

People v. Price, No. F065516 (Cal. Ct. App. Oct. 22, 2014).

Quas, J. A., Goodman, G. S., Ghetti, S., Alexander, K. W., Edelstein, R., Redlich, A. D., … Haugaard, J. J. (2005). Childhood sexual assault victims: Long-term outcomes after testifying in criminal court. *Monographs of the Society for Research in Child Development*, i–139.

Quas, J. A., & Goodman, G. S. (2012). Consequences of criminal court involvement for child victims. *Psychology, Public Policy, & Law, 18*(3), 392.

Quas, J. A., & McAuliff, B. D. (2009). Accommodating child witnesses in the criminal justice system: Implications for death penalty cases. In *Mental Disorder & Criminal Law* (pp. 79–102). New York, NY: Springer.

Quas, J. A., Wallin, A. R., Horwitz, B., Davis, E., & Lyon, T. D. (2009). Maltreated children's understanding of and emotional reactions to dependency court involvement. *Behavioral Sciences & the Law, 27*(1), 97–117.

Rainville, C. (2013). Prosecuting cases for children on the autism spectrum. *Child Law Practice, 32*(4).

Regan, P. C., & Baker, S. J. (1998). The impact of child witness demeanor on perceived credibility and trial outcome in sexual abuse cases. *Journal of Family Violence, 18*, 187–195. http://dx.doi.org/10.1023/A:1022845724226

Russell, A. J., Mataix-Cols, D., Anson, M., & Murphy, D. G. (2005). Obsessions and compulsions in Asperger syndrome and high-functioning Autism. *The British Journal of Psychiatry, 186*(6), 525–528.

Sas, L. (1997). *Sexually abused children as witnesses: Progress and pitfalls* (pp. 248–267). Thousand Oaks, CA: Sage Publications, Inc.

Sas, L., Hurley, P., Austin, G., & Wolfe, D. (1991). Reducing the system-induced trauma for child sexual abuse victims through court preparation, assessment and follow-up. *Ontario, Canada: London Family Court Clinic.*

Sas, L. D., & London Family Court Clinic. Child Witness Project. (1993). *Three years after the verdict: A longitudinal study of the social and psychological adjustment of child witnesses referred to the child witness project.* London, Ontario: Child Witness Project, London Family Court Clinic.

Sas, L. D., Wolfe, D. A., & Gowdey, K. (1996). Children in the courts in Canada. *Criminal Justice & Behavior, 23*, 338–357.

Saywitz, K. J., & Nathanson, R. (1993). Children's testimony and their perceptions of stress in and out of the courtroom. *Child Abuse & Neglect, 17*(5), 613–622.

Spragins v. State of Minnesota (2015). Court of Appeals of Minnesota.

State v. Burr, 948 A.2d 627, 195 N.J. 119 (2008).

State of Oregon v. Lorraine Elizabeth Sarich, 291 P.3d 647, 352 Or. 601 (2012).

Stewart, M. E., Barnard, L., Pearson, J., Hasan, R., & O'Brien, G. (2006). Presentation of depression in autism and Asperger syndrome: A review. *Autism, 10*(1), 103–116.

Stolzenberg, S. N., & Lyon, T. D. (2014). How attorneys question children about the dynamics of sexual abuse and disclosure in criminal trials. *Psychology, Public Policy, & Law, 20*(1), 19.

Sullivan, P. M., & Knutson, J. F. (2000). Maltreatment and disabilities: A population-based epidemiological study. *Child Abuse & Neglect, 24*(10), 1257–1273.

Szarko, J. E., Brown, A. J., & Watkins, M. W. (2013). Examiner familiarity effects for children with autism spectrum disorders. *Journal of Applied School Psychology*, *29*(1), 37–51.

Talwar, V., Zwaigenbaum, L., Goulden, K. J., Manji, S., Loomes, C., & Rasmussen, C. (2012). Lie-telling behavior in children with autism and its relation to false-belief understanding. *Focus on Autism & Other Developmental Disabilities*, *27*(2), 122–129.

Washington v. Tanner J., Court of Appeals of Washington (2015).

Wendrow v. Michigan Department of Human Services, No. 12-1496 (6th Cir. Aug. 28, 2013).

Wissink, I. B., Van Vugt, E., Moonen, X., Stams, G. J. J., & Hendriks, J. (2015). Sexual abuse involving children with an intellectual disability (ID): A narrative review. *Research in Developmental Disabilities*, *36*, 20–35.

Zajac, R., & Hayne, H. (2003). I don't think that's what really happened: The effect of cross-examination on the accuracy of children's reports. *Journal of Experimental Psychology: Applied*, *9*(3), 187–195. doi:10.1037/1076-898X.9.3.187

Zajac, R., & Hayne, H. (2006). The negative effect of cross-examination style questioning on children's accuracy: Older children are not immune. *Applied Cognitive Psychology*, *20*(1), 3–16. doi:10.1002/acp.1169

Zajac, R., Irvine, B., Ingram, J. M., & Jack, F. (2016). The diagnostic value of children's responses to cross-examination questioning. *Behavioral Sciences & the Law*, *34*(1), 160–177. doi:10.1002/bsl.2215.725 ILCS 5/106B-10

Index

The Wiley Handbook of Memory, Autism Spectrum Disorder, and the Law, First Edition.
Edited by Jonni L. Johnson, Gail S. Goodman, and Peter C. Mundy.